the Essential *Air Fryer* Cookbook

the Essential *Air Fryer* Cookbook

THE ONLY BOOK YOU NEED
FOR YOUR SMALL, MEDIUM, OR LARGE AIR FRYER

Bruce Weinstein and Mark Scarbrough

Photographs by Eric Medsker

VORACIOUS

LITTLE, BROWN AND COMPANY

NEW YORK BOSTON LONDON

Voracious / Little, Brown and Company
Hachette Book Group
1290 Avenue of the Americas, New York, NY 10104
littlebrown.com

First Edition: November 2019

Voracious is an imprint of Little, Brown and Company, a division of Hachette Book Group, Inc. The Voracious name and logo are trademarks of Hachette Book Group, Inc.

The publisher is not responsible for websites (or their content) that are not owned by the publisher.

The Hachette Speakers Bureau provides a wide range of authors for speaking events. To find out more, go to hachettespeakersbureau.com or call (866) 376-6591.

Photographs copyright © 2019 by Eric Medsker
Interior design by Laura Palese
Cover design © Hachette Book Group

ISBN 978-0-316-42564-3
LCCN 2019945556

10 9 8 7 6 5 4 3 2 1

LSC-C

Printed in the United States of America

Contents

CHAPTER 2: Thirty-Four Soups & Sandwiches

CHAPTER 3: Forty-Two Chicken, Turkey & Duck Main Courses

CHAPTER 4: Forty-Five Beef, Pork, Veal & Lamb Main Courses

CHAPTER 7: Thirty-Four Desserts & Sweets

Introduction

Ready for the next home cooking revolution? It's begun! Millions of people are using air fryers to make crisp, crunchy, delicious fare without the mess, expense, or health concerns associated with deep-frying.

Maybe you already know all that and you're an air fryer fanatic looking for new recipes. Maybe you've heard about these hot new appliances that can make shatteringly crunchy treats with just a few teaspoons of oil—and you're wondering if all the fuss is justified. (It is.) Or maybe you've just unboxed your new fryer and don't know where to start. No worries: Whatever your level of expertise, we're here to guide you.

The promise of air-frying is pretty simple: crunchy food that can be healthier than deep-fried, is often easier to prepare, and certainly calls for less cleanup afterwards. Although guilt-free French fries are the grail, you can make a lot more in an air fryer. The machine is actually a countertop convection oven that can make nachos and pork loin roasts in about half the time they'd take in the oven or on the stove. And it's something like a turbocharged broiler that can cook a strip steak in less time than it takes to heat up the grill. It can even reheat a store-bought rotisserie chicken, frozen dumplings, or yesterday's leftovers in less time and with better results than your oven or microwave.

Sounds too good to be true? At first, all revolutions do.

And we know a thing or two about revolutions. Over the course of more than 30 cookbooks, we've left no stone unturned in our search for tools that can save you time, effort, and hassle in the kitchen. We've written pressure-cooker books galore, a slow-cooker book, and even one for making desserts in a turbo blender. So take it from us: The air fryer really delivers. Even better (and despite our love of gadgets), you won't need any other specialty appliances or fancy tools to complete the recipes in this book. We wanted to focus on what the air fryer does well, with no gimmicks or clickbait-y tricks. Listen, air fryers are like spouses. They can't do everything, even though we want them to.

And like spouses, they come in lots of sizes. Most air fryers run around 3 to 4 quarts, although there are small 2-quart models on the market and giant 6-quart ones. We recently spotted a 10-quart model! Despite this array of sizes, almost none of the recipes written for air fryers account for the differences in cooking time or portion size for each model. We get why. A recipe that handles the size variable is hard to write.

But *not impossible*. That's where we come in, the guys who've already written a slow-cooker book with the recipes sized for every pot and *The Instant Pot Bible* with recipes calibrated for every size of the beloved multi-cooker.

So we did it again: This is an air-fryer book with every recipe tailored for almost every size of air fryer on the market. We'll get to how this

works in the next section. But we've got you covered, no matter which model you've bought.

With one exception: Lately, a very small 1.2-quart air fryer has shown up in stores. It's so little, it won't even handle a large bone-in chicken breast or two standard chicken thighs. It can't make more than a few French fries at a time, not enough for one serving (at least in our opinion). Unfortunately, it can't handle most of the recipes in this book. Sorry about that. But this book is good to go for all the other machines, from 2-quart minis on up to the biggest counter-space eaters.

So here's what's ahead. There's an introduction laying out the rules of the road. **Don't skip the five-step how-to that comes next!** It will show you how to use this book for maximum success. After that, there are 305 recipes in seven chapters, plus more than 150 narrative recipes for delicious ways to take your meals to the next level, including everything from a sweet-tart Pineapple Barbecue Sauce (page 174) to a classic Cream Gravy (page 211), along with lots of easy salads and over a dozen specialty cocktails and mocktails.

You thought you were holding the only book you need to make hundreds of air fryer recipes for snacks, soups, sandwiches, mains, roasts, and even desserts. You didn't know there were still dozens more recipe ideas to go along with all that great, crunchy fare. The revolution just got better. Join us!

A Five-Step How-To for This Book

① How do these recipes work?
Each recipe has a title, a set of tags to categorize it (more on those just below), a headnote that explains the dish or offers a trick to making it a success, a chart with ingredients sized for almost all air fryers (more, too, on that below), a recipe method that details the preparation of the dish, and one or more *Then*s that offer you serving suggestions, simple salads, additional recipes for sauces and the like, or further ways to use whatever's just come out of the machine. Everything in the *Then* section is for what happens *after* you complete the main recipe.

You might think that we have omitted the serving size, which is usually found by the recipe name. Since our ingredient charts are sized for various air fryers, you'll end up with a varying number of servings, depending on how much your fryer can handle *and* what quantity of ingredients you decide to work with. Look for the number of servings for each specific amount of ingredients below the list of those ingredients in the charts. (Admittedly, this sounds a little confusing. As you'll see in a bit, you *can* make a smaller number of servings in a larger machine—or, of course, a large number of servings in a large machine. But you can *never* make a large number of servings in a small machine without working in discrete—and often time-consuming—batches.)

The tags at the start of each recipe offer you a set of specs to guide you as you flip through the book. Is this recipe *fast* or *easy*? Is it *vegetarian* or *vegan*, or can it be either with some simple modifications that we always include in the list of ingredients? Is it *gluten-free*, or can it be with some modifications, again always given in the ingredient list? And finally, *how many ingredients* does the recipe require? The most is thirteen; the fewest, one.

As to that "gluten-free" or "can be gluten-free" tag: Although we've marked ingredients that are notorious problems (for example: bread crumbs, bacon, sausage meat, purchased mayonnaise), there are others that are *generally* gluten-free (for example: Dijon mustard, hot red pepper sauce, barbecue sauce, and even rolled oats) but which in some brands may be found with glutens, gluten derivatives, or cross contamination from gluten-laced products that are made in the same facility. If you're extremely sensitive, we trust you know to watch out for these "maybes."

❷ Should I bother to read the headnotes?
Yes! They often offer a specific tip to make the recipe a success. Lots of the recipes have little secrets that we discovered in our testing. We've put those in the headnotes, too.

The headnotes also include explanations of potentially unfamiliar ingredients. And a few have optional narrative recipes for specialty items like garam masala on page 156 or our favorite jerk dried seasoning blend on page 298, if you want to make your own.

❸ How do I read the charts for the ingredients?
Safe to say, these are the most innovative part of the book. They require a little explanation.

The leftmost column is the list of ingredients the dish requires. In the columns to the right of the ingredients are the amounts for each based on *both* the size of the batch *and* what a specific model can hold.

We've divided all air fryers into three groups: *2-quart or larger, 3.5-quart or larger,* and *5.25-quart or larger.* Almost always, each gets a column in the chart. (More on the exceptions in a bit.)

The first column of amounts *can* be made in a small 2-quart machine *or* in any larger machine *if* you own a larger appliance but want to make a smaller amount .

The second column of quantities, the *3.5-quart or larger* category, tells you that you *cannot* make this batch in a machine smaller than 3.5 quarts but you *can* make this moderate number of servings in a 3.5-quart machine *or* in any larger machine.

And finally, the last designation, *5.25-quart or larger,* is for the biggest machines and the most number of servings. These larger quantities *cannot* be made in smaller machines *unless* you work in batches.

And you can. Sometimes. It's easy to make several batches of Shrimp "Scampi" (page 301) in a small machine since each batch only takes 5 minutes. It's *much* harder to make several batches of country-style pork ribs when each batch takes 30 minutes. Some hungry family members or friends will be hanging out a long time after others have finished and gone to bed.

Please allow us to state all that one more time, in one sentence, just for clarity's sake: **You *can* make a smaller quantity in a larger machine, but you *cannot* make a larger quantity in a smaller machine *unless* you work in batches.**

Here's why: An air fryer is essentially a countertop convection oven. It works by heated air currents—which means it *only* works well when there's good air circulation around the items in the basket. When food pieces crowd against each other, they do not cook evenly and—the real shame—they do not get crunchy. So space between those items is of supreme importance. Sometimes, you may see an ingredient in a list—let's say, a 1-pound bone-in chicken breast—and say to yourself, "Shoot, I could fit more of them in my little machine." Don't! We sized these recipes for air flow as well as volume.

Now that we've got the batch sizes down, let's look at the exceptions. A few recipes have their ingredients sized for only two types of machines—for example, for a small machine (or, as we stated, for a small batch in a larger machine) and for a large machine. In these recipes, the amount of air space in the medium-size machines was not enough to make an intermediary amount without crowding items against each other in the basket. So the chart has been written only for small or large quantities. If you have a 3.5-quart machine, you can either make the small quantity in your machine (just as if you had a smaller model) or prepare the larger quantity and air-fry it *in batches*.

In a *very* few recipes, there's only one column for all machines. In these recipes, we assume you *must* air-fry in batches, even in the largest models. So these recipes have a one-size-fits-all approach, with the only variable being the number of times you'll have to air-fry something, remove it, and air-fry more of it in subsequent batches.

Some of the charts' ingredient sizes have been a matter of simple math, despite our testing variations galore. Others are trickier because, say, the flavor of garlic powder compounds exponentially. You can't just multiply it up for a bigger batch without killing off all the sexy vampires in your life. That said, cooking isn't rocket surgery (or brain science). If you like a little more garlic, have at it. (Baking, however, is another matter. Follow these recipes scrupulously.)

❹ Do I set the time from when I start to heat the machine?
Many recipes outside of this book tell you to fill the basket, put it in the machine, and turn the machine on. *Ours do not.* Air-fried foods come out better if they start in a hot machine. Coatings set more quickly for a better crunch; marinades caramelize more quickly for deeper flavor.

In testing, we put a breaded pork chop in a cold machine, turned it on, and watched the fan blow the panko coating off the chop and onto the basket's walls. But such pork-chop carnage didn't happen when the machine was first heated. In fact, it *never* happened when the machine was properly heated. Therefore, our timings are almost always set, not from when you turn the machine on, but from when you put something in the basket or a pan to cook. (There are a couple of rare exceptions in the book, but we'll be careful to call them out.)

Don't *solely* trust the timings we give. We also offer visual cues to tell you when your food is done. Open the drawer or the door. Check the basket or tray. See how things are cooking. Calibrations may vary among models. Trust your eyes. And when necessary, use an instant-read meat thermometer to ensure your food is safe to eat (more on that below).

And while we're on questions of timing, pay attention to a recipe's last step about letting foods rest when they come out of an air fryer. Such advice may seem like cookbook boilerplate. It's not. What comes out of the air fryer is superheated. A crisp crust needs to set; the juices need to reincorporate into a cut of meat. We'll let you know if you need to wait a couple of minutes, 5 minutes, 10 minutes, or more. For the best meal, don't cheat this step.

On the other hand, don't wait too long before digging in. Many coatings get soggy after half an hour, sometimes even after 15 minutes. Like anything deep-fried, air-fried food is crunchy for a bit, then it's sadly not. In most cases, plan on enjoying the meal pretty soon after you make it. Or if you've got tardy friends or a family member kept at the office past dinnertime, re-air-fry an item at the same temperature it was cooked at for 2 to 3 minutes to crisp it again.

⑤ How do I use the *Then* after each recipe? These bullet points are often serving suggestions. But they also include almost 160 optional narrative recipes that you *can*—but don't have to—add on to the main recipe. Many of these additional recipes will go with more than one dish in this book. For example, the Jalapeño Jam (page 58) is welcome with lots of snacky fare. We hope you'll find many more uses for this "bonus" content: 22 dips, almost 40 condiments and sauces, 34 salads, 16 cocktails and mocktails, and lots more.

The Sixteen Rules of the Road

① We use words like "fried," "roasted," and "barbecued" with a knowing wink.
We mean that something has a "fried" texture or a "roasted" feel or a "barbecued" flavor, although nothing in this book is "fried" or "barbecued" in the traditional sense. If you want to get technical, everything in this book is "convection baked," although the machine's convection fan is more powerful than the one in a convection oven— which is why the air fryer is a great tool for quicker cooking.

② Use the appropriate cooking fats.
There's a myth that air-frying doesn't require additional fat. Not true. Sure, you *can* cook a plain chicken breast in the machine. We hope you enjoy your chicken shards. Successfully air-fried foods require some fat, *but not much*. You'll see over and over that we ask you to spray food with vegetable oil, olive oil, or (rarely) coconut oil. This spritz of oil, less than 1 teaspoon per serving in most cases, helps set the coating, get it crunchy, and protect the food underneath. That little bit of oil also adds lots of flavor because it carries forward the notes from the herbs and spices in the coating. And the smidgen of oil allows the food to cook more evenly. Don't neglect that little bit of fat, but at the same time . . .

③ Almost never use aerosol nonstick sprays.
The problem with aerosol sprays is that they're not very directional. Bits of oil spew out in a fan pattern, most of it getting on the target food but some of it ending up all over the innards of an air fryer. That residual oil can start to gunk up the machine. It's the main reason an air fryer will start to smoke (more on that below). And there's some evidence that over time the propellants—that is, the chemicals that create the aerosol spray—may degrade the nonstick coating on the machine's basket. No manufacturer recommends these sprays. Take their word for it. Which means you should . . .

④ Buy little spritzer bottles for oils.
We have two on our counter right now: one for vegetable oil and one for olive oil. We used them constantly in testing the recipes for this book.

Ours are small, hand-sized plastic bottles with a bulbous body and a hand-pump spritzer. We got them for about a buck each at a dollar store. Yes, you can find more expensive ones. They'll work just as well. But we cheaped out and haven't noticed any difference. We filled them with their respective oils, then wrote on each with an indelible marker so we'd know which was which.

The one exception is for coconut oil spray. Most coconut oil is solid at room temperature. Unfortunately, we had to use an aerosol can to get the fat onto whatever we were cooking. In this case, make sure you spray the coconut oil away from the machine and onto the food itself.

That said, filling our two little spritzers with our own oil gave us another benefit over most aerosol cans. Let's face it: The oil in many aerosol sprays is not of the highest quality. Although we didn't put an expensive olive oil in our spritzer, the oil was still better than the stuff in most commercially packaged cans.

We can't stress how important these spritzers are. Unfortunately (or really, fortunately for your health), most of the coatings in this book are low-fat—which means they're delicate and their ingredients don't cohere as easily with each other or even adhere to the food underneath as readily as high-fat coatings would. You can't really brush oil onto these coatings without knocking them off. If you've only got a commercially packaged nonstick spray, go ahead and use it until you can get online and order a spritzer bottle or two.

And while we're on the matter of spritzers (or even aerosol sprays)...

❺ Never spray oil directly into the basket while it's set in the machine.
For one thing, you'll get oil all over the inside of the drawer and other internal parts. You'll soon have a machine that sets off the fire alarm.

What's more, spraying oil into the machine is dangerous. Would you do so into a 400°F oven? Absolutely not. And if you do use an aerosol spray (which, except for coconut oil, you shouldn't!), you're really asking for a nasty burn, as the atomized oil can easily ignite.

Discussing the matter of spraying oil actually brings us to the question of smoking, the bane of air-frying. We learned lots of lessons while we were testing these recipes but the most important one was this: **Once we stopped spraying food with oil as it sat in the basket, our machine stopped smoking**. The problem wasn't the food. It was the residual oil on the basket and even inside the machine. The proper order of operation is 1) spray the food (if necessary), *then* 2) set it in the basket.

Air fryers don't smoke on their own. If yours does, it's got a serious mechanical problem. Unplug it immediately and return it. Air fryers smoke because there's built-up oil and food gunk in the machine. You must clean it after every use. And you must also never spray any food while it's in the basket.

True, a few high-fat coatings do produce some smoke. And while we've mostly opted for lower-fat coatings, we did go all out a few times. For high-fat coatings, we opened a window and turned on the stove vent.

❻ Toaster oven–style air fryers work a bit differently than the more standard drawer-style models.
Most toaster oven–style air fryers have racks inside, some of which can be swapped out for other attachments. For almost every recipe in this book, slip the basket attachment into the slot nearest the middle of the machine. Then slip a tray into a lower slot to catch the inevitable drips.

The few exceptions are recipes that use cake pans. In these, you'll need to skip the basket attachment and set one of the trays or racks lower in the machine so the cake pan will fit comfortably with some head space left over. In any event, read your instruction manual to operate your appliance properly. Better yet, read the manual, then go online and watch the manufacturer's instructional videos.

❼ Heat the air fryer to the appropriate temperature.

Sounds easy, right? Unfortunately, it isn't, at least not for a book that's been designed to cover a wide array of models. Here's the problem: Some air fryers only offer temperatures in 10°F increments, not 5°F: 300°F, 310°F, 320°F, etc. And a few air fryers only offer temperatures in 30°F increments: 300°F, 330°F, 360°F, etc. So when we call for 325°F, we have to mark an alternate temperature in a parenthetical note like this: *With the basket (or basket attachment) in the air fryer, heat it to 400°F (or 390°F, if that's the closest setting)*. And sometimes, things get a little more confusing: *With the basket (or basket attachment) in the air fryer, heat it to 375°F (or 370°F or 360°F, if one of these is the closest setting)*.

Always go with the first temperature, if you can. Go with the parenthetical temperature only if you must. If the lower temperature makes a significant difference, we modify the cook time later in the recipe.

❽ Use pans approved for the air fryer (or a high-heat convection oven).

In a few recipes, we call for round or square baking pans, sized to fit into the machine you have on your counter. Make sure your cookware is approved for cooking in this high-heat environment. Most glazes are not. Much stoneware is not. Serving dishes and platters mostly are not. We assume you're using metal cake or baking pans. But even these may have a coating that should not be exposed to 400°F temperatures. Check your brand to be sure.

❾ Use more flour and dry coating ingredients than you need.

Food waste is a legitimate issue; but we can't solve it in one section of these recipes. You need *a lot* of flour, cornmeal, crushed corn chips (just wait), or crushed pork rinds (seriously, just wait) to get a good coating on a chicken thigh or a fish fillet. You have to use more of the dry stuff than merely coats the food because 1) some of the coating mixture gets soggy and unusable after repeated dips into it and 2) you need to be able to turn the food several times in the dry ingredients with room to spare. So yes, we call for, say, ⅓ cup all-purpose flour when you really only need 1½ tablespoons to coat two pork chops. The abundance will allow you to work efficiently and assure that the meat or vegetable or Twinkie (yup) is well coated before it gets dipped into the wet ingredient that will turn that flour (or cookie crumbs) into an irresistible coating. We hope you'll forgive this waste for the promise of crunch. Hey, at least you're not wasting all the oil that deep-frying requires.

❿ Use the kind of bread crumb we list in the ingredients.

We work with five types: 1) plain dried bread crumbs; 2) seasoned Italian-style dried bread crumbs; 3) plain panko bread crumbs; 4) seasoned panko bread crumbs; and 5) fresh bread crumbs (in only one recipe and one variation of one recipe). That's not counting other kinds of crumbs you might use as a coating, like potato chip crumbles. (See the chart on page 21.)

Let's start at the top: **plain dried bread crumbs**. You can make your own, although it's a pain. To do so, toast 4 to 8 slices of old but not stale white bread. We find that most bread is at the right stage after three days at room temperature (but sealed up, as if we were saving the bread for toast). Toast this bread lightly. Tear up the slices and either grate them through the large holes of a box grater or pulse them in a food processor until coarsely ground. Spread these bread crumbs on a large lipped baking sheet and bake in a 200°F oven for 30 minutes. Stir well and continue baking until evenly browned, 20 to 40 minutes more. (The exact timing will depend on the moisture content of the bread.) Cool the crumbs on the baking sheet for 20 minutes or up to 1 hour, then pour these bread crumbs into a food processor and pulse until they are about the consistency of coarse sand. Cool completely and store in a sealed container at room temperature for 3 days or in the freezer for up to 3 months. (Use them right out of the freezer for these recipes.)

See what we mean: They're a pain to make. That's why we used purchased dried bread crumbs for every recipe we tested. That said, purchased dried bread crumbs vary dramatically in quality. You'll do yourself a big favor by spending ten or fifteen bucks and taste-testing a few different brands. Some are wheaty; some, sweet; some, flavorless. You'll soon know exactly which brand you prefer.

The only sort of **seasoned dried bread crumbs** we call for are *Italian-style*, meaning there are Italian herbs and probably garlic powder in the mix.

Panko bread crumbs are a specialty product, once a Japanese staple, now an international one. Panko was traditionally made from bread baked on electrical wires that dried it out. But not anymore. These days, panko mostly means a slightly larger, much paler, softer version of dried bread crumbs.

Seasoned panko bread crumbs have salt and dried spices in the mix. Most are Italian-style; a few are more Asian in their flavors. In truth, you can use any sort of seasoned panko bread crumb here, although we tested all these recipes using the ones with Italian-style flavorings.

Finally, one bit of bad news: Bread crumbs, even dried ones, go stale just like bread. Sure, the processed ones last longer, maybe a month or more. But they eventually get a funky smell. No amount of dried herbs and good oils can overcome the taste of stale bread crumbs.

⓫ Space food out in the air fryer's basket or on the baking tray.

As we've indicated, air has to flow around food for it to get crunchy. Yes, there are exceptions, as you'll see in the recipes. And sometimes, we can take care of the problem of air flow around lots of ingredients (let's say, French fries) by tossing the things in the basket once (or several times) to rearrange them during cooking. But most things need space. We'll let you know if that amount of space is set, mostly when it comes to larger items that need a little extra room between them for proper air flow—say, 1 inch between larger bone-in chicken thighs. But the operative norm is often space itself without a fussy, exact designation. Look at the big surface area of the air fryer's basket. Use all of it.

⓬ Shake or rearrange items in the basket as necessary—or sometimes not at all.

There are two ways to air-fry food: *undisturbed,* or *tossing and rearranging what's in the basket*. We'll always indicate which is the method for a specific recipe.

You air-fry something undisturbed because the coating is very delicate, or the food gets enough air flow around it to need no further adjustments, or the food is in the air fryer such a short amount of time that messing with it would be beside the point.

When it comes to tossing and rearranging items in the basket, you're trying to get all surfaces exposed to the hot air. With a big pile of sweet potato fries or a bunch of pita chips, the point is to rearrange the items so they cook evenly and/or get crisp evenly. When we were testing recipes, we often pulled the basket out of the machine and tossed the basket like a chef with a skillet at the stove. You don't have to be so TV ready. (Or so chef coordinated.) You can use nonstick-safe kitchen tongs or even silicone baking mitts to rearrange the items in the basket or on the tray.

Here's the basic rule: bottom on top. And here's another: Use your eyes. In most cases, if something has browned and/or crisp, it's now okay to be covered. If it hasn't, it should stay exposed to the hot air.

You'll notice that sometimes we're very precise about this tossing and rearranging step: *tossing and rearranging at the 4- and 8-minute marks* or perhaps *tossing and rearranging after 5 minutes*. But at other times, we're loosey-goosey: *tossing and rearranging halfway through*. In the latter case, we're working with less temperamental items that can be exposed to the currents a minute more here, a minute less there.

⓭ Remember that an air fryer is as hot as your oven.
Everything is superheated inside, even the drawer and the basket. Most models have handles that are heat resistant. But always use hot pads for safety's sake. Keep children and furry well-wishers out of the way.

We did invest in one "gadget" as we tested these recipes: silicone baking mitts. They were invaluable because we could grab hot steaks out of the basket or gently pick up crusted chicken wings to transfer them to a wire rack. Even better, we clean the mitts with dishwashing soap in the sink. In fact, ours can even go in the washing machine on a cold cycle.

⓮ Clean the air fryer after every use.
We've already covered this a bit elsewhere, but it bears repeating. Grease builds up, even from low-fat foods. A thin coating of caked-on oil is the main reason your machine might smoke. Because we can't give the cleaning specifics for every model, read your instruction manual. A dirty machine is a smoke alarm nightmare.

⓯ Don't forget that an air fryer can reheat dinner in minutes.
If you bring a rotisserie chicken home from the store, you can cut it into quarters or smaller parts and heat these up in the basket for 5 minutes at 400°F. The air fryer is often as fast as the microwave. Better yet, it won't turn food gummy. Needless to say, you can't put a plate of food in an air fryer basket to heat it up. The plate won't fit and is probably not safe for an air fryer's intense heat. In like manner, don't reheat things in Tupperware or plastic containers. Instead, just put quesadillas or egg rolls right in the basket and let the machine do its thing.

⓰ And finally, one quirky bit of advice: You can indeed refreeze frozen puff pastry.
Why don't people know this? As long as you've thawed the puff pastry in the fridge and not on the counter, and as long as you've kept it wrapped until you're ready to use it, you can indeed rewrap any leftovers and refreeze them. No, they will not bake up quite as puffy after the second thawing. And all-butter puff pastry suffers a little more than one made with vegetable shortening. But they'll all work

fine for our purposes in this book. (Unfortunately, you can't then re-refreeze puff pastry—one refreezing and the puff pastry's done after the next use.)

By the way, the same goes for phyllo dough: Refreeze it if you've thawed it in the fridge and kept it covered. But once it dries out, it can't be refrozen. (And it's never much good after a third freezing.)

Four Special Tools

As we've stated, we don't call for many specialty gadgets. That said, we repeatedly call for these four common kitchen tools.

❶ Nonstick-safe kitchen tongs

Food in the machine will burn you as quickly as food in a 400°F oven. You need to be able to get a grip on a piece of pork or a scallop to get it out of the basket when the fare is ready. Sometimes, we tell you to dump the contents of the basket onto a wire rack, especially if the items do not have a delicate coating or are themselves fairly sturdy (like the shishito peppers on page 29 or falafel balls on page 146). But we *highly* recommend that you get kitchen tongs with nonstick-safe pinchers for everything else. Yes, these tongs will protect the nonstick coating on the basket. More importantly, the pinchers are a little more cushioned (with silicone or plastic edges) so they won't as easily break crisp coatings apart. Metal tongs can ruin the nonstick coating *and* shred your meal.

❷ A nonstick-safe spatula

Some items are too delicate to get out of the basket with tongs. These items must be lifted out with a spatula—and one that's nonstick-safe, to boot, given the coating on almost all baskets. Use a flatware fork or kitchen tongs in the other hand for balance.

❸ An instant-read meat thermometer

This tool is the *only* way to tell if proteins are cooked through. No amount of prodding a steak will tell you whether it's done, no matter what TV chefs say. Notice the professionals in their kitchens. They carry a meat thermometer in their chef's coats. And for good reason: No one should cut into a lamb chop to check if it's done, thereby destroying that crunchy coating or releasing the juices before the cut's ready to be enjoyed. We'll tell you in the recipes when we believe this thermometer is necessary.

❹ A wire cooling rack

Hot air-fried foods continue to release steam—the enemy of crispness—even when they've been removed from the machine. If you set a perfect chicken thigh or a crunchy air-fried shrimp on a serving plate, steam will turn the underside coating gummy. You went to too much effort for that! So invest in a wire rack that can hold foods as they cool with proper air circulation underneath. The best racks are a wire mesh, not just wire slats between which small items can sag or fall through.

A Crumb Equivalency Chart

In the recipes, we give you a weight equivalent for the various sorts of crumbs we use to coat air-fried food. In other words, we tell you how much of the original item you need (say, gingersnap cookies) to produce a certain amount of crumbs. But here's a handy chart that puts all that information in one place.

The best way to make crumbs is either in a food processor (but take care that you make *crumbs*, not powder; we'll often give you a visual cue for how finely ground the crumbs should look) or in a heavy zip-closed plastic bag that you roll over with a rolling pin or bash (lightly!) with the bottom of a small heavy saucepan or the smooth side of a meat mallet, repeatedly turning the bag over, as well as this way and that, to ensure everything is evenly pulverized. You can often eyeball the weight amount of the original ingredient (before it's crushed) by figuring how much of the bag or box you have in hand that would make the appropriate number of ounces. Close enough is fair enough, although this chart will help you be absurdly accurate.

Take note: Corn flake crumbs and graham cracker crumbs are widely available in boxes at the supermarket, with gluten-free alternatives to boot.

CRUMB EQUIVALENCIES

	This much of its weight	yields this volume of crumbs
Corn flake cereal	3 ounces	1 cup
Cheerios or round oat cereal	3 ounces	1 cup
Cheetos or cheese puffs	2 ounces	1¼ cups
Doritos or other corn tortilla chips	4 ounces (¼ pound)	1 cup
Fritos or similar corn chips	4 ounces (¼ pound)	¾ cup
Gingersnaps	6 ounces	1 cup
Graham crackers	4¾ ounces	1 cup
Nilla wafers or other vanilla wafer cookies	4 ounces (¼ pound)	1 cup
Potato chips	4 ounces (¼ pound)	1 cup
Pretzels	4 ounces (¼ pound)	1 cup
Rice Krispies or other rice-puff cereal	2½ ounces	¾ cup

In Conclusion ...

There's not a lot to say except "Happy air-frying." The promise of crunch is too alluring to wait any longer.

If you've got further questions, contact us through our website: bruceandmark.com. Or look us up on Facebook (Bruce Weinstein from New York, New York, and Mark Scarbrough from Dallas, Texas), on Twitter (@bruceweinstein and @markscarbrough), and/or on Instagram (@bruceaweinstein and @markscarbrough). And check out our YouTube channel, *Cooking with Bruce and Mark,* for air-frying videos, many of which take on specific recipes in this book. We'd love to hear from you.

1

SIXTY-FOUR

Nibbles, Snacks & Appetizers

We've got a hunch that recipes like these are the main reason you bought an air fryer. Eggplant fries, crisp spring rolls, kale chips, and warm, spicy chickpeas: These alone are enough for anyone to spring for this appliance.

But we take the notion of snacks further. Much further. All the way to our arancini, crunchy rice balls stuffed with mozzarella or meatballs. To Scotch eggs and shawarma bites, pub food to go with your favorite beer. To dip and spreads like our fine rendition of **Baba Ghanouj** (page 79) or our new take on caponata (page 82). To throwback tiki-bar classics like **Crab Rangoon** (page 65) as well as state fair–inspired favorites like **Corn Dog Bites** (page 43). And to surprises like **Pão de Queijo** (page 75), the gluten-free cheese balls from Brazil. Or **Smoked Whitefish Spread** (page 84), better (we dare say) than the stuff at your local deli.

No wonder, then, that this chapter is the longest in the book! It's made for nibblers and grazers, created with patios in mind, crafted for summer afternoons, and perfect for cocktails of all sorts. We have plenty of additional recipes in the *Then* sections of the larger recipes, even mocktails for those of us who don't imbibe.

If you're hankering for a snack, you're either hungry now or prepping like mad to feed your company, whether drop-ins, invited guests, or weekend squatters. (Living two hours from New York City, we know about those!) So this chapter is about instant gratification. Sure, you can't stuff an egg roll or a Middle Eastern phyllo roll without a little work. But most of these recipes are straightforward: pretzel bites, vegetable chips, pizzas with purchased dough, or crunchy tortellini nibbles made with a bag of the frozen stuffed pasta.

In other words, gratification just got, um, *instant-er*, thanks to the air fryer, which heats up in minutes and cooks things more quickly than a standard oven. And gratification got *better*, too, because these snacks are by and large healthier than their deep-fried counterparts.

Although we've classified everything here as a small bite, some recipes produce more substantial fare. A few are an easy dinner, particularly with a prepared salad or two from the supermarket. We'll let you know which can easily move beyond deck food, which can be combined for a fuller meal, and which make for tasty, light fare so you can skip a sit-down dinner and keep your day going long after you've settled in for the evening.

See: We *were* right. These recipes *are* why you got an air fryer.

Pita Chips

Bagged pita chips can be oily and salty, without much flavor other than their (admittedly great) crunch. The air fryer to the rescue! It can render wheaty pita rounds into terrific, flavorful chips.

That is, with one small trick: Use *pocketless* pita bread. Its thicker edges won't curl and burn in the machine's hot sirocco whirl.

You *must* spray the rounds with oil. Otherwise, they'll dry out—and blacken. A little oil also helps the salt stick. Use any sort of salt you like, even a salt-free spice blend substitute. Or go all out and use a flavored salt like lemon-pepper seasoning. Treat this recipe as a road map for your signature chips.

Note that this ingredient chart is only for two sizes of air fryers. The pita wedges need to be able to experience the hot air flow. Very large air fryers with deep baskets can indeed hold more pita wedges than this recipe calls for. Unfortunately, the wedges are then piled so high that they impede the air and never get crisp, no matter how much shaking and rearranging you do during cooking.

INGREDIENTS	2-quart or larger air fryer	3.5-quart or larger air fryer
Pocketless pita bread	1 round	2 rounds
Olive oil spray or any flavor spray you prefer, even coconut oil spray	As needed	As needed
Fine sea salt, garlic salt, onion salt, or other flavored salt	Up to ½ teaspoon	Up to 1 teaspoon
MAKES	8 chips	16 chips

1. With the basket (or basket attachment) in the air fryer, heat it to 400°F (or 390°F, if that's the closest setting).

2. Lightly coat the pita round(s) on both sides with olive oil spray, then lightly sprinkle each side with salt.

3. Cut each coated pita round into 8 even wedges. Lay these in the basket in as close to a single even layer as possible. Many will overlap or even be on top of each other, depending on the exact size of your machine.

4. Air-fry for 6 minutes, shaking the basket and rearranging the wedges at the 2- and 4-minute marks, until the wedges are crisp and brown. Turn them out onto a wire rack to cool a few minutes or to room temperature before digging in.

Then...

- Make LEMONY HUMMUS as a dip. Drain and rinse *one 15-ounce can chickpeas*. Put the chickpeas in a large blender or a food processor with *¼ cup tahini (see page 79), ¼ cup olive oil, 2 teaspoons finely grated lemon zest, ¼ cup lemon juice, 2 peeled medium garlic cloves or 2 teaspoons minced garlic, ½ teaspoon table salt*, and *½ teaspoon ground black pepper*. Cover and blend or process until smooth, stopping the machine at least once to scrape down the inside of the canister.

- Or serve them with **Muhamarra** (page 25) or **Sriracha-Yogurt Dip** (page 36).

- Or serve these chips with room-temperature Brie or soft goat cheese.

- Or float the edges in **Blistered Tomato Soup** (page 106).

Bagel Chips

FAST / EASY / VEGAN / 2 INGREDIENTS

What could be easier or more satisfying than making your own bagel chips? These are a little thicker than the standard, supermarket varieties. They'll be better able to stand up to dips and spreads. Once cooled, they can be sealed in a zip-closed plastic bag and stored at room temperature for up to 2 days (provided the humidity's low).

One important note: Do not use bagels with blueberries, raisins, or other fruit; or those with chocolate chips. These items will burn in the air fryer as the bagel chips dry out. And don't use bagels with seed or spice coatings like a poppy seed bagel or an everything bagel. These seeds and spices will burn before the chip is crisp.

INGREDIENTS	2-quart or larger air fryer	3.5-quart or larger air fryer	5.25-quart or larger air fryer
Plain, whole-wheat, pumpernickel, or salt bagel(s)	1	2	3
Vegetable oil or olive oil spray	As needed	As needed	As needed
MAKES	2 servings	3 servings	4 servings

1. With the basket (or basket attachment) in the air fryer, heat it to 400°F (or 390°F, if that's the closest setting).

2. Lay a bagel flat on a cutting board. Slice it across its circular surface into ⅛-inch-wide strips. Dump these strips into a bowl; make more bagel strips as needed. (Some strips will be cut through the hole and thus end up as two smaller strips; some will be short because they are at one end or the other as you're cutting across the bagel.)

3. Lightly coat the strips with vegetable or olive oil spray, toss well, and coat again (or a couple of times more), tossing until every piece is evenly coated but not greasy.

4. Pour the strips into the basket. Air-fry, tossing the basket and rearranging the strips three or four times, for 8 minutes, or until lightly browned, even a little blackened at the edges. Watch out: The chips can burn quickly. Do not step away from the machine.

5. When the chips are ready, pour them onto a wire rack. Cool for a few minutes before serving warm. Or cool to room temperature, about 1 hour.

Then...

- Serve these chips with a Middle Eastern favorite: MUHAMARRA. Place *¾ cup walnut pieces or whole almonds, 3 tablespoons olive oil, 1 jarred roasted red pepper, 1 small shallot (peeled and quartered), ½ small pocketless pita bread round (torn to bits), 1 tablespoon balsamic vinegar, 1 teaspoon ground cumin, up to 1 teaspoon table salt,* and *up to 1 teaspoon red pepper flakes* in a food processor. Cover and process until almost smooth, just a little grainy, stopping the machine at least once to scrape down the inside of the canister.

- Try these bagel chips with **Chimichurri** (page 94), **Tangy Jalapeño Dip** (page 151), or **Basil and Red Pepper Mayonnaise** (page 273).

- For a fast appetizer, smear the chips with a little cream cheese, then top each with a small piece of smoked salmon.

Sweet-and-Salty Pretzels

FAST / EASY / 5 INGREDIENTS

When we were teenagers in the '70s, everyone served toasted pretzel nuggets at their mod parties—except no one used smoked paprika in the coating, because it was unknown in most of North America back then. Too bad, because it adds a mild smoky flavor to all that crunch.

Since pretzel nuggets can be a little hard to measure by volume, err on the side of a rounded cup, rather than a scant one.

Watch the nuggets carefully as they air-fry. The coating should be quite brown but there's a fine line between *done* and *burned*.

Unfortunately, gluten-free pretzel "thins" will not work in this recipe.

INGREDIENTS	2-quart or larger air fryer	3.5-quart or larger air fryer	5.25-quart or larger air fryer
Plain pretzel nuggets	1 cup	2 cups	3 cups
Worcestershire sauce	1½ teaspoons	1 tablespoon	1½ tablespoons
Granulated white sugar	1 teaspoon	2 teaspoons	1 tablespoon
Mild smoked paprika	½ teaspoon	1 teaspoon	1½ teaspoons
Garlic or onion powder	¼ teaspoon	½ teaspoon	Rounded ½ teaspoon
MAKES	*2 servings*	*4 servings*	*6 servings*

1. With the basket (or basket attachment) in the air fryer, heat it to 350°F (or 360°F, if that's the closest setting).

2. Put the pretzel nuggets, Worcestershire sauce, sugar, smoked paprika, and garlic or onion powder in a large bowl. Toss gently until the nuggets are well coated.

3. When the machine is at temperature, pour the nuggets into the basket, spreading them into as close to a single layer as possible. Air-fry, shaking the basket three or four times to rearrange the nuggets, for 5 minutes, or until the nuggets are toasted and aromatic. Although the coating will darken, don't let it burn, especially if the machine's temperature is 360°F.

4. Pour the nuggets onto a wire rack and gently spread them into one layer. (A rubber spatula does a good job.) Cool for 5 minutes before serving.

Then...

- For a SPICY MUSTARD DIP with these nuggets, mix *regular, low-fat, or fat-free mayonnaise* and *hot brown mustard* in a 2-to-1 ratio by volume, adding *a little minced red onion* and/or *a pinch of garlic powder*, if desired.

- We also love to dip these into a sauce that mimics the one served at Shake Shack (page 134).

- Use these nuggets as croutons in any well-stocked, full-flavored salad, such as **Jicama and Mango Salad** (page 279).

See photo in insert.

Crunchy Spicy Chickpeas

EASY / VEGAN / GLUTEN-FREE / 4 INGREDIENTS

There may be no better accompaniment to a cold beer or a glass of iced tea than these warm chickpeas, especially when the sunlight is long in the sky. Although we suggest a Cajun or jerk dried seasoning blend, use just about any dried spice blend you like, even **curry powder** (see page 363 for a homemade blend) or **garam masala** (see page 156 for an explanation and a homemade blend). But avoid spice blends made with dried leafy herbs. These can singe in the intense heat without a more protective coating than the one offered here.

INGREDIENTS	2-quart or larger air fryer	3.5-quart or larger air fryer	5.25-quart or larger air fryer
Canned chickpeas, drained and rinsed	1¾ cups (one 15-ounce can)	2½ cups	3½ cups (two 15-ounce cans)
Vegetable or canola oil	1½ tablespoons	2½ tablespoons	3 tablespoons
Cajun or jerk dried seasoning blend (see page 279 for a Cajun blend, page 298 for a jerk blend)	up to 2 teaspoons	up to 1 tablespoon	up to 1½ tablespoons
Table salt (optional)	up to ½ teaspoon	up to ¾ teaspoon	up to 1 teaspoon
MAKES	*4 servings*	*6 servings*	*8 servings*

1. With the basket (or basket attachment) in the air fryer, heat it to 400°F (or 390°F, if that's the closest setting).

2. Toss the chickpeas, oil, seasoning blend, and salt (if using) in a large bowl until the chickpeas are evenly coated.

3. When the machine is at temperature, pour the chickpeas into the basket. Air-fry for 12 minutes, removing the basket at the 4- and 8-minute marks to toss and rearrange the chickpeas, until very aromatic and perhaps sizzling but not burned.

4. Pour the chickpeas into a large serving bowl. Cool for a couple of minutes, gently stirring once, before you dive in.

Then...

- These chickpeas are great with PERFECT FROZEN DAIQUIRIS. For two drinks, put *3 cups (about 13 ounces) ice* in a large blender, then add *4 ounces (½ cup) silver rum, 2½ ounces (5 tablespoons) lime juice, 1 ounce (2 tablespoons) Triple Sec,* and *1 tablespoon granulated white sugar, preferably superfine.* Cover and blend until slushy, shaking the canister as needed to get the ice to blend.

- Sprinkle the crunchy chickpeas over baked potatoes with sour cream.

- Or use the chickpeas as a garnish on **Creamy Roasted Potato and Bacon Soup** (page 102).

- Or use them as a garnish on top of stews or braises, particularly those with a Middle Eastern bent, like a tagine (which, with these chickpeas, would be mind blowing).

Warm and Salty Edamame

FAST / EASY / VEGAN / GLUTEN-FREE / 3 INGREDIENTS

Edamame—or soy beans—are a starter at many Japanese American restaurants. They're flavorfully sweet, a little herbaceous, and salty (mostly thanks to the salt on the exterior of the fibrous pods). Don't eat those pods. Put one in your mouth, then close your teeth so that one little bit sticks out. Pull the pod through your teeth, catching some of its salt as you release the sweet, green soy beans inside. Have a Japanese beer like Kirin Ichiban on hand!

And here's a time-saving hack: you can use unshelled edamame straight from the freezer for this recipe. If so, increase the air-frying time to 10 minutes.

INGREDIENTS	2-quart or larger air fryer	3.5-quart or larger air fryer	5.25-quart or larger air fryer
Unshelled edamame	¾ pound	1 pound	1½ pounds
Vegetable oil spray	As needed	As needed	As needed
Coarse sea salt or kosher salt	½ teaspoon	¾ teaspoon	1 teaspoon
MAKES	3 servings	4 or 5 servings	6 servings

1. With the basket (or basket attachment) in the air fryer, heat it to 400°F (or 390°F, if that's the closest setting).

2. Place the edamame in a large bowl and lightly coat them with vegetable oil spray. Toss well, spray again, and toss until they are evenly coated.

3. When the machine is at temperature, pour the edamame into the basket and air-fry, tossing the basket quite often to rearrange the edamame, for 7 minutes, or until warm and aromatic. (Air-fry for 10 minutes if the edamame were frozen and not thawed.)

4. Pour the edamame into a bowl and sprinkle the salt on top. Toss well, then set aside for a couple of minutes before serving with an empty bowl on the side for the pods.

Then...

- Gussy up the pods before air-frying them by tossing them with the salt and a little bit of a thin spicy or sweet condiment like sriracha, a hot red pepper sauce, balsamic vinegar, Thai sweet chili sauce, or pomegranate molasses (all of which can be gluten-free, if a concern). There's no need to spray the pods before air-frying with the addition of these wet coatings. If you use one of these wet coatings, you must shake the basket and rearrange the pods at least once a minute as they cook because the sugars in the condiments can begin to burn.

Blistered Shishito Peppers

FAST / EASY / VEGAN / GLUTEN-FREE / 3 INGREDIENTS

Shishito peppers are seasonal, available only in the summer months in North America (unless you shop at a high-end market that imports them all year). The peppers make a terrific snack before dinner: mildly spicy, a little sweet, and with a slight bitter edge, which we tame with lemon juice. Eat them seeds and all, right down to the stem. But keep in mind that about one in ten shishitos can be absurdly hot. The burn will be tamed by whole milk, not water, iced tea, or even beer.

INGREDIENTS	2-quart or larger air fryer	3.5-quart or larger air fryer	5.25-quart or larger air fryer
Shishito peppers	¼ pound (about 12)	6 ounces (about 18)	½ pound (about 24)
Vegetable oil spray	As needed	As needed	As needed
Coarse sea or kosher salt and lemon wedges	For garnishing	For garnishing	For garnishing
MAKES	2 servings	3 servings	4 servings

1. With the basket (or basket attachment) in the air fryer, heat it to 400°F (or 390°F, if that's the closest setting).

2. Put the peppers in a bowl and lightly coat them with vegetable oil spray. Toss gently, spray again, and toss until the peppers are glistening but not drenched.

3. Pour the peppers into the basket, spread them into as close to one layer as you can, and air-fry for 5 minutes, tossing and rearranging the peppers at the 2- and 4-minute marks, until the peppers are blistered and even blackened in spots.

4. Pour the peppers into a bowl, add salt to taste, and toss gently. Serve the peppers with lemon wedges to squeeze over them.

Then...

- Skip the salt and lemon juice garnishes. Instead, drizzle the blistered peppers with bottled yuzu sauce.

- Or make EASY HOMEMADE YUZU DRESSING by whisking *1½ tablespoons regular or low-sodium soy sauce or gluten-free tamari sauce, 1½ tablespoons mirin (see page 176), 1 tablespoon lemon juice, 2 teaspoons minced peeled fresh ginger, 1½ teaspoons toasted sesame oil,* and *up to 1 teaspoon wasabi paste* in a small bowl.

- Or try them with **Sriracha-Yogurt Dip** (page 36) or **Tangy Goat Cheese Dip** (page 230).

Sweet Chili Peanuts

FAST / EASY / VEGAN / CAN BE GLUTEN-FREE / 3 INGREDIENTS

There's one important trick to this easy recipe for a great snack with drinks or during a movie: You must use *raw* shelled peanuts, not roasted ones. The roasted ones (that is, the most common kind in our supermarkets) will burn before this simple coating caramelizes. Raw peanuts are pale, almost beige (about the same color as raw cashews). Look for raw peanuts in Asian supermarkets, at most health food stores, and from grocery suppliers online.

INGREDIENTS	2-quart or larger air fryer	3.5-quart or larger air fryer	5.25-quart or larger air fryer
Shelled raw peanuts	1 cup (5 ounces)	2 cups (10 ounces)	3 cups (slightly less than 1 pound)
Granulated white sugar	1 tablespoon	2 tablespoons	3 tablespoons
Hot red pepper sauce, such as Cholula or Tabasco (gluten-free, if a concern)	1 teaspoon	2 teaspoons	1 tablespoon
MAKES	*3 servings*	*6 servings*	*9 servings*

1. With the basket (or basket attachment) in the air fryer, heat it to 400°F (or 390°F, if that's the closest setting).

2. Toss the peanuts, sugar, and hot pepper sauce in a bowl until the peanuts are well coated.

3. When the machine is at temperature, pour the peanuts into the basket, spreading them into one layer as much as you can. Air-fry undisturbed for 3 minutes.

4. Shake the basket to rearrange the peanuts. Continue air-frying for 2 minutes more, shaking and stirring the peanuts every 30 seconds, until golden brown.

5. Pour the peanuts onto a large lipped baking sheet. Spread them into one layer and cool for 5 minutes before serving.

Then...

- To make a **PERFECT MANHATTAN** to go with these spicy peanuts, stir *(do not shake) 2 ounces (¼ cup) rye or bourbon whiskey, 1 ounce (2 tablespoons) dry vermouth, ½ ounce (1 tablespoon) sweet vermouth,* and *a dash of bitters, preferably orange bitters,* with *ice cubes* in a cocktail shaker or small pitcher until cold. Strain into a martini glass and twist *a strip of lemon zest* over the cocktail to release its oils before dropping the zest into the drink.

- Use these peanuts as a garnish over Chinese take-out. They're particularly good over orange chicken or sesame beef.

Buttery Spiced Pecans

FAST / EASY / VEGETARIAN / GLUTEN-FREE / 6 INGREDIENTS

Splurge on pecan halves for this tasty snack. For one thing, smaller pecan pieces can fall through the basket's mesh. For another, pecan halves are thicker and have less chance of burning as they roast.

Speaking of the chance they can burn, toss the pecans once a minute as they air-fry. You can even do so more often after the second minute in the machine to make sure the nuts don't blacken and turn bitter.

To preserve the freshness of pecan halves before you air-fry them, freeze them in a sealed bag or container for up to 6 months. Use them straight out of the freezer for this recipe, but increase the time in the air fryer to about 5 minutes.

INGREDIENTS	2-quart or larger air fryer	3.5-quart or larger air fryer	5.25-quart or larger air fryer
Pecan halves	1 cup (¼ pound)	2 cups (½ pound)	3 cups (¾ pound)
Butter, melted	1 tablespoon	2 tablespoons	3 tablespoons
Mild paprika	½ teaspoon	1 teaspoon	1½ teaspoons
Ground cumin	¼ teaspoon	½ teaspoon	Rounded ½ teaspoon
Cayenne	Up to ¼ teaspoon	Up to ½ teaspoon	Up to a rounded ½ teaspoon
Table salt	¼ teaspoon	½ teaspoon	Rounded ½ teaspoon
MAKES	3 servings	6 servings	9 servings

1. With the basket (or basket attachment) in the air fryer, heat it to 400°F (or 390°F, if that's the closest setting).

2. Toss the pecans, butter, paprika, cumin, cayenne, and salt in a bowl until the nuts are evenly coated.

3. When the machine is at temperature, pour the nuts into the basket, spreading them into as close to one layer as you can. Air-fry for 4 minutes, tossing after every minute, and perhaps even more frequently for the last minute if the pecans are really browning, until the pecans are warm, dark brown in spots, and very aromatic.

4. Pour the contents of the basket onto a lipped baking sheet and spread the nuts into one layer. Cool for at least 5 minutes before serving. The nuts can be stored at room temperature in a sealed container for up to 1 week.

Then...

- One of our favorite mocktails is a MANGO MULE. Muddle *a couple of thin slices of cucumber* with *a drizzle of honey* in a cocktail shaker. Add *2 ounces (¼ cup) mango juice* and *1 ounce (2 tablespoons) lime juice*. Add *lots of ice*, cover, and shake until very cold. Strain over *fresh ice* in a tall glass, then top with *ginger beer* and stir to incorporate.

- Toss these spiced nuts with dried cranberries for a more substantial snack.

- Use these as a garnish on **Spinach Salad** (page 265).

Sugar-Glazed Walnuts

FAST / VEGETARIAN / GLUTEN-FREE / 4 INGREDIENTS

These sweet-and-salty walnut halves require a little more effort than the peanuts or pecans in the two previous recipes. For one thing, the walnut halves can get swamped by the egg whites and turn (blech-ly) slimy. To combat the problem, you *must* remove some of the foamy beaten egg whites for both the small and large batches before you add the nuts so there's not too much of that slimy stuff in the bowl. (The medium batch has just the right amount of egg whites.)

Why use egg whites in the first place? Done correctly, they add an even crunchier texture to the walnuts.

These walnuts can also burn even more quickly than pecan halves, particularly after the 2-minute mark in the second cooking in step 5, mostly because the sugar coating gets superhot. Watch the walnuts carefully during that last minute of cooking and be ready to remove them the moment they turn dark brown. Remember, too, that the hot oils in the nuts will continue to "cook" them for a few seconds, even outside the machine.

INGREDIENTS	2-quart or larger air fryer	3.5-quart or larger air fryer	5.25-quart or larger air fryer
Large egg white(s)	1	1	2
Granulated white sugar	1 tablespoon	2 tablespoons	3 tablespoons
Table salt	A pinch	⅛ teaspoon	¼ teaspoon
Walnut halves	1 cup (3½ ounces)	2 cups (7 ounces)	3 cups (10½ ounces)
MAKES	3 servings	6 servings	9 servings

1. With the basket (or basket attachment) in the air fryer, heat it to 400°F (or 390°F, if that's the closest setting).

2. Use a whisk to beat the egg white(s) in a large bowl until quite foamy, more so than just well combined but certainly not yet a meringue.

- If you're working with the quantities for a small batch, remove half of the foamy egg white.

- If you're working with the quantities for a large batch, remove a quarter of it. It's fine to eyeball the amounts.

You can store the removed egg white in a sealed container to save for another use. (But seriously?)

3. Stir in the sugar and salt. Add the walnut halves and toss to coat evenly and well, including the nuts' crevasses.

4. When the machine is at temperature, use a slotted spoon to transfer the walnut halves to the basket, taking care not to dislodge any coating. Gently spread the nuts into as close to one layer as you can. Air-fry undisturbed for 2 minutes.

5. Break up any clumps, toss the walnuts gently but well, and air-fry for 3 minutes more, tossing after 1 minute, then every 30 seconds thereafter, until the nuts are browned in spots and very aromatic. Watch carefully so they don't burn.

6. Gently dump the nuts onto a lipped baking sheet and spread them into one layer. Cool for at least 10 minutes before serving, separating any that stick together. The walnuts can be stored in a sealed container at room temperature for up to 5 days.

Then...

- Use these glazed nuts to garnish frosted cakes or cupcakes.

- Chop them and serve over scoops of vanilla or chocolate ice cream. Try our **No-Churn Vanilla Ice Cream** (page 378).

See photo in insert.

Okra Chips

EASY / VEGAN / GLUTEN-FREE / 3 INGREDIENTS

These are an air-fryer version of the fried okra chips or whole pods you can buy in most supermarkets these days. Notice that the okra is cut into 1-inch pieces. We find these slightly larger pieces take a little longer in the machine and therefore have a better chance to get tender in their inner fibrous bits as they crisp on the outside.

One important warning: Some okra pods are naturally drier than others—which means they can burn more quickly. Watch the basket, paying attention each time you toss its contents. Use kitchen tongs to pick out any pods that are becoming too dark.

INGREDIENTS	2-quart or larger air fryer	3.5-quart or larger air fryer	5.25-quart or larger air fryer
Thin fresh okra pods, cut into 1-inch pieces	¾ pound	1¼ pounds	2 pounds
Vegetable or canola oil	1 tablespoon	1½ tablespoons	2 tablespoons
Coarse sea salt or kosher salt	½ teaspoon	¾ teaspoon	1 teaspoon
MAKES	*2 or 3 servings*	*4 or 5 servings*	*6 or 7 servings*

1. With the basket (or basket attachment) in the air fryer, heat it to 400°F (or 390°F, if that's the closest setting).

2. Toss the okra, oil, and salt in a large bowl until the pieces are well and evenly coated.

3. When the machine is at temperature, pour the contents of the bowl into the basket. Air-fry, tossing several times, for 16 minutes, or until crisp and quite brown (maybe even a little blackened on the thin bits).

4. Pour the contents of the basket onto a wire rack. Cool for a couple of minutes before serving.

Then...

- To make a batch of SMOKY DIPPING SAUCE for these chips, whisk *½ cup regular or low-fat mayonnaise, 1 tablespoon ketchup, 1 teaspoon Dijon mustard, ½ teaspoon honey,* and *½ teaspoon mild smoked paprika* in a small bowl until smooth. Use only gluten-free condiments, if that's a concern.

- Or try these with **Spicy Mustard Dip** (page 26), **Fiery Sour Cream Dip** (page 44), or **Spicy Cajun Dipping Sauce** (page 365).

Carrot Chips

EASY / VEGAN / GLUTEN-FREE / 3 INGREDIENTS

These crunchy little carrot "coins" are irresistible, particularly if you up your salt game. We call for regular table salt because we didn't want to fuss up this recipe. But the carrot slices will be tastier if you use an artisanal salt, particularly a finely ground sea salt. That said, don't use a coarse salt. The chips need a finer, more even coating.

This recipe calls for frozen carrots. *Don't thaw them.* The steam created as the carrots thaw in the machine leads to a softer internal texture and better caramelization of the natural sugars.

One other important note: These carrot chips don't last. Serve them while they're still warm.

INGREDIENTS	2-quart or larger air fryer	3.5-quart or larger air fryer	5.25-quart or larger air fryer
Frozen sliced carrots, preferably crinkle cut	¾ pound	1¼ pounds	2½ pounds
Vegetable oil spray	As needed	As needed	As needed
Table salt	1 teaspoon	1½ teaspoons	2 teaspoons
MAKES	*4 servings*	*6 servings*	*8 servings*

1. With the basket (or basket attachment) in the air fryer, heat it to 400°F (or 390°F, if that's the closest setting).

2. Place the carrots in a bowl. Generously coat them with vegetable oil spray, then toss well, making sure none are stuck together. Spray again, add the salt, and toss well until all the carrots are coated.

3. When the machine is at temperature, pour the carrots into the basket. Air-fry for 38 minutes, shaking the basket at the 10-, 15-, and 20-minute marks, then about every 3 minutes thereafter, until the chips are crisp and golden brown.

4. Pour the carrots onto a wire rack in one layer. Cool for at least 5 minutes before serving.

Then...

• Serve these with FROZEN PEACH SUNSETS, a blender drink without any buzz. For two drinks, put *1½ cups small ice cubes, ¾ cup peach nectar,* and *1 tablespoon lime juice* in a blender. Add *1 ripe peach (peeled and pitted).* Cover and blend until icy-smooth. Pour *1 tablespoon nonalcoholic grenadine syrup* into each of two tall glasses, then pour in the peach mixture; the syrup should then make stripes up the sides of the glasses. Garnish with *mint sprigs,* if desired. (To make this a boozy cocktail, add *3 ounces (6 tablespoons) white rum* and *1 ounce (2 tablespoons) Southern Comfort* with the peach nectar.)

Kale Chips

FAST / EASY / VEGAN / CAN BE GLUTEN-FREE / 3 INGREDIENTS

Although our recipe doesn't make many chips at one time, they get crunchier than they would if we'd let them overlap in the basket or (God forbid!) if we'd stacked them on top of each other. If you're hankering for more chips than a single batch provides, make multiple batches, with the next ready to go when one is finished.

Although the leaves are coated in soy sauce—or gluten-free tamari sauce—some people (like us) might still want a little more salt. Either sprinkle a little extra over the bowlful or pass extra salt when serving for those who want to indulge.

INGREDIENTS	2-quart or larger air fryer	3.5-quart or larger air fryer	5.25-quart or larger air fryer
Medium kale leaves, about 1 ounce each	2	4	6
Olive oil	1 teaspoon	2 teaspoons	1 tablespoon
Regular or low-sodium soy sauce or gluten-free tamari sauce	1 teaspoon	2 teaspoons	1 tablespoon
MAKES	1 serving	2 servings	3 servings

1. With the basket (or basket attachment) in the air fryer, heat it to 400°F (or 390°F, if that's the closest setting).

2. Cut the stems from the leaves (all the stems, all the way up the leaf). Tear each leaf into three pieces. Put them in a large bowl.

3. Add the olive oil and soy or tamari sauce. Toss well to coat. You can even gently rub the leaves along the side of the bowl to get the liquids to stick to them.

4. When the machine is at temperature, put the leaf pieces in the basket in one layer. Air-fry for 5 minutes, turning and rearranging with kitchen tongs once halfway through, until the chips are dried out and crunchy. Watch carefully so they don't turn dark brown at the edges.

5. Gently pour the contents of the basket onto a wire rack. Cool for at least 5 minutes before serving. The chips can keep for up to 8 hours uncovered on the rack (provided it's not a humid day).

Then...

- Serve these with a buzz-free BERRY BRAIN FREEZE. For two drinks, put *½ cup raspberries, ½ cup blueberries, ½ cup blackberries, ½ cup Concord grape juice, ½ cup bottled sour mix or Collins mix*, and *2 teaspoons superfine granulated white sugar* in a large blender. Cover and blend briefly. Then add *2 cups small ice cubes*, re-cover, and blend until icy-smooth. Divide between two tall glasses. (For a boozy version, add *3 ounces (6 tablespoons) vodka* and *1 ounce (2 tablespoons) raspberry liqueur* with the berries.)

Zucchini Chips

FAST / EASY / VEGAN / GLUTEN-FREE / 3 INGREDIENTS

Zucchini is a very wet vegetable! So for the best zucchini chips, look for small, 1-inch-diameter zucchini. These have less internal moisture and (thus) become crisper in the air fryer. No, zucchini chips will never get as crisp as **Carrot Chips** (page 34) or **Kale Chips** (page 35), just because of the nature of the vegetable. But the chips sure make an easy snack, especially good with creamy dips.

INGREDIENTS	2-quart or larger air fryer	3.5-quart or larger air fryer	5.25-quart or larger air fryer
Zucchini, washed but not peeled, and cut into ¼-inch-thick rounds	1 small (about 1 cup)	1½ small (about 1½ cups)	2½ small (about 2½ cups)
Olive oil spray	As needed	As needed	As needed
Table salt	⅛ teaspoon	¼ teaspoon	½ teaspoon
MAKES	*2 servings*	*3 servings*	*5 servings*

1. With the basket (or basket attachment) in the air fryer, heat it to 375°F (or 370°F or 360°F, if one of these is the closest setting).

2. Lay some paper towels on your work surface. Set the zucchini rounds on top, then set more paper towels over the rounds. Press gently to remove some of the moisture. Remove the top layer of paper towels and lightly coat the rounds with olive oil spray on both sides.

3. When the machine is at temperature, set the rounds in the basket, overlapping them a bit as needed. (They'll shrink as they cook.) Air-fry for 15 minutes, tossing and rearranging the rounds at the 5- and 10-minute marks, until browned, soft, yet crisp at the edges. (You'll need to air-fry the rounds 1 or 2 minutes more if the temperature is set at 360°F.)

4. Gently pour the contents of the basket onto a wire rack. Cool for at least 10 minutes or up to 2 hours before serving.

Then...

• Make SRIRACHA-YOGURT DIP by whisking *½ cup plain Greek yogurt, 1 tablespoon regular or low-sodium soy sauce or gluten-free tamari sauce, 1 tablespoon sriracha, and ¼ teaspoon lemon juice* in a small bowl.

• Or serve these with purchased French onion dip (gluten-free, if a concern), **Fiery Sour Cream Dip** (page 44), **Salty Sour Cream Dip** (page 49), or **Creamy Tomato Dip** (page 63).

• Or go all out and put a tiny dollop of sour cream or crème fraîche on each round, then top with salmon roe, tobiko (flying fish roe), or even caviar.

Sweet Plantain Chips

EASY / VEGAN / GLUTEN-FREE / 4 INGREDIENTS

Be forewarned: These plantain chips will never get crunchy. Instead, they will condense and become more flavorful, a good base for the maple syrup glaze. In other words, they'll be sweet if still a little savory, mildly herbaceous with a salty finish.

Use a very ripe plantain, one that has lots of blackened bits across its yellow skin and is a bit soft to the touch. Ripen plantains by sealing them in a paper bag and leaving them on the counter for a day or two.

INGREDIENTS	2-quart or larger air fryer	3.5-quart or larger air fryer	5.25-quart or larger air fryer
Very ripe plantain(s), peeled and sliced into 1-inch pieces	1	2	3
Vegetable oil spray	As needed	As needed	As needed
Maple syrup	1½ tablespoons	3 tablespoons	¼ cup
Coarse sea salt or kosher salt	For garnishing	For garnishing	For garnishing
MAKES	2 servings	4 servings	6 servings

1. Pour about ½ cup water into the bottom of your air fryer basket or into a metal tray on a lower rack in some models. With the basket (or basket attachment) in the air fryer, heat it to 400°F (or 390°F, if that's the closest setting).

2. Put the plantain pieces in a bowl, coat them with vegetable oil spray, and toss gently, spraying at least one more time and tossing repeatedly, until the pieces are well coated.

3. When the machine is at temperature, arrange the plantain pieces in the basket in one layer. Air-fry undisturbed for 5 minutes.

4. Remove the basket from the machine and spray the back of a metal spatula with vegetable oil spray. Use the spatula to press down on the plantain pieces, spraying it again as needed, to flatten the pieces to about half their original height. Brush the plantain pieces with maple syrup, then return the basket to the machine and continue air-frying undisturbed for 6 minutes, or until the plantain pieces are soft and caramelized.

5. Use kitchen tongs to transfer the pieces to a serving platter. Sprinkle the pieces with salt and cool for a couple of minutes before serving. Or cool to room temperature before serving, about 1 hour.

Then...

- Substitute any kind of flavored salt as a garnish for the sweet chips.

- Skip the salt as a garnish and drizzle them with Thai sweet chili sauce while they're still warm.

- Serve these as a side to **Carne Asada** (page 216) along with cooked long-grain white rice and warmed canned, drained, and rinsed black beans.

- Or serve them on top of **Jamaican Rice and Peas** (page 160) as a vegetarian main course.

Fried Dill Pickle Chips

FAST / VEGETARIAN / CAN BE GLUTEN-FREE / 6 INGREDIENTS

You'll need to hold back your friends when these are ready. Or brandish a baseball bat to calm the crowd. (Don't write us. It's a joke.)

The rounds are best when they're still warm, because the coating is crunchy and the pickle inside is soft and luxurious. If the chips sit around too long (but they won't), the pickle will release moisture that ruins the coating.

INGREDIENTS	2-quart or larger air fryer	3.5-quart or larger air fryer	5.25-quart or larger air fryer
All-purpose flour or tapioca flour	1 cup	1 cup	1 cup
Large egg white(s)	1	1	2
Brine from a jar of dill pickles	1 tablespoon	1 tablespoon	2 tablespoons
Seasoned Italian-style dried bread crumbs (gluten-free, if a concern)	1 cup	1 cup	1½ cups
Large dill pickle(s) (8 to 10 inches long), cut into ½-inch-thick rounds	1	2	3
Vegetable oil spray	As needed	As needed	As needed
MAKES	2 servings	4 servings	6 servings

1. With the basket (or basket attachment) in the air fryer, heat it to 400°F (or 390°F, if that's the closest setting).

2. Set up and fill three shallow soup plates or small pie plates on your counter: one for the flour, one for the egg white(s) whisked with the pickle brine, and one for the bread crumbs.

3. Set a pickle round in the flour and turn it to coat all sides, even the edge. Gently shake off the excess flour, then dip the round into the egg-white mixture and turn to coat both sides and the edge. Let any excess egg white mixture slip back into the rest, then set the round in the bread crumbs and turn it to coat both sides as well as the edge. Set aside on a cutting board and soldier on, dipping and coating the remaining rounds. Lightly coat the coated rounds on both sides with vegetable oil spray.

4. Set the pickle rounds in the basket in one layer. Air-fry undisturbed for 7 minutes, or until golden brown and crunchy. Cool in the basket for a few minutes before using kitchen tongs to transfer the (still hot) rounds to a serving platter.

Then...

- Smear the warm rounds with softened chive cream cheese.

- On their own, these rounds love a PERFECT GIN AND TONIC, made with tonic water and gin in 2-to-1 ratio. Stir (don't shake!) in a pitcher with ice, then strain and serve over fresh ice with a slice of lemon or a lemon zest twist.

See photo in insert.

Fried Olives

VEGETARIAN / CAN BE GLUTEN-FREE / 6 INGREDIENTS

We prefer pimiento-stuffed green olives for this tasty treat. Green olives themselves are brinier than black, a better contrast to the bread-crumb coating. And the pimiento strips inside offer a hint of sweetness. If you buy stuffed olives in bulk off the supermarket's salad bar, make sure you get a little of the brine into the container, enough so you can whisk it with the egg whites for more flavor. (If you forget or don't have any brine, water will work fine.)

One important note: Because olives are salty (and their brine, sometimes even more so), only use plain dried bread crumbs in the coating.

INGREDIENTS	2-quart or larger air fryer	3.5-quart or larger air fryer	5.25-quart or larger air fryer
All-purpose flour or tapioca flour	¼ cup	⅓ cup	½ cup
Large egg white(s)	1	1	2
Brine from the olive jar	1 tablespoon	1 tablespoon	2 tablespoons
Plain dried bread crumbs (gluten-free, if a concern)	½ cup	⅔ cup	¾ cup
Large pimiento-stuffed green olives	12	15	21
Olive oil spray	As needed	As needed	As needed
MAKES	4 servings	5 servings	7 servings

1. With the basket (or basket attachment) in the air fryer, heat it to 400°F (or 390°F, if that's the closest setting).

2. Pour the flour in a medium-size zip-closed plastic bag. Whisk the egg white and pickle brine in a medium bowl until foamy. Spread out the bread crumbs on a dinner plate.

3. Pour all the olives into the bag with the flour, seal, and shake to coat the olives. Remove a couple of olives, shake off any excess flour, and drop them into the egg white mixture. Toss gently but well to coat. Pick them up one at a time and roll each in the bread crumbs until well coated on all sides, even the ends. Set them aside on a cutting board as you finish the rest. When done, coat the olives with olive oil spray on all sides.

4. Place the olives in the basket in one layer. Air-fry for 8 minutes, gently shaking the basket once halfway through the cooking process to rearrange the olives, until lightly browned.

5. Gently pour the olives onto a wire rack and cool for at least 10 minutes before serving. Once cooled, the olives may be stored in a sealed container in the fridge for up to 2 days. To rewarm them, set them in the basket of a heated 400°F (or 390°F, if that's the closest setting) air fryer undisturbed for 1 to 2 minutes.

Then...

- Serve these olives as part of an antipasto platter with sun-dried tomatoes, marinated artichokes, sliced salami, cubed provolone, and **Roasted Peppers with Balsamic Vinegar and Basil** (page 309). Add crunchy crackers and the platter becomes a meal.

Fiery Bacon-Wrapped Dates

FAST / CAN BE GLUTEN-FREE / 4 INGREDIENTS

Stuffed dates are often made with cheese or chiles. But why choose when they're terrific with both? Vinegary pickled jalapeño rings make the sweet dates seem even sweeter. And the chile's burn is tempered (a bit) by the cheese.

Medjool dates are thicker and sweeter than the standard, hard, *deglet noor dates* (the generic pitted date in North American supermarkets). You'll pay a little more for Medjools, but the difference will make for all the success in the recipe.

For an even sweeter finish, use maple-cured bacon. Or brush the bacon wrapper with a little maple syrup before air-frying.

INGREDIENTS	2-quart or larger air fryer	3.5-quart or larger air fryer	5.25-quart or larger air fryer
Thin-cut bacon strips, halved widthwise (gluten-free, if a concern)	5	8	12
Medium or large Medjool dates, pitted	10	16	24
Shredded semi-firm mozzarella	2 tablespoons (about ½ ounce)	3 tablespoons (about ¾ ounce)	¼ cup (1 ounce)
Pickled jalapeño rings	20	32	48
MAKES	*10 pieces*	*16 pieces*	*24 pieces*

1. With the basket (or basket attachment) in the air fryer, heat it to 400°F (or 390°F, if that's the closest setting).

2. Lay a bacon strip half on a clean, dry work surface. Split one date lengthwise without cutting through it, so that it opens like a pocket. Set it on one end of the bacon strip and open it a bit. Place 1 teaspoon of the shredded cheese and 2 pickled jalapeño rings in the date, then gently squeeze it together without fully closing it (just to hold the stuffing inside). Roll up the date in the bacon strip and set it bacon seam side down on a cutting board. Repeat this process with the remaining bacon strip halves, dates, cheese, and jalapeño rings.

3. Place the bacon-wrapped dates bacon seam side down in the basket. Air-fry undisturbed for 6 minutes, or until crisp and brown.

4. Use kitchen tongs to gently transfer the wrapped dates to a wire rack or serving platter. Cool for a few minutes before serving.

Then...

- Use these stuffed dates to garnish a wild version of a turkey club sandwich. Split a few lengthwise after air-frying, then set them stuffing side down on top of sliced turkey, sliced tomato, and shredded iceberg lettuce, all set inside slices of toasted white bread that have been smeared with plenty of mayonnaise (gluten-free, if a concern).

- These sweet-and-hot dates pair perfectly with a salty drink. For the PERFECT BLOODY MARY MIX, stir all this in a large pitcher: *3 cups tomato juice, ¼ cup jarred prepared white horseradish, 2 tablespoons lemon juice, 2 tablespoons*

Worcestershire sauce, 1 teaspoon celery salt, and several dashes of hot red pepper sauce, such as Cholula or Tabasco (gluten-free, if a concern). Cover and refrigerate for up to 1 week. To make a single

Bloody Mary, fill a tall glass with *small ice cubes*, add *1½ ounces (3 tablespoons) vodka* and *½ cup Bloody Mary mix*. Stir well with a *celery stalk*.

Bacon Candy

FAST / EASY / CAN BE GLUTEN-FREE / 4 INGREDIENTS

These sweet bits of bacon goodness are a great snack for your day off! The little bit of vinegar in the glaze gives the salty pork a sweet-sour balance that makes these little bites irresistible.

Feel free to use any honey you like, even one far beyond the standard "wildflower" or "clover" honey. Dark-colored honeys from bees that feast on trees or grains, like eucalyptus or even buckwheat, are slightly less sweet and make a terrific contrast to the salty bacon bits.

INGREDIENTS	2-quart or larger air fryer	3.5-quart or larger air fryer	5.25-quart or larger air fryer
Honey	1 tablespoon	1½ tablespoons	2 tablespoons
White wine vinegar	½ teaspoon	1 teaspoon	1¼ teaspoons
Extra thick–cut bacon strips, halved widthwise (gluten-free, if a concern)	2	3	4
Ground black pepper	½ teaspoon	½ teaspoon	1 teaspoon
MAKES	*4 pieces*	*6 pieces*	*8 pieces*

1. With the basket (or basket attachment) in the air fryer, heat it to 350°F (or 360°F, if that's the closest setting).

2. Whisk the honey and vinegar in a small bowl until incorporated.

3. When the machine is at temperature, remove the basket. Lay the bacon strip halves in the basket in one layer. Brush the tops with the honey mixture; sprinkle each bacon strip evenly with black pepper.

4. Return the basket to the machine and air-fry undisturbed for 6 minutes, or until the bacon is crunchy. Or a little less time if you prefer bacon that's still pliable, an extra minute if you want the bacon super crunchy. Take care that the honey coating

doesn't burn. Remove the basket from the machine and set aside for 5 minutes. Use kitchen tongs to transfer the bacon strips to a serving plate.

Then...

- Crumble these bits of bacon candy over salads or slaws.

- Use them as the bacon in any sandwich, from grilled cheese to a turkey club.

- Crumble them on top of warmed sweet rolls or pecan rolls before serving.

- Crumble them on vanilla ice cream for a holy-moly dessert.

Jalapeño Poppers

CAN BE GLUTEN-FREE / 7 INGREDIENTS

The problem with jalapeño poppers is that bready, thick batter on them. We'd much rather savor the fresh (hot!) flavor of the chile. And we prefer a decently spiced bread-crumb stuffing. To that end, we split the chiles and fill them, rather than trying our—and everyone's—patience to get some filling inside a whole chile.

For the easiest preparation, buy raw chorizo as bulk meat sausage, not stuffed into casings. You can often find the bulk variety in the butcher case. It's sometimes called "Mexican chorizo" to differentiate it from dried, hard Spanish chorizo.

If you'd prefer a *much* plainer popper, substitute lean ground pork and a dash of ground cumin for the chorizo sausage meat.

INGREDIENTS	2-quart or larger air fryer	3.5-quart or larger air fryer	5.25-quart or larger air fryer
Bulk raw chorizo sausage meat or raw chorizo sausages, casings removed (gluten-free, if a concern)	2 ounces	¼ pound	5 ounces
Medium scallions, trimmed and thinly sliced	2	4	5
Shredded semi-firm mozzarella or Swiss cheese	¼ cup (about 1 ounce)	7 tablespoons (a little less than 2 ounces)	⅔ cup (about 2½ ounces)
Seasoned Italian-style panko bread crumbs (gluten-free, if a concern)	3 tablespoons	⅓ cup	½ cup
Olive oil	2 tablespoons	3½ tablespoons	5 tablespoons
Medium-size fresh jalapeño chiles (2 to 2½ inches long), stemmed	4	7	10
Olive oil spray	As needed	As needed	As needed
MAKES	8 pieces	14 pieces	20 pieces

1. With the basket (or basket attachment) in the air fryer, heat it to 400°F (or 390°F, if that's the closest setting).

2. Set a medium skillet over medium heat for a couple of minutes. Add the chorizo and cook for 3 minutes, stirring often, until well browned. Scrape the sausage and any juices from the skillet into a medium bowl. Stir in the scallion, cheese, bread crumbs, and olive oil until incorporated.

3. Split the jalapeños lengthwise; scoop out and discard the seeds. Lightly coat the skin side (not the cut side) of each chile half with olive oil spray. Set the halves cut side up on a cutting board and fill each with about 1 tablespoon of the chorizo mixture, mounding it as necessary and using up any excess to further build the mounds. Lightly coat the filling and any exposed bits of the chile around it with olive oil spray.

4. Arrange the jalapeño halves stuffed side up in the basket in a single layer. Air-fry undisturbed for 8 minutes, or until the stuffing has browned and chiles are a little blistered.

5. Use a nonstick-safe spatula, and perhaps a flatware fork for balance, to transfer the jalapeño poppers to a serving platter. Cool a couple of minutes before serving.

Then...

- These poppers are fabulous on top of baked potatoes along with a healthy dollop of sour cream.

- On their own as snacks, the poppers need the PERFECT MARGARITA. Our preferred ratio for each drink is *1 part tequila, 1 part orange-flavored* *liqueur (such as Triple Sec or Cointreau), and 1 part lime juice with a pinch of granulated white sugar, preferably superfine, or more if you like a sweet drink—or even a little stevia or Splenda. Shake with lots of ice in a covered cocktail shaker. Strain over fresh ice into lowball glasses.*

Corn Dog Bites

EASY / CAN BE VEGETARIAN / 5 INGREDIENTS

Here's a surprise: Purchased cornbread stuffing mix makes for an easy coating, sort of like the one on traditional corn dogs, but tastier thanks to the herbs and spices in the mix. Rather than making corn dogs themselves—which, admittedly, you can buy in the freezer case and air-fry as is—we cut hot dogs into pieces to turn into a fabulously crunchy little nibble.

One warning: Do not use crumbled cornbread or a plain bread stuffing mix. Both will burn with the time and temperature given.

Dipping and coating the hot dog bits is messy work. Even so, we prefer our clean and dry hands to kitchen tongs for the task.

INGREDIENTS	2-quart or larger air fryer	3.5-quart or larger air fryer	5.25-quart or larger air fryer
Purchased cornbread stuffing mix	2 cups	3 cups	4 cups
All-purpose flour	¼ cup	⅓ cup	½ cup
Large egg(s), well beaten	1	2	2
Hot dogs, cut into 2-inch pieces (vegetarian hot dogs, if preferred)	2	3	4
Vegetable oil spray	As needed	As needed	As needed
MAKES	2 servings	3 servings	4 servings

1. With the basket (or basket attachment) in the air fryer, heat it to 375°F (or 370°F or 360°F, if one of these is the closest setting).

2. Put the cornbread stuffing mix in a food processor. Cover and pulse to grind into a mixture like fine bread crumbs.

3. Set up and fill three shallow soup plates or small pie plates on your counter: one for the flour, one for the egg(s), and one for the stuffing mix crumbs.

4. Dip a hot dog piece in the flour to coat it completely, then gently shake off any excess. Dip the hot dog piece into the egg(s) and gently roll it around to coat all surfaces, then pick it up and allow any

continues

excess egg to slip back into the rest. Set the hot dog piece in the stuffing mix crumbs and roll it gently to coat it evenly and well on all sides, even the ends. Set it aside on a cutting board and continue dipping and coating the remaining hot dog pieces.

5. Give the coated hot dog pieces a generous coating of vegetable oil spray on all sides, then set them in the basket in one layer with some space between them. Air-fry undisturbed for 10 minutes, or until golden brown and crunchy. (You'll need to add 1 or 2 minutes in the air fryer if the temperature is at 360°F.)

6. Use a nonstick-safe spatula, and perhaps a flatware fork for balance, to transfer the corn dog bites to a wire rack. Cool for 5 minutes before serving.

Then...

- For FIERY SOUR CREAM DIP to go with these nibbles, whisk *hot or chile mustard* of any sort, *mayonnaise*, and *sour cream* in equal parts until uniform. For a sweeter (and pink!) version, add *ketchup*, also in an equal proportion.

Crunchy Lobster Bites

CAN BE GLUTEN-FREE / 10 INGREDIENTS

Like the recipe for **Chicken Shawarma Bites** (page 47), these could become a light dinner, set atop a chopped salad or served alongside a platter of grilled summer vegetables.

As an app or a snack, these nibbles need a creamy dip or a hot pepper dip. We suggest **Lemon Aioli**. But you could skip the extra prep and use Thai sweet chili sauce, salsa of just about any sort, or even just melted butter seasoned with a dash of Tabasco sauce.

The trick is to find very small lobster tails. The thin strip of tail meat will be cut into smaller chunks to cook more evenly as the coating quickly sets. Larger chunks of lobster will need more time in the machine and the coating will burn at the edges.

INGREDIENTS	2-quart or larger air fryer	3.5-quart or larger air fryer	5.25-quart or larger air fryer
Large egg white(s)	1	1	2
Water	2 tablespoons	2 tablespoons	2 tablespoons
All-purpose flour or gluten-free all-purpose flour	⅓ cup	½ cup	¾ cup
Yellow cornmeal	⅓ cup	½ cup	¾ cup
Mild paprika	½ teaspoon	1 teaspoon	1½ teaspoons
Garlic powder	½ teaspoon	1 teaspoon	1½ teaspoons
Onion powder	½ teaspoon	1 teaspoon	1½ teaspoons
Table salt	½ teaspoon	1 teaspoon	1½ teaspoons
Small (3- to 4-ounce) lobster tails	2	4	6
Vegetable oil spray	As needed	As needed	As needed
MAKES	2 servings	3 servings	4 servings

1. With the basket (or basket attachment) in the air fryer, heat it to 400°F (or 390°F, if that's the closest setting).

2. Whisk the egg white(s) and water in a shallow soup plate or small pie plate until foamy.

3. Stir the flour, cornmeal, paprika, garlic powder, onion powder, and salt in a large bowl until uniform.

4. Slice each lobster tail (shell and all) in half lengthwise, then pull the meat out of each half of the tail shell. Cut each strip of meat into 1-inch segments (2 or 3 segments per strip).

5. Dip a piece of lobster meat in the egg white mixture to coat it on all sides, letting any excess egg white slip back into the rest. Drop the piece of lobster meat into the bowl with the flour mixture. Continue on with the remaining pieces of lobster meat, getting them all in that bowl. Gently toss them all in the flour mixture until well coated.

6. Use two flatware forks to transfer the lobster pieces to a cutting board with the coating intact. Coat them on all sides with vegetable oil spray.

7. Set the lobster pieces in the basket in one layer. Air-fry undisturbed for 6 minutes, or until golden brown and crunchy. Gently dump the contents of the basket onto a wire rack and cool for 2 or 3 minutes before serving.

Then...

- These bites are terrific with LEMON AIOLI. Whisk all of the following in a medium bowl until smooth: *1 large egg yolk*; *2 tablespoons lemon juice*; *1 teaspoon Worcestershire sauce (gluten-free, if a concern)*; *up to 1 teaspoon minced garlic*; *up to 1 teaspoon hot red pepper sauce, such as Cholula or Tabasco (gluten-free, if a concern)*; *and ¼ teaspoon table salt*. Whisk in *⅔ cup olive oil* in a slow steady stream until creamy and thick. Save any extra in the fridge in a covered nonreactive container for up to 3 days.

- Or skip the creamy dip and serve the bits with **Spicy Cocktail Sauce** (page 294).

Crispy Tofu Bites

EASY / VEGAN / GLUTEN-FREE / 2 INGREDIENTS

It's so easy to make this velvety, satisfying deck fare! The tofu gets crunchy on the outside but stays creamy, even decadent underneath.

Don't use extra firm *silken* tofu. Rather, use regular extra firm tofu, usually found in the produce section's refrigerator case—and of course, at any Asian supermarket.

A snack like this one is all about the dip. Check out our ideas below—or come up with your own. You can find all sorts of purchased condiments that would work well with these: Red Duck Curry Ketchup, Patak's Lime Pickle, Brooklyn Delhi Tomato Achaar, Momofuku Spicy Ssäm Sauce, or even white barbecue sauce, bottled or homemade (see page 121).

INGREDIENTS	2-quart or larger air fryer	3.5-quart or larger air fryer	5.25-quart or larger air fryer
Extra firm unflavored tofu	¾ pound	1 pound	1½ pounds
Vegetable oil spray	As needed	As needed	As needed
MAKES	3 servings	4 servings	6 servings

1. Wrap the piece of tofu in a triple layer of paper towels. Place it on a wooden cutting board and set a large pot on top of it to press out excess moisture. Set aside for 10 minutes.

2. With the basket (or basket attachment) in the air fryer, heat it to 400°F (or 390°F, if that's the closest setting).

3. Remove the pot and unwrap the tofu. Cut it into 1-inch cubes. Place these in a bowl and coat them *generously* with vegetable oil spray. Toss gently, then spray generously again before tossing, until all are glistening.

4. Gently pour the tofu pieces into the basket, spread them into as close to one layer as possible, and air-fry for 20 minutes, using kitchen tongs to *gently* rearrange the pieces at the 7- and 14-minute marks, until light brown and crisp.

5. Gently pour the tofu pieces onto a wire rack. Cool for 5 minutes before serving warm.

Then...

- Serve these little chunks on toothpicks with a purchased peanut or Thai dipping sauce.

- Substitute these crunchy tofu bits for the cooked chicken in **Kung Pao Chicken** (page 184) to make Kung Pao Tofu.

- Or serve the bites with CHILE-PEANUT SAUCE. Whisk *⅓ cup natural-style creamy peanut butter, 1 tablespoon Lao Gan Ma Spicy Chili Crisp, 1 tablespoon regular or low-sodium soy sauce or gluten-free tamari sauce, 1 tablespoon unseasoned rice vinegar (see page 70), and 1 teaspoon granulated white sugar* until smooth. Make it more complex by adding up to *1 tablespoon balsamic vinegar.*

Chicken Shawarma Bites

EASY / GLUTEN-FREE / 10 INGREDIENTS

You could make a light dinner out of these bites, particularly with a chopped salad on the side—or even underneath them (see page 90 for the **Classic Greek Diner Dressing** to go on that salad). These chicken snacks are super crunchy, partly because they cook long enough for the air fryer to give them (almost) a deep-fried texture.

You can skip all the spices in this recipe and substitute bottled shawarma seasoning or even a north African blend like *ras al hanout*. You'll need 2 teaspoons for the small batch, 1 tablespoon for the medium batch, and 4 teaspoons for the large batch. Check to see if the blend includes salt; keep the salt in the mix if it does not.

And one more thing: Do not substitute chicken breasts for the thighs. You'll be disappointed and blame us. But we warned you!

INGREDIENTS	2-quart or larger air fryer	3.5-quart or larger air fryer	5.25-quart or larger air fryer
Boneless skinless chicken thighs, trimmed of any fat and cut into 1-inch pieces	1 pound	1½ pounds	2 pounds
Olive oil	1 tablespoon	1½ tablespoons	2 tablespoons
Minced garlic	Up to 1 tablespoon	Up to 1½ tablespoons	Up to 2 tablespoons
Table salt	½ teaspoon	Rounded ½ teaspoon	1 teaspoon
Ground cardamom	¼ teaspoon	Rounded ¼ teaspoon	½ teaspoon
Ground cinnamon	¼ teaspoon	Rounded ¼ teaspoon	½ teaspoon
Ground cumin	¼ teaspoon	Rounded ¼ teaspoon	½ teaspoon
Mild paprika	¼ teaspoon	Rounded ¼ teaspoon	½ teaspoon
Grated nutmeg	Up to ¼ teaspoon	Up to a rounded ¼ teaspoon	Up to ½ teaspoon
Ground black pepper	¼ teaspoon	Rounded ¼ teaspoon	½ teaspoon
MAKES	*4 servings*	*6 servings*	*8 servings*

1. With the basket (or basket attachment) in the air fryer, heat it to 400°F (or 390°F, if that's the closest setting).

2. Mix all the ingredients in a large bowl until the chicken is thoroughly and evenly coated in the oil and spices.

3. When the machine is at temperature, scrape the coated chicken pieces into the basket and spread them out into one layer as much as you can. Air-fry for 22 minutes, shaking the basket at least three times during cooking to rearrange the pieces, until well browned and crisp.

4. Pour the chicken pieces onto a wire rack. Cool for 5 minutes before serving.

continues

Then...

- Serve these bites with toothpicks and TANGY
  TAHINI DIP, made by whisking *tahini* (see page 79),
  regular or low-fat sour cream, and *regular or low-
  fat mayonnaise (gluten-free, if a concern)* in equal

proportions by volume until smooth, then whisking
in *a drizzle of lemon juice* for a tart finish.

- These shawarma bites can be turned into a
  sandwich. Pack them into an open pita pocket with
  chopped iceberg lettuce, chopped tomato, and a
  hearty drizzle of **Tzatziki Sauce** (page 120).

Onion Puffs

EASY / VEGETARIAN / 9 INGREDIENTS

These nibbles taste like a cross between onion rings and hush puppies. They're a bit salty, a bit oniony, and quite
crunchy on the outside with a soft, tender center. In other words, they're *so* tempting when they're warm from the
air fryer.

Start them out on a sheet of aluminum foil that you can then remove after they've begun to set. Make sure
there's a space between the piece of foil in the basket (or the basket attachment) and the machine's walls so air
can continue to circulate in the machine.

You can indeed just set them right on the basket's mesh, but the wet batter will drip down like little
stalactites between the lattice, not exactly making a mess but certainly making the puffs less attractive. The foil
lets them set before they finishing "baking" with good air circulation around each for a crisp texture, even on their
undersides.

INGREDIENTS	2-quart or larger air fryer	3.5-quart or larger air fryer	5.25-quart or larger air fryer
Vegetable oil spray	As needed	As needed	As needed
Chopped yellow or white onion	½ cup (1 small onion)	¾ cup	1 cup (1 medium onion)
Seasoned Italian-style panko bread crumbs	⅓ cup	½ cup	⅔ cup
All-purpose flour	3 tablespoons	4½ tablespoons	¼ cup plus 2 tablespoons
Whole, low-fat, or fat-free milk	3 tablespoons	4½ tablespoons	¼ cup plus 2 tablespoons
Yellow cornmeal	1 tablespoon	1½ tablespoons	2 tablespoons
Granulated white sugar	1 teaspoon	1¼ teaspoons	1½ teaspoons
Baking powder	½ teaspoon	Rounded ½ teaspoon	1 teaspoon
Table salt	¼ teaspoon	Rounded ¼ teaspoon	½ teaspoon
MAKES	*About 9 puffs*	*About 14 puffs*	*About 18 puffs*

1. Cut or tear a piece of aluminum foil so that it lines the air fryer's basket with a ½-inch space on each of its four sides. Lightly coat the foil with vegetable oil spray, then set the foil sprayed side up inside the basket.

2. With the basket (or basket attachment) in the air fryer, heat it to 400°F (or 390°F, if that's the closest setting).

3. Stir the onion, bread crumbs, flour, milk, cornmeal, sugar, baking powder, and salt in a bowl to form a thick batter.

4. Remove the basket from the machine. Drop the onion batter by 2-tablespoon measures onto the foil, spacing the mounds evenly across its surface. Return the basket to the machine and air-fry undisturbed for 4 minutes.

5. Remove the basket from the machine. Lightly coat the puffs with vegetable oil spray. Use kitchen tongs to pick up a corner of the foil, then gently pull it out of the basket, letting the puffs slip onto the basket directly. Return the basket to the machine and continue air-frying undisturbed for 8 minutes, or until brown and crunchy.

6. Use kitchen tongs to transfer the puffs to a wire rack or a serving platter. Cool for 5 minutes before serving.

Then...

• Although these are great with ketchup as a dip, try them with SALTY SOUR CREAM DIP made by mixing *3 parts sour cream* and *1 part ketchup* with *a dash of Worcestershire sauce*. Or replace the ketchup with a *red ketchup-like chili sauce, such as Heinz.*

Sweet Apple Fries

EASY / VEGETARIAN / CAN BE GLUTEN-FREE / 5 INGREDIENTS

We debated putting this recipe in the dessert chapter, but we set it here because these tasty apple slices are a great afternoon snack, particularly for kids returning home from school. The slices are coated in gingersnap crumbs, giving them a spicy bite that pairs better with sweet apples, not tart ones. Make sure the apples are firm, not mushy.

The easiest way to core an apple is to peel it first, then cut it in quarters through the stem. Lay a quarter cut side down on your cutting board (and also cut side up because of the way the cuts lie on the wedge). Slice off the thin edge of the quarter, thereby removing any seeds and their hard white sockets. (For this recipe, each quarter would then need to be cut lengthwise into three slices.)

INGREDIENTS	2-quart or larger air fryer	3.5-quart or larger air fryer	5.25-quart or larger air fryer
Medium-size sweet apple(s), such as Gala or Fuji	1	2	3
Large egg white(s)	1	1	2
Water	2 tablespoons	2 tablespoons	2 tablespoons
Finely ground gingersnap crumbs (gluten-free, if a concern)	1 cup	1½ cups	2 cups
Vegetable oil spray	As needed	As needed	As needed
MAKES	2 servings	3 servings	4 servings

1. With the basket (or basket attachment) in the air fryer, heat it to 375°F (or 370°F or 360°F, if one of these is the closest setting).

2. Peel and core an apple, then cut it into 12 slices (see the headnote for more information). Repeat with more apples as necessary.

3. Whisk the egg white(s) and water in a medium bowl until foamy. Add the apple slices and toss well to coat.

4. Spread the gingersnap crumbs across a dinner plate. Using clean hands, pick up an apple slice, let any excess egg white mixture slip back into the rest, and dredge the slice in the crumbs, coating it lightly but evenly on all sides. Set it aside and continue coating the remaining apple slices.

5. Lightly coat the slices on all sides with vegetable oil spray, then set them curved side down in the basket in one layer. Air-fry undisturbed for 6 minutes, or until browned and crisp. You may need to air-fry the slices for 1 or 2 minutes longer if the temperature is at 360°F.

6. Use kitchen tongs to transfer the slices to a wire rack. Cool for 2 to 3 minutes before serving.

Then...

- For MAPLE SOUR CREAM DIP, mix in *1 tablespoon maple syrup* for every *½ cup sour cream*. If desired, and for a more savory edge, stir in up to *a little ground black pepper* or even *a little garam masala* (page 156).

- Or skip the sauce and serve these fries alongside cubes or slices of sharp Cheddar cheese.

Eggplant Fries

FAST / VEGETARIAN / CAN BE GLUTEN-FREE / 6 INGREDIENTS

Could there be a better tide-you-over snack before an outdoor barbecue with friends? These eggplant fries—more like sticks—are crunchy and luxurious, especially when warm. They are also terrific with burgers!

You can double or even triple the amounts for any machine, although you'll have to work in batches to air-fry them. Or you can prepare the quantities for a large machine and cook them in batches in a small or medium air fryer. In any event, dip and coat each batch of eggplant strips just before frying. If they sit around, the coating can dry out and get detached from the vegetable before the strips are put in the air fryer.

INGREDIENTS	2-quart or larger air fryer	3.5-quart or larger air fryer	5.25-quart or larger air fryer
All-purpose flour or tapioca flour	½ cup	¾ cup	1 cup
Large egg(s), well beaten	1	1	2
Seasoned Italian-style dried bread crumbs (gluten-free, if a concern)	¾ cup	1 cup	1½ cups
Finely grated Asiago or Parmesan cheese	2 tablespoons (about ⅓ ounce)	3 tablespoons (about ½ ounce)	¼ cup (about ¾ ounce)
Peeled ½-inch-thick eggplant slices (each about 3 inches in diameter)	2	3	4
Olive oil spray	As needed	As needed	As needed
MAKES	12 fries	18 fries	24 fries

1. With the basket (or basket attachment) in the air fryer, heat it to 375°F (or 380°F or 390°F, if one of these is the closest setting).

2. Set up and fill three shallow soup plates or small pie plates on your counter: one for the flour, one for the egg(s), and one for the bread crumbs mixed with the cheese until well combined.

3. Cut each eggplant slice into six ½-inch-wide strips or sticks. Dip one strip in the flour, coating it well on all sides. Gently shake off the excess flour, then dip the strip in the beaten egg(s) to coat it without losing the flour. Let any excess egg slip back into the rest, then roll the strip in the bread-crumb mixture to coat evenly on all sides, even the ends. Set the strips aside on a cutting board and continue dipping and coating the remaining strips as you did the first one.

4. Generously coat the strips with olive oil spray on all sides. Set them in the basket in one layer and air-fry undisturbed for 10 minutes, or until golden brown and crisp. If the machine is at 390°F, the strips may be done in 8 minutes.

5. Remove the basket from the machine and cool for a couple of minutes. Then use kitchen tongs to transfer the eggplant fries to a wire rack to cool for only a minute or two more before serving.

Then...

- While the fries are still hot, sprinkle finely shredded mozzarella over them and let it melt a bit.
- Use purchased marinara sauce as a dip. Or make a simple marinara with the fast recipe in our book *The Kitchen Shortcut Bible*.

Avocado Fries

FAST / VEGAN / CAN BE GLUTEN-FREE / 9 INGREDIENTS

You simply haven't lived until you've had avocado fries! The trick is to use a ripe but still-firm avocado: neither a hard one nor a squishy, blackening one. If the avocado is too ripe—if it's, say, perfect for guacamole—it will be hard to cut into wedges and will almost melt under the coating as it cooks.

Notice the ingredient chart. The first column is for small or medium air fryers; the second column is *only* for a larger machine. Of course, you can always make the larger quantities for a small machine, but you then must cook the avocado fries in batches. Since these fries need space to get crisp, there was really no difference in the available real estate between a small and a medium machine.

INGREDIENTS	2-quart or larger air fryer	5.25-quart or larger air fryer
Large Hass avocado(s) (not too ripe)	1	2
All-purpose flour or gluten-free all-purpose flour	1 cup	1 cup
Orange juice	½ cup	¾ cup
Lime juice	2 tablespoons	3 tablespoons
Plain dried bread crumbs (gluten-free, if a concern)	¾ cup	1¼ cups
Yellow cornmeal	½ cup	1 cup
Chile powder	2 teaspoons	1½ tablespoons
Vegetable oil spray	As needed	As needed
Coarse sea salt or kosher salt	For garnishing	For garnishing
MAKES	*6 fries*	*12 fries*

1. With the basket (or basket attachment) in the air fryer, heat it to 400°F (or 390°F, if that's the closest setting).

2. Cut the avocado in half, then remove the pit. Use a large spoon to scoop the flesh out of the peel in one piece. Discard that peel, then cut each half lengthwise into thirds (that is, into longish wedges).

3. Set up and fill three shallow soup plates or small pie plates on your counter: one for the flour; one for the orange and lime juices, whisked together; and one for the bread crumbs, cornmeal, and chile powder, whisked until well combined.

4. Dredge an avocado wedge in the flour so that it's evenly coated on all sides. Set it in the juice mixture and turn gently without knocking off the flour. Pick it up and set it in the bread-crumb mixture. Gently roll it on all sides until evenly coated. Set the wedge aside on a cutting board and continue with the triple-dip process for the remaining wedges.

5. Generously coat the avocado wedges on all sides with vegetable oil spray. Arrange the wedges in the basket in one layer and air-fry undistributed for 8 minutes, or until crisp and brown.

6. Use a nonstick-safe spatula, and perhaps a flatware fork for balance, to transfer the (hot!) wedges to a wire rack or a serving platter. Sprinkle with salt, then cool for about 5 minutes before serving.

Then...

- Serve these fries with lime wedges to squeeze over each.

- Place these avocado fries as a garnish on tuna or salmon salad.

- For a new take on avocado toast, stir together room-temperature butter and sriracha into a spread,

then smear a light coating on a piece of white or whole-wheat toast (gluten-free, if a concern). Top with several avocado fries and some minced chives.

- Use these avocado fries as a vegan substitute for the fried fish in fish tacos, setting them in flour tortillas with plenty of salsa, some drained and rinsed canned black beans, some pickled onion rings, and maybe a little vegan sour cream.

Scotch Eggs

CAN BE GLUTEN-FREE / 5 INGREDIENTS

This pub food—a hard-cooked egg wrapped in sausage and then deep fried—is well known in the United Kingdom but needs to make more of a show in the United States. That said, even the standard could use a little improvement. Our problem with Scotch eggs is that the yolks are almost always overcooked, even green and sulfurous. Our solution is to boil the eggs just until the whites set, but not the yolks. They will set a little more as the eggs air-fry in their sausage coating.

All that said, take care when you peel the eggs. A not-set yolk will run out if you break the white.

INGREDIENTS	2-quart or larger air fryer	3.5-quart or larger air fryer	5.25-quart or larger air fryer
Large eggs	5	7	10
Corn flake crumbs (gluten-free, if a concern)	1 cup	1½ cups	2 cups
Bulk mild or hot breakfast sausage meat (gluten-free, if a concern)	1 pound	1½ pounds	2 pounds
Vegetable oil spray	As needed	As needed	As needed
Coarse sea salt or kosher salt	For garnishing	For garnishing	For garnishing
MAKES	4 to 5 servings	6 to 7 servings	8 to 10 servings

1. Bring a little more than 1 inch of water to a boil in a large saucepan set over high heat. Meanwhile, prepare a big bowl of ice water.

2. Set 4, 6, or 8 of the eggs in a vegetable steamer basket and lower them into the pot. Cover, reduce the heat to low, and steam for 10 minutes. Drain the eggs into a colander set in the sink, then put them in the ice water. Cool for 10 minutes, then peel the

eggs. (Be careful: the whites are set but not the yolks!)

3. With the basket (or basket attachment) in the air fryer, heat it to 375°F (or 380°F or 390°F, if one of these is the closest setting).

continues

4. Lay a sheet of plastic wrap on a clean, dry work surface. Place ¼ pound (4 ounces) of the sausage meat in the center of the sheet, then press the sausage into an oval 7 inches long and about 5 inches wide at its widest part. Place a peeled egg in the center of the sausage, then carefully and gently (no awards for speed!) use the plastic wrap to fold the sausage up and around the egg. Remove the plastic wrap, dampen your clean hands, then smooth and seal the sausage over the egg. Repeat with the remaining sausage and eggs, using a fresh sheet of plastic wrap each time.

5. Set up and fill two shallow soup plates or small pie plates on your counter: one with the remaining egg(s) in it, well beaten until uniform, and the other with the corn flake crumbs. Roll the sausage-covered egg in the beaten egg. Let the excess slip back into the rest, then set the coated egg in the corn flake crumbs. Roll the egg in the corn flake crumbs to coat it evenly and well, even on the ends. Set aside, then coat the remaining sausage-covered eggs.

6. Give the crumbed eggs a generous coating of vegetable oil spray. Set them in the basket in one layer and air-fry undisturbed for 12 minutes, or until the coating is well browned. If the air fryer is at 390°F, the Scotch eggs may be done in 10 minutes.

7. Use kitchen tongs to transfer the eggs to a wire rack. Cool for at least 5 minutes or up to 30 minutes before serving. Split the eggs in half, sprinkle them with salt, and relish every bite.

Then...

- Serve the eggs with beer and chutney of just about any sort (even **Blueberry Chutney**, page 73), purchased pickled onions, and a small wedge of Cheddar cheese.

- Go all out and crumble **Bacon Candy** (page 41) over each halved Scotch egg.

- Drizzle the finished eggs with Thai sweet chili sauce, Worcestershire sauce, or even *kecap manis* (a sweet Indonesian condiment).

Avocado Toast with Lemony Shrimp

EASY / CAN BE GLUTEN-FREE / 8 INGREDIENTS

This recipe is more than a nibble, more like a substantial snack, even a light meal with a salad on the side.

Use any sort of bread, although we recommend rye or whole-grain bread (even gluten-free) for the best texture with the creamy avocado.

The shrimp set on top will offer a sweet-and-sour bite. Make them even zestier by garnishing with a little more finely grated lemon zest along with the salt.

INGREDIENTS	2-quart or larger air fryer	3.5-quart or larger air fryer	5.25-quart or larger air fryer
Raw medium shrimp (30 to 35 per pound), peeled and deveined	3 ounces	6 ounces	9 ounces
Finely grated lemon zest	1 teaspoon	1½ teaspoons	2 teaspoons
Lemon juice	1 teaspoon	2 teaspoons	1 tablespoon
Minced garlic	1 teaspoon	1½ teaspoons	2 teaspoons
Ground black pepper	1 teaspoon	1½ teaspoons	2 teaspoons
Rye or whole-wheat bread slices (gluten-free, if a concern)	2	4	6
Ripe Hass avocado(s), halved, pitted, peeled and roughly chopped	1	2	3
Coarse sea salt or kosher salt	For garnishing	For garnishing	For garnishing
MAKES	2 pieces	4 pieces	6 pieces

1. With the basket (or basket attachment) in the air fryer, heat it to 400°F (or 390°F, if that's the closest setting).

2. Toss the shrimp, lemon zest, lemon juice, garlic, and pepper in a bowl until the shrimp are evenly coated.

3. When the machine is at temperature, use kitchen tongs to place the shrimp in a single layer in the basket. Air-fry undisturbed for 4 minutes, or until the shrimp are pink and barely firm. Use kitchen tongs to transfer the shrimp to a cutting board.

4. Working in batches, set as many slices of bread as will fit in the basket in one layer. Air-fry undisturbed

for 1 to 2 minutes, just until warmed through and crisp. The bread will not brown much.

5. Arrange the bread slices on a clean, dry work surface. Divide the avocado bits among them and gently smash the avocado into a coarse paste with the tines of a flatware fork. Top the toasts with the shrimp and sprinkle with salt as a garnish.

Then...

- Drizzle the finished toasts with sriracha, or even **Sriracha-Yogurt Dip** (page 36).

- Add toasted pine nuts or toasted sliced almonds to the toasts with the salt.

Eggs in Avocado Halves

EASY / VEGETARIAN / GLUTEN-FREE / 6 INGREDIENTS

Here's another recipe that can work just as well for a light lunch or quick meal as it does for an appetizer. It's a riff on shirred eggs, usually baked in ramekins with a touch of cream. Here, we let an avocado half stand in for that ramekin, turning the ordinary into something that would make a rustic but refined first course for a dinner with friends, especially if you garnished the cooked eggs in some way—with crumbled **Bacon Candy** (page 41), crumbled crunchy **Pita Chips** (page 24), or crumbled soft goat cheese.

Notice that this recipe calls for *medium* eggs, not exactly the cookbook standard. A large egg will overflow the indentation where the avocado pit was. You can indeed use a large egg and let the excess white flow over the avocado half, but you must then wipe the cut side of the avocado to remove any egg white sticking to it. And if the cavity is very small, scoop out a little more of the avocado flesh so it will indeed hold a medium egg.

For more pizzazz, cut a thin slice of prosciutto into small strips, then lay these over the avocado half for the last minute or two of cooking to let the prosciutto frizzle and get crisp.

INGREDIENTS	2-quart or larger air fryer	3.5-quart or larger air fryer	5.25-quart or larger air fryer
Hass avocados, halved and pitted but not peeled	2	3	4
Medium eggs	4	6	8
Vegetable oil spray	As needed	As needed	As needed
Heavy or light cream (*not* fat-free cream)	2 tablespoons	3 tablespoons	¼ cup
Table salt	To taste	To taste	To taste
Ground black pepper	To taste	To taste	To taste
Makes	*2 servings*	*3 servings*	*4 servings*

1. With the basket (or basket attachment) in the air fryer, heat it to 350°F (or 360°F, if that's the closest setting).

2. Slice a small amount off the rounded (skin) side of each avocado half so it can sit stable, without rocking. Lightly coat the skin of the avocado half (the side that will now sit stable) with vegetable oil spray.

3. Arrange the avocado halves open side up on a cutting board, then crack an egg into the indentation in each where the pit had been. If any white overflows the avocado half, wipe that bit of white off the cut edge of the avocado before proceeding.

4. Remove the basket (or its attachment) from the machine and set the filled avocado halves in it in one layer. Return it to the machine without pushing it in. Drizzle each avocado half with about 1½ teaspoons cream, a little salt, and a little ground black pepper.

5. Air-fry undisturbed for 10 minutes for a soft-set yolk, or air-fry for 12 to 13 minutes for more-set eggs.

6. Use a nonstick-safe spatula and a flatware fork for balance to transfer the avocado halves to serving plates. Cool a minute or two before serving.

Then...

- Pile pickled jalapeño slices over each serving.

- Or use a large serving spoon to scoop out the avocado half with its egg from the shell. Set the filled avocado half on a piece of toast (gluten-free, if a concern)—or even **Texas Toast** (page 321). Use a flatware fork to mash the avocado and egg onto the bread for a new, richer take on avocado toast.

Fried Goat Cheese

FAST / VEGETARIAN / CAN BE GLUTEN-FREE / 4 INGREDIENTS

Crunchy little rounds of goat cheese are a great treat! The cheese melts fairly quickly in the air fryer. As with the **Mozzarella Sticks** (page 58), freezing the goat cheese gives it a leg up on the cooking process. Even so, the goat cheese will undoubtedly leak under the coating. A puncture or two is no worry. More and you should remove the basket from the machine at once. But don't be too concerned—we fortify the coating's structure by double-dipping in the egg and bread crumbs. Even so, don't let timing be your only guide. Keep a watchful eye on the rounds.

　　Make sure the diameter of the goat cheese log is what we call for. If you can only find longer logs (which weigh more), slice off the amount you need for the batch you're making. And feel free to use any sort of soft goat cheese log you like: plain, herbed, truffled, or rolled in ground chiles. We left the coating plain to accommodate these sorts of variations.

INGREDIENTS	2-quart or larger air fryer	3.5-quart or larger air fryer	5.25-quart or larger air fryer
1- to 1½-inch-diameter goat cheese log	4 ounces (¼ pound)	7 ounces	11 ounces
Large egg(s)	1	2	3
Plain dried bread crumbs (gluten-free, if a concern)	1 cup	1¾ cups	2½ cups
Vegetable oil spray	As needed	As needed	As needed
MAKES	2 servings	3 servings	5 servings

1. Slice the goat cheese log into ½-inch-thick rounds. Set these flat on a small cutting board, a small baking sheet, or a large plate. Freeze uncovered for 30 minutes.

2. With the basket (or basket attachment) in the air fryer, heat it to 400°F (or 390°F, if that's the closest setting).

3. Set up and fill two shallow soup plates or small pie plates on your counter: one in which you whisk the egg(s) until uniform and the other for the bread crumbs.

continues

4. Take the goat cheese rounds out of the freezer. With clean, dry hands, dip one round in the egg(s) to coat it on all sides. Let the excess egg slip back into the rest, then dredge the round in the bread crumbs, turning it to coat all sides, even the edges. Repeat this process—egg, then bread crumbs—for a second coating. Coat both sides of the round and its edges with vegetable oil spray, then set it aside. Continue double-dipping, double-dredging, and spraying the remaining rounds.

5. Place the rounds in one layer in the basket. Air-fry undisturbed for 4 minutes, or until lightly browned and crunchy. Do not overcook. Some of the goat cheese may break through the crust. A few little breaks are fine but stop the cooking before the coating reaches structural failure.

6. Remove the basket from the machine and set aside for 3 minutes. Use a nonstick-safe spatula, and maybe a flatware fork for balance, to transfer the rounds to a wire rack. Cool for 5 minutes more before serving.

Then...

- Serve these rounds with hot pepper jelly, jalapeño jam, or any sweet-and-spicy condiment, even Thai sweet chili sauce.

- To make your own JALAPEÑO JAM, put *3 or 4 medium-size fresh jalapeño chiles (stemmed, seeded, and chopped)*, *1 large green bell pepper (stemmed, cored, and chopped)*, and *1 tablespoon lemon juice* in a food processor. Cover and process until finely chopped. Scrape this mixture into a medium saucepan and add *1 cup granulated white sugar*, *¼ cup apple cider vinegar*, and *1 teaspoon table salt*. Bring to a boil over medium heat, stirring often. Reduce the heat to low and simmer for 5 minutes, or until somewhat thickened. Scrape the mixture into a heat-safe bowl, cover the bowl with plastic wrap, and refrigerate for at least 3 hours before serving, or up to 1 week.

Fried Mozzarella Sticks

VEGETARIAN / CAN BE GLUTEN-FREE / 5 INGREDIENTS

Bring back the '80s! Not the hair. Nor the shoulder pads. But do bring back what we called "mozz sticks" back in the day. They were a favorite in every fern bar. It's high time they were on your table, no ferns necessary.

Freezing the cheese lets it endure the heat of the air fryer without turning gooey and runny too quickly. With the traditional method, the sticks spend much less time in a deep fryer, so the cheese has less of a chance to run out from the coating. Here, we have to wait for the coating to set. In fact, a little of the cheese may run out in spots. Check carefully as the sticks air-fry, particularly in the last few minutes. A spot or two is fine. More could mean imminent structural failure. Then your friends will abandon you over your broken promise of a tasty snack and you'll end up alone, watering your ferns.

You can make these sticks in advance. Once cooked, set them aside, uncovered, at room temperature for up to 3 hours, then give them another spritz with olive oil spray and reheat them in the 400°F air fryer (or 390°F, if that's the closest setting) undisturbed for 1 to 2 minutes.

INGREDIENTS	2-quart or larger air fryer	3.5-quart or larger air fryer	5.25-quart or larger air fryer
1-ounce string cheese sticks, unwrapped	5	7	9
All-purpose flour or tapioca flour	½ cup	½ cup	½ cup
Large egg(s), well beaten	1	2	2
Seasoned Italian-style dried bread crumbs (gluten-free, if a concern)	1½ cups	2¼ cups	3 cups
Olive oil spray	As needed	As needed	As needed
MAKES	5 sticks	7 sticks	9 sticks

1. Unwrap the string cheese and place the pieces in the freezer for 20 minutes (but not longer, or they will be too frozen to soften in the time given in the air fryer).

2. With the basket (or basket attachment) in the air fryer, heat it to 400°F (or 390°F, if that's the closest setting).

3. Set up and fill three shallow soup plates or small pie plates on your counter: one for the flour, one for the egg(s), and one for the bread crumbs.

4. Dip a piece of cold string cheese in the flour until well coated (keep the others in the freezer). Gently tap off any excess flour, then set the stick in the egg(s). Roll it around to coat, let any excess egg mixture slip back into the rest, and set the stick in the bread crumbs. Gently roll it around to coat it evenly, even the ends. Now dip it *back* in the egg(s), then *again* in the bread crumbs, rolling it to coat well and evenly. Set the stick aside on a cutting board and coat the remaining pieces of string cheese in the same way.

5. Lightly coat the sticks all over with olive oil spray. Place them in the basket in one layer and air-fry undisturbed for 5 minutes, or until golden brown and crisp.

6. Remove the basket from the machine and cool for 5 minutes. Use a nonstick-safe spatula to transfer the mozzarella sticks to a serving platter. Serve hot.

Then...

- Serve these sticks with purchased marinara sauce, purchased pesto, **Spicy Ketchup Dip** (page 66), or **Ranch Dip** (page 293).

- To make 2 or 3 servings of CREAM CHEESE AND SPINACH DIP for the sticks, mix *4 ounces (¼ pound) softened cream cheese (gluten-free, if a concern), ¼ cup frozen chopped spinach (thawed and squeezed to remove moisture), ¼ cup regular or low-fat mayonnaise (gluten-free, if a concern), 1 teaspoon onion powder, ½ teaspoon garlic powder, and ¼ teaspoon table salt* in a bowl until smooth.

Halloumi Fries

EASY / VEGETARIAN / GLUTEN-FREE / 7 INGREDIENTS

A Cypriot favorite, halloumi (sometimes called "grilling cheese" in the United States) seems to be made for the air fryer! It doesn't melt quickly (the way, say, goat cheese does). It holds it shape and still gets gooey. And it has a mild, pleasant flavor.

We kept the coating fairly simple, just dried herbs without added bread crumbs, mostly because we wanted the mellow flavor of the cheese to show through. These little "fries" are best when they're warm.

INGREDIENTS	2-quart or larger air fryer	3.5-quart or larger air fryer	5.25-quart or larger air fryer
Olive oil	1 tablespoon	1½ tablespoons	2 tablespoons
Minced garlic	1 teaspoon	1½ teaspoons	2 teaspoons
Dried oregano	⅛ teaspoon	Rounded ⅛ teaspoon	¼ teaspoon
Dried thyme	⅛ teaspoon	Rounded ⅛ teaspoon	¼ teaspoon
Table salt	⅛ teaspoon	Rounded ⅛ teaspoon	¼ teaspoon
Ground black pepper	⅛ teaspoon	Rounded ⅛ teaspoon	¼ teaspoon
Halloumi	½ pound	¾ pound	1 pound
MAKES	2 servings	3 servings	4 servings

1. With the basket (or basket attachment) in the air fryer, heat it to 400°F (or 390°F, if that's the closest setting).

2. Whisk the oil, garlic, oregano, thyme, salt, and pepper in a medium bowl.

3. Lay the piece of halloumi flat on a cutting board. Slice it widthwise into ½-inch-thick sticks. Cut each stick lengthwise into ½-inch-thick batons.

4. Put these batons into the olive oil mixture. Toss gently but well to coat.

5. Place the batons in the basket in a single layer. Air-fry undisturbed for 12 minutes, or until lightly browned, particularly at the edges.

6. Dump the fries out onto a wire rack. They may need a little coaxing with a nonstick-safe spatula to come free. Cool for a couple of minutes before serving hot.

Then...

- Serve these fries along with chilled ouzo or retsina.

- They're particularly good alongside stuffed grape leaves. The best might be found on your supermarket's salad bar (rather than in a can or a jar, because you can pick through at the salad bar and take the whole, juicy ones).

Garlic Breadsticks

FAST / EASY / CAN BE VEGAN / 5 INGREDIENTS

Pizza dough makes the easiest breadsticks! You can buy the dough in tubes or bags in the refrigerator case at most supermarkets. You can also freeze the dough, if you want to buy it in bulk to have on hand for breadsticks in the future (or, as you'll see, for upcoming recipes).

If you want to make more breadsticks than we recommend for your model, remember this: You can always prepare more for a smaller machine and air-fry the breadsticks in batches. In any event, make sure there's an inch between the breadsticks in the basket so they have room to expand and brown on all sides.

And one more thing: Basket sizes do vary, even in large models. The important thing here is the air space between the breadsticks. If you can't fit all eight in your model with the appropriate distance between them, then you *must* cook them in batches.

INGREDIENTS	2-quart or larger air fryer	3.5-quart or larger air fryer	5.25-quart or larger air fryer
Olive oil	1 tablespoon	1½ tablespoons	2 tablespoons
Minced garlic	1 teaspoon	1½ teaspoons	2 teaspoons
Table salt	¼ teaspoon	Rounded ¼ teaspoon	½ teaspoon
Ground black pepper	¼ teaspoon	Rounded ¼ teaspoon	½ teaspoon
Purchased pizza dough (vegan dough, if that's a concern)	¼ pound	6 ounces	½ pound
MAKES	8 breadsticks	12 breadsticks	16 breadsticks

1. With the basket (or basket attachment) in the air fryer, heat it to 400°F (or 390°F, if that's the closest setting). Mix the oil, garlic, salt, and pepper in a small bowl.

2. Divide the pizza dough into 4 balls for a small air fryer, 6 for a medium machine, or 8 for a large, each ball about the size of a walnut in its shell. (Each should weigh 1 ounce, if you want to drag out a scale and get obsessive.) Roll each ball into a 5-inch-long stick under your clean palms on a clean, dry work surface. Brush the sticks with the oil mixture.

3. When the machine is at temperature, place the prepared dough sticks in the basket, leaving a 1-inch space between them. Air-fry undisturbed for 7 minutes, or until puffed, golden, and set to the touch.

4. Use kitchen tongs to gently transfer the breadsticks to a wire rack and repeat step 3 with the remaining dough sticks.

Then...

- We're partial to this super creamy TOFU AND ARUGULA DIP. For six servings, whir *¾ pound (12 ounces) soft silken tofu, 4 ounces (¼ pound) packed arugula leaves, 2 tablespoons olive oil, 1 tablespoon lemon juice, 1 teaspoon granulated white sugar,* and *¼ teaspoon table salt* in a food processor until smooth, stopping the machine at least once to scrape down the inside of the canister. Store any leftover dip in a covered glass or nonreactive container in the fridge for up to 5 days.

Crispy Ravioli Bites

EASY / CAN BE VEGETARIAN / 5 INGREDIENTS

Crunchy ravioli are a great snack, perfect for a midafternoon pick-me-up when you don't want anything sweet on the platter. Use any sort of frozen ravioli you like, even ones filled with a vegan meat mixture, provided the ravioli are quite small, about ½ ounce each.

They should lie in as close to one layer in the basket as you can manage. They *can* overlap, as long as they do so only along their edges. You can even lean some of them up against the side of the basket.

INGREDIENTS	2-quart or larger air fryer	3.5-quart or larger air fryer	5.25-quart or larger air fryer
All-purpose flour	¼ cup	⅓ cup	½ cup
Large egg(s), well beaten	1	1	2
Seasoned Italian-style dried bread crumbs	½ cup	⅔ cup	1¼ cups
Frozen mini ravioli, meat or cheese, thawed	6 ounces (about 12)	10 ounces (about 20)	1 pound (about 32)
Olive oil spray	As needed	As needed	As needed
MAKES	3 appetizer servings	5 appetizer servings	8 appetizer servings

1. With the basket (or basket attachment) in the air fryer, heat it to 400°F (or 390°F, if that's the closest setting).

2. Pour the flour into a medium bowl. Set up and fill two shallow soup plates or small pie plates on your counter: one with the beaten egg(s) and one with the bread crumbs.

3. Pour all the ravioli into the flour and toss well to coat. Pick up 1 ravioli, gently shake off any excess flour, and dip the ravioli in the egg(s), coating both sides. Let any excess egg slip back into the rest, then set the ravioli in the bread crumbs, turning it several times until lightly and evenly coated on all sides. Set aside on a cutting board and continue on with the remaining ravioli.

4. Lightly coat the ravioli on both sides with olive oil spray, then set them in the basket in as close to a single layer as you can. Some can lean up against the side of the basket. Air-fry for 7 minutes, tossing the basket at the 4-minute mark to rearrange the pieces, until brown and crisp.

5. Pour the contents of the basket onto a wire rack. Cool for 5 minutes before serving.

Then...

- Traditionally, these need marinara for a dip, whether purchased or homemade. By the way, the best way to dip them in the sauce is with chopsticks.

- Or drizzle them with—or dip them into—a LEMON BUTTER–BASIL SAUCE. For 3 or 4 servings, melt *4 tablespoons (½ stick) butter* in a small saucepan over low heat. Stir in *1 tablespoon minced fresh basil leaves*, *up to 1 tablespoon minced shallot*, *2 teaspoons lemon juice*, *1 teaspoon finely grated lemon zest*, and *a pinch of table salt*. Remove from the heat and stir in up to *2 tablespoons finely grated Parmesan cheese*. Serve warm with the crisp ravioli.

- Or try them with **Roasted Red Pepper Dip** (page 81), **Sage Pesto** (page 111), or **Buttermilk Dip** (page 331).

Crunchy Tortellini Bites

EASY / VEGETARIAN / 6 INGREDIENTS

Unlike the previous recipe for ravioli, these tortellini need a quick boil before they turn crisp in the air fryer. The pasta dough for tortellini is usually made with egg, as opposed to a ravioli dough that is often just flour and water. The egg makes for a denser, thicker dough which doesn't perform as well in the air fryer. In fact, it tends to get hard, rather than tender, under the intense air circulation. Boiling the tortellini takes care of the problem, adding moisture to the dough and giving it a head start on getting tender.

INGREDIENTS	2-quart or larger air fryer	3.5-quart or larger air fryer	5.25-quart or larger air fryer
Cheese tortellini	6 ounces (about 1½ cups)	10 ounces (about 2½ cups)	14 ounces (about 3½ cups)
Yellow cornmeal	¼ cup	⅓ cup	½ cup
Seasoned Italian-style dried bread crumbs	¼ cup	⅓ cup	½ cup
Finely grated Parmesan cheese	¼ cup (about ¾ ounce)	⅓ cup (about 1 ounce)	½ cup (about 1½ ounces)
Large egg	1	1	1
Olive oil spray	As needed	As needed	As needed
MAKES	3 servings	5 servings	7 servings

1. Bring a large pot of water to a boil over high heat. Add the tortellini and cook for 3 minutes. Drain in a colander set in the sink, then spread out the tortellini on a large baking sheet and cool for 15 minutes.

2. With the basket (or basket attachment) in the air fryer, heat it to 400°F (or 390°F, if that's the closest setting).

3. Mix the cornmeal, bread crumbs, and cheese in a large zip-closed plastic bag.

4. Whisk the egg in a medium bowl until uniform. Add the tortellini and toss well to coat, even along the inside curve of the pasta. Use a slotted spoon or kitchen tongs to transfer 5 or 6 tortellini to the plastic bag, seal, and shake gently to coat thoroughly and evenly. Set the coated tortellini aside on a cutting board and continue coating the rest in the same way.

5. Generously coat the tortellini on all sides with the olive oil spray, then set them in one layer in the basket. Air-fry undisturbed for 10 minutes, gently tossing the basket and rearranging the tortellini at the 4- and 7-minute marks, until brown and crisp.

6. Pour the contents of the basket onto a wire rack. Cool for 5 minutes before serving.

Then...

- For CREAMY TOMATO DIP, mix purchased *pizza sauce* with *room-temperature cream cheese* in a 4-to-1 ratio by volume until smooth and creamy.

- Or for unusual combinations, try these crunchy tortellini with **Horseradish Sauce** (page 116), **Chipotle Salsa Dip** (page 262), or **Rémoulade Sauce** (page 291).

Cheese Straws

VEGETARIAN / 6 INGREDIENTS

Crunchy cheese straws must be made in batches in the air fryer, no matter what size model you have. They're too long to fit more than a few in a single layer in any basket at one time. Given that, you might consider making a large quantity, even if you have a small machine, since you'll probably be working in batches anyway.

Gussy up these straws by substituting any hard aged grating cheese for the Parmesan. Consider a well-aged goat gouda, a dry Boerenkaas, or an aged Asiago. Or sprinkle dried spices over the strips with the ground black pepper—try ground dried ginger, ground coriander, and/or ground cumin. If desired, also sprinkle them with small amounts of garlic or onion powder.

For more about the myth that you can't refreeze puff pastry, see page 19.

INGREDIENTS	2-quart or larger air fryer	3.5-quart or larger air fryer	5.25-quart or larger air fryer
All-purpose flour	For dusting	For dusting	For dusting
A 17.25-ounce box frozen puff pastry	One quarter of one thawed sheet (wrap and refreeze the remainder)	Two quarters of one thawed sheet (that is, a half of the sheet cut into two even pieces; wrap and refreeze the remainder)	One sheet, cut into four quarters
Large egg(s)	1	1	2
Water	2 tablespoons	2 tablespoons	¼ cup
Finely grated Parmesan cheese	2 tablespoons (about ⅓ ounce)	¼ cup (about ¾ ounce)	½ cup (about 1½ ounces)
Ground black pepper	up to ½ teaspoon	up to 1 teaspoon	up to 2 teaspoons
MAKES	4 straws	8 straws	16 straws

1. With the basket (or basket attachment) in the air fryer, heat it to 400°F (or 390°F, if that's the closest setting).

2. Dust a clean, dry work surface with flour. Set one of the pieces of puff pastry on top, dust the pastry lightly with flour, and roll with a rolling pin to a 6-inch square.

3. Whisk the egg(s) and water in a small or medium bowl until uniform. Brush the pastry square(s) generously with this mixture. Sprinkle each square with 2 tablespoons grated cheese and up to ½ teaspoon ground black pepper.

4. Cut each square into 4 even strips. Grasp each end of 1 strip with clean, dry hands; twist it into a cheese straw. Place the twisted straws on a baking sheet.

5. Lay as many straws as will fit in the air-fryer basket—as a general rule, 4 of them in a small machine, 5 in a medium model, or 6 in a large. There should be space for air to circulate around the straws. Set the baking sheet with any remaining straws in the fridge.

6. Air-fry undisturbed for 7 minutes, or until puffed and crisp. Use tongs to transfer the cheese straws to a wire rack, then make subsequent batches in the same way (keeping the baking sheet with the remaining straws in the fridge as each batch cooks). Serve warm.

Then...

- Serve these with a pitcher of PINEAPPLE MARGARITA PUNCH. Put about *6 cups small ice cubes* in a pitcher, then add *2½ cups pineapple juice, 10 ounces (1¼ cups) white tequila, 8 ounces (1 cup)*

orange liqueur (such as Cointreau), 1 cup lime juice, 1 cup orange juice, and 3 tablespoons granulated white sugar, preferably superfine. Stir well until the sugar melts, then strain the punch over *fresh ice* in tall glasses.

Crab Rangoon

7 INGREDIENTS

These retro wontons were once the rage at tiki bars and Polynesian restaurants. Bring them back with this fairly easy version made with wonton wrappers. Since the wrappers are not deep-fried, they easily retain the traditional shape, sort of like the petals of little flowers with a crab and cream cheese bundle at the center. (They have a tendency to collapse in a deep fryer in the oil's hot dance.)

Crab rangoon is often made with imitation crab meat. For the best flavor, spring for the real thing, not in cans on the store's shelf but in the refrigerator case in the fish department.

INGREDIENTS	2-quart or larger air fryer	3.5-quart or larger air fryer	5.25-quart or larger air fryer
Crabmeat, preferably backfin or claw, picked over for shells and cartilage	3 tablespoons (about 3 ounces)	4½ tablespoons (a little more than ¼ pound)	6 tablespoons (about 6 ounces)
Regular or low-fat cream cheese (*not fat-free*), softened to room temperature	1 ounce (2 tablespoons)	1½ ounces (3 tablespoons)	2 ounces (¼ cup)
Minced scallion	1 tablespoon	1½ tablespoons	2 tablespoons
Minced garlic	1 teaspoon	1½ teaspoons	2 teaspoons
Worcestershire sauce	1 teaspoon	1½ teaspoons	2 teaspoons
Wonton wrappers (thawed, if necessary)	12	18	24
Vegetable oil spray	As needed	As needed	As needed
MAKES	12 wontons	18 wontons	24 wontons

1. With the basket (or basket attachment) in the air fryer, heat it to 400°F (or 390°F, if that's the closest setting).

2. Gently stir the crab, cream cheese, scallion, garlic, and Worcestershire sauce in a medium bowl until well combined.

3. Set a bowl of water on a clean, dry work surface or next to a large cutting board. Set one wonton wrapper on the surface, then put a rounded teaspoonful of the crab mixture in the center of the wrapper. Dip your clean finger in the water and run it around the edge of the wrapper. Bring all four sides up to the center and over the filling, and pinch them together in the

continues

middle to seal without covering all of the filling. The traditional look is for the corners of the filled wonton to become four open "flower petals" radiating out from the filled center. Set the filled wonton aside and continue making more as needed. (If you want a video tutorial on filling these, see ours at our YouTube channel, *Cooking with Bruce and Mark*.)

4. Generously coat the filled wontons with vegetable oil spray. Set them sealed side up in the basket with a little room among them. Air-fry undisturbed for 6 minutes, or until golden brown and crisp.

5. Use a nonstick-safe spatula to gently transfer the wontons to a wire rack. Cool for 5 minutes before serving warm.

Then...

- The simplest dip is purchased duck sauce, Saucy Susan, or Thai sweet chili sauce.

- For SPICY KETCHUP DIP, whisk equal parts *ketchup, unseasoned rice vinegar* (see page 70), *brown sugar*, and *sriracha* by volume until uniform.

See photo in insert.

Vegetable Spring Rolls

EASY / VEGETARIAN / CAN BE GLUTEN-FREE / 9 INGREDIENTS

You'll need spring roll wrappers to make these crisp rolls, not the opaque rice-paper wrappers that must be soaked in warm water to become pliable. Instead, use translucent spring roll wrappers that are pliable and ready to roll from the get-go. Most are made from rice flour, a few from tapioca flour (which will also work here) or from wheat flour (which end up tough with this technique). These wrappers are most often found in the freezer case of large supermarkets—and of course, in the freezer case of almost all Asian supermarkets.

Thaw frozen spring roll wrappers overnight in the fridge. Keep the wrappers covered with a loose sheet of plastic wrap as you work with them. If they dry out, they can become brittle. Any remaining wrappers can be sealed in plastic wrap and refrozen.

For the best success, squeeze the marinated vegetables so they don't carry too much liquid into the wrapper. No worries over the moisture loss: The liquids will have already imparted a lot of flavor.

If you want to make vegan spring rolls, omit the beaten egg and instead brush water on the edges of each wrapper to seal it.

INGREDIENTS	2-quart or larger air fryer	3.5-quart or larger air fryer	5.25-quart or larger air fryer
Fresh bean sprouts	½ cup (about 1¾ ounces)	¾ cup (a little more than 2½ ounces)	1 cup (about 3½ ounces)
Shredded carrots	¼ cup	6 tablespoons	½ cup
Slivered, drained, sliced canned bamboo shoots	¼ cup	6 tablespoons	½ cup
Regular or low-sodium soy sauce or gluten-free tamari sauce	1 tablespoon	1½ tablespoons	2 tablespoons
Granulated white sugar	1 teaspoon	1½ teaspoons	2 teaspoons
Toasted sesame oil	1 teaspoon	1½ teaspoons	2 teaspoons
Spring roll wrappers (gluten-free, if a concern)	4	6	8
Large egg, well beaten	1	1	1
Vegetable oil spray	As needed	As needed	As needed
MAKES	4 spring rolls	6 spring rolls	8 spring rolls

1. Gently stir the bean sprouts, carrots, bamboo shoots, soy or tamari sauce, sugar, and oil in a large bowl until the vegetables are evenly coated. Set aside at room temperature for 10 to 15 minutes.

2. With the basket (or basket attachment) in the air fryer, heat it to 400°F (or 390°F, if that's the closest setting).

3. Set a spring roll wrapper on a clean, dry work surface. Pick up about ¼ cup of the vegetable mixture and gently squeeze it in your clean hand to release most of the liquid. Set this bundle of vegetables along one edge of the wrapper.

4. Fold two opposing sides (at right angles to the filling) up and over the filling, concealing part of it and making a folded-over border down two sides of the wrapper. Brush the top half of the wrapper (including the folded parts) with beaten egg so it will seal when you roll it closed.

5. Starting with the side nearest the filling, roll the wrapper closed, working to make a tight fit,

eliminating as much air as possible from inside the wrapper. Set it aside seam side down and continue making more filled rolls using the same techniques.

6. Lightly coat all the sealed rolls with vegetable oil spray on all sides. Set them seam side down in the basket and air-fry undisturbed for 8 minutes, or until golden brown and very crisp.

7. Use a nonstick-safe spatula and a flatware fork for balance to transfer the rolls to a wire rack. Cool for at least 5 minutes or up to 15 minutes before serving.

Then...

- Serve these spring rolls with **Chile-Peanut Sauce** (page 46), **Soy-and-Sour Dip** (page 70), **Sweet-and-Sour Ketchup Dip** (page 71), **No-Cook Spicy Soy Dipping Sauce** (page 253), or **Wasabi Mayonnaise** (page 296).

Fried Wontons

FAST / 7 INGREDIENTS

Crisp, tender, irresistible wontons: They're surely the reason you bought an air fryer.

In many North American supermarkets, wonton wrappers are in the refrigerator case of the produce section, near the fresh Asian noodles and Asian produce.

Use only *lean* ground meat here, so excess grease doesn't turn the bottom of the wrappers soggy as they cook.

White pepper may seem a fussy ingredient, but it gives the filling the characteristic musky flavor prized in Chinese American cooking. If you'd like a hotter filling, add some red pepper flakes to the ground meat mixture—or even a small spoonful of a hot chile paste or oil, especially the hot and garlicky Lao Gan Ma Spicy Chili Crisp. Look for that specialty condiment at Asian markets or from online suppliers. If you like spicy fare as much as we do, you won't regret springing for a jar.

INGREDIENTS	2-quart or larger air fryer	3.5-quart or larger air fryer	5.25-quart or larger air fryer
Lean ground beef, pork, or turkey	¼ pound	6 ounces	½ pound
Regular or reduced-sodium soy sauce or tamari sauce	2 teaspoons	1 tablespoon	2 tablespoons
Minced garlic	1 teaspoon	1½ teaspoons	2 teaspoons
Ground dried ginger	½ teaspoon	¾ teaspoon	1 teaspoon
Ground white pepper	Rounded ¼ teaspoon	½ teaspoon	1 teaspoon
Wonton wrappers (thawed, if necessary)	16	24	32
Vegetable oil spray	As needed	As needed	As needed
MAKES	*16 wontons*	*24 wontons*	*32 wontons*

1. With the basket (or basket attachment) in the air fryer, heat it to 350°F (or 360°F, if that's the closest setting).

2. Stir the ground meat, soy or tamari sauce, garlic, ginger, and white pepper in a bowl until the spices are uniformly distributed in the mixture.

3. Set a small bowl of water on a clean, dry surface or next to a clean, dry cutting board. Set one wonton wrapper on the surface. Dip your clean finger in the water, then run it along the edges of the wrapper. Set 1 rounded teaspoon of the ground meat mixture in the center of the wrapper. Fold it over, corner to corner, to create a filled triangle. Press to seal the edges, then pull the corners on the longest side up and together over the filling to create the classic wonton shape. Press the corners together to seal. Set aside and continue filling and making more filled wontons.

4. Generously coat the filled wontons on all sides with vegetable oil spray. Arrange them in the basket in one layer and air-fry for 6 minutes, shaking the basket gently at the 2- and 4-minute marks to rearrange the wontons (but always making sure they're still in one layer), until golden brown and crisp.

5. Pour the wontons in the basket onto a wire rack or even into a serving bowl. Cool for 2 or 3 minutes (but not much longer) and serve hot.

Then...

- Serve these wontons with PEANUT-SESAME SAUCE. Whisk *3 parts unseasoned rice vinegar* (see page 70), *2 parts natural-style creamy peanut butter, 2 parts toasted sesame oil, 1 part minced peeled fresh ginger, 1 part regular or reduced-sodium soy sauce or tamari sauce*, and *1 part granulated*

white sugar by volume until smooth. If desired, whisk in a splash of *sriracha* for heat.

- Or swap around the flavors and try them with **Chile-Peanut Sauce** (page 46), **Buffalo Sauce** (page 187), or **No-Cook Spicy Soy Dipping Sauce** (page 253).

See photo in insert.

Fried Gyoza

8 INGREDIENTS

These gyoza are stuffed with an aromatic mixture made with ground pork. Leaner ground pork is better because it releases less fat as it cooks, resulting in gyoza that stay crunchier longer.

The air fryer is a great tool to make the gyoza crunchy. They're almost always pan-fried for a crunchy bottom but the machine makes them crunchy all over. No, they won't have that darkly browned bottom with a soft dough top, their characteristic appeal in Japanese restaurants. But as compensation, these are much less oily and much crunchier—which frankly suits us to a T.

INGREDIENTS	2-quart or larger air fryer	3.5-quart or larger air fryer	5.25-quart or larger air fryer
Lean ground pork	¼ pound	5 ounces	6 ounces
Very thinly sliced scallion	2 tablespoons	2½ tablespoons	3 tablespoons
Minced peeled fresh ginger	4 teaspoons	1 tablespoon plus 2 teaspoons	2 tablespoons
Toasted sesame oil	1 teaspoon	1¼ teaspoons	1½ teaspoons
Table salt	Pinch	⅛ teaspoon	¼ teaspoon
Ground black pepper	Pinch	⅛ teaspoon	¼ teaspoon
Round gyoza or square wonton wrappers (thawed, if necessary)	14	18	24
Vegetable oil spray	As needed	As needed	As needed
MAKES	*14 gyoza*	*18 gyoza*	*24 gyoza*

1. With the basket (or basket attachment) in the air fryer, heat it to 350°F (or 360°F, if that's the closest setting).

2. Mix the ground pork, scallion, ginger, sesame oil, salt, and pepper in a bowl until well combined.

3. Set a bowl of water on a clean, dry surface or next to a clean, dry cutting board. Set one gyoza or wonton wrapper on that surface. Dip your clean finger in the water and run it around the perimeter of the gyoza wrapper or the edge of the wonton wrapper.

continues

Put about 1 ½ teaspoons of the meat mixture in the center of the wrapper.

For the gyoza wrapper, fold the wrapper in half to close, pressing the edge to seal, then wet the outside of the edge of both sides of the seam and pleat it into little ridges to seal.

For the wonton wrapper, fold it in half lengthwise to make a rectangle, then seal the sides together, flattening the packet a bit as you do.

Set the filled wrapper aside and continue making more in the same way. When done, generously coat them on all sides with vegetable oil spray.

4. Place the gyoza in the basket in one layer and air-fry undisturbed for 6 minutes, or until browned and crisp at the edges.

5. Use kitchen tongs or a nonstick-safe spatula to gently transfer the gyoza to a wire rack. Cool for only 2 or 3 minutes before serving hot.

Then...

- The CLASSIC DIPPING SAUCE FOR GYOZA is a combination of *regular or reduced-sodium soy sauce or tamari sauce* and *mirin* (see page 176), often in a 4-to-5 ratio. Add a *spritz of lemon juice* for a tart finish, if desired.

- For a complex SOY-AND-SOUR DIP, mix *unseasoned rice vinegar* (see below) and *regular or reduced-sodium soy sauce or tamari sauce* in equal proportions, then stir in *a little minced garlic, a bit more minced peeled fresh ginger*, as well as *some minced scallion (green part only)*. Add a *splash of toasted sesame oil* before serving.

- Or use the **Easy Homemade Yuzu Dressing** (page 29) for these gyoza.

- For a larger appetizer tray, serve these gyoza with **Warm and Salty Edamame** (page 28) and **Blistered Shishito Peppers** (page 29).

Shrimp Egg Rolls

EASY / 9 INGREDIENTS

With bagged slaw mix and purchased cooked shrimp, egg rolls are within reach on any weeknight. We nixed any ground pork here because we found that it caused the egg roll wrappers to get soggy in the air fryer unless the meat was cooked in advance—and turning on the stove is a bit of a stretch when someone wants egg rolls in a hurry.

Of course, you can double or even triple this recipe, making as many egg rolls as you like. The only limit is your patience in stuffing them, then air-frying them in batches.

Look for egg roll wrappers in the refrigerator case of the supermarket's produce section, usually near the tofu.

One ingredient note: **Unseasoned rice vinegar** is a low-acid vinegar, favored in Asian cooking and found with the other vinegars in most North American supermarkets these days. Rice vinegar actually comes in two varieties: seasoned, which is sweetened in some way, and unseasoned, which is *not* sweetened. Seasoned rice vinegar is almost always so labeled; unfortunately, unseasoned is rarely so labeled. You'll need to check the ingredient list on the bottle to make sure the one in hand is not sweetened. We only call for *unseasoned* (that is, unsweetened) rice vinegar in this book.

INGREDIENTS	2-quart or larger air fryer	3.5-quart or larger air fryer	5.25-quart or larger air fryer
Bagged shredded slaw mix	1½ cups	2 cups	3 cups
Cooked, peeled, and deveined cocktail shrimp, very finely chopped	3 ounces	¼ pound	6 ounces
Regular or reduced-sodium soy sauce or tamari sauce	1 teaspoon	1½ teaspoons	2 teaspoons
Unseasoned rice vinegar (see headnote)	1 teaspoon	1½ teaspoons	2 teaspoons
Cornstarch or tapioca starch	1 teaspoon	1¼ teaspoons	1½ teaspoons
Onion powder	¼ teaspoon	rounded ¼ teaspoon	½ teaspoon
Five-spice powder (see page 258)	⅛ teaspoon	¼ teaspoon	Rounded ¼ teaspoon
Garlic powder	⅛ teaspoon	¼ teaspoon	½ teaspoon
Egg roll wrappers	3	4	6
MAKES	3 egg rolls	4 egg rolls	6 egg rolls

1. With the basket (or basket attachment) in the air fryer, heat it to 400°F (or 390°F, if that's the closest setting).

2. Mix the slaw mix, shrimp, soy or tamari sauce, vinegar, cornstarch or tapioca starch, onion powder, five-spice powder, and garlic powder in a bowl until well combined.

3. Set a bowl of water on a clean, dry work surface or next to a clean, dry cutting board. Place an egg roll wrapper on the surface. Moisten your clean finger, then run it around all four edges of the wrapper. Place about ⅓ cup filling in the center of the wrapper. Fold two opposing sides up and over the filling before rolling the egg roll closed from one of the remaining sides of the wrapper (like rolling a burrito). Press gently to make sure the moistened wrapper seals. Set aside seam side down and continue making more egg rolls, following this technique.

4. Generously coat the egg rolls on all sides with vegetable oil spray. Set them seam side down in the basket in one layer. Air-fry undisturbed for 10 minutes, or until brown and very crisp. They may get fairly dark in spots (depending on the coating of spray).

5. Use kitchen tongs to gently transfer the egg rolls to a wire rack. Don't squeeze hard or the wrapper will break into shards. Cool for 2 or 3 minutes before serving hot.

Then...

• Go beyond duck sauce with SWEET-AND-SOUR KETCHUP DIP for the egg rolls. Mix *6 tablespoons granulated white sugar, ⅓ cup water, 3 tablespoons ketchup,* and *2 teaspoons regular or reduced-sodium soy sauce or tamari sauce* in a small saucepan. Simmer over low heat until bubbling and even thickened a bit, stirring fairly often, about 4 minutes. Whisk *¼ cup apple cider vinegar, 2 tablespoons water,* and *2 tablespoons cornstarch* in a small bowl, then whisk this mixture into the simmering sauce. Continue cooking, whisking all the while, until thickened, 1 to 2 minutes.

Potato Samosas

EASY / VEGAN / 7 INGREDIENTS

Our version of this crunchy South Asian stuffed pocket is in essence a shortcut recipe. We call for instant mashed potato flakes (which are just dehydrated potatoes) for the filling, as well as a ready-made pie crust to create the wrappers. In other words, you don't have to make mashed potatoes or a complicated dough.

Our samosas are also a little smaller than those served in Indian restaurants, better for a snack rather than a first course (although you could make dinner out of them with a salad on the side, like our **Carrot Slaw** on page 115).

You'll notice that the purchased, refrigerator pie crusts come in various sizes and densities, depending on the brand. We tested this recipe with the crusts from a 14.1-ounce box, although any will work. Larger boxes will have leftover (and, yes, wasted) dough when you've cut out as many wrappers as you need.

You can vary these samosas by swapping various sorts of curry powder for the more standard yellow variety; by adding more ground dried ginger and/or cayenne to any curry powder; by making your own curry powder (page 363); or by using garam masala (page 156) instead of curry powder for a milder flavor with lots of "warming" spices.

INGREDIENTS	2-quart or larger air fryer	3.5-quart or larger air fryer	5.25-quart or larger air fryer
Instant mashed potato flakes	½ cup	¾ cup	1 cup
Boiling water	½ cup	¾ cup	1 cup
Plain full-fat or low-fat yogurt (*not* Greek yogurt or fat-free yogurt)	¼ cup	⅓ cup	½ cup
Yellow curry powder, purchased or homemade (see page 363)	Rounded ½ teaspoon	1 teaspoon	1¼ teaspoons
Table salt	¼ teaspoon	½ teaspoon	¾ teaspoon
Purchased refrigerated pie crust(s), from a minimum 14.1-ounce box	1	1½	2
All-purpose flour	As needed	As needed	As needed
Vegetable oil spray	As needed	As needed	As needed
MAKES	*8 samosas*	*12 samosas*	*16 samosas*

1. Put the potato flakes in a medium bowl and pour the boiling water over them. Stir well to form a mixture like thick mashed potatoes. Cool for 15 minutes.

2. With the basket (or basket attachment) in the air fryer, heat it to 400°F (or 390°F, if that's the closest setting).

3. Stir the yogurt, curry powder, and salt into the potato mixture until smooth and uniform.

4. Unwrap and unroll the sheet(s) of pie crust dough onto a clean, dry work surface. Cut out as many 4-inch circles as you can with a big cookie cutter or a giant sturdy water glass, or even by tracing the circle with the rim of a 4-inch plate. Gather up the scraps of dough. Lightly flour your work surface and

set the scraps on top. Roll them together into a sheet that matches the thickness of the original crusts and cut more circles until you have the number you need—8 circles for the small batch, 12 for the medium batch, or 16 for the large.

5. Pick up one of the circles and create something like an ice cream cone by folding and sealing the circle together so that it is closed at the bottom and flared open at the top, in a conical shape. Put 1 tablespoon of the potato filling into the open cone, then push the filling into the cone toward the point. Fold the top over the filling and press to seal the dough into a triangular shape with rounded corners, taking care to seal those corners all around. Set aside and continue forming and filling the remainder of the dough circles as directed.

6. Lightly coat the filled dough pockets with vegetable oil spray on all sides. Set them in the basket in one layer and air-fry undisturbed for 10 minutes, or until lightly browned and crisp.

7. Gently turn the contents of the basket out onto a wire rack. Use kitchen tongs to gently set all the samosas seam side up. Cool for 10 minutes before serving.

Then...

- Serve these samosas with any chutney you prefer. Look beyond the standard mango chutney for, say, cranberry or plum chutney.

- To make an easy BLUEBERRY CHUTNEY, mix *2½ cups fresh blueberries, ½ cup minced red onion, ½ cup packed light brown sugar, ⅓ cup apple cider vinegar, 1 tablespoon minced peeled fresh ginger, 1 teaspoon minced garlic, up to ½ teaspoon cayenne, ½ teaspoon table salt*, and *one 4-inch cinnamon stick* in a large saucepan. Bring to a simmer over medium heat, stirring often. Cook, still stirring often, for 3 minutes; then stir in *2 tablespoons cornstarch*. Bring back to a boil and cook until thickened, stirring constantly, about 1 minute. Remove the pan from the heat and cool for at least 20 minutes or to room temperature. Remove the cinnamon stick before serving. Save any leftover chutney in a sealed nonreactive container in the fridge for up to 2 weeks.

Middle Eastern Phyllo Rolls

11 INGREDIENTS

Sometimes called "lamb cigars," these crunchy rolls with an aromatic filling are a staple in Middle Eastern restaurants. Traditionally, they're made with ground lamb, of course; you can use ground beef for a milder flavor.

Roll the cigars into fairly tight tubes without breaking the phyllo dough. Always have many more phyllo sheets out than you'll need. If a sheet tears, you might be able to save the cigar by patching it and sealing it back together, although it's (sorry) probably best just to start over. Keep the phyllo sheets under a clean kitchen towel so they don't dry out.

For far fewer ingredients, substitute bottled *ras al hanout*, a common North African spice blend, for the cinnamon, coriander, cumin, turmeric, and pepper. You'll need 1¼ teaspoons for a small batch, 2 teaspoons for a medium batch, or 1 tablespoon for a large batch. You still need to add the salt, as directed, unless the ras al hanout you have includes salt. (Most don't.)

INGREDIENTS	2-quart or larger air fryer	3.5-quart or larger air fryer	5.25-quart or larger air fryer
Lean ground beef or ground lamb	¼ pound	6 ounces	½ pound
Sliced almonds	2 tablespoons	3 tablespoons	¼ cup
Chutney (any variety), finely chopped	2½ teaspoons	1 tablespoon	1½ tablespoons
Ground cinnamon	¼ teaspoon	Rounded ¼ teaspoon	½ teaspoon
Ground coriander	¼ teaspoon	Rounded ¼ teaspoon	½ teaspoon
Ground cumin	¼ teaspoon	Rounded ¼ teaspoon	½ teaspoon
Ground dried turmeric	¼ teaspoon	Rounded ¼ teaspoon	½ teaspoon
Table salt	¼ teaspoon	Rounded ¼ teaspoon	½ teaspoon
Ground black pepper	¼ teaspoon	Rounded ¼ teaspoon	½ teaspoon
18 × 14-inch phyllo sheets (thawed, if necessary)	4	6	8
Olive oil spray	As needed	As needed	As needed
MAKES	4 rolls	6 rolls	8 rolls

1. Set a medium skillet over medium heat for a minute or two, then crumble in the ground meat. Cook for 3 minutes, stirring often, or until well browned. Stir in the almonds, chutney, cinnamon, coriander, cumin, turmeric, salt, and pepper until well combined. Remove from the heat, scrape the cooked ground meat mixture into a bowl, and cool for 15 minutes.

2. With the basket (or basket attachment) in the air fryer, heat it to 400°F (or 390°F, if that's the closest setting).

3. Place one sheet of phyllo dough on a clean, dry work surface. (Keep the others covered.) Lightly coat it with olive oil spray, then fold it in half by bringing the short ends together. Place about 3 tablespoons of the ground meat mixture along one of the longer edges, then fold both of the shorter sides of the dough up and over the meat to partially enclose it (and become a border along the sheet of dough). Roll the dough closed, coat it with olive oil spray on all sides, and set it aside seam side down. Repeat this filling and spraying process with the remaining phyllo sheets.

4. Set the rolls seam side down in the basket in one layer with some air space between them. Air-fry undisturbed for 5 minutes, or until very crisp and golden brown.

5. Use kitchen tongs to transfer the rolls to a wire rack. Cool for only 2 or 3 minutes before serving hot.

Then...

- Make CREAMY HARISSA DIP for the rolls. Whisk together ½ cup plain Greek yogurt, 1 teaspoon purchased harissa (a Tunisian chile paste, now favored across North Africa and the Middle East), and 1 teaspoon lemon juice.

- Or try the rolls with **Mint Tahini Sauce** (page 164).

- Or smear each bite with **Muhamarra** (page 25).

Pão de Queijo

VEGETARIAN / GLUTEN-FREE / 6 INGREDIENTS

These crunchy, cheesy balls (*pown-deh-KAY-zho*) are a favorite Brazilian street food—and gluten-free, to boot. Vary this recipe at will, using whatever sort of hard grating cheese you prefer, even taking them far away from Brazil with a caramelized Boerenkaas, for example.

Essentially, you make a gluten-free version of *pâte à choux*, the dough often used to make cream puffs. Doing so is admittedly time-consuming, so we didn't scale the ingredients out for various machines. That means you'll need to work in batches (perhaps three in a small machine or two in a medium machine). Don't worry about a batch not being hot when you serve them. They're better slightly warm. And they get crunchier as they sit!

INGREDIENTS	For any air fryer
Whole, low-fat, or fat-free milk	½ cup
Butter	2 tablespoons, plus more for greasing
Table salt	½ teaspoon
Tapioca flour or starch	1½ cups
Large egg	1
Finely grated aged Asiago cheese	⅔ cup (about 2 ounces)
MAKES	12 balls

1. Heat the milk and butter in a medium saucepan set over medium heat, stirring occasionally, just until the mixture reaches a low boil. Remove the pan from the heat and stir in the tapioca flour or starch to form a soft dough. Scrape this mixture into a medium bowl, cover with plastic wrap, and cool for 15 minutes.

2. Use an electric mixer at medium speed to beat the egg into the tapioca mixture until it becomes a thick,

smooth dough, about 2 minutes. Turn off the mixer, then scrape down and remove the beaters. Stir the cheese into the dough. Set aside, covered again in plastic wrap, for 10 minutes.

3. With the basket (or basket attachment) in the air fryer, heat it to 375°F (or 370°F or 360°F, if one of these is the closest setting).

continues

4. Generously butter the inside of a 6- to 8-inch cake pan (whatever fits in your machine). Scoop up 2 tablespoons of the tapioca dough and set it in the pan. Continue making more dollops, spacing them 1 ½ inches apart. Place the pan in the basket and air-fry for 12 minutes, or until the balls are puffed, lightly browned, round, and crunchy.

5. Use kitchen tongs to remove the cake pan from the basket and turn the balls out onto a wire rack. Cool the balls and the cake pan for 5 minutes, then butter the inside of the pan again before making more balls, in as many batches as necessary.

Then...

- Traditionally, these pão are served with either butter to smear on them bite by bite or *goiabada cremosa* (like a guava marmalade).

- Serve the pão with a pitcher of CAIPIRINHA PUNCH. Wash *12 medium limes*, then cut them into eighths. Put them in a large bowl and add *½ cup granulated white sugar, preferably superfine*. Use a potato masher or the back of a wooden spoon to smash the limes into the sugar, carrying on until the sugar has mostly dissolved. Scrape and pour this mixture into a pitcher, then add about *half a 750 ml bottle of cachaça* and *8 to 10 cups small ice cubes*. Stir well, then strain over fresh ice in tall glasses.

Cheese Arancini

VEGETARIAN / CAN BE GLUTEN-FREE / 8 INGREDIENTS

Although often served alongside a roast or a stew in a traditional Italian meal, these crunchy rice balls (*ah-run-CHEE-nee*, "little oranges") make a great snack or appetizer before almost anything off the grill.

Because of the intense heat in the air fryer, they can't be overstuffed with cheese. It'll run out and cause the ball to collapse. What's more, the balls set much more quickly when they're dropped in a deep fryer, the traditional cooking method. So we make slightly smaller arancini than you may have seen in Italian restaurants, the size of a golf ball instead of a softball, to deliver a decent cheese-to-rice ratio in the ball without any worries of collapse.

INGREDIENTS	2-quart or larger air fryer	3.5-quart or larger air fryer	5.25-quart or larger air fryer
Water	⅔ cup	1 cup	1⅓ cups
Raw white Arborio rice	⅓ cup	½ cup	⅔ cup
Butter	1 teaspoon	1½ teaspoons	2 teaspoons
Table salt	¼ teaspoon	Rounded ¼ teaspoon	½ teaspoon
¾-inch semi-firm mozzarella cubes (*not* fresh mozzarella)	5	8	10
Large egg(s), well beaten	1	2	2
Seasoned Italian-style dried bread crumbs (gluten-free, if a concern)	⅔ cup	1 cup	1¼ cups
Olive oil spray	As needed	As needed	As needed
MAKES	*5 arancini*	*8 arancini*	*10 arancini*

1. Combine the water, rice, butter, and salt in a small saucepan. Bring to a boil over medium-high heat, stirring occasionally. Cover, reduce the heat to very low, and simmer very slowly for 20 minutes.

2. Take the saucepan off the heat and let it stand, covered, for 10 minutes. Uncover it and fluff the rice. Cool for 20 minutes. (The rice can be made up to 1 hour in advance; keep it covered in its saucepan.)

3. With the basket (or basket attachment) in the air fryer, heat it to 375°F (or 370°F or 360°F, if one of these is the closest setting).

4. Set up and fill two shallow soup plates or small bowls on your counter: one with the beaten egg(s) and one with the bread crumbs.

5. With clean but wet hands, scoop up about 2 tablespoons of the cooked rice and form it into a ball. Push a cube of mozzarella into the middle of the ball and seal the cheese inside. Dip the ball in the egg(s) to coat completely, letting any excess egg slip back into the rest. Roll the ball in the bread crumbs to coat evenly but lightly. Set aside and continue making more rice balls.

6. Generously spray the balls with olive oil spray, then set them in the basket in one layer. They must not touch. Air-fry undisturbed for 10 minutes, or until crunchy and golden brown. If the machine is at 360°F, you may need to add 1 or 2 minutes to the cooking time.

7. Use a nonstick-safe spatula, and maybe a flatware spoon for balance, to gently transfer the balls to a wire rack. Cool for at least 5 minutes or up to 20 minutes before serving.

Then...

- Some arancini are stuffed with cooked eggplant—or even an eggplant stew. To replicate that taste, serve these with purchased caponata as a dip or spread. See our **Caponata Salsa** (page 82) as one option.

- Cheese arancini are often served with marinara sauce or even ragù, but we love them when they're served with BÉCHAMEL SAUCE. To make four servings, heat *1¼ cups whole or low-fat milk* in a bowl in the microwave until steaming. Melt *2 tablespoons butter* in a small saucepan set over low heat, then whisk in *2 tablespoons all-purpose flour* until dissolved and somewhat like a paste; do not let it brown. Slowly whisk the hot milk into this butter mixture and bring to a simmer, stirring constantly. Add *grated nutmeg* and *table salt* to taste, then continue cooking, stirring all the while, until thickened and creamy, 2 to 3 minutes. Serve warm, ladled over the arancini.

See photo in insert.

Meatball Arancini

EASY / CAN BE VEGETARIAN / CAN BE GLUTEN-FREE / 9 INGREDIENTS

Italian grandmothers would start making these rice balls by making meatballs from scratch. We've got an easier way. Frozen meatballs become the center of the rice ball in a snap.

Use any sort of meatball you like, even vegan "meatballs." Then get ready to serve these smaller-than-normal, tangerine-size arancini as an afternoon snack when dinner's still a ways off.

INGREDIENTS	2-quart or larger air fryer	3.5-quart or larger air fryer	5.25-quart or larger air fryer
Water	¾ cup	1⅓ cups	1½ cups
Raw white Arborio rice	6 tablespoons	⅔ cup	¾ cup
Butter	1½ teaspoons	2 teaspoons	1 tablespoon
Table salt	¼ teaspoon	Rounded ¼ teaspoon	½ teaspoon
Large egg(s), well beaten	1	2	2
Seasoned Italian-style dried bread crumbs (gluten-free, if a concern)	½ cup	¾ cup	1 cup
Finely grated Parmesan cheese	¼ cup (about ¾ ounce)	⅓ cup (about 1 ounce)	½ cup (about 1½ ounces)
½-ounce "bite-size" frozen meatballs (any variety, even vegan and/or gluten-free, if a concern), thawed	4	6	8
Olive oil spray	As needed	As needed	As needed
MAKES	4 arancini	6 arancini	8 arancini

1. Combine the water, rice, butter, and salt in a small saucepan. Bring to a boil over medium-high heat, stirring occasionally. Cover, reduce the heat to very low, and simmer very slowly for 20 minutes.

2. Take the saucepan off the heat and let it stand, covered, for 10 minutes. Uncover it and fluff the rice. Cool for 20 minutes. (The rice can be made up to 1 hour in advance; keep it covered in its saucepan.)

3. With the basket (or basket attachment) in the air fryer, heat it to 375°F (or 370°F or 360°F, if one of these is the closest setting).

4. Set up and fill two shallow soup plates or small bowls on your counter: one with the beaten egg(s) and one with the bread crumbs mixed with the grated cheese.

5. With clean but wet hands, scoop up about 3 tablespoons of the cooked rice and form it into a ball around a mini meatball, forming a sealed casing. Dip the ball in the egg(s) to coat completely, letting any excess egg slip back into the rest. Set the ball in the bread-crumb mixture and roll it gently to coat evenly but lightly all over. Set aside and continue making more rice balls.

6. Generously spray the balls with olive oil spray, then set them in the basket in one layer. They must not touch. Air-fry undisturbed for 10 minutes, or until crunchy and golden brown. Use kitchen tongs to gently transfer the balls to a wire rack. Cool for at least 5 minutes before serving.

Then...

- Serve with warmed purchased or homemade marinara sauce for dipping.

- Or make a COOKED TOMATO DIP, with its more summery flavor than marinara sauce. Heat *1 tablespoon olive oil* in a large skillet set over medium heat. Add *1 cup finely chopped fresh* tomatoes and cook, stirring often, until soft, about 5 minutes. Stir in *⅓ cup tomato paste, up to ⅓ cup minced scallions, up to 2 tablespoons minced fresh basil leaves, up to ½ teaspoon red pepper flakes,* and *table salt* and *ground black pepper* to taste. Scrape this mixture into a bowl and cool for 10 minutes. Serve warm or at room temperature.

See photo in insert.

Baba Ghanouj

EASY / VEGAN / GLUTEN-FREE / 7 INGREDIENTS

This Middle Eastern eggplant dip just got a whole lot better! The air fryer slowly blackens the eggplant, allowing the charred flavor to permeate the vegetable while leaving the inner parts of the vegetable more "cooked" than dehydrated for a silkier finish.

Be careful when you take the eggplant(s) out of the basket. They are quite soft and can split open with the slightest pressure.

One ingredient note: **Tahini** is a paste made from ground sesame seeds. It can be found in the international aisle of most supermarkets, often in cans. Once opened, reseal the can or jar and store in the refrigerator for up to 3 months—or freeze a portion of the paste in a sealed container for up to 1 year.

INGREDIENTS	2-quart or larger air fryer	3.5-quart or larger air fryer	5.25-quart or larger air fryer
Small (12-ounce) purple Italian eggplant(s)	1	2	3
Olive oil	2 tablespoons	¼ cup	6 tablespoons
Tahini	2 tablespoons	¼ cup	6 tablespoons
Ground black pepper	¼ teaspoon	½ teaspoon	¾ teaspoon
Onion powder	⅛ teaspoon	¼ teaspoon	Rounded ¼ teaspoon
Mild smoked paprika (optional)	⅛ teaspoon	¼ teaspoon	Rounded ¼ teaspoon
Table salt	Up to ½ teaspoon	Up to 1 teaspoon	Up to 1½ teaspoons
MAKES	1 cup	2 cups	3 cups

1. With the basket (or basket attachment) in the air fryer, heat it to 400°F (or 390°F, if that's the closest setting).

2. Prick the eggplant(s) on all sides with a fork. When the machine is at temperature, set the eggplant(s) in the basket in one layer. Air-fry undisturbed for 40 minutes, or until blackened and soft.

continues

3. Remove the basket from the machine. Cool the eggplant(s) in the basket for 20 minutes.

4. Use a nonstick-safe spatula, and perhaps a flatware tablespoon for balance, to gently transfer the eggplant(s) to a bowl. The juices will run out. Make sure the bowl is close to the basket. Split the eggplant(s) open.

5. Scrape the soft insides of half an eggplant into a food processor. Repeat with the remaining piece(s). Add any juices from the bowl to the eggplant in the food processor, but discard the skins and stems.

6. Add the olive oil, tahini, pepper, onion powder, and smoked paprika (if using). Add about half the salt, then cover and process until smooth, stopping the machine at least once to scrape down the inside of the canister. Check the spread for salt and add more as needed. Scrape the baba ghanouj into a bowl and serve warm, or set aside at room temperature for up to 2 hours, or cover and store in the refrigerator for up to 4 days.

Then...

- Serve this extra smoky baba ghanouj with **Pita Chips** (page 24) or **Bagel Chips** (page 25).

- This dip makes a nice "sauce" or even a bed for **Lemon-Roasted Salmon Fillets** (page 284).

- It's also a fine condiment on **Lamb Burgers** (page 135).

- For a mezze platter, include this dip with **Muhamarra** (page 25), **Middle Eastern Phyllo Rolls** (page 74), and **Crunchy Falafel Balls** (page 146) with **Tzatziki Sauce** (page 120).

Roasted Red Pepper Dip

EASY / VEGAN / GLUTEN-FREE / 7 INGREDIENTS

While you can make a decent red pepper dip with jarred red peppers, they'll never have that slightly citrusy, mildly charred flavor of those you roast yourself. An air fryer makes it easy because you don't mess up your stove trying to blister the peppers.

Although you don't need to tend the peppers constantly the way you would if you were charring them over an open flame, you should check on them after about 10 minutes in the machine. If they're already blackened and blistered (if they had less moisture in their skins from having sat on the grocery store's shelf for a while), you'll need to remove them a bit before we suggest. But remember: Blackened color means deeper flavor (within limits, of course).

INGREDIENTS	2-quart or larger air fryer	3.5-quart or larger air fryer
Medium-size red bell pepper(s)	1	2
Canned white beans, drained and rinsed	¾ cup plus 2 tablespoons	1¾ cups (one 15-ounce can)
Fresh oregano leaves, packed	1½ teaspoons	1 tablespoon
Olive oil	2 tablespoons	3 tablespoons
Lemon juice	2 teaspoons	1 tablespoon
Table salt	¼ teaspoon	½ teaspoon
Ground black pepper	¼ teaspoon	½ teaspoon
MAKES	1 cup	2 cups

1. With the basket (or basket attachment) in the air fryer, heat it to 400°F (or 390°F, if that's the closest setting).

2. Set the pepper(s) in the basket and air-fry undisturbed for 15 minutes, until blistered and even blackened.

3. Use kitchen tongs to transfer the pepper(s) to a zip-closed plastic bag or small bowl. Seal the bag or cover the bowl with plastic wrap. Set aside for 20 minutes.

4. Peel each pepper, then stem it, cut it in half, and remove all its seeds and their white membranes.

5. Set the pieces of the pepper in a food processor. Add the beans, oregano, olive oil, lemon juice, salt, and pepper. Cover and process until smooth, stopping the machine at least once to scrape down the inside of the canister. Scrape the dip into a bowl and serve warm, or cover and refrigerate for up to 3 days (although the dip tastes best if it's allowed to come back to room temperature).

Then...

- Serve this dip with **Pita Chips** (page 24).

- Or use it as a spread in wraps, especially those with lots of chopped vegetables and sprouts.

- Or mix equal parts of this dip with regular or low-fat mayonnaise (gluten-free, if a concern) and use it as a spread in roast beef sandwiches.

- Or use it as a spread underneath sliced avocado on toasted bread for a new take on avocado toast.

Caponata Salsa

EASY / VEGAN / GLUTEN-FREE / 10 INGREDIENTS

Our air-fried version of this classic eggplant condiment is not an oily mess the way some jarred caponata is. The summery vegetables retain their fresh flavor and some of their texture without getting a "stewed" taste—which is ultimately why we refer to this dish as a salsa.

We don't peel the eggplant because we like the slightly bitter flavor and chewy texture the peel adds to the final dish. If you don't, peel the eggplant before you dice it.

Plan on making this dish in advance because the dip needs a couple of hours in the fridge to mellow.

INGREDIENTS	2-quart or larger air fryer	3.5-quart or larger air fryer	5.25-quart or larger air fryer
Purple Italian eggplant(s), stemmed and diced (no need to peel)	3 cups (one 12-ounce eggplant)	4 cups (one 1-pound eggplant)	6 cups (two 12-ounce eggplants)
Olive oil spray	As needed	As needed	As needed
Celery, thinly sliced	1 cup	1½ cups	2¼ cups
Cherry or grape tomatoes, halved	12 (about 6 ounces)	16 (about ½ pound)	24 (about ¾ pound)
Drained and rinsed capers, chopped	2 teaspoons	1 tablespoon	1½ tablespoons
Minced fresh rosemary leaves	Up to 2 teaspoons	Up to 1 tablespoon	Up to 1½ tablespoons
Red wine vinegar	1 tablespoon	1½ tablespoons	2 tablespoons
Granulated white sugar	1 teaspoon	1½ teaspoons	2 teaspoons
Table salt	½ teaspoon	¾ teaspoon	1 teaspoon
Ground black pepper	½ teaspoon	¾ teaspoon	1 teaspoon
MAKES	4 servings	6 servings	8 servings

1. With the basket (or basket attachment) in the air fryer, heat it to 350°F (or 360°F, if that's the closest setting).

2. Put the eggplant pieces in a bowl and generously coat them with olive oil spray. Toss and stir, spray again, and toss some more, until the pieces are glistening.

3. When the machine is at temperature, pour the eggplant pieces into the basket and spread them out into an even layer. Air-fry for 8 minutes, tossing and rearranging the pieces twice.

4. Meanwhile, put the celery and tomatoes in the same bowl the eggplant pieces had been in. Generously coat them with olive oil spray; then toss well, spray again, and toss some more, until the vegetables are well coated.

5. When the eggplant has cooked for 8 minutes, pour the celery and tomatoes on top in the basket. Air-fry undisturbed for 8 minutes more, until the tomatoes have begun to soften.

6. Pour the contents of the basket back into the same bowl. Add the capers, rosemary, vinegar, sugar, salt, and pepper. Toss well to blend, breaking up the tomatoes a bit to create more moisture in the mixture.

7. Cover and refrigerate for 2 hours to blend the flavors. Serve chilled or at room temperature. The caponata salsa can stay in its covered bowl

in the fridge for up to 2 days before the vegetables weep too much moisture and the dish becomes too wet.

Then...

- Serve it as a condiment for **Pita Chips** (page 24) or **Bagel Chips** (page 25).

- Spoon some over burrata or full-fat ricotta as a more elegant spread or dip.

- Spread some of the caponata salsa on slices of toasted bread or toasted garlic bread for an easy take on bruschetta. If desired, top the salsa with bits of torn fresh basil leaves and/or a drizzle of balsamic vinegar. Or even a tinned anchovy fillet, particularly a white anchovy fillet.

- Spoon the caponata salsa over steaks from the grill—or over **Perfect Strip Steaks** (page 208).

- Or spoon it over the **Tuscan Chimichangas** (page 265).

- Or over slices of hot meatloaf—or slices of **Glazed Meatloaf** (page 227).

See photo in insert.

Green Olive and Mushroom Tapenade

FAST / EASY / VEGAN / GLUTEN-FREE / 5 INGREDIENTS

A tapenade is a finely minced olive paste or condiment, made from a wide variety of olives (although black olives are the most common). But we love green olive tapenade because it's sharper, a better contrast with cocktails and crackers before dinner.

Green olives can have a strong flavor. So we've included air-fried mushrooms in the dip. The mushrooms mellow the briny flavor with sweet notes. Brown mushrooms (sometimes called "Baby Bella" or "cremini") work best since they have an earthier flavor. They're a better contrast to the olives and aromatic oregano.

All in all, this recipe is a bit of a flight of fancy on our part, a creative fusion that we can only do with an air fryer.

INGREDIENTS	2-quart or larger air fryer	3.5-quart or larger air fryer	5.25-quart or larger air fryer
Brown or Baby Bella mushrooms, sliced	½ pound	¾ pound	1 pound
Pitted green olives	1 cup (about 5½ ounces)	1½ cups (about ½ pound)	2 cups (about 11 ounces)
Olive oil	2 tablespoons	3 tablespoons	¼ cup
Fresh oregano leaves, loosely packed	1 tablespoon	1½ tablespoons	2 tablespoons
Ground black pepper	¼ teaspoon	Rounded ¼ teaspoon	½ teaspoon
MAKES	1 cup	1 ½ cups	2 cups

1. With the basket (or basket attachment) in the air fryer, heat it to 400°F (or 390°F, if that's the closest setting).

2. When the machine is at temperature, arrange the mushroom slices in as close to an even layer as possible in the basket. They will overlap and even stack on top of each other.

continues

3. Air-fry for 10 minutes, tossing the basket and rearranging the mushrooms every 2 minutes, until shriveled but with still-noticeable moisture.

4. Pour the mushrooms into a food processor. Add the olives, olive oil, oregano leaves, and pepper. Cover and process until grainy, not too much, just not fully smooth for better texture, stopping the machine at least once to scrape down the inside of the canister. Scrape the tapenade into a bowl and serve warm, or cover and refrigerate for up to 4 days. (The tapenade will taste better if it comes back to room temperature before serving.)

Then...

- Serve the tapenade with **Bagel Chips** (page 25). Even better, spread a little sour cream on the chip, then top with this tapenade.

- Set a log of room-temperature plain fresh goat cheese on a serving plate, then top with generous spoonfuls of this tapenade. Scoop up the cheese and tapenade with crunchy crackers.

- Or serve the tapenade as a base on toast rounds (gluten-free, if a concern) topped with tinned sardines. While there's a rather mundane assortment of them at most supermarkets, check out the astounding array of imported tinned fish that you can order through the website of the Boston wine bar haley.henry (www.haleyhenry.com).

Smoked Whitefish Spread

EASY / CAN BE GLUTEN-FREE / 8 INGREDIENTS

Here's our version of whitefish salad, a delicatessen favorite now easy to make at home with a little liquid smoke and the help of the air fryer. Because we don't call for standard whitefish, but for hake or trout, our version is less fishy than some—and smokier, too. Cut the amount of liquid smoke in half if you'd like a milder flavor.

INGREDIENTS	2-quart or larger air fryer	3.5-quart or larger air fryer	5.25-quart or larger air fryer
Boneless skinless white-flesh fish fillets, such as hake or trout	½ pound	¾ pound	1 pound
Liquid smoke	2 tablespoons	3 tablespoons	¼ cup
Regular, low-fat, or fat-free mayonnaise (gluten-free, if a concern)	2 tablespoons	3 tablespoons	¼ cup
Jarred prepared white horseradish (optional)	1 teaspoon	2 teaspoons	1 tablespoon
Onion powder	¼ teaspoon	Rounded ¼ teaspoon	½ teaspoon
Celery seeds	¼ teaspoon	Rounded ¼ teaspoon	½ teaspoon
Table salt	¼ teaspoon	Rounded ¼ teaspoon	½ teaspoon
Ground black pepper	¼ teaspoon	Rounded ¼ teaspoon	½ teaspoon
MAKES	¾ cup	1 cup	1½ cups

1. Put the fish fillets in a zip-closed bag, add the liquid smoke, and seal closed. Rub the liquid smoke all over the fish (be gentle!), then refrigerate the sealed bag for 2 hours.

2. With the basket (or basket attachment) in the air fryer, heat it to 400°F (or 390°F, if that's the closest setting).

3. Set a 12-inch piece of aluminum foil on your work surface. Remove the fish fillets from the bag and set them in the center of this piece of foil (the fillets can overlap). Fold the long sides of the foil together and crimp them closed. Make a tight seam so no steam can escape. Fold up the ends and crimp to seal well.

4. Set the packet in the basket and air-fry undisturbed for 10 minutes.

5. Use kitchen tongs to transfer the foil packet to a wire rack. Cool for a minute or so. Open the packet, transfer the fish to a plate, and refrigerate for 30 minutes.

6. Put the cold fish in a food processor. Add the mayonnaise, horseradish (if using), onion powder, celery seeds, salt, and pepper. Cover and pulse to a slightly coarse spread, certainly not fully smooth.

For a more traditional texture, put the fish fillets in a bowl, add the other ingredients, and stir with a wooden spoon, mashing the fish with everything else to make a coarse paste.

7. Scrape the spread into a bowl and serve at once, or cover with plastic wrap and store in the fridge for up to 4 days.

Then...

- Serve on whole-wheat crackers, topped with pickled jalapeño rings. (Trust us.)

- Or serve on cucumber slices with a drizzle of syrupy balsamic vinegar over each. And maybe some toasted sesame seeds, if you want to get fancy.

- Or hollow out cherry tomatoes with a melon baller, then stuff each with a little smoked fish spread and a sprinkle of chopped fresh parsley leaves.

Antipasto-Stuffed Cherry Tomatoes

FAST / VEGETARIAN / CAN BE GLUTEN-FREE / 8 INGREDIENTS

We developed this recipe so that you could raid the salad bar at the supermarket and make a great filling from some of the ingredients you can find there, a sort of Italian American version of stuffed mushrooms (but with cherry tomatoes as the shell).

The best tomatoes for this recipe are Campari tomatoes. They often show up in a plastic clam shell in the produce section, all still attached to their stems. They are slightly larger than a standard cherry tomato but not as large as a plum tomato. They're also quite juicy, with thick walls that are better at holding the stuffing than some more delicate cherry tomatoes.

Note that you must use some of the marinade that the artichoke hearts have been stored in. If you scoop the artichoke heart quarters off the salad bar, get some of their marinade in the container, too, so you'll have a little for the recipe's requirements.

INGREDIENTS	2-quart or larger air fryer	3.5-quart or larger air fryer	5.25-quart or larger air fryer
Large cherry tomatoes, preferably Campari tomatoes (about 1½ ounces each and the size of golf balls)	8	12	16
Seasoned Italian-style dried bread crumbs (gluten-free, if a concern)	6 tablespoons	½ cup	¾ cup
Finely grated Parmesan cheese	3 tablespoons (about ½ ounce)	¼ cup (about ¾ ounce)	⅓ cup (about 1 ounce)
Finely chopped pitted black olives	2½ tablespoons	¼ cup	⅓ cup
Finely chopped marinated artichoke hearts	2½ tablespoons	¼ cup	⅓ cup
Marinade from the artichokes	1½ tablespoons	2 tablespoons	2½ tablespoons
Sun-dried tomatoes (dry, not packed in oil), finely chopped	2	4	5
Olive oil spray	As needed	As needed	As needed
MAKES	8 stuffed tomatoes	12 stuffed tomatoes	16 stuffed tomatoes

1. With the basket (or basket attachment) in the air fryer, heat it to 400°F (or 390°F, if that's the closest setting).

2. Cut the top off of each fresh tomato, exposing the seeds and pulp. (The tops can be saved for a snack, sprinkled with some kosher salt, to tide you over while the stuffed tomatoes cook.) Cut a very small slice off the bottom of each tomato (no cutting into the pulp) so it will stand up flat on your work surface.

Use a melon baller to remove and discard the seeds and pulp from each tomato.

3. Mix the bread crumbs, cheese, olives, artichoke hearts, marinade, and sun-dried tomatoes in a bowl until well combined. Stuff this mixture into each prepared tomato, about 1½ tablespoons in each. Generously coat the tops of the tomatoes with olive oil spray.

4. Set the tomatoes stuffing side up in the basket. Air-fry undisturbed for 9 minutes, or until the stuffing has browned a bit and the tomatoes are blistered in places.

5. Remove the basket and cool the tomatoes in it for 5 minutes. Then use kitchen tongs to gently transfer the tomatoes to a serving platter.

Then...

- Serve these as a side dish with **Steakhouse Filets Mignons** (page 209), **Smokehouse-Style Beef Ribs** (page 213), or **Three Seed–Coated Pork Loin** (page 249).

- These stuffed tomatoes are great in a pasta salad, either gently tossed with the dressing, pasta, and other vegetables, or simply set on top as a garnish.

- They can also become a more elegant first course by setting them on top of cooked spaghetti, linguine, or fettuccine that's been tossed with a little olive oil, butter, minced garlic, and red pepper flakes.

Stuffed Mushrooms

VEGETARIAN / CAN BE GLUTEN-FREE / 6 INGREDIENTS

Hands down, these are our favorite app from the air fryer. They're old school, sure. Something out of a steakhouse in the 1960s, maybe. But the combination of the sweet mushroom base and the cheesy filling is hard to beat.

You can, of course, double the recipe for any size machine—or use, say, the large ingredient list for a smaller machine. But then you'll need to work in batches, not to dehydrate the mushroom stems and aromatics (although these may take a little longer and require you to shake the basket once or twice), but to air-fry the stuffed mushrooms in a single layer.

Spice up the stuffing by adding red pepper flakes or cayenne, from a pinch on up, depending on your tolerance. We prefer to drizzle them with sriracha after they've cooked.

INGREDIENTS	2-quart or larger air fryer	3.5-quart or larger air fryer	5.25-quart or larger air fryer
Peeled medium white or brown mushrooms	10	16	20
Medium garlic clove(s)	1	2	2 or 3
Shallot(s), thinly sliced	1 small	1 medium	2 small
Seasoned Italian-style dried bread crumbs (gluten-free, if a concern)	¼ cup	6 tablespoons	½ cup
Olive oil	¼ cup	5 tablespoons	¼ cup plus 2 tablespoons
Finely grated Parmesan cheese	¼ cup (about ¾ ounce)	¼ cup plus 2 tablespoons (about 1 ounce)	½ cup (about 1½ ounces)
MAKES	10 stuffed mushrooms	16 stuffed mushrooms	20 stuffed mushrooms

continues

1. With the basket (or basket attachment) in the air fryer, heat it to 400°F (or 390°F, if that's the closest setting).

2. Remove the stems from the mushrooms. When the machine is at temperature, put the stems with the garlic and shallots in the basket. Air-fry undisturbed for 5 minutes.

3. Remove the basket and pour out the contents onto a cutting board. Cool for 5 minutes. Reduce the air fryer's temperature to 325°F (or 330°F, if that's the closest setting).

4. Chop the mushroom stems, garlic, and shallots into very small bits, like minced garlic. Scrape these into a bowl. Stir in the bread crumbs, oil, and cheese until well combined. Divide this mixture among the mushroom caps, overfilling them to mound the mixture up just a bit.

5. Set the mushroom caps stuffing side up in the basket in one layer. Air-fry undisturbed for 12 minutes, or until the stuffing is browned and the mushroom caps have softened a bit. Use kitchen tongs to gently transfer the caps to a serving platter. Cool for a couple of minutes before serving.

Then...

- Serve these as a side dish to **Perfect Strip Steaks** (page 208).
- Or with **Roasted Turkey Breast** (page 200).
- Or add them to a platter with prosciutto slices, stuffed grape leaves, **Roasted Peppers with Balsamic Vinegar and Basil** (page 309), and chunks of Parmesan cheese drizzled with a syrupy balsamic vinegar.

Individual Pizzas

FAST / VEGETARIAN / 4 INGREDIENTS

First off, a warning: This recipe makes *one* pizza (of different sizes) in each of our three air fryer sizes. You *can* double or *even* triple the amounts for any size air fryer, provided you keep to the instructions for the size of your model and air-fry the pizzas one at a time.

Although the pizza here is classic, just tomato sauce and cheese, you can add lots more toppings: sliced pitted black or green olives, anchovy fillets (minced or whole), pepperoni slices, crumbled cooked sausage meat, sliced mushrooms, sun-dried tomatoes, or marinated artichoke hearts. Put any (or several) of these on the dough *after* the sauce but *before* the cheese.

These recipe ingredients for the small and medium air fryer use less than the full amount of pizza dough (often sold in 1 pound bags or 11- or 13.8-ounce tubes). Wrap the remainder of the dough in plastic wrap and store it in the fridge for up to 1 week. (For more pizzas, of course!)

INGREDIENTS	2-quart or larger air fryer	3.5-quart or larger air fryer	5.25-quart or larger air fryer
Purchased fresh pizza dough (not a prebaked crust)	¼ pound	6 ounces	½ pound
Olive oil spray	As needed	As needed	As needed
Purchased pizza sauce or purchased pesto	3 tablespoons	4½ tablespoons	6 tablespoons
Shredded semi-firm mozzarella	⅓ cup (about 1½ ounces)	½ cup (about 2 ounces)	⅔ cup (about 3 ounces)
MAKES	*1 serving*	*2 servings*	*3 servings*

1. With the basket (or basket attachment) in the air fryer, heat it to 400°F (or 390°F, if that's the closest setting).

2. Press the pizza dough into a 5-inch circle for a small air fryer, a 6-inch circle for a medium air fryer, or a 7-inch circle for a large machine. Generously coat the top of the dough with olive oil spray.

3. Remove the basket from the machine and set the dough oil side down in the basket. Smear the sauce or pesto over the dough, then sprinkle with the cheese.

4. Return the basket to the machine and air-fry undisturbed for 7 minutes, or until the dough is puffed and browned and the cheese has melted. (Extra toppings will not increase the cooking time, provided you add no extra cheese.)

5. Remove the basket from the machine and cool the pizza in it for 5 minutes. Use a large nonstick-safe spatula to transfer the pizza from the basket to a wire rack. Cool for 5 minutes more before serving.

Then...

• Pizza needs a great chopped salad. The CLASSIC GREEK DINER DRESSING is made by whisking *olive oil* and *red wine vinegar* in a 4-to-1 ratio with *a generous sprinkling of dried oregano*, *a smaller amount of ground black pepper*, and *a still smaller amount of table salt* to taste. Use it on a salad of chopped iceberg lettuce, sliced cucumbers, sliced celery, sliced radishes, and/or chopped tomatoes.

Thick-Crust Pepperoni Pizza

FAST / EASY / 5 INGREDIENTS

For those who love pizza crust, we haven't stinted in this recipe. To get the best results, we've set the thick-crust pie in a cake pan so that dough, formed to the edges, rises up inside like a pillow. Because of the convection air currents, the dough gets so puffed it can barely hold onto its toppings.

To make sure that the center of the pie is not underdone, coat the cake pan generously with the spray, thereby giving it a good medium to transfer heat to the dough inside.

Of course, there's no reason to limit yourself to our suggested toppings. Try chopped prosciutto, crumbled cooked sausage meat, thinly sliced deli ham, or sliced salami in equivalent amounts.

INGREDIENTS	2-quart or larger air fryer	3.5-quart or larger air fryer	5.25-quart or larger air fryer
Purchased fresh pizza dough (not a prebaked crust)	½ pound	10 ounces	¾ pound (slightly more than an 11-ounce tube)
Olive oil spray	As needed	As needed	As needed
Purchased pizza sauce	3 tablespoons	¼ cup	⅓ cup
Sliced pepperoni	8 slices	10 slices	12 slices
Purchased shredded Italian 3- or 4-cheese blend	¼ cup	⅓ cup	½ cup
MAKES	1 servings	2 servings	3 servings

1. With the basket (or basket attachment) in the air fryer, heat it to 400°F (or 390°F, if that's the closest setting).

2. Generously coat the inside of a 6-inch round cake pan for a small air fryer, a 7-inch round cake pan for a medium air fryer, or an 8-inch round cake pan for a large model with olive oil spray.

3. Set the dough in the pan and press it to fill the bottom in an even, thick layer. Spread the sauce over the dough, then top with the pepperoni and cheese.

4. When the machine is at temperature, set the pan in the basket and air-fry undisturbed for 10 minutes, or until puffed, brown, and bubbling.

5. Use kitchen tongs to transfer the cake pan to a wire rack. Cool for only a minute or so. Use a spatula to loosen the pizza from the pan and lift it out and onto the rack. Continue cooling for a few minutes before cutting into wedges to serve.

Then...

• If desired, sprinkle the top of the pie with finely grated Parmesan cheese right after removing it from the air fryer. The heat of the pie will melt the cheese.

Pizza Bagel Bites

FAST / EASY / VEGETARIAN / 3 INGREDIENTS

We intentionally kept these pizza bagels simple. Their success will depend on the cheese. Don't just think of purchased grated Parmesan cheese—try a blend of cheeses. Or if you intend to serve these to adults, mix in a little crumbled Gorgonzola or maybe some partially-frozen-then-diced Brie.

Yes, you can add other toppings. Maybe a couple of slices of pepperoni per bagel half? Or a shredded fresh basil leaf? A couple of olive slices? But keep it simple.

Gluten-free *mini* bagels are hard to find, usually only at very high-end supermarkets. If you can track some down, this recipe becomes gluten-free (so long as the pizza sauce is also gluten-free).

INGREDIENTS	2-quart or larger air fryer	3.5-quart or larger air fryer	5.25-quart or larger air fryer
Mini bagel(s), split into two rings	1	2	3
Purchased pizza sauce	2 tablespoons	¼ cup	6 tablespoons
Finely grated or shredded cheese, such as Parmesan cheese, semi-firm mozzarella, fontina, or (preferably) a cheese blend	¼ cup	½ cup	¾ cup
MAKES	*1 serving*	*2 servings*	*3 servings*

1. With the basket (or basket attachment) in the air fryer, heat it to 375°F (or 370°F or 360°F, if one of these is the closest setting).

2. Spread the cut side of each bagel half with 1 tablespoon pizza sauce; top each half with 2 tablespoons shredded cheese.

3. When the machine is at temperature, put the bagels cheese side up in the basket in one layer. Air-fry undisturbed for 4 minutes, or until the cheese has melted and is gooey. You may need to air-fry the pizza bagel bites for 1 minute extra if the temperature is at 360°F.

4. Use a nonstick-safe spatula to transfer the topped bagel halves to a wire rack. Cool for at least 5 minutes before serving.

Then...

- To make these bagel bites into a full meal, make SUMMERY WATERCRESS SALAD. Toss *thin peach slices* and *small cubes of seeded and peeled honeydew melon or cantaloupe* with *stemmed watercress* (and maybe a little *chopped romaine lettuce*, just to even out the flavors). Add some *walnut pieces* (or even **Sugar-Glazed Walnuts**, page 32) for crunch, then dress the salad with *a little olive oil, much less lemon juice, a little table salt*, and *some ground black pepper*.

Cauliflower-Crust Pizza

VEGETARIAN / GLUTEN-FREE / 9 INGREDIENTS

Of course, you could always buy a small cauliflower crust to make a pie in your air fryer; but here's a relatively easy way to *make* a crust with purchased riced cauliflower (almost always available in the produce section refrigerator case). The crust must be baked in advance to set before any toppings are added.

We add a little potato starch to the crust ingredients. The starch gets sticky in the presence of moisture, so it helps the riced cauliflower hold together and create a more traditional crunch. Look for potato starch in the baking aisle or among the Jewish foods in the supermarket, often near the matzo meal.

INGREDIENTS	2-quart or larger air fryer	3.5-quart or larger air fryer	5.25-quart or larger air fryer
Riced cauliflower	¾ pound	1 pound 2 ounces	1½ pounds
Large egg(s)	1	1 plus 1 large egg yolk	2
Finely grated Parmesan cheese	2 tablespoons (about ⅓ ounce)	3 tablespoons (a little more than ½ ounce)	¼ cup (about ¾ ounce)
Potato starch	1 tablespoon	1½ tablespoons	2 tablespoons
Dried oregano	½ teaspoon	¾ teaspoon	1 teaspoon
Table salt	½ teaspoon	¾ teaspoon	1 teaspoon
Vegetable oil spray	As needed	As needed	As needed
Purchased pizza sauce	2 tablespoons	3 tablespoons	¼ cup
Shredded semi-firm mozzarella	¼ cup (about 1 ounce)	6 tablespoons (about 1½ ounces)	½ cup (about 2 ounces)
MAKES	2 servings	3 servings	4 servings

1. Pour the riced cauliflower into a medium microwave-safe bowl. Microwave on high for 4 minutes. Stir well, then cool for 15 minutes.

2. With the basket (or basket attachment) in the air fryer, heat it to 400°F (or 390°F, if that's the closest setting).

3. Pour the riced cauliflower into a clean kitchen towel or a large piece of cheesecloth. Gather the towel or cheesecloth together. Working over the sink, squeeze the moisture out of the cauliflower, getting out as much of the liquid as you can.

4. Pour the squeezed cauliflower back into that same medium bowl and stir in the egg, egg yolk (if using), cheese, potato starch, oregano, and salt to form a loose, uniform "dough."

5. Cut a piece of aluminum foil or parchment paper into a 6-inch circle for a small pizza, a 7-inch circle for a medium one, or an 8-inch circle for a large one. Coat the circle with vegetable oil spray, then place it in the air-fryer basket. Using a small offset spatula or the back of a flatware tablespoon, spread and smooth the cauliflower mixture onto the circle right to the edges. Air-fry undisturbed for 10 minutes.

6. Remove the basket from the air fryer. Reduce the machine's temperature to 350°F (or 360°F, if that's the closest setting).

7. Using a large nonstick-safe spatula, flip over the cauliflower circle along with its foil or parchment paper right in the basket. Peel off and discard the foil or parchment paper. Spread the pizza sauce evenly over the crust and sprinkle with the cheese.

8. Air-fry undisturbed for 4 minutes, or until the cheese has melted and begun to bubble. Remove the basket from the machine and cool for 5 minutes. Use the same spatula to transfer the pizza to a wire rack to cool for 5 minutes more before cutting the pie into wedges to serve.

Then...

• Once the pizza is out of the basket, top it with baby arugula that's been dressed with a little olive oil and white balsamic vinegar (see page 203), as well as some table salt and ground black pepper.

Small Chicken Empanadas

8 INGREDIENTS

Here's a great recipe for leftover chicken! Although we recommend using rotisserie chicken breast meat (because it's less fatty), you can mix in some thigh meat, although the empanadas will be a bit softer on their bottoms and not quite as crisp (because of the released fat).

These empanadas are finger food, not the standard, large, knife-and-fork empanadas you might get from a Hispanic grocery store or Tex-Mex restaurant. Ours are better with drinks!

INGREDIENTS	2-quart or larger air fryer	5.25-quart or larger air fryer
Deboned, skinned roast or rotisserie chicken breast meat, very finely chopped	½ cup	1 cup
Shredded Cheddar cheese	⅓ cup (about 1½ ounces)	⅔ cup (about 3 ounces)
Purchased salsa verde	2 tablespoons	¼ cup
Ground cumin	½ teaspoon	1 teaspoon
Ground black pepper	½ teaspoon	1 teaspoon
Purchased refrigerated pie crust(s), from a minimum 14.1-ounce box	1	2
All-purpose flour	For dusting	For dusting
Large egg	1	1
Water	2 tablespoons	2 tablespoons
MAKES	6 empanadas	12 empanadas

continues

1. With the basket (or basket attachment) in the air fryer, heat it to 350°F (or 360°F, if that's the closest setting).

2. Mix the chicken, cheese, salsa verde, cumin, and pepper in a bowl until well combined.

3. Unwrap and unroll the sheet(s) of pie crust dough onto a clean, dry work surface. Cut out 3½-inch circles with a large cookie cutter or giant sturdy drinking glass—or use a 3½-inch plate to trace and cut out a circle in the dough. Gather up the scraps of dough. Lightly flour your work surface and set the scraps on top. Roll them together into a sheet that matches the thickness of the original dough and cut more circles until you have 6 for the small batch or 12 circles for the larger batch.

4. Place 1½ tablespoons of the chicken mixture in the center of each circle. Wet the perimeter of a circle with a finger dipped in cold water and fold the dough over the filling to make a half-moon. Seal the edge by pressing the tines of a flatware fork along the edge.

5. Set the filled empanadas in the basket in one layer and air-fry undisturbed for 6 minutes. Meanwhile, whisk the egg and water in a small bowl until uniform.

6. Remove the basket from the machine. Brush the tops of the empanadas with the egg mixture and continue air-frying undisturbed for 6 minutes, or until shiny, golden brown, and firm to the touch.

7. Gently dump the contents of the basket onto a wire rack and turn the (hot!) empanadas so they're all brushed side up. Cool for at least 5 minutes before serving.

Then...

- Serve these with **Spicy Ketchup Dip** (page 66) or **Tangy Jalapeño Dip** (page 151).
- Make CHIMICHURRI as a dip. For 4 to 6 servings, put the following in a food processor: *½ cup chopped fresh parsley leaves, ⅓ cup chopped fresh cilantro leaves, ¼ cup chopped fresh oregano leaves, ¼ cup red wine vinegar, 2 tablespoons lemon juice, 2 chopped medium scallions, up to 5 chopped medium garlic cloves, up to 1 teaspoon red pepper flakes,* and *½ teaspoon table salt.* Cover and process, drizzling *up to ½ cup olive oil* through the feed tube to make a thick, coarse sauce (not a puree). Store any leftover chimichurri in a sealed nonreactive container in the fridge for up to 2 days. Let it come back to room temperature before serving.

See photo in insert.

Meatball Bread

EASY / CAN BE VEGETARIAN / 6 INGREDIENTS

Essentially, this recipe gives you a loaf that's stuffed with the makings of a meatball sub. With a good salad on the side, this could certainly be more than an app or a snack, probably dinner.

If desired, add more to the roll—minced fresh basil leaves, minced oregano leaves, minced garlic, red pepper flakes, and/or an anchovy fillet. Just remember to seal the ends well so that the filling doesn't leak out during cooking.

INGREDIENTS	2-quart or larger air fryer	5.25-quart or larger air fryer
Purchased pizza dough (not a prebaked crust)	½ pound	1 pound
Purchased pizza sauce	2 tablespoons	¼ cup
½-ounce "bite-size" frozen meatballs (any variety, even vegan, if a concern), thawed	7	14
1-ounce string cheese stick(s), unwrapped and cut into ½-inch pieces	1	2
Seasoned Italian-style dried bread crumbs	2 teaspoons	4 teaspoons
Vegetable oil spray	As needed	As needed
MAKES	2 servings	4 servings

1. With the basket (or basket attachment) in the air fryer, heat it to 350°F (or 360°F, if that's the closest setting).

2. If you're working with a 1-pound piece of dough, divide it in half and set aside one piece. Set a ½-pound piece of dough on a clean, dry work surface.

3. Using a rolling pin, roll the dough into a 4 x 6-inch rectangle. Spread 2 tablespoons sauce over the dough, then top with 7 meatballs. Set half of the cheese bits among the meatballs and sprinkle with half of the bread crumbs, or use all the cheese and all the crumbs if you're making only one loaf.

4. Starting with one long side of the rectangle, roll the dough up and over the sauce and fillings. Seal the tube at both ends by pinching the dough together. Generously coat the loaf on all sides with vegetable oil spray.

5. Repeat steps 3 and 4 if you have a second ½-pound lump of dough, using up the sauce, meatballs, cheese, and crumbs.

6. Set the loaf or loaves seam side down in the basket with at least ½-inch space between them. Air-fry undisturbed for 10 minutes, or until golden brown and puffed.

7. Use a nonstick-safe spatula and kitchen tongs for balance to transfer the loaf or loaves to a wire rack. Cool for at least 10 minutes, then cut a loaf into 4 slices—or just tear it apart—to serve.

Then...

- If you want to take this over the top, drizzle the slices with **Blue Cheese Dressing** (page 172).

- For a great frozen concoction to go on the side, try our STRAWBERRY COOLER. Put the following in a large blender in this order: *1½ cups frozen hulled strawberries* (do not thaw), *2 ounces (¼ cup) orange juice*, *1½ ounces (3 tablespoons) gin*, *1½ ounces (3 tablespoons) Aperol*, *1 ounce (2 tablespoons) amaretto*, and *a pinch of table salt*. Cover and blend until slushy smooth, then divide between two glasses.

Sausage and Cheese Rolls

FAST / 3 INGREDIENTS

Rolling string cheese and link sausage in puff pastry is not something you do every day. But maybe you should. These open-ended sausage rolls are so tasty, they might even become a weekend breakfast staple, not just deck fare.

Although we suggest Italian links for a savory snack, you can use just about any sort of sausage link, even chicken or turkey sausages.

INGREDIENTS	2-quart or larger air fryer	3.5-quart or larger air fryer	5.25-quart or larger air fryer
3- to 3½-ounce sweet or hot Italian sausage links	2	3	4
1-ounce string cheese stick(s), unwrapped and cut in half lengthwise	1	2	2
A 17.25-ounce box frozen puff pastry	Two quarters of one thawed sheet (that is, a half of the sheet cut into two even pieces; wrap and refreeze the remainder)	Three quarters from one thawed sheet (cut the sheet into four quarters; wrap and refreeze one of them)	One sheet, cut into four quarters
MAKES	*2 servings*	*3 servings*	*4 servings*

1. With the basket (or basket attachment) in the air fryer, heat it to 400°F (or 390°F, if that's the closest setting).

2. When the machine is at temperature, set the sausage links in the basket and air-fry undisturbed for 12 minutes, or until cooked through.

3. Use kitchen tongs to transfer the links to a wire rack. Cool for 15 minutes. (If necessary, pour out any rendered fat that has collected below the basket in the machine.)

4. Cut the sausage links in half lengthwise. Sandwich half a string cheese stick between two sausage halves, trimming the ends so the cheese doesn't stick out beyond the meat.

5. Roll each piece of puff pastry into a 6 x 6-inch square on a clean, dry work surface. Set the sausage-cheese sandwich at one edge and roll it up in the dough. The ends will be open like a pig-in-a-blanket. Repeat with the remaining puff pastry, sausage, and cheese.

6. Set the rolls seam side down in the basket. Air-fry undisturbed for 6 minutes, or until puffed and golden brown.

7. Use a nonstick-safe spatula, and perhaps a flatware fork for balance, to transfer the rolls to a wire rack. Cool for at least 5 minutes before serving.

Then...

- These rolls need to go with an APEROL SPRITZ. For one drink, fill a red wine glass halfway with *small ice cubes*. Add *1 ounce (2 tablespoons) Aperol*, then *3 ounces (6 tablespoons) Prosecco or other sparkling wine*. Top up the glass with *plain seltzer* and serve.

Smoked Salmon Puffs

FAST / 7 INGREDIENTS

These are like a savory smoked salmon version of a turnover. After baking, each one can be cut in half to make two smaller nibbles—each half may be a single serving, depending on what else you're serving with them. As always, feel free to use the larger amounts for a smaller machine—or even double the larger amounts for a large machine—as long as you work in batches to get good air flow around the packets as they cook.

INGREDIENTS	2-quart or larger air fryer	3.5-quart or larger air fryer
A 17.25-ounce box frozen puff pastry	One quarter of one thawed sheet (wrap and refreeze the remainder)	Two quarters of one thawed sheet (that is, a half of the sheet; wrap and refreeze the remainder)
½-ounce smoked salmon slices	2	4
Softened regular or low-fat cream cheese (*not* fat-free)	1 tablespoon	2 tablespoons
Drained and rinsed capers, minced	Up to 1 teaspoon	Up to 2 teaspoons
Minced red onion	Up to 1 teaspoon	Up to 2 teaspoons
Large egg white	1	1
Water	1 tablespoon	1 tablespoon
MAKES	*1 puff*	*2 puffs*

1. With the basket (or basket attachment) in the air fryer, heat it to 400°F (or 390°F, if that's the closest setting).

2. For a small air fryer, roll the piece of puff pastry into a 6 x 6-inch square on a clean, dry work surface.
   For a medium or larger air fryer, roll each piece of puff pastry into a 6 x 6-inch square.

3. Set 2 salmon slices on the diagonal, corner to corner, on each rolled-out sheet. Smear the salmon with cream cheese, then sprinkle with capers and red onion. Fold the sheet closed by picking up one corner that *does not* have an edge of salmon near it and folding the dough across the salmon to its opposite corner. Seal the edges closed by pressing the tines of a flatware fork into them.

4. Whisk the egg white and water in a small bowl until uniform. Brush this mixture over the top(s) of the packet(s).

5. Set the packet(s) in the basket (if you're working with more than one, they cannot touch). Air-fry undisturbed for 8 minutes, or until golden brown and flaky.

6. Use a nonstick-safe spatula to transfer the packet(s) to a wire rack. Cool for 5 minutes before serving.

Then...

- For a small amount of SWEET-AND-SOUR DRIZZLE to go over the puffs, whisk ¼ cup honey, 1 tablespoon prepared white horseradish, and 1 tablespoon coarse-grained Dijon mustard until uniform.

Onion Ring Nachos

FAST / EASY / VEGETARIAN / 3 INGREDIENTS

Here's a flight of fancy, certainly not your everyday plate of nachos. We replaced the chips with onion rings (just because we could), then added cheese and jalapeños for a crazy cross-cultural snack that's almost impossible to turn down. This one doesn't last. You want that hot, melty cheese. Just be careful that you don't take off the roof of your mouth.

INGREDIENTS	2-quart or larger air fryer	3.5-quart or larger air fryer	5.25-quart or larger air fryer
Frozen breaded (not battered) onion rings (do not thaw)	½ pound	¾ pound	1 pound
Shredded Cheddar, Monterey Jack, or Swiss cheese, or a purchased Tex-Mex blend	1 cup (about ¼ pound)	1½ cups (about 6 ounces)	2 cups (about ½ pound)
Pickled jalapeño rings	Up to 6	Up to 12	Up to 18
MAKES	2 servings	3 servings	4 servings

1. With the basket (or basket attachment) in the air fryer, heat it to 400°F (or 390°F, if that's the closest setting).

2. When the machine is at temperature, spread the onion rings in the basket in a fairly even layer. Air-fry undisturbed for 6 minutes, or until crisp. Remove the basket from the machine.

3. Cut a circle of parchment paper to line a 6-inch round cake pan for a small air fryer, a 7-inch round cake pan for a medium air fryer, or an 8-inch round cake pan for a large machine.

4. Pour the onion rings into a fairly even layer in the cake pan, then sprinkle the cheese evenly over them. Dot with the jalapeño rings.

5. Set the pan in the basket and air-fry undisturbed for 1 to 2 minutes, until the cheese has melted and is bubbling.

6. Remove the pan from the basket. Cool for 5 minutes before serving.

Then...

- Dollop the cooked nachos with sour cream and/or purchased salsa or even **Salsa Fresca** (page 167), once they've cooled a bit.

- Although pretty fine on their own, you can pull the rings apart and use them (cheese, jalapeños, and all) as a topper on burgers, maybe along with a very thin tomato slice.

See photo in insert.

Barbecue Chicken Nachos

FAST / EASY / CAN BE GLUTEN-FREE / 7 INGREDIENTS

These nachos come close to being dinner, especially if the day's been packed and you're out of time for much else. The recipe calls for rotisserie chicken meat—which will give you the best flavor. But you can buy a roasted chicken breast at the deli counter and chop the meat up into little bits to top the nachos.

INGREDIENTS	2-quart or larger air fryer	3.5-quart or larger air fryer	5.25-quart or larger air fryer
Corn tortilla chips (gluten-free, if a concern)	2 heaping cups (a little more than 2 ounces)	3 heaping cups (a little more than 3 ounces)	4 heaping cups (a little more than ¼ pound)
Shredded deboned and skinned rotisserie chicken meat (gluten-free, if a concern)	½ cup	¾ cup	1 cup
Canned black beans, drained and rinsed	2 tablespoons	3 tablespoons	¼ cup
Pickled jalapeño slices	6 rings	9 rings	12 rings
Small pickled cocktail onions, halved	3	4	6
Barbecue sauce (any sort)	2 tablespoons	3 tablespoons	¼ cup
Shredded Cheddar cheese	½ cup (about 2 ounces)	¾ cup (about 3 ounces)	1 cup (about ¼ pound)
MAKES	2 servings	3 servings	4 servings

1. With the basket (or basket attachment) in the air fryer, heat it to 400°F (or 390°F, if that's the closest setting).

2. Cut a circle of parchment paper to line a 6-inch round cake pan for a small air fryer, a 7-inch round cake pan for a medium air fryer, or an 8-inch round cake pan for a large machine.

3. Fill the pan with an even layer of about two-thirds of the chips. Sprinkle the chicken evenly over the chips. Set the pan in the basket and air-fry undisturbed for 2 minutes.

4. Remove the basket from the machine. Scatter the beans, jalapeño rings, and pickled onion halves over the chicken. Drizzle the barbecue sauce over everything, then sprinkle the cheese on top.

5. Return the basket to the machine and air-fry undisturbed for 3 minutes, or until the cheese has melted and is bubbly. Remove the pan from the machine and cool for a couple of minutes before serving.

Then...

- We love these nachos with **FROZEN SANGRIA**. For 2 to 4 servings, put the following in a large blender in this order: *3 cups frozen peach slices, 2 cups small ice cubes, 12 ounces (1½ cups) chilled white wine (preferably a Riesling), 1½ ounces (3 tablespoons) orange juice, 1 ounce (2 tablespoons) orange-flavored liqueur (preferably Triple Sec or Cointreau), ½ ounce (1 tablespoon) peach-flavored liqueur, ¼ ounce (½ tablespoon) lemon juice,* and *1 tablespoon granulated white sugar, preferably superfine.* Cover and blend for about 1 minute, until slushy thick and pale yellow, stopping the blender once to shake the contents so they fall down onto the blades. Divide between red wine glasses.

2

THIRTY-FOUR
Soups &
Sandwiches

Surprise! Soup from an air fryer! Well, okay, most of these soups are not *finished* in the machine (although we do make a fine **French Onion Soup** in a pan set in the machine's basket on page 103). But we can quickly roast vegetables and caramelize onions to create full-flavored soups without turning on the oven.

And here's another surprise: sandwiches! You may not think of an air fryer as a sandwich machine. But it's like a panini press without, well, the press: a high-heat appliance that toasts buns, cooks burgers, and serves up some fine renditions of favorites like **Tuna Melts** (page 130) and **Eggplant Parmesan Subs** (page 143).

When it comes to sandwiches, let's make one thing clear: No amount of careful cooking can make up for inferior bread and buns. True, you don't necessarily get what you pay for. Some firmer, more roll-like hamburger and slider buns are relatively inexpensive yet a much better choice than soft, overly sweet, and strangely expensive buns. The best bread and buns for these recipes are probably found at a bakery, even if most of us don't have the time to drive to a separate store and select the finest before we endure a meltdown from a car seat or pass out from sheer exhaustion at 5:59 p.m. So search around the grocery store for better options. A one-minute expedition will set you up for better sandwiches down the road.

We tested most of these recipes with whole-wheat bread or buns—and often whole-grain bread or buns, especially for easy sandwiches like the **Super Crunchy Grilled Cheese** (page 113—which, as you'll see, is made with a little trick that you'll want to keep hidden from prying second-grade eyes but that guarantees a delicious sandwich every time).

Some of these recipes can cause a bit of a greasy mess in the machine: burger patties and the like, as well as sausages and hot dogs. That's why we prefer to air-fry leaner meats. They are healthier, sure; but they also create less mess because there are fewer grease spatters. A grease buildup is the main reason an air fryer sets off the smoke alarm. If you go with lower-fat alternatives like lean ground beef or leaner sausages, you'll end up with a quicker cleanup and more time to enjoy whatever remains of your day after 6:00 p.m.

So here we go—first seven soups, then twenty-five sandwiches, ending with quesadillas and falafel. Maybe you didn't think about these sorts of things when you bought an air fryer. It's high time you did.

Creamy Roasted Potato and Bacon Soup

EASY / CAN BE GLUTEN-FREE / 10 INGREDIENTS

When you start with frozen hash brown cubes, this winter warmer couldn't be easier. Make sure they're unseasoned because you don't want any competing flavors in the mix. The potato cubes cook with the bacon and onion, offering a roasted flavor to an otherwise simple soup. Of course, you can omit the cream, although we don't know why you would.

INGREDIENTS	2-quart or larger air fryer	3.5-quart or larger air fryer	5.25-quart or larger air fryer
Frozen unseasoned hash brown cubes (do not thaw)	2 cups	3 cups	4 cups
Thin-cut bacon, roughly chopped (gluten-free, if a concern)	1½ ounces (about 1½ strips)	2 ounces (about 2 strips)	3 ounces (about 3 strips)
Roughly chopped yellow or white onion	¼ cup	⅓ cup	½ cup (1 small onion)
Chicken or vegetable broth	2 cups	3 cups	4 cups (1 quart)
Chopped jarred roasted red peppers	⅓ cup	½ cup	¾ cup
Dried thyme	Rounded ¼ teaspoon	½ teaspoon	¾ teaspoon
Celery seeds	⅛ teaspoon	Rounded ⅛ teaspoon	¼ teaspoon
Table salt	Pinch	⅛ teaspoon	¼ teaspoon
Ground black pepper	⅛ teaspoon	Rounded ⅛ teaspoon	¼ teaspoon
Heavy or light cream (*not* fat-free)	2 tablespoons	3 tablespoons	¼ cup
MAKES	*2 hearty servings*	*3 hearty servings*	*4 hearty servings*

1. With the basket (or basket attachment) in the air fryer, heat it to 400°F (or 390°F, if that's the closest setting).

2. When the machine is at temperature, put the potatoes, bacon, and onion in the basket. Air-fry undisturbed for 13 minutes, then shake the basket, rearranging all the ingredients. Continue air-frying undisturbed for 12 minutes, until the potatoes are crisp at the edges and lightly browned.

3. Pour the contents of the basket into a large saucepan set over medium-high heat. Stir in the broth, roasted red pepper, thyme, celery seeds, salt, and pepper. Bring to a simmer; then cover, reduce the heat to low, and simmer slowly for

10 minutes, or until the potato cubes are very tender.

4. Use the back of a wooden spoon to smash some of the potato cubes against the side of the saucepan, stirring these into the soup to thicken it a bit. Stir in the cream, cover, and continue cooking, stirring occasionally, for 3 minutes to blend the flavors. Serve hot. Any leftover soup can be stored in a sealed container in the fridge for up to 3 days.

Then...

- If you like a little heat, add a dollop of sour cream and bit of jalapeño relish, or even **Jalapeño Jam** (page 58), to each bowlful.

- Or top the servings with shredded sharp Cheddar cheese and minced chives or scallions (green part only).

- Leftovers will thicken considerably as they sit in the fridge. You'll need to thin the soup out with more broth before reheating it.

French Onion Soup

EASY / 9 INGREDIENTS

There are a few ways to make French Onion Soup in an air fryer. Many recipes ask you to caramelize the onions in the machine, then finish the soup on the stove. But we think it's simpler to do the whole operation in a baking pan set right in the appliance.

Remember that the pan is superhot after cooking. Use silicone baking mitts or thick hot pads to remove it from the machine. Or leave it be and simply dish the soup up right out of the pan in the basket.

One more thing: Thinly slice the onions so they'll caramelize in the time stated. While paper thin may be too far, they should be thin enough to be limp and wiggly even before air-frying. Stir the onions in the butter more than you might think because they can begin to burn, particularly any edges closest to the perimeter of the pan.

INGREDIENTS	2-quart or larger air fryer	3.5-quart or larger air fryer	5.25-quart or larger air fryer
Thinly sliced yellow or white onions	3 cups (2 large onions)	4½ cups (3 large onions)	6 cups (4 large onions)
Butter	1½ tablespoons	2 tablespoons	3 tablespoons
Beef broth	2½ cups	4 cups (1 quart)	5 cups (1 quart plus 1 cup)
Brandy or unsweetened apple juice	2 tablespoons	3 tablespoons	¼ cup
Dried thyme	½ teaspoon	¾ teaspoon	1 teaspoon
Table salt	¼ teaspoon	Rounded ¼ teaspoon	½ teaspoon
Ground black pepper	¼ teaspoon	Rounded ¼ teaspoon	½ teaspoon
½-inch-thick slices French or Italian bread	2	3	4
Finely grated Gruyère or ½-ounce slices Swiss cheese	¼ cup or 2 slices	6 tablespoons or 3 slices	½ cup or 4 slices
MAKES	2 servings	3 servings	4 servings

1. With the basket (or basket attachment) in the air fryer, heat it to 325°F (or 330°F, if that's the closest setting).

2. Place the onions and butter in a 6-inch square or round baking pan for a smaller batch, a 7-inch square or round baking pan for a medium batch, or an 8-inch square or round baking pan for a large batch.

continues

3. When the machine is at temperature, set the baking pan in the basket and air-fry for 30 minutes, tossing four or five times, maybe even more as the onions begin to soften, until they're golden brown and sweet.

4. Stir in the broth, brandy or apple juice, thyme, salt, and pepper. Raise the temperature to 400°F (or 390°F, if that's the closest setting). Air-fry undisturbed for 15 minutes, or until bubbling.

5. Set the bread slices in the soup in the pan. Top each with 2 tablespoons of the grated cheese or a slice of

Swiss cheese. Continue air-frying for 1 to 2 minutes, or until the cheese has melted. Ladle the soup with a bread slice into individual serving bowls.

Then...

- Serve this soup alongside **Green Bean and Tomato Salad** (page 119), **Herb Salad** (page 249), or **Tricolore Salad** (page 274).

See photo in insert.

Roasted Cauliflower Soup

EASY / CAN BE VEGETARIAN / GLUTEN-FREE / 9 INGREDIENTS

Because cauliflower is a fairly low-moisture vegetable (especially when it sits on the grocery store's shelf for a week or more), it needs a little boost to cook well in the air fryer. Make sure you coat the vegetable well with the olive oil spray to give it a good head start on getting brown and tender before it dries out. Or skip the olive oil spray and add up to 1 tablespoon olive oil to the bowl with the vegetables. But one warning: Adding olive oil (rather than spraying) may cause the air fryer to smoke. Set the machine under a turned-on vent hood or beside an open window to help cut down on the smoke in your house.

INGREDIENTS	2-quart or larger air fryer	3.5-quart or larger air fryer	5.25-quart or larger air fryer
Small cauliflower florets, any large ones cut into 1-inch pieces	3 rounded cups	4 rounded cups	6 rounded cups
Roughly chopped yellow or white onion	½ cup (1 small onion)	¾ cup	1 cup (1 medium onion)
Medium garlic cloves, peeled	Up to 2	Up to 3	Up to 4
Olive oil spray	As needed	As needed	As needed
Chicken or vegetable broth	2½ cups	3¼ cups	5 cups (1 quart plus 1 cup)
Stemmed fresh thyme leaves	1 teaspoon	1½ teaspoons	2 teaspoons
Heavy or light cream (*not* fat-free)	¼ cup	⅓ cup	½ cup
Table salt	Up to ½ teaspoon	Up to ¾ teaspoon	Up to 1 teaspoon
Ground black pepper	Up to ½ teaspoon	Up to ¾ teaspoon	Up to 1 teaspoon
MAKES	*4 servings*	*6 servings*	*8 servings*

1. With the basket (or basket attachment) in the air fryer, heat it to 400°F (or 390°F, if that's the closest setting).

2. Put the cauliflower, onion, and garlic in a large bowl. Generously spray the vegetables with olive oil spray, then toss to coat, spraying more as needed until the vegetables are glistening. Pour the vegetables into the basket.

3. Air-fry for 16 minutes, tossing at least three times to rearrange all the pieces, or until the cauliflower is golden brown and fragrant.

4. Save back a few of the florets for a garnish, then pour the remaining contents of the basket into a medium or large saucepan. Stir in the broth and thyme. Bring to a simmer over medium-high heat, stirring often. Cover, reduce the heat to low, and simmer slowly for 5 minutes, or until the cauliflower is very soft.

5. Remove the pan from the heat. Stir in the cream, salt, and pepper. Use an immersion blender to puree the soup in the saucepan until creamy. Or pour the contents of the saucepan into a large blender (working in batches, as necessary). Cover the canister but remove the center knob from the lid of the blender and place a clean kitchen towel over the opening (to avoid a pressure buildup and an explosion of soup on your cabinets). Blend until smooth, turning off the machine and scraping down the sides of the canister at least once. No matter which method you've used, stir the soup and serve it warm, garnished with a couple of roasted cauliflower florets.

Then...

- Top the servings with crumbled **Bacon Candy** (page 41).

- Dollop a little **Muhamara** (page 25) on top.

- Garnish with **Crunchy Spicy Chickpeas** (page 27) or **Buttery Spiced Pecans** (page 31).

Blistered Tomato Soup

EASY / CAN BE VEGAN / GLUTEN-FREE / 7 INGREDIENTS

Nothing beats a bowl of warm tomato soup. And now that soup is even better because the air fryer concentrates the tomatoes' natural flavors in a fraction of the time it would take to get the same results on a sheet pan in the oven. Even better, because the hot air dries out the surface of the tomatoes before they soften, they retain more of their natural juice than they would in an oven. And as a capper to the greatness here, this technique makes even off-season long-haul tomatoes shine in the soup.

INGREDIENTS	2-quart or larger air fryer	3.5-quart or larger air fryer	5.25-quart or larger air fryer
Small round tomatoes (about 5 ounces each), cut in halves through their "equators" (that is, not their stems)	2	4	5
Small single-lobe shallot(s), peeled and halved lengthwise	1	2	2
Medium garlic clove(s), peeled	1	2	2
Chicken or vegetable broth	1 cup	2 cups	2½ cups
Loosely packed fresh basil leaves	¼ cup	½ cup	⅔ cup
Table salt	¼ teaspoon	½ teaspoon	¾ teaspoon
Ground black pepper	¼ teaspoon	½ teaspoon	¾ teaspoon
MAKES	2 servings	3 servings	4 servings

1. With the basket (or basket attachment) in the air fryer, heat it to 400°F (or 390°F, if that's the closest setting).

2. When the machine is at temperature, put the tomatoes cut side up in the basket, stacking them as necessary. Scatter the shallot(s) and garlic in the basket among the tomato halves. Air-fry undisturbed for 20 minutes, until the tomatoes are softened and beginning to blister.

3. Dump the contents of the basket into a medium or large saucepan (depending on the batch size) and add the broth. Bring to a simmer over medium-high heat, stirring occasionally. Cover, reduce the heat to low, and simmer slowly for 10 minutes.

4. Stir in the basil, salt, and pepper. Use an immersion blender to puree the soup in the pan. Or pour the contents of the saucepan into a large blender (working in batches, as necessary). Cover the canister, but remove the center knob from the lid of the blender and place a clean kitchen towel over the opening (to avoid a pressure buildup and an explosion of tomato soup on your cabinets). Blend until smooth, turning off the machine and scraping down the sides of the canister at least once. No matter which method you've used, stir the soup well and serve it warm.

Then...

- Put a pat of butter on each bowlful.
- Or drizzle it with a little aromatic olive oil.
- Swirl a little cream into each bowlful.
- Or add a dollop of crème fraîche.
- This soup's got to have a **Super Crunchy Grilled Cheese** sandwich for dunking (page 113).

Roasted Beet Soup

CAN BE VEGETARIAN / GLUTEN-FREE / 10 INGREDIENTS

This soup is an update of hot borscht, a Russian classic. Our version uses potatoes as well as beets to give the soup a milder flavor, if still that dark purple color. (Beware your linens!) The spuds also thicken the soup a bit as they release their starch. We prefer this silky but not thick texture, but you could make the soup even thicker by removing some of the potato pieces (they'll have turned purple and are hard to spot), working them into a paste with a potato masher, and stirring them back into the soup in step 4 with the broth and other ingredients.

Use fresh beets only. Supermarkets sell packaged peeled beets in the produce section. Unfortunately, these are often fully cooked and will not stand up to the fairly long cooking here.

INGREDIENTS	2-quart or larger air fryer	3.5-quart or larger air fryer	5.25-quart or larger air fryer
Diced (¾-inch) peeled beets	3 cups (about 1 pound trimmed beets)	4½ cups (about 1½ pounds trimmed beets)	6 cups (about 2 pounds trimmed beets)
Diced (¾-inch) yellow potatoes, such as Yukon Golds (no need to peel)	1 cup (about ½ pound)	1½ cups (about ¾ pound)	2 cups (about 1 pound)
Medium single-lobe shallot(s), roughly chopped	1	1½	2
Olive oil spray	As needed	As needed	As needed
Chicken or vegetable broth	3½ cups	5 cups	7 cups
Finely chopped fresh dill fronds	1 tablespoon	1½ tablespoons	2 tablespoons
Red wine vinegar	2 teaspoons	1 tablespoon	1½ tablespoons
Table salt	½ teaspoon	¾ teaspoon	1 teaspoon
Ground black pepper	½ teaspoon	¾ teaspoon	1 teaspoon
Caraway seeds	¼ teaspoon	Rounded ¼ teaspoon	½ teaspoon
MAKES	*4 servings*	*6 servings*	*8 servings*

1. With the basket (or basket attachment) in the air fryer, heat it to 400°F (or 390°F, if that's the closest setting).

2. Put the beets, potatoes, and shallot(s) in a large bowl. Generously coat the vegetables with olive oil spray, then toss well, spraying more as needed until the vegetables are glistening. Pour them into the basket.

3. Air-fry for 20 minutes, tossing at least four times—or more—to rearrange all the pieces, particularly as the vegetables soften, until they are tender yet crisp at the edges.

4. Pour the contents of the basket into a medium or large saucepan. Stir in the broth, dill, vinegar, salt, pepper, and caraway seeds. Bring to a simmer over medium-high heat, stirring often.

continues

5. Cover, reduce the heat to as low as you can to maintain the simmer, and cook very slowly for 10 minutes to blend the flavors. Serve warm.

Then...

- Puree the soup for a smoother finish, using an immersion blender in the pan or working in batches in a blender.

- Serve the hot soup with thick slices of pumpernickel (gluten-free, if a concern) and lots of butter.

- Top each bowlful with sour cream.

- For the full "borscht" effect, boil or steam medium-size peeled white or yellow potatoes until tender, then set one in the center of each bowlful and garnish with lots of sour cream and some minced chives.

Hearty Roasted Vegetable Soup

CAN BE VEGETARIAN / GLUTEN-FREE / 9 INGREDIENTS

Consider this a road map for a hearty vegetable soup. Although we offer three vegetables in this recipe, you could use just about any root or winter-keeping vegetable in equivalent proportions, even potatoes, cutting any roots or tubers into ½-inch dice and any winter squash into 1-inch cubes. Try parsnips, potatoes, and butternut squash for another appealing combination. The point is to get the vegetables into a softened state so that their flavors concentrate and they thicken the soup a bit when some are smashed at the end of cooking.

You can also add *drained* diced tomatoes to the soup, up to 1 cup, with the broth, herbs, and spices. Drained canned *fire-roasted* diced tomatoes would be even better.

INGREDIENTS	2-quart or larger air fryer	3.5-quart or larger air fryer	5.25-quart or larger air fryer
Peeled and diced (½-inch) sweet potato	1 cup (about ½ pound)	1½ cups (about ¾ pound)	2 cups (about 1 pound)
"Baby" carrots, halved widthwise	1 cup (about 6 ounces)	1½ cups (about 9 ounces)	2 cups (about ¾ pound)
Peeled, seeded, and diced (1-inch) butternut squash	1 cup (about 6 ounces)	1½ cups (about 9 ounces)	2 cups (about ¾ pound)
Olive oil spray	As needed	As needed	As needed
Chicken or vegetable broth	3 cups	4½ cups (1 quart plus ½ cup)	6 cups (1½ quarts)
Dried thyme	½ teaspoon	¾ teaspoon	1 teaspoon
Ground allspice	¼ teaspoon	Rounded ¼ teaspoon	½ teaspoon
Table salt	¼ teaspoon	Rounded ¼ teaspoon	½ teaspoon
Ground black pepper	¼ teaspoon	Rounded ¼ teaspoon	½ teaspoon
MAKES	*3 servings*	*4 servings*	*6 servings*

1. With the basket (or basket attachment) in the air fryer, heat it to 400°F (or 390°F, if that's the closest setting).

2. Put the sweet potato, carrots, and butternut squash in a large bowl. Generously coat the vegetables with olive oil spray, then toss well, spraying more as needed until the vegetables are glistening. Pour the vegetables into the basket.

3. Air-fry for 25 minutes, tossing at least three times—or more—to rearrange all the pieces, until the vegetables are tender and lightly browned.

4. Pour the contents of the basket into a medium or large saucepan. Stir in the broth, thyme, allspice, salt, and pepper. Bring to a simmer over medium-high heat, stirring occasionally.

5. Cover, reduce the heat to low, and simmer slowly for 10 minutes. Use the back of a wooden spoon to smash some of the soft vegetables into a paste against the side of the pan. Stir the soup well so that this paste thickens it somewhat. Serve hot.

Then...

• Make GARLIC BREAD CROUTONS. For 4 servings, put *3 cups 1-inch cubes of fresh Italian or French bread (gluten-free, if a concern)* in a bowl and stir in *4 tablespoons (¼ cup/½ stick) melted butter, up to 3 medium garlic cloves put through a garlic press,* and *½ teaspoon table salt* until the bread is evenly and well coated. Heat the air fryer to 400°F (or 390°F, if that's the closest setting). Pour the bread cubes into the basket and air-fry, tossing to rearrange the croutons frequently, for 5 minutes, or until crisp and golden brown.

Roasted Vegetable Minestrone

CAN BE VEGETARIAN / CAN BE GLUTEN-FREE / 11 INGREDIENTS

As you know, air-frying vegetables intensifies their sweetness, the swirl of heat acting like a dehydrator to concentrate the flavors. That said, there are two tricks to this recipe.

One, make sure the vegetables are chopped to the size we indicate so that they don't fall through the basket mesh and also so they cook evenly.

Two, air-fry the vegetables until they're a little blackened at the edges, particularly the onions. Doing so takes the caramelization process a little further than in some other vegetable soup recipes. But it yields an incredibly deep, sophisticated, roasted flavor to the minestrone.

And one note: Some Italian-style seasoning blends include salt. If yours does, go easy on the additional table salt.

INGREDIENTS	2-quart or larger air fryer	3.5-quart or larger air fryer	5.25-quart or larger air fryer
Peeled and diced (¾-inch) carrots	1 cup (about 7 ounces)	1½ cups (about 10 ounces)	2 cups (about 14 ounces)
Diced (¾-inch) zucchini	1 cup (about 6 ounces)	1½ cups (about 9 ounces)	2 cups (about ¾ pound)
Diced (¾-inch) yellow or summer crookneck squash	1 cup (about 6 ounces)	1½ cups (about 9 ounces)	2 cups (about ¾ pound)
Roughly chopped yellow or white onion	½ cup (1 small onion)	¾ cup	1 cup (1 medium onion)
Sliced (½-inch-thick) celery	½ cup	¾ cup	1 cup
Olive oil spray	As needed	As needed	As needed
Chicken or vegetable broth	3 cups	4½ cups (1 quart plus ½ cup)	6 cups (1½ quarts)
Canned diced tomatoes (do not drain)	1¼ cups	One 14-ounce can (1¾ cups)	2¼ cups
Uncooked small shell or elbow pasta (gluten-free, if a concern)	¼ cup	⅓ cup	½ cup
Italian-style dried herb seasoning blend	1½ teaspoons	2¼ teaspoons	1 tablespoon
Table salt	½ teaspoon	¾ teaspoon	1 teaspoon
MAKES	4 servings	6 servings	8 servings

1. With the basket (or basket attachment) in the air fryer, heat it to 400°F (or 390°F, if that's the closest setting).

2. Put the carrots, zucchini, yellow squash, onion, and celery in a large bowl. Generously coat the vegetables with olive oil spray, then toss well, spraying a few times until the vegetables are glistening. Pour the vegetables into the basket.

3. Air-fry for 15 minutes, tossing the basket at the 5- and 10-minute marks to rearrange the vegetables, then about once a minute thereafter, until the vegetables are tender and a little charred at their edges.

4. Pour the contents of the basket into a medium or large saucepan. Stir in the broth, tomatoes, pasta, seasoning blend, and salt. Bring to a simmer over medium-high heat, stirring often. Cover, reduce the heat to low, and simmer for 15 minutes, or until the pasta is tender. Serve hot.

Then...

- Shave or grate Parmesan cheese or aged Asiago over each bowlful.

- Garnish each bowlful with purchased pesto.

- Better yet, make SAGE PESTO as a garnish. For 2½ cups, put *1 cup loosely packed fresh sage leaves, 1 cup loosely packed fresh parsley leaves, ½ cup walnut pieces, ½ cup finely grated Parmesan, 1 tablespoon lemon juice,* and *½ teaspoon table salt* in a food processor. Cover and process until a coarse paste, then with the motor running slowly pour in *⅓ cup olive oil* until fairly smooth. Use as much pesto as you like; store the remainder in a small container in the fridge with some *olive oil* poured over the top to keep the pesto from oxidizing, covering the container with its lid or plastic wrap.

Chili Cheese Dogs

EASY / CAN BE GLUTEN-FREE / 7 INGREDIENTS

When the dogs are this loaded, those of us from the South know they should be called "chili cheese *dawgs*." For this recipe, you'll make a quick and easy chili with ground beef, chile powder, and jarred sofrito (a mix of tomatoes, onions, aromatics, and spices).

Of course, you could skip the whole process and use canned chili. But why not try this super easy version for a real treat? The lean ground beef keeps the chili from being too oily.

These dogs can be a vegetarian entrée, if you substitute textured vegetable protein (TVP) for the ground beef and use vegan hot dogs. (There's cheese, so the fully loaded dogs aren't vegan unless you also sub in vegan cheese.)

INGREDIENTS	2-quart or larger air fryer	3.5-quart or larger air fryer	5.25-quart or larger air fryer
Lean ground beef	½ pound	¾ pound	1 pound
Chile powder	1 tablespoon	1½ tablespoons	2 tablespoons
Jarred sofrito	¾ cup	1 cup plus 2 tablespoons	One 12-ounce jar (1½ cups)
Hot dogs (gluten-free, if a concern)	2	3	4
Hot dog buns (gluten-free, if a concern), split open lengthwise	2	3	4
Finely chopped scallion	2 tablespoons	3 tablespoons	¼ cup
Shredded Cheddar cheese	6 tablespoons (about 1½ ounces)	9 tablespoons (a little more than 2 ounces)	¾ cup (about 3 ounces)
MAKES	2 chili dogs	3 chili dogs	4 chili dogs

1. Crumble the ground beef into a medium or large saucepan set over medium heat. Brown well, stirring often to break up the clumps. Add the chile powder and cook for 30 seconds, stirring the whole time. Stir in the sofrito and bring to a simmer. Reduce the heat to low and simmer, stirring occasionally, for 5 minutes. Keep warm.

2. With the basket (or basket attachment) in the air fryer, heat it to 400°F (or 390°F, if that's the closest setting).

3. When the machine is at temperature, put the hot dogs in the basket and air-fry undisturbed for 10 minutes, or until the hot dogs are bubbling and blistered, even a little crisp.

4. Use kitchen tongs to put the hot dogs in the buns. Top each with a rounded ½ cup of the ground beef mixture, 1 tablespoon of the minced scallion, and 3 tablespoons of the cheese. (The scallion should go under the cheese so it superheats and wilts a bit.) Set the filled hot dog buns in the basket and air-fry undisturbed for 2 minutes, or until the cheese has melted.

5. Remove the basket from the machine. Cool the chili cheese dogs in the basket for 5 minutes before serving.

Then...

- Top the chili cheese dogs with pickled jalapeño rings, jalapeño relish, chowchow, or even minced, fresh jalapeño chiles.

- Serve these "dawgs" with **Carrot Chips** (page 34) or **Onion Puffs** (page 48).

- Or offer **Radish Slaw** (page 117) or **Celery Root Slaw** (page 205) on the side.

Super Crunchy Grilled Cheese

FAST / EASY / VEGETARIAN / CAN BE GLUTEN-FREE / 3 INGREDIENTS

Mayonnaise on the outside of the bread for a grilled cheese sandwich lets that bread get super crunchy in the air fryer. Don't hesitate, even if you're not sure you like mayo. The results are worth the risk!

Keep in mind that some types of bread toast more quickly than others. Oatmeal bread, some whole-wheat breads, and any other sliced breads with a higher sugar content will toast much more quickly than, say, rye, dense whole-grain, or even many types of plain white bread. Although we give a general notion of the timing here, check the basket a few times to make sure the bread is browning, not burning.

INGREDIENTS	2-quart or larger air fryer	5.25-quart or larger air fryer
Sandwich bread slices: white, whole-wheat, whole-grain, rye, oatmeal, or any variety you prefer, even gluten-free	2	4
Regular or low-fat mayonnaise (*not* fat-free; gluten-free, if a concern)	2 tablespoons	¼ cup
Sliced semi-firm cheese of any variety you prefer, such as Cheddar, Swiss, Monterey Jack, or Colby	3 ounces (3 to 4 slices)	6 ounces (6 to 8 slices)
MAKES	1 sandwich	2 sandwiches

1. With the basket (or basket attachment) in the air fryer, heat it to 400°F (or 390°F, if that's the closest setting).

2. Spread 1 tablespoon mayonnaise over one side of each slice of bread. Turn one slice of bread over, top the unspread side with cheese, then set another slice of bread on top, mayonnaise side up. Repeat if you're making two sandwiches.

3. When the machine is at temperature, put the sandwich(es) in the basket. Air-fry undisturbed for 5 minutes, or until browned and crunchy on the outside. Use kitchen tongs to transfer the

sandwich(es) to a cutting board, cool for a few minutes, then cut in half to serve.

Then...

- Doesn't a grilled cheese *need* **Blistered Tomato Soup** (page 106)?

- A pickle on the side is traditional, but we also like a few pickled onion slices scattered over the sandwich halves.

- Smear a thin spread of hot brown mustard (gluten-free, if a concern) over the top of the sandwich as it cools.

Philly Cheesesteak Sandwiches

EASY / CAN BE GLUTEN-FREE / 8 INGREDIENTS

Making this classic sandwich couldn't be easier with an air fryer. You'll build the filling in the basket, then transfer it to rolls or even hot dog buns for serving.

You can often find shaved beef in the butcher or meat case at your supermarket. It's very thinly sliced rib-eye steak or other leaner cuts (too much fat makes the beef too greasy as it cooks), often used for French dip sandwiches and even some recent pressure-cooker favorites like Mongolian beef. Shaved beef is sometimes sold in the freezer case as "beef for cheesesteak sandwiches," but this specialty labeling inflates the price considerably.

INGREDIENTS	2-quart or larger air fryer	3.5-quart or larger air fryer	5.25-quart or larger air fryer
Shaved beef	½ pound	¾ pound	1 pound
Worcestershire sauce (gluten-free, if a concern)	2 teaspoons	1 tablespoon	4 teaspoons
Garlic powder	¼ teaspoon	Rounded ¼ teaspoon	½ teaspoon
Mild paprika	¼ teaspoon	Rounded ¼ teaspoon	½ teaspoon
Frozen bell pepper strips (do not thaw)	¼ cup (1 ounce)	6 tablespoons (1½ ounces)	½ cup (2 ounces)
Very thin yellow or white medium onion slice(s)	1 slice, broken into rings	2 slices, broken into rings	3 slices, broken into rings
Provolone cheese slices	4 ounces (4 to 6 slices)	6 ounces (6 to 8 slices)	½ pound (10 to 12 slices)
Long soft rolls such as hero, hoagie, or Italian sub rolls, or hot dog buns (gluten-free, if a concern), split open lengthwise	2	3	4
MAKES	2 sandwiches	3 sandwiches	4 sandwiches

1. With the basket (or basket attachment) in the air fryer, heat it to 400°F (or 390°F, if that's the closest setting).

2. When the machine is at temperature, spread the shaved beef in the basket, leaving a ½-inch perimeter around the meat for good air flow. Sprinkle the meat with the Worcestershire sauce, paprika, and garlic powder. Spread the peppers and onions on top of the meat.

3. Air-fry undisturbed for 6 minutes, or until cooked through. Set the cheese on top of the meat. Continue air-frying undisturbed for 2 to 3 minutes, or until the cheese has melted.

4. Use kitchen tongs to divide the meat and cheese layers in the basket between the rolls or buns. Serve hot.

Then...

- Before you pick up the meat and cheese with tongs, or just after you set it on the bottom half of the roll, top it with pickle relish, jalapeño relish, chowchow, or even carrot slaw.

- To make CARROT SLAW from scratch, mix *grated or shredded carrots* with *a little minced scallion* and *minced fresh parsley leaves*. Dress with *equal parts olive oil* and *lemon juice*, plus a *touch of honey* and *Dijon mustard (gluten-free, if a concern)* as well as some *table salt* to taste.

Best-Ever Roast Beef Sandwiches

EASY / CAN BE GLUTEN-FREE / 11 INGREDIENTS

Here you'll make a flavorful, fairly inexpensive beef roast in the air fryer that you can slice for sandwiches while the beef is warm. Or store the beef in the fridge for cold sandwiches in the days ahead.

In truth, you can skip the whole sandwich-making process here and slice this roast beef onto chopped salads for a quick dinner (especially if you've made the beef ahead and kept it in the fridge) or onto an antipasto platter to fill it out enough to make a meal.

INGREDIENTS	2-quart or larger air fryer	3.5-quart or larger air fryer	5.25-quart or larger air fryer
Olive oil	1½ teaspoons	2½ teaspoons	1 tablespoon
Dried oregano	1 teaspoon	1½ teaspoons	2 teaspoons
Dried thyme	1 teaspoon	1½ teaspoons	2 teaspoons
Onion powder	1 teaspoon	1½ teaspoons	2 teaspoons
Table salt	1 teaspoon	1½ teaspoons	2 teaspoons
Ground black pepper	1 teaspoon	1½ teaspoons	2 teaspoons
Beef eye of round	2 pounds	3 pounds	4 pounds
Round soft rolls, such as Kaiser rolls or hamburger buns (gluten-free, if a concern), split open lengthwise	4	6	8
Regular, low-fat, or fat-free mayonnaise (gluten-free, if a concern)	½ cup	¾ cup	1 cup
Romaine lettuce leaves, rinsed	4	6	8
Round tomato slices (¼ inch thick)	4	6	8
MAKES	4 sandwiches	6 sandwiches	8 sandwiches

1. With the basket (or basket attachment) in the air fryer, heat it to 350°F (or 360°F, if that's the closest setting).

2. Mix the oil, oregano, thyme, onion powder, salt, and pepper in a small bowl. Spread this mixture all over the eye of round.

continues

3. When the machine is at temperature, set the beef in the basket and air-fry for 30 to 50 minutes (the range depends on the size of the cut), turning the meat twice, until an instant-read meat thermometer inserted into the thickest piece of the meat registers 130°F for rare, 140°F for medium, or 150°F for well-done.

4. Use kitchen tongs to transfer the beef to a cutting board. Cool for 10 minutes. If serving now, carve into ⅛-inch-thick slices. Spread each roll with 2 tablespoons mayonnaise and divide the beef slices between the rolls. Top with a lettuce leaf and a tomato slice and serve. Or set the beef in a container, cover, and refrigerate for up to 3 days to make cold roast beef sandwiches anytime.

Then...

- To make 2 cups HORSERADISH SAUCE for the sandwiches, whisk *1 cup jarred prepared white horseradish, ½ cup regular or low-fat sour cream, ½ cup regular or low-fat mayonnaise (gluten-free, if a concern), ½ teaspoon table salt, ½ teaspoon ground black pepper,* and *several dashes of hot red pepper sauce (such as Cholula or Tabasco; gluten-free if a concern)* in a bowl until creamy. Skip the plain mayonnaise and slather this sauce on the sandwiches, storing the remainder in a covered glass or other nonreactive container in the fridge for up to 1 week.

Chicken Club Sandwiches

FAST / EASY / CAN BE GLUTEN-FREE / 6 INGREDIENTS

Rather than layering bacon and chicken breast slices in a sandwich—and adding a third and totally unnecessary slice of bread in the middle—why not let the air fryer cook the bacon right on the chicken, which protects the poultry from the onslaught of intense heat and gives it some of that bacon-y goodness along the way?

We gave you the classic combo of toppers for this sandwich (mayonnaise, lettuce, and tomato), but you could vary it in dozens of ways: with pickle relish, cole slaw, and mustard; or with sauerkraut, sliced tomatoes, and honey mustard, just to name two possibilities.

INGREDIENTS	2-quart or larger air fryer	3.5-quart or larger air fryer	5.25-quart or larger air fryer
5- to 6-ounce boneless skinless chicken breasts	2	3	4
Thick-cut bacon strips (gluten-free, if a concern)	4	6	8
Long soft rolls, such as hero, hoagie, or Italian sub rolls (gluten-free, if a concern)	2	3	4
Regular, low-fat, or fat-free mayonnaise (gluten-free, if a concern)	2 tablespoons	3 tablespoons	¼ cup
Lettuce leaves, preferably romaine or iceberg	2	3	4
¼-inch-thick tomato slices	4	6	8
MAKES	*2 sandwiches*	*3 sandwiches*	*4 sandwiches*

1. With the basket (or basket attachment) in the air fryer, heat it to 375°F (or 370°F or 360°F, if one of these is the closest setting).

2. Wrap each chicken breast with 2 strips of bacon, spiraling the bacon around the meat, slightly overlapping the strips on each revolution. Start the second strip of bacon farther down the breast but on a line with the start of the first strip so they both end at a lined-up point on the chicken breast.

3. When the machine is at temperature, set the wrapped breasts bacon-seam side down in the basket with space between them. Air-fry undisturbed for 12 minutes, until the bacon is browned, crisp, and cooked through and an instant-read meat thermometer inserted into the center of a breast registers 165°F. You may need to add 1 to 2 minutes in the air fryer if the temperature is at 360°F.

4. Use kitchen tongs to transfer the breasts to a wire rack. Split the rolls open lengthwise and set them cut side down in the basket. Air-fry for 1 minute, or until warmed through.

5. Use kitchen tongs to transfer the rolls to a cutting board. Spread 1 tablespoon mayonnaise on the cut side of one half of each roll. Top with a chicken breast, lettuce leaf, and tomato slice. Serve warm.

Then...

- Sliced pitted and peeled avocado is particularly delicious on these sandwiches.

- Try these sandwiches with RADISH SLAW. Trim and very thinly slice *radishes*, then mix them with *a little minced scallion* and *minced fresh cilantro leaves*. Dress the slaw with *olive oil* and *lime juice* in a 2-to-1 ratio, whisked with *a little table salt* to taste.

Chicken Saltimbocca Sandwiches

These sandwiches replicate the flavors of the classic prosciutto-topped veal entrée served in Italian-American restaurants. We went with chicken, simply because it's easier to find and work with.

We've simplified things considerably by using purchased pesto as a condiment, but you can make your own. For BASIL PESTO, our best volume ratio is *4 parts loosely packed fresh basil leaves* to *1 part olive oil, 1 part finely grated Parmesan cheese*, and *1 part pine nuts*. Add *a little minced garlic*, if desired, and *table salt* and *ground black pepper* to taste. Whir these ingredients in a food processor, stopping the machine once or twice to scrape down the inside of the canister, and adding *a little more olive oil* if the mixture needs help, until fairly smooth if still a tad grainy. Store any leftover pesto in a covered glass or other nonreactive container in the fridge for a day or two. Putting a thin layer of olive oil on top of it will preserve its green color.

INGREDIENTS	2-quart or larger air fryer	3.5-quart or larger air fryer	5.25-quart or larger air fryer
5- to 6-ounce boneless skinless chicken breasts	2	3	4
Thin prosciutto slices	4	6	8
Provolone cheese slices	4	6	8
Long soft rolls, such as hero, hoagie, or Italian sub rolls (gluten-free, if a concern), split open lengthwise	2	3	4
Pesto, purchased or homemade (see the headnote)	2 tablespoons	3 tablespoons	¼ cup
MAKES	2 sandwiches	3 sandwiches	4 sandwiches

1. With the basket (or basket attachment) in the air fryer, heat it to 400°F (or 390°F, if that's the closest setting).

2. Wrap each chicken breast with 2 prosciutto slices, spiraling the prosciutto around the breast and overlapping the slices a bit to cover the breast. The prosciutto will stick to the chicken more readily than bacon does.

3. When the machine is at temperature, set the wrapped chicken breasts in the basket and air-fry undisturbed for 10 minutes, or until the prosciutto is frizzled and the chicken is cooked through.

4. Overlap 2 cheese slices on each breast. Air-fry undisturbed for 1 minute, or until melted. Take the basket out of the machine.

5. Smear the insides of the rolls with the pesto, then use kitchen tongs to put a wrapped and cheesy chicken breast in each roll.

Then...

- Sage is the traditional herb in saltimbocca. You can skip the pesto called for in this recipe and use **Sage Pesto** (page 111) for a more traditional flavor.

- This GREEN BEAN AND TOMATO SALAD will turn this easy sandwich into a full meal. Trim *green beans* and cut them into 3-inch pieces before blanching them for 1 minute in boiling water. Drain and rinse under cool running water. Drain well, then combine in a bowl with *chopped cherry tomatoes*. Dress with *olive oil* and *balsamic vinegar* in a 2-to-1 ratio. If desired, press a *garlic clove* and/or a *tinned anchovy fillet* through a garlic press. Season the salad with *table salt* and *ground black pepper* to taste.

Chicken Gyros

EASY / CAN BE GLUTEN-FREE / 11 INGREDIENTS

We offer the easiest, air-fryer way to make a gyro (pronounced exactly like the word "hero" in most of the country, but as *JEYE-roh* on the East Coast). We use chicken thighs, some lettuce, and pita pockets. Honestly, the sky's then the limit as to how you can customize these things: Add minced red onion, diced cucumber, shredded lettuce, shredded carrots, even a tart slaw like our **Radish Slaw** (page 117), along with **Tzatziki Sauce** (next page), all put right into the pita pocket with the chicken.

Traditionally, gyros are served in pocketless pita that's folded over the filling, kind of like a taco shell. We advocate for pita pockets because we think there's less mess involved. But go traditional, if you prefer.

INGREDIENTS	2-quart or larger air fryer	3.5-quart or larger air fryer	5.25-quart or larger air fryer
4- to 5-ounce boneless skinless chicken thighs, trimmed of any fat blobs	2	4	6
Lemon juice	1½ tablespoons	2 tablespoons	3 tablespoons
Red wine vinegar	1 tablespoon	2 tablespoons	3 tablespoons
Olive oil	1 tablespoon	2 tablespoons	3 tablespoons
Dried oregano	1 teaspoon	2 teaspoons	1 tablespoon
Minced garlic	1 teaspoon	2 teaspoons	2½ teaspoons
Table salt	½ teaspoon	1 teaspoon	1¼ teaspoons
Ground black pepper	½ teaspoon	1 teaspoon	1¼ teaspoons
Pita pockets (gluten-free, if a concern)	2	4	6
Chopped tomatoes	¼ cup	½ cup	¾ cup
Bottled regular, low-fat, or fat-free ranch dressing (gluten-free, if a concern)	¼ cup	½ cup	¾ cup
MAKES	2 gyros	4 gyros	6 gyros

continues

1. Mix the thighs, lemon juice, vinegar, oil, oregano, garlic, salt, and pepper in a zip-closed bag. Seal, gently massage the marinade into the meat through the plastic, and refrigerate for at least 2 hours or up to 6 hours. (Longer than that and the meat can turn rubbery.)

2. Set the plastic bag out on the counter (to make the contents a little less frigid). With the basket (or basket attachment) in the air fryer, heat it to 375°F (or 370°F or 360°F, if one of these is the closest setting).

3. When the machine is at temperature, use kitchen tongs to place the thighs in the basket in one layer. Discard the marinade. Air-fry the chicken thighs undisturbed for 12 minutes, or until browned and an instant-read meat thermometer inserted into the thickest part of one thigh registers 165°F. You may need to air-fry the chicken 1 to 2 minutes longer if the machine's temperature is 360°F.

4. Use kitchen tongs to transfer the thighs to a cutting board. Cool for 5 minutes, then set one thigh in each of the pita pockets. Top each with 2 tablespoons chopped tomatoes and 2 tablespoons dressing. Serve warm.

Then...

• Skip the ranch dressing and top these with TZATZIKI SAUCE. Mix *1¼ cups plain full-fat or low-fat yogurt or Greek yogurt (not fat-free), 1 cup finely chopped peeled cucumber, 1 tablespoon lemon juice, ½ teaspoon finely minced garlic, ½ teaspoon table salt,* and *½ teaspoon ground black pepper* in a small bowl. Garnish the pita pockets with this sauce, saving back any remainder in a covered container in the fridge for up to 3 days.

Chicken Spiedies

EASY / CAN BE GLUTEN-FREE / 13 INGREDIENTS

Spiedies (*SPEE-dees*) are a Binghamton, New York, specialty, an Italian-American sandwich made with pork or beef, or chicken as we do here. The meat is usually skewered because it's grilled or cooked on a grill pan. We don't need the skewers for the air fryer because the basket will hold the chicken thighs without any added fuss.

Spiedies often don't have any sauce—or maybe just a little mayonnaise or ranch dressing (gluten-free, if a concern). We give these a riff on Alabama white barbecue sauce instead. The sauce needs lots of ground black pepper to give it a pop.

INGREDIENTS	2-quart or larger air fryer	3.5-quart or larger air fryer	5.25-quart or larger air fryer
Boneless skinless chicken thighs, trimmed of any fat blobs and cut into 2-inch pieces	¾ pound	1¼ pounds	1½ pounds
Red wine vinegar	2 tablespoons	3 tablespoons	¼ cup
Olive oil	1 tablespoon	2 tablespoons	3 tablespoons
Minced fresh mint leaves	1 tablespoon	2 tablespoons	3 tablespoons
Minced fresh parsley leaves	1 tablespoon	2 tablespoons	3 tablespoons
Minced fresh dill fronds	1½ teaspoon	2 teaspoons	1 tablespoon
Fennel seeds	½ teaspoon	¾ teaspoon	1 teaspoon
Table salt	½ teaspoon	¾ teaspoon	1 teaspoon
Red pepper flakes	Up to ¼ teaspoon	Up to a rounded ¼ teaspoon	Up to ½ teaspoon
Long soft rolls, such as hero, hoagie, or Italian sub rolls (gluten-free, if a concern), split open lengthwise	2	3	4
Regular or low-fat mayonnaise (*not* fat-free; gluten-free, if a concern)	3 tablespoons	4½ tablespoons	6 tablespoons
Distilled white vinegar	1 tablespoon	1½ tablespoons	2 tablespoons
Ground black pepper	1 teaspoon	1½ teaspoons	2 teaspoons
MAKES	*2 sandwiches*	*3 sandwiches*	*4 sandwiches*

1. Mix the chicken, vinegar, oil, mint, parsley, dill, fennel seeds, salt, and red pepper flakes in a zip-closed plastic bag. Seal, gently massage the marinade ingredients into the meat, and refrigerate for at least 2 hours or up to 6 hours. (Longer than that and the meat can turn rubbery.)

2. Set the plastic bag out on the counter (to make the contents a little less frigid). With the basket (or basket attachment) in the air fryer, heat it to 400°F (or 390°F, if that's the closest setting).

continues

3. When the machine is at temperature, use kitchen tongs to set the chicken thighs in the basket (discard any remaining marinade) and air-fry undisturbed for 6 minutes. Turn the thighs over and continue air-frying undisturbed for 4 to 6 minutes more, until well browned, cooked through, and even a little crunchy.

4. Dump the contents of the basket onto a wire rack and cool for 2 or 3 minutes. Divide the chicken evenly between the rolls. Whisk the mayonnaise, vinegar, and black pepper in a small bowl until smooth. Drizzle this sauce over the chicken pieces in the rolls.

Then...

- Skip the mayonnaise sauce and smear the insides of the rolls with marinara sauce. Add some grated Parmesan or provolone slices.

Thanksgiving Turkey Sandwiches

CAN BE GLUTEN-FREE / 11 INGREDIENTS

Nope, these sandwiches are not made with leftover turkey. Rather, they start with air-fried turkey cutlets that are breaded with ground stuffing mix. Then the sandwiches get cranberry sauce and Brussels sprouts, turning them into a lunch reminiscent of the sort served the day after the holiday feast.

Look for shredded Brussels sprouts in the produce section of almost all supermarkets. Failing that, shred large Brussels sprouts through the large holes of a box grater. Or punt and substitute bagged slaw mix.

INGREDIENTS	2-quart or larger air fryer	3.5-quart or larger air fryer	5.25-quart or larger air fryer
Herb-seasoned stuffing mix (*not* cornbread-style; gluten-free, if a concern)	1 cup	1½ cups	2 cups
Large egg white(s)	1	1	2
Water	2 tablespoons	2 tablespoons	2 tablespoons
5- to 6-ounce turkey breast cutlets	2	3	4
Vegetable oil spray	As needed	As needed	As needed
Purchased cranberry sauce, preferably whole berry	3 tablespoons	4½ tablespoons	6 tablespoons
Ground cinnamon	⅛ teaspoon	Rounded ⅛ teaspoon	¼ teaspoon
Ground dried ginger	⅛ teaspoon	Rounded ⅛ teaspoon	¼ teaspoon
Regular, low-fat, or fat-free mayonnaise (gluten-free, if a concern)	3 tablespoons	4½ tablespoons	6 tablespoons
Shredded Brussels sprouts	¼ cup	6 tablespoons	½ cup
Kaiser rolls (gluten-free, if a concern), split open	2	3	4
MAKES	2 sandwiches	3 sandwiches	4 sandwiches

1. With the basket (or basket attachment) in the air fryer, heat it to 375°F (or 370°F or 360°F, if one of these is the closest setting).

2. Put the stuffing mix in a heavy zip-closed bag, seal it, lay it flat on your counter, and roll a rolling pin over the bag to crush the stuffing mix to the consistency of rough sand. (Or you can pulse the stuffing mix to the desired consistency in a food processor.)

3. Set up and fill two shallow soup plates or small pie plates on your counter: one for the egg white(s), whisked with the water until foamy; and one for the ground stuffing mix.

4. Dip a cutlet in the egg white mixture, coating both sides and letting any excess egg white slip back into the rest. Set the cutlet in the ground stuffing mix and coat it evenly on both sides, pressing gently to coat well on both sides. Lightly coat the cutlet on both sides with vegetable oil spray, set it aside, and continue dipping and coating the remaining cutlets in the same way.

5. Set the cutlets in the basket and air-fry undisturbed for 10 minutes, or until crisp and brown. Use kitchen tongs to transfer the cutlets to a wire rack to cool for a few minutes.

6. Meanwhile, stir the cranberry sauce with the cinnamon and ginger in a small bowl. Mix the shredded Brussels sprouts and mayonnaise in a second bowl until the vegetable is evenly coated.

7. Build the sandwiches by spreading about 1½ tablespoons of the cranberry mixture on the cut side of the bottom half of each roll. Set a cutlet on top, then spread about 3 tablespoons of the Brussels sprouts mixture evenly over the cutlet. Set the other half of the roll on top and serve warm.

Then...

• Get the full holiday vibe with a side of SWEET POTATO SALAD. Peel one or more *sweet potatoes* and cut them into 1-inch cubes. Boil them in a pot of salted water over high heat until tender, about 20 minutes. Drain in a colander set in the sink, then mix them with *minced red onion*, *thinly sliced celery*, and *chopped thin (and raw) green beans*. Dress them with *regular, low-fat, or fat-free bottled French dressing* to taste.

Cuban Sandwiches

FAST / EASY / CAN BE GLUTEN-FREE / 5 INGREDIENTS

Here's a New York favorite, served up hot by street vendors and at deli counters. For an even more authentic take, use half thinly sliced ham and half thinly sliced roast pork (see **Three Seed–Coated Pork Loin** on page 249).

Remember: The success of this sandwich lies mostly with the pickle. Choose one that has a tart, crisp bite for the best contrast against the meat and cheese.

INGREDIENTS	2-quart or larger air fryer	5.25-quart or larger air fryer
Long soft rolls such as hero, hoagie, or Italian sub rolls, or soft sandwich roll(s) (gluten-free, if a concern), split open lengthwise	1	2
Yellow prepared mustard (gluten-free, if a concern)	1 tablespoon	2 tablespoons
Thinly sliced deli ham	6 ounces	¾ pound
Long dill pickle sandwich slices (gluten-free, if a concern)	2	4
Cheddar cheese slices	1 ounce (2 to 3 slices)	2 ounces (2 to 4 slices)
MAKES	1 sandwich	2 sandwiches

1. With the basket (or basket attachment) in the air fryer, heat it to 375°F (or 370°F or 360°F, if one of these is the closest setting).

2. Smear the inside of the roll(s) with the mustard. If making one sandwich, pile the ham, pickle, and cheese in the roll. If making two sandwiches, divide these equally between the rolls. Gently press the sandwich(es) closed.

3. When the machine is at temperature, set the sandwich(es) in the basket and air-fry undisturbed for 4 minutes, until the cheese has melted and the roll is crisp.

4. Use a nonstick-safe spatula, and perhaps a flatware fork for balance, to transfer the sandwich(es) to a wire rack. Cool for 5 minutes before serving.

Then...

- Serve these with a CUBAN SALAD. Rather than tossing these together, line the following down a serving platter: *pitted, peeled, and thinly sliced avocados; roughly chopped large tomatoes; stemmed fresh watercress; peeled and chopped fresh pineapple;* and *very thinly sliced red onion.* (You can alter their proportions based on your taste). Make a dressing by whisking *olive oil, lime juice,* and *white wine vinegar* in a 3-to-1-to-1 proportion, adding *a little minced garlic* if desired, as well as *table salt* and *ground black pepper* to taste. Drizzle this dressing over the salad.

Croque Monsieur

FAST / EASY / CAN BE GLUTEN-FREE / 5 INGREDIENTS

The best bread for this classic bistro sandwich is a hearty, thick sandwich bread such as Pepperidge Farm (not the thin-sliced loaf but the more standard slices). Once the sandwich has been dipped in the beaten egg, it must be set aside so the egg soaks through the bread, allowing the slices to get crunchy on the outside but still stay soft on the "underside."

INGREDIENTS	2-quart or larger air fryer	5.25-quart or larger air fryer
White or oat sandwich bread slices (gluten-free, if a concern)	2	4
Thin Swiss cheese slices	2	4
Thinly sliced deli ham (gluten-free, if a concern)	3 ounces	6 ounces
Large egg(s)	1	2
Vegetable oil spray	As needed	As needed
MAKES	*1 sandwich*	*2 sandwiches*

1. With the basket (or basket attachment) in the air fryer, heat it to 375°F (or 370°F or 360°F, if one of these is the closest setting).

2. Build a sandwich by setting a slice of cheese on a slice of bread, then 3 ounces ham, then another slice of cheese, and finally a second slice of bread. (The point is that bread is always against the cheese.) Repeat if making two sandwiches.

3. Whisk the egg(s) in a shallow soup plate or small pie plate until uniform. Set the sandwich in the beaten egg(s), then turn it over, coating both sides. Allow the excess egg to slip back into the rest, then set the sandwich on a cutting board for 3 minutes to let the egg soak in. Repeat with the second sandwich, as necessary.

4. Lightly coat both sides of the sandwich(es) with vegetable oil spray. Set the sandwich(es) in the basket and air-fry undisturbed for 6 minutes, or until the bread has browned and the cheese has melted.

5. Use a nonstick-safe spatula, and perhaps a flatware fork for balance, to transfer the sandwich(es) to a wire rack. Cool for 5 minutes before slicing in half and serving.

Then...

- Serve these sandwiches with **FENNEL-PEAR SALAD**. Trim a *head of fennel* of its stalks, fronds, and thick bottom, then thinly slice the bulb before chopping it into bite-size pieces. Toss these with *peeled, cored, and thinly sliced pear* and *thinly shaved Parmesan*. Whisk a dressing of *olive oil* and *lemon juice* in equal proportions. Drizzle over the salad and season with *table salt* and *ground black pepper* to taste.

Reuben Sandwiches

EASY / 5 OR 6 INGREDIENTS

By using purchased corned beef, sauerkraut, and Russian dressing, you can make the crunchiest, tastiest reubens in minutes. For the best sauerkraut, skip the cans and look for the bags of it near the hot dogs or packaged sausages at the supermarket.

You'll note that the cheese is optional. Nine zillion kosher delis can't be wrong. But cheese is now traditional in the American version. Go ahead, ruin tradition, and make your kosher grandmother cry. We have in countless recipes.

For a super quick, streamlined version of Russian dressing, whisk *regular, low-fat, or fat-free mayonnaise* and *red ketchup-like chili sauce (such as Heinz)* in a 3-to-1 ratio, adding *a little jarred prepared white or red horseradish* and *a touch of Worcestershire sauce* to taste. Save any extra in a covered container in the refrigerator for up to 1 week.

And one final note: most corned beef is gluten-free, but some has been injected with fillers that can include wheat starches. Buy certified gluten-free corned beef if this is a concern.

INGREDIENTS	2-quart or larger air fryer	3.5-quart or larger air fryer
Sliced deli corned beef	¼ pound	½ pound
Regular or low-fat mayonnaise (*not* fat-free)	2 teaspoons	4 teaspoons
Rye bread slices	2	4
Russian dressing	4 teaspoons	2 tablespoons plus 2 teaspoons
Purchased sauerkraut, squeezed by the handful over the sink to get rid of excess moisture	¼ cup	½ cup
Swiss cheese slices (optional)	1 ounce (1 to 2 slices)	2 ounces (2 to 4 slices)
MAKES	*1 sandwich*	*2 sandwiches*

1. Set the corned beef in the basket, slip the basket into the machine, and heat the air fryer to 400°F (or 390°F, if that's the closest setting). Air-fry undisturbed for 3 minutes from the time the basket is put in the machine, just to warm up the meat.

2. Use kitchen tongs to transfer the corned beef to a cutting board. Spread 1 teaspoon mayonnaise on one side of each slice of rye bread, rubbing the mayonnaise into the bread with a small flatware knife.

3. Place the bread slices mayonnaise side down on a cutting board. Spread the Russian dressing over the "dry" side of each slice. For one sandwich, top one slice of bread with the corned beef, sauerkraut, and cheese (if using). For two sandwiches, top two slices of bread each with half of the corned beef, sauerkraut, and cheese (if using). Close the sandwiches with the remaining bread, setting it mayonnaise side up on top.

4. Set the sandwich(es) in the basket and air-fry undisturbed for 8 minutes, or until browned and crunchy.

5. Use a nonstick-safe spatula, and perhaps a flatware fork for balance, to transfer the sandwich(es) to a cutting board. Cool for 2 or 3 minutes before slicing in half and serving.

Then...

- Serve this sandwich with a BROCCOLI AND GRAPE SALAD. Toss *broccoli florets, halved seedless red grapes, some thinly sliced celery,* and *a little chopped scallion* in a bowl, then dress with *regular or low-fat* *mayonnaise (gluten-free, if a concern)* and *regular or low-fat sour cream* in equal proportions by volume, as well as *a splash of apple cider vinegar, table salt,* and *ground black pepper* to taste.

See photo in insert.

Chicken Apple Brie Melt

FAST / EASY / CAN BE GLUTEN-FREE / 7 INGREDIENTS

Here's a hearty sandwich that can be gussied up any number of ways: Use honey mustard instead of Dijon, add one or two fresh basil leaves on top of the apple slices and under the cheese, or swap the Brie out for Camembert or even Cambozola.

There are two tricks to success. One, make sure the apple slices are quite thin. If you buy presliced apples, the wedges will need to be cut thinner so they lie flat on the chicken breast. Figure on each slice being about 1/8 inch wide.

And two, freeze a soft cheese like Brie for 30 minutes before you prepare the sandwich. You'll then be able to slice the cheese easily into strips.

INGREDIENTS	2-quart or larger air fryer	3.5-quart or larger air fryer	5.25-quart or larger air fryer
5- to 6-ounce boneless skinless chicken breasts	2	3	4
Vegetable oil spray	As needed	As needed	As needed
Dried herbes de Provence	1 teaspoon	1½ teaspoons	2 teaspoons
Brie, rind removed, thinly sliced	2 ounces	3 ounces	¼ pound
Thin cored apple slices	4	6	8
French rolls (gluten-free, if a concern)	2	3	4
Dijon mustard (gluten-free, if a concern)	4 teaspoons	2 tablespoons	2 tablespoons plus 2 teaspoons
MAKES	2 sandwiches	3 sandwiches	4 sandwiches

1. With the basket (or basket attachment) in the air fryer, heat it to 375°F (or 370°F or 360°F, if one of these is the closest setting).

2. Lightly coat all sides of the chicken breasts with vegetable oil spray. Sprinkle the breasts evenly with the herbes de Provence.

3. When the machine is at temperature, set the breasts in the basket and air-fry undisturbed for 10 minutes.

4. Top the chicken breasts with the apple slices, then the cheese. Air-fry undisturbed for 2 minutes, or until the cheese is melty and bubbling.

continues

5. Use a nonstick-safe spatula and kitchen tongs, for balance, to transfer the breasts to a cutting board. Set the rolls in the basket and air-fry for 1 minute to warm through. (Putting them in the machine without splitting them keeps the insides very soft while the outside gets a little crunchy.)

6. Transfer the rolls to the cutting board. Split them open lengthwise, then spread 1 teaspoon mustard on each cut side. Set a prepared chicken breast on the bottom of a roll and close with its top, repeating as necessary to make additional sandwiches. Serve warm.

Then...

- Serve these with SIMPLE ARUGULA SALAD. Mix *baby arugula* with some *chopped walnuts*, *finely grated Parmesan*, and perhaps a couple of *thinly sliced strawberries*. Squeeze a little *lemon juice* over the salad, then drizzle it with a *syrupy aged balsamic vinegar*, seasoning it with *table salt* and *ground black pepper* to taste.

Patty Melt

CAN BE GLUTEN-FREE / 9 INGREDIENTS

This diner classic is much better in the air fryer because the bread dries out and toasts beautifully. Admittedly, the recipe is a two-step process: first one or more patties and the onions, then the sandwich as a whole in the basket. But doing so keeps the juices from the meat from soaking into the bread and turning it soggy.

INGREDIENTS	2-quart or larger air fryer	5.25-quart or larger air fryer
Lean ground beef	¼ pound	½ pound
Worcestershire sauce (gluten-free, if a concern)	2 teaspoons	4 teaspoons
Yellow prepared mustard (gluten-free, if a concern)	1 teaspoon	2 teaspoons
Ground black pepper	¼ teaspoon	½ teaspoon
Small yellow or white onion(s), cut into ½-inch-thick slices, these broken into individual rings	1	2
Vegetable oil spray	As needed	As needed
Rye bread slices (gluten-free, if a concern)	2	4
Butter, at room temperature	4 teaspoons	2½ tablespoons
Cheddar cheese slices	2 thin slices (about 1½ ounces)	4 thin slices (about 3 ounces)
MAKES	1 sandwich	2 sandwiches

1. With the basket (or basket attachment) in the air fryer, heat it to 400°F (or 390°F, if that's the closest setting).

2. Mix the ground beef, Worcestershire sauce, mustard, and black pepper in a medium bowl until well combined. Form into one or two patties (depending on the size of the batch), each patty about ½-inch thick but slightly larger than one of the rye bread slices.

3. Lightly coat the onion rings with vegetable oil spray. Set the patty (or patties) in the basket; scatter the onions all around. Air-fry undisturbed for 5 minutes.

4. Butter one side of each slice of bread. Turn one slice buttered side down on a cutting board, then top with a patty and all or half of the onions in the basket, depending on which size batch you're making. Top the onions with all or half of the cheese (again, depending on the batch size), then set a second slice of bread, buttered side up, on top. Repeat if you're building a second sandwich. Use a metal spatula to press down on each sandwich, compacting it a bit.

5. Put the sandwich(es) in the basket and air-fry undisturbed for 3 minutes, or until the cheese has melted and the bread is crunchy.

6. Use a nonstick-safe spatula, and perhaps a flatware spoon for balance, to transfer the sandwich(es) to a wire rack. Cool for 5 minutes before slicing in half and serving.

Then...

- For an easy side of ASIAN SEASONED SUGAR SNAP PEAS, blanch *sugar snap peas* in boiling water for no more than 1 minute, then drain them in a colander set in the sink and rinse with cold running water. Drain well, then toss them with a *little minced peeled fresh ginger* and perhaps *some finely grated lemon zest*. Drizzle with *very small amounts of toasted sesame oil* and *unseasoned rice vinegar* (see page 70) in about equal proportions. (Figure that 2 cups sugar snaps will get about 2 teaspoons toasted sesame oil and 2 teaspoons unseasoned rice vinegar.) Toss again and add a small splash of *regular or low-sodium soy sauce or gluten-free tamari sauce* before serving.

Tuna Melt

FAST / EASY / CAN BE GLUTEN-FREE / 9 INGREDIENTS

This erstwhile diner favorite deserves a comeback at home, especially when the air fryer makes it so easy. We use English muffins for the melts because all those nooks and crannies soak up the juices better than, say, sliced sandwich bread would. You can use any sort of English muffin you prefer: plain, whole-wheat, even sourdough.

Notice that the celery and scallion are minced, not just chopped or sliced. There should be no noticeable bits in the overall texture of the tuna topper. And we love yellowfin tuna packed in oil. It's more expensive, yes—but it's low in mercury, more sustainably caught, and milder than some other varieties.

Just a note: We consider one English muffin—that is, two small, round open-face tuna melts—to be one serving.

INGREDIENTS	2-quart or larger air fryer	5.25-quart or larger air fryer
6-ounce can tuna, preferably yellowfin packed in oil, drained	1	2
Regular, low-fat, or fat-free mayonnaise (gluten-free, if a concern)	2½ tablespoons	⅓ cup
Minced celery	1 tablespoon	2 tablespoons
Minced scallion	1 tablespoon	2 tablespoons
Dijon mustard (gluten-free, if a concern)	1½ teaspoons	1 tablespoon
Lemon juice	1 teaspoon	2 teaspoons
Ground black pepper	½ teaspoon	1 teaspoon
English muffin (gluten-free, if a concern)	1	2
Shredded Cheddar cheese	½ cup (about 2 ounces)	1 cup (about 4 ounces)
MAKES	1 serving	2 servings

1. With the basket (or basket attachment) in the air fryer, heat it to 400°F (or 390°F, if that's the closest setting).

2. Meanwhile, gently stir the tuna, mayonnaise, celery, scallion, mustard, lemon juice, and pepper in a bowl until well combined but not mush.

3. Split the English muffin(s) and set the halves cut side up in the basket. Air-fry undisturbed for 2 minutes to warm them up.

4. Top the English muffins with equal portions of the tuna mixture. Top evenly with equal portions of the cheese. Air-fry undisturbed for 3 minutes or until the cheese has melted and is gooey.

5. Use a nonstick-safe spatula, and perhaps a flatware fork for balance, to transfer the tuna melts to a wire rack. Cool for 5 minutes before serving.

Then...

- Keep a bowl of VINEGARY CUCUMBERS on hand to offer with creamy, rich sandwiches like these. To make 8 servings, thinly slice *3 large cucumbers* and *1 medium red onion*; toss them in a large nonreactive bowl, such as a stainless-steel or glass bowl. Pour in *¾ cup white wine vinegar* and stir in *2 tablespoons granulated white sugar* and about *2 teaspoons table salt*. Fill the bowl with *water* to cover the vegetables by about 1 inch, then stir well. Cover and refrigerate for at least 48 hours. Store covered in the fridge for up to 10 days. Serve by scooping out cucumbers and onions with a slotted spoon.

Perfect Burgers

FAST / EASY / CAN BE GLUTEN-FREE / 4 INGREDIENTS

Although we like much fattier ground beef for burgers on the grill (around 80% lean, to be honest), we prefer leaner ground beef in an air fryer. For one thing, the meat doesn't throw off as much fat, so the machine doesn't turn into a smoker. For another, the burger stays more compact as it cooks. And with a leaner burger, we feel free to load up on condiments to our heart's content!

Since air fryers are an intense heat source that dries out the surface before the inside of the burgers cook, you must put a thumb indentation into the center of each one to keep it from puffing up as it cooks.

The timing we've given is in compliance with the USDA standards for cooking ground beef. If you want a less "done" burger, we recommend using only organic grass-finished beef from a reputable supplier. Frankly, we like burgers at about 127°F, super rare—but then we shake the hand of the farmer with every package we buy in rural New England.

INGREDIENTS	2-quart or larger air fryer	3.5-quart or larger air fryer	5.25-quart or larger air fryer
90% lean ground beef	¾ pound	1 pound 2 ounces	1½ pounds
Worcestershire sauce (gluten-free, if a concern)	1 tablespoon	1½ tablespoons	2 tablespoons
Ground black pepper	½ teaspoon	Rounded ½ teaspoon	1 teaspoon
Hamburger buns (gluten-free if a concern), split open	2	3	4
MAKES	*2 burgers*	*3 burgers*	*4 burgers*

1. With the basket (or basket attachment) in the air fryer, heat it to 375°F (or 370°F or 360°F, if one of these is the closest setting).

2. Gently mix the ground beef, Worcestershire sauce, and pepper in a bowl until well combined but preserving as much of the meat's fibers as possible.

Divide this mixture into two 5-inch patties for the small batch, three 5-inch patties for the medium, or four 5-inch patties for the large. Make a thumbprint indentation in the center of each patty, about halfway through the meat.

continues

3. Set the patties in the basket in one layer with some space between them. Air-fry undisturbed for 10 minutes, or until an instant-read meat thermometer inserted into the center of a burger registers 160°F (a medium-well burger). You may need to add 1 to 2 minutes cooking time if the air fryer is at 360°F.

4. Use a nonstick-safe spatula, and perhaps a flatware fork for balance, to transfer the burgers to a cutting board. Set the buns cut side down in the basket in one layer (working in batches as necessary) and air-fry undisturbed for 1 minute, to toast a bit and warm up. Serve the burgers in the warm buns.

Then...

- Of course, burgers need condiments. Think beyond mayo, mustard, or ketchup. Try chutney, lime pickle, cole slaw, or chowchow. Or try unusual combinations like sour cream and purchased sofrito; sauerkraut, deli mustard, and jalapeño relish; or our favorite: mayonnaise (gluten-free, if a concern) and kimchi.

- For a big spread, serve these burgers with **Roasted Peppers with Balsamic Vinegar and Basil** (page 309), **Zucchini Fries** (page 330), **Air-Fried Potato Salad** (page 338), and/or **Perfect Broccolini** (page 347).

Inside-Out Cheeseburgers

CAN BE GLUTEN-FREE / 7 INGREDIENTS

Here's our version of the Jucy Lucy. (Or the Juicy Lucy, if you insist on spelling purity.) Actually, we prefer this inside-out preparation because cheese laid on top of a burger can drip off—or even slip off—in the machine. Make sure you *seal* the cheese into the burger so none of it leaks out.

You'll note that we've seasoned the meat more heavily for this recipe than for Perfect Burgers (previous page). We wanted to add some contrast to the cheese inside, a flavor punch that actually helps balance the sweet flavors in a cheeseburger.

INGREDIENTS	2-quart or larger air fryer	3.5-quart or larger air fryer	5.25-quart or larger air fryer
90% lean ground beef	¾ pound	1 pound 2 ounces	1½ pounds
Dried oregano	½ teaspoon	¾ teaspoon	1 teaspoon
Table salt	½ teaspoon	¾ teaspoon	1 teaspoon
Ground black pepper	½ teaspoon	¾ teaspoon	1 teaspoon
Garlic powder	¼ teaspoon	Rounded ¼ teaspoon	½ teaspoon
Shredded Cheddar, Swiss, or other semi-firm cheese, or a purchased blend of shredded cheeses	¼ cup (about 1 ounce)	6 tablespoons (about 1½ ounces)	½ cup (about 2 ounces)
Hamburger buns (gluten-free, if a concern), split open	2	3	4
MAKES	*2 burgers*	*3 burgers*	*4 burgers*

1. With the basket (or basket attachment) in the air fryer, heat it to 375°F (or 370°F or 360°F, if one of these is the closest setting).

2. Gently mix the ground beef, oregano, salt, pepper, and garlic powder in a bowl until well combined without turning the mixture to mush. Form it into two 6-inch patties for the small batch, three for the medium, or four for the large.

3. Place 2 tablespoons of the shredded cheese in the center of each patty. With clean hands, fold the sides of the patty up to cover the cheese, then pick it up and roll it gently into a ball to seal the cheese inside. Gently press it back into a 5-inch burger without letting any cheese squish out. Continue filling and preparing more burgers, as needed.

4. Place the burgers in the basket in one layer and air-fry undisturbed for 8 minutes for medium or 10 minutes for well-done. (An instant-read meat thermometer won't work for these burgers because it will hit the mostly melted cheese inside and offer a hotter temperature than the surrounding meat.)

5. Use a nonstick-safe spatula, and perhaps a flatware fork for balance, to transfer the burgers to a cutting board. Set the buns cut side down in the basket in one layer (working in batches as necessary) and air-fry undisturbed for 1 minute, to toast a bit and warm up. Cool the burgers a few minutes more, then serve them warm in the buns.

Then...

- Use **Muhamarra** (page 25) as a condiment with sliced tomatoes and crisp lettuce leaves.

- Mix regular or low-fat mayonnaise, barbecue sauce, and pickle relish in a 4-to-2-to-1 ratio by volume for a great topper. Use gluten-free condiments, if a concern.

- Or mix ranch dressing, regular or low-fat mayonnaise (gluten-free, if a concern), and pickle relish in equal proportions.

- Or mix purchased pesto and sriracha in a 3-to-1 ratio by volume.

See photo in insert.

Turkey Burgers

EASY / CAN BE GLUTEN-FREE / 9 INGREDIENTS

Because of the air fryer's convection currents, turkey burgers can dry out even more in the machine than they do on the grill. We've got a solution! We add frozen chopped spinach and bread crumbs to the burger mix, thereby keeping the meat juicy—and more flavorful!—through the cooking process. In fact, because of the added "moisture enhancers," you can feel free to use lean all-white-meat ground turkey for these burgers.

INGREDIENTS	2-quart or larger air fryer	3.5-quart or larger air fryer	5.25-quart or larger air fryer
Ground turkey	¾ pound	1 pound 2 ounces	1½ pounds
Frozen chopped spinach, thawed and squeezed dry	¼ cup	6 tablespoons	½ cup
Plain panko bread crumbs (gluten-free, if a concern)	2 tablespoons	3 tablespoons	¼ cup
Dijon mustard (gluten-free, if a concern)	2 teaspoons	1 tablespoon	1½ tablespoons
Minced garlic	1 teaspoon	1½ teaspoons	2 teaspoons
Table salt	½ teaspoon	¾ teaspoon	1 teaspoon
Ground black pepper	½ teaspoon	¾ teaspoon	1 teaspoon
Olive oil spray	As needed	As needed	As needed
Kaiser rolls (gluten-free, if a concern), split open	2	3	4
MAKES	2 burgers	3 burgers	4 burgers

1. With the basket (or basket attachment) in the air fryer, heat it to 375°F (or 370°F or 360°F, if one of these is the closest setting).

2. Gently mix the ground turkey, spinach, bread crumbs, mustard, garlic, salt, and pepper in a large bowl until well combined, trying to keep some of the fibers of the ground turkey intact. Form into two 5-inch-wide patties for the small batch, three 5-inch patties for the medium batch, or four 5-inch patties for the large. Coat each side of the patties with olive oil spray.

3. Set the patties in in the basket in one layer and air-fry undisturbed for 20 minutes, or until an instant-read meat thermometer inserted into the center of a burger registers 165°F. You may need to add 1 to 2 minutes to the cooking time if the air fryer is at 360°F.

4. Use a nonstick-safe spatula, and perhaps a flatware fork for balance, to transfer the burgers to a cutting board. Set the buns cut side down in the basket in one layer (working in batches as necessary) and air-fry for 1 minute, to toast a bit and warm up. Serve the burgers warm in the buns.

Then...

- Whip up a SPECIAL SAUCE inspired by Shake Shack. Whisk ½ cup regular, low-fat, or fat-free mayonnaise; 2 tablespoons pickle relish (or jalapeño relish, if you want to go over the top); 1 tablespoon ketchup; 1 tablespoon yellow prepared mustard; ½ teaspoon mild paprika; and ¼ teaspoon garlic powder until uniform. Use gluten-free condiments, if a concern. Save any remainder in a covered glass or nonreactive container in the fridge for up to 1 week.

Lamb Burgers

EASY / CAN BE GLUTEN-FREE / 8 OR 9 INGREDIENTS

These lamb burgers have a Greek twist. They could easily be served on top of a chopped salad, rather than in a bun. For the best dressing for that salad, see the **Classic Greek Diner Dressing** on page 90.

For even more flavor in the patties, add a little finely grated lemon zest, dried thyme, and/or dried oregano to the ground meat mixture. Note that the table salt is optional here, because feta is fairly salty.

For the best feta, look for cubes packed in brine, rather than the dry, prepackaged crumbles that often lack that characteristic zip.

And one final note: Ground lamb can be very fatty. It will make a bit of a mess in the air fryer and can cause some smoking. If that's a bother for you, mix equal parts ground lamb and very lean ground beef.

INGREDIENTS	2-quart or larger air fryer	3.5-quart or larger air fryer	5.25-quart or larger air fryer
Ground lamb	¾ pound	1 pound 2 ounces	1½ pounds
Crumbled feta	2 tablespoons	3 tablespoons	¼ cup
Minced garlic	½ teaspoon	1 teaspoon	1½ teaspoons
Tomato paste	½ teaspoon	1 teaspoon	1½ teaspoons
Ground coriander	½ teaspoon	¾ teaspoon	1 teaspoon
Ground dried ginger	½ teaspoon	¾ teaspoon	1 teaspoon
Cayenne	Up to ⅛ teaspoon	Up to rounded ⅛ teaspoon	Up to ¼ teaspoon
Table salt (optional)	Up to ⅛ teaspoon	Up to a rounded ⅛ teaspoon	Up to ¼ teaspoon
Kaiser rolls or hamburger buns (gluten-free, if a concern), split open	2	3	4
MAKES	2 burgers	3 burgers	4 burgers

1. With the basket (or basket attachment) in the air fryer, heat it to 375°F (or 370°F or 360°F, if one of these is the closest setting).

2. Gently mix the ground lamb, feta, garlic, tomato paste, coriander, ginger, cayenne, and salt (if using) in a bowl until well combined, trying to keep the bits of cheese intact. Form this mixture into two 5-inch patties for the small batch, three 5-inch patties for the medium, or four 5-inch patties for the large.

3. Set the patties in the basket in one layer and air-fry undisturbed for 16 minutes, or until an instant-read meat thermometer inserted into one burger registers 160°F. (The cheese is not an issue with the temperature probe in this recipe as it was for the Inside-Out Cheeseburgers, because the feta is so well mixed into the ground meat.)

continues

4. Use a nonstick-safe spatula, and perhaps a flatware fork for balance, to transfer the burgers to a cutting board. Set the buns cut side down in the basket in one layer (working in batches as necessary) and air-fry undisturbed for 1 minute, to toast a bit and warm up. Serve the burgers warm in the buns.

Then...

• Make **YOGURT-CILANTRO SAUCE** for these burgers. Process *cilantro leaves* with *some minced fresh jalapeño, a little lemon juice, a little granulated white sugar,* and *even less minced peeled fresh ginger.* Add *a little water* if the mixture is not processing properly. Scrape into a bowl, cover, and refrigerate for at least 2 hours or up to 2 days to mellow the flavors. Stir this paste into *plain Greek yogurt (full-fat, low-fat, or fat-free)* for a spread on the patties.

Salmon Burgers

FAST / CAN BE GLUTEN-FREE / 9 INGREDIENTS

Rather than using canned salmon, which can be too strongly flavored for successful burgers, we go the extra step and grind raw salmon fillet in a food processor. Yes, it's messy. But it's worth the effort both for texture and for flavor.

Be careful you don't turn the fillet into salmon paste. Pulse the processor a couple of times, then scrape down the inside of the canister to rearrange pieces before pulsing again. In no case should you just process the fish outright. Pulse and pulse, scraping down the canister as necessary, to get the right texture: smooth throughout with lots of bits that look like fresh salmon itself, with none larger than a corn kernel and most about the size of raw rice grains.

Atlantic salmon is better here than Pacific, because the Atlantic fish is fattier and stands up better to the intense heat inside the machine.

INGREDIENTS	2-quart or larger air fryer	3.5-quart or larger air fryer	5.25-quart or larger air fryer
Skinless salmon fillet, preferably fattier Atlantic salmon	¾ pound	1 pound 2 ounces	1½ pounds
Minced chives or the green part of a scallion	1 tablespoon	1½ tablespoons	2 tablespoons
Plain panko bread crumbs (gluten-free, if a concern)	⅓ cup	½ cup	⅔ cup
Dijon mustard (gluten-free, if a concern)	1 teaspoon	1½ teaspoons	2 teaspoons
Drained and rinsed capers, minced	1 teaspoon	1½ teaspoons	2 teaspoons
Lemon juice	1 teaspoon	1½ teaspoons	2 teaspoons
Table salt	¼ teaspoon	Rounded ¼ teaspoon	½ teaspoon
Ground black pepper	¼ teaspoon	Rounded ¼ teaspoon	½ teaspoon
Vegetable oil spray	As needed	As needed	As needed
MAKES	*2 patties*	*3 patties*	*4 patties*

1. With the basket (or basket attachment) in the air fryer, heat it to 375°F (or 370°F or 360°F, if one of these is the closest setting).

2. Cut the salmon into pieces that will fit in a food processor. Cover and pulse until coarsely chopped. Add the chives and pulse to combine, until the fish is ground but not a paste. (See the headnote for more information.)

3. Scrape down and remove the blade. Scrape the salmon mixture into a bowl. Add the bread crumbs, mustard, capers, lemon juice, salt, and pepper. Stir gently until well combined.

4. Use clean and dry hands to form the mixture into two 5-inch patties for a small batch, three 5-inch patties for a medium batch, or four 5-inch patties for a large one.

5. Coat both sides of each patty with vegetable oil spray. Set them in the basket in one layer and air-fry undisturbed for 8 minutes, or until browned and an instant-read meat thermometer inserted into the center of a burger registers 145°F.

6. Use a nonstick-safe spatula, and perhaps a flatware fork for balance, to transfer the burgers to a wire rack. Cool for 2 or 3 minutes before serving.

Then...

- Set these burgers in toasted hamburger buns, toasted English muffins, or between toasted rye bread slices. The best condiments are mustard, mayonnaise, and/or kimchi. Mayonnaise and chutney also make a great combination. Use gluten-free condiments, if a concern.

- Or go all out and make **Chimichurri** (page 94) or **Yogurt-Cilantro Sauce** (page 136) as a condiment for the burgers.

- Salmon burgers are great with **Moroccan-Spiced Carrots** (page 348).

- And they're terrific bunless, atop a chopped salad with a vinegary dressing.

Sausage and Pepper Heros

EASY / CAN BE GLUTEN-FREE / 6 INGREDIENTS

These sandwiches are a fairly simple version of the Italian-American classic, but you could add a lot more to them, including pizza sauce (for an easy homemade recipe, see page 143) and shredded semi-firm mozzarella. All of that should go in the bun *after* it's been toasted, rather than in the air fryer, since they will heat up and start to run.

One note: These are fat sausage links, not thin breakfast links. They're usually sold four or five to a 19- or 20-ounce package. Check the weight to be sure.

INGREDIENTS	2-quart or larger air fryer	3.5-quart or larger air fryer	5.25-quart or larger air fryer
Sweet Italian sausages (gluten-free, if a concern)	2 links (about 6 ounces total)	3 links (about 9 ounces total)	4 links (about ¾ pound total)
Medium red or green bell pepper(s), stemmed, cored, and cut into ½-inch-wide strips	1	1½	2
Yellow or white onion(s), peeled, halved, and sliced into thin half-moons	1 small	1 medium	2 small
Long soft rolls, such as hero, hoagie, or Italian sub rolls (gluten-free, if a concern), split open lengthwise	2	3	4
Balsamic vinegar	For garnishing	For garnishing	For garnishing
Fresh basil leaves	For garnishing	For garnishing	For garnishing
MAKES	*2 heros*	*3 heros*	*4 heros*

1. With the basket (or basket attachment) in the air fryer, heat it to 400°F (or 390°F, if that's the closest setting).

2. When the machine is at temperature, set the sausage links in the basket in one layer and air-fry undisturbed for 5 minutes.

3. Add the pepper strips and onions. Continue air-frying, tossing and rearranging everything about once every minute, for 5 minutes, or until the sausages are browned and an instant-read meat thermometer inserted into one of the links registers 160°F.

4. Use a nonstick-safe spatula and kitchen tongs to transfer the sausages and vegetables to a cutting board. Set the rolls cut side down in the basket in one layer (working in batches as necessary) and air-fry undisturbed for 1 minute, to toast the rolls a bit and warm them up. Set 1 sausage with some pepper strips and onions in each warm roll, sprinkle balsamic vinegar over the sandwich fillings, and garnish with basil leaves.

Then...

- Make a fresh green salad with BUTTERMILK DRESSING. Whisk *buttermilk* and *regular, low-fat, or fat-free sour cream* in equal proportions by volume, thinning the mixture with *a few drops of apple cider vinegar* until smooth. Whisk in *a little minced garlic, fresh thyme leaves, table salt* and *ground black pepper* to taste. Heat it up with *a couple of dashes of hot red pepper sauce (gluten-free, if a concern)*.

Thai-Style Pork Sliders

CAN BE GLUTEN-FREE / 8 INGREDIENTS

These mini burgers are best with cold beer on a hot day. They're a bit spicy—and they can be even more so, depending on the Thai curry paste you use. First, look for Thai curry pastes in tubs or jars in the Asian aisle of the supermarket. They're wetter than many other curry pastes. Next, figure out which one you want to buy. By and large, yellow Thai curry pastes are the mildest, followed by green, then red—although brands differ considerably. Check the label to see where chiles fall in the list of ingredients. If chiles are at the top, the brand is super spicy.

If you want to get experimental in your culinary endeavors, search out sour vegetable curry pastes online or at Asian supermarkets. These will make the sliders much less sweet, a little funky—even musky—because of all the shrimp paste and fermented vegetables. Sliders made with sour vegetable curry paste are best with a splash of lime juice on them after air-frying.

INGREDIENTS	2-quart or larger air fryer	3.5-quart or larger air fryer	5.25-quart or larger air fryer
Ground pork	½ pound	11 ounces	1 pound
Very thinly sliced scallions, white and green parts	2 tablespoons	2½ tablespoons	¼ cup
Minced peeled fresh ginger	1 tablespoon	4 teaspoons	2 tablespoons
Fish sauce (gluten-free, if a concern)	2 teaspoons	2½ teaspoons	1½ tablespoons
Thai curry paste (see the headnote; gluten-free, if a concern)	1½ teaspoons	2 teaspoons	1 tablespoon
Light brown sugar	1½ teaspoons	2 teaspoons	1 tablespoon
Ground black pepper	½ teaspoon	¾ teaspoon	1 teaspoon
Slider buns (gluten-free, if a concern)	3	4	6
MAKES	3 sliders	4 sliders	6 sliders

1. With the basket (or basket attachment) in the air fryer, heat it to 375°F (or 370°F or 360°F, if one of these is the closest setting).

2. Gently mix the pork, scallions, ginger, fish sauce, curry paste, brown sugar, and black pepper in a bowl until well combined. With clean, wet hands, form about ⅓ cup of the pork mixture into a slider about 2½ inches in diameter. Repeat until you use up all the meat—3 sliders for the small batch, 4 for the medium, and 6 for the large. (Keep wetting your hands to help the patties adhere.)

3. When the machine is at temperature, set the sliders in the basket in one layer. Air-fry undisturbed for 14 minutes, or until the sliders are golden brown and caramelized at their edges and an instant-read meat thermometer inserted into the center of a slider registers 160°F.

4. Use a nonstick-safe spatula, and perhaps a flatware fork for balance, to transfer the sliders to a cutting board. Set the buns cut side down in the basket in one layer (working in batches as necessary) and air-fry undisturbed for 1 minute, to toast a bit and warm up. Serve the sliders warm in the buns.

continues

Then...

- The most common condiment for these sliders is mayonnaise of any sort (gluten-free, if a concern), but particularly the sweet Kewpie mayonnaise favored in Japanese cooking.

- Use sliced radishes tossed with toasted sesame oil and unseasoned rice vinegar (see page 70) as a topper for these sliders.

- Or mix sprouts—particularly Brussels sprout sprouts or radish sprouts—with mayonnaise of any sort and perhaps a little sriracha as a topper.

Black Bean Veggie Burgers

VEGETARIAN / CAN BE GLUTEN-FREE / 11 INGREDIENTS

Although these burgers are great in buns as a main course, we often serve them as a side dish with shell-on shrimp or fish fillets off the grill. The bunless burgers also make a nice alternative to potatoes alongside steaks, especially if the beef has been given a Southwestern rub.

Unfortunately, none of these batches can use a whole egg or even a whole can of beans. The "paste" then makes too many burgers to fit in any machine in one batch. So we have to resort to pasteurized egg substitutes to make the necessary paste for the burgers. Of course, if you want to whisk a large egg until uniform, then measure out what you need, you're welcome to the extra work.

INGREDIENTS	2-quart or larger air fryer	3.5-quart or larger air fryer	5.25-quart or larger air fryer
Drained and rinsed canned black beans	⅔ cup	1 cup	1⅓ cups
Pecan pieces	¼ cup	⅓ cup	½ cup
Rolled oats (*not* quick-cooking or steel-cut; gluten-free, if a concern)	¼ cup	⅓ cup	½ cup
Pasteurized egg substitute, such as Egg Beaters (gluten-free, if a concern)	1½ tablespoons	2 tablespoons (or 1 small egg)	3 tablespoons (or 1 medium egg)
Red ketchup-like chili sauce, such as Heinz	1½ teaspoons	2 teaspoons	1 tablespoon
Ground cumin	¼ teaspoon	Rounded ¼ teaspoon	½ teaspoon
Dried oregano	¼ teaspoon	Rounded ¼ teaspoon	½ teaspoon
Table salt	¼ teaspoon	Rounded ¼ teaspoon	½ teaspoon
Ground black pepper	¼ teaspoon	Rounded ¼ teaspoon	½ teaspoon
Olive oil	As needed	As needed	As needed
Olive oil spray	As needed	As needed	As needed
MAKES	*2 burgers*	*3 burgers*	*4 burgers*

1. With the basket (or basket attachment) in the air fryer, heat it to 400°F (or 390°F, if that's the closest setting).

2. Put the beans, pecans, oats, egg substitute or egg, chili sauce, cumin, oregano, salt, and pepper in a food processor. Cover and process to a coarse paste that will hold its shape like sugar-cookie dough, adding olive oil in 1-teaspoon increments to get the mixture to blend smoothly. The amount of olive oil is actually dependent on the internal moisture content of the beans and the oats. Figure on about 1 tablespoon (three 1-teaspoon additions) for the smaller batch, with proportional increases for the other batches. A little too much olive oil can't hurt, but a dry paste will fall apart as it cooks and a far-too-wet paste will stick to the basket.

3. Scrape down and remove the blade. Using clean, wet hands, form the paste into two 4-inch patties for the small batch, three 4-inch patties for the medium, or four 4-inch patties for the large batch, setting them one by one on a cutting board. Generously coat both sides of the patties with olive oil spray.

4. Set them in the basket in one layer. Air-fry undisturbed for 10 minutes, or until lightly browned and crisp at the edges.

5. Use a nonstick-safe spatula, and perhaps a flatware fork for balance, to transfer the burgers to a wire rack. Cool for 5 minutes before serving.

Then...

- These burgers are great on toasted whole-wheat Kaiser rolls (or gluten-free whole-grain rolls, if a concern). Top the burgers with purchased cole slaw or **Carrot Slaw** (page 115), with a drizzle of sriracha on top either way.

- Serve with **Sweet Plantain Chips** (page 37) and **Eggplant Fries** (page 51).

- Or serve the patties with **Yogurt-Cilantro Sauce** (page 136) on top of a chopped salad of romaine lettuce, cucumbers, radishes, and carrots.

White Bean Veggie Burgers

VEGETARIAN / CAN BE GLUTEN-FREE / 10 INGREDIENTS

These bean burgers hold together because of the oats and don't dry out because of the walnuts. The texture is crunchy on the outside but creamy and rich on the inside. Despite the presence of the sweet beans, the burgers are actually savory, thanks to the nuts, mustard, and oil. In other words, these are not just bean dip turned into a burger.

For a bun-free meal, generously coat portobello mushroom caps with olive oil spray and air-fry them gill (very dark brown) side down for 5 minutes at 400°F. Set a cooked white bean burger on top of each cap.

INGREDIENTS	2-quart or larger air fryer	3.5-quart or larger air fryer	5.25-quart or larger air fryer
Drained and rinsed canned white beans	1 cup	1⅓ cups	One 15-ounce can (1¾ cups)
Rolled oats (*not* quick-cooking or steel-cut; gluten-free, if a concern)	2 tablespoons	3 tablespoons	¼ cup
Chopped walnuts	2 tablespoons	3 tablespoons	¼ cup
Olive oil	1½ teaspoons	2 teaspoons	1 tablespoon
Lemon juice	1½ teaspoons	2 teaspoons	1 tablespoon
Dijon mustard (gluten-free, if a concern)	1 teaspoon	1½ teaspoons	2 teaspoons
Dried sage leaves	½ teaspoon	¾ teaspoon	1 teaspoon
Table salt	¼ teaspoon	Rounded ¼ teaspoon	½ teaspoon
Olive oil spray	As needed	As needed	As needed
Whole-wheat buns or gluten-free whole-grain buns (if a concern), split open	2	3	4
MAKES	*2 burgers*	*3 burgers*	*4 burgers*

1. With the basket (or basket attachment) in the air fryer, heat it to 400°F (or 390°F, if that's the closest setting).

2. Place the beans, oats, walnuts, oil, lemon juice, mustard, sage, and salt in a food processor. Cover and process to make a coarse paste that will hold its shape, about like wet sugar-cookie dough, stopping the machine to scrape down the inside of the canister at least once.

3. Scrape down and remove the blade. With clean and wet hands, form the bean paste into two 4-inch

patties for the small batch, three 4-inch patties for the medium, or four 4-inch patties for the large batch. Generously coat the patties on both sides with olive oil spray.

4. Set them in the basket with some space between them and air-fry undisturbed for 12 minutes, or until lightly brown and crisp at the edges. The tops of the burgers will feel firm to the touch.

5. Use a nonstick-safe spatula, and perhaps a flatware fork for balance, to transfer the burgers to a cutting board. Set the buns cut side down in the basket in one

layer (working in batches as necessary) and air-fry undisturbed for 1 minute, to toast a bit and warm up. Serve the burgers warm in the buns.

Then...

- Make FENNEL AND BLOOD ORANGE SALAD as a side dish for these burgers. Mix *thinly sliced, trimmed fennel* with *blood orange segments, toasted pine nuts*, and *baby arugula*. The easiest

way to get segments from a blood orange is to slice off the rind as if you were peeling an apple. Then use a paring knife to cut down along each membrane, releasing the segments one by one. Hold the blood orange over the salad bowl to catch the extra drips of juice. Dress the salad with *walnut oil or olive oil* (but no vinegar) and sprinkle it with *crumbled feta or goat cheese*, as well as *table salt* and *ground black pepper* to taste.

Eggplant Parmesan Subs

EASY / VEGETARIAN / CAN BE GLUTEN-FREE / 5 INGREDIENTS

These eggplant subs skip the breading to let the flavors of the eggplant show through. We didn't even coat the eggplant slices in bread crumbs, because we wanted a cleaner, brighter taste.

You can alter the sandwich's flavors to your heart's content by using any pizza sauce you prefer, except those that are "alfredo" style or creamy—those will run as they heat and muck up the appliance.

If you want to make homemade PIZZA SAUCE, whisk *a 15-ounce can tomato sauce, a 6-ounce can tomato paste, Italian-style dried herb seasoning to taste,* and *table salt to taste* in a bowl until smooth. For more flavor, add *minced garlic* and/or *a tiny bit of onion powder to taste*. Use at will and store in a sealed nonreactive container in the fridge for up to 10 days. (It's terrific on pizzas, like those starting on page 89!)

INGREDIENTS	2-quart or larger air fryer	3.5-quart or larger air fryer	5.25-quart or larger air fryer
Peeled eggplant slices (about ½ inch thick and 3 inches in diameter)	2	4	6
Olive oil spray	As needed	As needed	As needed
Jarred pizza sauce, any variety except creamy	4 teaspoons	2 tablespoons plus 2 teaspoons	¼ cup
Finely grated Parmesan cheese	2 tablespoons (about ⅓ ounce)	¼ cup (about ⅔ ounce)	6 tablespoons (about 1 ounce)
Small, long soft rolls, such as hero, hoagie, or Italian sub rolls (gluten-free, if a concern), split open lengthwise	1	2	3
MAKES	1 sub	2 subs	3 subs

continues

1. With the basket (or basket attachment) in the air fryer, heat it to 350°F (or 360°F, if that's the closest setting).

2. When the machine is at temperature, coat both sides of the eggplant slices with olive oil spray. Set them in the basket in one layer and air-fry undisturbed for 10 minutes, until lightly browned and softened.

3. Increase the machine's temperature to 375°F (or 370°F, if that's the closest setting—unless the machine is already at 360°F, in which case leave it alone). Top each eggplant slice with 2 teaspoons pizza sauce, then 1 tablespoon cheese. Air-fry undisturbed for 2 minutes, or until the cheese has melted.

4. Use a nonstick-safe spatula, and perhaps a flatware fork for balance, to transfer the eggplant slices cheese side up to a cutting board. Set the roll(s) cut side down in the basket in one layer (working in batches as necessary) and air-fry undisturbed for 1 minute, to toast the rolls a bit and warm them up. Set 2 eggplant slices in each warm roll.

Then...

- Serve these subs with our version of a **THREE BEAN SALAD**. Bring equal proportions of *apple cider vinegar*, *vegetable oil*, and *granulated white sugar* (or perhaps a splash more vinegar) to a boil in a small saucepan over high heat. Pour this mixture over *trimmed and chopped fresh green beans*, *trimmed and chopped fresh wax beans*, *drained and rinsed canned kidney beans*, and *thinly sliced red onion* in a big bowl. Set aside for 1 hour at room temperature, then season with *table salt* and dish up the veggies with a slotted spoon.

Customize-Your-Own Quesadillas

FAST / EASY / CAN BE VEGETARIAN / AT LEAST 3 INGREDIENTS

Because quesadillas need to lie flat and cannot be stacked for proper cooking in the air fryer's basket, you can only make one at a time, no matter what size machine you have. So yes, you must work in batches, even if you want to make several. Have them prepared and lined up on the counter, ready to go into the basket one after the other. Better yet, set up an add-in bar and let your friends or family make their own!

INGREDIENTS	2-quart or larger air fryer
6- to 7-inch flour tortillas (sometimes called mini tortillas)	2
Shredded Monterey Jack cheese	3 tablespoons (a little less than 1 ounce)
Add-ins: drained and rinsed canned black beans; finely chopped and drained jarred pimientos; thinly sliced pitted black or green olives; minced pickled jalapeño rings; finely chopped, deboned and skinned rotisserie chicken meat; finely chopped deli ham; finely chopped barbecued brisket	Up to 2 tablespoons total volume
MAKES	*1 quesadilla*

1. With the basket (or basket attachment) in the air fryer, heat it to 400°F (or 390°F, if that's the closest setting).

2. Put one tortilla on a clean, dry work surface. Top with half the cheese, any add-ins, and then the remainder of the cheese. Top with a second tortilla and gently press down to compact the tortillas onto the filling without squishing any out.

3. When the machine is at temperature, use a nonstick-safe spatula to transfer the quesadilla to the basket. Air-fry undisturbed for 3 minutes, or until lightly browned.

4. Use a nonstick-safe spatula to transfer the quesadilla to a wire rack. Cool for at least 5 minutes before cutting into quarters to serve.

Then...

- **PERFECT FROZEN MARGARITAS** are made by putting the following in a blender in this order: *1 pound 2 ounces (about 4 cups) small ice cubes, 3 ounces (6 tablespoons) silver tequila, 3 ounces (6 tablespoons) Triple Sec or Cointreau, 3 ounces (6 tablespoons)* fresh *lime juice* (or better yet, *Key lime juice*), and *1½ tablespoons superfine granulated white sugar* in a blender. Cover and blend until slushy smooth, then divide between two or three lowball glasses.

Crunchy Falafel Balls

EASY / VEGAN / 8 INGREDIENTS

Traditional falafel is made from soaked, dried chickpeas. The shortcut is to use canned chickpeas, but doing so requires us to add a little flour to the mix to help keep it dry. Our version won't win any authenticity awards but it will get the job done with minimal fuss.

Drain the canned chickpeas, then rinse them well to get rid of any slime (the excess natural sugars left over from the canning process). Drain them again. It's important that they be fairly dry when they go in the food processor. You don't have to pat them dry, but shake the colander or sieve a few times to get rid of as much water as you can.

This recipe will make only crunchy falafel balls. What you do with them after they come out of the air fryer depends on what you want. We suggest options with pita pockets after the recipe. But you could serve the balls on their own with any number of dips, including **Lemony Hummus** (page 24), **Muhamarra** (page 25), or **Tangy Tahini Dip** (page 48)—in which case this recipe might be better suited as a snack or an app.

If you want to cut down on the number of ingredients—and give the falafel a more characteristic flavor—omit the dried oregano, sage, and thyme; instead, substitute 1 tablespoon *za'atar* (a Middle Eastern dried herb-and-spice blend) for the small batch, 1½ tablespoons za'atar for the medium batch, or 2 tablespoons za'atar for the large.

INGREDIENTS	2-quart or larger air fryer	3.5-quart or larger air fryer	5.25-quart or larger air fryer
Drained and rinsed canned chickpeas	One 15-ounce can (1¾ cups)	2½ cups	Two 15-ounce cans (3½ cups)
Olive oil	3 tablespoons	¼ cup	¼ cup plus 2 tablespoons
All-purpose flour	2 tablespoons	3 tablespoons	¼ cup
Dried oregano	1 teaspoon	1½ teaspoons	2 teaspoons
Dried sage leaves	1 teaspoon	1½ teaspoons	2 teaspoons
Dried thyme	1 teaspoon	1½ teaspoons	2 teaspoons
Table salt	½ teaspoon	¾ teaspoon	1 teaspoon
Olive oil spray	As needed	As needed	As needed
MAKES	*10 balls*	*16 balls*	*20 balls*

1. With the basket (or basket attachment) in the air fryer, heat it to 400°F (or 390°F, if that's the closest setting).

2. Place the chickpeas, olive oil, flour, oregano, sage, thyme, and salt in a food processor. Cover and process into a paste, stopping the machine at least once to scrape down the inside of the canister.

3. Scrape down and remove the blade. Using clean, wet hands, form 2 tablespoons of the paste into a ball, then continue making 9 more balls for a small batch, 15 more for a medium one, and 19 more for a large batch. Generously coat the balls in olive oil spray.

4. Set the balls in the basket in one layer with a little space between them and air-fry undisturbed for 16 minutes, or until well browned and crisp.

5. Dump the contents of the basket onto a wire rack. Cool for 5 minutes before serving.

Then...

- Serve the falafel balls in pita pockets with chopped lettuce, chopped tomato, thinly sliced red onion, and purchased tahini sauce.

- To make about ¾ cups homemade TAHINI SAUCE, whisk *½ cup tahini* (see page 79), *¼ cup plain full-fat or low-fat yogurt* (not fat-free), *2 tablespoons lemon juice, ½ teaspoon table salt,* and *½ teaspoon ground black pepper* in a bowl, whisking in *water* in 1-tablespoon increments until it's the consistency of ranch dressing. For more flavor, whisk in up *to ⅛ teaspoon garlic* and/or *onion powder.* Save any extra sauce in a covered glass or nonreactive container in the fridge for up to 1 week.

3

FORTY-TWO

Chicken, Turkey & Duck Main Courses

If you didn't buy an air fryer for the promise of crunchy nibbles, you bought one for boneless skinless chicken breasts. Let's face it: They're *always* a problem. They end up bland and are too easy to dry out. The hope that they can become crunchy and irresistible is enough to get anyone to buy just about any appliance.

We've got lots of answers in the recipes ahead for not only those boneless skinless breasts but also chicken thighs and wings, as well as lots of turkey bits, with a couple of recipes for duck thrown in for good measure. Hey, in our opinion crunchy duck skin on a thigh-and-leg quarter is worth the price of the machine any day.

All that good news aside, we've got a couple of issues we'd like to get out of the way right up front. Not to sound schoolmarmish, but **please pay attention to the size of the cut of chicken or turkey in each recipe**. The sizes are *not* consistent (not all the chicken breast recipes use the same size of chicken breasts, for example). Here's why: Some coatings burn when subjected to longer times in an air fryer and so work better on smaller cuts that cook more quickly. And some coatings or marinades take longer to set or caramelize and so are better on larger cuts that spend longer in the heat.

As long as you take the size of the cut into consideration (and keep the difference between *bone-in* and *boneless* sacrosanct), you can do a bit of mix-and-match with these recipes, swapping one coating for another, if one is more to your taste. There's a big range of coatings here, from ground cheese puffs to ground cornbread stuffing mix, from ground vinegar-and-salt potato chips on chicken breasts (yum!) to ground pork rinds on chicken thighs (yummer!).

No recipe in this chapter calls for you to brine a piece of poultry. We felt it was too much effort for this book. But every recipe would be better if you *did* brine the cut. To do so, dissolve 2 tablespoons kosher salt for every 1 cup water, then submerge the chicken, turkey, or duck piece in that brine and refrigerate for 2 hours but not more than 5 hours. If you brine the cut, omit any salt from the coating. The meat will stay juicier and be more tender.

There's also an easy workaround for brining. If you want the juiciest chicken, buy kosher chicken. Because of religious dietary laws, it's essentially already brined. You needn't worry about its drying out. (But as we said, omit the salt from the coating mixture.)

So there you have it: the skinny on poultry in the air fryer. Now to the recipes, which promise a better boneless skinless chicken breast and so much more. That all still seems like a pipe dream. Nope, just an air-fryer one.

Buttery Popcorn Chicken

EASY / CAN BE GLUTEN-FREE / 8 INGREDIENTS

Here's kid food! (And grown-up food, too.) Corn flake crumbs give these chicken nuggets a crisp, light coating, the better to let their buttery taste shine through. (For a handy chart on crumb equivalents, see page 21.) There's no need to coat the pieces with vegetable oil spray because the butter will help "fry" the crumb mixture as the air heats it up and dries it out on the meat.

There's no way to get all these pieces in a single layer in the basket. You must work carefully to rearrange the little pieces in the basket. Be gentle: the coating is fragile, particularly early on. It can come off the nuggets. In this case, don't shake the basket. Use kitchen tongs to rearrange the little pieces.

INGREDIENTS	2-quart or larger air fryer	3.5-quart or larger air fryer	5.25-quart or larger air fryer
Boneless skinless chicken breasts, cut into 1-inch pieces	¾ pound	1¼ pounds	1¾ pounds
Butter, melted and cooled for 5 minutes	2 tablespoons	3 tablespoons	4 tablespoons (¼ cup/½ stick)
Corn flake crumbs (gluten-free, if a concern)	½ cup	¾ cup	1¼ cups
Dried thyme	1 teaspoon	1½ teaspoons	2 teaspoons
Dried oregano	1 teaspoon	1½ teaspoons	2 teaspoons
Mild paprika	1 teaspoon	1½ teaspoons	2 teaspoons
Table salt	1 teaspoon	1½ teaspoons	2 teaspoons
Garlic powder	¼ teaspoon	Rounded ¼ teaspoon	½ teaspoon
MAKES	2 servings	4 servings	6 servings

1. With the basket (or basket attachment) in the air fryer, heat it to 375°F (or 370°F or 360°F, if one of these is the closest setting).

2. Toss the chicken and butter in a bowl until the meat is evenly coated.

3. Put the corn flake crumbs, thyme, oregano, paprika, salt, and garlic powder in a large zip-closed plastic bag. Seal it closed and shake gently a few times to mix everything up. Add the chicken. If all the butter has been absorbed by the meat, you can dump the chicken right into the bag; otherwise, you'll have to pick out the small pieces with kitchen tongs and set them in the bag with the crumb mixture. (Excess butter will make the crumbs clump.) Seal the bag but leave air in it so there's room for the chicken to move around. Shake gently many times to make sure every piece is evenly coated.

4. Put the chicken pieces in the basket, spreading them out into as close to an even layer as you can, although they will most likely overlap a bit and even stack on top of each other (depending on the size of your basket and the batch size you've made). Air-fry for 10 minutes, using kitchen tongs to *gently* rearrange the pieces twice, until they are lightly browned and crunchy.

5. Gently pour the contents of the basket onto a wire rack. Cool for 5 minutes before serving.

Then...

- Although these chicken pieces are pretty rich, we also like them served on toothpicks as a nibble with **Smoky Dipping Sauce** (page 33) or **Avocado Ranch Dip** (page 223).

- Or make TANGY JALAPEÑO DIP by whirring *a fresh seeded and stemmed jalapeño chile* with *lots of cilantro, some regular or low-fat sour cream, up to 2 tablespoons lime juice, a generous amount of olive oil,* and *a little table salt* in a food processor. Experiment with the proportions for your taste, but remember you can always add more lime juice and sour cream a little at a time. It's hard to balance them once you've added too much.

Cheesy Chicken Nuggets

FAST / CAN BE GLUTEN-FREE / 6 INGREDIENTS

By mixing ground Cheetos or cheese puff snacks with bread crumbs, you can create a cheesy, crunchy coating for chicken nuggets, soon to be a favorite in your house.

The smaller amounts here are so that the nuggets can be set in a single layer in the basket. Because of all that air circulation, these nuggets cook more quickly than those in the **Buttery Popcorn Chicken** recipe (previous page).

While you can coat the little pieces of chicken in two batches—provided that the bowls for the coating ingredients are large enough to hold that many nuggets—you'll probably have to work in three or four batches for the larger quantities. Be fairly conservative in estimating how many can get coated at any one go, if only to make sure all the pieces are evenly covered.

INGREDIENTS	2-quart or larger air fryer	3.5-quart or larger air fryer	5.25-quart or larger air fryer
All-purpose flour or tapioca flour	½ cup	⅔ cup	¾ cup
Large egg white(s), well beaten	1	1	2
Finely ground Cheetos or cheese puffs (gluten-free, if a concern)	¾ cup (a little less than 1 ounce)	1 cup (a little more than 1 ounce)	1½ cups (about 1¼ ounces)
Plain dried bread crumbs (gluten-free, if a concern)	6 tablespoons	½ cup	¾ cup
Boneless skinless chicken breasts, cut into 1-inch cubes	6 ounces	½ pound	¾ pound
Vegetable oil spray	As needed	As needed	As needed
MAKES	2 servings	3 servings	4 servings

1. With the basket (or basket attachment) in the air fryer, heat it to 375°F (or 370°F or 360°F, if one of these is the closest setting).

2. Set up and fill three shallow soup plates or small pie plates on your counter: one for the flour; one for the egg white(s); and one for the ground Cheetos and bread crumbs, stirred until well combined.

continues

3. Put about half the chicken pieces in the flour and toss them around until well coated. Transfer them to the egg white(s) and toss gently to coat while preserving the flour on them. Use a slotted spoon to pick them up, letting any excess egg white slip back into the rest. Transfer the pieces to the Cheetos mixture. Turn and toss them gently to coat evenly. Transfer the pieces to a cutting board, then repeat with the remaining chicken nuggets.

4. Lightly coat the pieces with vegetable spray on all sides, then set them in the basket in one layer. Air-fry undisturbed for 8 minutes, or until lightly browned and cooked through.

5. Gently dump the contents of the basket onto a wire rack. Cool for 5 minutes before serving.

Then...

- Serve these with a whole-wheat pasta salad that includes black beans. Cook up some *whole-wheat farfalle or ziti* according to the package's instructions; drain in a colander in the sink, then transfer to a large bowl. Stir in *drained and rinsed canned black beans, chopped tomatoes, canned artichoke hearts (cut into quarters),* and *shredded Swiss cheese.* Season the whole thing with *olive oil, lemon juice,* and *ground black pepper.* Then spoon the chicken nuggets on top of— or next to—each serving.

See photo in insert.

Fried Chicken Tenders

EASY / CAN BE GLUTEN-FREE / 10 INGREDIENTS

Here's something everyone loves! And why not? Tasty, crunchy, juicy chicken you can eat with your hands—what's not to like? The amount here may seem small in each batch, but the tenders need lots of air flow around them to get crisp. Make sure you have plenty of room around each piece of meat in the basket. Figure on at least a ½-inch gap. If you're hankering for more tenders, double any one set of quantities for a second batch.

By using potato starch instead of flour, the coating becomes *very* crunchy. Flour blends beautifully with chicken skin for a crust; but since tenders are skinless, they need help getting that prized texture. Thus, the alternate starch. It'll pay off. We know. We ate the whole batch in one sitting.

And here's one strange twist: Because the spices are going into a single egg that's enough for any size batch given here, the spice amounts don't change in the chart. If you want to make your life easier, substitute 2½ teaspoons dried poultry seasoning blend for the onion powder, paprika, garlic powder, and pepper. Check to see if the blend contains salt. If so, omit the salt as well.

INGREDIENTS	2-quart or larger air fryer	3.5-quart or larger air fryer	5.25-quart or larger air fryer
2-ounce chicken tenders	4	6	8
Potato starch	1 tablespoon	1½ tablespoons	2 tablespoons
Large egg	1	1	1
Onion powder	1 teaspoon	1 teaspoon	1 teaspoon
Table salt	1 teaspoon	1 teaspoon	1 teaspoon
Mild paprika	½ teaspoon	½ teaspoon	½ teaspoon
Garlic powder	½ teaspoon	½ teaspoon	½ teaspoon
Ground black pepper	½ teaspoon	½ teaspoon	½ teaspoon
Plain panko bread crumbs (gluten-free, if a concern)	¾ cup	1¼ cups	2 cups
Vegetable oil spray	As needed	As needed	As needed
MAKES	4 tenders	6 tenders	8 tenders

1. With the basket (or basket attachment) in the air fryer, heat it to 400°F (or 390°F, if that's the closest setting).

2. Toss the chicken tenders in a bowl with the potato starch until the tenders are evenly and thoroughly coated.

3. Whisk the egg, onion powder, salt, paprika, garlic powder, and pepper in a large bowl until uniform. Add the coated tenders and toss gently to coat.

4. Spread the bread crumbs on a plate. Transfer the tenders one by one to the bread crumbs, turning and pressing gently to coat all sides. Transfer them one by one to a cutting board. When you're done, coat them on all sides with vegetable oil spray.

continues

5. Set them in the basket in one layer with at least a ½-inch space (or more) between them. Air-fry undisturbed for 12 minutes, until crunchy and browned.

6. Use kitchen tongs to gently transfer the tenders to a wire rack. Cool for 5 minutes before serving.

Then...

- Duck sauce is probably the best condiment for these. It's a sweet, sticky sauce, found in the Jewish or ethnic food section of a supermarket.

- Or doctor duck sauce (or even the throwback condiment Saucy Susan) by whisking 1 cup of it with 2 teaspoons unseasoned rice vinegar (see page 70) to make the sauce a little less sweet.

See photo in insert.

Classic Buttermilk Fried Chicken

EASY / CAN BE GLUTEN-FREE / UP TO 8 INGREDIENTS

Soaking chicken in buttermilk tenderizes the skin and renders it crunchier in the air fryer. But trim off any large blobs of fat or thick bits of excess skin before dropping the thighs in the buttermilk.

If you don't want to dirty a bowl for the buttermilk, pour it into a large zip-closed plastic bag, add the chicken, seal, and shake gently to coat. Refrigerate as directed, turning the bag and rearranging the meat occasionally.

You can also substitute other chicken parts for the thighs: four skin-on chicken legs for a small or medium batch or six legs for a large batch—or one *large* (1-pound) bone-in skin-on chicken breast, halved widthwise for the small or medium batch or 2 halved breasts of the same size for the large batch.

Of course, you can double or triple any of these amounts for crowds, but you must then air-fry the pieces in batches because they must lie in a single layer in the basket. (Or buy a second air fryer. We did. Several, in fact.)

INGREDIENTS	2-quart or larger air fryer	3.5-quart or larger air fryer	5.25-quart or larger air fryer
Bone-in skin-on ½-pound chicken thighs, trimmed of any fat blobs	2	3	4
Buttermilk	1 cup	1 cup	1½ cups
All-purpose flour or tapioca flour	½ cup	¾ cup	1 cup
Mild paprika	1 teaspoon	1½ teaspoons	2 teaspoons
Table salt	1 teaspoon	1½ teaspoons	2 teaspoons
Onion powder (optional)	1 teaspoon	1½ teaspoons	2 teaspoons
Garlic powder (optional)	½ teaspoon	¾ teaspoon	1 teaspoon
Vegetable oil spray	As needed	As needed	As needed
MAKES	*2 servings*	*3 servings*	*4 servings*

1. Put the chicken thighs in a bowl, pour in the buttermilk, toss well to coat, and refrigerate for 30 minutes, tossing occasionally to coat the chicken pieces.

2. With the basket (or basket attachment) in the air fryer, heat it to 350°F (or 360°F, if that's the closest setting).

3. Whisk the flour, paprika, salt, onion powder (if using), and garlic powder (if using) in a medium bowl. Use kitchen tongs to transfer one chicken thigh from the buttermilk bowl to the flour mixture. Turn several times to coat evenly on all sides. Gently shake off any excess flour coating, set the thigh on a cutting board, and continue on with the remaining thigh(s).

4. Generously coat the thighs with vegetable oil spray on both sides, then set them in the basket so there's as much air space around each thigh as possible. They should not overlap or even touch. Air-fry undisturbed for 25 minutes, or until the thighs are golden and an instant-read meat thermometer inserted into the thickest section of one thigh (without touching bone) registers 165°F.

5. Use kitchen tongs to transfer the thighs to a wire rack and sprinkle with additional salt, if desired. Cool for 5 to 10 minutes before serving.

Then...

- Serve these with purchased cole slaw, **Carrot Slaw** (page 115), or **Radish Slaw** (page 117).
- Or make QUICK MASHED POTATOES. After boiling *peeled small, white potatoes* in *water or a mixture of water and chicken broth* until tender, use a potato masher to mash them into a fairly smooth puree along with *butter, milk, cream, more broth,* and/or *sour cream. Salt* and *pepper* to taste.

See photo in insert.

Indian-Style Butter Chicken

FAST / EASY / GLUTEN-FREE / 6 INGREDIENTS

Here's an air-fryer version of a recipe that became an internet sensation for the Instant Pot. (We share our version in *The Instant Pot Bible*.) The traditional recipe is a saucy braise. Here, you'll make a buttery blend of spices with curry powder and garam masala to coat the chicken.

GARAM MASALA is a South Asian blend of "warming" spices (not hot but rather autumnal, like the smell of cinnamon apples on an October morning). There are lots of bottlings on the market; but to make your own garam masala, toast *2 tablespoons coriander seeds, 1½ tablespoons cumin seeds, 1 teaspoon black peppercorns, 1 teaspoon whole cloves, 1 teaspoon fennel seeds,* and *one 2-inch cinnamon stick* in a small skillet over medium-low heat, stirring often, until fragrant, about 2 minutes. Cool a few minutes, then pour everything into a small food processor or a large spice grinder. Add *½ teaspoon grated nutmeg* and *up to ¼ teaspoon cayenne.* Cover and grind to a powder. Store the spice mixture sealed in a glass bottle or container in a cool, dry pantry for up to 3 months.

INGREDIENTS	2-quart or larger air fryer	3.5-quart or larger air fryer	5.25-quart or larger air fryer
10- to 12-ounce (¾-pound) bone-in skin-on chicken breast(s)	1	2	3
Butter, melted and cooled	1 tablespoon	2 tablespoons	3 tablespoons
Mild yellow or spicy red curry powder, or homemade curry powder (see page 363)	½ teaspoon	1 teaspoon	1½ teaspoons
Garam masala (see the headnote)	½ teaspoon	1 teaspoon	1½ teaspoons
Table salt	¼ teaspoon	½ teaspoon	½ teaspoon
Ground black pepper	¼ teaspoon	½ teaspoon	½ teaspoon
MAKES	*2 breast halves*	*4 breast halves*	*6 breast halves*

1. With the basket (or basket attachment) in the air fryer, heat it to 375°F (or 370°F or 360°F, if one of these is the closest setting).

2. Remove the skin from the chicken breasts by nicking it up with a knife at the small, pointy end of the breast, then peeling the skin off the breast. Remove any blobs of fat and split the breast widthwise into two equal halves. Repeat with any remaining breasts.

3. Mix the butter, curry powder, garam masala, salt, and pepper in a large bowl. Add the chicken and toss repeatedly until the meat and even the bones underneath are well coated.

4. When the machine is at temperature, set the breast halves in the basket with as much air space around them as possible. Air-fry undisturbed for 12 minutes, or until lightly browned and an instant-read meat thermometer inserted into the thickest part of a breast (without touching bone) registers 165°F. If the machine's temperature is at 360°F, you may need to add 1 to 2 minutes to the cooking time.

5. Use kitchen tongs to gently transfer the breasts to a wire rack. Cool for 5 minutes before serving.

Then...

- Serve these with purchased naan (a South Asian flatbread) as well as purchased lime chutney and/or lime pickle.

- And perhaps with the cooling yogurt dip **Cucumber and Cilantro Raita** (page 179).

Crunchy Vinegar-and-Salt Chicken Breasts

FAST / EASY / CAN BE GLUTEN-FREE / 3 INGREDIENTS

These are salty and sour chicken breasts with a very crunchy coating made from vinegar-and-salt potato chips, an incredible treat. Crush the chips until they're the consistency of panko bread crumbs. You can pulse them in a food processor or seal the chips in a large zip-closed plastic bag and roll them repeatedly with a rolling pin, turning the bag over and in different directions to get an even consistency throughout.

INGREDIENTS	2-quart or larger air fryer	3.5-quart or larger air fryer	5.25-quart or larger air fryer
Large egg white(s), well beaten	1	2	2
Vinegar-and-salt potato chips (gluten-free, if a concern), crushed to crumbs	Half of a 5-ounce bag	Two-thirds of a 5-ounce bag	One 5-ounce bag
5- to 6-ounce boneless skinless chicken breasts	2	3	4
MAKES	2 servings	3 servings	4 servings

1. With the basket (or basket attachment) in the air fryer, heat it to 375°F (or 370°F or 360°F, if one of these is the closest setting).

2. Set up and fill two shallow soup plates or small pie plates on your counter: one for the beaten egg white(s) and one for the crushed potato chips.

3. Use kitchen tongs to dip one breast in the egg white(s), turning it to coat all sides. Let the excess egg white slip back into the rest, then set the breast in the crushed chips. Turn several times to coat evenly on all sides, pressing gently to get the crumbs to adhere. Set the coated breast aside and coat the remaining chicken breast(s).

4. Set them in the basket with as much air space around each as possible and air-fry undisturbed

for 10 minutes, or until golden brown and cooked through. You may need to add 1 minute to the cooking time if the air fryer is at 360°F.

5. Use kitchen tongs to gently transfer the breasts to a wire rack. Cool for 5 to 10 minutes before serving.

Then...

- These salty-sour chicken breasts are particularly good with **Spicy Mustard Dip** (page 26) or **Cooked Tomato Dip** (page 79) as a sauce alongside them.

- They're also great served with **Fried Green Tomatoes** (page 313), **Beet Fries** (page 331), or **Crispy Brussels Sprouts** (page 367).

Tamale-Style Chicken Breasts

EASY / CAN BE GLUTEN-FREE / 5 INGREDIENTS

By crushing Fritos and using them as a coating on chicken breasts that have already been coated in purchased salsa verde, we replicate the flavors of chicken tamales for a crunchy, satisfying main course any night of the week.

You'll get the most even crumbs from Fritos if you seal them in a large zip-closed plastic bag, then set the bag on the counter and press your palms gently but firmly against it. Turn the bag over and in multiple directions, pressing each time to crush the chips. You don't want crumbs. You don't even want the bits to be as small as panko bread crumbs. They should still look like crushed-up Fritos.

INGREDIENTS	2-quart or larger air fryer	3.5-quart or larger air fryer	5.25-quart or larger air fryer
All-purpose flour or gluten-free all-purpose flour	½ cup	½ cup	½ cup
Purchased salsa verde	½ cup	¾ cup	1 cup
Fritos (original flavor) or generic corn chip equivalent, crushed to crumbs	Half of a 9¼-ounce bag	Two-thirds of a 9¼-ounce bag	One 9¼-ounce bag
5- to 6-ounce boneless skinless chicken breasts	2	3	4
Vegetable oil spray	As needed	As needed	As needed
MAKES	2 servings	3 servings	4 servings

1. With the basket (or basket attachment) in the air fryer, heat it to 375°F (or 370°F or 360°F, if one of these is the closest setting).

2. Set up and fill three shallow soup plates or small pie plates on your counter: one for the flour; one for the salsa verde; and one for the Fritos crumbs or crushed corn chips.

3. Use kitchen tongs to dip one breast in the flour, turning it to coat all sides evenly. Shake off any excess, then dip the breast gently in the salsa verde, coating it on all sides by turning it several times. Finally, set the breast in the Fritos or corn chip crumbs and turn it several times to coat evenly but not too thickly. Set the breast on a cutting board and continue coating the remaining breast(s).

4. Generously coat the chicken breasts on both sides with vegetable oil spray. Set them in the basket with as much air space around them as possible. They can be close (especially if a larger batch) but they should not touch. Air-fry undisturbed for 10 minutes, or until golden brown and cooked through. You may need to add 1 minute to the cooking time if the air fryer is at 360°F.

5. Use kitchen tongs to gently transfer the breasts to a wire rack. Cool for 5 to 10 minutes before serving.

Then...

- Serve these chicken breasts with sour cream, pickled jalapeño rings, minced red onion, and/or chopped fresh cilantro leaves.

- Make STREAMLINED SPANISH RICE. For 4 servings, heat *1 tablespoon olive oil* in a medium saucepan set over medium heat. Add about *¼ cup chopped yellow or white onion* and cook, stirring often, until softened, about 3 minutes. Add *1½ cups raw long-grain white rice, 2 cups chicken or vegetable broth*, and *1 cup chunky red salsa*. Stir well and bring to a simmer. Cover, reduce the heat to low, and cook for 15 minutes, or until the liquids have been absorbed. Set aside covered, off the heat, for 10 minutes before serving.

Fiery Coconut Fried Chicken

EASY / CAN BE GLUTEN-FREE / 5 OR 6 INGREDIENTS

These chicken breasts can be quite fiery, depending on the brand of jerk dried seasoning blend you use. Some bottlings are mostly cayenne; others, more aromatic. Read the label to make sure your bottling is not just searing fire (unless that's what you want).

Take note: This recipe calls for *unsweetened* shredded coconut, not the sweetened stuff found in the baking aisle. Sometimes called "desiccated coconut," unsweetened coconut can often be found in the health-food or "organic" sections of your supermarket, and is easily ordered online.

INGREDIENTS	2-quart or larger air fryer	3.5-quart or larger air fryer	5.25-quart or larger air fryer
5- to 6-ounce boneless skinless chicken breasts	2	3	4
Regular or low-fat coconut milk	2 tablespoons	3 tablespoons	¼ cup
Unsweetened shredded coconut	¼ cup	6 tablespoons	½ cup
Jerk dried seasoning blend (for a homemade blend, see page 298)	2 teaspoons	1 tablespoon	1½ tablespoons
Vegetable oil or coconut oil spray	As needed	As needed	As needed
Table salt (optional)	For garnishing	For garnishing	For garnishing
MAKES	*2 servings*	*3 servings*	*4 servings*

1. With the basket (or basket attachment) in the air fryer, heat it to 375°F (or 370°F or 360°F, if one of these is the closest setting).

2. Toss the chicken and coconut milk in a bowl until the meat is evenly coated.

3. Mix the shredded coconut and seasoning blend on a large plate until well combined. Use kitchen tongs to set one of the chicken breasts in the shredded coconut mixture, turning it several times to coat it evenly on all sides, pressing gently to get the coconut to adhere. Set aside and coat the remaining breast(s).

continues

4. Lightly coat the breasts on all sides with vegetable or coconut oil spray, then set them in the basket with as much air space around each of them as possible. They may be close but should not touch. Air-fry undisturbed for 12 minutes, or until browned, crisp, and cooked through. You may need to add 1 minute to the cooking time if the air fryer is at 360°F.

5. Use kitchen tongs to gently transfer the breasts to a wire rack. Season with salt to taste (if using) and cool for 5 minutes before serving.

Then...

- Check out the **Asian Carrot Slaw** (page 250) as a side for these crunchy chicken breasts.

- Or serve them alongside **Blistered Green Beans** (page 344).

- Or try this version of JAMAICAN RICE AND PEAS. For 6 servings, melt *2 tablespoons butter* in a large saucepan, then add *1 small yellow or white onion, chopped.* Cook a minute or two, just to soften; then stir in *2 cups raw long-grain white rice, up to 1 tablespoon minced garlic, up to 1 tablespoon minced peeled fresh ginger,* and *½ teaspoon table salt.* Stir in the pan for just a bit to warm up, then pour in *1 quart (4 cups) vegetable or chicken broth* and stir in *1 small or large fresh jalapeño, cut in half lengthwise* (or just about any chile you like). Bring to a simmer, cover, reduce the heat to low, and simmer until the rice is tender, 15 to 20 minutes. Remove the chile from the rice, then stir in *one 15-ounce can dark red kidney beans (drained and rinsed),* as well as *2 teaspoons minced fresh thyme.* Cover and set aside for a few minutes before serving (perhaps with a little more *salt,* to taste).

Sugar-Glazed Walnuts (page 32) and Sweet-and-Salty Pretzels (page 26)

Crab Rangoon (page 65) and Fried Wontons (page 68)

Fried Dill Pickle Chips
(page 38)

Small Chicken Empanadas
with Chimichurri (pages 93–94)
and Spicy Ketchup Dip (page 66)

Cheese Arancini (page 76) with
Caponata Salsa (page 82) and
Meatball Arancini (page 78)
with marinara sauce

Onion Ring Nachos (page 98)

French Onion Soup (page 103)

Reuben Sandwiches
(page 126)

Inside-Out Cheeseburgers (page 132)

**Cheesy Chicken Nuggets
(page 151) and Fried
Chicken Tenders (page 153)
with pasta salad**

Chicken Souvlaki (page 163)
with Tahini Sauce (page 147)

Classic Buttermilk Fried Chicken
(page 154) with cole slaw

Chicken Taquitos (page 168)

Chicken 65 with Cucumber and Cilantro Raita (pages 178–79)

Better-Than-Chinese-Take-Out
Orange Chicken (page 180)

Crunchy Chicken Wings with Buffalo Sauce (page 187) and blue cheese

**Italian Meatballs (page 223)
served as a submarine sandwich
with marinara sauce and cheese**

Cornbread-Crusted Chicken Breasts

EASY / CAN BE GLUTEN-FREE / 4 INGREDIENTS

No, these chicken breasts aren't coated with cornbread crumbs. Those are fragile and burn too quickly in the air fryer. Instead, these breasts are coated with ground cornbread stuffing mix, which (as a bonus) has all the seasoning—and salt—you need.

These are larger boneless skinless breasts than those in some other recipes in this chapter. We needed extra time to get the coating crisp, and the smaller 5-ounce breasts dry out too quickly when they have to sit in an air fryer that long.

Notice that the volume amount for the stuffing mix is given for the stuff *before* it's crushed to crumbs. When you crush it, go for a fairly fine consistency, certainly smaller than panko bread crumbs, more like traditional dried bread crumbs.

INGREDIENTS	2-quart or larger air fryer	3.5-quart or larger air fryer	5.25-quart or larger air fryer
Buttermilk	½ cup	1 cup	1 cup
Purchased cornbread stuffing mix (gluten-free, if a concern), crushed	2 cups	3 cups	4 cups
10-ounce boneless skinless chicken breast(s)	1	2	3
Vegetable oil spray	As needed	As needed	As needed
MAKES	*1 to 2 servings*	*2 to 3 servings*	*3 to 4 servings*

1. With the basket (or basket attachment) in the air fryer, heat it to 350°F (or 360°F, if that's the closest setting).

2. Set up and fill two shallow soup plates or pie plates on your counter: one for the buttermilk and one for the crushed stuffing mix.

3. Use kitchen tongs to dip a breast in the buttermilk, turning it several times to coat it on all sides. Set it in the cornbread stuffing mix crumbs and turn several times to coat thoroughly, even on the ends, pressing gently so the crumbs adhere. Set the breast on a cutting board and coat additional breasts as needed.

4. Lightly coat the breast(s) on both sides with vegetable oil spray, then set the breast(s) in the basket with as much air space around those in the larger batches as possible. Air-fry undisturbed for 18 minutes, or until golden brown with a crisp coating and an instant-read meat thermometer inserted into the center of one breast registers 160°F. (Checking the internal temperature is important because these are larger chicken breasts.)

5. Use kitchen tongs to gently transfer the breast(s) to a wire rack. Cool for 5 to 10 minutes before serving.

Then...

- Make a vegetable salad with a CRANBERRY VINAIGRETTE. For 4 servings, whisk ⅓ cup cranberry sauce, 2 tablespoons red wine vinegar, 1 tablespoon olive oil, and 1 teaspoon regular or low-sodium soy sauce or gluten-free tamari sauce in a small bowl. This flavorful dressing will stand up to diced bell peppers, sliced radishes, and sugar snap peas.

Chicken Pastrami

GLUTEN-FREE / 11 INGREDIENTS

This recipe uses a large amount of spices. There's method to this madness: By dipping chicken breasts in an egg-white mixture, then coating them in that spice blend, you can create a really good version of pastrami without brining, smoking, or roasting the meat for hours in very low heat. What's more, this is chicken pastrami, not beef brisket pastrami, and so a healthier treat.

Once cooked, these "pastramied" chicken breasts can be saved in the fridge for lunches and dinners in the days ahead. Or seal them in a heavy zip-closed plastic bag and freeze them for up to 3 months.

INGREDIENTS	2-quart or larger air fryer	3.5-quart or larger air fryer	5.25-quart or larger air fryer
Large egg white	1	1	1
Liquid smoke	1 tablespoon	1 tablespoon	1 tablespoon
Light brown sugar	1½ teaspoons	2 teaspoons	1 tablespoon
Ground coriander	1 teaspoon	1½ teaspoons	2 teaspoons
Ground dried ginger	¾ teaspoon	1 teaspoon	1½ teaspoons
Ground mustard	¾ teaspoon	1 teaspoon	1½ teaspoons
Table salt	½ teaspoon	¾ teaspoon	1 teaspoon
Ground black pepper	½ teaspoon	¾ teaspoon	1 teaspoon
Garlic powder	¼ teaspoon	Rounded ¼ teaspoon	½ teaspoon
½-*pound* boneless skinless chicken breasts	2	3	4
Vegetable oil spray	As needed	As needed	As needed
MAKES	*2 to 3 servings*	*3 to 4 servings*	*4 to 6 servings*

1. With the basket (or basket attachment) in the air fryer, heat it to 350°F (or 360°F, if that's the closest setting).

2. Whisk the egg white and liquid smoke in a shallow soup plate or a small pie plate.

3. Mix the brown sugar, coriander, ginger, mustard, salt, pepper, and garlic powder in a small bowl until well combined.

4. Dip a chicken breast in the egg white mixture, turning and coating it evenly all over. Sprinkle the chicken breast evenly with the brown sugar mixture on both sides. Lightly coat the breast on both sides

with the vegetable oil spray. Set aside on a cutting board and coat the remaining chicken breast(s).

5. Set the chicken breasts in the basket with as much air space between them as possible. They may be close in larger batches but should not touch. Air-fry undisturbed for 16 minutes, until browned and an instant-read meat thermometer inserted into the center of one of the breasts registers 160°F.

6. Use kitchen tongs to transfer the breasts to a wire rack. Cool for at least 20 minutes before serving or before wrapping in plastic wrap and refrigerating for up to 4 days.

Then...

- To make CHICKEN REUBEN SANDWICHES, slice *cooked Chicken Pastrami*, then layer the meat with *purchased sauerkraut* and **Russian Dressing** *(see page 314)* on *rye bread*. Add some *deli mustard*, too, if desired. Toast the sandwiches in a nonstick skillet set over medium-high heat or on a grill over direct high heat for about 3 minutes, turning once. For ways to toast a reuben in the air fryer, see page 126.

- For a REUBEN SALAD, dice some of the *cooked Chicken Pastrami meat* and toss it with *bagged slaw mix* and *a little drained purchased sauerkraut*. Add *small Swiss cheese cubes*, then toss with *Russian dressing*.

Chicken Souvlaki

EASY / GLUTEN-FREE / 9 INGREDIENTS PLUS BAMBOO SKEWERS

These skewers make a tasty dinner, but they'd also be a great appetizer or snack with **Tahini Sauce** (page 147) or **Tzatziki Sauce** (page 120) on the side. The meat should have blackened bits. If you're worried about it drying out, even after marinating, omit the salt and use kosher (and thus already brined) boneless skinless chicken breasts.

The bamboo skewers can only be 4 inches long to fit in the machine's basket. You can look for short skewers or trim longer ones to the right size with kitchen shears.

There's no need to soak the skewers in water. They don't spend enough time in the heat to be a problem, although the tips may blacken.

INGREDIENTS	2-quart or larger air fryer	3.5-quart or larger air fryer	5.25-quart or larger air fryer
Boneless skinless chicken breasts, cut into 2-inch cubes	10 ounces	1 pound	1½ pounds
Olive oil	1 tablespoon	4 teaspoons	2 tablespoons
Lemon juice	1 tablespoon	4 teaspoons	2 tablespoons
Fresh oregano leaves, finely chopped	1 teaspoon	1½ teaspoons	2½ teaspoons
Fresh thyme leaves, finely chopped	1 teaspoon	1½ teaspoons	2½ teaspoons
Minced garlic	1 teaspoon	1½ teaspoons	2½ teaspoons
Mild paprika	½ teaspoon	¾ teaspoon	1 teaspoon
Table salt	½ teaspoon	¾ teaspoon	1 teaspoon
Red pepper flakes	Up to ½ teaspoon	Up to ¾ teaspoon	Up to 1 teaspoon
MAKES	*2 servings*	*3 servings*	*4 servings*

continues

1. Stir the chicken cubes, oil, lemon juice, oregano, thyme, garlic, paprika, salt, and red pepper flakes in a large bowl. Cover and refrigerate for at least 1 hour or up to 6 hours, stirring the chicken in the marinade at least once.

2. Remove the bowl from the fridge and let it sit on the counter while the air fryer heats. With the basket (or basket attachment) in the air fryer, heat it to 400°F (or 390°F, if that's the closest setting).

3. When the machine is at temperature, divide the chicken pieces evenly between 2, 3, or 4 bamboo or wooden skewers, packing the chicken pieces together on each skewer. Set the skewers in the basket in one layer and air-fry undisturbed for 16 minutes, or until well browned, almost charred, and sizzling.

4. Use kitchen tongs to transfer the skewers to a wire rack. Cool for 5 minutes before serving.

Then...

- Serve the skewers over sliced tomatoes with minced fresh cilantro and mint leaves sprinkled on top. You'll need pita bread on the side, too!

- Or set them over cooked long-grain white or brown rice. Or perhaps a whole grain like cooked and drained wheat berries or spelt berries.

- Or skip the mint in the garnish and make MINT TAHINI SAUCE for the skewers. Whisk *plain full-fat or low-fat yogurt* (not Greek yogurt) and *tahini* (see page 79) in a 7-to-1 or 8-to-1 ratio by volume with *a little lemon juice* and a fair amount of *minced fresh mint leaves*.

See photo in insert.

Chicken Kiev

For this throwback recipe, chicken breasts are pounded thin, seasoned, stuffed with butter, then rolled closed and wrapped in a crunchy bread-crumb coating. When you cut one open, the butter runs out, forming the "sauce." How did *this* ever go out of style?

The easiest way to make butter batons is to take a stick of butter, slice it in half lengthwise, slice each of these two pieces in half widthwise, and finally slice each of these four pieces in half lengthwise. You can then use as many of the batons as you need, saving the rest in the fridge—or even the freezer—for another round of Chicken Kiev, or simply using them as you would butter in any recipe (since each one is now a premeasured 1 tablespoon).

INGREDIENTS	2-quart or larger air fryer	3.5-quart or larger air fryer	5.25-quart or larger air fryer
1-tablespoon butter batons (see the headnote)	2	3	4
5- to 6-ounce boneless skinless chicken breasts	2	3	4
Onion powder	¼ teaspoon	Rounded ¼ teaspoon	½ teaspoon
Mild paprika	¼ teaspoon	Rounded ¼ teaspoon	½ teaspoon
Table salt	¼ teaspoon	Rounded ¼ teaspoon	½ teaspoon
Ground black pepper	¼ teaspoon	Rounded ¼ teaspoon	½ teaspoon
All-purpose flour	1 cup	1⅓ cups	2 cups
Large eggs, well beaten	2	2	3
Plain dried bread crumbs	1½ cups	2 cups	2½ cups
Vegetable oil spray	As needed	As needed	As needed
MAKES	*2 servings*	*3 servings*	*4 servings*

1. Freeze the butter batons for 30 minutes.

2. Meanwhile, put a chicken breast between two sheets of plastic wrap on your work surface. Flatten the meat by knocking it (through the plastic wrap) with the smooth side of a meat mallet or the bottom of a heavy saucepan until the meat is about ¼ inch thick. Work with glancing blows, striking the meat in an arc so that the meat is pulled a bit with each blow. Peel off the top layer of plastic, set the breast aside on its bottom piece of plastic wrap, and continue on flattening more breasts.

3. With the basket (or basket attachment) in the air fryer, heat it to 400°F (or 390°F, if that's the closest setting).

4. Set up and fill three shallow soup plates or small pie plates on your counter: one for the flour, one for the beaten eggs, and one for the bread crumbs.

continues

5. Take one flattened chicken breast and set the frozen butter baton in its center so that the baton lies parallel to the longer sides of the meat. Season the breast with ⅛ teaspoon each of the onion powder, paprika, salt, and pepper. Fold the shorter (if ragged) sides of the breast up and over the butter, then roll the meat closed into a fat tube, starting at one of the longer sides.

6. Holding the roll tightly closed with your clean hand, dip it in the flour to coat it on all sides. Then dip it in the beaten eggs to coat all sides, even the ends. Let any excess egg slip back into the rest, then (still holding it tightly closed) set the tube in the bread crumbs and coat it on all sides with an even and fairly thick coating. Dip the tube back into the egg as before, then back into the bread crumbs, turning it to coat all sides on this second dip. Set the tube aside on a cutting board and continue making and coating the remaining chicken tube(s) as detailed in steps 5 and 6.

7. Lightly coat the tubes on all sides with vegetable oil spray. Set them in the basket with as much air space around them as possible. Air-fry undisturbed for 14 minutes, or until browned and crisp across the crust.

8. Use kitchen tongs to transfer the tubes to serving plates and cool for 5 minutes before serving. Some butter may leak out during cooking; pour any melted butter at the bottom of the machine (or on the tray, in some models) over the stuffed chicken breasts on the plates.

Then...

- Serve these with **Steak Fries** (page 327), **Steakhouse Baked Potatoes** (page 333), **Honey-Roasted Parsnips** (page 343), **Blistered Green Beans** (page 344), **Perfect Broccoli** (page 345), or **Crispy, Cheesy Leeks** (page 350).

Chicken Fajitas

EASY / CAN BE GLUTEN-FREE / 6 INGREDIENTS

By air-frying chicken tenders for fajitas, they become a little crunchier than they would with standard skillet-frying. The meat also retains more juiciness and ends up better all around in the tortillas. In other words, we're sold on this process and don't make chicken fajitas any other way.

This recipe is only for the meat. See the ideas for serving the fajitas at the end.

INGREDIENTS	2-quart or larger air fryer	3.5-quart or larger air fryer	5.25-quart or larger air fryer
Chicken tenders	1 pound	1½ pounds	2 pounds
Olive oil	1 tablespoon	1½ tablespoons	2 tablespoons
Dried taco seasoning blend (gluten-free, if a concern)	2 teaspoons	1 tablespoon	1½ tablespoons
Medium red or yellow bell pepper(s), stemmed, cored, and cut into 1-inch-thick strips	1	2	2
Small yellow or white onion(s), peeled and halved	1	1	2
Vegetable oil spray	As needed	As needed	As needed
MAKES	2 servings	3 servings	4 servings

1. With the basket (or basket attachment) in the air fryer, heat it to 375°F (or 370°F or 360°F, if one of these is the closest setting).

2. Toss the chicken tenders with the oil and seasoning blend in a bowl until evenly coated.

3. Set the tenders in the basket, overlapping them if necessary. Air-fry for 10 minutes, tossing and rearranging the tenders at the 5-minute mark.

4. After 10 minutes, toss and rearrange the tenders again. Lightly coat the peppers and onion with vegetable oil spray. Add them to the basket and continue air-frying for 12 minutes, gently tossing things in the basket twice, until the vegetables are soft and the tenders are cooked through.

5. Pour the contents of the basket into a large bowl. Cool for 5 minutes before serving.

Then...

- Fajitas should be served with flour or corn tortillas, lots of sour cream, shredded cheese, and pico de gallo or salsa fresca.

- To make about 2 cups of SALSA FRESCA, soak *¼ cup chopped red onion* in a small bowl of *water* with *1 tablespoon white wine vinegar* for 1 hour. Drain in a colander set in the sink, then stir the onion in a large bowl with about *¾ pound Roma or plum tomatoes, chopped; up to 3 tablespoons minced fresh cilantro leaves; 1½ tablespoons lime juice;* and *part or all of 1 medium fresh jalapeño chile, stemmed, seeded, and minced.* Season with *table salt* and *ground black pepper* to taste. Store any remainder in a covered glass or nonreactive container in the fridge for up to 3 days.

Chicken Taquitos

FAST / EASY / 5 INGREDIENTS

These fried little rolled tortilla tubes are not only a full meal but also a great snack or a light lunch on a weekday when you've got some leftover rotisserie chicken to use up. These taquitos are made with small flour tortillas so they'll fit in the basket. If you've got larger flour tortillas on hand—even the 12-inch, burrito-size ones—you can always cut a 6-inch circle out of the middle of each (with quite a bit of food waste but the right size tortilla). In fact, with a 12-inch flour tortilla, you can cut out two 6-inch circles side by side.

INGREDIENTS	2-quart or larger air fryer	3.5-quart or larger air fryer	5.25-quart or larger air fryer
Chopped deboned and skinned rotisserie chicken meat	⅓ cup	⅔ cup	1 cup
Shredded Cheddar or Tex-Mex blend cheese	¼ cup (about 1 ounce)	½ cup (about 2 ounces)	¾ cup (about 3 ounces)
Purchased salsa verde	1 tablespoon	2 tablespoons	3 tablespoons
5- to 6-inch flour tortillas	2	4	6
Vegetable oil spray	As needed	As needed	As needed
MAKES	2 taquitos	4 taquitos	6 taquitos

1. With the basket (or basket attachment) in the air fryer, heat it to 375°F (or 370°F or 360°F, if one of these is the closest setting).

2. Mix the chicken, cheese, and salsa verde in a bowl until well combined.

3. Microwave a tortilla on high for 10 seconds to soften it. Set it on a clean, dry work surface. Place a heaping ¼ cup of the chicken mixture in the center of the tortilla, then roll it up tightly like a cigar. Spray the roll with vegetable spray on all sides. Set it aside seam side down; microwave and fill more tortillas as needed.

4. Set the filled tortillas seam side down in the basket with as much air space between them as possible. Air-fry undisturbed for 8 minutes, or until speckled brown and crunchy at the edges. You may need to add an extra minute to the air-frying if the machine is at 360°F.

5. Use kitchen tongs to transfer the taquitos to a wire rack. Cool for 2 or 3 minutes before serving.

Then...

- Although there's salsa verde in the taquitos, you could make a simple dip by mixing more salsa verde into sour cream or yogurt.

- Or make a dip by whisking equal amounts of sour cream and room-temperature cream cheese until smooth, adding either a little dried taco seasoning blend or chile powder.

- Serve these with **Mexican-Style Roasted Corn** (page 358).

- And don't forget the **Perfect Frozen Margaritas** (page 145)!

See photo in insert.

Barbecue Chicken Flautas

FAST / EASY / CAN BE GLUTEN-FREE / 5 INGREDIENTS

Traditionally, flautas are deep-fried stuffed corn tortillas. We kept this air-fryer version simple so you could make them on a whim (whenever you have leftover rotisserie chicken) without having to heat a vat of oil on the stove.

These flautas are great for a party. You can make several batches a bit in advance because the flautas reheat well. Once cooked, they can stay at room temperature for up to 1 hour or sit in the fridge, covered once cooled, for up to 8 hours. Heat the air fryer to 375°F (or 370°F or 360°F, if one of these is the closest setting), then stack the flautas in the basket like Lincoln Logs and cook for 1 to 2 minutes, until crisp and hot.

INGREDIENTS	2-quart or larger air fryer	3.5-quart or larger air fryer	5.25-quart or larger air fryer
Chopped deboned and skinned rotisserie chicken meat, preferably dark meat	¼ cup	½ cup	¾ cup
Shredded Cheddar cheese	¼ cup (about 1 ounce)	½ cup (about 2 ounces)	¾ cup (about 3 ounces)
Purchased barbecue sauce, any sort (gluten-free, if a concern)	2 teaspoons	1½ tablespoons	2 tablespoons
Vegetable oil spray	As needed	As needed	As needed
6-inch corn tortillas (gluten-free, if a concern)	2	4	4
MAKES	2 flautas	4 flautas	6 flautas

1. With the basket (or basket attachment) in the air fryer, heat it to 375°F (or 370°F or 360°F, if one of these is the closest setting).

2. Mix the chicken, cheese, and barbecue sauce in a bowl until well combined.

3. Microwave the corn tortillas on high for 20 seconds, or until soft.

4. Lay the tortillas on a clean, dry work surface. Top each with about ¼ cup of the filling. Roll the tortillas closed like a cigar. Coat them on all sides with vegetable oil spray.

5. When the machine is at temperature, set the rolled filled tortillas seam side down in the basket with as much air space between them as possible. They should not be touching. Air-fry undisturbed for 8 minutes, or until brown and crunchy. You may need to add an extra minute to the air-frying if the machine is at 360°F.

6. Use kitchen tongs to transfer the flautas to a wire rack. Cool for 5 minutes before serving.

Then...

• To make 4 servings of QUESO SAUCE to dip the flautas in or to pour over them, put *½ pound grated white Cheddar cheese, 6 tablespoons whole milk,* and *3 tablespoons butter* in a small saucepan set over low heat. Cook, stirring often, until melted and smooth. Stir in *¼ cup canned hot or mild diced green chiles, ½ teaspoon garlic powder,* and a *pinch of cayenne.* Taste for salt and serve warm.

Crunchy Barbecue-Style Chicken Thighs

EASY / CAN BE GLUTEN-FREE / 3 INGREDIENTS

This recipe represents the sort of nifty trick that has made the air fryer an American favorite. No, the chicken is not "barbecued" in any standard sense of the word. Instead, it's coated in crushed barbecue-flavored potato chips and turned into a crunchy wonder. The best way to crush the chips is to seal them in a large zip-closed plastic bag, set the bag on your counter, and press against it with the bottom of a heavy saucepan, turning the bag this way and that, even over, to get the chips evenly crushed to about the size of panko bread crumbs.

INGREDIENTS	2-quart or larger air fryer	3.5-quart or larger air fryer	5.25-quart or larger air fryer
Large egg white(s)	1	2	2
Crushed barbecue-flavored potato chips (gluten-free, if a concern)	1 cup (from about 4 ounces chips)	1½ cups (from about 6 ounces chips)	2 cups (from about 8 ounces chips)
½-pound bone-in skin-on chicken thighs, trimmed of fat blobs and excess skin	2	3	4
MAKES	2 servings	3 servings	4 servings

1. With the basket (or basket attachment) in the air fryer, heat it to 350°F (or 360°F, if that's the closest setting).

2. Whisk the egg white(s) in a shallow soup plate or small pie plate until foamy. Pour the crushed chips into an even layer in a second soup plate or pie plate.

3. Use kitchen tongs to dip a chicken thigh in the egg white(s), turning it to coat all sides, then letting any excess egg white slip back into the rest. Set it in the crushed chips and turn repeatedly to coat all sides. Set it aside and continue coating the remaining thigh(s).

4. Set the thighs in the basket with as much air space between them as possible. Air-fry undisturbed for 16 minutes, turning once, until crunchy and an instant-read meat thermometer inserted into the center of one thigh (without touching bone) registers 160°F.

5. Use kitchen tongs to gently transfer the thighs to a wire rack. Cool for 5 minutes before serving.

Then...

- These chicken thighs are great with pickled green tomatoes, which you can sometimes find in the deli case of a large supermarket.

- Serve these chicken thighs with **Fried Corn on the Cob** (page 357).

- And/or serve them with purchased potato salad or **Air-Fried Potato Salad** (page 338).

Crispy Ranch Chicken Thighs

EASY / CAN BE GLUTEN-FREE / 4 INGREDIENTS

Ranch dressing is buttermilk-based, so it can easily become a marinade for fried chicken. Doing so renders these little thighs super tasty (so long as they are evenly coated in the bread crumbs). There shouldn't be a thick layer of crumbs, but it should definitely conceal the meat underneath.

Ranch dressing is pretty salty, especially the purchased stuff. We didn't add any extra salt to this recipe, but you could pass more at the table.

To make homemade RANCH DRESSING, chop a *medium garlic clove* and a *very thin slice of yellow or white onion* into small bits on a cutting board; then add *¼ teaspoon ground mustard*, *¼ teaspoon table salt*, and *⅛ teaspoon ground black pepper*. Continue chopping and mixing together, wiping the mixture against the board occasionally, to create a paste. Whisk this paste in a bowl with *¼ cup regular or low-fat buttermilk*, *¼ cup regular or low-fat mayonnaise (gluten-free, if a concern)*, *1 tablespoon minced fresh parsley leaves*, and *1 tablespoon minced fresh dill fronds*. Store any excess dressing in a small covered nonreactive container in the fridge for up to a couple of days.

INGREDIENTS	2-quart or larger air fryer	3.5-quart or larger air fryer	5.25-quart or larger air fryer
5- to 6-ounce boneless skinless chicken thighs, trimmed of any fat blobs	2	3	4
Purchased ranch dressing	¼ cup	⅓ cup	½ cup
Plain panko bread crumbs (gluten-free, if a concern)	1 cup	1½ cups	2 cups
Vegetable oil spray	As needed	As needed	As needed
MAKES	2 chicken thighs	3 chicken thighs	4 chicken thighs

1. With the basket (or basket attachment) in the air fryer, heat it to 375°F (or 370°F or 360°F, if one of these is the closest setting).

2. Place the chicken in a bowl and add the dressing. Stir and toss well to coat evenly.

3. Spread the bread crumbs on a plate. Use kitchen tongs to pick up one chicken thigh and set it in the bread crumbs, turning it several times to coat it evenly. Gently shake off any excess bread crumbs, set the thigh on a cutting board, and continue coating the remaining thigh(s).

4. Lightly coat the thighs on both sides with vegetable oil spray, then set them in the basket with as much air space between them as possible. They should not touch. Air-fry undisturbed for 12 minutes, or until golden brown and crisp at the edges.

5. Use kitchen tongs to gently transfer the thighs to a wire rack. Cool for 5 minutes before serving.

Then...

- Try these with a large ORANGE-ROMAINE SALAD. Whisk *⅓ cup olive oil*, *¼ cup red wine vinegar*, *1 tablespoon honey*, *½ teaspoon table salt*, and *½ teaspoon ground black pepper* in a large bowl. Add *1 large head of romaine lettuce, chopped*, and *up to 3 oranges, peeled, any white pith removed, and cut into small segments.* You can also add *up to ¼ cup thinly sliced scallions* to the salad.

Pickle-Brined Fried Chicken Thighs

EASY / CAN BE GLUTEN-FREE / 4 INGREDIENTS

The liquid in a jar of pickles is a highly flavored combination of vinegar, water, and spices that *must* not be wasted, especially since it's a great marinade for chicken, here given a crust with instant mashed potato flakes (sometimes called just "instant mashed potatoes"). Potato flakes give a sweet and crisp finish to the chicken, a nice contrast to the vinegary brine.

Use any pickle brine you like—garlic, dill, sweet, whatever—or a combination of brines, or even the brine from a jar of pickled jalapeño rings, if you like things spicy. If you're not ready to make fried chicken when you finish a jar of pickles, just strain and freeze the brine in a zip-closed plastic bag or a small nonreactive container.

INGREDIENTS	2-quart or larger air fryer	3.5-quart or larger air fryer	5.25-quart or larger air fryer
5- to 6-ounce boneless skinless chicken thighs, trimmed of any fat blobs	2	3	4
Brine from a jar of pickles (gluten-free, if a concern)	½ cup	¾ cup	1 cup
Instant mashed potato flakes	⅔ cup	1 cup	1⅓ cups
Vegetable oil spray	As needed	As needed	As needed
MAKES	2 small thighs	3 small thighs	4 small thighs

1. Put the thighs in a large zip-closed plastic bag, add the pickle brine, and seal the bag. Gently massage the brine into the meat through the plastic, then refrigerate (maybe on a plate in case there are any drips) for at least 2 hours or up to 6 hours, turning the bag and rearranging the chicken pieces occasionally.

2. With the basket (or basket attachment) in the air fryer, heat it to 375°F (or 370°F or 360°F, if one of these is the closest setting).

3. Spread the potato flakes on a large plate. Use kitchen tongs to remove one of the chicken pieces from its bag and set it on the potato flakes. Turn to coat all sides, gently shake off any excess, and set aside. Continue coating the remaining thigh(s).

4. Lightly coat the thighs on both sides with vegetable oil spray. Set them in the basket with as much air space between them as possible. They should not

touch. Air-fry undisturbed for 12 minutes, or until well browned and crisp at the edges.

5. Use kitchen tongs to gently transfer the thighs to a wire rack. Cool for 5 minutes before serving.

Then...

- These thighs would be great drizzled with **Tangy Tahini Dip** (page 48) or served with **Sweet-and-Sour Ketchup Dip** (page 71).

- Try our favorite version of BLUE CHEESE DRESSING on a side salad. Whisk *mayonnaise of any sort (gluten-free, if a concern)* and *crumbled blue cheese* in 2-to-1 volume amounts, then whisk in *a little sour cream* to smooth out the flavors, as well as *a splash of white wine vinegar* and *a dash of Worcestershire sauce (gluten-free, if a concern)*.

Coconut Curry Chicken Thighs

EASY / CAN BE GLUTEN-FREE / 6 INGREDIENTS

In this dish, you can vary the flavors endlessly by using different sorts of Thai curry paste (for more information on them, see page 139). We preferred *massaman* when we were testing the recipes because it offered a milder, more aromatic flavor with a decidedly coconut finish. But you could go with any Thai curry paste, even a fiery red one that will take the skin off of your tongue.

You can also vary the flavors here by using fish sauce rather than soy or tamari sauce. Fish sauce will offer a brinier, muskier finish, a nice contrast to the chicken and coconut milk.

One note: bone-in *skinless* chicken thighs are rarely sold in the U.S. To remove the skin, grasp one bit near a "corner" of the thigh with a paper towel, then peel the skin back and off the meat. Or ask your butcher if she or he would do this job for you. (Tip well!)

INGREDIENTS	2-quart or larger air fryer	3.5-quart or larger air fryer	5.25-quart or larger air fryer
Regular or low-fat coconut milk	¼ cup	6 tablespoons	½ cup
Thai curry paste, preferably *massaman* or yellow curry paste (gluten-free, if a concern)	1 tablespoon	1½ tablespoons	2 tablespoons
Dark brown sugar	2 teaspoons	1 tablespoon	1½ tablespoons
Regular or low-sodium soy sauce, gluten-free tamari sauce, or fish sauce	2 teaspoons	1 tablespoon	1½ tablespoons
Lime juice	1 teaspoon	1½ teaspoons	2 teaspoons
½-pound bone-in skinless chicken thighs, trimmed of any fat blobs	2	3	4
MAKES	*2 large thighs*	*3 large thighs*	*4 large thighs*

1. With the basket (or basket attachment) in the air fryer, heat it to 375°F (or 370°F or 360°F, if one of these is the closest setting).

2. Mix the coconut milk, curry paste, brown sugar, soy or tamari or fish sauce, and lime juice in a bowl. Add the chicken and toss to coat well and evenly.

3. When the machine is at temperature, put the chicken thighs in the basket with as much air space between them as possible. They should not touch. Air-fry undisturbed for 12 minutes, or until well browned and an instant-read meat thermometer inserted into the thickest part of one thigh (without touching bone) registers 165°F.

4. Use kitchen tongs to transfer the thighs to a wire rack. Cool for 5 minutes before serving.

Then...

• Make a SHREDDED MIXED VEGETABLE SALAD by shredding *carrots*, *stemmed radishes*, and *cored cabbage quarters* through the large holes of a box grater. Dress the shreds with *unseasoned rice vinegar* (see page 70) whisked with *granulated white sugar* in a 3-to-1 proportion by volume. Drizzle *toasted sesame oil* over the salad just before serving.

• Or serve these thighs with **Asian Carrot Slaw** (page 250) or even **Sushi Rice** (page 263).

Chicharrones-Crusted Chicken Thighs

CAN BE GLUTEN-FREE / 8 INGREDIENTS

We should have called this recipe "the crispest fried chicken ever." Or maybe "the best chicken recipe ever, no doubt." By grinding pork rinds with bread crumbs, you can create a coating that's absurdly tasty and ridiculously crunchy.

You'll make more coating than the recipe needs, but it's important to have enough so that the thighs get good, even coverage across the meat.

INGREDIENTS	2-quart or larger air fryer	3.5-quart or larger air fryer	5.25-quart or larger air fryer
Pork rinds (chicharrones)	1½ ounces	2 ounces	3 ounces
Plain dried bread crumbs (gluten-free, if a concern)	1½ tablespoons	2 tablespoons	3 tablespoons
Table salt	½ teaspoon	¾ teaspoon	1 teaspoon
Garlic powder	¼ teaspoon	Rounded ¼ teaspoon	½ teaspoon
Cayenne	¼ teaspoon	Rounded ¼ teaspoon	½ teaspoon
5- to 6-ounce boneless skinless chicken thighs, trimmed of any fat blobs	2	3	4
Large egg white(s)	1	1	2
Water	2 tablespoons	2 tablespoons	2 tablespoons
MAKES	*2 small thighs*	*3 small thighs*	*4 small thighs*

1. With the basket (or basket attachment) in the air fryer, heat it to 375°F (or 370°F or 360°F, if one of these is the closest setting).

2. Combine the pork rinds, bread crumbs, salt, garlic powder, and cayenne in a food processor. (You may have to break up the pork rinds so they'll fit.) Cover and process until the pork rinds are coarsely but evenly ground, about like panko bread crumbs. Spread this mixture on a large plate.

3. Beat the egg white(s) and water in a shallow soup plate or small pie plate until foamy. Use kitchen tongs to dip a chicken thigh into the egg white mixture, coating well all over. Set the chicken thigh in the pork rind mixture, turning several times and pressing gently to coat evenly. Set the thigh on a cutting board and continue dipping and coating the remaining chicken thigh(s).

4. Set the chicken thighs in the basket with as much air space between them as possible. They should not touch. Air-fry undisturbed for 14 minutes, or until very crisp and brown.

5. Use kitchen tongs to transfer the thighs to a wire rack. Cool for 5 minutes before serving.

Then...

- You'll want a **Perfect Margarita** (page 43), for sure!
- For a little more than ¾ cup PINEAPPLE BARBECUE SAUCE to serve as a dip with these crunchy thighs, whisk *½ cup ketchup (gluten-free, if a concern), ¼ cup pineapple juice; 1 tablespoon regular or low-sodium soy sauce or gluten-free tamari sauce, 1 teaspoon ground dried ginger,* and up to *¼ teaspoon cayenne* in a small bowl until smooth.

Korean-Style Fried Chicken Thighs

CAN BE GLUTEN-FREE / 11 INGREDIENTS

These sweet-and-salty chicken thighs—an aromatic mix of garlic, ginger, chile paste, and sesame oil—would also be great as a snack for a crowd before dinner. Just cut each cooked thigh half into two or three pieces and serve them on toothpicks.

The marinade is particularly flavorful. As the chicken gets a little dried out by the air fryer, it will absorb every remaining drop. If you run out of marinade and find you need more to brush them with, substitute Thai sweet chili sauce for the remainder in step 5.

INGREDIENTS	2-quart or larger air fryer	3.5-quart or larger air fryer	5.25-quart or larger air fryer
Regular or low-sodium soy sauce or gluten-free tamari sauce	1½ tablespoons	2 tablespoons	¼ cup
Minced garlic	2 teaspoons	1 tablespoon	2 tablespoons
Minced peeled fresh ginger	2 teaspoons	1 tablespoon	2 tablespoons
Sambal oelek or other pulpy hot red pepper sauce (see page 184)	Up to 2 teaspoons	Up to 1 tablespoon	Up to 2 tablespoons
Light brown sugar	2 teaspoons	1 tablespoon	1½ tablespoons
Unseasoned rice vinegar (see page 70)	2 teaspoons	1 tablespoon	1½ tablespoons
Toasted sesame oil	2 teaspoons	1 tablespoon	1½ tablespoons
Boneless skinless chicken thighs, trimmed of any fat blobs and cut in half	¾ pound	1¼ pounds	2 pounds
All-purpose flour or gluten-free all-purpose flour	1 cup	1 cup	1½ cups
Cornstarch	¼ cup	¼ cup	6 tablespoons
Vegetable oil spray	As needed	As needed	As needed
MAKES	2 servings	4 servings	6 servings

1. Mix the soy sauce, garlic, ginger, sambal oelek, brown sugar, vinegar, and sesame oil in a bowl. Add the chicken and toss well to coat. Set aside on the counter for 20 minutes, tossing once.

2. With the basket (or basket attachment) in the air fryer, heat it to 375°F (or 370°F or 360°F, if one of these is the closest setting).

3. Whisk the flour and cornstarch in a large bowl. Use kitchen tongs to transfer the chicken pieces from the marinade to this bowl. Toss until well coated. Shake off any excess. Coat each piece of chicken on all sides with vegetable oil spray.

4. Set the chicken pieces in the basket in as close to one layer as you can. Air-fry undisturbed for 10 minutes.

continues

5. Brush the thighs in the machine with any remaining marinade left in the bowl. If any thighs have overlapped, rearrange them so those covered bits are now exposed. Continue air-frying undisturbed for 5 minutes, or until crisp and aromatic.

6. Use kitchen tongs to transfer the chicken pieces to a wire rack. Cool for 5 minutes before serving.

Then...

- Serve these with cooked white rice, garnished with kimchi.

- If you're lucky enough to live near an H Mart, you'll find a wide range of vinegary Korean condiments that will work perfectly with these thighs. Set out the condiments in bowls so everyone can pick and choose at will.

Chicken Yakitori Skewers

CAN BE GLUTEN-FREE / 7 INGREDIENTS PLUS BAMBOO SKEWERS

Although true Japanese sweet-and-salty yakitori skewers are grilled over charcoal, they can get done in much less time and with a cleaner flavor in the air fryer. You must brush the glaze on the skewered meat as it cooks. Use a pastry brush to get the sauce down into all the nooks and crannies. And don't forget to brush the scallions, too!

One ingredient note: **Mirin** is a rice wine, favored in cooking, sort of like sake, but with a lower alcohol content and a higher sugar content. A good substitute for each tablespoon is 1 tablespoon fruity white wine (like Pinot Grigio) and ¼ teaspoon granulated white sugar—or if you don't want the alcohol, then an equivalent amount of white grape juice (preferably) or unsweetened apple juice.

INGREDIENTS	2-quart or larger air fryer	3.5-quart or larger air fryer	5.25-quart or larger air fryer
Regular or low-sodium soy sauce or gluten-free tamari sauce	¼ cup	6 tablespoons	½ cup
Mirin (see the headnote)	¼ cup	6 tablespoons	½ cup
Dry sake or dry white wine	2 tablespoons	3 tablespoons	¼ cup
Light brown sugar	1½ teaspoons	2½ teaspoons	1 tablespoon
Boneless skinless chicken thighs, cut into 1½-inch pieces, trimmed of any fat blobs	¾ pound	1 pound	1½ pounds
Trimmed medium scallions, cut into 1½-inch pieces	2	3	4
Vegetable oil spray	As needed	As needed	As needed
MAKES	2 servings	3 servings	4 servings

1. Stir the soy or tamari sauce, mirin, sake or wine, and brown sugar in a small saucepan set over medium heat. Bring to a boil, stirring quite often. Boil for 1 minute for a small batch, 1½ minutes for a medium batch, or 2 minutes for a large batch, stirring frequently, until slightly thickened. Remove the pan from the heat.

2. With the basket (or basket attachment) in the air fryer, heat it to 400°F (or 390°F, if that's the closest setting).

3. Alternate the chicken pieces and scallions (these, widthwise) on 4-inch bamboo skewers. Lightly coat both sides of the meat and scallions with vegetable oil spray.

4. When the machine is at temperature, pile the skewers into the basket, overlapping as necessary. Air-fry undisturbed for 5 minutes.

5. Brush all of the skewers in the machine all over (not just the tops of some of them) with the soy sauce mixture. Rearrange the skewers and continue air-frying undisturbed for 5 minutes.

6. Brush the chicken and scallions again, then air-fry undisturbed for 5 minutes more, until the chicken and scallions have caramelized at the edges.

7. Use kitchen tongs to transfer the skewers to a wire rack. Cool for 5 minutes before serving.

Then...

- Yakitori should be served over cooked rice— but don't stick with the standard. Go with white medium-grain rice (like Arborio) or even short-grain white sticky rice. Or serve the skewers over **Sushi Rice** (page 263).

- Although it's not traditional, we like these skewers with **Vinegary Cucumbers** (page 131).

Chicken 65

GLUTEN-FREE / 11 INGREDIENTS

There are a million stories about how this dish got its name. While most indicate it was created by A. M. Buhari of the eponymous Buhari Hotel in Chennai, India, there are myriad stories for *why* the dish ended up with this strange name. Some claim it's because the original required sixty-five chiles; others, because it was served to weary Indian soldiers in 1965; and still others, because it was the sixty-fifth item on the menu.

Whatever its origins, there are now two versions of this deeply flavored dish: one done in a skillet with a spicy sauce and one that features highly spiced fried chicken pieces. This second version is ripe for an air-fryer adaptation.

The dish isn't complete after the chicken and chiles come out of the machine. It still needs condiments and accompaniments, as you'll see in the note following the recipe.

INGREDIENTS	2-quart or larger air fryer	3.5-quart or larger air fryer	5.25-quart or larger air fryer
Boneless skinless chicken thighs, trimmed of any fat blobs and cut into 1½-inch pieces	¾ pound	1 pound	1½ pounds
Ground coriander	Rounded ¼ teaspoon	½ teaspoon	¾ teaspoon
Ground cumin	Rounded ¼ teaspoon	½ teaspoon	¾ teaspoon
Ground dried ginger	Rounded ¼ teaspoon	½ teaspoon	¾ teaspoon
Garam masala (see page 156)	Rounded ¼ teaspoon	½ teaspoon	¾ teaspoon
Garlic powder	Rounded ¼ teaspoon	½ teaspoon	¾ teaspoon
Table salt	Rounded ¼ teaspoon	½ teaspoon	¾ teaspoon
Cayenne	Up to ¼ teaspoon	Up to ½ teaspoon	Up to ¾ teaspoon
Distilled white vinegar	¾ teaspoon	1 teaspoon	1½ teaspoons
Tapioca flour	1½ teaspoons	2 teaspoons	2½ teaspoons
Small fresh jalapeño chile(s), stemmed and sliced into ½-inch-thick rings	1	2	2
MAKES	*2 to 3 servings*	*3 to 4 servings*	*5 to 6 servings*

1. With the basket (or basket attachment) in the air fryer, heat it to 400°F (or 390°F, if that's the closest setting).

2. Mix the chicken pieces, coriander, cumin, ginger, garam masala, garlic powder, salt, and cayenne in a bowl until the chicken is evenly coated in the spices.

3. Add the vinegar and toss well to blend. Finally, add the tapioca flour and mix well until the chicken is evenly coated.

4. When the machine is at temperature, pour the chicken into the basket and spread the pieces out in as close to a single layer as you can. Air-fry for 10 minutes, tossing the basket and rearranging the pieces at the 5-minute mark so that any covered parts are now exposed.

5. After 10 minutes, toss again, add the jalapeño slices, and air-fry undisturbed for 5 minutes more, or until the chicken is crisp and brown. Pour the contents of the basket onto a serving platter. Serve hot.

Then...

- Serve this dish with cooked long-grain white rice as well as a chutney of some sort and CUCUMBER AND CILANTRO RAITA. For 4 servings, mix together *1 or 2 medium cucumbers, peeled, halved, seeded, and chopped; 2 to 2½ cups plain full-fat yogurt; 2 to 3 tablespoons minced fresh cilantro leaves; 1 to 1½ teaspoons cumin seeds; 1 to 1½ teaspoons minced garlic; and a little table salt.* Have naan on the side, too!

See photo in insert.

Better-Than-Chinese-Take-Out Orange Chicken

CAN BE GLUTEN-FREE / 13 INGREDIENTS

This recipe is the first of several that uses a combination of the air fryer and a wok on the stove to create a Chinese-American classic. In the traditional method, the chicken is breaded and deep-fried, then stir-fried with the other ingredients. Here, you air-fry the chicken until it is crisp without having to waste time—and calories—with breading and deep-frying. Then head to the wok to turn that chicken into a dish worth the best cooked white rice you can comfortably afford.

One ingredient note: **Hoisin sauce** is a sweet condiment, often made from soy beans or sweet potatoes, usually with molasses, vinegar, and chiles in the mix. There are gluten-free versions on the market, if this is a concern.

INGREDIENTS	2-quart or larger air fryer	3.5-quart or larger air fryer	5.25-quart or larger air fryer
Boneless skinless chicken thighs, trimmed of any fat blobs and cut into 1-inch pieces	¾ pound	1 pound	1½ pounds
Regular or low-sodium soy sauce or gluten-free tamari sauce	2 tablespoons	2 tablespoons plus 2 teaspoons	¼ cup
Cornstarch	1¼ teaspoons	1 tablespoon	1½ tablespoons
Small broccoli florets	9 ounces (2¼ cups)	¾ pound (about 3 cups)	1¼ pounds (about 4½ cups)
Water	1½ teaspoons	1 tablespoon	1½ tablespoons
Orange juice	3 tablespoons	¼ cup	6 tablespoons
Unseasoned rice vinegar (see page 70)	1½ tablespoons	2 tablespoons	3 tablespoons
Hoisin sauce (see the headnote; gluten-free, if a concern)	1½ tablespoons	2 tablespoons	3 tablespoons
Sambal oelek or other pulpy hot red pepper sauce (see page 184)	Up to 1½ tablespoons	Up to 2 tablespoons	Up to 3 tablespoons
Honey	2 teaspoons	1 tablespoon	1½ tablespoons
Vegetable oil spray	As needed	As needed	As needed
Medium scallions, trimmed and thinly sliced	3	4	6
Minced peeled fresh ginger	2 teaspoons	1 tablespoon	1½ tablespoons
MAKES	2 to 3 servings	3 to 4 servings	5 to 6 servings

1. In a bowl, toss the chicken pieces with 1½ teaspoons of the soy sauce and ½ teaspoon of the cornstarch for a small batch, 2 teaspoons of the soy sauce and 1 teaspoon of the cornstarch for a medium batch, or 2 tablespoons of the soy sauce and 1½ teaspoons of the cornstarch for a large batch. Set aside while the machine heats.

2. With the basket (or basket attachment) in the air fryer, heat it to 400°F (or 390°F, if that's the closest setting).

3. When the machine is at temperature, put the chicken pieces in the basket and air-fry for 15 minutes, breaking them up and tossing them after 5 minutes and then tossing them again at the 10-minute mark, until brown and crisp. Transfer the chicken pieces to a clean bowl.

4. Put the broccoli florets in the basket and air-fry undisturbed for 4 minutes, or until slightly softened but still crunchy overall. Pour the florets into the bowl with the chicken. Turn off the air fryer.

5. *For a small batch*, whisk the remaining ¾ teaspoon cornstarch with the water in a small bowl until smooth. Whisk the remaining 1½ tablespoons soy sauce with the orange juice, rice vinegar, hoisin sauce, sambal oelek, and honey in a second bowl until uniform.

For a medium batch, whisk the remaining 2 teaspoons cornstarch with the water in a small bowl until smooth. Whisk the remaining 2 tablespoons soy sauce with the orange juice, rice vinegar, hoisin sauce, sambal oelek, and honey in a second bowl until uniform.

For a large batch, whisk the remaining 1 tablespoon cornstarch with the water in a small bowl until smooth. Whisk the remaining 2 tablespoons soy sauce with the orange juice, rice vinegar, hoisin sauce, sambal oelek, and honey in a second bowl until uniform.

6. Coat the inside of a large wok with vegetable oil spray, then set it over high heat for a couple of minutes. Add the scallion and ginger; stir-fry for 20 seconds, until fragrant. Add the chicken and broccoli; stir-fry for 1 minute to heat through.

7. Add the soy sauce mixture and stir-fry until bubbling, just a few seconds. Add the cornstarch slurry and stir-fry until thickened, less than 1 minute. Remove from the heat and serve hot.

Then...

- To go over the top, skip the cooked rice and serve this stir-fry over boiled and drained rice noodles, cooked according to the package directions.

- Garnish the servings with sesame seeds, minced fresh scallions, toasted sesame oil, and/or fresh cilantro leaves.

See photo in insert.

Better-Than-Chinese-Take-Out Chicken and Asparagus

CAN BE GLUTEN-FREE / 11 INGREDIENTS

This recipe's a little different from the Orange Chicken stir-fry riff (page 180). For one thing, it's easier! You'll start with chicken already cut for stir-fries, available in almost all supermarkets. (Discard any seasoning packet.) Then you'll make the entire dish right in the machine by turning a cake pan into a makeshift wok.

Although you can make a small two-serving batch in a large machine, use only the cake pan size designated for the smaller batch, since the smaller cake pan will hold the ingredients without letting them get too dried out because they're spread out too much. Some air fryer models come with an accessory that's a bread pan or cake pan. Feel free to use that instead of a more standard cake pan.

You can substitute crunchy peanut butter for the smooth, if you'd prefer little bits of peanut in the stir-fry.

INGREDIENTS	2-quart or larger air fryer	3.5-quart or larger air fryer	5.25-quart or larger air fryer
Toasted sesame oil	2 teaspoons	1 tablespoon	1½ tablespoons
Natural-style creamy peanut butter	1½ teaspoons	2 teaspoons	1 tablespoon
Unseasoned rice vinegar (see page 70)	1½ teaspoons	2 teaspoons	1 tablespoon
Worcestershire sauce (gluten-free, if a concern)	1 teaspoon	1½ teaspoons	2 teaspoons
Granulated white sugar	1 teaspoon	1½ teaspoons	2 teaspoons
Sriracha	½ teaspoon	1 teaspoon	1 teaspoon
Thin asparagus spears, cut into 1½-inch pieces	1 cup (5 ounces)	1½ cups (7½ ounces)	2 cups (10 ounces)
Boneless skinless chicken breast cut for stir-fry	¾ pound	1 pound	1½ pounds
Minced peeled fresh ginger	1 tablespoon	1½ tablespoons	2 tablespoons
Large single-lobe shallot, peeled and thinly sliced	½	1	1
Medium garlic clove(s), peeled and thinly sliced	1	1	2
MAKES	2 servings	3 servings	4 servings

1. With the basket (or basket attachment) in the air fryer, heat it to 400°F (or 390°F, if that's the closest setting).

2. Whisk the oil, peanut butter, vinegar, Worcestershire sauce, sugar, and sriracha in a large bowl until as smooth as possible.

3. When the machine is at temperature, put the asparagus pieces in the basket. Air-fry undisturbed for 5 minutes, or until crisp-tender but a bit softened. Pour the spears from the basket into the oil mixture.

4. Set a 6-inch round cake pan in a small model's basket or a 7-inch round cake pan in a medium or large model's basket. Put the chicken, ginger, shallot, and garlic in the pan. Air-fry for 12 minutes, stirring twice, until the chicken has cooked through.

5. Pour and scrape the asparagus and other contents of the bowl into the cake pan. Toss well. Air-fry undisturbed for 1 minute, or until the sauce is bubbling. Remove the pan from the machine using kitchen tongs and serve the stir-fry hot.

Then...

- Although stir-fries are most often served over cooked rice in North America, they're sometimes served over wilted greens in China. This "stir-fry" would be a great candidate to go over wilted spinach, baby kale, or even chopped bok choy.

- Or try it over **Crispy Noodle Salad** (page 317).

Better-Than-Chinese-Take-Out Kung Pao Chicken

CAN BE GLUTEN-FREE / 13 INGREDIENTS

This spicy, peanut-laced stir-fry favorite is yet a third technique for stir-fries from the air fryer. Here, you'll cook the chicken in the appliance until quite crisp, then you'll make a fairly traditional sauce on the stove to spoon over the chicken on a platter just before serving. The results are dramatic. Make sure someone posts a shot of the dish (and tags you).

Sambal oelek is one of dozens of pulpy hot red pepper sauces popular in Indonesia, Brunei, and Sri Lanka, grouped under the name "sambal." Sambal oelek is the most common varietal found in North America, a bright red pepper sauce usually made with plenty of salt and lime juice. It's super hot, so use it sparingly until you get the hang of it. Almost any sambal would work in the recipes in this book. *Sambal bajak* is particularly appealing, with lots of garlic and a little sugar, but it can be hard to find outside of specialty markets.

INGREDIENTS	2-quart or larger air fryer	3.5-quart or larger air fryer	5.25-quart or larger air fryer
Boneless skinless chicken thighs, trimmed of any fat blobs and cut into 1-inch pieces	1 pound	1½ pounds	2 pounds
Vegetable or canola oil	1½ teaspoons	2 teaspoons	1 tablespoon
Table salt	½ teaspoon	¾ teaspoon	1 teaspoon
Chicken broth	¼ cup plus 2 tablespoons	⅔ cup	¾ cup
Diced carrots	¼ cup	¼ cup plus 2 tablespoons	½ cup
Unsalted peanuts	2 tablespoons	3 tablespoons	¼ cup
Regular or low-sodium soy sauce or gluten-free tamari sauce	1½ tablespoons	2½ tablespoons	3 tablespoons
Unseasoned rice vinegar (see page 70)	1½ tablespoons	2½ tablespoons	3 tablespoons
Granulated white sugar	2 teaspoons	1 tablespoon	1½ tablespoons
Minced peeled fresh ginger	1½ teaspoons	2½ teaspoons	1 tablespoon
Sambal oelek or other pulpy hot red pepper sauce	1½ teaspoons	1 tablespoon	1½ tablespoons
Cornstarch	1½ teaspoons	2 teaspoons	1 tablespoon
Water	2 teaspoons	1 tablespoon	1½ tablespoons
MAKES	*3 servings*	*4 servings*	*6 servings*

1. With the basket (or basket attachment) in the air fryer, heat it to 400°F (or 390°F, if that's the closest setting).

2. When the machine is at temperature, mix the chicken pieces, oil, and salt in a large bowl. Dump this mixture into the basket. Air-fry for 25 minutes, tossing and rearranging the pieces twice, until *very* brown and crunchy.

3. Meanwhile, mix the broth, carrots, peanuts, soy or tamari sauce, vinegar, sugar, ginger, and sambal oelek in a small or medium saucepan. Set over medium heat and bring to a simmer, stirring occasionally. Whisk the cornstarch into the water in a small bowl, then stir this slurry into the simmering broth mixture. Cook, stirring constantly, until somewhat thickened, about 1 minute. Cover and keep warm until the chicken is ready in the air fryer.

4. Pour the chicken from the basket onto a platter. Pour and scrape the sauce from the saucepan over the chicken just before serving.

Then...

• Garnish the platter with minced fresh cilantro leaves and/or minced chives or the green parts of a scallion.

• Serve this "stir-fry" over a combination of cooked rice and millet. You can substitute millet for half the raw white rice in any batch, using the same amount of water or broth you would have used for all rice. The millet will taste better if the small grains are toasted for a minute or two in a dry saucepan before you add the rice and broth.

Tandoori Chicken Legs

EASY / GLUTEN-FREE / 10 INGREDIENTS

An air fryer is *not* a tandoori oven. But because the air moves at such a fast rate and at such a close range, the coating for these chicken legs gets bound up with the natural juices to create an irresistible if healthier version of the South Asian favorite.

Finding *skinless* bone-in chicken legs is next to impossible. You can ask the butcher at your supermarket to remove the skin for you. Or do it yourself by grasping the skin with a paper towel at the thick end of the leg and then stripping the skin along the leg and "inside out" over the small end.

INGREDIENTS	2-quart or larger air fryer	3.5-quart or larger air fryer	5.25-quart or larger air fryer
Plain full-fat or low-fat yogurt	¼ cup	6 tablespoons	½ cup
Buttermilk	2 tablespoons	3 tablespoons	¼ cup
Minced garlic	1 teaspoon	1½ teaspoons	2 teaspoons
Minced peeled fresh ginger	1 teaspoon	1½ teaspoons	2 teaspoons
Ground cinnamon	1 teaspoon	1½ teaspoons	2 teaspoons
Ground coriander	1 teaspoon	1½ teaspoons	2 teaspoons
Mild paprika	1 teaspoon	1½ teaspoons	2 teaspoons
Table salt	½ teaspoon	¾ teaspoon	1 teaspoon
Hot red pepper sauce, such as Cholula or Tabasco (gluten-free, if a concern)	Up to ½ teaspoon	Up to ½ teaspoon	Up to 1 teaspoon
4- to 5-ounce skinless bone-in chicken legs	4	6	8
MAKES	*2 servings*	*3 servings*	*4 servings*

1. Mix the yogurt, buttermilk, garlic, ginger, cinnamon, coriander, paprika, salt, and hot pepper sauce in a large bowl. Add the chicken legs and toss well to coat. Cover and refrigerate for 1 hour, tossing once.

2. With the basket (or basket attachment) in the air fryer, heat it to 375°F (or 370°F or 360°F, if one of these is the closest setting).

3. When the machine is at temperature, arrange the legs in the basket in one layer with as much air space between them as you can leave open. Air-fry undisturbed for 14 minutes, or until brown and an instant-read meat thermometer inserted into the center of the thickest part of a leg (without touching bone) registers 160°F.

4. Use kitchen tongs to transfer the legs to a wire rack. Cool for 5 minutes before serving.

Then...

- Serve these legs with cooked long-grain white rice and chutney (even **Blueberry Chutney**, page 73) as well as **Cucumber and Cilantro Raita** (page 179).

- To make your own version of the aromatic Indian rice often favored with tandoori dishes, cook *long-grain white rice* with a bit of *cinnamon stick*, a few *cardamom pods*, and a little *ground dried turmeric*. When done, discard the cinnamon stick and cardamom pods, then toss the rice with *toasted unsalted cashews* and *raisins*

Crunchy Chicken Wings

EASY / GLUTEN-FREE / 5 INGREDIENTS

Rather than air-frying whole wings, you'll get them crunchier if you work with only drumettes and winglets, the two parts of the wing often sold separately. If you have to buy whole wings and separate them yourself, buy an additional ¼ to ½ pound wings, since you'll be removing and discarding the flapper portion of each wing.

Although these wings are tasty on their own, check out the two saucing options that follow.

INGREDIENTS	2-quart or larger air fryer	3.5-quart or larger air fryer	5.25-quart or larger air fryer
Chicken wing drumettes and/or winglets	2 pounds	3 pounds	4 pounds
Mild paprika	1 teaspoon	1½ teaspoons	2 teaspoons
Table salt	1 teaspoon	1½ teaspoons	2 teaspoons
Ground black pepper	½ teaspoon	¾ teaspoon	1 teaspoon
Garlic powder	½ teaspoon	¾ teaspoon	1 teaspoon
MAKES	*4 servings*	*6 servings*	*8 servings*

1. With the basket (or basket attachment) in the air fryer, heat it to 400°F (or 390°F, if that's the closest setting).

2. Toss the wing pieces, paprika, salt, pepper, and garlic powder in a bowl until the chicken is evenly coated in the spices.

3. When the machine is at temperature, dump the wing pieces into the basket. Air-fry for 25 minutes, tossing and rearranging the chicken pieces twice so that covered parts get exposed, until dark brown and crisp.

4. Dump the contents of the basket onto a wire rack. Cool for 5 minutes before serving.

Then...

- Make **BUFFALO SAUCE**. Whisk *melted butter* and *Frank's RedHot* in a 4-to-3 proportion by volume in a large bowl. When the wings are done, dump them (while hot) in this sauce and toss until thoroughly coated. Pour the sauced wings onto a platter and crumble *blue cheese* over the top.

- Or make an aromatic dip by whisking *Thai sweet chili sauce* and *minced fresh cilantro leaves* in a 2-to-1 proportion by volume in a large bowl. When the wings are done, dump them (while hot) into this sauce and toss until thoroughly coated. Pour the sauced wings onto a platter and sprinkle with chopped unsalted peanuts.

See photo in insert.

Barbecue-Style Chicken Wings

EASY / CAN BE GLUTEN-FREE / 3 INGREDIENTS

By mixing the brine from a jar of dill pickles with barbecue sauce, we moderate the sweetness of the sauce as it condenses in the air fryer, thereby creating more flavorful wings that aren't just a sticky mess. You can use any smooth barbecue sauce you like, but remember that the brine is highly flavored. Plainer is probably better.

There's a lower cooking temperature in this recipe than in the one for **Crunchy Chicken Wings** (previous page). The problem is the coating, which can burn fairly quickly. These wings need to go longer at a lower temperature to get the coating to turn into a lacquered glaze.

INGREDIENTS	2-quart or larger air fryer	3.5-quart or larger air fryer	5.25-quart or larger air fryer
Chicken wing drumettes and/or winglets	1 pound	1¾ pounds	2½ pounds
Purchased smooth barbecue sauce, any sort (gluten-free, if a concern)	1 tablespoon	2 tablespoons	3 tablespoons
Brine from a jar of dill pickles (gluten-free, if a concern)	1 tablespoon	2 tablespoons	3 tablespoons
MAKES	3 servings	4 servings	6 servings

1. With the basket (or basket attachment) in the air fryer, heat it to 350°F (or 360°F, if that's the closest setting).

2. Toss the wing pieces, barbecue sauce, and brine in a bowl until the meat is evenly coated.

3. When the machine is at temperature, transfer the wing pieces to the basket. Air-fry for 35 minutes, tossing and rearranging the wing pieces three times so that covered parts get exposed, until very brown and lacquered.

4. Dump the contents of the basket onto a wire rack. Cool for 5 minutes before serving.

Then...

- Serve these with **Tangy Jalapeño Dip** (page 151) or **Blue Cheese Dressing** (page 172).
- And with **Lime-Cumin Slaw** (page 276).

Balsamic–Brown Sugar Chicken Wings

CAN BE GLUTEN-FREE / 4 INGREDIENTS

If you're hankering for sweet and sticky wings, this is your recipe. The same concerns are here as in the other wing recipes—that is, that winglet and drumette pieces work better than whole wings. That's because pieces cook more evenly and because whole wings are closed up so you can't get sauce into the spaces between the parts, which means they can't get crunchy along all their exterior surfaces.

INGREDIENTS	2-quart or larger air fryer	3.5-quart or larger air fryer	5.25-quart or larger air fryer
Chicken wing drumettes and/or winglets	1 pound	1¾ pounds	2½ pounds
Balsamic vinegar	1 tablespoon	2 tablespoons	3 tablespoons
Dark brown sugar	1 tablespoon	2 tablespoons	3 tablespoons
Dijon mustard (gluten-free, if a concern)	1 teaspoon	2 teaspoons	1 tablespoon
MAKES	3 servings	4 servings	6 servings

1. With the basket (or basket attachment) in the air fryer, heat it to 350°F (or 360°F, if that's the closest setting).

2. Toss the wing pieces, vinegar, brown sugar, and mustard in a bowl until the pieces are evenly coated.

3. When the machine is at temperature, transfer the wing pieces to the basket. Air-fry for 35 minutes, tossing and rearranging the wing pieces three times so that covered parts get exposed, until dark brown and crisp.

4. Dump the contents of the basket onto a wire rack and cool for 5 minutes before serving.

Then...

- These wings would be tasty alongside **Green Bean and Tomato Salad** (page 119) or **Honey Mustard Cole Slaw** (page 215).

- Go over the top with BUTTERY GARLIC DIP on the side. Mix together *melted butter*, *minced garlic*, *red pepper flakes*, and *a pinch of salt*. For more flavor, also add *dried oregano*. If you have some warmed potato rolls on the side, it wouldn't be a shame if a little corner or two fell in that dip along with the wings.

Crispy Chicken Gizzards

CAN BE GLUTEN-FREE / 4 INGREDIENTS

Don't get squeamish. Chicken gizzards are an amazing treat: meaty, chewy, and a little gamy. They can make a great dinner with a vinegary salad on the side. Or they can be a nibble on the patio when the summer's heat tones down a bit in the evening. In that case, cut the gizzards into small bits after cooking and serve them on toothpicks.

Make sure you buy cleaned gizzards. Most of those in a supermarket are split open and cleaned; ask to be sure. If you buy the gizzards at a farmers' market, they may still be whole and filled with grass and grit. Split them open, peel off the tough inner layer of tissue, and wash out their inner chambers.

Because gizzards are tough, they need a head start before they get in the air fryer, a bit of time boiling in a saucepan on the stove, so they can get tender before any coating burns.

INGREDIENTS	2-quart or larger air fryer	3.5-quart or larger air fryer	5.25-quart or larger air fryer
Cleaned chicken gizzards (about ¾ ounce each)	½ pound	¾ pound	1 pound
Buttermilk	2 tablespoons	3 tablespoons	¼ cup
Seasoned Italian-style dried bread crumbs (gluten-free, if a concern)	¾ cup	1 cup	1½ cups
Olive oil spray	As needed	As needed	As needed
MAKES	2 servings	3 servings	4 servings

1. Place the gizzards in a medium saucepan and cover them with water until they're submerged by an inch or so. Bring to a boil over high heat, stirring occasionally. Cover, reduce the heat to low, and simmer slowly for 30 minutes. Drain the gizzards in a colander set in the sink and cool for 20 minutes.

2. With the basket (or basket attachment) in the air fryer, heat it to 400°F (or 390°F, if that's the closest setting).

3. Toss the gizzards in a bowl with the buttermilk until they are evenly coated.

4. Pour the bread crumbs into a second bowl. Use a slotted spoon to pick up a few gizzards, letting the excess buttermilk drip off, and transfer them to the bread crumbs. Continue transferring all the gizzards to the bread crumbs, then toss well until the gizzards are evenly coated.

5. Set the coated gizzards on a cutting board and lightly coat them all over with olive oil spray.

6. Put them in the basket in as close to a single layer as you can. Air-fry undisturbed for 6 minutes, then toss gently and rearrange the pieces so that the covered parts have now been exposed. Continue air-frying for 6 minutes more, or until well browned and crisp.

7. Gently pour the gizzards onto a wire rack (to keep the coating intact). Cool for 5 minutes before serving.

Then...

- Chicken gizzards are often sold with chicken hearts. If you've got some hearts left, too, turn them into ANTICUCHOS, a Peruvian delicacy. Toss the hearts with a little *red wine vinegar* and *olive oil*, as well *dried oregano*, *minced garlic*, and *red pepper flakes*. Refrigerate to marinate for 1 hour, tossing occasionally. Then skewer the hearts and grill them over high heat for 7 minutes, turning occasionally, or until well browned. Or put them in the air fryer basket with the machine at 400°F (or 390°F, if that's the closest setting) and air-fry for 10 minutes, tossing twice, until well browned and even a little crunchy.

Rotisserie-Style Air-Roasted Chicken

GLUTEN-FREE / 7 INGREDIENTS

Why would you use an air fryer to cook a whole chicken? Because doing so is like putting the bird in the most intense convection oven ever. The skin gets crisp while the meat stays juicy.

If you're working with a small air fryer, you'll only be able to cook half a chicken. It should be split so that each half has a thigh, a leg, a breast, and a wing. Put the chicken breast side up on a cutting board. Insert a large knife into the large cavity and slice down on either side of the spine. Turn the chicken over and open it out flat. Then slice down on either side of the breast bone to create the two halves. Or hand a whole chicken to the butcher at your market and ask her or him to do the deed for you.

One note: There can be a fair amount of smoking with all the chicken fat that gets rendered. If your air fryer allows it, pour ½ cup water in the drawer underneath the basket to mitigate the grease's burning. Some air fryers use racks and trays; these could never handle this much water. You'll either need to skip the water and open the windows for the smoke or keep adding water in small amounts to a tray set under the rack with the chicken.

INGREDIENTS	2-quart or larger air fryer	3.5-quart or larger air fryer	5.25-quart or larger air fryer
Whole chicken, giblets and neck removed from the inner cavities as well as any fat blobs	Half a 3½-pound chicken	One 3- to 3½-pound chicken	One 4- to 4½-pound chicken
Olive oil spray	As needed	As needed	As needed
Mild paprika	¼ teaspoon	½ teaspoon	¾ teaspoon
Onion powder	¼ teaspoon	½ teaspoon	¾ teaspoon
Garlic powder	¼ teaspoon	Rounded ¼ teaspoon	½ teaspoon
Table salt	¼ teaspoon	½ teaspoon	1 teaspoon
Ground black pepper	¼ teaspoon	½ teaspoon	1 teaspoon
MAKES	*2 servings*	*4 servings*	*6 servings*

continues

1. With the basket (or basket attachment) in the air fryer, heat it to 375°F (or 370°F or 360°F, if one of these is the closest setting).

2. Generously coat the chicken all over with olive oil spray. Set it breast side up on a cutting board and sprinkle it with the paprika, onion powder, garlic powder, salt, and pepper.

3. When the machine is at temperature, if cooking a whole chicken set it *breast side down* in the basket. If making a small batch (that is, half a chicken), set it *skin side down* in the basket. Air-fry the small batch undisturbed for 20 minutes, the medium batch undisturbed for 30 minutes, or the large batch undisturbed for 40 minutes.

4. Use kitchen tongs and a metal spatula to turn the chicken over in the basket. Continue air-frying the small batch undisturbed for another 20 minutes, the medium batch undisturbed for another 30 minutes, or the large batch undisturbed for another 40 minutes, or until the chicken is golden brown and an instant-read meat thermometer inserted into the breast and the thigh (without touching bone) registers 160°F. If the machine is at 360°F, you may need to add up to 5 minutes to the cooking time.

5. Use kitchen tongs and a nonstick-safe spatula to transfer the chicken to a cutting board. Be very careful of hot juices inside the whole chicken, juices that can pour out onto the counter—or worse, scald pets underfoot. Cool the bird for 10 minutes, then carve and serve.

Then...

- The easiest way to carve a chicken is with poultry or kitchen shears. You can cut between the thighs and legs, between the thighs and breast, and even cut the breast into chunks if you want.

- Serve this roast chicken with **Perfect Asparagus** (page 342), **Perfect Broccolini** (page 347), and/or **Charred Radicchio Salad** (page 352).

- Roast a chicken, then cool it for 20 minutes and store in the fridge for the week ahead. Now you've got chicken for chicken salad, sandwiches, and dishes like **Taquitos** (page 168) and **Flautas** (page 169).

Nacho Turkey Cutlets

FAST / EASY / CAN BE GLUTEN-FREE / 5 INGREDIENTS

By using ground nacho-flavored corn chips, you can turn everyday turkey cutlets into something special, a sort of cross between our favorite Tex-Mex snack and dinner. There's no added salt here because the chips carry plenty.

The best way to grind the chips is in a food processor, so long as you're willing to stop the machine a couple of times to rearrange the chips. The final consistency should be something like panko bread crumbs, not as tiny as traditional dried bread crumbs.

INGREDIENTS	2-quart or larger air fryer	3.5-quart or larger air fryer	5.25-quart or larger air fryer
Large egg white(s)	1	1	2
Lime juice	1 tablespoon	1 tablespoon	2 tablespoons
Ground Nacho Cheese Doritos or other nacho-flavored corn chips (gluten-free, if a concern)	1 cup (from about 4 ounces chips)	1½ cups (from about 6 ounces chips)	2½ cups (from about 10 ounces chips)
6-ounce turkey cutlet(s)	1	2	3
Vegetable oil spray	As needed	As needed	As needed
MAKES	1 serving	2 servings	3 servings

1. With the basket (or basket attachment) in the air fryer, heat it to 375°F (or 370°F or 360°F, if one of these is the closest setting).

2. Set up and fill two shallow soup plates or small pie plates on your counter: the first for the egg white(s) whisked with the lime juice until foamy; the second for the crushed chips.

3. Use kitchen tongs to pick up a cutlet and dip it in the egg white mixture on both sides. Pick the cutlet up to let any excess egg white slip back into the rest, then set the cutlet in the ground chips. Turn it a couple of times to coat all sides (even around the edges), pressingly gently to get the ground chips to adhere. Lightly coat the cutlet on both sides with vegetable oil spray. If necessary, set it aside and continue dipping and coating more cutlets.

4. Set the cutlet(s) in the basket so that there's as much air space between them as possible in the larger batches. Air-fry undisturbed for 8 minutes, or until lightly browned and very crisp. If the machine is at 360°F, you may need to add 1 to 2 minutes to the cooking time—but be careful, the cheesy coating on the cutlet(s) can burn quickly.

5. Use kitchen tongs to transfer the cutlet(s) to a wire rack. Cool for 5 minutes before serving.

Then...

- Serve these with **Cuban Salad** (page 124).

- Make TEX-MEX WEDGE SALAD. Whisk *mayonnaise of any sort (gluten-free, if a concern)* and *salsa* in equal proportions by volume, then drizzle this mixture over wedges of iceberg lettuce. Top with *fresh corn kernels* (no need to cook), *finely diced avocado*, and/or *crumbled queso Cotija*.

Fried Turkey Tenders

FAST / 9 INGREDIENTS

Turkey tenderloin cooks beautifully in an air-fryer. The naturally lean meat doesn't render its crust soggy with excess grease, and the meat's mild flavor doesn't take away from the zip the buttermilk leaves behind. Don't be afraid of that buttermilk. It adds a slightly tangy richness to the meat, a nice contrast to the simple flour coating.

By the way, you can freeze buttermilk so you don't waste it. We suggest freezing it in ¼- or ½-cup portions. Make sure there's enough headspace in the container for when the buttermilk expands as it freezes.

To slice the turkey tenderloin into medallions, lay it flat on a clean cutting board, then slice it widthwise but a little on the diagonal so that you're cutting (sort of) across the meat's fibers. On the diagonal, you're also making slightly longer medallions than you would if you cut it straight across. These slightly longer medallions are more like the more familiar chicken tenders.

INGREDIENTS	2-quart or larger air fryer	3.5-quart or larger air fryer	5.25-quart or larger air fryer
Turkey tenderloin, cut into 1-inch-thick medallions (see the headnote)	¾ pound	1 pound	1½ pounds
Buttermilk	½ cup	⅔ cup	¾ cup
All-purpose flour	¾ cup	1 cup	1½ cups
Celery seeds	1 teaspoon	1½ teaspoons	2 teaspoons
Onion powder	1 teaspoon	1½ teaspoons	2 teaspoons
Table salt	1 teaspoon, plus more as needed	1½ teaspoons, plus more as needed	2 teaspoons, plus more as needed
Garlic powder	½ teaspoon	¾ teaspoon	1 teaspoon
Ground black pepper	1 teaspoon	1½ teaspoons	2 teaspoons
Vegetable oil spray	As needed	As needed	As needed
MAKES	2 servings	3 servings	4 servings

1. Stir the turkey pieces and buttermilk in a bowl. Cover and refrigerate for 1 hour, stirring once.

2. With the basket (or basket attachment) in the air fryer, heat it to 400°F (or 390°F, if that's the closest setting).

3. Whisk the flour, celery seeds, onion powder, the measured amount of salt, the garlic powder, and pepper in a bowl until well combined. Spread evenly on a large plate.

4. Use kitchen tongs to grab a piece of turkey, gently shake off any excess buttermilk, and set the turkey in the flour mixture. Turn it several times to coat every bit of surface evenly. Lift it up and coat it with vegetable oil spray on all sides. Set it aside on a cutting board and continue on with the rest of the turkey pieces.

5. Set the turkey pieces in the basket in one layer with as much air space as possible between them. (Even ¼ inch is fine.) Air-fry undisturbed for 12 minutes, or until golden brown and crisp.

6. Gently pour the contents of the basket onto a wire rack. Cool for 5 minutes before serving. Season with additional salt, if desired.

Then...

- Make **Carrot Chips** (page 34) or **Okra Chips** (page 33) as the tenders cool.

- Serve these with **Broccoli and Grape Salad** (page 127).

- Go all out with ENDIVE, WALNUT, AND BLUE CHEESE SALAD. Toss cored and chopped *Belgian endive* and perhaps *radicchio* with *chopped walnuts* and *dried cranberries*. Whisk together a dressing of *olive oil* and *red wine vinegar or sherry vinegar* in a 3-to-1 proportion, along with a smidgen of *Dijon mustard* and *salt* and *pepper* to taste. Pour over the salad, toss gently, and add a little *crumbled Gorgonzola or other blue cheese*.

Peanut Curry Turkey Cutlets

FAST / CAN BE GLUTEN-FREE / 7 INGREDIENTS

This recipe is like some strange, new take on satay, no dipping sauce required, what with the peanuts and curry ground into a coating along with bread crumbs, all put onto the meat after it takes a bath in coconut milk.

Notice that the coating mixture includes no salt because we've called for salted, roasted peanuts. If you use unsalted peanuts, add ½ teaspoon table salt to the small batch, ¾ teaspoon table salt to the medium one, and 1 teaspoon table salt to the large batch.

INGREDIENTS	2-quart or larger air fryer	3.5-quart or larger air fryer	5.25-quart or larger air fryer
Plain dried bread crumbs (gluten-free, if a concern)	½ cup	⅔ cup	1⅓ cups
Roasted, salted shelled peanuts	¼ cup	⅓ cup	⅔ cup
Dark brown sugar	2 teaspoons	1 tablespoon	1½ tablespoons
Mild yellow or spicy red curry powder, or homemade curry powder (page 363)	1 teaspoon	1½ teaspoons	2½ teaspoons
6-ounce turkey cutlet(s)	1	2	3
Regular or low-fat coconut milk	½ cup	⅔ cup	¾ cup
Vegetable oil spray	As needed	As needed	As needed
MAKES	*1 serving*	*2 servings*	*3 servings*

1. With the basket (or basket attachment) in the air fryer, heat it to 350°F (or 360°F, if that's the closest setting).

2. Place the bread crumbs, peanuts, brown sugar, and curry powder in a food processor. Cover and process until finely ground.

continues

3. Pour the coconut milk into a shallow soup plate or a small pie plate. Pour the bread-crumb mixture into a second shallow soup plate or small pie plate.

4. Use kitchen tongs to dip a turkey cutlet into the coconut milk. Turn a couple of times to coat both sides, then pick it up and let the excess slip back into the rest. Set the turkey cutlet in the bread-crumb mixture and turn it several times to coat evenly and thoroughly (even around its edges), pressing gently so that the coating adheres. Pick up the cutlet with tongs and lightly coat both sides with vegetable oil spray. If necessary, set the cutlet aside, then dip and coat more cutlets.

5. Set the cutlet(s) in the basket so there's as much air space as possible between them in the larger batches.

Air-fry undisturbed for 10 minutes, or until lightly browned and crisp.

6. Use kitchen tongs to transfer the cutlet(s) to a wire rack. Cool for 5 minutes before serving.

Then...

• Did you know you can make a wedge salad out of very small heads of white cabbage? The small heads are the most tender. Remove the outer layer of leaves, then cut the head(s) into wedges. To go with these cutlets, dress them with **Yogurt-Cilantro Sauce** (page 136) or **Chile-Peanut Sauce** (page 46).

Garlic and Herb Turkey Tenderloin

EASY / GLUTEN-FREE / 7 INGREDIENTS

This classic preparation for a whole turkey tenderloin is elegant enough to serve as the entrée at a simple dinner party. You can even work in advance, smearing the garlic paste on the turkey tenderloin up to 3 hours before you're ready to cook it and storing it on a cutting board under plastic wrap in the fridge.

The technique for creating the garlic paste is pretty cheffy. Basically, you'll mince the ingredients, occasionally wiping the side of the knife's blade over them and pressing down against the cutting board; then you'll gather the ingredients together and continue to mince them, all until the mixture is a coarse paste. (By the way, this technique will ruin the edge of a decent knife if you work with a glass cutting board. Use a wooden cutting board, if possible.)

INGREDIENTS	2-quart or larger air fryer	3.5-quart or larger air fryer	5.25-quart or larger air fryer
Medium garlic cloves, peeled	2	3	4
Coriander seeds	½ teaspoon	¾ teaspoon	1 teaspoon
Fennel seeds	½ teaspoon	¾ teaspoon	1 teaspoon
Table salt	½ teaspoon	¾ teaspoon	1 teaspoon
Red pepper flakes	Up to ¼ teaspoon	Up to a rounded ¼ teaspoon	Up to ½ teaspoon
Olive oil	1½ tablespoons	2 tablespoons	3 tablespoons
¾-pound turkey tenderloin(s)	1	1½	2
MAKES	2 servings	3 servings	4 servings

1. With the basket (or basket attachment) in the air fryer, heat it to 400°F (or 390°F, if that's the closest setting).

2. Chop the garlic cloves on a cutting board with a large knife, then add the coriander seeds, fennel seeds, salt, and red pepper flakes. Continue chopping the mixture into a finely minced paste, occasionally pressing and wiping the side of the knife across the ingredients to squash them. Scrape this mixture into a small bowl and stir in the olive oil. Rub this paste all over the turkey tenderloin(s).

3. Set the coated tenderloin(s) in the basket with as much air space as possible between the pieces in the larger or batches. Air-fry undisturbed for 20 minutes, or until browned and an instant-read meat thermometer inserted into the meat at the thickest point registers 160°F.

4. Use kitchen tongs to transfer the turkey tenderloin(s) to a cutting board, cool for a few minutes, then slice into ½-inch-thick medallions to serve.

Then...

- Serve the turkey with a chopped salad tossed with **Classic Greek Diner Dressing** (page 90).

- Make **ARUGULA AND PISTACHIO SALAD.** Whisk *olive oil*, *sherry vinegar*, and *orange juice* in a 2-to-1-to-1 ratio by volume in a large serving bowl until well blended. Taste and season with *table salt* and *ground black pepper*. Then add *baby arugula*, *chopped pitted and peeled avocado,* and *chopped shelled pistachios*. Toss gently. Add *chopped dried cranberries*, if desired.

Fried Turkey Thighs

EASY / 7 INGREDIENTS

Turkey thighs are a wonderfully juicy and flavorful treat. One hundred percent dark meat and quite rich, they're made for air-frying.

You'll notice that the dry ingredients are the same amounts for all sizes. You have to have enough to coat the thighs without getting too much of that coating mix wet at any one time and thus rendering it unusable, in little damp globs rather than a dry mixture.

One other note: The thighs here are a tad small (a lot of turkey thighs run around 1 pound each). We kept them small because 1) they need to fit in the basket with plenty of room to spare between them (at least ½ inch) and 2) smaller thighs cook more quickly, so the coating doesn't have a chance to burn.

INGREDIENTS	2-quart or larger air fryer	3.5-quart or larger air fryer	5.25-quart or larger air fryer
All-purpose flour	1 cup	1 cup	1 cup
Table salt	2 teaspoons	2 teaspoons	2 teaspoons
Mild paprika	1 teaspoon	1 teaspoon	1 teaspoon
Garlic powder	1 teaspoon	1 teaspoon	1 teaspoon
Celery seeds	½ teaspoon	½ teaspoon	½ teaspoon
10- to 12-ounce bone-in skin-on turkey thighs, trimmed of any fat blobs	2	3	4
Olive oil spray	As needed	As needed	As needed
MAKES	2 servings	3 servings	4 servings

1. With the basket (or basket attachment) in the air fryer, heat it to 350°F (or 360°F, if that's the closest setting).

2. Whisk the flour, salt, paprika, garlic powder, and celery seeds in a medium bowl until well combined.

3. Use kitchen tongs to dip a turkey thigh into the flour mixture, turning it several times to coat evenly and well on all sides, pressing gently so the coating adheres. Lightly coat all sides of the thigh with olive oil spray. Set it aside and continue coating more thighs.

4. Set the thighs in the basket with at least ½ inch between them (or more space, if possible). Air-fry undisturbed for 25 minutes, or until crisp and an instant-read meat thermometer inserted into the center of a thigh (without touching bone) registers 160°F.

5. Use kitchen tongs to transfer the thighs to a wire rack. Cool for 5 minutes before serving.

Then...

- These turkey thighs would be great with WILTED BABY SPINACH SALAD. Put lots of *baby spinach* in a large, heat-proof bowl, then heat some *olive oil* in a skillet set over medium heat. Add a good helping of *cherry or grape tomatoes* and a little *minced garlic* to the oil. Also add a *minced tinned anchovy fillet*, if you like. Cook, stirring occasionally, until the tomatoes start to burst and give off their juices. Pour this hot mixture from the skillet over the baby spinach and toss to wilt. Season with *table salt* and *ground black pepper*, then garnish with *finely grated Parmesan*.

- Or serve the thighs with **Air-Fried Potato Salad** (page 338) and/or **Roasted Yellow Squash and Onions** (page 349).

State Fair Turkey Wings

EASY / CAN BE GLUTEN-FREE / 7 INGREDIENTS

Unfortunately, the results from air-frying *whole* turkey wings are not as great as when you deep-fry them. The wings' inner parts don't get crunchy and irresistible. And if you air-fry the whole wings long enough so that those parts are crunchy, the rest of the meat gets dried out and tough.

The only solution is to treat them as we do chicken wings: to *divide* the wings into their separate pieces. But don't toss out the so-called flappers, the thinnest section of the wing. With a turkey, there's still some meat on it.

INGREDIENTS	2-quart or larger air fryer	3.5-quart or larger air fryer	5.25-quart or larger air fryer
6-ounce turkey wings	2	3	4
Olive oil	1 tablespoon	1½ tablespoons	2 tablespoons
Worcestershire sauce (gluten-free, if a concern)	1 tablespoon	1½ tablespoons	2 tablespoons
Mild smoked paprika	1 teaspoon	1½ teaspoons	2 teaspoons
Garlic powder	½ teaspoon	½ teaspoon	1 teaspoon
Hot red pepper sauce, such as Cholula or Tabasco (gluten-free, if a concern)	Up to ½ teaspoon	Up to ½ teaspoon	Up to 1 teaspoon
Table salt	½ teaspoon	1 teaspoon	1 teaspoon
MAKES	6 pieces	9 pieces	12 pieces

1. With the basket (or basket attachment) in the air fryer, heat it to 350°F (or 360°F, if that's the closest setting).

2. Divide the wings into their drumettes, winglets, and flappers. The easiest way to do the deed is with the tip of a sharp paring knife, inserting the tip right into the joint and wedging it around to find the point between the bones that can then be sliced through to pry the wing into separate parts.

continues

3. Put the wing pieces in a large bowl. Whisk the olive oil, Worcestershire sauce, smoked paprika, garlic powder, hot pepper sauce, and salt in a small bowl. Pour this mixture over the wing pieces and toss well to coat.

4. When the machine is at temperature, transfer the wing pieces to the basket. They will overlap in places. Air-fry undisturbed for 20 minutes, tossing and rearranging the pieces twice so that any covered parts are exposed, until browned and crisp.

5. Dump the contents of the basket onto a wire rack. Cool for at least 5 minutes before serving.

Then...

- Serve these with **Spicy Ketchup Dip** (page 66) or **Sriracha-Yogurt Dip** (page 36).
- Offer **Strawberry Coolers** (page 95) as a cocktail.
- Or whip up **Shoestring Butternut Squash Fries** (page 329) or **General Tso's Cauliflower** (page 361) for a full meal.

Roasted Turkey Breast

EASY / GLUTEN-FREE / 3 INGREDIENTS

This rather surprising recipe—a *whole* turkey breast?—comes with a few caveats. Although the footprint of small, medium, and large air fryers is fairly consistent within their respective categories, the depth of their baskets is *not* consistent. Put simply, some baskets are deep enough to hold a whole turkey breast—or a whole chicken (see page 191); others are not.

Even so, this recipe may not be out of your reach. If the basket in your machine is too shallow to fit the turkey breast, you can use the grilling tray accessory that comes with your machine or you can remove the basket and set the turkey breast in a 6-inch, 7-inch, or 8-inch round cake pan right in the bottom of the air-fryer drawer (provided there's no heating element down there).

All this said, there are a few air fryers on the market that are like souped-up toaster ovens. In these, you'll never fit a whole turkey breast or a whole chicken. Sorry about that. But there are three hundred other recipes in this book for you to enjoy.

INGREDIENTS	2-quart or larger air fryer	3.5-quart or larger air fryer	5.25-quart or larger air fryer
Bone-in skin-on turkey breast	Half of a 4-pound turkey breast, cut into two pieces to fit a smaller machine	One 4- to 4½-pound turkey breast	One 5- to 6-pound turkey breast
Table salt	½ teaspoon	1 teaspoon	1½ teaspoons
Ground black pepper	½ teaspoon	1 teaspoon	1 teaspoon
MAKES	*2 servings*	*4 servings*	*6 servings*

1. With the basket (or basket attachment) in the air fryer, heat it to 350°F (or 360°F, if that's the closest setting).

2. Set the breast skin side down on a cutting board. Note the two long sides of the turkey breast. One may have a part of the back bone as well as some small ribs attached. Slice off and discard this bit of back bone as well as any attached ribs.

3. Season the breast all over with the salt and pepper. Set it skin side down in the basket. Air-fry undisturbed for 35 minutes.

4. Use kitchen tongs and a nonstick-safe spatula to flip the breast upside down. Continue air-frying undisturbed for 30 minutes for a small batch, 35 minutes for a medium batch, or 40 minutes for a large batch, until an instant-read meat thermometer inserted into the thickest part of the breast (without touching bone) registers 160°F (or until the breast's timer insert pops up).

5. Use kitchen tongs and a nonstick-safe spatula for balance, or use silicone baking mitts, to transfer the breast to a cutting board. Cool for 10 minutes before carving.

Then...

- Serve the turkey breast with **Honey-Roasted Parsnips** (page 343) and **Perfect Asparagus** (page 342).

- The best turkey clubs are made with **Bacon Candy** (page 41), *toasted rye bread (gluten-free, if a concern), romaine lettuce leaves, thinly sliced tomatoes, cranberry chutney,* and *regular or low-fat mayonnaise (gluten-free, if a concern).*

Gluten-Free Turkey Meatloaf

GLUTEN-FREE / 12 INGREDIENTS

Although neither of us needs to avoid gluten, we both like this gluten-free turkey meatloaf better than ones we tested that had been made with bread crumbs. The riced cauliflower and almond flour here prove an unbeatable combination for keeping moisture inside the loaf *and* giving it a somewhat *less* sweet finish.

One note: You must take the meatloaf's temperature to make sure it is cooked through. This is the *only* way guaranteed to result in your and your family's safety.

INGREDIENTS	2-quart or larger air fryer	3.5-quart or larger air fryer	5.25-quart or larger air fryer
Lean ground turkey	1 pound	1½ pounds	2 pounds
Riced cauliflower	⅔ cup	1 cup	1⅓ cups
Chopped yellow or white onion	⅓ cup	½ cup (1 small onion)	⅔ cup
Almond flour	2 tablespoons	3 tablespoons	¼ cup
Large egg(s), lightly beaten	1	1	2
Minced garlic	1½ teaspoons	2 teaspoons	1 tablespoon
Ground coriander	½ teaspoon	¾ teaspoon	1 teaspoon
Ground cumin	½ teaspoon	¾ teaspoon	1 teaspoon
Ground dried turmeric	½ teaspoon	¾ teaspoon	1 teaspoon
Table salt	½ teaspoon	¾ teaspoon	1 teaspoon
Ground black pepper	½ teaspoon	¾ teaspoon	1 teaspoon
Vegetable oil spray	As needed	As needed	As needed
MAKES	2 to 3 servings	3 to 4 servings	5 to 6 servings

1. With the basket (or basket attachment) in the air fryer, heat it to 350°F (or 360°F, if that's the closest setting).

2. Mix the ground turkey, riced cauliflower, onion, almond flour, egg(s), garlic, coriander, cumin, turmeric, salt, and pepper in a bowl until well combined. Form this mixture into an oval loaf about 2 inches high. The exact dimensions will depend on the size of the batch, but the "depth" of meat (2 inches) is the most important factor. Do not taper the ends.

3. Generously coat the exposed surface of the loaf with vegetable spray, then use a large nonstick-safe spatula to pick it up. Spray the bottom of the loaf to coat it well, then set it in the basket.

4. Air-fry undisturbed for 25 minutes for a small meatloaf, 35 minutes for a medium one, or 45 minutes for a large, until an instant-read meat thermometer inserted into the center of the loaf registers 160°F.

5. Use a clean nonstick-safe spatula with the help of kitchen tongs for balance, or use silicone baking mitts, to transfer the meatloaf to a cutting board. Cool for 10 minutes before slicing and serving.

Then...

- Glaze the meatloaf by brushing it with duck sauce, Saucy Susan, barbecue sauce (gluten-free, if a concern), Thai sweet chili sauce, or a red ketchup-like chili sauce (such as Heinz) as soon as it comes out of the air fryer.

- **Roasted Fennel Salad** (page 351) or **Roasted Belgian Endive with Pistachios and Lemon** (page 353) would be terrific with slices of this meatloaf.

Duck Breasts with Orange-Pepper Glaze

EASY / GLUTEN-FREE / 5 INGREDIENTS

Since the air fryer is like a super-duper convection oven, it's perfect for duck breasts because it allows the skin to dry out and get crunchy as the meat stays juicy.

You can't put the glaze on early or at the start of the cooking process because the sugars will blacken and burn. Adding that glaze for the last few minutes allows the flavors to stay bright. The timing we give is for medium-rare duck with a decidedly pinkish hue. If you want to be USDA safe, cook the duck breasts for 13 minutes in step 3 before glazing them.

One ingredient note: **White balsamic vinegar** is a fairly low-acid, mildly sweet vinegar made from white Trebbiano grape must (that is, the crushed grapes with their skins, seeds, and even stems, remnants of the wine-making process). The must is then pressure-cooked to keep it from browning (as it would if allowed to age into more standard balsamic vinegar). The results are a cheffy favorite, a decidedly worth-it pantry splurge. But if you need a substitute, try 1 tablespoon white wine vinegar with ¼ teaspoon granulated white sugar for every 1 tablespoon vinegar.

INGREDIENTS	2-quart or larger air fryer	3.5-quart or larger air fryer	5.25-quart or larger air fryer
6-ounce skin-on duck breasts	2	3	4
Table salt	½ teaspoon	¾ teaspoon	1 teaspoon
Orange marmalade	2 tablespoons	3 tablespoons	¼ cup
White balsamic vinegar (see the headnote)	1½ teaspoons	2 teaspoons	1 tablespoon
Ground black pepper	¼ teaspoon	½ teaspoon	¾ teaspoon
MAKES	*2 servings*	*3 servings*	*4 servings*

continues

1. With the basket (or basket attachment) in the air fryer, heat it to 400°F (or 390°F, if that's the closest setting).

2. Score the skin of each breast in a diamond pattern, without cutting down into the meat, by cutting three diagonal lines across the breast, then three more lines at a 90-degree angle to these lines, as if you're making three X's in the skin. Salt both sides of each breast.

3. When the machine is at temperature, set the breasts skin side up in the basket with as much air space as possible between them. Air-fry undisturbed for 10 minutes.

4. Whisk the marmalade, vinegar, and pepper in a small bowl. Brush this mixture on the skin of each breast, coating it evenly. Continue air-frying undisturbed for 3 minutes, or until browned and even crunchy at the skin's edges.

5. Use kitchen tongs to transfer the breasts skin side up to a wire rack with a sheet of wax paper underneath it to catch the drips and make cleanup easier. Cool for 5 minutes before serving.

Then...

- For an elegant meal, serve these with **Crispy, Cheesy Leeks** (page 350) or **Roman Artichokes** (page 366).

- For a quick side, make SIMPLE ALMOND-RAISIN COUSCOUS. Substitute *vegetable or chicken broth* for the amount of water required by the package. Add *some sliced almonds*, *chopped golden raisins*, and *a little yellow curry powder* (See page 363 to make your own) to the saucepan with the *dry couscous*. Follow the package's instructions for cooking.

Perfect Duck Leg Quarters

EASY / GLUTEN-FREE / 4 INGREDIENTS

Unfortunately, duck leg quarters give off a lot of fat as they cook. Prepare for the cleanup. The bottom of the basket may be a mess. And the tray below the rack in some models of air fryers may become quite full of fat.

Don't pour the fat down the drain unless you're looking to call a plumber. Cool the fat to room temperature, then pour it into a bag that you can seal to throw it out. Or better yet, strain the rendered fat through a fine-mesh sieve and save it in a covered glass jar in the fridge for a terrific treat as the fat to use in soups or stews, or even for scrambled eggs.

INGREDIENTS	2-quart or larger air fryer	3.5-quart or larger air fryer	5.25-quart or larger air fryer
½-pound skin-on duck leg quarters	2	3	4
Medium garlic cloves, peeled and halved lengthwise	1	1	2
Table salt	¼ teaspoon	Rounded ¼ teaspoon	½ teaspoon
Ground black pepper	¼ teaspoon	Rounded ¼ teaspoon	½ teaspoon
MAKES	2 servings	3 servings	4 servings

1. With the basket (or basket attachment) in the air fryer, heat it to 300°F (all models we've seen can be set to this temperature).

2. Rub the leg quarters all over with the cut sides of the garlic cloves. Sprinkle them with the salt and pepper.

3. Add a little hot water to the fryer basket. If the air fryer has a lower heating element, add the water to the baking tray that can sit on a lower rack. Set the leg quarters skin side up in the basket or on a wire rack in the machine with as much air space between the pieces as possible. They should not touch. Air-fry undisturbed for 30 minutes.

4. Raise the machine heat to 375°F (or 370°F or 360°F, if one of these is the closest setting). Continue air-frying undisturbed for about 15 minutes, until very crisp and well-browned and the meat is almost falling off the bone.

5. Use kitchen tongs, and perhaps a flatware fork for balance, to transfer the leg quarters to a wire rack. Cool for 10 minutes before serving.

Then...

- Make CELERY ROOT SLAW. Spiralize a *peeled celery root (celeriac)* or shred it through the large holes of a box grater. Drop these bits into a large pot of *boiling water.* Blanch for 1 minute, then drain in a colander set in the sink. Rinse with cold water and drain very well. Make a dressing by whisking *1 tablespoon each granulated white sugar, lemon juice,* and *white wine vinegar* into every *½ cup regular or low-fat mayonnaise (gluten-free, if a concern)* you use, seasoned with a little *table salt* and *ground black pepper.* Or make it easier and use a bottled cole slaw dressing. Pour the dressing onto the celery root pieces and toss well to coat.

4

FORTY-FIVE

Beef, Pork, Veal & Lamb Main Courses

When you think of an air fryer, beef, pork, and the rest of these meats aren't necessarily the first thing that comes to mind. Sure, maybe chicken-fried steak or perhaps breaded pork chops, but probably not much else.

You should think of much more, because this chapter proves the versatility of this appliance that works like a broiler, a grill, and an oven, all in one. You can air-fry barbecue-style ribs, marinated pork tenderloins, and even some decidedly delicate veal chops in those high-powered convection currents.

But take our advice: Letting things cool after they come out of the machine really pays off with these recipes. Beef cuts and the rest are made of muscle fibers that often run parallel to one another. Those fibers tighten when heated, squeezing out their natural "juices" as they cook. In an air fryer, the juices that come up to the exposed surfaces quickly evaporate because of the flowing hot air. The only way any remaining juices can get back into the meat is to let the cut rest when it's out of the machine. The fibers need to relax and open up. Small amounts of their squeezed-out juices can get back in.

You won't find any recipes here for large cuts of meat—brisket or pork shoulder, for example. They're too big for all but the very largest machines. What's more, some larger cuts like beef short ribs or chuck roasts toughen long before they're done in an air fryer. These need a moist, slow heat for the best success. (Or maybe a dip in a sous vide bath.) That's why you'll find mostly smaller cuts here: strip steaks, filets mignons, pork cutlets, and lamb chops, although we do have one crazy-delicious recipe for Chinese-style roasted pork belly in the mix.

Even these smaller cuts are more likely to throw off fat as they cook, more so than chicken or turkey might. Make sure you clean the machine after each use. Although it may not smoke while you're making a pork tenderloin, chances are it will the next time you make something, if you haven't given it a good cleaning.

And one more thing: Get ready for some surprises in this chapter, like an easy rendition of **Vietnamese Shaking Beef** (page 217), tasty **Albóndigas** (little Mexican meatballs, page 261), and even a throwback to the mid-century-modern world with **Fried Spam** (page 262). Yes, we've got strip steaks and pork chops. But life's made of—and for—surprises, right?

Perfect Strip Steaks

EASY / GLUTEN-FREE / 5 INGREDIENTS

Although strip steaks are a smaller cut across the spectrum of beef cuts, this recipe calls for larger strip steaks than you sometimes find in the butcher case. Why? Because those steaks have more time to develop a crust while staying rare or medium-rare inside. If you don't see what you need, ask the butcher.

If you want even more crunch on the steak's exterior, use the machine's grill pan either in or instead of the basket. Or use the grill pan attachment for a toaster oven–style air fryer. Set the pan in the machine as the air fryer comes up to temperature. Set the steaks on the grill pan and cook as directed, turning once. The sear will work magic on the steaks!

Notice that this recipe calls for *at most* two steaks. We couldn't fit three in most large models without the crowding that prevents good air circulation—which means the steaks wouldn't cook properly. But since these are larger steaks, one might well serve two people. At least it does in our house.

INGREDIENTS	2-quart or larger air fryer	3.5-quart or larger air fryer
Olive oil	2 teaspoons	1½ tablespoons
Minced garlic	2 teaspoons	1½ tablespoons
Ground black pepper	1 teaspoon	2 teaspoons
Table salt	½ teaspoon	1 teaspoon
¾-pound boneless beef strip steak(s)	1	2
MAKES	1 to 2 servings	2 to 4 servings

1. With the basket (or basket attachment) in the air fryer, heat it to 375°F (or 380°F or 390°F, if one of these is the closest setting).

2. Mix the oil, garlic, pepper, and salt in a small bowl, then smear this mixture over both sides of the steak(s).

3. When the machine is at temperature, put the steak(s) in the basket with as much air space as possible between them for the larger batch. They should not overlap or even touch. That said, even just a ¼-inch between them will work. Air-fry for 12 minutes, turning once, until an instant-read meat thermometer inserted into the thickest part of a steak registers 127°F for rare (not USDA-approved). Or air-fry for 15 minutes, turning once, until an

instant-read meat thermometer registers 145°F for medium (USDA-approved). If the machine is at 390°F, the steaks may cook 1 to 2 minutes more quickly than the stated timing.

4. Use kitchen tongs to transfer the steak(s) to a wire rack. Cool for 5 minutes before serving.

Then...

- For 6 servings of HOMEMADE STEAK SAUCE, warm *1 tablespoon vegetable or canola oil* in a large skillet over medium heat; then add *¼ cup finely chopped onion* and *1 teaspoon minced garlic*. Cook, stirring often, until the onion is translucent, just a couple of minutes. Add *½ cup ketchup, 2 tablespoons lemon juice, 2 tablespoons white wine vinegar, 2 tablespoons water, 1 tablespoon Worcestershire sauce (gluten-free, if a concern), 1 tablespoon dark brown sugar, 2 teaspoons regular or low-sodium soy sauce or gluten-free tamari sauce,* and *2 teaspoons Dijon mustard (gluten-free, if a concern).* Reduce the heat to low and cook, stirring often, until thickened a bit, 15 to 20 minutes. Pour and scrape the contents of the skillet into a glass or nonreactive container and cool for 10 minutes. Serve at once or store, covered, in the refrigerator for up to 1 week.

Steakhouse Filets Mignons

EASY / CAN BE GLUTEN-FREE / 6 INGREDIENTS

A seasoning of ground dried mushrooms, white pepper, and a little sugar will make any steak taste as if it's been aged for weeks. This mixture adds a slightly musky, sweet flavor to the meat, almost exactly like the flavors prized in steakhouses.

Although the recipe calls for individual filets mignons, you can buy a tenderloin and cut your own steaks: a 1-pound piece for a small batch, a 1½-pound piece for a medium batch, or a 2-pound one for a large one. Try to get a center-cut tenderloin so that the steaks will all be the same diameter. Figure on steaks that are about as thick as a strip of bacon is wide.

The servings are given here in a range, depending on whether you think one filet or two is best on a plate.

INGREDIENTS	2-quart or larger air fryer	3.5-quart or larger air fryer	5.25-quart or larger air fryer
Dried porcini mushrooms	½ ounce	¾ ounce	1 ounce
Granulated white sugar	¼ teaspoon	Rounded ¼ teaspoon	½ teaspoon
Ground white pepper	¼ teaspoon	Rounded ¼ teaspoon	½ teaspoon
Table salt	¼ teaspoon	Rounded ¼ teaspoon	½ teaspoon
¼-pound filets mignons or beef tenderloin steaks	4	6	8
Thin-cut bacon strips (gluten-free, if a concern)	4	6	8
MAKES	*2 or 4 servings*	*3 or 6 servings*	*4 or 8 servings*

1. With the basket (or basket attachment) in the air fryer, heat it to 400°F (or 390°F, if that's the closest setting).

2. Grind the dried mushrooms in a clean spice grinder until powdery. Add the sugar, white pepper, and salt. Grind to blend.

3. Rub this mushroom mixture into both cut sides of each filet. Wrap the circumference of each filet with a strip of bacon. (It will loop around the beef about 1½ times.)

continues

4. Set the filets mignons in the basket on their sides with the bacon seam side down. Do not let the filets touch; keep at least ¼ inch open between them. Air-fry undisturbed for 12 minutes for rare, or until an instant-read meat thermometer inserted into the center of a filet registers 125°F (not USDA-approved); 13 minutes for medium-rare, or until an instant-read meat thermometer inserted into the center of a filet registers 132°F (not USDA-approved); or 15 minutes for medium, or until an instant-read meat thermometer inserted into the center of a filet registers 145°F (USDA-approved).

5. Use kitchen tongs to transfer the filets to a wire rack, setting them cut side down. Cool for 5 minutes before serving.

Then...

- A great filet demands **Steakhouse Baked Potatoes** (page 333). Since the baked potatoes take longer to cook, prepare them first, then reheat them in a 350°F air fryer (or 360°F, if that's the closest setting) for 5 minutes as the filets rest.

- For a sauce, consider **Horseradish Sauce** (page 116) or **Chimichurri** (page 94).

Chicken-Fried Steak

6 INGREDIENTS

If you don't know about chicken-fried steak, we pray for mercy on your Yankee soul. Let us explain this Texas wonder. First off, there's no chicken in chicken-fried steak. Instead, it's a thin cut of beef (sometimes cube steak, as here, sometimes chuck or even flank steak) fried in about the same way you might batter and fry chicken.

The best way to get a crunchy coating on a cube steak, one that mimics the sort of chicken-fried steak served at Texas roadhouses, is to dredge the piece of meat in flour twice, once before the egg wash and once after. The second time, the coating may get a little thick, depending on how you like it on the steak. (A sturdy but not too thick coating is prized by the fare's mavens.)

INGREDIENTS	2-quart or larger air fryer	3.5-quart or larger air fryer	5.25-quart or larger air fryer
All-purpose flour	1 cup	1½ cups	2 cups
Large egg(s)	1	2	2
Regular or low-fat sour cream	1 tablespoon	2 tablespoons	3 tablespoons
Worcestershire sauce	1 tablespoon	2 tablespoons	3 tablespoons
¼-pound thin beef cube steak(s)	1	2	3
Vegetable oil spray	As needed	As needed	As needed
MAKES	*1 serving*	*2 servings*	*3 servings*

1. With the basket (or basket attachment) in the air fryer, heat it to 400°F (or 390°F, if that's the closest setting).

2. Set up and fill two shallow soup plates or small pie plates on your counter: one for the flour; and one for the egg(s), whisked with the sour cream and Worcestershire sauce until uniform.

3. Dredge a piece of beef in the flour, coating it well on both sides and even along the edge. Shake off any excess; then dip the meat in the egg mixture, coating both sides while retaining the flour on the meat. Let any excess egg mixture slip back into the rest. Dredge the meat in the flour once again, coating all surfaces well. Gently shake off the excess coating and set the steak aside if you're coating another steak or two. Once done, coat the steak(s) on both sides with the vegetable oil spray.

4. Set the steak(s) in the basket. If there's more than one steak, make sure they do not overlap or even touch, although the smallest gap between them is enough to get them crunchy. Air-fry undisturbed for 6 minutes.

5. Use kitchen tongs to pick up one of the steaks. Coat it again on both sides with vegetable oil spray. Turn it upside down and set it back in the basket with that same regard for the space between them in larger batches. Repeat with any other steaks. Continue air-frying undisturbed for 6 minutes, or until golden brown and crunchy.

6. Use kitchen tongs to transfer the steak(s) to a wire rack. Cool for 5 minutes before serving.

Then...

- Although chicken-fried steak is often served with ketchup, the real deal comes with CREAM GRAVY. The easiest way to make 4 servings is to warm *2 cups whole or 2% milk* in a small saucepan set over medium-low heat. Meanwhile, melt *2 tablespoons butter* in a medium skillet set over medium heat. Whisk in *2 tablespoons all-purpose flour* until the mixture is like a white paste. Whisk in the warmed milk in a slow, steady stream, working to get that paste dissolved in the milk. Don't add the milk too quickly. Once smooth, raise the heat to medium-high and continue whisking until the gravy thickens, 2 to 3 minutes. Immediately remove from the heat. Season with *salt and pepper* before serving warm.

See photo in insert.

Barbecue-Style Beef Cube Steak

FAST / EASY / CAN BE GLUTEN-FREE / 3 INGREDIENTS

You might not know it on first glance at this recipe's title, but it's actually a bit of whimsy, a new riff on **Chicken-Fried Steak** (previous page). The cube steak is coated in a crazy mixture of barbecue sauce and ground corn chips for a sweet-and-salty crunch in every bite.

Note that the recipe calls for *a lot* of Fritos (or a generic corn chip equivalent). For the best crunch, we want a fairly heavy coating on the beef.

Note, too, that the smallest batch makes only one steak. To make multiple batches, put a large lipped baking sheet topped with an oven-safe wire rack in a 175°F oven, then set the air-fried steaks on the rack as you make more. (To assure crunch all around the steak, the wire rack lifts the cooked, crunched steaks off the hot surface of the baking sheet.)

INGREDIENTS	2-quart or larger air fryer	3.5-quart or larger air fryer	5.25-quart or larger air fryer
4-ounce beef cube steak(s)	1	2	3
Fritos (original flavor) or a generic corn chip equivalent, crushed to crumbs (see page 158)	1 cup (about 4 ounces)	2 cups (about 8 ounces)	3 cups (about 12 ounces)
Purchased smooth barbecue sauce, any flavor (gluten-free, if a concern)	3 tablespoons	6 tablespoons	½ cup
MAKES	1 serving	2 servings	3 servings

1. With the basket (or basket attachment) in the air fryer, heat it to 375°F (or 370°F or 360°F, if one of these is the closest setting).

2. Spread the Fritos crumbs in a shallow soup plate or a small pie plate. Rub the barbecue sauce onto both sides of the steak(s). Dredge the steak(s) in the Fritos crumbs to coat well and thoroughly, turning several times and pressing down to get the little bits to adhere to the meat.

3. When the machine is at temperature, set the steak(s) in the basket. Leave as much air space between them as possible if you're working with more than one piece of beef. Air-fry undisturbed for 12 minutes, or until lightly brown and crunchy.

If the machine is at 360°F, you may need to add 1 to 2 minutes to the cooking time.

4. Use kitchen tongs to transfer the steak(s) to a wire rack. Cool for 5 minutes before serving.

Then...

- Serve these steaks with more of the barbecue sauce on the side as a dip.

- Try them with **Radish Slaw** (page 117) or **Celery Root Slaw** (page 205).

- Or go the easy route and buy some cole slaw to serve on the side. Dill pickles would also be welcome, as well as thinly sliced red onion.

Smokehouse-Style Beef Ribs

EASY / GLUTEN-FREE / 6 INGREDIENTS

These are not beef *short* ribs but the meaty, fatty ribs that sit at the bottom of a bone-in standing rib roast and are sometimes served up for gnawing at state fairs.

Choose beef ribs with quite a bit of meat on them—not just ribs for making stock or treating the dogs, but those that would indeed make a meal. One per serving should do it.

The rub is a simple mixture to keep the flavor of the beef present in each bite. Note the slightly lower temperature here: The ribs need time to get tender before the fat turns crunchy.

And one more thing: The ribs must fit in the basket (or the basket attachment). If you're in doubt, measure your basket's dimensions, then take this figure to the supermarket. If you find beef ribs too large, have the butcher cut them down to size so they'll fit in your machine.

INGREDIENTS	2-quart or larger air fryer	3.5-quart or larger air fryer	5.25-quart or larger air fryer
Mild smoked paprika	¼ teaspoon	Rounded ¼ teaspoon	½ teaspoon
Garlic powder	¼ teaspoon	Rounded ¼ teaspoon	½ teaspoon
Onion powder	¼ teaspoon	Rounded ¼ teaspoon	½ teaspoon
Table salt	¼ teaspoon	Rounded ¼ teaspoon	½ teaspoon
Ground black pepper	¼ teaspoon	Rounded ¼ teaspoon	½ teaspoon
10- to 12-ounce beef back ribs (not beef short ribs)	2	3	4
MAKES	2 servings	3 servings	4 servings

1. With the basket (or basket attachment) in the air fryer, heat it to 350°F (or 360°F, if that's the closest setting).

2. Mix the smoked paprika, garlic powder, onion powder, salt, and pepper in a small bowl until uniform. Massage and pat this mixture onto the ribs.

3. When the machine is at temperature, set the ribs in the basket in one layer, turning them on their sides if necessary, sort of like they're spooning but with at least ¼ inch air space between them. Air-fry for 25 minutes, turning once, until deep brown and sizzling.

4. Use kitchen tongs to transfer the ribs to a wire rack. Cool for 5 minutes before serving.

Then...

• For a glaze on the ribs, whisk a dribble of *hot tap water* into some *orange marmalade* to loosen it up. After the ribs have cooled for 5 minutes, brush this mixture on them and put them back in a 400°F (or 390°F) air fryer for 3 minutes or so to turn the glaze into a crunch.

• For a steakhouse pasta side, prepare the **Blistered Tomatoes** (page 310), then toss them with *a little olive oil, a little minced garlic, a generous amount of grated Parmesan cheese, a little table salt,* and *even less ground black pepper.* Toss this mixture with *cooked, drained, and still-hot spaghetti.*

Barbecue-Style London Broil

FAST / EASY / GLUTEN-FREE / 8 INGREDIENTS

Of course, this isn't a "real" barbecue recipe. But the smoky flavor of the rub gives the London broil a barbecue flavor, even though the cut gets done in a fraction of the time it would take you to set up the grill, prepare the meat, and cook it outdoors.

Look for top round labeled *London broil*. The cut should be 1 to 1½ inches thick to work with our timing and to fit in the machine's basket, based on its weight.

To carve a London broil, you must work "against the grain." Run your clean fingers across the top of the cooked cut to discover the direction of the meat's fibers. Position your knife at a 90-degree angle to these fibers (so you're cutting across them, not with them—and thus, you're cutting "against the grain"). Carve the thinnest slice you can. A sharp knife is a must. For the best slices, slant the knife's blade to a 45-degree angle, thereby cutting wider—but still thin—slices.

INGREDIENTS	2-quart or larger air fryer	3.5-quart or larger air fryer	5.25-quart or larger air fryer
Mild smoked paprika	½ teaspoon	¾ teaspoon	1 teaspoon
Dried oregano	½ teaspoon	¾ teaspoon	1 teaspoon
Table salt	½ teaspoon	¾ teaspoon	1 teaspoon
Ground black pepper	½ teaspoon	¾ teaspoon	1 teaspoon
Garlic powder	¼ teaspoon	Rounded ¼ teaspoon	½ teaspoon
Onion powder	¼ teaspoon	Rounded ¼ teaspoon	½ teaspoon
Beef London broil (in one piece)	1 pound	1½ pounds	2 pounds
Olive oil spray	As needed	As needed	As needed
MAKES	3 to 4 servings	5 to 6 servings	7 to 8 servings

1. With the basket (or basket attachment) in the air fryer, heat it to 400°F (or 390°F, if that's the closest setting).

2. Mix the smoked paprika, oregano, salt, pepper, garlic powder, and onion powder in a small bowl until uniform.

3. Pat and rub this mixture across all surfaces of the beef. Lightly coat the beef on all sides with olive oil spray.

4. When the machine is at temperature, lay the London broil flat in the basket and air-fry undisturbed for 8 minutes for the small batch, 10 minutes for the medium batch, or 12 minutes for the large batch for medium-rare, until an instant-read meat thermometer inserted into the center of the meat registers 130°F (not USDA-approved). Add 1, 2, or 3 minutes, respectively (based on the size of the cut) for medium, until an instant-read meat thermometer registers 135°F (not USDA-approved). Or add 3, 4, or 5 minutes respectively for medium, until an instant-read meat thermometer registers 145°F (USDA-approved).

5. Use kitchen tongs to transfer the London broil to a cutting board. Let the meat rest for 10 minutes. It needs a long time for the juices to be reincorporated into the meat's fibers. Carve it against the grain into very thin (less than ¼-inch-thick) slices to serve. (See the headnote for more detailed carving instructions.)

Then...

- Serve this London broil with HONEY MUSTARD COLE SLAW. For 4 to 6 servings, mix *½ cup regular or low-fat mayonnaise, 2 tablespoons honey, 1 tablespoon apple cider vinegar, 1 tablespoon Dijon mustard, ½ teaspoon table salt, ½ teaspoon ground black pepper,* and *¼ teaspoon celery seeds* in a bowl until well combined. Use gluten-free condiments, if a concern. Add *one 1-pound bag cole slaw vegetables* (thinly sliced cabbage and carrots) and toss well to coat.

Carne Asada

EASY / CAN BE GLUTEN-FREE / 9 INGREDIENTS

A taqueria classic, *carne asada* is sometimes made with sirloin or flank steak, but these cuts are too large for the air fryer's basket. What's worse, they're too thick, resulting in a burned exterior before the meat's cooked inside.

Skirt steak is more forgiving—and better able to be cut into smaller segments. As a bonus, skirt steak is more strongly flavored and better able to stand up to this bold marinade of citrus juices and soy sauce or tamari sauce. Of course, fresh juices offer the best flavor. But bottled will do in a pinch.

Because of the fatty cut of beef, we have to offer one warning: If there's one recipe guaranteed to make your air fryer smoke, it's this one. Open a window and turn on the vent.

INGREDIENTS	2-quart or larger air fryer	3.5-quart or larger air fryer	5.25-quart or larger air fryer
Orange juice	3 tablespoons	¼ cup	⅓ cup
Regular or low-sodium soy sauce or gluten-free tamari sauce	2 tablespoons	3 tablespoons	¼ cup
Lemon juice	1 tablespoon	1½ tablespoons	2 tablespoons
Lime juice	1 tablespoon	1½ tablespoons	2 tablespoons
Minced garlic	1 teaspoon	1½ teaspoons	2 teaspoons
Ground cumin	½ teaspoon	¾ teaspoon	1 teaspoon
Dried oregano	½ teaspoon	¾ teaspoon	1 teaspoon
Red pepper flakes	Up to ½ teaspoon	Up to ¾ teaspoon	Up to 1 teaspoon
Beef skirt steak	½ pound	¾ pound	1¼ pounds
MAKES	2 servings	3 servings	4 servings

1. Mix the orange juice, soy or tamari sauce, lemon juice, lime juice, garlic, cumin, oregano, and red pepper flakes in a large bowl. Add the steak and turn several time to coat. Cover and refrigerate for at least 2 hours or up to 6 hours, turning the meat in the marinade twice or more.

2. With the basket (or basket attachment) in the air fryer, heat it to 400°F (or 390°F, if that's the closest setting).

3. Meanwhile, remove the steak from the marinade, discard any remaining marinade, and cut the steak into pieces that will fit in the basket in one layer.

Leave these out at room temperature as the machine heats.

4. When the machine is at temperature, set the steak pieces in the basket, overlapping them as necessary without letting any climb up the side of the basket. Air-fry for 12 minutes, turning and rearranging the pieces once so that any covered bits are exposed, until browned and sizzling.

5. Use kitchen tongs to transfer the pieces of skirt steak to a cutting board. Cool for 5 minutes, then carve against the grain into ½-inch-thick strips. (For tips on cutting against the grain, see page 214.)

- Serve the skirt steak strips as you would fajitas: with flour or corn tortillas, diced avocado, sour cream, shredded cheese, thinly sliced scallions, and/or chopped tomatoes. Consider adding sliced radishes and fresh cilantro leaves to the mix of accompaniments. In any event, always offer lime wedges to squeeze over the meat.

- Try the strips with **Jalapeño Jam** (page 58) or **Salsa Fresca** (page 167).

- If you have any leftover, use it as the filling for **Customize-Your-Own Quesadillas** (page 145).

See photo in insert.

Vietnamese Shaking Beef

EASY / CAN BE GLUTEN-FREE / 8 INGREDIENTS

In the traditional preparation of buttery *bo luc lac*, you must shake the pan constantly so that the ingredients don't burn. Nobody wants to stand by an air fryer that long. And nobody needs to. The hot-air circulation keeps the meat from burning as it might over a stovetop burner. Until, that is, the very end of the cooking process. We also add the scallions and garlic late to keep their flavors fresher, less "cooked."

Just one note: The longer you let the meat marinate, the better-tasting the dish will be.

INGREDIENTS	2-quart or larger air fryer	3.5-quart or larger air fryer	5.25-quart or larger air fryer
Beef tenderloin, cut into 1-inch cubes	¾ pound	1 pound	1½ pounds
Regular or low-sodium soy sauce or gluten-free tamari sauce	2½ teaspoons	1 tablespoon	1½ tablespoons
Fish sauce (gluten-free, if a concern)	2½ teaspoons	1 tablespoon	1½ tablespoons
Dark brown sugar	2½ teaspoons	1 tablespoon	1½ tablespoons
Ground black pepper	1 teaspoon	1½ teaspoons	2 teaspoons
Medium scallions, trimmed and thinly sliced	2	3	4
Butter	1½ tablespoons	2 tablespoons	3 tablespoons
Minced garlic	1 teaspoon	1½ teaspoons	2 teaspoons
MAKES	2 servings	3 servings	4 servings

1. Mix the beef, soy or tamari sauce, fish sauce, and brown sugar in a bowl until well combined. Cover and refrigerate for at least 2 hours or up to 8 hours, tossing the beef at least twice in the marinade.

2. Put a 6-inch round or square cake pan in an air-fryer basket for a small batch, a 7-inch round or square cake pan for a medium batch, or an 8-inch round or square cake pan for a large one. Or put one of these on the rack of a toaster oven–style air

continues

fryer. Heat the machine with the pan in it to 400°F (or 390°F, if that's the closest setting). When the machine it at temperature, let the pan sit in the heat for 2 to 3 minutes so that it gets very hot.

3. Use a slotted spoon to transfer the beef to the pan, leaving any marinade behind in the bowl. Spread the meat into as close to an even layer as you can. Air-fry undisturbed for 5 minutes. Meanwhile, discard the marinade, if any.

4. Add the scallions, butter, and garlic to the beef. Air-fry for 2 minutes, tossing and rearranging the beef and scallions repeatedly, perhaps every 20 seconds.

5. Remove the basket from the machine and let the meat cool in the pan for a couple of minutes before serving.

Then...

- Because the dish is sweet, we prefer it over cooked long-grain *brown* rice (which adds a nutty finish to each bite).

- Sprinkle servings with crunchy chow mein noodles. Or even with the **Sweet Chili Peanuts** on page 30.

- You can also serve the dish on top of a bed of stemmed watercress leaves. (The stems can be quite woody, even on small leaves, and so should be removed.) The hot beef dish will partially wilt the watercress on the plates.

Better-Than-Chinese-Take-Out Sesame Beef

CAN BE GLUTEN-FREE / 13 INGREDIENTS

Like the **Better-Than-Chinese-Take-Out Orange Chicken** (page 180), this recipe is *not* completed in the air fryer. You air-fry the beef and vegetables, then make a quick stir-fry in a wok. Air-frying the ingredients gives them the texture they would have gotten if they were deep-fried, usually the traditional method for a stir-fry like this one.

Admittedly, the process is complicated. Plan on extra time until you get the hang of this recipe. But the results are amazing: Since the strips of beef aren't deep-fried, they end up crunchy but not oily, without as much fat and with a ton more flavor.

INGREDIENTS	2-quart or larger air fryer	3.5-quart or larger air fryer	5.25-quart or larger air fryer
Beef flank steak	¾ pound	1¼ pounds	1¾ pounds
Regular or low-sodium soy sauce or gluten-free tamari sauce	2 tablespoons	2½ tablespoons	3½ tablespoons
Toasted sesame oil	4 teaspoons	2 tablespoons	3 tablespoons
Cornstarch	1½ teaspoons	2½ teaspoons	3½ teaspoons
Frozen mixed vegetables for stir-fry, thawed, seasoning packet discarded	¾ pound (about 3 cups)	1 pound 2 ounces (about 4½ cups)	1½ pounds (about 6 cups)
Unseasoned rice vinegar (see page 70)	2 tablespoons	3 tablespoons	¼ cup
Thai sweet chili sauce	2 tablespoons	3 tablespoons	¼ cup
Light brown sugar	1½ tablespoons	2 tablespoons	3 tablespoons plus 1 teaspoon
White sesame seeds	1 tablespoon	2 tablespoons	3 tablespoons
Water	1½ teaspoons	2 teaspoons	1 tablespoon
Vegetable oil spray	As needed	As needed	As needed
Minced peeled fresh ginger	1 tablespoon	1½ tablespoons	2 tablespoons
Minced garlic	2 teaspoons	1 tablespoon	1½ tablespoons
MAKES	*3 servings*	*4 servings*	*6 servings*

1. Set the flank steak on a cutting board and run your clean fingers across it to figure out which way the meat's fibers are running. (Usually, they run the long way from end to end, or perhaps slightly at an angle lengthwise along the cut.) Cut the flank steak into three pieces *parallel to the meat's grain*. Then cut each of these pieces into ½-inch-wide strips *against the grain*.

2. Put the meat strips in a large bowl. For a small batch, add 2 teaspoons of the soy or tamari sauce, 2 teaspoons of the sesame oil, and ½ teaspoon of the cornstarch; for a medium batch, add 1 tablespoon of the soy or tamari sauce, 1 tablespoon of the sesame oil, and 1 teaspoon of the cornstarch; and for a large batch, add 1½ tablespoons of the soy or tamari sauce, 1½ tablespoons of the sesame oil, and

continues

1½ teaspoons of the cornstarch. Toss well until the meat is thoroughly coated in the marinade. Set aside at room temperature.

3. With the basket (or basket attachment) in the air fryer, heat it to 400°F (or 390°F, if that's the closest setting).

4. When the machine is at temperature, place the beef strips in the basket in as close to one layer as possible. The strips will overlap or even cover each other. Air-fry for 10 minutes, tossing and rearranging the strips three times so that the covered parts get exposed, until browned and even a little crisp. Pour the strips into a clean bowl.

5. Spread the vegetables in the basket and air-fry undisturbed for 3 to 4 minutes, just until they are heated through and somewhat softened. Pour these into the bowl with the meat strips. Turn off the air fryer.

6. Whisk the rice vinegar, sweet chili sauce, brown sugar, sesame seeds, the remaining soy sauce, and the remaining sesame oil in a small bowl until well combined. For a small batch, whisk the remaining 1 teaspoon cornstarch with the water in a second small bowl to make a smooth slurry; for medium batch, whisk the remaining 1½ teaspoons cornstarch with the water in a second small bowl to make a smooth slurry; and for a large batch, whisk the remaining 2 teaspoons cornstarch with the water in a second small bowl to make a smooth slurry.

7. Generously coat the inside of a large wok with vegetable oil spray, then set the wok over high heat for a few minutes. Add the ginger and garlic; stir-fry for 10 seconds or so, just until fragrant. Add the meat and vegetables; stir-fry for 1 minute to heat through.

8. Add the rice vinegar mixture and continue stir-frying until the sauce is bubbling, less than 1 minute. Add the cornstarch slurry and stir-fry until the sauce has thickened, just a few seconds. Remove the wok from the heat and serve hot.

Then...

- While this stir-fry would traditionally be served over cooked white rice—a medium-grain rice like Arborio would be terrific, if not traditional—it can also be set over wilted stemmed, chopped spinach or even wilted baby kale. Lightly coat a skillet (or the wok) with *vegetable oil spray,* then set it over high heat for a couple of minutes. Add *a little minced garlic* and/or *minced peeled fresh ginger.* Stir-fry for a few seconds, then add the *greens* as well as *a little water* or *broth.* Stir-fry as the liquid boils away. Use kitchen tongs to transfer the greens to serving plates as a bed for the stir-fried beef, its vegetables, and sauce.

Corned Beef Hash

FAST / EASY / GLUTEN-FREE / 8 INGREDIENTS

Here's a *very* easy recipe that uses frozen hash brown cubes and deli corned beef for a pretty spectacular hash. And you don't even have to thaw those hash brown cubes!

Have the person at the deli counter slice the corned beef into ¾-inch strips. You can cube these at home so they're about the size of the hash brown cubes. You'll then toss those meat and potatoes with roughly chopped vegetables before it all goes in the basket. Make sure the vegetable pieces are fairly large, at least ½ inch each, so they can withstand the heat in the machine as the potatoes get tender.

INGREDIENTS	2-quart or larger air fryer	3.5-quart or larger air fryer	5.25-quart or larger air fryer
Frozen unseasoned hash brown cubes (no need to thaw)	2 cups (about 9 ounces)	3 cups (about 14 ounces)	4 cups (about 1 pound 2 ounces)
Deli corned beef, cut into ¾-inch-thick slices, then cubed	6 ounces	9 ounces	¾ pound
Roughly chopped yellow or white onion	½ cup (1 small onion)	¾ cup	1 cup (1 medium onion)
Stemmed, cored, and roughly chopped red bell pepper	½ cup (1 small bell pepper)	¾ cup	1 cup (1 medium bell pepper)
Olive oil	1½ tablespoons	2½ tablespoons	3 tablespoons
Dried thyme	¼ teaspoon	Rounded ¼ teaspoon	½ teaspoon
Dried sage leaves	¼ teaspoon	Rounded ¼ teaspoon	½ teaspoon
Cayenne	Up to ⅛ teaspoon	Up to a rounded ⅛ teaspoon	Up to ¼ teaspoon
MAKES	4 servings	6 servings	8 servings

1. With the basket (or basket attachment) in the air fryer, heat it to 400°F (or 390°F, if that's the closest setting).

2. Mix all the ingredients in a large or very large bowl until the potato cubes and corned beef are coated in the spices.

3. Spread the mixture in the basket in as close to an even layer as you can. Air-fry for 15 minutes, tossing and rearranging the pieces at the 5- and 10-minute marks to expose covered bits, until the potatoes are browned, even crisp, and the mixture is very fragrant.

4. Pour the contents of the basket onto a serving platter or divide between serving plates. Cool for a couple of minutes before serving.

Then...

- This hash could use a little acid to brighten the flavors on the plate. Drizzle the servings with syrupy balsamic vinegar or white balsamic vinegar (see page 203).

- Top the hash with a fried egg. Even better, fry the eggs and drizzle them with a touch of white wine or white balsamic vinegar before transferring them from the skillet to the servings.

Easy Tex-Mex Chimichangas

EASY / CAN BE GLUTEN-FREE / 8 INGREDIENTS

By using purchased ingredients like deli roast beef and canned refried beans, you can make a chimichanga in no time without all the fat (and mess) of deep-frying it. If you don't know, a chimichanga is sort of like a deep-fried burrito—although when air-fried it's a much lighter meal with all the crunch of the original.

Because a chimichanga cooks so quickly, feel free to make additional ones, air-frying them in batches. If some get cold, they can be reheated at a similar air fryer heat for 2 to 3 minutes.

INGREDIENTS	2-quart or larger air fryer	3.5-quart or larger air fryer
Thinly sliced deli roast beef, chopped	2 ounces	¼ pound
Shredded Cheddar cheese or shredded Tex-Mex cheese blend	¼ cup (about 1 ounce)	½ cup (about 2 ounces)
Jarred salsa verde or salsa rojo	2 tablespoons	¼ cup
Ground cumin	¼ teaspoon	½ teaspoon
Dried oregano	¼ teaspoon	½ teaspoon
Burrito-size (12-inch) flour tortilla(s), *not* corn tortillas (gluten-free, if a concern)	1	2
Canned refried beans	⅓ cup	⅔ cup
Vegetable oil spray	As needed	As needed
MAKES	*1 chimichanga*	*2 chimichangas*

1. With the basket (or basket attachment) in the air fryer, heat it to 375°F (or 370°F or 360°F, if one of these is the closest setting).

2. Stir the roast beef, cheese, salsa, cumin, and oregano in a bowl until well mixed.

3. Lay a tortilla on a clean, dry work surface. Spread ⅓ cup of the refried beans in the center lower third of the tortilla(s), leaving an inch on either side of the spread beans.

For one chimichanga, spread all of the roast beef mixture on top of the beans. For two, spread half of the roast beef mixture on each tortilla.

At either "end" of the filling mixture, fold the sides of the tortilla up and over the filling, partially covering it. Starting with the unfolded side of the tortilla just below the filling, roll the tortilla closed. Fold and roll the second filled tortilla, as necessary.

4. Coat the exterior of the tortilla(s) with vegetable oil spray. Set the chimichanga(s) seam side down in the basket, with at least ½ inch air space between them if you're working with two. Air-fry undisturbed for 8 minutes, or until the tortilla is lightly browned and crisp.

5. Use kitchen tongs to gently transfer the chimichanga(s) to a wire rack. Cool for at last 5 minutes or up to 20 minutes before serving.

Then...

- Although chimichangas are traditionally served with salsa or even **Salsa Fresca** (page 167) spooned on top, they're pretty fine with **AVOCADO RANCH DIP.** For 4 to 6 servings, mash and mix *1 pitted and peeled ripe Hass avocado, 1 cup plain Greek yogurt, ¼ cup buttermilk, 1 tablespoon powdered ranch dressing mix, up to ½ cup minced fresh parsley and/ or cilantro leaves;* and *the juice of 1 lemon* in a small bowl until smooth and uniform.

Italian Meatballs

FAST / EASY / CAN BE GLUTEN-FREE / 6 INGREDIENTS

We've made meatballs *easier* by using Italian sausage meat and seasoned bread crumbs alongside ground beef, thus eliminating the need for any dried or fresh spices in this recipe. There's also no added salt, since sausage meat and seasoned bread crumbs are pretty salty. (Check the labels to be sure. You can add ½ to 1 teaspoon table salt, if you like.)

If you can't find bulk Italian sausage meat, buy an equivalent weight of Italian sausage links or even the fatter Italian sausages made for the grill. Slit the casings and pull them off the filling. Crumble this filling a bit so it has more of the texture of ground meat.

The sausage meat is fatty, so the leaner the ground beef, the better.

INGREDIENTS	2-quart or larger air fryer	3.5-quart or larger air fryer	5.25-quart or larger air fryer
Lean ground beef	½ pound (gluten-free, if a concern)	¾ pound	1 pound
Bulk mild or hot Italian sausage meat	¼ pound (gluten-free, if a concern)	6 ounces	½ pound
Seasoned Italian-style dried bread crumbs	⅓ cup	½ cup	⅔ cup
Large egg	1 white only	1	1
Whole or low-fat milk	2 tablespoons	3 tablespoons	¼ cup
Olive oil spray	As needed	As needed	As needed
MAKES	*6 meatballs*	*8 meatballs*	*12 meatballs*

1. With the basket (or basket attachment) in the air fryer, heat it to 375°F (or 370°F or 360°F, if one of these is the closest setting).

2. Mix the ground beef, Italian sausage meat, bread crumbs, egg, and milk in a bowl until well combined. Using clean hands, form this mixture into large meatballs, using a rounded ¼ cup for each. Set the meatballs on a large cutting board and coat them on all sides with olive oil spray. Be gentle when you turn them. They're fragile.

continues

3. When the machine is at temperature, set them in the basket with as much space between them as possible. The important thing is that they should not touch, even if there's only a fraction of an inch between them. Air-fry undisturbed for 12 minutes, or until an instant-read meat thermometer inserted into the center of a meatball registers 165°F.

4. Use kitchen tongs to gently pick up the meatballs one by one and transfer them to a cutting board or a serving platter. Cool for a few minutes before serving.

Then...

- Drop the air-fried meatballs right into a pot of simmering marinara or alfredo sauce.

- Pour *marinara sauce* into a 9-inch round or 9 x 13-inch rectangular baking pan, then add the *meatballs* and cover them with *shredded semi-firm mozzarella* and *finely grated Parmesan*. Bake in a 375°F oven until bubbling and gooey, about 15 minutes.

- Serve them warm right on top of **Wilted Baby Spinach Salad** (page 199).

- Or save some of the meatballs in a covered bowl in the fridge and use them in the next couple of days to make meatball subs. Line them up in a split-open *long, soft roll, such as hero, hoagie, or Italian sub roll (gluten-free, if a concern)* with warmed *marinara sauce* and *shredded semi-firm mozzarella cheese*.

See photo in insert.

Beef Empanadas

12 INGREDIENTS

Here's our (relatively) easy way to make empanadas with purchased pie crust. These are fairly small, certainly not the big hand pies you can get at some Mexican bakeries. Figure on two or three per serving. But you can make the large batch for a small air-fryer and cook the empanadas in two stages for the proper air circulation around the pastries.

These empanadas freeze well *after* they've cooked. Cool them on the rack to room temperature (about 30 minutes), then store them in a heavy zip-closed plastic bag in the freezer for up to 4 months. To reheat, transfer them straight from the freezer to a 300°F air fryer and air-fry for 8 to 10 minutes, until they are heated through and crisp again.

INGREDIENTS	2-quart or larger air fryer	5.25-quart or larger air fryer
Olive oil	1 tablespoon	2 tablespoons
Lean ground beef	2 ounces	¼ pound
Medium scallion(s), trimmed and thinly sliced	1	2
Raisins, chopped	1 tablespoon	2 tablespoons
Drained and rinsed capers, chopped	1 teaspoon	2 teaspoons
Tomato paste	1 teaspoon	2 teaspoons
Dried oregano	½ teaspoon	1 teaspoon
Table salt	¼ teaspoon	½ teaspoon
Ground black pepper	¼ teaspoon	½ teaspoon
Purchased refrigerated pie crust(s), from a minimum 14.1-ounce box	1	2
Large egg	1	1
Water	2 tablespoons	2 tablespoons
MAKES	*6 empanadas*	*12 empanadas*

1. Set a medium or large skillet over medium heat for a couple of minutes. Swirl in the oil, then crumble in the ground beef. Cook, stirring often, until browned, 3 to 4 minutes.

2. Remove the skillet from the heat and stir in the scallion(s), raisins, capers, tomato paste, oregano, salt, and pepper. Set the filling mixture aside to cool for 15 minutes.

3. With the basket (or basket attachment) in the air fryer, heat it to 350°F (or 360°F, if that's the closest setting).

4. Unwrap and unroll the sheet(s) of pie crust dough onto a clean, dry work surface. Cut out 3½-inch circles with a large cookie cutter or giant sturdy drinking glass—or use a 3½-inch plate to trace and cut the circles in the dough. Gather up the scraps of

continues

dough. Lightly flour your work surface and set the scraps on top. Roll them together into a sheet that matches the thickness of the original dough and cut more circles until you have 6 for the small batch or 12 circles for the larger batch.

5. Place 1½ tablespoons of the filling mixture in the center of each circle. Wet the perimeter of a circle with a clean finger dipped in cold water and fold the circle in half, making a half-moon. Press to seal the edge. Even better, seal the edge by pressing the tines of a flatware fork along it. Continue folding and sealing the remainder of the circles.

6. Set the filled empanadas in the basket in one layer with as much air space between them as possible. Air-fry undisturbed for 6 minutes.

7. Meanwhile, whisk the egg and water in a small bowl until uniform.

8. Remove the basket from the machine. Use a pastry brush to coat the tops of the empanadas with the egg mixture. Continue air-frying undisturbed for 6 minutes more, or until golden brown and flaky.

9. Use a nonstick-safe spatula to transfer the empanadas to a wire rack. Cool for at least 5 minutes or up to 30 minutes before serving.

Then...

- Serve these with **Avocado Ranch Dip** (page 223), **Salsa Fresca** (page 167), or **Fiery Sour Cream Dip** (page 44).

- Or make CURTIDO DE CEBOLLA Y TOMATE (onion and tomato salsa), a Latin American favorite. For 4 to 6 servings, slice *2 small red onions* into paper-thin rings. Set them in a bowl and toss well with *1 tablespoon table salt* (or better, *kosher salt*). Set aside for 10 minutes, then cover the onions with *lukewarm tap water* and set aside for another 10 minutes. Drain the onions in a colander set in the sink and rinse them well with cold water; drain them well to get most of the water off of them. Set them in a bowl and add *the juice of 3 limes*. Toss well and set aside for 30 minutes, tossing frequently. Add *4 diced Roma or plum tomatoes*, *1 to 2 tablespoons minced fresh cilantro leaves,* and *1 to 2 tablespoons olive oil*. Toss well, taste for salt, and season again, if the salsa needs it.

Glazed Meatloaf

CAN BE GLUTEN-FREE / 12 INGREDIENTS

If we nix the loaf pan and make a meatloaf right in the air fryer's basket, the entire surface of the loaf gets a tasty crust. We've glazed the meatloaf with a sweet, sticky mix that includes hoisin sauce. If you don't want to spring for a jar, substitute equal parts regular or low-sodium soy sauce or gluten-free tamari sauce and molasses to come to the same volume amount as stated for the hoisin sauce.

Please use an instant-read meat thermometer. It's the only way to tell if the meatloaf has cooked through and is safe to eat.

INGREDIENTS	2-quart or larger air fryer	3.5-quart or larger air fryer	5.25-quart or larger air fryer
Seasoned Italian-style panko bread crumbs (gluten-free, if a concern)	¼ cup	½ cup	¾ cup
Whole or low-fat milk	2 tablespoons	¼ cup	6 tablespoons
Lean ground beef	½ pound	1 pound	1½ pounds
Bulk mild Italian sausage meat (gluten-free, if a concern)	½ pound	1 pound	1½ pounds
Large egg(s), well beaten	1 white only	1	1 plus 1 additional egg white
Dried thyme	½ teaspoon	1 teaspoon	1½ teaspoons
Onion powder	½ teaspoon	1 teaspoon	1½ teaspoons
Garlic powder	½ teaspoon	1 teaspoon	1½ teaspoons
Vegetable oil spray	As needed	As needed	As needed
Ketchup (gluten-free, if a concern)	1½ teaspoons	1 tablespoon	1½ tablespoons
Hoisin sauce (see page 180; gluten-free, if a concern)	1½ teaspoons	1 tablespoon	1½ tablespoons
Pickle brine, preferably from a jar of jalapeño rings (gluten-free, if a concern)	1 teaspoon	2 teaspoons	1 tablespoon
MAKES	2 servings	4 servings	6 servings

1. Pour the bread crumbs into a large bowl, add the milk, stir gently, and soak for 10 minutes.

2. With the basket (or basket attachment) in the air fryer, heat it to 350°F (or 360°F, if that's the closest setting).

3. Add the ground beef, Italian sausage meat, egg(s), thyme, onion powder, and garlic powder to the bowl with the bread crumbs. Blend gently until well combined. (Clean, dry hands work best!) Form this mixture into an oval loaf about 2 inches tall (its length

continues

will vary depending on the amount of ingredients) but with a flat bottom. Generously coat the top, bottom, and all sides of the loaf with vegetable oil spray.

4. Use a large, nonstick-safe spatula or perhaps silicone baking mitts to transfer the loaf to the basket. Air-fry undisturbed for 30 minutes for a small meatloaf, 40 minutes for a medium one, or 50 minutes for a large, until an instant-read meat thermometer inserted into the center of the loaf registers 165°F.

5. Whisk the ketchup, hoisin, and pickle brine in a small bowl until smooth. Brush this over the top and sides of the meatloaf and continue air-frying undisturbed for 5 minutes, or until the glaze has browned a bit. Use that same spatula or those same baking mitts to transfer the meatloaf to a cutting board. Cool for 10 minutes before slicing.

Then...

- Serve this meatloaf with **Charred Radicchio Salad** (page 352) and **Fried Corn on the Cob** (page 357).

- Or make **Air-Fried Potato Salad** (page 338).

- If you're looking for a gluten-free meatloaf—or just a turkey meatloaf—check the recipe on page 202.

Cinnamon-Stick Kofta Skewers

EASY / GLUTEN-FREE / 9 INGREDIENTS

A stick of kofta is something like a Middle Eastern meatloaf: a spiced ground meat mixture, sometimes cooked on its own when shaped like little tubes, sometimes wrapped around skewers before cooking, or (as here) put on cinnamon sticks for an added flavor boost.

Make sure you adequately *form* the meat *around* the cinnamon stick, pressing the mixture so it adheres to the stick and holds together.

For a more traditional flavor, substitute ground lamb (or even ground goat, if you can find it) for the ground beef. Or use a 50-50 combo of ground beef and ground lamb.

Cinnamon sticks can be expensive in the spice rack. Look for them in bulk containers, often in the produce section, if not in the bulk ingredient section. Or order them in bulk from online suppliers. If you can only find long cinnamon sticks, break them into 4-inch sections so they can fit in the basket.

INGREDIENTS	2-quart or larger air fryer	3.5-quart or larger air fryer	5.25-quart or larger air fryer
Lean ground beef	¾ pound	1 pound	1½ pounds
Ground cumin	¼ teaspoon	½ teaspoon	1 teaspoon
Onion powder	¼ teaspoon	½ teaspoon	1 teaspoon
Ground dried turmeric	¼ teaspoon	½ teaspoon	¾ teaspoon
Ground cinnamon	¼ teaspoon	½ teaspoon	¾ teaspoon
Table salt	¼ teaspoon	½ teaspoon	¾ teaspoon
Cayenne	Up to ⅛ teaspoon	Up to a rounded ⅛ teaspoon	Up to ¼ teaspoon
3½- to 4-inch-long cinnamon sticks (see the headnote)	6	8	12
Vegetable oil spray	As needed	As needed	As needed
MAKES	6 koftas	8 koftas	12 koftas

1. With the basket (or basket attachment) in the air fryer, heat it to 375°F (or 370°F or 360°F, if one of these is the closest setting).

2. Gently mix the ground beef, cumin, onion powder, turmeric, cinnamon, salt, and cayenne in a bowl until the meat is evenly mixed with the spices. (Clean, dry hands work best!) Divide this mixture into 2-ounce portions, each about the size of a golf ball.

3. Wrap one portion of the meat mixture around a cinnamon stick, using about three-quarters of the length of the stick, covering one end but leaving a little "handle" of cinnamon stick protruding from the other end. Set aside and continue making more kofta skewers.

continues

4. Generously coat the formed kofta skewers on all sides with vegetable oil spray. Set them in the basket with as much air space between them as possible. Air-fry undisturbed for 13 minutes, or until browned and cooked through. If the machine is at 360°F, you may need to add 2 minutes to the cooking time.

5. Use a nonstick-safe spatula, and perhaps kitchen tongs for balance, to gently transfer the kofta skewers to a wire rack. Cool for at least 5 minutes or up to 20 minutes before serving.

Then...

- Serve these with **Tangy Tahini Dip** (page 48) or just **Tahini Sauce** (page 147).

- Or make 4 servings of TANGY GOAT CHEESE DIP by whisking *3 ounces crumbled soft goat cheese (chèvre), 2½ tablespoons buttermilk (or whole milk for less tang), 1 teaspoon granulated white sugar, up to ½ teaspoon table salt,* and *¼ teaspoon garlic powder* in a medium bowl until smooth.

Tuscan Veal Chops

FAST / GLUTEN-FREE / 8 INGREDIENTS

Veal chops are a luxury that the air fryer does right. For the best results, look for meaty chops without much fat. We prefer pink or so-called pastured veal, rather than the pure white meat that was once prized in French restaurants. The pink meat is simply more flavorful. It can stand up to a bold rub.

Crush the fennel seeds in a mortar with a pestle, in a spice grinder with just a couple of pulses (but not until they're dust), or between sheets of plastic wrap on a cutting board underneath a heavy, small saucepan.

INGREDIENTS	2-quart or larger air fryer	3.5-quart or larger air fryer	5.25-quart or larger air fryer
Olive oil	2 teaspoons	4 teaspoons	2 tablespoons
Finely minced garlic	1 teaspoon	2 teaspoons	1 tablespoon
Finely minced fresh rosemary leaves	1 teaspoon	2 teaspoons	1 tablespoon
Finely grated lemon zest	½ teaspoon	1 teaspoon	1½ teaspoons
Crushed fennel seeds	½ teaspoon	1 teaspoon	1½ teaspoons
Table salt	½ teaspoon	1 teaspoon	1½ teaspoons
Red pepper flakes	Up to ⅛ teaspoon	Up to ¼ teaspoon	Up to ½ teaspoon
10-ounce bone-in veal loin or rib chop(s), about ½ inch thick	1	2	3
MAKES	*1 veal chop*	*2 veal chops*	*3 veal chops*

1. With the basket (or basket attachment) in the air fryer, heat it to 400°F (or 390°F, if that's the closest setting).

2. Mix the oil, garlic, rosemary, lemon zest, fennel seeds, salt, and red pepper flakes in a small bowl. Rub this mixture onto both sides of the veal chop(s). Set aside at room temperature as the machine comes to temperature.

3. Set the chop(s) in the basket. If you're cooking more than one chop, leave as much air space between them as possible. Air-fry undisturbed for 12 minutes for medium-rare, or until an instant-read meat thermometer inserted into the center of a chop (without touching bone) registers 135°F (not USDA-approved). Or air-fry undisturbed for 15 minutes for medium-well, or until an instant-read meat thermometer registers 145°F (USDA-approved).

4. Use kitchen tongs to transfer the chops to a cutting board or a wire rack. Cool for 5 minutes before serving.

Then...

- Serve these with **Steak Fries** (page 327) or **Hasselback Garlic-and-Butter Potatoes** (page 337).

- Try our **EASY RED WINE SAUCE.** For 4 servings, boil *2 cups dry red wine* (such as Cabernet Sauvignon or Pinot Noir) and *1 medium single-lobe shallot, finely chopped,* in a small saucepan over high heat until reduced to about ½ cup. Remove from the heat. Melt *2 tablespoons butter* in a small skillet over medium heat. Whisk (do not stir) *2 tablespoons all-purpose flour* into the butter until the mixture makes a blond paste. Slowly whisk in the hot wine mixture until the flour mixture dissolves. Reduce the heat to low and continue cooking, whisking often, until thickened, about 5 minutes. Season with *table salt* to taste and serve warm.

Pesto-Rubbed Veal Chops

FAST / EASY / GLUTEN-FREE / 3 INGREDIENTS

It doesn't get much easier than this! Of course, you can gussy the chops up by making pesto from scratch. Consider either our **Basil Pesto** (page 118) or the more unusual **Sage Pesto** (page 111). But honestly, these may not be worth the effort when the sun's setting and a summer evening is well underway.

INGREDIENTS	2-quart or larger air fryer	3.5-quart or larger air fryer	5.25-quart or larger air fryer
Purchased pesto	2 tablespoons	¼ cup	6 tablespoons
10-ounce bone-in veal loin or rib chop(s)	1	2	3
Ground black pepper	¼ teaspoon	½ teaspoon	¾ teaspoon
MAKES	1 veal chop	2 veal chops	3 veal chops

1. With the basket (or basket attachment) in the air fryer, heat it to 400°F (or 390°F, if that's the closest setting).

2. Rub the pesto onto both sides of the veal chop(s). Sprinkle one side of the chop(s) with the ground black pepper. Set aside at room temperature as the machine comes up to temperature.

3. Set the chop(s) in the basket. If you're cooking more than one chop, leave as much air space between them as possible. Air-fry undisturbed for 12 minutes for medium-rare, or until an instant-read meat thermometer inserted into the center of a chop (without touching bone) registers 135°F (not USDA-approved). Or air-fry undisturbed for 15 minutes for medium-well, or until an instant-read meat thermometer registers 145°F (USDA-approved).

4. Use kitchen tongs to transfer the chops to a cutting board or a wire rack. Cool for 5 minutes before serving.

Then...

- Because of the subtle flavors in the pesto, these veal chops are best with a vinegary salad. Consider **Fennel-Pear Salad** (page 125), **Orange-Romaine Salad** (page 171), **Arugula and Pistachio Salad** (page 197), or **Caprese Pasta Salad** (page 252).

Crunchy Veal Cutlets

FAST / CAN BE GLUTEN-FREE / 6 INGREDIENTS

Veal cutlets make a great dinner in an air fryer because the coating gets crisp while the meat stays tender. If you can't find already-pounded-thin veal cutlets, set a 2-ounce cutlet between sheets of plastic wrap on a cutting board or counter, then gently but firmly pound it to the desired thickness with the smooth side of a meat mallet or the bottom of a heavy saucepan.

The servings here are given as a twofer, depending on whether you believe one or two veal cutlets are a serving. (Two in our household, but tastes—and appetites—vary.)

INGREDIENTS	2-quart or larger air fryer	3.5-quart or larger air fryer	5.25-quart or larger air fryer
All-purpose flour or tapioca flour	¼ cup	½ cup	⅔ cup
Large egg(s), well beaten	1	1	2
Seasoned Italian-style dried bread crumbs (gluten-free, if a concern)	½ cup	¾ cup	1 cup
Yellow cornmeal	1 tablespoon	2 tablespoons	3 tablespoons
Thinly pounded 2-ounce veal leg cutlets (less than ¼ inch thick)	2	4	6
Olive oil spray	As needed	As needed	As needed
MAKES	1 or 2 servings	2 or 4 servings	3 or 6 servings

1. With the basket (or basket attachment) in the air fryer, heat it to 400°F (or 390°F, if that's the closest setting).

2. Set up and fill three shallow soup plates or small pie plates on your counter: one for the flour; one for the egg(s); and one for the bread crumbs, whisked with the cornmeal until well combined.

3. Dredge a veal cutlet in the flour, coating it on both sides. Gently shake off any excess flour, then gently dip it in the beaten egg(s), coating both sides. Let the excess egg slip back into the rest. Dip the cutlet in the bread-crumb mixture, turning it several times and pressing gently to make an even coating on both sides. Coat it on both sides with olive oil spray, then set it aside and continue dredging and coating more cutlets.

4. When the machine is at temperature, set the cutlets in the basket so that they don't touch each other. Air-fry undisturbed for 5 minutes, or until crisp and brown. (If only some of the veal cutlets will fit in one layer for any selected batch—the sizes of air fryer baskets vary dramatically—work in batches as necessary.)

5. Use kitchen tongs to transfer the cutlets to a wire rack. Cool for only 1 to 2 minutes before serving.

continues

Then...

- Make BALSAMIC SAUCE for these cutlets. For 2 to 4 servings, melt *2 tablespoons butter* in a small skillet set over medium heat. Add *1 tablespoon minced fresh sage leaves* and *2 teaspoons minced garlic.* Cook for a few seconds, stirring often, until fragrant. Stir in *½ cup chicken broth* and *1 teaspoon dark brown sugar.* Bring to a full boil, then cook, stirring often, until reduced to about ⅓ cup. Stir in *2 tablespoons balsamic vinegar,* bring back to a simmer, remove from the heat, and season with table salt to taste.

- Or turn the cutlets into VEAL PARMESAN. Set the cooked cutlets in a large baking dish. Top each cutlet with *2 tablespoons jarred pizza sauce,* then *2 tablespoons shredded semi-firm mozzarella* and *1 tablespoon finely grated Parmesan cheese.* If desired, add *a pinch of red pepper flakes.* Bake in a 400°F oven for 2 minutes to melt the cheese and heat the sauce.

Lemon-Butter Veal Cutlets

FAST / EASY / GLUTEN-FREE / 3 INGREDIENTS

Here's a super easy recipe that doesn't even involve breading veal cutlets. They're actually cooked under a thin strip of butter, which will melt and (mostly) run to the bottom of the drawer or onto the tray below the basket attachment in a toaster oven–style air fryer.

Don't worry. The butter won't go to waste. It'll brown down there as the cutlets cook. You can then pour it over them as a brown butter "sauce."

But watch out. The drawer may have a bottom insert that can come loose. Pour gently and carefully, holding the basket's bottom in place with a wooden spoon.

There's no salt in this recipe. Many brands of lemon-pepper seasoning include salt. If yours doesn't, season the cutlets with salt at the table after cooking.

INGREDIENTS	2-quart or larger air fryer	3.5-quart or larger air fryer	5.25-quart or larger air fryer
Butter (see step 2)	2 strips	3 strips	4 strips
Thinly pounded 2-ounce veal leg cutlets (less than ¼ inch thick)	2	3	4
Lemon-pepper seasoning	¼ teaspoon	Rounded ¼ teaspoon	½ teaspoon
MAKES	1 serving	2 servings	3 servings

1. With the basket (or basket attachment) in the air fryer, heat it to 400°F (or 390°F, if that's the closest setting).

2. Run a vegetable peeler lengthwise along a hard, cold stick of butter, making 2, 3, or 4 long strips as the recipe requires for the number of cutlets you're making.

3. Lay the veal cutlets on a clean, dry cutting board or work surface. Sprinkle about ⅛ teaspoon lemon-pepper seasoning over each. Set a strip of butter on top of each cutlet.

4. When the machine is at temperature, set the topped cutlets in the basket so that they don't overlap or even touch. Air-fry undisturbed for 4 minutes without turning.

5. Use a nonstick-safe spatula to transfer the cutlets to a serving plate or plates, taking care to keep as much of the butter on top as possible. Remove the basket from the drawer or from over the baking tray. Carefully pour the browned butter over the cutlets.

Then...

- These cutlets would be great with **Beet Fries** (page 331) or **Zucchini Fries** (page 330).

- Or make **Simple Roasted Sweet Potatoes** (page 341), then pour that browned butter over the sweet potatoes.

- Or get more elegant with **Crispy, Cheesy Leeks** (page 350).

Crunchy Fried Pork Loin Chops

FAST / CAN BE GLUTEN-FREE / 5 INGREDIENTS

Remember those breaded, oven-baked Shake-'N-Bake pork chops advertised incessantly on TV? Our version is tastier because the coating is less processed and because the air fryer lets that coating get crunchy on all sides of the chops, not just on the tops.

In this recipe, we use smaller boneless pork loin chops than in some of the other recipes. These 4- to 5-ounce chops cook quickly without burning the bread-crumb coating. For a kick in that coating, add some hot red pepper sauce (gluten-free, if a concern), such as Cholula or Tabasco, to the beaten eggs.

INGREDIENTS	2-quart or larger air fryer	3.5-quart or larger air fryer	5.25-quart or larger air fryer
All-purpose flour or tapioca flour	1 cup	1 cup	1 cup
Large egg(s), well beaten	1	1	2
Seasoned Italian-style dried bread crumbs (gluten-free, if a concern)	1 cup	1½ cups	2 cups
4- to 5-ounce boneless center-cut pork loin chops	2	3	4
Vegetable oil spray	As needed	As needed	As needed
MAKES	2 servings	3 servings	4 servings

1. With the basket (or basket attachment) in the air fryer, heat it to 350°F (or 360°F, if that's the closest setting).

2. Set up and fill three shallow soup plates or small pie plates on your counter: one for the flour, one for the beaten egg(s), and one for the bread crumbs.

3. Dredge a pork chop in the flour, coating both sides as well as around the edge. Gently shake off any excess, then dip the chop in the egg(s), again coating both sides and the edge. Let any excess egg slip back into the rest, then set the chop in the bread crumbs, turning it and pressing gently to coat well on both sides and the edge. Coat the pork chop all over with vegetable oil spray and set aside so you can dredge, coat, and spray the additional chop(s).

4. Set the chops in the basket with as much air space between them as possible. Air-fry undisturbed for 12 minutes, or until brown and crunchy and an instant-read meat thermometer inserted into the center of a chop registers 145°F.

5. Use kitchen tongs to transfer the chops to a wire rack. Cool for 5 minutes before serving.

Then...

- Serve these pork chops with **Roasted Peppers with Balsamic Vinegar and Basil** (page 309) or **Perfect Broccolini** (page 347).

- Or make a TOMATO-PEACH SALAD. Toss *thin wedges of peeled, pitted peaches* and *round tomatoes* with *very thin red onion slices* and *stemmed fresh thyme leaves*. Dress the salad with a *drizzle of olive oil* and *balsamic vinegar* as well as *table salt* and *ground black pepper*, to taste. A smattering of *red pepper flakes* would also be welcome.

Wasabi-Coated Pork Loin Chops

FAST / 5 INGREDIENTS

A crust of ground wasabi peas is one of the craziest things we can make happen in an air fryer. This crust is best with pork because the meat is sweeter than, say, chicken or even beef. Since the peas are fairly oily, there's no need to spray the chops. And the results are unexpected: a sweet, nose-prickling satisfaction.

Unfortunately, almost all wasabi peas contain flour in their coating. So unless you're up for a long internet-retailer search, this recipe cannot be gluten-free.

INGREDIENTS	2-quart or larger air fryer	3.5-quart or larger air fryer	5.25-quart or larger air fryer
Wasabi peas	1 cup	1½ cups	2 cups
Plain panko bread crumbs	3 tablespoons	¼ cup	⅓ cup
Large egg white(s)	1	1	2
Water	2 tablespoons	2 tablespoons	2 tablespoons
5- to 6-ounce boneless center-cut pork loin chops (about ½ inch thick)	2	3	4
MAKES	2 servings	3 servings	4 servings

1. With the basket (or basket attachment) in the air fryer, heat it to 375°F (or 370°F or 360°F, if one of these is the closest setting).

2. Put the wasabi peas in a food processor. Cover and process until finely ground, about like panko bread crumbs. Add the bread crumbs and pulse a few times to blend.

3. Set up and fill two shallow soup plates or small pie plates on your counter: one for the egg white(s), whisked with the water until uniform; and one for the wasabi pea mixture.

4. Dip a pork chop in the egg white mixture, coating the chop on both sides as well as around the edge. Allow any excess egg white mixture to slip back into the rest, then set the chop in the wasabi pea mixture. Press gently and turn it several times to coat evenly on both sides and around the edge. Set aside, then dip and coat the remaining chop(s).

5. Set the chops in the basket with as much air space between them as possible. Air-fry, turning once at the 6-minute mark, for 12 minutes, or until the chops are crisp and browned and an instant-read meat thermometer inserted into the center of a chop registers 145°F. If the machine is at 360°F, you may need to add 1 to 2 minutes to the cooking time.

6. Use kitchen tongs to transfer the chops to a wire rack. Cool for a couple of minutes before serving.

Then...

- Start this meal with **Warm and Salty Edamame** (page 28).

- Serve these chops alongside cooked white rice (preferably medium- or even short-grain) and pickled ginger for sushi.

- These chops would also be great with **Vinegary Cucumbers** (page 131).

Perfect Pork Chops

FAST / EASY / GLUTEN-FREE / 8 INGREDIENTS

We think the perfect pork chops in the air fryer are boneless center-cut pork loin chops. They have a little interstitial fat, just enough that they don't dry out. They're not so fatty they'll create a smoking hazard in the machine. And mostly, they're super meaty, essentially a round of meat from the pork loin. They even cut like a steak after air-frying. But pay careful attention to the size of these chops: *6 ounces.*

We suggest cooking them to the USDA standard of 145°F—which means they'll be slightly pink inside. If they've reached 145°F and rested at least 3 minutes after cooking, they should be perfectly safe. However, pink pork might not be to your taste (although it *is* much juicier). If you want the chops more well done, cook them for 12 minutes or until the internal temperature is 160°F.

You can also use a grill pan accessory for these chops. They will get crunchier (but not much, since there's no coating on the meat). If you use this accessory, turn the chops at the 5-minute mark, halfway through cooking.

INGREDIENTS	2-quart or larger air fryer	3.5-quart or larger air fryer	5.25-quart or larger air fryer
Mild paprika	½ teaspoon	¾ teaspoon	1 teaspoon
Dried thyme	½ teaspoon	¾ teaspoon	1 teaspoon
Onion powder	½ teaspoon	¾ teaspoon	1 teaspoon
Garlic powder	¼ teaspoon	Rounded ¼ teaspoon	½ teaspoon
Table salt	¼ teaspoon	Rounded ¼ teaspoon	½ teaspoon
Ground black pepper	¼ teaspoon	Rounded ¼ teaspoon	½ teaspoon
6-ounce boneless center-cut pork loin chops	2	3	4
Vegetable oil spray	As needed	As needed	As needed
MAKES	*2 pork chops*	*3 pork chops*	*4 pork chops*

1. With the basket (or basket attachment) in the air fryer, heat it to 400°F (or 390°F, if that's the closest setting).

2. Mix the paprika, thyme, onion powder, garlic powder, salt, and pepper in a small bowl until well combined. Massage this mixture into both sides of the chops. Generously coat both sides of the chops with vegetable oil spray.

3. When the machine is at temperature, set the chops in the basket with as much air space between them as possible. Air-fry undisturbed for 10 minutes, or until an instant-read meat thermometer inserted into the thickest part of a chop registers 145°F.

4. Use kitchen tongs to transfer the chops to a cutting board or serving plates. Cool for 5 minutes before serving.

Then...

- For a simple, healthy dinner, serve these chops with **Perfect Asparagus** (page 342), **Perfect Broccoli** (page 345), or **Perfect Broccolini** (page 347).

- Or try a SUMMER SQUASH AND ORZO SALAD. Cook *diced yellow squash, diced zucchini,* and *thinly sliced scallions* in *a little olive oil* in a large skillet set over medium heat, stirring until the vegetables soften just a bit. Scrape the contents of the skillet into a bowl and add *cooked and drained orzo, crumbled goat cheese,* perhaps some *minced fresh basil or dill,* as well as *table salt* and *ground black pepper* to taste.

Sweet Potato–Crusted Pork Rib Chops

EASY / CAN BE GLUTEN-FREE / 5 OR 6 INGREDIENTS

Here's a recipe for classic bone-in pork rib chops done in an updated style. Because the meat is not as dense and thus more easily overcooked, the coating has to be thicker to protect it. And because the thicker coating needs time to set, we call for slightly thicker bone-in chops than the standard ones sold in big packages at the supermarket. But all those considerations lead to a big payoff. Crushed sweet potato chips yield a super tasty coating, an autumnal dinner any time of the year, even when the summer heat is on.

Many brands of sweet potato chips are not salted, so the salt here is optional. Check the ingredient list to be sure. And many brands of sweet potato chips are made without any gluten-containing products but may be made in factories where cross contamination is possible; so use *certified* gluten-free chips, if this is a concern.

INGREDIENTS	2-quart or larger air fryer	3.5-quart or larger air fryer	5.25-quart or larger air fryer
Large egg white(s), well beaten	1	2	2
Crushed sweet potato chips (certified gluten-free, if a concern)	¾ cup (about 3 ounces)	1½ cups (about 6 ounces)	2½ cups (about 10 ounces)
Ground cinnamon	½ teaspoon	1 teaspoon	2 teaspoons
Ground dried ginger	½ teaspoon	1 teaspoon	2 teaspoons
Table salt (optional)	½ teaspoon	1 teaspoon	1½ teaspoons
10-ounce, 1-inch-thick bone-in pork rib chop(s)	1	2	3
MAKES	1 serving	2 servings	3 servings

1. With the basket (or basket attachment) in the air fryer, heat it to 375°F (or 370°F or 360°F, if one of these is the closest setting).

2. Set up and fill two shallow soup plates or small pie plates on your counter: one for the beaten egg white(s); and one for the crushed chips, mixed with the cinnamon, ginger, and salt (if using).

continues

3. Dip a chop in the egg white(s), coating it on both sides as well as the edges. Let the excess egg white slip back into the rest, then set it in the crushed chip mixture. Turn it several times, pressing gently, until evenly coated on both sides and the edges. If necessary, set the chop aside and coat the remaining chop(s).

4. Set the chop(s) in the basket with as much air space between them as possible. Air-fry undisturbed for 12 minutes, or until crunchy and browned and an instant-read meat thermometer inserted into the center of a chop (without touching bone) registers 145°F. If the machine is at 360°F, you may need to add 1 to 2 minutes to the cooking time.

5. Use kitchen tongs to transfer the chop(s) to a wire rack. Cool for 2 or 3 minutes before serving.

Then...

- These pork chops would be great with a SPICY BLACK-EYED PEA SALAD. First, whisk *olive oil* and *lemon juice* in a 1-to-1 ratio (or 2-to-1 for milder flavor) in a serving bowl, along with *a little garlic powder, a little ground cumin, table salt,* and *ground black pepper.* Add *canned black-eyed peas (drained and rinsed), very thinly sliced fresh jalapeño rings, diced tomato, thinly sliced red onion,* and *chopped fresh cilantro leaves.* Toss well and taste for salt before serving.

Crispy Smoked Pork Chops

FAST / CAN BE GLUTEN-FREE / 5 INGREDIENTS

Most smoked pork chops come ready to eat, so they only need a little time in the air fryer to get this coating crunchy and lightly browned.

Smoked pork chops are usually quite salty, so this sweet corn flake–crumb coating is a fine contrast. For an even bigger contrast, stir a little cayenne or some red pepper flakes into the corn flakes before you coat the chops.

INGREDIENTS	2-quart or larger air fryer	3.5-quart or larger air fryer	5.25-quart or larger air fryer
All-purpose flour or tapioca flour	½ cup	⅔ cup	¾ cup
Large egg white(s)	1	1	2
Water	2 tablespoons	2 tablespoons	2 tablespoons
Corn flake crumbs (gluten-free, if a concern)	1 cup	1½ cups	2 cups
½-pound, ½-inch-thick bone-in smoked pork chops	2	3	4
MAKES	2 servings	3 servings	4 servings

1. With the basket (or basket attachment) in the air fryer, heat it to 375°F (or 370°F or 360°F, if the closest setting).

2. Set up and fill three shallow soup plates or small pie plates on your counter: one for the flour; one for the egg white(s), whisked with the water until foamy; and one for the corn flake crumbs.

3. Set a chop in the flour and turn it several times, coating both sides and the edges. Gently shake off any excess flour, then set it in the beaten egg white mixture. Turn to coat both sides as well as the edges. Let any excess egg white slip back into the rest, then set the chop in the corn flake crumbs. Turn it several times, pressing gently to coat the chop evenly on both sides and around the edge. Set the chop aside and continue coating the remaining chop(s) in the same way.

4. Set the chops in the basket with as much air space between them as possible. Air-fry undisturbed for 8 minutes, or until the coating is crunchy and the chops are heated through.

5. Use kitchen tongs to transfer the chops to a wire rack and cool for a couple of minutes before serving.

Then...

- Keep that sweet contrast to the salty chops going by serving these with bread-and-butter pickles or sweet gherkins, purchased cole slaw, and/or chunky cranberry sauce.

- Try them with the **Broccoli and Grape Salad** (page 127) or **Orange-Romaine Salad** (page 171).

Pork Schnitzel

FAST / CAN BE GLUTEN-FREE / 6 INGREDIENTS

This recipe is an outlier in this book because it's one of only a few missing a complete chart. Because a pounded-thin cutlet has so much exposed area, you can only fit one at a time in even the largest air fryer basket (or basket attachment, as the case might be). So this recipe makes one cutlet, assuming that you'll probably double, triple, or quadruple the recipe for a meal with others and thus work in batches. You can keep the individual schnitzel warm on a baking sheet (or better yet, on an oven-safe wire rack set on a baking sheet) in a 175°F oven.

Before we get to the doubling issues, let's talk about the best way to get a cutlet thin enough for schnitzel. Place the pork between plastic wrap sheets, then *gently* pound the cutlet with the smooth side of a meat mallet or the bottom of a heavy saucepan, striking the meat in arcs near its center and then on out to the edges, so you pull its edges farther and farther out with each glancing blow.

As for sizing this recipe for multiple batches, you won't need to double the egg mixture, flour, or bread crumbs with a second cutlet; but you will need to *double* them if you're making *three or four* cutlets. Notice that this recipe requires a double-dipping process to get an even, thick coating.

Use this recipe as a template for any sort of schnitzel—veal, chicken, or turkey.

INGREDIENTS	2-quart or larger air fryer
All-purpose flour or tapioca flour	½ cup
Large egg	1
Water	2 tablespoons
Seasoned Italian-style panko bread crumbs (gluten-free, if a concern)	1 cup
8-ounce pork cutlet, pounded to ¼ inch thick	1
Vegetable oil spray	As needed
MAKES	*1 serving*

1. With the basket (or basket attachment) in the air fryer, heat it to 375°F (or 370°F or 360°F, if one of these is the closest setting).

2. Set up and fill three shallow soup plates or small pie plates on your counter: one for the flour; one for the egg, whisked with the water until uniform; and one for the bread crumbs.

3. Set the cutlet in the flour and turn to coat evenly on both sides. Gently shake off any excess flour, then set the cutlet in the egg mixture. Turn several times to coat the meat, then let any excess egg mixture slip back into the rest. Set the cutlet in the bread crumbs. Turn it several times, pressing gently to coat the cutlet. Return the cutlet to the egg mixture and coat it again on both sides. Then return it to the bread crumbs and again coat it evenly on both sides. Lightly coat the cutlet with vegetable oil spray.

4. Set it in the basket and air-fry undisturbed for 12 minutes, or until browned and crunchy.

5. Use kitchen tongs to transfer the cutlet to a wire rack and cool for a minute or two before serving (or keeping a cutlet warm as we suggest in the headnote of this recipe while you make more).

Then...

- Serve the schnitzel on top of baby arugula dressed with a little olive oil, table salt, and ground black pepper—then offer lemon wedges to squeeze over both the schnitzel and the salad.

- Go over the top by putting a fried egg on top of the schnitzel, itself set on top of this salad.

- Or set the schnitzel over egg noodles, cooked, drained, and tossed with melted butter, a little ground black pepper, and a few caraway seeds.

Tonkatsu

FAST / CAN BE GLUTEN-FREE / 5 INGREDIENTS

Tonkatsu is a Japanese classic, a fairly simple breaded boneless pork chop. The meat's a little thicker than that used for schnitzel (see previous page) and there's no seasoning in the coating because, well, the dish is as much about the sauce as it is about the meat.

Our version calls for pork loin chops that are a little smaller (and thinner) than you might find in the meat case. If you can't find what you need, buy a center-cut boneless pork loin roast and cut some chops from it. Or ask your butcher to slice it into the correctly sized pieces.

You can buy bottled tonkatsu sauce, but you don't have to stick to tradition. You can use a variety of bottled Asian sauces, even Thai sweet chili sauce or duck sauce. But see the *Then* recipe for our quirky take on the classic sauce.

INGREDIENTS	2-quart or larger air fryer	3.5-quart or larger air fryer	5.25-quart or larger air fryer
All-purpose flour or tapioca flour	½ cup	½ cup	⅔ cup
Large egg white(s), well beaten	1	1	2
Plain panko bread crumbs (gluten-free, if a concern)	⅔ cup	¾ cup	1 cup
4-ounce center-cut boneless pork loin chops (about ½ inch thick)	2	3	4
Vegetable oil spray	As needed	As needed	As needed
MAKES	2 servings	3 servings	4 servings

1. With the basket (or basket attachment) in the air fryer, heat it to 375°F (or 370°F or 360°F, if one of these is the closest setting).

2. Set up and fill three shallow soup plates or small pie plates on your counter: one for the flour, one for the beaten egg white(s), and one for the bread crumbs.

continues

3. Set a chop in the flour and roll it to coat all sides, even the ends. Gently shake off any excess flour and set it in the egg white(s). Gently roll and turn it to coat all sides. Let any excess egg white slip back into the rest, then set the chop in the bread crumbs. Turn it several times, pressing gently to get an even coating on all sides and the ends. Generously coat the breaded chop with vegetable oil spray, then set it aside so you can dredge, coat, and spray the remaining chop(s).

4. Set the chops in the basket with as much air space between them as possible. Air-fry undisturbed for 10 minutes, or until golden brown and crisp.

5. Use kitchen tongs to transfer the chops to a wire rack and cool for a couple of minutes before serving.

Then...

- Serve these chops with SWEET-AND-SALTY DIPPING SAUCE. Whisk *ketchup, oyster sauce,* and *Worcestershire sauce (gluten-free, if a concern)* in a 4-to-2-to-1 ratio by volume, then whisk in a little *ground mustard* and *granulated white sugar* to taste.

- This sauce can also be used as a dressing for shredded cabbage, shredded daikon radish, or even thinly sliced cucumbers. If you use it as the dressing on a side salad, add a splash or two of lemon juice to bring out the sweetness of the vegetables. Under no circumstances should this sweet sauce be put on (already sweet) cooked white rice.

Pork Cutlets with Almond-Lemon Crust

EASY / CAN BE GLUTEN-FREE / 10 INGREDIENTS

This dish is fairly fancy, great for a gathering of friends at a sit-down meal. You might be surprised that we call for almond flour, not all-purpose flour. The almond flour has a slightly sweeter flavor, a better contrast to the lemon in the coating. And the almond flour makes the dish easily gluten-free, *if* you also use gluten-free dried bread crumbs. Make sure you give the cutlets a generous dose of olive oil spray so the coating gets extra crunchy.

INGREDIENTS	2-quart or larger air fryer	3.5-quart or larger air fryer	5.25-quart or larger air fryer
Almond flour	½ cup	¾ cup	1 cup
Plain dried bread crumbs (gluten-free, if a concern)	½ cup	¾ cup	1 cup
Finely grated lemon zest	1 teaspoon	1½ teaspoons	2 teaspoons
Table salt	1 teaspoon	1¼ teaspoons	1½ teaspoons
Garlic powder	½ teaspoon	¾ teaspoon	1 teaspoon
Dried oregano	½ teaspoon	¾ teaspoon	1 teaspoon
Large egg white(s)	1	1	2
Water	2 tablespoons	2 tablespoons	2 tablespoons
6-ounce center-cut boneless pork loin chops (about ¾ inch thick)	2	3	4
Olive oil spray	As needed	As needed	As needed
MAKES	2 servings	3 servings	4 servings

1. With the basket (or basket attachment) in the air fryer, heat it to 375°F (or 370°F or 360°F, if one of these is the closest setting).

2. Mix the almond flour, bread crumbs, lemon zest, salt, garlic powder, and dried oregano in a large bowl until well combined.

3. Whisk the egg white(s) and water in a shallow soup plate or small pie plate until uniform.

4. Dip a chop in the egg white mixture, turning it to coat all sides, even the ends. Let any excess egg white mixture slip back into the rest, then set it in the almond flour mixture. Turn it several times, pressing gently to coat it evenly. Generously coat the chop with olive oil spray, then set aside to dip and coat the remaining chop(s).

5. Set the chops in the basket with as much air space between them as possible. Air-fry undisturbed for 12 minutes, or until browned and crunchy. You may need to add 1 to 2 minutes to the cooking time if the machine is at 360°F.

continues

6. Use kitchen tongs to transfer the chops to a wire rack. Cool for a few minutes before serving.

Then...

- Serve these chop with lemon wedges. A little squeeze of the juice will brighten the flavors considerably.

- Also consider serving **Honey Mustard Cole Slaw** (page 215), **Sweet Potato Salad** (page 123), or **Fennel-Pear Salad** (page 125).

- Or make ZUCCHINI SLAW. Shred *zucchini* through the large holes of a box grater, then squeeze the shreds dry by handfuls over the sink. Set them in a serving bowl and toss with *toasted sliced almonds*, then dress with *a drizzle of olive oil* and *white balsamic vinegar (see page 203)*, as well as *table salt* and *ground black pepper* to taste.

Pretzel-Coated Pork Tenderloin

FAST / CAN BE GLUTEN-FREE / 5 INGREDIENTS

Pretzels make an excellent coating for pork: salty, a little sweet, with that characteristic beer hall flavor. The best pretzels to grind into crumbs are nuggets, rather than the more familiar ties. In any event, choose hard, crunchy pretzels, not soft ballpark ones. Better yet, look for "extra dark" pretzel nuggets.

This recipe is one of only two for pork tenderloin. Although lots of people throw pork tenderloins in the air fryer, we had little success with most techniques. For one thing, the typical pork tenderloin is too large to fit in most baskets. For another, the meat often dries out and gets tough, no matter which technique we used. In the end, we got the best results with this fairly thick coating that protects the cut-up tenderloin while it's inside the high-powered machine.

One note: We added no salt to this recipe because we used salted pretzel nuggets. If you use salt-free pretzels, you'll need to add up to 1 teaspoon table salt to the crushed pretzel crumbs.

INGREDIENTS	2-quart or larger air fryer	3.5-quart or larger air fryer	5.25-quart or larger air fryer
Large egg white(s)	1	1	2
Dijon mustard (gluten-free, if a concern)	2 teaspoons	2 teaspoons	1½ tablespoons
Crushed pretzel crumbs (see the headnote; gluten-free, if a concern)	1 cup (about 4 ounces)	1½ cups (about 6 ounces)	2 cups (about 8 ounces)
Pork tenderloin, cut into ¼-pound (4-ounce) sections	¾ pound (3 sections)	1 pound (4 sections)	1½ pounds (6 sections)
Vegetable oil spray	As needed	As needed	As needed
MAKES	*3 servings*	*4 servings*	*6 servings*

1. With the basket (or basket attachment) in the air fryer, heat it to 350°F (or 360°F, if that's the closest setting).

2. Set up and fill two shallow soup plates or small pie plates on your counter: one for the egg white(s), whisked with the mustard until foamy; and one for the pretzel crumbs.

3. Dip a section of pork tenderloin in the egg white mixture and turn it to coat well, even on the ends. Let any excess egg white mixture slip back into the rest, then set the pork in the pretzel crumbs. Roll it several times, pressing gently, until the pork is evenly coated, even on the ends. Generously coat the pork section with vegetable oil spray, set it aside, and continue coating and spraying the remaining sections.

4. Set the pork sections in the basket with at least ¼ inch between them. Air-fry undisturbed for 10 minutes, or until an instant-read meat thermometer inserted into the center of one section registers 145°F.

5. Use kitchen tongs to transfer the pieces to a wire rack. Cool for 3 to 5 minutes before serving.

Then...

- Serve these pork tenderloin pieces on warmed purchased sauerkraut. The best sort is found in bags in the meat case or perhaps a refrigerator case nearby.

- And offer boiled white potatoes with spicy deli mustard (gluten-free, if a concern).

- Or serve the pork with **Wilted Brussels Sprouts Slaw** (page 368). Make the slaw before you cook the pork tenderloin pieces so their coating won't sit around and get soggy.

City "Chicken"

FAST / CAN BE GLUTEN-FREE / 6 INGREDIENTS PLUS BAMBOO SKEWERS

There's no chicken in City "Chicken." Rather, the dish is from the era of the Great Depression. (No, not your mother's.) Chicken was expensive back in the days before factory poultry farming, so breaded pork—or sometimes veal, believe it or not—was substituted as an economical alternative, with traditional poultry seasonings in the mix to make the pork or veal "taste like chicken." While the skewers are traditionally pan-fried in a fair amount of oil, the air fryer makes the crunchy with only a spritz of vegetable oil.

INGREDIENTS	2-quart or larger air fryer	3.5-quart or larger air fryer	5.25-quart or larger air fryer
Pork tenderloin, cut into 2-inch cubes	¾ pound	1 pound	1½ pounds
All-purpose flour or tapioca flour	¼ cup	½ cup	¾ cup
Large egg(s)	1	1	2
Dried poultry seasoning blend	1 teaspoon	1 teaspoon	2 teaspoons
Plain panko bread crumbs (gluten-free, if a concern)	1 cup	1¼ cups	2 cups
Vegetable oil spray	As needed	As needed	As needed
MAKES	2 or 3 servings	3 or 4 servings	5 or 6 servings

1. With the basket (or basket attachment) in the air fryer, heat it to 350°F (or 360°F, if that's the closest setting).

2. Thread 3 or 4 pieces of pork on a 4-inch bamboo skewer. You'll need 2 or 3 skewers for a small batch, 3 or 4 for a medium, and up to 6 for a large batch.

3. Set up and fill three shallow soup plates or small pie plates on your counter: one for the flour; one for the egg(s), beaten with the poultry seasoning until foamy; and one for the bread crumbs.

4. Dip and roll one skewer into the flour, coating all sides of the meat. Gently shake off any excess flour, then dip and roll the skewer in the egg mixture. Let any excess egg mixture slip back into the rest, then set the skewer in the bread crumbs and roll it around, pressing gently, until the exterior surfaces of the meat are evenly coated. Generously coat the meat on the skewer with vegetable oil spray. Set aside and

continue dredging, dipping, coating, and spraying the remaining skewers.

5. Set the skewers in the basket in one layer and air-fry undisturbed for 10 minutes, or until brown and crunchy.

6. Use kitchen tongs to transfer the skewers to a wire rack. Cool for a minute or two before serving.

Then...

- Serve these with **Summer Squash and Orzo Salad** (page 239) or even on top of **Jamaican Rice and Peas** (page 160).

- These would also be good with large round *tomatoes, sliced* and a smattering of *very thinly sliced shallots,* all sprinkled with *coarse sea salt (or even kosher salt)* and set aside for 10 minutes at room temperature. Drizzle the vegetables with *olive oil* and *white wine or champagne vinegar* and garnish with *minced fresh mint leaves.*

Three Seed–Coated Pork Loin

EASY / GLUTEN-FREE / 8 INGREDIENTS

Why would you cook a pork loin roast in the air fryer and not in the oven? It's all about the slight crust the meat gets while it stays juicy inside.

Because the roast cooks more quickly in an air fryer, we can coat it in crushed seeds that might otherwise burn in the oven. Make sure those seeds are crushed but not pulverized. Better to spread them on a cutting board and use the edge of a saucepan or the smooth side of a meat mallet, rather than whirring them in a spice grinder.

Notice that this recipe will make one roast in any but the largest machines. Only those monster appliances have enough space to fit two roasts in the basket and allow adequate air flow.

INGREDIENTS	2-quart or larger air fryer	5.25-quart or larger air fryer
Olive oil	1 tablespoon	2 tablespoons
Minced garlic	2 teaspoons	1½ tablespoons
Caraway seeds, crushed	1 teaspoon	2 teaspoons
Coriander seeds, crushed	1 teaspoon	2 teaspoons
Fennel seeds, crushed	1 teaspoon	2 teaspoons
Table salt	½ teaspoon	1 teaspoon
Ground black pepper	½ teaspoon	1 teaspoon
2-pound boneless center-cut pork loin roast(s)	1	2
MAKES	3 to 4 servings	6 to 8 servings

1. With the basket (or basket attachment) in the air fryer, heat it to 350°F (or 360°F, if that's the closest setting).

2. Mix the oil, garlic, crushed seeds, salt, and pepper in a small bowl. Rub this mixture over the outside of the pork loin roast(s).

3. When the machine is at temperature, set the roast(s) in the basket. If working with two roasts, make sure there's at least ½ inch of air space between them. Air-fry undisturbed for 40 minutes, turning once, until an instant-read meat thermometer inserted into the center of the pork registers 145°F.

4. Use kitchen tongs to transfer the roast(s) to a carving board. Let stand for 5 minutes before carving into ½-inch-thick slices.

Then...

- Try this roast with an **HERB SALAD**. Whisk *olive oil* and *lemon juice* in a 2-to-1 ratio in a large bowl. Then add (in diminishing quantities) *torn fresh basil leaves, chopped fresh dill fronds, finely chopped fresh chives,* and *chopped fresh oregano leaves,* as well as *a good amount of baby lettuce leaves, even a mesclun mix.* Season with *table salt* and *ground black pepper* to taste before serving.

Barbecue Country-Style Pork Ribs

EASY / GLUTEN-FREE / 7 INGREDIENTS

Here's a streamlined recipe for country-style pork ribs. Now a favorite in the United States, these ribs are cut from the blade end of the loin, combining the best of both the leaner loin and fattier shoulder.

Some country-style ribs have bits of the shoulder bones still in them. If possible, buy boneless country-style ribs. There's no sense in paying money for the bone unless it provides a good opportunity for slurping. Those shards don't.

You can make your life even easier by skipping all the dried spices, even the salt, and substituting a dried barbecue seasoning blend: 1 tablespoon for the small batch, 1½ tablespoons for the medium batch, and 2 tablespoons for the large.

INGREDIENTS	2-quart or larger air fryer	3.5-quart or larger air fryer	5.25-quart or larger air fryer
8-ounce boneless country-style pork ribs	2	3	4
Mild smoked paprika	1 teaspoon	1½ teaspoons	2 teaspoons
Light brown sugar	1 teaspoon	1½ teaspoons	2 teaspoons
Onion powder	½ teaspoon	¾ teaspoon	1 teaspoon
Ground black pepper	½ teaspoon	¾ teaspoon	1 teaspoon
Table salt	¼ teaspoon	Rounded ¼ teaspoon	½ teaspoon
Vegetable oil spray	As needed	As needed	As needed
MAKES	2 servings	3 servings	4 servings

1. With the basket (or basket attachment) in the air fryer, heat it to 350°F (or 360°F, if that's the closest setting). Set the ribs in a bowl on the counter as the machine heats.

2. Mix the smoked paprika, brown sugar, onion powder, pepper, and salt in a small bowl until well combined. Rub this mixture over all the surfaces of the country-style ribs. Generously coat the country-style ribs with vegetable oil spray.

3. Set the ribs in the basket with as much air space between them as possible. Air-fry undisturbed for 30 minutes, or until browned and sizzling and an instant-read meat thermometer inserted into one rib registers at least 145°F.

4. Use kitchen tongs to transfer the country-style ribs to a wire rack. Cool for 5 minutes before serving.

Then...

- Serve these ribs with an ASIAN CARROT SLAW. Blanch *thawed frozen pearl onions* in boiling water for 1 minute, then drain in a colander set in the sink, cool a bit, and chop them into small bits. Mix these with *shredded carrots* and *chopped unsalted cashews*. Dress the mixture with *unseasoned rice vinegar* (see page 70), *regular or low-sodium soy sauce or gluten-free tamari sauce,* and *minced peeled fresh ginger* in a 2-to-1-to-1 ratio by volume.

Baby Back Ribs

EASY / CAN BE GLUTEN-FREE / 3 INGREDIENTS

It's easy to make great baby back ribs in an air fryer. In fact, you can use this recipe as a road map, substituting any spice blend you like (Tex-Mex, herbes de Provence, even standard chile powder) and any thick glazing liquid (Thai sweet chili sauce, a mustard/ketchup combo, duck sauce, or hoisin sauce, as examples).

The trick is to cook the ribs in the hot air flow while creating steam to keep the ribs from drying out. In many machines, you can pour the water into the bottom of the drawer that holds the basket. In others, you'll need to put the water in a lipped tray on a level below the basket attachment that holds the ribs. You need to watch this tray—add more water if it dries out or empty it if the rendered fat from the ribs threatens to overflow. Never pour the water onto a heating element or other electrical system in the machine.

INGREDIENTS	2-quart or larger air fryer	3.5-quart or larger air fryer	5.25-quart or larger air fryer
Pork baby back rib rack(s)	1½ pounds	2¼ pounds	3 pounds
Dried barbecue seasoning blend or rub (gluten-free, if a concern)	2 teaspoons	1 tablespoon	1½ tablespoons
Water	1 cup	1 cup	1 cup
Purchased smooth barbecue sauce (gluten-free, if a concern)	2 tablespoons	3 tablespoons	¼ cup
MAKES	3 servings	4 servings	6 servings

1. With the basket (or basket attachment) in the air fryer, heat it to 350°F (or 360°F, if that's the closest setting).

2. Cut the racks into 4- to 5-bone sections, about two sections for the small batch, three for the medium, and four for the large. Sprinkle both sides of these sections with the seasoning blend.

3. Pour the water into the bottom of the air-fryer drawer or into a tray placed under the rack. (The rack cannot then sit in water—adjust the amount of water for your machine.) Set the rib sections in the basket so that they're not touching. Air-fry for 30 minutes, turning once.

If using a tray with water, check it a couple of times to make sure it still has water in it or hasn't overflowed from the rendered fat.

4. Brush half the barbecue sauce on the exposed side of the ribs. Air-fry undisturbed for 3 minutes. Turn the racks over (but make sure they're still not touching), brush with the remaining sauce, and air-fry undisturbed for 3 minutes more, or until sizzling and brown.

5. Use kitchen tongs to transfer the racks to a cutting board. Let stand for 5 minutes, then slice between the bones to serve.

continues

Then...

- Serve these ribs with **Beet Fries** (page 331), **Homemade Potato Puffs** (page 332), or **Air-Fried Potato Salad** (page 338).

- Or make a CAPRESE PASTA SALAD. Toss together *cooked and drained penne pasta (gluten-free, if that's a concern), diced sun-dried tomatoes, diced fresh mozzarella or small fresh mozzarella balls, halved cherry tomatoes, chopped fresh basil leaves, toasted pine nuts,* and *thinly sliced red onion.* Dress the salad with *olive oil* and *balsamic vinegar,* as well as *table salt* and *ground black pepper* to taste.

Better-Than-Chinese-Take-Out Pork Ribs

EASY / CAN BE GLUTEN-FREE / 7 INGREDIENTS

Here's a version of the Chinese-American take-out classic, developed specifically for the air fryer. The baby back rib racks are cut into small 2-bone sections so they can get crunchy across lots of surfaces as they cook.

The secret to the flavor, with the fewest possible ingredients, is to use purchased hoisin sauce and ground white pepper—a bit of an unusual ingredient but necessary for the slightly musky notes so prized in the more traditional versions of this dish. (As a bonus, you'll have white pepper on hand for **Steakhouse Filets Mignons** on page 209.)

Although this recipe falls among the main courses, it could certainly do good service as an appetizer before dinner.

INGREDIENTS	2-quart or larger air fryer	3.5-quart or larger air fryer	5.25-quart or larger air fryer
Hoisin sauce (see page 180; gluten-free, if a concern)	1 tablespoon	1½ tablespoons	2 tablespoons
Regular or low-sodium soy sauce or gluten-free tamari sauce	1 tablespoon	1½ tablespoons	2 tablespoons
Shaoxing (Chinese cooking rice wine), dry sherry, or white grape juice	1 tablespoon	1½ tablespoons	2 tablespoons
Minced garlic	1 teaspoon	1½ teaspoons	2 teaspoons
Ground dried ginger	½ teaspoon	¾ teaspoon	1 teaspoon
Ground white pepper	½ teaspoon	¾ teaspoon	1 teaspoon
Pork baby back rib rack(s), cut into 2-bone pieces	1 pound	1½ pounds	2½ pounds
MAKES	*2 servings*	*3 servings*	*4 servings*

1. Mix the hoisin sauce, soy or tamari sauce, Shaoxing or its substitute, garlic, ginger, and white pepper in a large bowl. Add the rib sections and stir well to coat. Cover and refrigerate for at least 2 hours or up to 24 hours, stirring the rib sections in the marinade occasionally.

2. With the basket (or basket attachment) in the air fryer, heat it to 350°F (or 360°F, if that's the closest setting). Set the ribs in their bowl on the counter as the machine heats.

3. When the machine is at temperature, set the rib pieces *on their sides* in a single layer in the basket with as much air space between them as possible. Air-fry for 35 minutes, turning and rearranging the pieces once, until deeply browned and sizzling.

4. Use kitchen tongs to transfer the rib pieces to a large serving bowl or platter. Wait a minute or two before serving them so the meat can reabsorb some of its own juices.

Then...

- Make a **NO-COOK SPICY SOY DIPPING SAUCE** for the ribs. For 3 to 4 servings, whisk *¼ cup regular or low-sodium soy sauce or gluten-free tamari sauce, ¼ cup unseasoned rice vinegar* (see page 70), *1 tablespoon Worcestershire sauce (gluten-free, if a concern), up to 1 tablespoon sriracha, 2 teaspoons dark brown sugar,* and *1 teaspoon ground dried ginger* in a bowl until smooth.

- Serve the dish with wilted pea shoots or sliced bok choy. Warm a wok or skillet over medium-high heat for a minute or two, add some *toasted sesame oil,* then add the washed (but not drained) *pea shoots* or *bok choy.* Cook, stirring constantly, for 1 minute, letting the steam wilt the vegetables a bit, just until they're somewhat softened. Season with *table salt* to taste before serving.

See photo in insert.

Teriyaki Country-Style Pork Ribs

EASY / CAN BE GLUTEN-FREE / 6 INGREDIENTS

Why buy bottled teriyaki sauce when it's so easy to make your own without the chemical shenanigans in some bottlings, not to mention their overly sweet flavor? Good teriyaki sauce should be a balance between salty and sweet, with hints of ginger and garlic. It doesn't take much to make it and will then make these country-style ribs exceptional.

You might want to make a double batch of this teriyaki sauce, then save the rest in a covered glass or other nonreactive container in the refrigerator for up to 1 week. It's terrific as a glaze on grilled chicken.

INGREDIENTS	2-quart or larger air fryer	3.5-quart or larger air fryer	5.25-quart or larger air fryer
Regular or low-sodium soy sauce or gluten-free tamari sauce	2 tablespoons	3 tablespoons	¼ cup
Honey	2 tablespoons	3 tablespoons	¼ cup
Ground dried ginger	½ teaspoon	¾ teaspoon	1 teaspoon
Garlic powder	½ teaspoon	¾ teaspoon	1 teaspoon
8-ounce boneless country-style pork ribs	2	3	4
Vegetable oil spray	As needed	As needed	As needed
MAKES	2 servings	3 servings	4 servings

1. With the basket (or basket attachment) in the air fryer, heat it to 350°F (or 360°F, if that's the closest setting).

2. Mix the soy or tamari sauce, honey, ground ginger, and garlic powder in another bowl until uniform.

3. Smear about half of this teriyaki sauce over all sides of the country-style ribs. Reserve the remainder of the teriyaki sauce. Generously coat the meat with vegetable oil spray.

4. When the machine is at temperature, place the country-style ribs in the basket with as much air space between them as possible. Air-fry undisturbed for 15 minutes. Turn the country-style ribs (but keep the space between them) and brush them all over with the remaining teriyaki sauce. Continue air-frying undisturbed for 15 minutes, or until an instant-read

meat thermometer inserted into the center of one rib registers at least 145°F.

5. Use kitchen tongs to transfer the country-style ribs to a wire rack. Cool for 5 minutes before serving.

Then...

- With the Asian flavors, serve these with **Asian Carrot Slaw** (page 250) and/or **Sushi Rice** (page 263).

- Or make this BEAN SPROUT SALAD. Toss *fresh bean sprouts* with *a drizzle of toasted sesame oil, a drizzle of regular or low-sodium soy sauce or gluten-free tamari sauce, a little thinly sliced scallion,* and *a touch of minced garlic.*

Extra Crispy Country-Style Pork Riblets

EASY / GLUTEN-FREE / 4 OR 5 INGREDIENTS

Here, the country-style ribs are cut into small chunks for more crunch per bite. The secret to all that crunch is tapioca flour, often called for as a gluten-free substitute in these recipes but here given a star turn. Because it's a root starch, rather than a wheat starch, it dries out pretty quickly for crunchy results that are sublime, so long as you give those pork chunks generous spritzes of vegetable oil spray.

The salt is optional in the coating because most standard chile powders include salt. Check the label on your bottling to see if you need to add salt.

INGREDIENTS	2-quart or larger air fryer	3.5-quart or larger air fryer	5.25-quart or larger air fryer
Tapioca flour	¼ cup	⅓ cup	½ cup
Chile powder	2 tablespoons	2½ tablespoons	3 tablespoons
Table salt (optional)	½ teaspoon	¾ teaspoon	1 teaspoon
Boneless country-style pork ribs, cut into 1½-inch chunks	¾ pound	1¼ pounds	2 pounds
Vegetable oil spray	As needed	As needed	As needed
MAKES	2 servings	3 servings	4 servings

1. With the basket (or basket attachment) in the air fryer, heat it to 375°F (or 370°F or 360°F, if one of these is the closest setting).

2. Mix the tapioca flour, chile powder, and salt (if using) in a large bowl until well combined. Add the country-style rib chunks and toss well to coat thoroughly.

3. When the machine is at temperature, gently shake off any excess tapioca coating from the chunks. Generously coat them on all sides with vegetable oil spray. Arrange the chunks in the basket in one (admittedly fairly tight) layer. The pieces may touch. Air-fry for 30 minutes, rearranging the pieces at the 10- and 20-minute marks to expose any touching bits, until very crisp and well browned.

4. Gently pour the contents of the basket onto a wire rack. Cool for 5 minutes before serving.

Then...

- Serve these riblets with **Creamy Tomato Dip** (page 63), **Jalapeño Jam** (page 58), **Spicy Ketchup Dip** (page 66), or **Sweet-and-Sour Ketchup Dip** (page 71).

- Or use them instead of bacon chunks in a FRISÉE BISTRO SALAD. Heat some *olive oil* in a nonstick skillet set over medium heat, then add *thinly sliced shallots* and cook, stirring often, until tender, just a minute or two. Add *a little white wine vinegar* and some *table salt*. Remove from the heat and use a slotted spoon to transfer the softened shallots to a bowl of *stemmed and torn frisée leaves*. Add a little of the residual oil in the skillet to dress the salad. Toss well, then divide it between serving plates and top with the crunchy country-style riblets.

Easy Carnitas

GLUTEN-FREE / 8 INGREDIENTS

One warning right up front: this recipe yields only the chunks of meaty carnitas themselves—not a full meal. But we have plenty of suggestions below.

Although carnitas are sometimes made with a pork butt or a picnic ham, those cuts are too large for modern air fryers. That's why we use 2-inch pieces of country-style ribs, which have the right ratio of fat to meat, ensuring that the pieces will be juicy when they come out of the machine.

This recipe can be altered endless by the sort of pickle brine you use. If you choose the brine from bread-and-butter pickles, the bits of pork will be sweet and more deeply colored. If you use the brine from dill pickles, the pork will be more herbaceous with a sour finish. And if you use the liquid from a jar of giardiniera (Italian marinated vegetables), the pork will taste lighter and more savory.

INGREDIENTS	2-quart or larger air fryer	3.5-quart or larger air fryer	5.25-quart or larger air fryer
Boneless country-style pork ribs, cut into 2-inch pieces	1 pound	1½ pounds	2½ pounds
Orange juice	3 tablespoons	¼ cup	⅓ cup
Brine from a jar of pickles, any type, even pickled jalapeño rings (gluten-free, if a concern)	1½ tablespoons	2 tablespoons	3 tablespoons
Minced garlic	1½ teaspoons	2 teaspoons	1 tablespoon
Minced fresh oregano leaves	1½ teaspoons	2 teaspoons	1 tablespoon
Ground cumin	½ teaspoon	¾ teaspoon	1 teaspoon
Table salt	½ teaspoon	¾ teaspoon	1 teaspoon
Ground black pepper	½ teaspoon	¾ teaspoon	1 teaspoon
MAKES	2 or 3 servings	3 or 4 servings	5 or 6 servings

1. Mix the country-style pork rib pieces, orange juice, pickle brine, garlic, oregano, cumin, salt, and pepper in a large bowl. Cover and refrigerate for at least 2 hours or up to 10 hours, stirring the mixture occasionally.

2. With the basket (or basket attachment) in the air fryer, heat it to 400°F (or 390°F, if that's the closest setting). Set the rib pieces in their bowl on the counter as the machine heats.

3. Use kitchen tongs to transfer the rib pieces to the basket, arranging them in one layer. Some may touch. Air-fry for 25 minutes, turning and rearranging the pieces at the 10- and 20-minute marks to make sure all surfaces have been exposed to the air currents, until browned and sizzling.

4. Use clean kitchen tongs to transfer the rib pieces to a wire rack. Cool for a couple of minutes before serving.

Then...

- To make a full meal, carnitas need flour or corn tortillas, chopped tomatoes, chopped iceberg lettuce, pickled jalapeño rings, regular or low-fat sour cream, grated Cheddar or Monterey Jack cheese, and/or pitted, peeled, and thinly sliced avocado. Also have lots of bottled hot red pepper sauces (gluten-free, if a concern) on hand for garnishing the meat and its condiments either folded into the tortillas or served with a tortilla on the side.

- Or offer them on top of **Streamlined Spanish Rice** (page 159), garnished with sour cream and jalapeño or pickle relish.

Crispy Five-Spice Pork Belly

GLUTEN-FREE / 5 INGREDIENTS

Here's a simplified, air-fryer version of a Chinese classic that usually takes days—quite literally—to make. In this version, you'll end up with porky bliss for little effort: incredibly crisp skin, juicy meat, all wrapped in a good amount of fat for the best flavor.

Look for a piece of pork belly that's not too fatty, with a good strip of meat under the skin. (And yes, it must be a skin-on piece, sometimes difficult to track down. Check in an Asian market or ask the butcher at your supermarket.) Some belly pieces are so fatty, there's not much meat to be had. You want to serve dinner, not just a bit of crisp skin.

One ingredient note: **Five-spice powder** is a blend of ground, dried spices, often (in North America) with cinnamon, cloves, fennel, star anise, and Sichuan peppercorns. Asian bottlings usually include Chinese cassia instead of the cinnamon and may also include ground dried orange peel, licorice, nutmeg, ground dried turmeric, and/or ground dried ginger. It's available in more run-of-the-mill bottlings in the spice aisle of most supermarkets; it's available in a more astounding array from online spice purveyors and Chinese grocers.

INGREDIENTS	2-quart or larger air fryer	3.5-quart or larger air fryer	5.25-quart or larger air fryer
Pork belly with skin	1 pound	1½ pounds	2 pounds
Shaoxing (Chinese cooking rice wine), dry sherry, or white grape juice	2 tablespoons	3 tablespoons	¼ cup
Granulated white sugar	1 teaspoon	1½ teaspoons	2 teaspoons
Five-spice powder (see the headnote)	½ teaspoon	¾ teaspoon	1 teaspoon
Coarse sea salt or kosher salt	¾ cup	1¼ cups	1½ cups
MAKES	4 servings	6 servings	8 servings

1. With the basket (or basket attachment) in the air fryer, heat it to 350°F (or 360°F, if that's the closest setting).

2. Set the pork belly skin side up on a cutting board. Use a meat fork to make dozens and dozens of tiny holes all across the surface of the skin. You can hardly make too many holes. These will allow the skin to bubble up and keep it from becoming hard as it roasts.

3. Turn the pork belly over so that one of its longer sides faces you. Make four evenly spaced vertical slits in the meat. The slits should go about halfway into the meat toward the fat.

4. Mix the Shaoxing or its substitute, sugar, and five-spice powder in a small bowl until the sugar dissolves. Massage this mixture across the meat and into the cuts.

5. Turn the pork belly over again. Blot dry any moisture on the skin. Make a double-thickness aluminum foil tray by setting two 10-inch-long pieces of foil on top of another. Set the pork belly skin side up in the center of this tray. Fold the sides of the tray up toward the pork, crimping the foil as you work to make a high-sided case all around the pork belly. Seal the foil to the meat on all sides so that only the skin is exposed.

6. Pour the salt onto the skin and pat it down and in place to create a crust. Pick up the foil tray with the pork in it and set it in the basket.

7. Air-fry undisturbed for 35 minutes for a small batch, 45 minutes for a medium batch, or 50 minutes for a large batch.

8. Remove the foil tray with the pork belly still in it. Warning: The foil tray is full of scalding-hot fat. Discard the fat in the tray (not down the drain!), as well as the tray itself. Transfer the pork belly to a cutting board.

9. Raise the air fryer temperature to 375°F (or 380°F or 390°F, if one of these is the closest setting). Brush the salt crust off the pork, removing any visible salt from the sides of the meat, too.

10. When the machine is at temperature, return the pork belly skin side up to the basket. Air-fry undisturbed for 25 minutes, or until crisp and very well browned. If the machine is at 390°F, you may be able to shave 5 minutes off the cooking time so that the skin doesn't blacken.

11. Use a nonstick-safe spatula, and perhaps a silicone baking mitt, to transfer the pork belly to a wire rack. Cool for 10 minutes before serving.

Then...

- To slice the pork belly, turn it skin side down on a carving board. Use a very sharp, heavy knife to cut through the meat and skin, making 1-inch-wide slices the short way across the meat. Then slice each of these "columns" into two or three pieces.

- You can serve the pork with a bottled condiment like Thai sweet chili sauce, duck sauce, or Saucy Susan. Or you can make your own: **No-Cook Spicy Soy Dipping Sauce** (page 253), **Peanut-Sesame Sauce** (page 69), or **Sweet-and-Salty Dipping Sauce** (page 244).

Crispy Ham and Eggs

FAST / EASY / CAN BE GLUTEN-FREE / 7 INGREDIENTS

Coating a ham steak in ground rice cereal gives it a delicately sweet flavor after frying, a great contrast to the salty, smoky meat. Watch the ham steak carefully—it is already fully cooked, so you're just heating it up and setting the coating, which must not burn.

This recipe is a two-step with the ham in the air fryer and the eggs in a skillet. We couldn't skip those fried eggs. We think they're the perfect way to set off that ham steak for a fantastic brunch.

INGREDIENTS	2-quart or larger air fryer	3.5-quart or larger air fryer	5.25-quart or larger air fryer
Rice-puff cereal, such as Rice Krispies	1¾ cups	2 cups	2⅓ cups
Maple syrup	3 tablespoons	¼ cup	6 tablespoons
¼- to ½-inch-thick ham steak (gluten-free, if a concern)	6 ounces	½ pound	¾ pound
Unsalted butter	2 teaspoons	1 tablespoon	1½ tablespoons
Large eggs	2	3	4
Table salt	⅛ teaspoon	Rounded ⅛ teaspoon	¼ teaspoon
Ground black pepper	⅛ teaspoon	Rounded ⅛ teaspoon	¼ teaspoon
MAKES	*2 servings*	*3 servings*	*4 servings*

1. With the basket (or basket attachment) in the air fryer, heat it to 400°F (or 390°F, if that's the closest setting).

2. Pour the cereal into a food processor, cover, and process until finely ground. Pour the ground cereal into a shallow soup plate or a small pie plate.

3. Smear the maple syrup on both sides of the ham, then set the ham into the ground cereal. Turn a few times, pressing gently, until evenly coated.

4. Set the ham steak in the basket and air-fry undisturbed for 5 minutes, or until browned.

5. Meanwhile, melt the butter in a medium or large nonstick skillet set over medium heat. Crack the eggs into the skillet and cook until the whites are set and the yolks are hot, about 3 minutes (or 4 minutes for a more set yolk.) Season with the salt and pepper.

6. When the ham is ready, transfer it to a serving platter, then slip the eggs from the skillet on top of it. Divide into portions to serve.

Then...

- Make sure there's lots of hot red pepper sauce (gluten-free, if a concern) on the table. It's great on the eggs and cuts through the sweetness of the pork.

- Make **CINNAMON TOAST** in the air fryer! Mash together *room-temperature butter, granulated white sugar,* and *ground cinnamon* in your preferred proportions. (We prefer 1 tablespoon butter to 1½ teaspoons sugar and a little cinnamon.) Spread it on one side of *white or whole-wheat bread slices,* then set the slices spread side up in the basket of a 400°F air fryer until crunchy, 3 to 4 minutes.

Albóndigas

CAN BE GLUTEN-FREE / 11 INGREDIENTS

These little pork meatballs are often served in soup in Mexican cooking, but we feel they make a pretty fine dinner on their own. They're not spicy, so feel free to offer lots of minced fresh chiles, pickled jalapeños, or even jalapeño relish on the side.

They're also fragile when they first come out of the air fryer. Work carefully to transfer them to a wire rack.

INGREDIENTS	2-quart or larger air fryer	3.5-quart or larger air fryer	5.25-quart or larger air fryer
Lean ground pork	¾ pound	1 pound	1½ pounds
Very finely chopped trimmed scallions	2 tablespoons	3 tablespoons	¼ cup
Finely chopped fresh cilantro leaves	2 tablespoons	3 tablespoons	¼ cup
Plain panko bread crumbs (gluten-free, if a concern)	2 tablespoons	3 tablespoons	¼ cup
Dry white wine, dry sherry, or unsweetened apple juice	2 tablespoons	3 tablespoons	¼ cup
Minced garlic	1 teaspoon	1½ teaspoons	2 teaspoons
Mild smoked paprika	1 teaspoon	1¼ teaspoons	2 teaspoons
Dried oregano	½ teaspoon	¾ teaspoon	1 teaspoon
Table salt	½ teaspoon	¾ teaspoon	1 teaspoon
Ground black pepper	¼ teaspoon	Rounded ¼ teaspoon	½ teaspoon
Olive oil spray	As needed	As needed	As needed
MAKES	3 servings	4 servings	6 servings

1. With the basket (or basket attachment) in the air fryer, heat it to 400°F (or 390°F, if that's the closest setting).

2. Mix the ground pork, scallions, cilantro, bread crumbs, wine or its substitute, garlic, smoked paprika, oregano, salt, and pepper in a bowl until the herbs and spices are evenly distributed in the mixture.

3. Lightly coat your clean hands with olive oil spray, then form the ground pork mixture into balls, using 2 tablespoons for each one. Spray your hands frequently so that the meat mixture doesn't stick.

4. Set the balls in the basket so that they're not touching, even if they're close together. Air-fry undisturbed for 15 minutes, or until well browned and an instant-read meat thermometer inserted into one or two balls registers 165°F.

5. Use a nonstick-safe spatula and kitchen tongs for balance to gently transfer the fragile balls to a wire rack to cool for 5 minutes before serving.

continues

Then...

- Serve these meatballs over **Jamaican Rice and Peas** (page 160) or even inside a baked potato garnished with a little butter and sour cream.

- Or make CHIPOTLE SALSA DIP for them. For 4 to 6 servings, put all of the following in a food processor: *one 10-ounce can Rotel original diced tomatoes and green chiles, 2 tablespoons minced yellow onion, 2 tablespoons lime juice, 1 stemmed and seeded canned chipotle in adobo sauce, ½ teaspoon ground cumin, ½ teaspoon granulated white sugar,* and *½ teaspoon table salt.* Cover and process until smooth, scraping down the inside of the canister at least once. Store any leftovers in a sealed glass or other nonreactive container in the fridge for up to 1 week.

Fried Spam

FAST / EASY / CAN BE GLUTEN-FREE / 6 INGREDIENTS

Anyone who knows Spam knows that you can fry it in a skillet. But frying it with a crunchy coating is another thing entirely! Here, you'll whisk eggs with wasabi paste to create a nose-spanking topping to mix with panko bread crumbs, a nice contrast to this much-maligned if also much-loved food.

Wasabi paste is sold in tubes in the Asian aisle of almost all supermarkets.

INGREDIENTS	2-quart or larger air fryer	3.5-quart or larger air fryer	5.25-quart or larger air fryer
All-purpose flour or gluten-free all-purpose flour	⅓ cup	½ cup	⅔ cup
Large egg(s)	1	1	2
Wasabi paste	2 teaspoons	1 tablespoon	1½ tablespoons
Plain panko bread crumbs (gluten-free, if a concern)	⅔ cup	1⅓ cups	2 cups
½-inch-thick Spam slices	2	4	6
Vegetable oil spray	As needed	As needed	As needed
MAKES	1 serving	2 servings	3 servings

1. With the basket (or basket attachment) in the air fryer, heat it to 400°F (or 390°F, if that's the closest setting).

2. Set up and fill three shallow soup plates or small pie plates on your counter: one for the flour; one for the egg(s), whisked with the wasabi paste until uniform; and one for the bread crumbs.

3. Dip a slice of Spam in the flour, coating both sides. Slip it into the egg mixture and turn to coat on both sides, even along the edges. Let any excess egg mixture slip back into the rest, then set the slice in the bread crumbs. Turn it several times, pressing gently to make an even coating on both sides. Generously coat both sides of the slice with vegetable oil spray. Set aside so you can dip, coat, and spray the remaining slice(s).

4. Set the slices in the basket in a single layer so that they don't touch (even if they're close together). Air-fry undisturbed for 12 minutes, or until very brown and quite crunchy.

5. Use kitchen tongs to transfer the slices to a wire rack. Cool for a minute or two before serving.

Then...

- Given the wasabi finish to these slices, we suggest a sprinkle of unseasoned rice vinegar (see page 70) just before serving. Or try the slices with **Sweet-and-Salty Dipping Sauce** (page 244).

- And given that wasabi finish, serve the slices with SUSHI RICE. For 4 servings, mix *2 cups raw sushi rice* (a specific type of short-grain white rice) with *2¼ cups water* in a medium saucepan. Bring to a boil over high heat, stirring occasionally. Cover, reduce the heat to low, and barely simmer until the water has been absorbed, about 20 minutes. Turn the hot rice out into a large, shallow bowl. Spread the rice out and cool for 5 minutes, then sprinkle it with *¼ cup unseasoned rice vinegar* (see page 70), *1 tablespoon granulated white sugar,* and *1 teaspoon table salt.* Toss gently to incorporate the seasonings into the rice. Serve warm.

Crispy Pierogi with Kielbasa and Onions

EASY / 4 INGREDIENTS

Frozen pierogi are a treat! They get crunchier in the air fryer than they would in a skillet—and better than if they'd come out of a deep fryer because the dough retains just a little bit of chewy goodness after they're done. We've combined them with smoked kielbasa and onions, so they become a full meal right out of the machine's basket. Look for pierogi in the freezer case of most large supermarkets.

INGREDIENTS	2-quart or larger air fryer	3.5-quart or larger air fryer	5.25-quart or larger air fryer
Frozen potato and cheese pierogi, thawed (about 12 pierogi to 1 pound)	4	6	8
Smoked kielbasa, sliced into ½-inch-thick rounds	6 ounces	½ pound	¾ pound
Very roughly chopped sweet onion, preferably Vidalia	½ cup	¾ cup	1 cup
Vegetable oil spray	As needed	As needed	As needed
MAKES	2 servings	3 servings	4 servings

1. With the basket (or basket attachment) in the air fryer, heat it to 375°F (or 370°F or 360°F, if one of these is the closest setting).

2. Put the pierogi, kielbasa rounds, and onion in a large bowl. Coat them with vegetable oil spray, toss well, spray again, and toss until everything is glistening.

3. When the machine is at temperature, dump the contents of the bowl it into the basket. (Items may be leaning against each other and even on top of each other.) Air-fry, tossing and rearranging everything twice so that all covered surfaces get exposed, for 20 minutes, or until the sausages have begun to brown and the pierogi are crisp.

4. Pour the contents of the basket onto a serving platter. Wait a minute or two just to take make sure nothing's searing hot before serving.

Then...

- Serve with prepared horseradish and coarse Dijon mustard, as well as rye bread slices.

- And add **Vinegary Cucumbers** (page 131) to the offerings.

Tuscan Chimichangas

FAST / EASY / 7 INGREDIENTS

One last pork recipe—and one that's a bit out of the ordinary. We've stuffed a tortilla with deli and pantry items to morph a Tex-Mex staple into a simple Italian meal.

If you want to take this concoction over the top, substitute chopped thinly sliced prosciutto for the deli ham. And add a few more ingredients like sliced pitted black olives; chopped drained marinated artichoke hearts; and/or drained minced jarred pimientos. Also, consider substituting a shredded four-cheese cheese blend for the mozzarella.

INGREDIENTS	2-quart or larger air fryer	3.5-quart or larger air fryer
Thinly sliced deli ham, chopped	2 ounces	¼ pound
Drained and rinsed canned white beans	½ cup	1 cup
Shredded semi-firm mozzarella	¼ cup (about 1 ounce)	½ cup (about 2 ounces)
Chopped sun-dried tomatoes	2 tablespoons	¼ cup
Bottled Italian salad dressing, vinaigrette type	2 tablespoons	¼ cup
Burrito-size (12-inch) flour tortilla(s)	1	2
Olive oil spray	As needed	As needed
MAKES	1 chimichanga	2 chimichangas

1. With the basket (or basket attachment) in the air fryer, heat it to 375°F (or 370°F or 360°F, if one of these is the closest setting).

2. Mix the ham, beans, cheese, tomatoes, and salad dressing in a bowl.

3. Lay a tortilla on a clean, dry work surface. Put all of the ham mixture in a narrow oval in the middle of the tortilla, if making one burrito; or half of this mixture, if making two. Fold the parts of the tortilla that are closest to the ends of the filling oval up and over the filling, then roll the tortilla tightly closed, but don't press down hard. Generously coat the tortilla with olive oil spray. Make a second filled tortilla, if necessary.

4. Set the filled tortilla(s) seam side down in the basket, with at least ½ inch between them, if making two. Air-fry undisturbed for 8 minutes, or until crisp and lightly browned.

5. Use kitchen tongs and a nonstick-safe spatula to transfer the chimichanga(s) to a wire rack. Cool for 5 minutes before serving.

Then...

- For a great SPINACH SALAD on the side, whisk *walnut oil* and *red wine vinegar* in a 2-to-1 ratio with *a little minced shallot, table salt,* and *ground black pepper* in a bowl. Add *baby spinach leaves* and some *walnut pieces*. Toss well, then crumble in some *goat cheese* and toss gently.

- And maybe continue the Tuscan theme by making a pesto mayonnaise to dip the chimichangas in. Stir *regular or low-fat mayonnaise* and *purchased pesto* in a 2-to-1 ratio by volume until smooth.

Korean-Style Lamb Shoulder Chops

EASY / CAN BE GLUTEN-FREE / 9 INGREDIENTS

This quick, sweet-salty, and very aromatic marinade add lots of flavor to the chops. But the real star of the recipe is the tapioca flour. It turns into a super crunchy coating in an air fryer.

For the best results, make sure the chops are evenly coated and well sprayed. And don't wait too long after they come out of the fryer. The coating is crisp for a while—and then quickly gets soggy as the natural juices of the meat loosen it up again.

INGREDIENTS	2-quart or larger air fryer	3.5-quart or larger air fryer	5.25-quart or larger air fryer
Regular or low-sodium soy sauce or gluten-free tamari sauce	¼ cup	⅓ cup	½ cup
Toasted sesame oil	1 tablespoon	1½ tablespoons	2 tablespoons
Granulated white sugar	1 tablespoon	1½ tablespoons	2 tablespoons
Minced peeled fresh ginger	1½ teaspoons	2 teaspoons	1 tablespoon
Minced garlic	½ teaspoon	1 teaspoon	1½ teaspoons
Red pepper flakes	¼ teaspoon	Rounded ¼ teaspoon	½ teaspoon
6-ounce bone-in lamb shoulder chops, any excess fat trimmed	2	3	4
Tapioca flour	½ cup	⅔ cup	1 cup
Vegetable oil spray	As needed	As needed	As needed
MAKES	2 servings	3 servings	4 servings

1. Put the soy or tamari sauce, sesame oil, sugar, ginger, garlic, and red pepper flakes in a large, heavy zip-closed plastic bag. Add the chops, seal, and rub the marinade evenly over them through the bag. Refrigerate for at least 2 hours or up to 6 hours, turning the bag at least once so the chops move around in the marinade.

2. Set the bag out on the counter as the air fryer heats. With the basket (or basket attachment) in the air fryer, heat it to 375°F (or 370°F or 360°F, if one of these is the closest setting).

3. Pour the tapioca flour on a dinner plate or in a small pie plate. Remove a chop from the marinade and dredge it on both sides in the tapioca flour,

coating it evenly and well. Coat both sides with vegetable oil spray, set it in the basket, and dredge and spray the remaining chop(s), setting them in the basket in a single layer with space between them. Discard the bag with the marinade.

4. Air-fry, turning once, for 25 minutes, or until the chops are well browned and tender when pierced with the point of a paring knife. If the machine is at 360°F, you may need to add up to 3 minutes to the cooking time.

5. Use kitchen tongs to transfer the chops to a wire rack. Cool for just a couple of minutes before serving.

Then...

- Serve these chops with kimchi, pickled ginger, and cooked long-grain white rice, or perhaps even **Sushi Rice** (page 263).

- Or serve the chops with SOBA NOODLE SALAD. Toss cooked and drained *soba noodles* with *unseasoned rice vinegar, regular or low-sodium soy sauce or gluten-free tamari sauce, a bit of minced scallion,* and *some chopped unsalted shelled peanuts.*

Garlic and Oregano Lamb Chops

FAST / EASY / GLUTEN-FREE / 8 INGREDIENTS

In North America, lamb chops come in three varieties: rib, loin, and shoulder. Rib chops are individual chops from a rack of lamb, each chop one bone of the rack. These are thin and will quickly overcook in an air fryer. By contrast, loin chops, the ones called for here, are like little lamb T-bones. They tend to be thicker and hold up better to the machine's heat. (Our other two lamb chop recipes are for fattier shoulder chops.)

We chose this super simple method as a way to highlight the savory flavor of loin chops. For a deeper flavor, you can cover the bowl and refrigerate them in the marinade for up to 24 hours, stirring the chops occasionally. If you opt for this longer marination, leave the bowl on the counter for 20 minutes before you even turn on the air fryer so the chops have a chance to get closer to room temperature before they undergo the cooking process.

INGREDIENTS	2-quart or larger air fryer	3.5-quart or larger air fryer	5.25-quart or larger air fryer
Olive oil	1 tablespoon	1½ tablespoons	2 tablespoons
Minced garlic	2 teaspoons	1 tablespoon	1½ tablespoons
Dried oregano	½ teaspoon	1 teaspoon	1¼ teaspoons
Finely minced orange zest	½ teaspoon	1 teaspoon	1¼ teaspoons
Fennel seeds	½ teaspoon	¾ teaspoon	1 teaspoon
Table salt	½ teaspoon	¾ teaspoon	1 teaspoon
Ground black pepper	½ teaspoon	¾ teaspoon	1 teaspoon
4-ounce, 1-inch-thick lamb loin chops	4	6	8
MAKES	*2 servings*	*4 servings*	*6 servings*

1. Mix the olive oil, garlic, oregano, orange zest, fennel seeds, salt, and pepper in a large bowl. Add the chops and toss well to coat. Set aside as the air fryer heats, tossing one more time.

2. With the basket (or basket attachment) in the air fryer, heat it to 400°F (or 390°F, if that's the closest setting).

continues

3. Set the chops bone side down in the basket (that is, so they stand up on their bony edge) with as much air space between them as possible. Air-fry undisturbed for 14 minutes for medium-rare, or until an instant-read meat thermometer inserted into the thickest part of a chop (without touching bone) registers 132°F (not USDA-approved). Or air-fry undisturbed for 17 minutes for well done, or until an instant-read meat thermometer registers 145°F (USDA-approved).

4. Use kitchen tongs to transfer the chops to a wire rack. Cool for 5 minutes before serving.

Then...

- Serve these simple chops with **Broccoli and Grape Salad** (page 127); **Endive, Walnut, and Blue Cheese Salad** (page 195); **Tomato-Peach Salad** (page 236); or **Spinach Salad** (page 265).

- Or make **Air-Fried Potato Salad** (page 338).

See photo in insert.

Crispy Lamb Shoulder Chops

EASY / CAN BE GLUTEN-FREE / 7 INGREDIENTS

Lamb shoulder chops are fattier than loin chops. Shoulder chops are often chopped into smaller bits to be used in braises and stews. But because of the way the air fryer cooks, they come out wonderfully juicy and irresistible, an economical treat any weeknight.

Make sure you turn them once in the middle of cooking. Doing so requires a light touch. Don't knock off the crust. Grasp them gently with kitchen tongs and use a nonstick-safe spatula in your other hand for balance.

INGREDIENTS	2-quart or larger air fryer	3.5-quart or larger air fryer	5.25-quart or larger air fryer
All-purpose flour or gluten-free all-purpose flour	½ cup	¾ cup	1 cup
Mild paprika	1½ teaspoons	2 teaspoons	1 tablespoon
Table salt	1½ teaspoons	2 teaspoons	1 tablespoon
Garlic powder	1 teaspoon	1½ teaspoons	2 teaspoons
Dried sage leaves	1 teaspoon	1½ teaspoons	2 teaspoons
6-ounce bone-in lamb shoulder chops, any excess fat trimmed	2	3	4
Olive oil spray	As needed	As needed	As needed
MAKES	2 servings	3 servings	4 servings

1. Whisk the flour, paprika, salt, garlic powder, and sage in a large bowl until the mixture is of a uniform color. Add the chops and toss well to coat. Transfer them to a cutting board.

2. With the basket (or basket attachment) in the air fryer, heat it to 375°F (or 370°F or 360°F, if one of these is the closest setting).

3. When the machine is at temperature, *again* dredge the chops one by one in the flour mixture. Lightly coat both sides of each chop with olive oil spray before putting it in the basket. Continue on with the remaining chop(s), leaving air space between them in the basket.

4. Air-fry, turning once, for 25 minutes, or until the chops are well browned and tender when pierced with the point of a paring knife. If the machine is at 360°F, you may need to add up to 3 minutes to the cooking time.

5. Use kitchen tongs to transfer the chops to a wire rack. Cool for 5 minutes before serving.

Then...

- Serve these with classic TABBOULEH. Cook *bulgur wheat* as the package directs; then cool and put in a bowl with *toasted pine nuts, thinly sliced scallions, lots of minced fresh parsley,* and *a little minced fresh mint.* Add *a generous splash of olive oil* and *a little lemon juice,* as well as *table salt* and *ground black pepper* to taste. For a fuller salad, add *chopped tomatoes.*

- Or try these chops with **Roasted Broccoli and Red Bean Salad** (page 346) or **Crispy Brussels Sprouts** (page 367).

THIRTY

Fish & Shellfish Main Courses

Sure, you probably know about purchased fish sticks from an air fryer. And maybe breaded shrimp, too. But how about **Salmon Croquettes** (page 288) or simple but elegant **Lemon-Roasted Salmon Fillets** (page 284)? And we can safely say you haven't lived until you've tried **Crispy Smelts** (page 293).

In many ways, these fish and shellfish recipes are the fastest in this book. There's really not much effort to air-frying seafood. It's done in minutes.

Without a doubt, cooking fish and shellfish makes a bit of odor in the kitchen. That smell is mostly the result of the natural oils getting volatilized and then landing on counters and walls. Fortunately, the air fryer is a very contained environment. The volatilized oils stay mostly in the machine. Yes, you must clean it up afterwards. But our experience has consistently been that the kitchen itself suffered from fewer fish smells the next day.

Although these recipes may be some of the fastest in the book, they're unfortunately not the easiest. And speed is the culprit in their difficulty. There's a razor-thin line between when seafood is right and when it's overcooked. This difference will particularly come into play with anything breaded or coated in this chapter.

Here's why: fish and shellfish, like other proteins, tighten over the heat. All's well until the moment they tighten too much and release too much liquid, turning tough and (worse yet) rendering any coating soggy.

So pay attention to what's happening in the basket. Don't walk away. Check several times, even for the speediest recipe. Keep in mind the visual cues we give. Prod the fish or shellfish, not with a fork, and maybe not with your finger (unless you have asbestos chef fingers), but perhaps with the back side of a flatware spoon. You'll be able to tell if the seafood is firm or if it's starting to get hard. Get it out of the drawer the moment it's firm and the coating is set. There's no point in going to the trouble of getting a good coating on a piece of fish only to have it ruined.

More than the recipes in any other chapter, these recipes are made for sales at the supermarket. Check out the packages of fish fillets or scallops in the freezer section. When you see them for (relatively) cheap, grab a couple of bags and stash them in your freezer. We've developed a lot of these recipes for fish in exactly the size of the fillets in those frozen packages. If you've got a bag of fish fillets or shrimp at home, you've got an easy dinner without having to think about it.

We run through a lot of sauces in the *Then* sections after these recipes because salty fish and shellfish really take to condiments. And no amount of careful attention to the crust will ever make up for sugary-sweet, inferior cocktail sauce. A word to the wise: Nothing beats homemade.

Fish-In-Chips

FAST / CAN BE GLUTEN-FREE / 4 INGREDIENTS

No, not fish *and* chips. Instead, cod fillets coated *in* crushed potato chips, so you get the flavor of fish and chips in every bite. The coating requires a double dip in the egg and crushed potato chips to be thick enough to stand in for the missing French fries!

Crush potato chips right in their opened bag; or put the amount you need in a heavy zip-closed plastic bag, seal it well, and roll over it with a rolling pin, turning the bag repeatedly and working gently so it doesn't open. You're looking for little shards that still look like potato chips, not dust.

The serving sizes here are a bit light, on the assumption that these fish fillets are part of a larger meal. If not, consider two fillets as one serving.

INGREDIENTS	2-quart or larger air fryer	3.5-quart or larger air fryer	5.25-quart or larger air fryer
All-purpose flour or potato starch	¾ cup	1 cup	1 cup
Large egg(s), well beaten	1	2	3
Crushed plain potato chips, preferably thick-cut or ruffled (gluten-free, if a concern)	1 cup (4 ounces)	1½ cups (6 ounces)	2 cups (8 ounces)
4-ounce skinless cod fillets	2	4	6
MAKES	2 pieces	4 pieces	6 pieces

1. With the basket (or basket attachment) in the air fryer, heat it to 400°F (or 390°F, if that's the closest setting).

2. Set up and fill three shallow soup plates or small pie plates on your counter: one for the flour, one for the beaten egg(s), and one for the crushed potato chips.

3. Dip a piece of cod in the flour, turning it to coat on all sides, even the ends and sides. Gently shake off any excess flour, then dip it in the beaten egg(s). Gently turn to coat it on all sides, then let any excess egg slip back into the rest. Set the fillet in the crushed potato chips and turn several times and onto all sides, pressing gently to coat the fish. Dip it back in the egg(s), coating all sides but taking care that the coating doesn't slip off; then dip it back in the potato chips for a thick, even coating. Set it aside and coat more fillets in the same way.

4. When the machine is at temperature, set the fillets in the basket with as much air space between them as possible. Air-fry undisturbed for 11 minutes, until golden brown and firm but not hard.

5. Use kitchen tongs to transfer the fillets to a wire rack. Cool for just a minute or two before serving.

Then...

- For a dip, try **Avocado Ranch Dip** (page 223), **Spicy Ketchup Dip** (page 66), or **Sweet-and Sour Ketchup Dip** (page 71).

- Or for SWEET TARTAR SAUCE, combine *regular or low-fat mayonnaise (gluten-free, if a concern)* and *sweet pickle relish* in a 2-to-1 ratio by volume.

- For a side salad, try **Green Bean and Tomato Salad** (page 119), **Spicy Black-Eyed Pea Salad** (page 240), or **Three Bean Salad** (page 144).

See photo in insert.

Better Fish Sticks

FAST / EASY / CAN BE GLUTEN-FREE / 5 INGREDIENTS

So much better than heavily breaded, highly processed fish sticks, ours are light but flavorful, thanks to both the seasoning and the small amount of cheese in the coating. But what makes these fish sticks so crunchy is the combo of mayonnaise and vegetable oil spray, a double hit that crisps the coating from inside and out.

The only trick is cutting the fillets lengthwise into 1-inch-wide strips. You'll need a sharp knife to keep the fish intact.

INGREDIENTS	2-quart or larger air fryer	3.5-quart or larger air fryer	5.25-quart or larger air fryer
Seasoned Italian-style dried bread crumbs (gluten-free, if a concern)	½ cup	¾ cup	1 cup
Finely grated Parmesan cheese	2 tablespoons (about ⅓ ounce)	3 tablespoons (about ½ ounce)	¼ cup (about ¾ ounce)
Skinless cod fillets, cut lengthwise into 1-inch-wide pieces	6 ounces	10 ounces	1 pound
Regular or low-fat mayonnaise (*not* fat-free; gluten-free, if a concern)	2 tablespoons	3 tablespoons	¼ cup
Vegetable oil spray	As needed	As needed	As needed
MAKES	*2 servings*	*3 servings*	*4 servings*

1. With the basket (or basket attachment) in the air fryer, heat it to 400°F (or 390°F, if that's the closest setting).

2. Mix the bread crumbs and grated Parmesan in a shallow soup bowl or a small pie plate.

3. Smear the fish fillet sticks completely with the mayonnaise, then dip them one by one in the bread-crumb mixture, turning and pressing gently to make an even and thorough coating. Coat each stick on all sides with vegetable oil spray.

4. Set the fish sticks in the basket with at least ¼ inch between them. Air-fry undisturbed for 8 minutes, or until golden brown and crisp.

5. Use a nonstick-safe spatula to gently transfer them from the basket to a wire rack. Cool for only a minute or two before serving.

Then...

- Although ketchup or tartar sauce seems natural, for a more sophisticated treat try these with BASIL AND RED PEPPER MAYONNAISE. For 4 servings, whisk *1 cup regular, low-fat, or fat-free mayonnaise (gluten-free, if a concern); ¼ cup finely minced fresh basil leaves; ¼ cup minced drained jarred pimientos; and ½ teaspoon table salt* in a bowl until well combined. Store the remainder in a covered container in the fridge for up to 4 days.

Beer-Battered Cod

FAST / 6 INGREDIENTS

Since we can't use very wet batters in an air fryer (they drip off), it'll take several back-and-forths between a flour coating and an egg coating to get a proper, thick crust on the cod that replicates this bar-food staple.

Be warned: The batter won't puff up the way beer batter does in a deep fryer. However, the crust will have more of its characteristic "beer" flavor, rather than taste mostly like oil.

Check the fillets as they cook. When the coating's right, they're right. Don't let the coating darken or (heaven forfend!) burn.

INGREDIENTS	2-quart or larger air fryer	3.5-quart or larger air fryer	5.25-quart or larger air fryer
All-purpose flour	1 cup	1½ cups	2 cups
Old Bay seasoning	2 tablespoons	3 tablespoons	¼ cup
Large egg(s)	1	1	2
Amber beer, pale ale, or IPA	¼ cup	¼ cup	½ cup
4-ounce skinless cod fillets	2	3	4
Vegetable oil spray	As needed	As needed	As needed
MAKES	*2 pieces*	*3 pieces*	*4 pieces*

1. With the basket (or basket attachment) in the air fryer, heat it to 400°F (or 390°F, if that's the closest setting).

2. Set up and fill two shallow soup plates or small pie plates on your counter: one with the flour, whisked with the Old Bay until well combined; and one with the egg(s), whisked with the beer until foamy and uniform.

3. Dip a piece of cod in the flour mixture, turning it to coat on all sides (not just the top and bottom). Gently shake off any excess flour and dip the fish in the egg mixture, turning it to coat. Let any excess egg mixture slip back into the rest, then set the fish back in the flour mixture and coat it again, *then back* in the egg mixture for a second wash, *then back* in the flour mixture for a *third* time. Coat the fish on all sides with vegetable oil spray and set it aside. "Batter" the remaining piece(s) of cod in the same way.

4. Set the coated cod fillets in the basket with as much space between them as possible. They should not touch. Air-fry undisturbed for 12 minutes, or until brown and crisp.

5. Use kitchen tongs to gently transfer the fish to a wire rack. Cool for only a couple of minutes before serving.

Then...

- These crunchy fillets deserve a TRICOLORE SALAD. Whisk *olive oil* and *balsamic vinegar* in a 3-to-1 ratio in a big bowl. Add *chopped trimmed radicchio* and *Belgian endive,* as well as *stemmed arugula* (or better, baby arugula, which doesn't need to be stemmed). Toss well and season with *table salt* and *ground black pepper* to taste.

Crispy Sweet-and-Sour Cod Fillets

FAST / EASY / CAN BE GLUTEN-FREE / 4 INGREDIENTS

Why have tartar sauce on the side when you can put it right in the coating?

Okay, no one's ever asked that question! But we've answered it with these cod fillets that are rubbed with homemade tartar sauce, then coated in panko bread crumbs.

As with other coatings in this book, you can't use fat-free mayonnaise. Its stabilizers will break in the heat, resulting in a soggy and unappealing coating.

INGREDIENTS	2-quart or larger air fryer	3.5-quart or larger air fryer	5.25-quart or larger air fryer
Plain panko bread crumbs (gluten-free, if a concern)	1 cup	1½ cups	2 cups
Regular or low-fat mayonnaise (*not* fat-free; gluten-free, if a concern)	1½ tablespoons	2 tablespoons	3 tablespoons
Sweet pickle relish	3 tablespoons	¼ cup	6 tablespoons
4- to 5-ounce skinless cod fillets	2	3	4
MAKES	*2 fillets*	*3 fillets*	*4 fillets*

1. With the basket (or basket attachment) in the air fryer, heat it to 400°F (or 390°F, if that's the closest setting).

2. Pour the bread crumbs into a shallow soup plate or a small pie plate. Mix the mayonnaise and relish in a small bowl until well combined. Smear this mixture all over the cod fillets. Set them in the crumbs and turn until evenly coated on all sides, even on the ends.

3. Set the coated cod fillets in the basket with as much air space between them as possible. They should not touch. Air-fry undisturbed for 12 minutes, or until browned and crisp.

4. Use a nonstick-safe spatula to transfer the cod pieces to a wire rack. Cool for only a minute or two before serving hot.

Then...

- Serve these fillets with **Roasted Fennel Salad** (page 351), **Charred Radicchio Salad** (page 352), or **Roman Artichokes** (page 366).

Tex-Mex Fish Tacos

FAST / EASY / CAN BE GLUTEN-FREE / 8 INGREDIENTS

A '90s fad, fish tacos are better nowadays with an air fryer. The fish can get a bit of a crust without any breading, just a spice mixture. We use mahi-mahi because its meaty texture offers more "bite" per taco.

You can either buy individual mahi-mahi "steaks" (often in the freezer case near the fish counter); or buy a single large mahi-mahi fillet for the total amount of fish you need (10 ounces, 15 ounces, or 1¼ pounds), then slice it in halves, thirds, or quarters, depending on the batch you're making.

INGREDIENTS	2-quart or larger air fryer	3.5-quart or larger air fryer	5.25-quart or larger air fryer
Chile powder	½ teaspoon	¾ teaspoon	1 teaspoon
Ground cumin	¼ teaspoon	Rounded ¼ teaspoon	½ teaspoon
Dried oregano	¼ teaspoon	Rounded ¼ teaspoon	½ teaspoon
5-ounce skinless mahi-mahi fillets	2	3	4
Vegetable oil spray	As needed	As needed	As needed
Corn or flour tortillas	2	3	4
Diced tomatoes	¼ cup	6 tablespoons	½ cup
Regular, low-fat, or fat-free sour cream	2 tablespoons	3 tablespoons	¼ cup
MAKES	2 tacos	3 tacos	4 tacos

1. With the basket (or basket attachment) in the air fryer, heat it to 400°F (or 390°F, if that's the closest setting).

2. Stir the chile powder, cumin, and oregano in a small bowl until well combined.

3. Coat each piece of fish all over (even the sides and ends) with vegetable oil spray. Sprinkle the spice mixture evenly over all sides of the fillets. Lightly spray them again.

4. When the machine is at temperature, set the fillets in the basket with as much air space between them as possible. Air-fry undisturbed for 7 minutes, until lightly browned and firm but not hard.

5. Use a nonstick-safe spatula to transfer the fillets to a wire rack. Microwave the tortillas on high for a few seconds, until supple. Put a fillet in each tortilla and top each with 2 tablespoons diced tomatoes and 1 tablespoon sour cream.

Then...

- Although we suggest chopped tomatoes and sour cream in the tacos, you can also add chopped iceberg lettuce, pickled jalapeño rings, and/or shredded Cheddar cheese.

- To make LIME-CUMIN SLAW to go with the tacos, mix *2 cups bagged slaw mix, ¼ cup minced fresh cilantro leaves, 2 tablespoons lime juice, 2 teaspoons honey, ¼ teaspoon ground cumin, ¼ teaspoon table salt,* and *¼ teaspoon ground black pepper* in a large bowl.

See photo in insert.

Mahi-Mahi "Burrito" Fillets

FAST / CAN BE GLUTEN-FREE / 6 INGREDIENTS

No, these aren't burritos with fried fish in them. They're mahi-mahi fillets that have been coated in the flavors—even some of the ingredients—of burritos. With chile powder, refried beans, and crushed tortilla chips on the outside, these fillets will take care of your Tex-Mex hankerings.

INGREDIENTS	2-quart or larger air fryer	3.5-quart or larger air fryer	5.25-quart or larger air fryer
Large egg white	1	1	1
Crushed corn tortilla chips (gluten-free, if a concern)	1 cup (4 ounces)	1½ cups (6 ounces)	2 cups (8 ounces)
Chile powder	2 teaspoons	1 tablespoon	4 teaspoons
5-ounce skinless mahi-mahi fillets	2	3	4
Canned refried beans	¼ cup	6 tablespoons	½ cup
Vegetable oil spray	As needed	As needed	As needed
MAKES	2 pieces	3 pieces	4 pieces

1. With the basket (or basket attachment) in the air fryer, heat it to 400°F (or 390°F, if that's the closest setting).

2. Set up and fill two shallow soup plates or small pie plates on your counter: one with the egg white, beaten until foamy; and one with the crushed tortilla chips.

3. Gently rub ½ teaspoon chile powder on each side of each fillet.

4. Spread (or maybe smear) 1 tablespoon refried beans over both sides and the edges of a fillet. Dip the fillet in the egg white, turning to coat it on both sides. Let any excess egg white slip back into the rest, then set the fillet in the crushed tortilla chips. Turn several times, pressing gently to coat it evenly. Coat the fillet on all sides with the vegetable oil spray, then set it aside. Prepare the remaining fillet(s) in the same way.

5. When the machine is at temperature, set the fillets in the basket with as much air space between them as possible. Air-fry undisturbed for 10 minutes, or until crisp and browned.

6. Use a nonstick-safe spatula to transfer the fillets to a serving platter or plates. Cool for only a minute or so, then serve hot.

Then...

- Top these fillets with PICO DE GALLO. For 4 to 6 servings, mix *4 chopped large tomatoes; 1 chopped small red onion; 1 stemmed, seeded, and diced fresh small jalapeño chile; ½ cup stemmed and chopped cilantro leaves; ¼ cup lime juice;* and *1 teaspoon table salt* in a bowl. Serve as a relish over the fillet. Cover and store any leftovers in a glass or other nonreactive container in the fridge for up to 2 days.

Super Crunchy Flounder Fillets

FAST / CAN BE GLUTEN-FREE / 8 INGREDIENTS

Flounder is mild and sweet—and not traditionally used for fish and chips because the flat fillets don't hold a wet coating very well. No worries: a crumb coating gives lots of crunch—in fact, a greater crunch-to-fish ratio than it would on a thicker fish fillet. Spritz the coating *well* with vegetable oil spray. For more flavor, use olive oil spray or even coconut oil spray.

Because flounder fillets are wide and flat, you won't be able to fit as many in the air fryer as some other sorts of fish fillets. However, every flounder fillet has a natural "seam" that runs down the center of the fillet. You can separate them at this seam before you bread them to make them fit more easily, if you'd like.

INGREDIENTS	2-quart or larger air fryer	3.5-quart or larger air fryer	5.25-quart or larger air fryer
All-purpose flour or tapioca flour	½ cup	½ cup	¾ cup
Large egg white(s)	1	1	2
Water	1 tablespoon	1 tablespoon	1 tablespoon
Table salt	½ teaspoon	¾ teaspoon	1 teaspoon
Plain panko bread crumbs (gluten-free, if a concern)	½ cup	1 cup	1½ cups
4-ounce skinless flounder fillet(s)	1	2	3
Vegetable oil spray	As needed	As needed	As needed
MAKES	*1 piece*	*2 pieces*	*3 pieces*

1. With the basket (or basket attachment) in the air fryer, heat it to 400°F (or 390°F, if that's the closest setting).

2. Set up and fill three shallow soup plates or small pie plates on your counter: one for the flour; one for the egg white(s), beaten with the water and salt until foamy; and one for the bread crumbs.

3. Dip one fillet in the flour, turning it to coat both sides. Gently shake off any excess flour, then dip the fillet in the egg white mixture, turning it to coat. Let any excess egg white mixture slip back into the rest, then set the fish in the bread crumbs. Turn it several times, gently pressing it into the crumbs to create an even crust. *Generously* coat both sides of the fillet with vegetable oil spray. If necessary, set it aside and continue coating the remaining fillet(s) in the same way.

4. Set the fillet(s) in the basket. If working with more than one fillet, they should not touch, although they may be quite close together, depending on the basket's size. Air-fry undisturbed for 6 minutes, or until lightly browned and crunchy.

5. Use a nonstick-safe spatula to transfer the fillet(s) to a wire rack. Cool for only a minute or two before serving.

Then...

- To make 4 servings of **SPICY TARTAR SAUCE** for the fillets, stir *½ cup regular, low-fat, or fat-free mayonnaise (gluten-free, if a concern); 2 tablespoons minced hot dill pickles; 1 tablespoon white wine vinegar; 1 teaspoon hot mustard (gluten-free, if a concern); ⅛ teaspoon table salt; and ⅛ teaspoon ground black pepper* in a small bowl.

Cajun Flounder Fillets

FAST / EASY / GLUTEN-FREE / 3 INGREDIENTS

By using a Cajun seasoning blend on the flounder, the sort of blend used to blacken the fish, we can turn these fillets into an easy, air-fryer version of the Cajun favorite without heating a cast-iron skillet to smelting levels.

For better flavor, make your own CAJUN DRIED SEASONING BLEND. For more than you'll need for this recipe, whisk *2 tablespoons mild paprika, 1 tablespoon mild smoked paprika, 2 teaspoons onion powder, 1 teaspoon dried basil, 1 teaspoon dried thyme, 1 teaspoon garlic powder, 1 teaspoon table salt,* and *up to 1 teaspoon cayenne* in a small bowl until well combined. Store in a covered glass container at room temperature, out of the light and in a cool place, for up to 6 months.

This recipe doesn't call for the more traditional catfish fillets because they can be hard to track down outside of the South. If you can find them, they are thicker, so they'll take an extra 2 minutes in the air fryer.

INGREDIENTS	2-quart or larger air fryer	3.5-quart or larger air fryer	5.25-quart or larger air fryer
4-ounce skinless flounder fillet(s)	1	2	3
Peanut oil	1 teaspoon	2 teaspoons	1 tablespoon
Purchased or homemade Cajun dried seasoning blend (see the headnote)	½ teaspoon	1 teaspoon	1½ teaspoons
MAKES	*1 piece*	*2 pieces*	*3 pieces*

1. With the basket (or basket attachment) in the air fryer, heat it to 400°F (or 390°F, if that's the closest setting).

2. Oil the fillet(s) by drizzling on the peanut oil, then gently rubbing in the oil with your clean, dry fingers. Sprinkle the seasoning blend evenly over both sides of the fillet(s).

3. When the machine is at temperature, set the fillet(s) in the basket. If working with more than one fillet, they should not touch, although they may be quite close together, depending on the basket's size. Air-fry undisturbed for 5 minutes, or until lightly browned and cooked through.

4. Use a nonstick-safe spatula to transfer the fillets to a serving platter or plate(s). Serve at once.

Then...

• Make JICAMA AND MANGO SALAD to go with these spicy fillets. Mix *peeled, pitted, and chopped mango; peeled and julienned jicama; some thinly sliced radish rounds;* and *chopped fresh cilantro leaves* in a large bowl. Add a little *ground cumin,* some *table salt,* and a *tiny sprinkle of cayenne.* Dress the salad with *olive oil* and *lime juice* in a 3-to-1 ratio. Toss well to blend the spices.

Crabmeat-Stuffed Flounder

9 INGREDIENTS

This recipe may be the fanciest in this chapter. It's an old-school preparation, the flounder fillets stuffed with a crabmeat mixture. Don't waste expensive lump crabmeat on this recipe. Less-expensive backfin or claw meat will be brinier, giving the flounder more flavor.

Getting the stuffed flounder out of the basket is a little tricky. First, remove the basket from the machine. Then use two thin nonstick-safe spatulas, coming at the fish from both longer sides. Don't lift the fillet up by two spatulas at once. Instead, use one spatula to slide the fillet onto the second spatula. If the ends of the fillet hang off the spatula, support them with the other spatula for transport to plates or serving platter.

INGREDIENTS	2-quart or larger air fryer	3.5-quart or larger air fryer	5.25-quart or larger air fryer
Purchased backfin or claw crabmeat, picked over for bits of shell and cartilage	3 ounces	4½ ounces	6 ounces
Saltine crackers, crushed into fine crumbs	4	6	8
Regular or low-fat mayonnaise (*not* fat-free)	1½ tablespoons	2 tablespoons plus 1 teaspoon	3 tablespoons
Yellow prepared mustard	½ teaspoon	¾ teaspoon	1 teaspoon
Worcestershire sauce	1 teaspoon	1½ teaspoons	2 teaspoons
Celery salt	⅛ teaspoon	Rounded ⅛ teaspoon	¼ teaspoon
5- to 6-ounce skinless flounder fillets	2	3	4
Vegetable oil spray	As needed	As needed	As needed
Mild paprika	As needed	As needed	As needed
MAKES	*2 pieces*	*3 pieces*	*4 pieces*

1. With the basket (or basket attachment) in the air fryer, heat it to 400°F (or 390°F, if that's the closest setting).

2. Gently mix the crabmeat, crushed saltines, mayonnaise, mustard, Worcestershire sauce, and celery salt in a bowl until well combined.

3. Generously coat the flat side of a fillet with vegetable oil spray. Set the fillet sprayed side down on your work surface. Cut the fillet in half widthwise, then cut one of the halves in half lengthwise. Set a scant ⅓ cup of the crabmeat mixture on top of the undivided half of the fish fillet, mounding the mixture to make an oval that somewhat fits the shape of the fillet with at least a ¼-inch border of fillet beyond the filling all around.

4. Take the two thin divided quarters (that is, the halves of the half) and lay them lengthwise over the filling, overlapping at each end and leaving a little space in the middle where the filling peeks through. Coat the top of the stuffed flounder piece with vegetable oil spray, then sprinkle paprika over the stuffed flounder fillet. Set aside and use the remaining fillet(s) to make more stuffed flounder "packets," repeating steps 3 and 4.

5. Use a nonstick-safe spatula to transfer the stuffed flounder fillets to the basket. Leave as much space between them as possible. Air-fry undisturbed for 12 minutes, or until lightly brown and firm (but not hard).

6. Use that same spatula, plus perhaps another one, to transfer the fillets to a serving platter or plates (see the headnote for more information). Cool for a minute or two, then serve hot.

Then...

- A fancy dish like these one needs a fancy side. Try **Roasted Belgian Endive with Pistachios and Lemon** (page 353) or **Roman Artichokes** (page 366).

- Try a salad on the side like **Broccoli and Grape Salad** (page 127), **Fennel-Pear Salad** (page 125), or **Spinach Salad** (page 265).

Sesame-Crusted Tuna Steaks

FAST / EASY / GLUTEN-FREE / 3 INGREDIENTS

This is about the easiest recipe for tuna steaks we've written in more than thirty cookbooks! Look for sesame seeds among the spices or sometimes the Asian foods in the supermarket. Or buy them in bulk from a spice store and keep them in a sealed container in the freezer for up to 1 year to preserve their freshness.

Be careful not to let the sesame seeds burn and become bitter. But do let those seeds brown and release some of their natural oils and flavor.

In a bid for good health, we call for a minimal amount of toasted sesame oil; but you don't really need to follow our guidelines. You can use a little more, if only to deepen the flavor it imparts to the tuna.

INGREDIENTS	2-quart or larger air fryer	3.5-quart or larger air fryer	5.25-quart or larger air fryer
Sesame seeds, preferably a blend of white and black	⅓ cup	½ cup	⅔ cup
Toasted sesame oil	1 tablespoon	1½ tablespoons	2 tablespoons
6-ounce skinless tuna steaks	2	3	4
MAKES	*2 servings*	*3 servings*	*4 servings*

1. With the basket (or basket attachment) in the air fryer, heat it to 400°F (or 390°F, if that's the closest setting).

2. Pour the sesame seeds on a dinner plate. Use ½ tablespoon of the sesame oil as a rub on both sides and the edges of a tuna steak. Set it in the sesame seeds, then turn it several times, pressing gently, to create an even coating of the seeds, including around the steak's edge. Set aside and continue coating the remaining steak(s).

3. When the machine is at temperature, set the steaks in the basket with as much air space between them as possible. Air-fry undisturbed for 10 minutes for medium-rare (not USDA-approved), or 12 to 13 minutes for cooked through (USDA-approved).

4. Use a nonstick-safe spatula to transfer the steaks to serving plates. Serve hot.

Then...

- Serve these tuna steaks with picked sushi ginger and **Sushi Rice** (page 263).

- Or go all out and serve them with **Kale Chips** (page 35) and **Avocado Fries** (page 52). Make the three dishes in this order: avocado, tuna, kale. Then recrisp the avocado pieces just before serving.

Butternut Squash–Wrapped Halibut Fillets

FAST / EASY / GLUTEN-FREE / 6 INGREDIENTS

Here we wrap halibut in spiralized vegetables to create a "crust"—no dredging or coating necessary. We use butternut squash strands for a sweet finish against the added butter.

Spiralized vegetables are available in the produce department of almost all large supermarkets. Some strands are short and others long, depending on which part of the vegetable was in the spiralizing machine at any given moment. Choose the longest strands you can, making sure they are all about the same length for each fillet.

If desired, substitute 5- to 6-ounce skinless mahi-mahi fillets for the halibut.

INGREDIENTS	2-quart or larger air fryer	3.5-quart or larger air fryer	5.25-quart or larger air fryer
Long spiralized peeled and seeded butternut squash strands	10	15	20
5- to 6-ounce skinless halibut fillets	2	3	4
Butter, melted	2 tablespoons	3 tablespoons	4 tablespoons (¼ cup/½ stick)
Mild paprika	½ teaspoon	¾ teaspoon	1 teaspoon
Table salt	½ teaspoon	¾ teaspoon	1 teaspoon
Ground black pepper	½ teaspoon	¾ teaspoon	1 teaspoon
MAKES	*2 servings*	*3 servings*	*4 servings*

1. With the basket (or basket attachment) in the air fryer, heat it to 375°F (or 370°F or 360°F, if one of these is the closest setting).

2. Hold 5 long butternut squash strands together and wrap them around a fillet. Set it aside and wrap any remaining fillet(s).

3. Mix the melted butter, paprika, salt, and pepper in a small bowl. Brush this mixture over the squash-wrapped fillets on all sides.

4. When the machine is at temperature, set the fillets in the basket with as much air space between them as possible. Air-fry undisturbed for 10 minutes, or until the squash strands have browned but not burned. If the machine is at 360°F, you may need to add 1 minute to the cooking time. In any event, watch the fish carefully after the 8-minute mark.

5. Use a nonstick-safe spatula to gently transfer the fillets to a serving platter or plates. Cool for only a minute or so before serving.

Then...

- This rather sweet entrée needs a full-flavored side. Try SPICY WAX BEAN SALAD. Blanch *trimmed and chopped wax beans* and *thinly sliced shallots* in *boiling water* for 1 minute. Drain in a colander set in the sink, then bring back down to room temperature under cool running water. Drain well and pour into a bowl. Dress with *a splash of olive oil, a smaller splash of white wine vinegar,* and a little *Creole mustard.* Season with *table salt* and *ground black pepper* before serving.

Lemon-Roasted Salmon Fillets

FAST / EASY / GLUTEN-FREE / 5 INGREDIENTS

This recipe is super simple, partly so that there's nothing to compete with the lemon flavor on the salmon. The lemon slices should be very thin, although not paper thin (in which case they'll burn).

If you want to make the recipe a little more complicated, sprinkle stemmed fresh thyme leaves on the fillets before you add the lemon slices, salt, and pepper. And for a fancier preparation, skip coating the tops of the fillets with olive oil spray and instead brush them with melted and cooled butter (about 2 teaspoons per fillet).

For more information on the types of salmon that work best in an air fryer, see the headnote on page 287.

INGREDIENTS	2-quart or larger air fryer	3.5-quart or larger air fryer	5.25-quart or larger air fryer
6-ounce skin-on salmon fillets	2	3	4
Olive oil spray	As needed	As needed	As needed
Very thin lemon slices	6	9	12
Ground black pepper	½ teaspoon	¾ teaspoon	1 teaspoon
Table salt	¼ teaspoon	Rounded ¼ teaspoon	½ teaspoon
MAKES	2 servings	3 servings	4 servings

1. With the basket (or basket attachment) in the air fryer, heat it to 400°F (or 390°F, if that's the closest setting).

2. Generously coat the skin of each of the fillets with olive oil spray. Set the fillets skin side down on your work surface. Place three overlapping lemon slices down the length of each salmon fillet. Sprinkle them with the pepper and salt. Coat lightly with olive oil spray.

3. Use a nonstick-safe spatula to transfer the fillets one by one to the basket, leaving as much air space between them as possible. Air-fry undisturbed for 7 minutes, or until cooked through.

4. Use a nonstick-safe spatula to transfer the fillets to serving plates. Cool for only a minute or two before serving.

Then...

- Serve these simple fillets with **Moroccan-Spiced Carrots** (page 348) or **Wilted Brussels Sprout Slaw** (page 368). Or make a fancier meal with **Stuffed Onions** (page 314).

- These are the best fillets to put over a Caesar salad, particularly a kale Caesar made with baby kale and bottled Caesar dressing.

Miso-Rubbed Salmon Fillets

FAST / EASY / 5 INGREDIENTS

Miso adds a savory and salty flavor to naturally sweet salmon fillets. That's all well and good, but trust us: You want the skin crisp, too. Coat it generously with spray so it won't stick to the basket. When the salmon's cooked, use a nonstick-safe spatula to loosen it little by little from the basket, starting at one corner, then working at another corner, and on around the fillet, all so that the skin comes up with the meat.

Miso is a fermented paste, often made from soy beans but also from grains (rice, millet, amaranth, barley, wheat, or rye). Unfortunately, most miso cannot be gluten-free, even if it's made with a gluten-free grain, because of trace amounts of other grains either by recipe ratios or by cross-contamination in the facility where it's made. Look for miso paste near the tofu in the refrigerator case. Covered, miso paste can last up to 3 months in the fridge; or it can be covered and frozen in small amounts for up to 1 year.

INGREDIENTS	2-quart or larger air fryer	3.5-quart or larger air fryer	5.25-quart or larger air fryer
White *(shiro)* miso paste (usually made from rice and soy beans)	2½ tablespoons	¼ cup	⅓ cup
Mirin or a substitute (see page 176)	1 tablespoon	1½ tablespoons	2 tablespoons
Unseasoned rice vinegar (see page 70)	1½ teaspoons	2½ teaspoons	1 tablespoon
Vegetable oil spray	As needed	As needed	As needed
6-ounce skin-on salmon fillets (for more information, see page 287)	2	3	4
MAKES	*2 servings*	*3 servings*	*4 servings*

1. With the basket (or basket attachment) in the air fryer, heat it to 400°F (or 390°F, if that's the closest setting).

2. Mix the miso, mirin, and vinegar in a small bowl until uniform.

3. Remove the basket from the machine. *Generously* spray the skin side of each fillet. Pick them up one by one with a nonstick-safe spatula and set them in the basket skin side down with as much air space between them as possible. Coat the top of each fillet with the miso mixture, dividing it evenly between them.

4. Return the basket to the machine. Air-fry undisturbed for 5 minutes, or until lightly browned and firm.

5. Use a nonstick-safe spatula to transfer the fillets to serving plates. Cool for only a minute or so before serving.

Then...

- Make a JAPANESE-INSPIRED RADISH SALAD as a side dish. Toss *trimmed and thinly sliced radishes* and *scallions* with *baby lettuce greens* in a large bowl. In a separate bowl, whisk *mirin (see page 176), unseasoned rice vinegar (see page 70), toasted sesame oil,* and *regular or low-sodium soy sauce or tamari sauce* in equal proportions until uniform. Add a little *minced peeled fresh ginger*, then pour as much as you like over the salad. Toss well before serving.

Horseradish-Crusted Salmon Fillets

FAST / EASY / 5 INGREDIENTS

This horseradish crust is amazing! It's a bit spicy but very buttery, a wonderful balance with the fish.

Note that recipe calls for *fresh* bread crumbs, not dried, an unusual move in this book. You can often find fresh bread crumbs in the bakery department of a large supermarket. Or you can make your own by pulsing torn pieces of stale baguette in a food processor until the consistency is like very coarse sand. (Don't process them too far, not to the size of dried bread crumbs.) Figure two 4-inch sections of stale baguette will give you about ½ cup fresh bread crumbs. For even more flavor, split the baguette sections in half and toast them on a baking sheet under a heated broiler for a couple of minutes before processing.

INGREDIENTS	2-quart or larger air fryer	3.5-quart or larger air fryer	5.25-quart or larger air fryer
Fresh bread crumbs (see the headnote)	¼ cup	6 tablespoons	½ cup
Butter, melted and cooled	2 tablespoons	3 tablespoons	4 tablespoons (¼ cup/½ stick)
Jarred prepared white horseradish	2 tablespoons	3 tablespoons	¼ cup
Vegetable oil spray	As needed	As needed	As needed
6-ounce skin-on salmon fillets (for more information, see page 287)	2	3	4
MAKES	2 servings	3 servings	4 serving

1. With the basket (or basket attachment) in the air fryer, heat it to 400°F (or 390°F, if that's the closest setting).

2. Mix the bread crumbs, butter, and horseradish in a bowl until well combined.

3. Take the basket out of the machine. *Generously* spray the skin side of each fillet. Pick them up one by one with a nonstick-safe spatula and set them in the basket skin side down with as much air space between them as possible. Divide the bread-crumb mixture between the fillets, coating the top of each fillet with an even layer. Generously coat the bread-crumb mixture with vegetable oil spray.

4. Return the basket to the machine and air-fry undisturbed for 8 minutes, or until the topping has lightly browned and the fish is firm but not hard.

5. Use a nonstick-safe spatula to transfer the salmon fillets to serving plates. Cool for 5 minutes before serving. Because of the butter in the topping, it will stay very hot for quite a while. Take care, especially if you're serving these fillets to children. (And if you're serving horseradish-coated salmon to kids, good on you!)

Then...

- Make MASHED POTATOES by boiling *small yellow potatoes* (peeled or not) in *lightly salted water* until tender, about 20 minutes. Drain in a colander set in the sink, then transfer to a bowl and use a potato masher or an electric mixer at medium speed to mash them with *a little chicken or vegetable broth*, *even less regular or low-fat sour cream*, and *a small dollop of Dijon mustard*. Season with *table salt* to taste.

Potato-Wrapped Salmon Fillets

FAST / GLUTEN-FREE / 5 INGREDIENTS

These are elegant fillets, each wrapped in thin strips of potato to make a crust. *Carefully* transfer the wrapped raw fillets to the machine: The potato "crust" can fall off before it's air-fried to the fish.

For a more professional look, use a mandoline with the slicing blade set at 1⁄16 inch to cut perfect, even strips from the potatoes. Grip a spud with the mandoline guard, then repeatedly run it the long way over the blade.

That said, you can get a fair approximation of that cheffy look with a vegetable peeler, so long as you make even, long strips. A standard peeler, one like a big, fat pen, is more maneuverable and makes consistently longer strips than a so-called Y peeler that has a blade stretched across two prongs out of the handle.

One final, important ingredient note: The best **salmon** for an air fryer is the fattier Atlantic or King salmon. Avoid Coho, Sockeye, or other super lean salmon, because the machine will unduly dry out the fish.

INGREDIENTS	2-quart or larger air fryer	3.5-quart or larger air fryer	5.25-quart or larger air fryer
Large 1-pound elongated yellow potato(es), peeled	1	1	2
6-ounce, 1½-inch-wide, quite thick skinless salmon fillets	2	3	4
Olive oil spray	As needed	As needed	As needed
Table salt	¼ teaspoon	Rounded ¼ teaspoon	½ teaspoon
Ground black pepper	¼ teaspoon	Rounded ¼ teaspoon	½ teaspoon
MAKES	2 servings	3 servings	4 servings

1. With the basket (or basket attachment) in the air fryer, heat it to 400°F (or 390°F, if that's the closest setting).

2. Use a vegetable peeler or mandoline to make long strips from the potato(es). You'll need anywhere from 8 to 12 strips per fillet, depending on the shape of the potato and of the salmon fillet.

3. Drape potato strips over a salmon fillet, overlapping the strips to create an even "crust." Tuck the potato strips under the fillet, overlapping the strips underneath to create as smooth a bottom as you can. Wrap the remaining fillet(s) in the same way.

4. Gently turn the fillets over. *Generously* coat the bottoms with olive oil spray. Turn them back seam side down and *generously* coat the tops with the oil spray. Sprinkle the salt and pepper over the wrapped fillets.

5. Use a nonstick-safe spatula to *gently* transfer the fillets seam side down to the basket. It helps to remove the basket from the machine and set it on your work surface (keeping in mind that the basket's hot). Leave as much air space as possible between the fillets. Air-fry undisturbed for 8 minutes, or until golden brown and crisp.

6. Use a nonstick-safe spatula to gently transfer the fillets to serving plates. Cool for a couple of minutes before serving.

Then...

- Try these wrapped fillets with **Arugula and Pistachio Salad** (page 197), **Green Bean and Tomato Salad** (page 119), or **Spicy Wax Bean Salad** (page 283).

Salmon Croquettes

FAST / EASY / CAN BE GLUTEN-FREE / 9 INGREDIENTS

A salmon croquette is a mid-century-modern favorite that needs a little updating. We've improved the flavor by calling for canned pink salmon, milder than other canned salmon on the market. We've also added panko bread crumbs (rather than regular dried bread crumbs) for a softer, smoother texture inside.

INGREDIENTS	2-quart or larger air fryer	3.5-quart or larger air fryer	5.25-quart or larger air fryer
5-ounce can or pouch pink salmon, drained if necessary	1	2	3
Plain panko bread crumbs (gluten-free, if a concern)	2½ tablespoons	⅓ cup	½ cup
Finely chopped stemmed and cored red bell pepper	2½ tablespoons	⅓ cup	½ cup
Regular or low-fat mayonnaise (*not* fat-free; gluten-free, if a concern)	1½ tablespoons	3½ tablespoons	⅓ cup
Worcestershire sauce (gluten-free, if a concern)	1 teaspoon	2 teaspoons	1 tablespoon
Garlic powder	¼ teaspoon	Rounded ¼ teaspoon	½ teaspoon
Table salt	¼ teaspoon	Rounded ¼ teaspoon	½ teaspoon
Ground black pepper	¼ teaspoon	Rounded ¼ teaspoon	½ teaspoon
Vegetable oil spray	As needed	As needed	As needed
MAKES	2 croquettes	4 croquettes	6 croquettes

1. With the basket (or basket attachment) in the air fryer, heat it to 375°F (or 370°F or 360°F, if one of these is the closest setting).

2. Gently stir the canned salmon, bread crumbs, bell pepper, mayonnaise, Worcestershire sauce, garlic powder, salt, and pepper in a bowl until well combined.

3. With clean but damp hands, form this mixture into 2 patties for a small batch, 4 patties for a medium batch, or 6 patties for a large batch. Dampen your hands after every one or two patties to keep the mixture from sticking to you. Generously coat both sides of each patty with vegetable oil spray.

4. Set the patties in the basket with as much air space between them as possible. Air-fry undisturbed for 8 minutes, or until lightly browned and firm.

5. Use a nonstick-safe spatula to transfer the croquettes to a wire rack. Cool for a couple of minutes before serving.

Then...

- Serve the croquettes in toasted Kaiser rolls with **Spicy Tartar Sauce** (page 278), shredded iceberg lettuce, and sprouts (particularly radish sprouts).

- Set these warm croquettes bunless over servings of a chopped salad tossed with **Classic Greek Diner Dressing** (page 90).

- Or serve them with mashed potatoes and **Perfect Broccolini** (page 347).

Better-Than-Chinese-Take-Out Pork Ribs (page 252) with duck sauce

Chicken-Fried Steak (page 210) with Crispy Brussels Sprouts (page 367)

Carne Asada (page 216) with all the fixings

Garlic and Oregano Lamb Chops (page 267) with Roasted Fennel Salad (page 351)

**Fish-In-Chips (page 272)
with Three Bean Salad
(page 144)**

Tex-Mex Fish Tacos
with Lime-Cumin
Slaw (page 276)

Shrimp Teriyaki with
Wasabi Mayonnaise
(pages 295–96)

Fried Scallops (page 303) with melted butter garnished with red pepper flakes

Crispy Noodle Salad (page 317)

Hasselback
Garlic-and-
Butter Potatoes
(page 337) with
lightly dressed
pea shoots

Air-Fried Potato Salad (page 338) and Buttery Rolls (page 322)

Perfect Asparagus (page 342) topped with a fried egg

Roasted Eggplant Halves with Herbed Ricotta (page 354)

Mexican-Style Roasted Corn
(page 358)

Fried Cheesecake (page 383)

Cinnamon Sugar Banana Rolls (page 385) and Sweet Potato Pie Rolls with Easy Salted Caramel Sauce (page 384)

Giant Buttery Chocolate
Chip Cookie (page 392) and
Giant Buttery Oatmeal
Cookie (page 396)

Fried Fruit Pies (page 411)

Classic Crab Cakes

EASY / CAN BE GLUTEN-FREE / 12 INGREDIENTS

Because we're not larding up these crab cakes with eggs or pouring a lot of oil into a skillet to fry them, they stay marvelously light in the air fryer, perhaps a surprising texture if you're used to the hockey-puck standard. The exterior will be slightly crisp, not crunchy—a more delicate finish against the soft interior.

Note that we call for lump crabmeat, not jumbo lump. The lump meat has a milder flavor than backfin or claw; but since the crabmeat is stirred with the other ingredients, the more expensive jumbo lump would be wasted in this recipe. For the best flavor, look for refrigerated containers of lump crabmeat near the fish counter (rather than the cans of crabmeat on supermarket shelves of pantry staples).

INGREDIENTS	2-quart or larger air fryer	3.5-quart or larger air fryer	5.25-quart or larger air fryer
Lump crabmeat, picked over for shell and cartilage	5 ounces	10 ounces	1 pound
Plain panko bread crumbs (gluten-free, if a concern)	3 tablespoons	6 tablespoons	½ cup plus 1 tablespoon
Chopped drained jarred roasted red peppers	3 tablespoons	6 tablespoons	½ cup
Medium scallions, trimmed and thinly sliced	2	4	6
Regular or low-fat mayonnaise (*not* fat-free; gluten-free, if a concern)	2 tablespoons	¼ cup	6 tablespoons
Dried dill	¼ teaspoon	Rounded ¼ teaspoon	½ teaspoon
Dried thyme	¼ teaspoon	Rounded ¼ teaspoon	½ teaspoon
Onion powder	¼ teaspoon	Rounded ¼ teaspoon	½ teaspoon
Table salt	¼ teaspoon	Rounded ¼ teaspoon	½ teaspoon
Celery seeds	⅛ teaspoon	Rounded ⅛ teaspoon	¼ teaspoon
Cayenne	Up to ⅛ teaspoon	Up to rounded ⅛ teaspoon	Up to ¼ teaspoon
Vegetable oil spray	As needed	As needed	As needed
MAKES	2 crab cakes	4 crab cakes	6 crab cakes

1. With the basket (or basket attachment) in the air fryer, heat it to 400°F (or 390°F, if that's the closest setting).

2. Gently mix the crabmeat, bread crumbs, red pepper, scallion, mayonnaise, dill, thyme, onion powder, salt, celery seeds, and cayenne in a bowl until well combined.

3. Use clean and dry hands to form ½ cup of this mixture into a *tightly packed* 1-inch-thick, 3- to 4-inch-wide patty. Coat the top and bottom of the patty with vegetable oil spray and set it aside. Continue making 1 more patty for a small batch, 3 more for a medium batch, or 5 more for a larger one, coating them with vegetable oil spray on both sides.

continues

4. Set the patties in one layer in the basket and air-fry undisturbed for 10 minutes, or until lightly browned and cooked through.

5. Use a nonstick-safe spatula to transfer the crab cakes to a serving platter or plates. Wait a couple of minutes before serving.

Then...

- These crab cakes would be great with **Lemon Aioli** (page 45), **Basil and Red Pepper Mayonnaise** (page 273), or **Spicy Tartar Sauce** (page 278).

- For a side dish, consider **Celery Root Slaw** (page 205) or **Herb Salad** (page 249).

Fried Oysters

FAST / 6 INGREDIENTS

In this recipe, you'll make a beer batter, dip the oysters in it, then coat them in a dried mixture laced with spices. Don't worry: You needn't shuck oysters for dinner. Look for shucked oysters in containers in the refrigerator section of your supermarket's fish counter, or maybe at the fish counter itself. These will be milder and sweeter than canned shucked oysters.

INGREDIENTS	2-quart or larger air fryer	3.5-quart or larger air fryer	5.25-quart or larger air fryer
All-purpose flour	1 cup	1½ cups	2 cups
Yellow cornmeal	1 cup	1½ cups	2 cups
Cajun dried seasoning blend (for a homemade blend, see page 279)	1 tablespoon	1½ tablespoons	2 tablespoons
Amber beer, pale ale, or IPA	1 cup, plus more if needed	1¼ cups, plus more if needed	1½ cups (one 12-ounce bottle or can), plus more needed
Large shucked oysters, any liquid drained off	8	12	16
Vegetable oil spray	As needed	As needed	As needed
MAKES	8 fried oysters	12 fried oysters	16 fried oysters

1. With the basket (or basket attachment) in the air fryer, heat it to 400°F (or 390°F, if that's the closest setting).

2. Whisk ⅔ cup of the flour, ½ cup of the cornmeal, and the seasoning blend in a bowl until uniform. Set aside.

3. Whisk the remaining ⅓ cup flour and the remaining ½ cup cornmeal with the beer in a second bowl, adding more beer in dribs and drabs until the mixture is the consistency of pancake batter.

4. Using a fork, dip a shucked oyster in the beer batter, coating it thoroughly. Gently shake off any excess batter, then set the oyster in the dry mixture and turn gently to coat well and evenly. Set the coated oyster on a cutting board and continue dipping and coating the remainder of the oysters.

5. Coat the oysters with vegetable oil spray, then set them in the basket with as much air space between them as possible. Air-fry undisturbed for 8 minutes, or until lightly browned and crisp.

6. Use a nonstick-safe spatula to transfer the oysters to a wire rack. Cool for a couple of minutes before serving.

Then...

- Rather than tartar sauce, consider serving these oysters with **Cucumber and Cilantro Raita** (page 179). The only side dish you need is **Simple Arugula Salad** (page 128).

- Or make a RÉMOULADE SAUCE. For 4 to 6 servings, whisk *1 cup regular, low-fat, or fat-free mayonnaise; 3 tablespoons Dijon mustard; 2 teaspoons brine from a pickle jar; 2 teaspoons minced drained and rinsed capers; 1 teaspoon minced garlic; 1 teaspoon jarred prepared white horseradish;* and *up to ¼ teaspoon cayenne* in a bowl until well combined. Store any leftovers under plastic wrap in the refrigerator for up to 3 days.

Perfect Soft-Shelled Crabs

EASY / 6 INGREDIENTS

If you live on the East Coast, you live for soft-shelled crabs to come in season during the late spring. These crabs have molted and are now missing their hard shells. You eat the whole crab, a knife-and-fork affair after it's been fried.

We call for *cleaned* soft-shelled crabs. Have the fishmonger at your market do this for you. (It can be a pain at home.) But take note: Once the crabs are cleaned, they should be kept in the refrigerator and cooked within a few hours. Never cook—or eat—a soft-shelled crab with a funky smell. They should be briny-sweet, a perfect meal when the weather starts to warm up.

INGREDIENTS	2-quart or larger air fryer	3.5-quart or larger air fryer	5.25-quart or larger air fryer
All-purpose flour	⅓ cup	½ cup	¾ cup
Old Bay seasoning	1½ teaspoons	1 tablespoon	1½ tablespoons
Large egg(s), well beaten	1	1	2
Ground oyster crackers	½ cup (about 1½ ounces)	1 cup (about 3 ounces)	1½ cups (about 4½ ounces)
2½-ounce *cleaned* soft-shelled crab(s), about 4 inches across	1	2	3
Vegetable oil spray	As needed	As needed	As needed
MAKES	*1 fried crab*	*2 fried crabs*	*3 fried crabs*

1. With the basket (or basket attachment) in the air fryer, heat it to 375°F (or 380°F or 390°F, if one of these is the closest setting).

2. Set up and fill three shallow soup plates or small pie plates on your counter: one for the flour, whisked with the Old Bay until well combined; one for the beaten egg(s); and one for the cracker crumbs.

3. Set a soft-shelled crab in the flour mixture and turn to coat evenly and well on all sides, even inside the legs. Dip the crab into the egg(s) and coat well, turning at least once, again getting some of the egg between the legs. Let any excess egg slip back into the rest, then set the crab in the cracker crumbs. Turn several times, pressing *very* gently to get the crab evenly coated with crumbs, even between the legs. Generously coat the crab on all sides with vegetable oil spray. Set it aside if

you're making more than one and coat these in the same way.

4. Set the crab(s) in the basket with as much air space between them as possible. They may overlap slightly, particularly at the ends of their legs, depending on the basket's size. Air-fry undisturbed for 12 minutes, or until very crisp and golden brown. If the machine is at 390°F, the crabs may be done in only 10 minutes.

5. Use kitchen tongs to gently transfer the crab(s) to a wire rack. Cool for a couple of minutes before serving.

Then...

* Although **Spicy Tartar Sauce** (page 278) is a natural with these crabs, try **Spicy Ketchup Dip** (page 66), **Sriracha-Yogurt Dip** (page 36), **Rémoulade Sauce** (page 291), or even **Tzatziki Sauce** (page 120). We even like them with **Chimichurri** (page 94).

- Or try VIETNAMESE BELL PEPPER SAUCE (*nuoc cham*) with these crabs. For each ½ *cup finely diced cored and stemmed yellow bell pepper, add 1 tablespoon granulated white sugar, 1 tablespoon fish sauce, 1 tablespoon distilled* *white vinegar, and 1½ teaspoons lime juice.* Stir together, then let sit, covered, at room temperature for 1 hour, or in the fridge for up to 24 hours, so the bell pepper begins to release its juices into the sauce.

Crispy Smelts

EASY / GLUTEN-FREE / 4 INGREDIENTS

Look for frozen cleaned smelts in the freezer case of large supermarkets. Thaw them in the fridge, then get ready for some of the best eating in this chapter! The smelts have a mild, briny flavor. Eat them all, fins, tails, the works.

INGREDIENTS	2-quart or larger air fryer	3.5-quart or larger air fryer	5.25-quart or larger air fryer
Cleaned smelts	¾ pound	1 pound	1½ pounds
Tapioca flour	2 tablespoons	3 tablespoons	⅓ cup
Vegetable oil spray	As needed	As needed	As needed
Coarse sea salt or kosher salt	To taste	To taste	To taste
MAKES	*2 to 3 servings*	*3 to 4 servings*	*5 to 6 servings*

1. With the basket (or basket attachment) in the air fryer, heat it to 400°F (or 390°F, if that's the closest setting).

2. Toss the smelts and tapioca flour in a large bowl until the little fish are evenly coated.

3. Lay the smelts out on a large cutting board. Lightly coat both sides of each fish with vegetable oil spray.

4. When the machine is at temperature, set the smelts close together in the basket, with a few even overlapping on top. Air-fry undisturbed for 20 minutes, until lightly browned and crisp.

5. Remove the basket from the machine and turn out the fish onto a wire rack. The smelts will most likely come out as one large block, or maybe in a couple of large pieces. Cool for a minute or two, then sprinkle the smelts with salt and break the block(s) into much smaller sections or individual fish to serve.

Then...

- Serve these with lemon wedges for a spritz of bright flavor over each bite.

- Or consider RANCH DIP the go-to dipping sauce. For 4 servings, whisk *½ cup regular, low-fat, or fat-free mayonnaise (gluten-free, if a concern); ½ cup buttermilk; 2 tablespoons minced chives or the green part of a scallion; 1 tablespoon finely chopped fresh dill fronds; 1 teaspoon minced garlic; 1 teaspoon granulated white sugar; ½ teaspoon ground mustard; ½ teaspoon table salt; and ¼ teaspoon ground black pepper* in a small bowl until well combined. Save any leftovers in a covered glass or other nonreactive container in the fridge for up to 4 days.

Crunchy Clam Strips

Fried clams used to be made from sliced strips of the "foot" of large sea clams. Nowadays, fried clams are usually made from sliced surf clams, the meat cut into thin strips. These sliced clams are often found in the refrigerator case near the fish counter of well-stocked supermarkets.

Unfortunately, because the clam strips need some space to fry up crunchy, you can't make many at a time. Even the large batch here may not be dinner for four if that's all you're offering. Or just offer the fried clams as a starter for a bigger meal.

INGREDIENTS	2-quart or larger air fryer	3.5-quart or larger air fryer	5.25-quart or larger air fryer
Clam strips, drained	6 ounces	½ pound	¾ pound
Large egg, well beaten	1	1	1
All-purpose flour	⅓ cup	½ cup	⅔ cup
Yellow cornmeal	⅓ cup	½ cup	⅔ cup
Table salt	1 teaspoon	1½ teaspoons	2 teaspoons
Ground black pepper	1 teaspoon	1½ teaspoons	2 teaspoons
Cayenne	Up to ½ teaspoon	Up to ¾ teaspoon	Up to 1 teaspoon
Vegetable oil spray	As needed	As needed	As needed
MAKES	2 servings	3 servings	4 servings

1. With the basket (or basket attachment) in the air fryer, heat it to 400°F (or 390°F, if that's the closest setting).

2. Toss the clam strips and beaten egg in a bowl until the clams are well coated.

3. Mix the flour, cornmeal, salt, pepper, and cayenne in a large zip-closed plastic bag until well combined. Using a flatware fork or small kitchen tongs, lift the clam strips one by one out of the egg, letting any excess egg slip back into the rest. Put the strips in the bag with the flour mixture. Once all the strips are in the bag, seal it and shake gently until the strips are well coated.

4. Use kitchen tongs to pick out the clam strips and lay them on a cutting board (leaving any extra flour mixture in the bag to be discarded). Coat the strips on both sides with vegetable oil spray.

5. When the machine is at temperature, spread the clam strips in the basket in one layer. They may touch in places, but try to leave as much air space as possible around them. Air-fry undisturbed for 8 minutes, or until brown and crunchy.

6. Gently dump the contents of the basket onto a serving platter. Cool for just a minute or two before serving hot.

Then...

- To make SPICY COCKTAIL SAUCE for these clam strips, whisk *1 cup red ketchup-like chili sauce (such as Heinz), 1 heaping tablespoon jarred prepared white horseradish, 2 teaspoons Worcestershire sauce, 2 teaspoons lemon juice,* and *several dashes of hot red pepper sauce (such as Cholula or Tabasco)* in a small bowl until uniform.

Shrimp Teriyaki

CAN BE GLUTEN-FREE / 7 INGREDIENTS PLUS BAMBOO SKEWERS

These skewered shrimp will make a simple meal or great deck food. Shrimp teriyaki is not usually breaded, but we wanted something crunchy with the aromatic marinade and felt this alteration of the classic was well suited to an air fryer.

Notice that the shrimp are straightened out along the length of the bamboo skewers so they cook evenly and can maintain an even coating all over them. These bamboo skewers may be shorter than the regular ones you find in the supermarket. Cut longer ones down to size with kitchen shears. There's no need to soak the skewers in water. They don't spend enough time in the heat to be a problem, although the tips may blacken.

The recipe includes ginger juice, available with the condiments in most supermarkets. You can also use the liquid in a jar of pickled ginger for a more sour finish.

INGREDIENTS	2-quart or larger air fryer	3.5-quart or larger air fryer	5.25-quart or larger air fryer
Regular or low-sodium soy sauce or gluten-free tamari sauce	1 tablespoon	1 tablespoon	1½ tablespoons
Mirin or a substitute (see page 176)	1 tablespoon	1 tablespoon	1½ tablespoons
Ginger juice (see the headnote)	1 teaspoon	1 teaspoon	1½ teaspoons
Large shrimp (20–25 per pound), peeled and deveined	8	10	12
Plain panko bread crumbs (gluten-free, if a concern)	½ cup	⅔ cup	¾ cup
Large egg	1	1	1
Vegetable oil spray	As needed	As needed	As needed
MAKES	8 skewered shrimp	10 skewered shrimp	12 skewered shrimp

1. Whisk the soy or tamari sauce, mirin, and ginger juice in an 8- or 9-inch square baking pan until uniform. Add the shrimp and toss well to coat. Cover and refrigerate for 1 hour, tossing the shrimp in the marinade at least twice.

2. With the basket (or basket attachment) in the air fryer, heat it to 400°F (or 390°F, if that's the closest setting).

3. Thread a marinated shrimp on a 4-inch bamboo skewer by inserting the pointy tip at the small end of the shrimp, then guiding the skewer along the shrimp so that the tip comes out the thick end and the shrimp is flat along the length of the skewer. Repeat with the remaining shrimp. (You'll need eight 4-inch skewers for the small batch, 10 skewers for the medium batch, and 12 for the large.)

continues

4. Pour the bread crumbs onto a dinner plate. Whisk the egg in the baking pan with any marinade that stayed behind. Lay the skewers in the pan, in as close to a single layer as possible. Turn repeatedly to make sure the shrimp is coated in the egg mixture.

5. One at a time, take a skewered shrimp out of the pan and set it in the bread crumbs, turning several times and pressing gently until the shrimp is evenly coated on all sides. Coat the shrimp with vegetable oil spray and set the skewer aside. Repeat with the remainder of the shrimp.

6. Set the skewered shrimp in the basket in one layer. Air-fry undisturbed for 6 minutes, or until pink and firm.

7. Transfer the skewers to a wire rack. Cool for only a minute or two before serving.

Then...

- Try these skewered shrimp with WASABI MAYONNAISE. For every ¼ cup of regular, low-fat, or fat-free mayonnaise (gluten-free, if a concern), whisk in 1 teaspoon prepared wasabi paste.

See photo in insert.

Sweet Potato–Wrapped Shrimp

GLUTEN-FREE / 6 INGREDIENTS

As you did for our wrapped halibut fillets (page 283), look for spiralized vegetables in the refrigerator case of the produce section of almost any large supermarket. You'll need to choose the longest strands from the package to wrap the shrimp. In this case, don't worry about an even wrapping, one strand after another, the way we encouraged you to do with the halibut. Instead, wrap the two strands around the shrimp so that they form a bit of a "nest" without being too thick at any one point.

Remember: Shrimp are sold by how many make up 1 pound—for example, 30 per pound for medium shrimp or 10 per pound for giant ones. Skip all other adjectives—"jumbo," "colossal"—and go with the more accurate measurement of count by weight.

INGREDIENTS	2-quart or larger air fryer	3.5-quart or larger air fryer	5.25-quart or larger air fryer
Long spiralized sweet potato strands	16	24	32
Olive oil spray	As needed	As needed	As needed
Garlic powder	¼ teaspoon	Rounded ¼ teaspoon	½ teaspoon
Table salt	¼ teaspoon	Rounded ¼ teaspoon	½ teaspoon
Cayenne	Up to ⅛ teaspoon	Up to a rounded ⅛ teaspoon	Up to ¼ teaspoon
Large shrimp (20–25 per pound), peeled and deveined	8	12	16
MAKES	2 servings	3 servings	4 servings

1. With the basket (or basket attachment) in the air fryer, heat it to 400°F (or 390°F, if that's the closest setting).

2. Lay the spiralized sweet potato strands on a large swath of paper towels and straighten out the strands to long ropes. Coat them with olive oil spray, then sprinkle them with the garlic powder, salt, and cayenne.

3. Pick up 2 strands and wrap them around the center of a shrimp, with the ends tucked under what now becomes the bottom side of the shrimp. Continue wrapping the remainder of the shrimp.

4. Set the shrimp bottom side down in the basket with as much air space between them as possible. Air-fry undisturbed for 6 minutes, or until the sweet potato strands are crisp and the shrimp are pink and firm.

5. Use kitchen tongs to transfer the shrimp to a wire rack. Cool for only a minute or two before serving.

Then...

• You may have a lot of spiralized strands left over from this recipe, as from the wrapped halibut recipe. To make VELVETY CURRIED VEGETABLE SOUP out of any or all of them, place them in a large saucepan and cover them with *3 to 5 cups of broth (any sort)*, so that the liquid comes to the top of the strands in the pot. Stir in *½ cup regular or low-fat coconut milk, ½ cup chopped yellow or white onion, 1 tablespoon curry powder (any sort; see page 363 to make your own), 1 tablespoon minced peeled fresh ginger,* and *½ teaspoon table salt.* Bring to a simmer over medium-high heat, stirring often. Then cover, reduce the heat to low, and simmer slowly for 15 minutes. Use an immersion blender to puree the soup in the pan. Or puree the soup in batches in a covered blender with the center knob removed from the lid and a clean kitchen towel draped over that opening (to avoid a pressure buildup and an explosion of soup on your cabinets).

Coconut Jerk Shrimp

CAN BE GLUTEN-FREE / 6 INGREDIENTS

By using *unsweetened shredded* coconut (see page 159) and a jerk dried seasoning blend, we can end up with a Caribbean flavor on air-fried shrimp. Don't use sweetened coconut, which will burn before the shrimp are done.

To make your own JERK DRIED SEASONING BLEND, mix *1 tablespoon ground allspice, 2 teaspoons dried thyme, ½ teaspoon ground cumin, ½ teaspoon red pepper flakes, ½ teaspoon ground cloves, ½ teaspoon ground cinnamon, ½ teaspoon grated nutmeg, ½ teaspoon garlic powder,* and *½ teaspoon table salt* in a small bowl until well combined. Use the equivalent amount of this blend for the jerk seasoning blend in the recipe. Store the remainder, covered, in a small glass container set in a cool, dark pantry for up to 6 months. (Label it so you remember what you have!)

INGREDIENTS	2-quart or larger air fryer	3.5-quart or larger air fryer	5.25-quart or larger air fryer
Large egg white(s)	1	1	2
Purchased or homemade jerk dried seasoning blend (see the headnote)	1 teaspoon	1 teaspoon	2 teaspoons
Plain panko bread crumbs (gluten-free, if a concern)	½ cup	¾ cup	1 cup
Unsweetened shredded coconut	½ cup	¾ cup	1 cup
Large shrimp (20–25 per pound), peeled and deveined	8	12	20
Coconut oil spray	As needed	As needed	As needed
MAKES	2 servings	3 servings	4—5 servings

1. With the basket (or basket attachment) in the air fryer, heat it to 375°F (or 370°F or 360°F, if one of these is the closest setting).

2. Whisk the egg white(s) and seasoning blend in a bowl until foamy. Add the shrimp and toss well to coat evenly.

3. Mix the bread crumbs and coconut on a dinner plate until well combined. Use kitchen tongs to pick up a shrimp, letting the excess egg white mixture slip back into the rest. Set the shrimp in the bread-crumb mixture. Turn several times to coat evenly and thoroughly. Set on a cutting board and continue coating the remainder of the shrimp.

4. Lightly coat all the shrimp on both sides with the coconut oil spray. Set them in the basket in one layer with as much space between them as possible. (You can even stand some up along the basket's wall in some models.) Air-fry undisturbed for 6 minutes, or until the coating is lightly browned. If the air fryer is at 360°F, you may need to add 1 to 2 minutes to the cooking time.

5. Use clean kitchen tongs to transfer the shrimp to a wire rack. Cool for only a minute or two before serving.

Then...

- Serve these shrimp with PERFECT MAI TAIS. For each drink, fill a cocktail shaker about three-quarters full of *ice.* Add 1½ ounces (3 tablespoons) white rum, 1 ounce (2 tablespoons) Grand Marnier, 2 teaspoons almond syrup (that is, orgeat), 1 teaspoon confectioners' sugar, 1 teaspoon grenadine syrup, and the juice of half a lime. Cover and shake well. Strain into a cocktail glass over *fresh ice.*

Fried Shrimp

FAST / CAN BE GLUTEN-FREE / 9 OR 10 INGREDIENTS

We've added a little cornmeal to the bread-crumb coating for fried shrimp because the cornmeal exponentially increases the crunch factor—which is the whole point of fried shrimp.

The quality of the shrimp factors into the equation, too. There are lots of inferior shrimp on the market—and a lot of them on the fish counter. Almost all shrimp sold have been frozen at harvest. Those that are on the counter have most likely been thawed in the back of the store. And as they sit around on the ice, they get mushy. So skip the extra expense of letting the store thaw the shrimp and buy frozen peeled and deveined shrimp. If you buy so-called IQFs (that is, "individually quick-frozen" shrimp), you can take out as many as you need, thaw them in the fridge, and use them long before they go mushy from being in a display case for too long.

When you buy shrimp already peeled and deveined, the little bit of shell on the tail fins is often still attached. No amount of bread coating will ever stick to that shell. Either remove the bit of shell for a fully breaded shrimp or leave it on for a more aesthetically pleasing look, a little red fan at the end of each shrimp, which also serves as a handle.

INGREDIENTS	2-quart or larger air fryer	3.5-quart or larger air fryer	5.25-quart or larger air fryer
Large egg white	1	1	1
Water	2 tablespoons	2 tablespoons	2 tablespoons
Plain dried bread crumbs (gluten-free, if a concern)	1 cup	1 cup	1 cup
All-purpose flour or almond flour	¼ cup	¼ cup	¼ cup
Yellow cornmeal	¼ cup	¼ cup	¼ cup
Celery salt	1 teaspoon	1 teaspoon	1 teaspoon
Mild paprika	1 teaspoon	1 teaspoon	1 teaspoon
Cayenne (optional)	Up to ¼ teaspoon	Up to ½ teaspoon	Up to ¾ teaspoon
Large shrimp (20–25 per pound), peeled and deveined	½ pound	¾ pound	1 pound
Vegetable oil spray	As needed	As needed	As needed
MAKES	*2 servings*	*3 servings*	*4 servings*

continues

1. With the basket (or basket attachment) in the air fryer, heat it to 400°F (or 390°F, if that's the closest setting).

2. Set two medium or large bowls on your counter. In the first, whisk the egg white and water until foamy. In the second, stir the bread crumbs, flour, cornmeal, celery salt, paprika, and cayenne (if using) until well combined.

3. Pour all the shrimp into the egg white mixture and stir gently until all the shrimp are coated. Use kitchen tongs to pick them up one by one and transfer them to the bread-crumb mixture. Turn each in the bread-crumb mixture to coat it evenly and thoroughly on all sides before setting it on a cutting board. When you're done coating the shrimp, coat them all on both sides with the vegetable oil spray.

4. Set the shrimp in as close to one layer in the basket as you can. Some may overlap. Air-fry for 7 minutes, gently rearranging the shrimp at the 4-minute mark to get covered surfaces exposed, until golden brown and firm but not hard.

5. Use kitchen tongs to *gently* transfer the shrimp to a wire rack. Cool for only a minute or two before serving.

Then...

- Serve the shrimp with **Horseradish Sauce** (page 116), **Spicy Tartar Sauce** (page 278), **Ranch Dip** (page 293), or **Spicy Cocktail Sauce** (page 294).

- For a '50s country-club surf-and-turf meal, serve these shrimp with **Barbecue-Style London Broil** (page 214) and **Perfect Broccoli** (page 345). Make the meal in this order: London broil, broccoli, shrimp. Then reheat the London broil in a 350°F (or 360°F, if the closest setting) air fryer for 3 to 4 minutes and serve the broccoli at room temperature.

Shrimp "Scampi"

FAST / EASY / GLUTEN-FREE / 7 INGREDIENTS

Although not a traditional preparation of the classic Italian-American favorite, our air-fryer version concentrates the shrimp and other flavors with the hot air, making the dish more garlicky, more intense. We've kept the preparation fairly simple, its flavors straightforward—all of which just means you'll need lots of Italian bread or (for a double whammy) toasted garlic bread on the side.

INGREDIENTS	2-quart or larger air fryer	3.5-quart or larger air fryer	5.25-quart or larger air fryer
Large shrimp (20–25 per pound), peeled and deveined	¾ pound	1½ pounds	2 pounds
Olive oil	2 tablespoons	¼ cup	⅓ cup
Minced garlic	1 tablespoon	2 tablespoons	2½ tablespoons
Dried oregano	½ teaspoon	1 teaspoon	1¼ teaspoons
Red pepper flakes	Up to ½ teaspoon	Up to 1 teaspoon	Up to 1¼ teaspoons
Table salt	¼ teaspoon	½ teaspoon	¾ teaspoon
White balsamic vinegar (see page 203)	1 tablespoon	2 tablespoons	2½ tablespoons
MAKES	2 to 3 servings	4 to 5 servings	5 to 6 servings

1. With the basket (or basket attachment) in the air fryer, heat it to 400°F (or 390°F, if that's the closest setting).

2. Stir the shrimp, olive oil, garlic, oregano, red pepper flakes, and salt in a large bowl until the shrimp are well coated.

3. When the machine is at temperature, transfer the shrimp to the basket. They will overlap and even sit on top of each other. Air-fry for 5 minutes, tossing and rearranging the shrimp twice to make sure the covered surfaces are exposed, until pink and firm.

4. Pour the contents of the basket into a serving bowl. Pour the vinegar over the shrimp while hot and toss to coat.

Then...

- For a more flavorful and richer dish, also pour 2 to 3 tablespoons melted butter over the shrimp with the vinegar.

- Serve the shrimp on top of a chopped salad, garnished with **Classic Greek Diner Dressing** (page 90).

- Or serve them on a classic **Spinach Salad** (page 265).

Easy Scallops with Lemon Butter

FAST / EASY / GLUTEN-FREE / 8 INGREDIENTS

This recipe is undoubtedly the easiest for scallops: just the sweet seafood in a simple, classic sauce. Look for bags of frozen scallops on sale, then squirrel them into your freezer for when you'd like to make this dish.

If you're buying fresh scallops (and at most seafood counters, you're not; you're buying frozen ones that were thawed in the back of the store), look for "dry-packed" scallops that haven't been doped with a solution to plump them up and help them retain water, so you're not paying for excess water weight.

INGREDIENTS	2-quart or larger air fryer	3.5-quart or larger air fryer	5.25-quart or larger air fryer
Olive oil	2 teaspoons	1 tablespoon	1½ tablespoons
Minced garlic	1 teaspoon	2 teaspoons	1 tablespoon
Finely grated lemon zest	½ teaspoon	1 teaspoon	1½ teaspoons
Red pepper flakes	¼ teaspoon	½ teaspoon	¾ teaspoon
Table salt	⅛ teaspoon	¼ teaspoon	Rounded ¼ teaspoon
Sea scallops	½ pound	1 pound	1½ pounds
Butter, melted	2 tablespoons	3 tablespoons	4 tablespoons (¼ cup/½ stick)
Lemon juice	1 tablespoon	1½ tablespoons	2 tablespoons
MAKES	2 servings	3 to 4 servings	5 to 6 servings

1. With the basket (or basket attachment) in the air fryer, heat it to 400°F (or 390°F, if that's the closest setting).

2. Gently stir the olive oil, garlic, lemon zest, red pepper flakes, and salt in a bowl. Add the scallops and stir very gently until they are evenly and well coated.

3. When the machine is at temperature, arrange the scallops in a single layer in the basket. Some may touch. Air-fry undisturbed for 4 minutes, or until the scallops are opaque and firm.

4. While the scallops cook, stir the melted butter and lemon juice in a serving bowl. When the scallops are ready, pour them from the basket into this bowl. Toss well before serving.

Then...

- Serve these scallops with **Radish Slaw** (page 117), **Caprese Pasta Salad** (page 252), or just **Simple Arugula Salad** (page 128).

- For a pasta dish, gently toss these scallops and *some finely grated Parmesan cheese* with *cooked and drained linguine*. Add *a little extra olive oil* if the pasta seems dry. Garnish the servings with *minced fresh parsley leaves*.

Fried Scallops

CAN BE GLUTEN-FREE / 8 INGREDIENTS

Fried scallops are one of life's better luxuries: crunchy, sweet, and mildly briny. Ours are coated in corn flake crumbs mixed with cayenne to give the scallops a little spicy kick. You can use much less cayenne than we recommend—or omit it entirely. But we think the spice works great with all those crumbs.

INGREDIENTS	2-quart or larger air fryer	3.5-quart or larger air fryer	5.25-quart or larger air fryer
All-purpose flour or tapioca flour	½ cup	½ cup	½ cup
Large egg(s), well beaten	1	1	2
Corn flake crumbs (gluten-free, if a concern)	1 cup	2 cups	2½ cups
Cayenne	Up to 1 teaspoon	Up to 2 teaspoons	Up to 2½ teaspoons
Celery seeds	½ teaspoon	1 teaspoon	1½ teaspoons
Table salt	½ teaspoon	1 teaspoon	1½ teaspoons
Sea scallops	½ pound	1 pound	1½ pounds
Vegetable oil spray	As needed	As needed	As needed
MAKES	2 servings	3 to 4 servings	5 to 6 servings

1. With the basket (or basket attachment) in the air fryer, heat it to 400°F (or 390°F, if that's the closest setting).

2. Set up and fill three shallow soup plates or small pie plates on your counter: one for the flour; one for the beaten egg(s); and one for the corn flake crumbs, stirred with the cayenne, celery seeds, and salt until well combined.

3. One by one, dip a scallop in the flour, turning it every way to coat it thoroughly. Gently shake off any excess flour, then dip the scallop in the egg(s), turning it again to coat all sides. Let any excess egg slip back into the rest, then set the scallop in the corn flake mixture. Turn it several times, pressing gently to get an even coating on the scallop all around. Generously coat the scallop with vegetable oil spray, then set it aside on a cutting board. Coat the remaining scallops in the same way.

4. Set the scallops in the basket with as much air space between them as possible. They should not touch. Air-fry undisturbed for 6 minutes, or until lightly browned and firm.

5. Use kitchen tongs to *gently* transfer the scallops to a wire rack. Cool for only a minute or two before serving.

Then...

- Serve these scallops with melted butter for a dip. Season the butter, if desired, with red pepper flakes, minced garlic, onion powder, and/or ground black pepper.

- For a full meal, try these alongside **Jicama and Mango Salad** (page 279).

See photo in insert.

Curried Sweet-and-Spicy Scallops

EASY / GLUTEN-FREE / 5 INGREDIENTS

These chili sauce–coated scallops get super crunchy, thanks to ground rice cereal. The coating is a little unstable after cooking and can slide off easily. Make sure you let it cool and set up for 2 minutes before you serve the scallops.

The coating is flavored with curry powder. You can stick with the standard yellow variety or make your own (page 363). Or skip the curry powder and use a **Cajun dried seasoning blend** (page 279) or **jerk dried seasoning blend** (page 298).

INGREDIENTS	2-quart or larger air fryer	3.5-quart or larger air fryer	5.25-quart or larger air fryer
Thai sweet chili sauce	¼ cup	6 tablespoons	½ cup
Crushed Rice Krispies or other rice-puff cereal	1 cup (from about 2½ cups cereal)	2 cups (from about 5 cups cereal)	2½ cups (from about 6¼ cups cereal)
Yellow curry powder, purchased or homemade (see page 363)	1 teaspoon	2 teaspoons	1 tablespoon
Sea scallops	½ pound	1 pound	1½ pounds
Vegetable oil spray	As needed	As needed	As needed
MAKES	2 servings	3 to 4 servings	5 to 6 servings

1. With the basket (or basket attachment) in the air fryer, heat it to 400°F (or 390°F, if that's the closest setting).

2. Set up and fill two shallow soup plates or small pie plates on your counter: one for the chili sauce and one for crumbs, mixed with the curry powder.

3. Dip a scallop into the chili sauce, coating it on all sides. Set it in the cereal mixture and turn several times to coat evenly. Gently shake off any excess and set the scallop on a cutting board. Continue dipping and coating the remaining scallops. Coat them all on all sides with the vegetable oil spray.

4. Set the scallops in the basket with as much air space between them as possible. Air-fry undisturbed for 5 minutes, or until lightly browned and crunchy.

5. Remove the basket. Set aside for 2 minutes to let the coating set up. Then gently pour the contents of the basket onto a platter and serve at once.

Then...

- To make a scallop roll, butter a toasted split hot dog bun (gluten-free, if a concern). Fill it with some of these scallops, diced cucumbers, and pickled onion rings.

- Or serve these scallops with **Jamaican Rice and Peas** (page 160).

Buttery Lobster Tails

FAST / GLUTEN-FREE / 7 INGREDIENTS

Lobster tails work well in an air fryer with two caveats. One, you have to work with *larger* tails than you might normally find at the supermarket. (The smaller ones overcook too quickly, drying out and turning rubbery.) And two, you must work with *raw* tails, not cooked.

Our technique will give you the classic steakhouse look with the tail meat sitting up and out of the shell.

INGREDIENTS	2-quart or larger air fryer	3.5-quart or larger air fryer	5.25-quart or larger air fryer
6- to 8-ounce shell-on raw lobster tails	2	4	6
Butter, melted and cooled	1 tablespoon	2 tablespoons	3 tablespoons
Lemon juice	½ teaspoon	1 teaspoon	1½ teaspoons
Finely grated lemon zest	¼ teaspoon	½ teaspoon	1 teaspoon
Garlic powder	¼ teaspoon	½ teaspoon	¾ teaspoon
Table salt	¼ teaspoon	½ teaspoon	¾ teaspoon
Ground black pepper	¼ teaspoon	½ teaspoon	¾ teaspoon
MAKES	*2 servings*	*4 servings*	*6 servings*

1. With the basket (or basket attachment) in the air fryer, heat it to 375°F (or 370°F or 360°F, if one of these is the closest setting).

2. To give the tails that restaurant look, you need to butterfly the meat. To do so, place a tail on a cutting board so that the shell is convex. Use kitchen shears to cut a line down the middle of the shell from the larger end to the smaller, cutting only the shell and not the meat below, and stopping before the back fins. Pry open the shell, leaving it intact. Use your clean fingers to separate the meat from the shell's sides and bottom, keeping it attached to the shell at the back near the fins. Pull the meat up and out of the shell through the cut line, laying the meat on top of the shell and closing the shell (as well as you can) under the meat. Make two equidistant cuts down the meat from the larger end to near the smaller end, each about ¼ inch deep, for the classic restaurant look on the plate. Repeat this procedure with the remaining tail(s).

3. Stir the butter, lemon juice, zest, garlic powder, salt, and pepper in a small bowl until well combined. Brush this mixture over the lobster meat set atop the shells.

4. When the machine is at temperature, place the tails shell side down in the basket with as much air space between them as possible. Air-fry undisturbed for 6 minutes, or until the lobster meat has pink streaks over it and is firm.

5. Use kitchen tongs to transfer the tails to a wire rack. Cool for only a minute or two before serving.

Then...

- Serve these with **Hasselback Garlic-and-Butter Potatoes** (page 337) and **Roman Artichokes** (page 366). You'll need to make both of these before you cook the tails in the machine. Reheat these two sides in the basket at the last minute before serving.

FIFTY-SIX

Vegetable & Side Dishes

Vegetables in an air fryer need little fuss. In fact, if you look at most of the booklets that come with the machines, they're loaded with vegetable recipes. Because of all that, we've kept things simple but skipped the most obvious choices like basic carrots or zucchini in favor of a little more flavor and creativity. And we've got lots of extra sauces for the fare.

One of the reasons that vegetables take so well to the appliance is that it's easy to cut them to make them fit in the basket or the basket attachment. Because of bones and many other factors, you can't very well cut a beef rib roast or a pork shoulder to fit and then expect it to cook evenly. But you can easily slice yellow squash or asparagus to fit for a batch.

In fact, you can get away with overpacking the basket a bit more with these recipes than with many others in this book. If more broccoli florets are piled on top, there's nothing to keep them from getting done if you shake the basket often enough.

Coated or breaded vegetables are another matter. By and large, these must not be stacked on each other if you want a crisp texture. But you can still overlap them a bit more than you would a batch of fish sticks and come out with a decent result—if you gently rearrange them after the coating has begun to set.

Unless we say otherwise, all vegetables used in this chapter are assumed to be fresh. Frozen vegetables are softer once thawed, often too soft to hold any coating or breading. Their texture is too compromised to make them successful in the machine.

The one stand-out exception is corn on the cob. Frozen 4-inch sections of corn work exceptionally well in the air fryer. Yes, you must thaw them but doing so doesn't ruin their texture when they're cooked in the air fryer.

In the end, we bet this chapter represents how you'll still be using your air fryer on a consistent basis a year from now. Many people buy an air fryer and soon discover it's a great tool for making sides while other things are coming out of the oven or off the grill grate. Some people even think of their air fryer as "the ultimate side maker." You should, too. Here are lots of ideas.

Roasted Garlic

EASY / VEGAN / GLUTEN-FREE / 2 INGREDIENTS

Who doesn't love the sweet, mellow flavor of roasted garlic? But instead of roasting whole heads, it's much easier to use the peeled cloves which you can find in jars or containers in almost every supermarket's produce section. Since the cloves are exposed, we have to seal them in a foil packet. But doing so allows us to add a little olive oil for better flavor. The softened, sweet, aromatic cloves can then be kept for a while in the fridge, the better to use them in the days ahead.

INGREDIENTS	2-quart or larger air fryer	3.5-quart or larger air fryer	5.25-quart or larger air fryer
Peeled medium garlic cloves	10	20	30
Olive oil	1 tablespoon, plus more as needed	2 tablespoons, plus more as needed	3 tablespoons, plus more as needed
MAKES	10 roasted cloves	20 roasted cloves	30 roasted cloves

1. With the basket (or basket attachment) in the air fryer, heat it to 400°F (or 390°F, if that's the closest setting).

2. Set a 10-inch sheet of aluminum foil on your work surface for a small batch, a 14-inch sheet for a medium batch, or a 16-inch sheet for a large batch. Put the garlic cloves in its center in one layer without bunching the cloves together. (Spread them out a little for even cooking.) Drizzle the small batch with 1 tablespoon oil, the medium batch with 2 tablespoons, or the large one with 3 tablespoons. Fold up the sides and seal the foil into a packet.

3. When the machine is at temperature, put the packet in the basket. Air-fry for 40 minutes, or until very fragrant. The cloves inside should be golden and soft.

4. Transfer the packet to a cutting board. Cool for 5 minutes, then open and use the cloves hot. Or cool them to room temperature, set them in a small container or jar, pour in enough olive oil to cover them, seal or cover the container, and refrigerate for up to 2 weeks.

Then...

- Set some roasted cloves on top of a pizza before baking. Or smear a clove on toasted bread for instant garlic bread.

- Or mix a clove or two with softened butter for a spread on bread or a topper for a grilled steak— or **Perfect Strip Steaks** (page 208).

- Chop them and toss them into almost any pasta sauce, even a creamy one, for a big hit of garlic flavor.

- Add the roasted garlic cloves to almost any stew or braise for a sweet, mellow garlic flavor that will infuse the liquids over the long cooking.

Roasted Peppers with Balsamic Vinegar and Basil

EASY / VEGAN / GLUTEN-FREE / 4 INGREDIENTS

Roasted bell peppers make an easy appetizer or a great side dish. They're also nice to have in the fridge so you can add them to sandwiches, wraps, or even tomato-based pasta sauces. (Do not add them to cream-based sauces because the vinegar will cause the sauce to curdle.)

There's no salt in this recipe on the assumption that you're going to store these for the days ahead. Salt will leach moisture out of the peppers, making them too limp and watery after storage. You can add salt when you serve or use them.

The little bits of basil leaves may blacken over a few days in the fridge. You can pick these off for pitch-perfect aesthetics. (We never do.)

INGREDIENTS	2-quart or larger air fryer	3.5-quart or larger air fryer	5.25-quart or larger air fryer
Small or medium red or yellow bell peppers	3	4	5
Olive oil	2 tablespoons	3 tablespoons	¼ cup
Balsamic vinegar	2 teaspoons	1 tablespoon	1½ tablespoons
Fresh basil leaves, torn up	Up to 4	Up to 6	Up to 8
MAKES	About 4 side-dish servings	About 6 side-dish servings	About 8 side-dish servings

1. With the basket (or basket attachment) in the air fryer, heat it to 400°F (or 390°F, if that's the closest setting).

2. When the machine is at temperature, put the peppers in the basket with at least ¼ inch between them. Air-fry undisturbed for 12 minutes, until blistered, even blackened in places.

3. Use kitchen tongs to transfer the peppers to a medium bowl. Cover the bowl with plastic wrap. Set aside at room temperature for 30 minutes.

4. Uncover the bowl and use kitchen tongs to transfer the peppers to a cutting board or work surface. Peel off the filmy exterior skin. If there are blackened bits under it, these can stay on the peppers. Cut off and remove the stem ends. Split open the peppers and discard any seeds and their spongy membranes. Slice the peppers into ½-inch- to 1-inch-wide strips.

5. Put these in a clean bowl and gently toss them with the oil, vinegar, and basil. Serve at once. Or cover and store at room temperature for up to 4 hours or in the refrigerator for up to 5 days.

Then...

- When serving the peppers, spoon them up with a slotted spoon and sprinkle coarse sea or kosher salt over them, to taste.

- These peppers would be welcome on an antipasto plate with stuffed grape leaves and little mozzarella balls. They're also terrific as a garnish over or next to steaks, chops, chicken thighs, and just about anything off the grill.

- Puree some of these pepper strips with drained and rinsed canned white or black beans and a little olive oil and table salt for an instant dip.

Blistered Tomatoes

EASY / VEGAN / GLUTEN-FREE / 5 INGREDIENTS

Blistered tomatoes make an easy side dish with steaks, chops, and fish, whether from the grill, oven, or air fryer. You can also use these tomatoes for so much more, as you'll see in the *Then* section.

You must check the tomatoes occasionally as they air-fry to make sure they're not burning. Cherry and grape tomatoes have varying amounts of internal and surface moisture, depending on the season. (They're drier, mostly, in the winter when they've endured long transportation.) Low-moisture tomatoes can burn more quickly, so it's best to stop the cooking before they become too blackened (although a little blackening adds a deeper, more sophisticated flavor).

INGREDIENTS	2-quart or larger air fryer	3.5-quart or larger air fryer	5.25-quart or larger air fryer
Cherry or grape tomatoes	1 pound	1½ pounds	2 pounds
Olive oil spray	As needed	As needed	As needed
Balsamic vinegar	1 teaspoon	1½ teaspoons	2 teaspoons
Table salt	¼ teaspoon	Rounded ¼ teaspoon	½ teaspoon
Ground black pepper	¼ teaspoon	Rounded ¼ teaspoon	½ teaspoon
MAKES	15 to 20 tomatoes	20 to 30 tomatoes	30 to 40 tomatoes

1. Put the basket in a drawer-style air fryer, or a baking tray in the lower third of a toaster oven–style air fryer. Place a 6-inch round cake pan in the basket or on the tray for a small batch, a 7-inch round cake pan for a medium batch, or an 8-inch round cake pan for a large one. Heat the air fryer to 400°F (or 390°F, if that's the closest setting) with the pan in the basket. When the machine is at temperature, keep heating the pan for 5 minutes more.

2. Place the tomatoes in a large bowl, coat them with the olive oil spray, toss gently, then spritz a couple of times more, tossing after each spritz, until the tomatoes are glistening.

3. Pour the tomatoes into the cake pan and air-fry undisturbed for 10 minutes, or until they split and begin to brown.

4. Use kitchen tongs and a nonstick-safe spatula, or silicone baking mitts, to remove the cake pan from the basket. Toss the hot tomatoes with the vinegar, salt, and pepper. Cool in the pan for a few minutes before serving.

Then...

- Spoon these tomatoes onto cooked and drained spaghetti, fettuccine, or other long pasta that's been dressed with olive oil, grated Parmesan, salt, and red pepper flakes.

- Toss the blistered tomatoes into vegetable soups, beef stews, or heavily flavored braises (all without any cream in the mix) for a concentrated pop of tomato flavor.

- While the tomatoes are still hot, add fresh herbs like stemmed thyme leaves or minced oregano leaves. Cool to room temperature and use the herbaceous tomatoes as a garnish for steaks or fish fillets.

Tomato Candy

EASY / VEGAN / GLUTEN-FREE / 2 INGREDIENTS

Rather than blistered, as in our other basic tomato recipe on the previous page, these are dried at a low temperature until they become *super* sweet, no hints of bitterness in the flavors.

The tomatoes store fairly well, so you can use them in dishes in the week ahead. Or you can serve a batch with a hunk of cheese and some crusty bread and call it all "dinner."

INGREDIENTS	2-quart or larger air fryer	3.5-quart or larger air fryer	5.25-quart or larger air fryer
Small Roma or plum tomatoes, halved lengthwise	4	6	8
Coarse sea salt or kosher salt	1 teaspoon	1½ teaspoons	2 teaspoons
MAKES	8 pieces	12 pieces	16 pieces

1. *Before you turn the machine on*, set the tomatoes cut side up in a single layer in the basket (or the basket attachment). They can touch each other, but try to leave at least a fraction of an inch between them (depending, of course, on the size of the basket or basket attachment). Sprinkle the cut sides of the tomatoes with the salt.

2. Set the machine to cook at 225°F (or 230°F, if that's the closest setting). Put the basket in the machine and air-fry for 2 hours, or until the tomatoes are dry but pliable, with a little moisture down in their centers.

3. Remove the basket from the machine and cool the tomatoes in it for 10 minutes before gently transferring them to a plate for serving, or to a shallow dish that you can cover and store in the refrigerator for up to 1 week.

Then...

- Cut up these dried tomatoes to toss them into salads, particularly chopped or pasta salads.

- They're also good as a baked potato topper, roughly chopped and mixed with lots of sour cream.

- Or set on top of pizzas before baking, particularly pies with white or garlic sauces.

Buttery Stuffed Tomatoes

These tomatoes are filled with a buttery stuffing that gets crisp on top while the tomato "shell" becomes soft, sweet, and mellow. If desired, add dried herbs to the filling—up to 1 tablespoon (for a large batch) of your favorite herb, a purchased blend, or a mix of dried herbs you concoct.

The tomatoes are quite delicate when they come out of the air fryer. Use a nonstick-safe spatula to pick them up and kitchen tongs to *gently* grasp them for safe transport.

These tomatoes are also great at room temperature. You can make them up to a couple of hours ahead, then leave them uncovered until you're ready to serve them.

INGREDIENTS	2-quart or larger air fryer	3.5-quart or larger air fryer	5.25-quart or larger air fryer
8-ounce round tomatoes	2	3	4
Plain panko bread crumbs (gluten-free, if a concern)	6 tablespoons	½ cup plus 1 tablespoon	¾ cup
Finely grated Parmesan cheese	2 tablespoons (about ⅓ ounce)	3 tablespoons (about ½ ounce)	¼ cup (about ¾ ounce)
Butter, melted and cooled	2 tablespoons	3 tablespoons	4 tablespoons (¼ cup/½ stick)
Stemmed and chopped fresh parsley leaves	1 tablespoon	4 teaspoons	1½ tablespoons
Minced garlic	½ teaspoon	1 teaspoon	1½ teaspoons
Table salt	¼ teaspoon	Rounded ¼ teaspoon	½ teaspoon
Red pepper flakes	Up to ⅛ teaspoon	Up to ¼ teaspoon	Up to ½ teaspoon
Olive oil spray	As needed	As needed	As needed
MAKES	*4 stuffed tomatoes*	*6 stuffed tomatoes*	*8 stuffed tomatoes*

1. With the basket (or basket attachment) in the air fryer, heat it to 375°F (or 370°F or 360°F, if one of these is the closest setting).

2. Cut the tomatoes in half through their "equators" (that is, not through the stem ends). One at a time, *gently* squeeze the tomato halves over a trash can, using a clean finger to gently force out the seeds and most of the juice inside, working carefully so that the tomato doesn't lose its round shape or get crushed.

3. Stir the bread crumbs, cheese, butter, parsley, garlic, salt, and red pepper flakes in a bowl until the bread crumbs are moistened and the parsley is uniform throughout the mixture. Pile this mixture into the spaces left in the tomato halves. Press gently to compact the filling. Coat the tops of the tomatoes with olive oil spray.

4. Place the tomatoes cut side up in the basket. They may touch each other. Air-fry for 15 minutes, or until the filling is lightly browned and crunchy.

5. Use nonstick-safe spatula and kitchen tongs for balance to *gently* transfer the stuffed tomatoes to a platter or a cutting board. (They're a bit too soft for a wire rack.) Cool for a couple of minutes before serving.

Then...

- Serve these stuffed tomatoes with **Pickle-Brined Fried Chicken Thighs** (page 172), **Rotisserie-Style Air-Roasted Chicken** (page 191), **State Fair Turkey Wings** (page 199), **Perfect Strip Steaks** (page 208), **Barbecue-Style London Broil** (page 214), or **Tuscan Veal Chops** (page 230).

Fried Green Tomatoes

VEGETARIAN / CAN BE GLUTEN-FREE / 9 INGREDIENTS

This strictly seasonal recipe is the best way to use up an overabundance of tomatoes in midsummer or even at the end of the growing season. You *cannot* use ripe green tomatoes, varietals that show up at farmers' markets or high-end supermarkets. Rather, these tomatoes *must* be underripe, would-be-red-but-are-not-yet tomatoes. They have a firm texture and a tart flavor that stand up well to air-frying.

INGREDIENTS	2-quart or larger air fryer	5.25-quart or larger air fryer
All-purpose flour or tapioca flour	⅓ cup	¾ cup
Large egg(s)	1	2
Buttermilk	3 tablespoons	6 tablespoons
Plain dried bread crumbs (gluten-free, if a concern)	¾ cup	1⅓ cups
Yellow cornmeal	¼ cup	½ cup
Table salt	1 teaspoon	1½ teaspoons
Ground black pepper	½ teaspoon	1 teaspoon
Small 6-ounce green tomato(es), cut into ¼-inch-thick rounds	1	2
Vegetable oil spray	As needed	As needed
MAKES	2 to 3 servings	4 to 5 servings

1. With the basket (or basket attachment) in the air fryer, heat it to 400°F (or 390°F, if that's the closest setting).

2. Set up and fill three shallow soup plates or small pie plates on your counter: one for the flour; one for the egg(s), whisked with the buttermilk until uniform; and one for bread crumbs stirred with the cornmeal, salt, and pepper until well combined.

continues

3. Set a tomato slice in the flour and turn it a couple of times to coat evenly. Gently shake off any excess flour, then dip the slice in the egg mixture. Turn a couple of times to coat well, then pick the slice up and let any excess egg mixture slip back into the rest. Set the slice in the bread-crumb mixture and turn it a couple of times, pressing gently, to coat evenly and well. Set aside on a cutting board and coat the remaining slices in the same way.

4. Lightly coat both sides of each slice with vegetable oil spray. Set them in the basket with as much air space between them as possible. Air-fry undisturbed for 8 minutes, or until browned and crunchy.

5. Use a nonstick-safe spatula to transfer the fried tomatoes to a wire rack. Cool for a couple of minutes before serving.

Then...

- Serve these with RUSSIAN DRESSING. For about 6 servings, whisk ½ cup regular, low-fat, or fat-free mayonnaise (gluten-free, if a concern); ¼ cup pickle relish; ¼ cup ketchup (gluten-free, if a concern); 1 tablespoon white wine vinegar; 1 tablespoon jarred prepared white horseradish; 1½ teaspoons Worcestershire sauce (gluten-free, if a concern); and 1 teaspoon onion powder in a bowl. Season with table salt to taste. Store any leftovers in a covered bowl or container in the refrigerator for up to 4 days.

Stuffed Onions

CAN BE GLUTEN-FREE / 6 INGREDIENTS

An old-school steakhouse favorite, these stuffed onions have a sausage-and-cheese filling, so they're both hearty and super aromatic. When you hollow out the onions, take care that there's enough structure left in the walls and bottom so the onion doesn't collapse as it softens in the heat.

Vidalia or other sweet onions may be best for this dish if it's a side. If it's a main course, use a less-sweet, more standard yellow onion.

INGREDIENTS	2-quart or larger air fryer	3.5-quart or larger air fryer	5.25-quart or larger air fryer
Small 3½- to 4-ounce yellow or white onions	4	6	8
Olive oil spray	As needed	As needed	As needed
Bulk sweet Italian sausage meat (gluten-free, if a concern)	¼ pound	6 ounces	½ pound
Cherry tomatoes, chopped	6	9	12
Seasoned Italian-style dried bread crumbs (gluten-free, if a concern)	2 tablespoons	3 tablespoons	¼ cup
Finely grated Parmesan cheese	2 tablespoons (about ⅓ ounce)	3 tablespoons (about ½ ounce)	¼ cup (about ¾ ounce)
MAKES	4 stuffed onions	6 stuffed onions	8 stuffed onions

1. With the basket (or basket attachment) in the air fryer, heat it to 325°F (or 330°F, if that's the closest setting).

2. Cut just enough off the root ends of the onions so they will stand up on a cutting board when this end is turned down. Carefully peel off just the brown, papery skin. Now cut the top quarter off each and place the onion back on the cutting board with this end facing up. Use a flatware spoon (preferably a serrated grapefruit spoon) or a melon baller to scoop out the "insides" (interior layers) of the onion, leaving enough of the bottom and side walls so that the onion does not collapse. Depending on the thickness of the layers in the onion, this may be one or two of those layers— or even three, if they're very thin.

3. Coat the insides and outsides of the onions with olive oil spray. Set the onion "shells" in the basket and air-fry for 15 minutes.

4. Meanwhile, make the filling. Set a medium skillet over medium heat for a couple of minutes, then crumble in the sausage meat. Cook, stirring often, until browned, about 4 minutes. Transfer the contents of the skillet to a medium bowl (leave the fat behind in the skillet or add it to the bowl, depending on your cross-trainer regimen). Stir in the tomatoes, bread crumbs, and cheese until well combined.

5. When the onions are ready, use a nonstick-safe spatula to gently transfer them to a cutting board. Increase the air fryer's temperature to 350°F (or 360°F, if that's the closest setting).

6. Pack the sausage mixture into the onion shells, gently compacting the filling and mounding it up at the top.

7. When the machine is at temperature, set the onions stuffing side up in the basket with at least ¼ inch between them. Air-fry for 12 minutes, or until lightly browned and sizzling hot.

8. Use a nonstick-safe spatula, and perhaps a flatware fork for balance, to transfer the onions to a cutting board or serving platter. Cool for 5 minutes before serving.

Then...

- Although these are a great side dish to beef, pork, and chicken off the grill, they can also be a meal on their own. Serve them with **Caprese Pasta Salad** (page 252); **Endive, Walnut, and Blue Cheese Salad** (page 195); or **Summery Watercress Salad** (page 91).

- For a main course, serve two stuffed onions per person. Cover with warmed marinara, pizza, or other tomato-based pasta sauce. Add more grated Parmesan on top, if desired.

Fried Mac-and-Cheese Balls

VEGETARIAN / CAN BE GLUTEN-FREE / 3 INGREDIENTS

This recipe seems like a state fair gimmick. Hardly! These little balls are so tasty, they'll be a hit no matter where you serve them. We tested this recipe using frozen regular mac and cheese, low-fat mac and cheese, and even gluten free mac and cheese. They all work.

But there are two tricks. One, the mac and cheese must be *very* cold so the cheese doesn't melt immediately. If you're a slow worker in the kitchen, consider putting the first coated balls in the refrigerator while you make more.

Two, dip and redip those balls until they begin to hold together. The pasta wants to "unravel" and stick out of a ball. Keep rolling the balls until it doesn't.

In the smallest air fryers, you may have to make even the small amount in batches. Make sure there's adequate air flow between the balls so they can get crisp.

INGREDIENTS	2-quart or larger air fryer	5.25-quart or larger air fryer
Seasoned Italian-style dried bread crumbs (gluten-free, if a concern)	1 cup	1½ cups
10- to 12-ounce package(s) frozen mac and cheese (gluten-free, if a concern), thawed but still cold	1	2
Olive oil spray	As needed	As needed
MAKES	About 8 balls	About 16 balls

1. With the basket (or basket attachment) in the air fryer, heat it to 400°F (or 390°F, if that's the closest setting).

2. Pour the bread crumbs into a medium bowl. Scoop up 2 tablespoons of the mac and cheese. Using clean hands, form it into a ball between your palms (it may not be perfect), then roll it in the bread crumbs to coat. Roll it again into a ball, then set it back into the bread crumbs, perhaps doing this a few times to make sure that the ball holds together, that it's compact and coated. Set aside and make more.

3. Coat the balls with olive oil spray, then set them in the basket with as much air space between them as possible. Air-fry undisturbed for 10 minutes, or *just* until browned and crisp. Be very careful: If you overcook these balls, the cheese will melt and start to run out.

4. Use a nonstick-safe spatula, and perhaps kitchen tongs for balance, to *gently* transfer the balls to a wire rack or a cutting board. Cool for 5 minutes before serving.

Then...

- Set these air-fried balls of cheese bliss in bowls of chili.

- Serve them slathered in **Spicy Ketchup Dip** (page 66).

- Offer **Arugula and Pistachio Salad** (page 197) or **Honey Mustard Cole Slaw** (page 215) on the side.

Crispy Noodle Salad

VEGAN / 9 INGREDIENTS

This crossover dish is often served as a side in Chinese-American restaurants or as a vegetarian main course in South Asian restaurants. When the noodles come out of the fryer basket, they'll be in one slab that you must then break up and toss in the dressing with the other ingredients. Look for fresh Asian noodles near the wonton or egg roll wrappers.

You can also use these crispy noodles alone as the base of a stir-fry: Omit all the ingredients except the noodles and cornstarch; follow only steps 1 through 3 of the recipe to get the noodles crunchy.

INGREDIENTS	2-quart or larger air fryer	3.5-quart or larger air fryer	5.25-quart or larger air fryer
Fresh Chinese-style stir-fry or lo mein wheat noodles	¼ pound	6 ounces	½ pound
Cornstarch	1 tablespoon	1½ tablespoons	2 tablespoons
Chopped stemmed and cored red bell pepper	½ cup (1 small bell pepper)	¾ cup	1 cup (1 medium bell pepper)
Medium scallion(s), trimmed and thinly sliced	1	2	3
Sambal oelek or other pulpy hot red pepper sauce (see page 184)	1½ teaspoons	2 teaspoons	1 tablespoon
Thai sweet chili sauce or red ketchup-like chili sauce, such as Heinz	1½ teaspoons	2 teaspoons	1 tablespoon
Regular or low-sodium soy sauce or tamari sauce	1½ teaspoons	2 teaspoons	1 tablespoon
Unseasoned rice vinegar (see page 70)	1½ teaspoons	2 teaspoons	1 tablespoon
White or black sesame seeds	2 teaspoons	1 tablespoon	4 teaspoons
MAKES	2 side-dish servings	3 side-dish servings	4 side-dish servings

1. Bring a large saucepan of water to a boil over high heat. Add the noodles and boil for 2 minutes. Drain in a colander set in the sink. Rinse several times with cold water, shaking the colander to drain the noodles very well. Spread the noodles out on a large cutting board and air-dry for 10 minutes.

2. With the basket (or basket attachment) in the air fryer, heat it to 400°F (or 390°F, if that's the closest setting).

3. Toss the noodles in a bowl with the cornstarch until well coated. Spread them out across the entire basket (although they will be touching and overlapping a bit). Air-fry for 6 minutes, then turn the solid mass of noodles over as one piece. If it cracks in half or smaller pieces, just fit these back together after turning. Continue air-frying for 6 minutes, or until golden brown and crisp.

continues

4. As the noodles cook, stir the bell pepper, scallion(s), sambal oelek, red chili sauce, soy sauce, vinegar, and sesame seeds in a serving bowl until well combined.

5. Turn the basket of noodles out onto a cutting board and cool for a minute or two. Break the mass of noodles into individual noodles and/or small chunks and add to the dressing in the serving bowl. Toss well to serve.

Then...

- Use the salad as a bed for **Korean-Style Fried Chicken Thighs** (page 175), **Chicken Yakitori Skewers** (page 176), **Peanut Curry Turkey Cutlets** (page 195), **Wasabi-Coated Pork Loin Chops** (page 237), **Tonkatsu** (page 243), **Sesame-Crusted Tuna Steaks** (page 282), or **Shrimp Teriyaki** (page 295). Make this salad first, then let it sit at room temperature while you prepare the main course to go on it.

See photo in insert.

Brown Rice and Goat Cheese Croquettes

VEGETARIAN / CAN BE GLUTEN-FREE / 10 INGREDIENTS

These crunchy and decidedly savory croquettes (or patties) can be made well in advance. After cooking store them uncovered at room temperature for a couple of hours, or covered in the refrigerator for up to 3 days. To make them hot and crisp again, coat them once again with olive oil spray, then put them in one layer in a 400°F air fryer (or 390°F, if that's the closest setting) and air-fry for 3 to 4 minutes, until heated through.

INGREDIENTS	2-quart or larger air fryer	3.5-quart or larger air fryer	5.25-quart or larger air fryer
Water	½ cup	¾ cup	1 cup
Raw medium-grain *brown* rice, such as brown Arborio	¼ cup	6 tablespoons	½ cup
Shredded carrot	⅓ cup	½ cup	⅔ cup
Walnut pieces	3 tablespoons	¼ cup	⅓ cup
Soft goat cheese	2 tablespoons (about 1 ounce)	3 tablespoons (about 1½ ounces)	¼ cup (about 2 ounces)
Pasteurized egg substitute, such as Egg Beaters (gluten-free, if a concern)	2 teaspoons	1 tablespoon	1½ tablespoons
Dried thyme	¼ teaspoon	Rounded ¼ teaspoon	½ teaspoon
Table salt	¼ teaspoon	Rounded ¼ teaspoon	½ teaspoon
Ground black pepper	¼ teaspoon	Rounded ¼ teaspoon	½ teaspoon
Olive oil spray	As needed	As needed	As needed
MAKES	*2 croquettes*	*3 croquettes*	*4 croquettes*

1. Combine the water, rice, and carrots in a *small* saucepan set over medium-high heat. Bring to a boil, stirring occasionally. Cover, reduce the heat to very low, and simmer *very* slowly for 45 minutes, or until the water has been absorbed and the rice is tender. Set aside, covered, for 10 minutes.

2. Scrape the contents of the saucepan into a food processor. Cool for 10 minutes.

3. With the basket (or basket attachment) in the air fryer, heat it to 400°F (or 390°F, if that's the closest setting).

4. Put the nuts, cheese, egg substitute, thyme, salt, and pepper into the food processor. Cover and pulse to a coarse paste, stopping the machine at least once to scrape down the inside of the canister.

5. Uncover the food processor; scrape down and remove the blade. Using wet, clean hands, form the mixture into two 4-inch-diameter patties for a small batch, three 4-inch-diameter patties for a medium batch, or four 4-inch-diameter patties for a large one. Generously coat both sides of the patties with olive oil spray.

6. Set the patties in the basket with as much air space between them as possible. Air-fry undisturbed for 8 minutes, or until brown and crisp.

7. Use a nonstick-safe spatula to transfer the croquettes to a wire rack. Cool for 5 minutes before serving.

Then...

- These croquettes are a great side dish to hearty entrées like **Three Seed–Coated Pork Loin** (page 249) or **Horseradish-Crusted Salmon Fillets** (page 286).

- They're also terrific as a main course on top of a simple salad, like the **Celery Root Slaw** (page 205) or **Herb Salad** (page 249).

- Or you can serve them in toasted buns, particularly whole-wheat buns (gluten-free, if a concern), which are less sweet than standard buns and a better match to the patties. Use deli mustard, chopped lettuce, and thinly sliced red onion as toppers.

Hush Puppies

VEGETARIAN / 11 INGREDIENTS

The air fryer makes light, crisp hush puppies, best with fried seafood and lots of **Spicy Cocktail Sauce** (page 294).

Because the batter is fairly wet, you'll need to make two adjustments you might not make if you were deep-frying the hush puppies. First, the batter must rest in the fridge so it can set up a bit before you roll it into balls. Second, you'll need to line the machine's basket (or basket attachment) with parchment paper so the balls don't ooze through the mesh before they've set.

INGREDIENTS	2-quart or larger air fryer	3.5-quart or larger air fryer	5.25-quart or larger air fryer
Whole or low-fat milk (*not* fat-free)	⅓ cup	½ cup	⅔ cup
Butter	1 tablespoon	1½ tablespoons	2 tablespoons
All-purpose flour	6 tablespoons, plus more as needed	½ cup plus 1 tablespoon, plus more as needed	¾ cup, plus more as needed
Yellow cornmeal	6 tablespoons	½ cup plus 1 tablespoon	¾ cup
Granulated white sugar	1½ teaspoons	2 teaspoons	1 tablespoon
Baking powder	1½ teaspoons	2 teaspoons	1 tablespoon
Baking soda	½ teaspoon	¾ teaspoon	1 teaspoon
Table salt	½ teaspoon	¾ teaspoon	1 teaspoon
Onion powder	¼ teaspoon	Rounded ¼ teaspoon	½ teaspoon
Pasteurized egg substitute, such as Egg Beaters	2 tablespoons (or 1 small egg, well beaten)	3 tablespoons (or 1 medium egg, well beaten)	¼ cup (or 1 large egg, well beaten)
Vegetable oil spray	As needed	As needed	As needed
MAKES	*About 6 hush puppies*	*About 8 hush puppies*	*About 12 hush puppies*

1. Heat the milk and butter in a small saucepan set over medium heat just until the butter melts and the milk is steamy. Do not simmer or boil.

2. Meanwhile, whisk the flour, cornmeal, sugar, baking powder, baking soda, salt, and onion powder in a large bowl until the mixture is a uniform color.

3. Stir the hot milk mixture into the flour mixture to form a dough. Set aside to cool for 5 minutes.

4. Mix the egg substitute or egg into the dough to make a thick, smooth batter. Cover and refrigerate for at least 1 hour or up to 4 hours.

5. With the basket (or basket attachment) in the air fryer, heat it to 350°F (or 360°F, if that's the closest setting).

6. Lightly flour your clean, dry hands. Roll 2 tablespoons of the batter into a ball between your floured palms. Set aside, flour your hands again if necessary, and continue making more balls with the remaining batter.

7. Coat the balls all over with the vegetable oil spray. Line the machine's basket (or basket attachment) with a piece of parchment paper. Set the balls on the parchment paper with as much air space between them as possible. Air-fry for 9 minutes, or until lightly browned and set.

8. Use kitchen tongs to gently transfer the hush puppies to a wire rack. Cool for at least 5 minutes before serving. Or cool to room temperature, about 45 minutes, and store in a sealed container at room temperature for up to 2 days. To crisp the hush puppies again, put them in a 350°F air fryer (or 360°F, if that's the closest setting) for 1 to 2 minutes. (There's no need for parchment paper in the machine during reheating.)

Then...

- You've got to have lots of butter to smear on the hot hush puppies when you serve them with **Better Fish Sticks** (page 273), **Crispy Smelts** (page 293), **Crunchy Clam Strips** (page 294), **Fried Shrimp** (page 299), or **Fried Scallops** (page 303).

- Hush puppies are also great with drinks before dinner. Try them with **Frozen Sangria** (page 99) or **Perfect Frozen Margaritas** (page 145).

Cheesy Texas Toast

VEGETARIAN / 4 INGREDIENTS

Texas toast was a thing in the '70s, a thick slice of oiled-up bread to go alongside steaks. We've morphed the classic a little, calling for butter rather than a tasteless oil and adding lots of cheese, in keeping with how the toast comes in some steakhouses these days.

Unfortunately, because of the size of the basket, you can't make many of these at once. So if you've got a crowd, cut the toasts into smaller pieces after they're done and let everyone dig in while you put another batch in the air fryer.

INGREDIENTS	2-quart or larger air fryer	3.5-quart or larger air fryer	5.25-quart or larger air fryer
1-inch-thick slice(s) Italian bread (each about 4 inches across)	1	2	3
Softened butter	2 teaspoons	4 teaspoons	2 tablespoons
Minced garlic	1 teaspoon	2 teaspoons	1 tablespoon
Finely grated Parmesan cheese	2 tablespoons (about ⅓ ounce)	¼ cup (about ¾ ounce)	6 tablespoons (a little more than 1 ounce)
MAKES	*1 toast*	*2 toasts*	*3 toasts*

continues

1. With the basket (or basket attachment) in the air fryer, heat it to 400°F (or 390°F, if that's the closest setting).

2. Spread one side of a slice of bread with 2 teaspoons butter. Sprinkle with 1 teaspoon minced garlic, followed by 2 tablespoons grated cheese. Repeat this process if you're making one or more additional toasts.

3. When the machine is at temperature, put the bread slice(s) cheese side up in the basket (with as much air space between them as possible if you're making more than one). Air-fry undisturbed for 4 minutes, or until browned and crunchy.

4. Use a nonstick-safe spatula to transfer the toasts cheese side up to a wire rack. Cool for 5 minutes before serving.

Then...

- Use a slice of Texas toast as a substitute for the bun to make an open-faced burger.

- Turn Texas toast into a bigger breakfast—or a fast lunch or dinner—by topping a slice with a fried egg or two.

- Put a slice of Texas toast in a bowl and ladle soup or stew on top, particularly a soup or stew without any cream in the mix.

Buttery Rolls

VEGETARIAN / 9 INGREDIENTS

You can indeed bake fine yeast rolls in an air fryer. Because the machine is a mini convection oven, the rolls come out light but with a good crust, ready to be split open for a pat of butter.

Note that the milk in this recipe *must be* at room temperature. You can heat it in a microwave, but you can't make it hot or it'll kill the yeast. And the melted butter must be cooled to at least body temperature or it, too, will kill the yeast; and it cannot be cold because the yeast will not activate.

We *strongly* recommend using instant yeast. It's reliable and doesn't require a complicated proofing step. Look for it at the supermarket or from an online supplier; keep it in the freezer for future batches.

We also call for a pasteurized egg substitute for the smaller batches since we need less than a whole large egg (although we also give you the equivalents for other sizes of eggs, just to cover all the bases).

INGREDIENTS	2-quart or larger air fryer	3.5-quart or larger air fryer	5.25-quart or larger air fryer
Room-temperature whole or low-fat milk	⅓ cup	6½ tablespoons	½ cup
Butter, melted and cooled	2 tablespoons plus 2 teaspoons	3 tablespoons plus 1 teaspoon	4 tablespoons (¼ cup/½ stick)
Pasteurized egg substitute, such as Egg Beaters	2 tablespoons plus 2 teaspoons (or 1 small egg, well beaten)	3 tablespoons plus 1 teaspoon (or 1 medium egg, well beaten)	¼ cup (or 1 large egg, well beaten)
Granulated white sugar	4 teaspoons	1½ tablespoons	2 tablespoons

	1 teaspoon	1¼ teaspoons	1½ teaspoons
Instant yeast	1 teaspoon	1¼ teaspoons	1½ teaspoons
Table salt	¼ teaspoon	Rounded ¼ teaspoon	½ teaspoon
All-purpose flour	1⅔ cups, plus more for dusting	2 cups, plus more for dusting	2½ cups, plus more for dusting
Vegetable oil	As needed	As needed	As needed
Additional melted butter, for brushing	As needed	As needed	As needed
MAKES	5 rolls	6 rolls	8 rolls

1. Stir the milk, melted butter, pasteurized egg substitute (or whole egg), sugar, yeast, and salt in a medium bowl to combine. Stir in the flour just until the mixture makes a soft dough.

2. Lightly flour a clean, dry work surface. Turn the dough out onto the work surface. Knead the dough for 5 minutes to develop the gluten.

3. Lightly oil the inside of a clean medium bowl. Gather the dough into a compact ball and set it in the bowl. Turn the dough over so that its surface has oil on it all over. Cover the bowl tightly with plastic wrap and set aside in a warm, draft-free place until the dough has doubled in bulk, about 1½ hours.

4. Punch down the dough, then turn it out onto a clean, dry work surface. Divide it into 5 even balls for a small batch, 6 balls for a medium batch, or 8 balls for a large one.

For a small batch, lightly oil the inside of a 6-inch round cake pan and set the balls around its perimeter, separating them as much as possible.

For a medium batch, lightly oil the inside of a 7-inch round cake pan and set the balls in it with one ball at its center, separating them as much as possible.

For a large batch, lightly oil the inside of an 8-inch round cake pan and set the balls in it with one at the center, separating them as much as possible.

Cover with plastic wrap and set aside to rise for 30 minutes.

5. With the basket (or basket attachment) in the air fryer, heat it to 350°F (or 360°F, if that's the closest setting).

6. Uncover the pan and brush the rolls with a little melted butter, perhaps ½ teaspoon per roll. When the machine is at temperature, set the cake pan in the basket. Air-fry undisturbed for 14 minutes, or until the rolls have risen and browned.

7. Using kitchen tongs and a nonstick-safe spatula, two hot pads, or silicone baking mitts, transfer the cake pan from the basket to a wire rack. Cool the rolls in the pan for a minute or two. Turn the rolls out onto a wire rack, set them top side up again, and cool for at least another couple of minutes before serving warm.

Then...

- Since fine rolls need a fine soup, may we recommend **Hearty Roasted Vegetable Soup** (page 108)?

- Use these rolls to make sandwiches with deli mustard and the **Three Seed–Coated Pork Loin** (page 249).

Buttermilk Biscuits

VEGETARIAN / 6 INGREDIENTS

An air fryer makes crazy-good biscuits. The tops are crunchy and brown; the insides, soft and moist. The only trick is the baking powder: It has to be fresh and active. Baking powder does lose its efficacy because of ambient humidity and temperature fluctuations. To test if yours is active, mix ¼ teaspoon into ⅓ cup boiling water. It should foam and froth. Or skip the chemical experiment and just buy a new can if yours is more than nine months old.

INGREDIENTS	2-quart or larger air fryer	3.5-quart or larger air fryer	5.25-quart or larger air fryer
All-purpose flour	1⅓ cups, plus more for dusting	1⅔ cups, plus more for dusting	2 cups, plus more for dusting
Baking powder	1¼ teaspoons	1½ teaspoons	2 teaspoons
Table salt	Pinch	¼ teaspoon	½ teaspoon
Butter, cold and cut into small pieces	2 tablespoons plus 2 teaspoons	3 tablespoons plus 1 teaspoon	4 tablespoons (¼ cup/½ stick)
Cold buttermilk, regular or low-fat	7 tablespoons	½ cup plus ½ tablespoon	⅔ cup
Butter, melted and cooled	2 tablespoons	2½ tablespoons	3 tablespoons
MAKES	*4 biscuits*	*5 biscuits*	*6 biscuits*

1. With the basket (or basket attachment) in the air fryer, heat it to 400°F (or 390°F, if that's the closest setting).

2. Mix the flour, baking powder, and salt in a large bowl. Use a pastry cutter or a sturdy flatware fork to cut the cold butter pieces into the flour mixture, working the fat through the tines again and again until the mixture resembles coarse dry sand. Stir in the buttermilk to make a dough.

3. Very lightly dust a clean, dry work surface with flour. Turn the dough out onto it, dip your clean hands into flour, and press the dough into a ¾-inch-thick circle. Use a 3-inch round cookie cutter or sturdy drinking glass to cut the dough into rounds. Gather the dough scraps together, lightly shape again into a ¾-inch-thick circle, and cut out a few more rounds. You'll end up with 4 raw biscuits for a small air fryer, 5 for a medium, or 6 for a large.

4. For a small air fryer, brush the inside of a 6-inch round cake pan with a little more than half of the melted butter, then set the 4 raw biscuits in it, letting them touch but without squishing them.

For a medium air fryer, do the same with half of the melted butter in a 7-inch round cake pan and 5 raw biscuits.

And for a large air fryer, use a little more than half the melted butter to brush the inside of an 8-inch round cake pan, and set the 6 raw biscuits in it in the same way.

Brush the tops of the raw biscuits with the remaining melted butter.

5. Air-fry undisturbed for 14 minutes, or until the biscuits are golden brown and dry to the touch.

6. Using kitchen tongs and a nonstick-safe spatula, two hot pads, or silicone baking mitts, remove the cake pan from the basket and set it on a wire rack. Cool undisturbed for a couple of minutes. Turn the biscuits out onto the wire rack to cool for a couple of minutes more before serving.

Then...

- **PERFECT SCRAMBLED EGGS** are made low and slow, not fast and hot as diner chefs often do.

Try it: a nonstick skillet, *a little melted butter, some whisked-up eggs*, and low heat. Stir and stir with a rubber spatula, gathering the curds as they (very slowly!) form. Four eggs will take up to 15 minutes but the texture will be nothing less than creamy custard.

- Split these biscuits each into two rounds and use them as a substitute for the English muffins in our **Tuna Melt** (page 130).

Perfect French Fries

VEGAN / GLUTEN-FREE / 3 INGREDIENTS

While there are lots of packaged frozen fries that will work great in the machine, here's a recipe for fries from scratch.

And here are our seven rules. Perfect fries are made from 1) russet potatoes (peeled or not, your choice) 2) that have been soaked to get rid of excess starch and then 3) carefully dried. They are cooked 4) at a low temperature without any oil to dry them out, then 5) at a moderately high temperature with a spritz of oil to crisp them, and finally 6) at a high temperature for a few minutes to brown them and get rid of the last bits of surface moisture. And all this cooking must happen with 7) frequent tossing and rearranging of the fries to make sure they all get an even chance at the heat. You can rearrange them with kitchen tongs or you can shake the basket, but make sure you reposition the fries each time.

INGREDIENTS	2-quart or larger air fryer	3.5-quart or larger air fryer	5.25-quart or larger air fryer
Large russet potato(es)	¾ pound	1 pound	1½ pounds
Vegetable oil or olive oil spray	As needed	As needed	As needed
Table salt	¼ teaspoon	½ teaspoon	1 teaspoon
MAKES	*2 servings*	*3 servings*	*4 to 5 servings*

1. Cut each potato lengthwise into ¼-inch-thick slices. Cut each of these lengthwise into ¼-inch-thick matchsticks.

2. Set the potato matchsticks in a big bowl of cool water and soak for 5 minutes. Drain in a colander set in the sink, then spread the matchsticks out on paper towels and dry them very well.

continues

3. With the basket (or basket attachment) in the air fryer, heat it to 225°F (or 230°F, if that's the closest setting).

4. When the machine is at temperature, arrange the matchsticks in an even layer (if overlapping but not compact) in the basket. Air-fry for 20 minutes, tossing and rearranging the fries twice.

5. Pour the contents of the basket into a big bowl. Increase the air fryer's temperature to 325°F (or 330°F, if that's the closest setting).

6. Generously coat the fries with vegetable or olive oil spray. Toss well, then coat them again to make sure they're covered on all sides, tossing (and maybe spraying) a couple of times to make sure.

7. When the machine is at temperature, pour the fries into the basket and air-fry for 12 minutes, tossing and rearranging the fries at least twice.

8. Increase the machine's temperature to 375°F (or 380°F or 390°F, if one of these is the closest setting). Air-fry for 5 minutes more (from the moment you raise the temperature), tossing and rearranging the fries at least twice to keep them from burning and to make sure they all get an even measure of the heat, until brown and crisp.

9. Pour the contents of the basket into a serving bowl. Toss the fries with the salt and serve hot.

Then...

- Although bottled ketchup is the go-to condiment, we'd also like to suggest **Cooked Tomato Dip** (page 79), **Creamy Harissa Dip** (page 75), **Lemon Aioli** (page 45), **Spicy Ketchup Dip** (page 66), or **Basil and Red Pepper Mayonnaise** (page 273).

- Although we suggest tossing them with salt, you don't have to stop there. In addition to the salt, add finely grated lemon zest and finely grated Parmesan cheese. Or a little dried thyme and lots of black pepper. Or just about any dried seasoning blend you like.

Steak Fries

VEGAN / GLUTEN-FREE / 4 INGREDIENTS

Although we use russet potatoes for French fries, the best steak fries are made with yellow potatoes like Yukon Golds, which have less starch and become creamy inside as the exterior browns. To make wedges, cut each potato in half lengthwise, then cut these halves lengthwise into three or four wedges.

INGREDIENTS	2-quart or larger air fryer	3.5-quart or larger air fryer	5.25-quart or larger air fryer
Medium Yukon Gold or other yellow potatoes (peeled or not—your choice)	1 pound	2 pounds	3 pounds
Olive oil	1 tablespoon	2 tablespoons	3 tablespoons
Table salt	¼ teaspoon, or more to taste	½ teaspoon, or more to taste	1 teaspoon, or more to taste
Ground black pepper	¼ teaspoon, or more to taste	½ teaspoon, or more to taste	1 teaspoon, or more to taste
MAKES	2 servings	4 servings	6 servings

1. With the basket (or basket attachment) in the air fryer, heat it to 350°F (or 360°F, if that's the closest setting).

2. Cut the potatoes lengthwise into wedges about 1 inch wide at the outer rounded edge. Toss these wedges in a bowl with the oil, salt, and pepper until the wedges are evenly coated in the oil. (Start with the minimum amounts of salt and pepper we recommend—you can always add more later.)

3. When the machine is at temperature, set the wedges in the basket in a crisscross stack, with about half of the wedges first lining in the basket's bottom, then others set on top of those at a 45-degree angle. Air-fry undisturbed for 15 minutes.

4. Increase the machine's temperature to 400°F (or 390°F, if that's the closest setting). Toss the fries so they're no longer in a crisscross pattern but more like a mound. Air-fry for 10 minutes more (from the moment you raise the temperature), tossing and rearranging the fries once, until they're crisp and brown.

5. Pour them onto a wire rack and cool for a few minutes before serving hot.

Then...

- You've got to serve these with **Perfect Strip Steaks** (page 208), **Barbecue-Style London Broil** (page 214), or **Pesto-Rubbed Veal Chops** (page 232).

- Skip the ketchup and try these with **Chimichurri** (page 94).

Sweet Potato Fries

VEGAN / GLUTEN-FREE / 3 INGREDIENTS

Sweet potato fries are not as temperamental as regular French fries and so may well be easier to pull off on a weeknight. Although we assume you'll cut the sweet potato with a (sharp!) chef's knife (a paring knife is too small to do a good, even job), it's easier to make those initial ¼-inch-thick slices if you use a mandoline with the slicing blade set at ¼ inch. (A high-end mandoline may even have a French fry setting.) Remember to use the guard as you run the sweet potato lengthwise over the super sharp blade.

INGREDIENTS	2-quart or larger air fryer	3.5-quart or larger air fryer	5.25-quart or larger air fryer
10-ounce sweet potato(es)	1	2	3
Vegetable oil spray	As needed	As needed	As needed
Coarse sea salt or kosher salt	To taste	To taste	To taste
MAKES	2 servings	3 to 4 servings	5 to 6 servings

1. With the basket (or basket attachment) in the air fryer, heat it to 400°F (or 390°F, if that's the closest setting).

2. Peel the sweet potato(es), then cut lengthwise into ¼-inch-thick slices. Cut these slices lengthwise into ¼-inch-thick matchsticks. Place these matchsticks in a bowl and coat them with vegetable oil spray. Toss well, spray them again, and toss several times to make sure they're all evenly coated.

3. When the machine is at temperature, pour the sweet potato matchsticks into the basket, spreading them out in as close to an even layer as possible. Air-fry for 20 minutes, tossing and rearranging the matchsticks every 5 minutes, until lightly browned and crisp.

4. Pour the contents of the basket into a bowl, add some salt to taste, and toss well to coat.

Then...

- There's no reason to stick with just salt for these fries. They're sweet, so a spicy dried seasoning blend works very well, like **Cajun dried seasoning blend** (page 279) or even just standard chile powder. Add a little, toss well, taste the fries, and add a little more if desired.

- Although fries are often served with burgers, we especially like sweet potato fries with grilled or broiled sausages such as kielbasa or even knackwurst—especially if there's spicy mustard to go with the sausages.

Shoestring Butternut Squash Fries

VEGAN / GLUTEN-FREE / 3 INGREDIENTS

Consider this easy recipe a road map for other spiralized root or "winter keeping" vegetables like turnips, rutabaga, sweet potatoes, or even regular potatoes. Since spiralized vegetables show up in the refrigerator case of most supermarkets these days, you'll never run out of possibilities.

Spiral-cut butternut squash and other hard winter squashes shrink a lot as they cook. The basket will be full when you start but much less crowded when you're done.

You can alter the flavor profile of the fries by swapping out the vegetable oil spray for olive oil spray or even coconut oil spray. Or skip the spray and toss the spiralized vegetable with up to 1 tablespoon nut oil. Walnut oil is particularly appealing on sweet vegetables like butternut squash or sweet potatoes.

INGREDIENTS	2-quart or larger air fryer	3.5-quart or larger air fryer	5.25-quart or larger air fryer
Spiralized butternut squash strands	¾ pound	1 pound 2 ounces	1½ pounds
Vegetable oil spray	As needed	As needed	As needed
Coarse sea salt or kosher salt	To taste	To taste	To taste
MAKES	2 or 3 servings	3 or 4 servings	4 or 5 servings

1. With the basket (or basket attachment) in the air fryer, heat it to 375°F (or 370°F or 360°F, if one of these is the closest setting).

2. Place the spiralized squash in a big bowl. Coat the strands with vegetable oil spray, toss well, coat again, and toss several times to make sure all the strands have been oiled.

3. When the machine is at temperature, pour the strands into the basket and spread them out into as even a layer as possible. Air-fry for 16 minutes, tossing and rearranging the strands every 4 minutes, or until they're lightly browned and crisp.

4. Pour the contents of the basket into a serving bowl, add salt to taste, and toss well before serving hot.

Then...

- Because butternut squash is sweet, try these shoestring fries with a spicy dip like **Buffalo Sauce** (page 187), **Chile-Peanut Sauce** (page 46), **Peanut-Sesame Sauce** (page 69), or even **Wasabi Mayonnaise** (page 296).

Zucchini Fries

VEGETARIAN / CAN BE GLUTEN-FREE / 5 INGREDIENTS

There are several ways to make zucchini fries—with zucchini rounds, with spiralized zucchini, or what we think is the best way: with the vegetable cut into little batons, because 1) there's more coating, even on the ends of the batons, so there's more crunch; and 2) the insides can become very creamy with no peel left on the vegetable. If you're hankering for **Zucchini Chips**, see page 36.

INGREDIENTS	2-quart or larger air fryer	3.5-quart or larger air fryer	5.25-quart or larger air fryer
Zucchini	1 medium	1 large	2 medium
All-purpose flour or tapioca flour	⅓ cup	½ cup	¾ cup
Large egg(s), well beaten	1	2	2
Seasoned Italian-style dried bread crumbs (gluten-free, if a concern)	¾ cup	1 cup	1½ cups
Olive oil spray	As needed	As needed	As needed
MAKES	2 servings	3 servings	4 servings

1. With the basket (or basket attachment) in the air fryer, heat it to 400°F (or 390°F, if that's the closest setting).

2. Trim the zucchini into a long rectangular block, taking off the ends and four "sides" to make this shape. Cut the block lengthwise into ½-inch-thick slices. Lay these slices flat and cut in half widthwise. Slice each of these pieces into ½-inch-thick batons.

3. Set up and fill three shallow soup plates or small pie plates on your counter: one for the flour, one for the beaten egg(s), and one for the bread crumbs.

4. Set a zucchini baton in the flour and turn it several times to coat all sides. Gently shake off any excess flour, then dip it in the egg(s), turning it to coat. Let any excess egg slip back into the rest, then set the baton in the bread crumbs and turn it several times, pressing gently to coat all sides, even the ends. Set aside on a cutting board and continue coating the remainder of the batons in the same way.

5. Lightly coat the batons on all sides with olive oil spray. Set them in two flat layers in the basket, the top layer at a 90-degree angle to the bottom one, with a little air space between the batons in each layer. In the end, the whole thing will look like a crosshatch pattern. Air-fry undisturbed for 6 minutes.

6. Use kitchen tongs to *gently* rearrange the batons so that any covered parts are now uncovered. The batons no longer need to be in a crosshatch pattern. Continue air-frying undisturbed for 6 minutes, or until lightly browned and crisp.

7. Gently pour the contents of the basket onto a wire rack. Spread the batons out and cool for only a minute or two before serving.

Then...

- Try these fries with **BUTTERMILK DIP**. Whisk ¼ cup plain full-fat or low-fat yogurt, ¼ cup regular or low-fat sour cream, 2 tablespoons buttermilk, 2 tablespoons minced chives, 1 tablespoon minced *fresh dill fronds, 1 tablespoon apple cider vinegar, ¼ teaspoon table salt,* and *¼ teaspoon ground black pepper* in a small bowl until well combined.

- Or serve the fries with **Lemon Aioli** (page 45) or **Sriracha-Yogurt Dip** (page 36).

Beet Fries

FAST / EASY / VEGAN / GLUTEN-FREE / 3 INGREDIENTS

Because beets are loaded with natural sugars, we felt any coating weighed them down, making them seem too sweet for a successful side dish.

And because beets stain your fingers (and your linens), it's best to eat these fries with a fork. If you stain your hands, you can follow one of two methods, both a bit harsh on your skin. Either rub lemon juice all over your hands repeatedly and rinse well until the stains are gone, or put some coarse salt in your hands and rub them together under running water, repeating until the stains are gone. In either case, use hand moisturizer afterwards.

INGREDIENTS	2-quart or larger air fryer	3.5-quart or larger air fryer	5.25-quart or larger air fryer
6-ounce red beets	2	3	4
Vegetable oil spray	As needed	As needed	As needed
Coarse sea salt or kosher salt	To taste	To taste	To taste
MAKES	2 servings	3 servings	4 servings

1. With the basket (or basket attachment) in the air fryer, heat it to 375°F (or 370°F or 360°F, if one of these is the closest setting).

2. Remove the stems from the beets and peel them with a knife or vegetable peeler. Slice them into ½-inch-thick circles. Lay these flat on a cutting board and slice them into ½-inch-thick sticks. Generously coat the sticks on all sides with vegetable oil spray.

3. When the machine is at temperature, drop them into the basket, shake the basket to even the sticks out into as close to one layer as possible, and air-fry for 20 minutes, tossing and rearranging the beet matchsticks every 5 minutes, or until brown and even crisp at the ends. If the machine is at 360°F, you may need to add 1 or 2 minutes to the cooking time.

4. Pour the fries into a big bowl, add the salt, toss well, and serve warm.

Then...

- Although these fries are great alongside burgers, we like them as a crunchy topping right on bunless beef, pork, or even lamb patties. Pile the beet fries high, then drizzle them with **Yogurt-Cilantro Sauce** (page 136).

Homemade Potato Puffs

EASY / VEGETARIAN / CAN BE GLUTEN-FREE / 9 INGREDIENTS

Here's our knock-off version of Tater Tots, a treat when you want to go to a little extra effort. Ours are made from instant mashed potato flakes, which are (after all) just dehydrated cooked potatoes. These flakes make great puffs without the unnecessary added moisture a batch of cooled mashed potatoes would bring to the mix (which would render the puffs unfortunately gummy).

INGREDIENTS	2-quart or larger air fryer	3.5-quart or larger air fryer	5.25-quart or larger air fryer
Water	1¼ cups	1¾ cups	2½ cups
Butter	3 tablespoons	4 tablespoons (¼ cup/½ stick)	6 tablespoons (¾ stick)
Instant mashed potato flakes	1½ cups	2 cups plus 2 tablespoons	3 cups
Table salt	1 teaspoon	1½ teaspoons	2 teaspoons
Ground black pepper	½ teaspoon	¾ teaspoon	1 teaspoon
Mild paprika	¼ teaspoon	Rounded ¼ teaspoon	½ teaspoon
Dried thyme	¼ teaspoon	Rounded ¼ teaspoon	½ teaspoon
Seasoned Italian-style dried bread crumbs (gluten-free, if a concern)	1 cup	1¼ cups	1½ cups
Olive oil spray	As needed	As needed	As needed
MAKES	*2 servings*	*4 servings*	*6 servings*

1. Heat the water with the butter in a medium saucepan set over medium-low heat just until the butter melts. Do not bring to a boil.

2. Remove the saucepan from the heat and stir in the potato flakes, salt, pepper, paprika, and thyme until smooth. Set aside to cool for 5 minutes.

3. With the basket (or basket attachment) in the air fryer, heat it to 400°F (or 390°F, if that's the closest setting). Spread the bread crumbs on a dinner plate.

4. Scrape up 2 tablespoons of the potato flake mixture and form it into a small, oblong puff, like a little cylinder about 1½ inches long. Gently roll the puff in the bread crumbs until coated on all sides. Set it aside and continue making more, about 12 for the small batch, 18 for the medium batch, or 24 for the large.

5. Coat the potato cylinders with olive oil spray on all sides, then arrange them in the basket in one layer with some air space between them. Air-fry undisturbed for 15 minutes, or until crisp and brown.

6. Gently dump the contents of the basket onto a wire rack. Cool for 5 minutes before serving.

Then...

- Turn potato puffs into **TOT NACHOS**. After they're done, line them up in a 6-, 7-, or 8-inch round cake pan. Cover the puffs with *shredded cheese, particularly a Tex-Mex blend*, and *pickled jalapeño rings*. Dot the tops with *green or red salsa*, then set the pan in a small, medium, or large air-fryer (depending on the pan size) set at 400°F until the cheese has melted and is bubbly, about 2 minutes.

Steakhouse Baked Potatoes

EASY / VEGAN / GLUTEN-FREE / 3 INGREDIENTS

These are *steakhouse* baked potatoes because they remind us of those terrific, crunchy/fluffy baked potatoes we got in American steakhouses when we were kids. The air fryer is far better than an oven for getting the potato's skin crisp while keeping the interior creamy. Who's got a steak or a slice of meatloaf for the plate?

INGREDIENTS	2-quart or larger air fryer	3.5-quart or larger air fryer	5.25-quart or larger air fryer
10-ounce russet potatoes	2	3	4
Olive oil	4 teaspoons	2 tablespoons	2 tablespoons plus 2 teaspoons
Table salt	½ teaspoon	1 teaspoon	1½ teaspoons
MAKES	*2 baked potatoes*	*3 baked potatoes*	*4 baked potatoes*

1. With the basket (or basket attachment) in the air fryer, heat it to 375°F (or 370°F or 360°F, if one of these is the closest setting).

2. Poke holes all over each potato with a fork. Rub the skin of each potato with 2 teaspoons of the olive oil, then sprinkle ¼ teaspoon salt all over each potato.

3. When the machine is at temperature, set the potatoes in the basket in one layer with as much air space between them as possible. Air-fry for 50 minutes, turning once, or until soft to the touch but with crunchy skins. If the machine is at 360°F, you may need to add up to 5 minutes to the cooking time.

4. Use kitchen tongs to gently transfer the baked potatoes to a wire rack. Cool for 5 or 10 minutes before serving.

Then...

- These need the traditional accompaniments: butter, sour cream, chives, and/or crisp bacon bits.

- Or split them open on plates and use them as the base of a stew or braise.

- For extra crunchy potato fries, cool the potatoes to room temperature, about 1½ hours. Wrap them in plastic wrap and store them in the fridge for at least 1 day or up to 4 days. Slice the potatoes into ¾-inch-thick rounds, coat them lightly with olive oil on all sides, and set them in as close to a single layer as possible in the basket of a 400°F air fryer (or 390°F, if that's the closest setting) for 20 minutes, rearranging after 10 minutes if there are any overlapping bits, until very brown and very crunchy.

Cheesy Potato Skins

EASY / VEGETARIAN / CAN BE GLUTEN-FREE / 9 INGREDIENTS

These potato skins are better than those from an oven because the air fryer dries out the skins to make them crunchy and hard to resist. Although a lot of people serve potato skins as a snack or as deck food, we think they're a terrific side dish to barbecue brisket or even **Barbecue-Style London Broil** (page 214)—or they can easily be a vegetarian main course with a side salad.

INGREDIENTS	2-quart or larger air fryer	3.5-quart or larger air fryer	5.25-quart or larger air fryer
6- to 8-ounce *small* russet potatoes	2	3	4
Thick-cut bacon strips, halved widthwise (gluten-free, if a concern)	2	3	4
Mild paprika	½ teaspoon	¾ teaspoon	1 teaspoon
Garlic powder	¼ teaspoon	Rounded ¼ teaspoon	½ teaspoon
Table salt	¼ teaspoon	Rounded ¼ teaspoon	½ teaspoon
Ground black pepper	¼ teaspoon	Rounded ¼ teaspoon	½ teaspoon
Shredded Cheddar cheese	6 tablespoons (about 1½ ounces)	½ cup plus 1 tablespoon (a little over 2 ounces)	¾ cup (about 3 ounces)
Thinly sliced trimmed chives	2 tablespoons	3 tablespoons	¼ cup
Finely grated Parmesan cheese	¼ cup (about ¾ ounce)	6 tablespoons (a little over 1 ounce)	½ cup (about 1½ ounces)
MAKES	4 stuffed potato halves	6 stuffed potato halves	8 stuffed potato halves

1. With the basket (or basket attachment) in the air fryer, heat it to 375°F (or 370°F or 360°F, if one of these is the closest setting).

2. Prick each potato in four places with a fork (not four places in a line but four places all around the potato). Set the potatoes in the basket with as much air space between them as possible. Air-fry undisturbed for 45 minutes, or until the potatoes are tender when pricked with a fork.

3. Use kitchen tongs to gently transfer the potatoes to a wire rack. Cool for 15 minutes. Maintain the machine's temperature.

4. Lay the bacon strip halves in the basket in one layer. They may touch but should not overlap. Air-fry undisturbed for 5 minutes, until crisp. Use those same tongs to transfer the bacon pieces to the wire rack. If there's a great deal of rendered bacon fat in the basket's bottom or on a tray under the basket attachment, pour this into a bowl, cool, and discard. Don't throw it down the drain!

5. Cut the potatoes in half lengthwise (not just slit them open but actually cut in half). Use a flatware spoon to scoop the hot, soft middles into a bowl, leaving ½ inch of potato all around the inside of the spud next to the skin. Sprinkle the inside of the potato "shells" evenly with paprika, garlic powder, salt, and pepper.

6. Chop the bacon pieces into small bits. Sprinkle these along with the Cheddar and chives evenly inside the potato shells. Crumble 2 to 3 tablespoons of the soft potato insides over the filling mixture. Divide the grated Parmesan evenly over the tops of the potatoes.

7. Set the stuffed potatoes in the basket with as much air space between them as possible. Air-fry undisturbed for 4 minutes, until the cheese melts and lightly browns.

8. Use kitchen tongs to gently transfer the stuffed potato halves to a wire rack. Cool for 5 minutes before serving.

Then...

- Save the leftover potato "insides" in a sealed container in the fridge. They'll keep for about 5 days. You can stir them into soups and stews as a last-minute thickener, mix them with yogurt and dried spices for a spread inside wraps, or thin them out with warmed milk and melted butter for "instant" mashed potatoes.

- The simplest way to serve these skins is to garnish the halves with sour cream.

- For even more cheese flavor, top them when done with **Tangy Goat Cheese Dip** (page 230). Or spike them with a little **Jalapeño Jam** (page 58).

Crunchy Roasted Potatoes

EASY / VEGAN / GLUTEN-FREE / 5 INGREDIENTS

Look no further for the best roasted potatoes. We use small potatoes and don't cut them into wedges or spears precisely because the intact skins will turn super crunchy while the insides stay soft and tender. No, they won't have browned edges like fries do. But we feel that luxurious texture inside each potato is worth sacrificing those ultra browned bits (just this once).

Use whatever fat you like: vegetable oil, a nut oil (especially walnut oil), sesame oil, or even a melted and cooled animal fat like bacon fat, chicken fat, or duck fat.

INGREDIENTS	2-quart or larger air fryer	3.5-quart or larger air fryer	5.25-quart or larger air fryer
Small (1- to 1½-inch-diameter) red, white, or purple potatoes	1½ pounds	2 pounds	3 pounds
Olive oil	4 teaspoons	2 tablespoons	2½ tablespoons
Table salt	1½ teaspoons	2 teaspoons	1 tablespoon
Garlic powder	½ teaspoon	¾ teaspoon	1 teaspoon
Ground black pepper	¼ teaspoon	½ teaspoon	1 teaspoon
MAKES	4 servings	5 to 6 servings	8 servings

1. With the basket (or basket attachment) in the air fryer, heat it to 400°F (or 390°F, if that's the closest setting).

2. Toss the potatoes, oil, salt, garlic powder, and pepper in a large bowl until the spuds are evenly and thoroughly coated.

3. When the machine is at temperature, pour the potatoes into the basket, spreading them into an even layer (although they may be stacked on top of each other). Air-fry for 25 minutes, tossing twice, until the potatoes are tender but crunchy.

4. Pour the contents of the basket into a serving bowl. Cool for 5 minutes before serving.

Then...

- Serve these with **Perfect Pork Chops** (page 238), **Barbecue Country-Style Pork Ribs** (page 250), or **Garlic and Oregano Lamb Chops** (page 267). Make the potatoes first, then the main course, then reheat the potatoes in a 400°F (or 390°F, if the closest setting) air fryer for 3 to 4 minutes, until hot and crisp.

- Cool the potatoes to room temperature and serve them with a dip for a snack before dinner. Try **Spicy Mustard Dip** (page 26), **Chimichurri** (page 94), or **Ranch Dip** (page 293).

Hasselback Garlic-and-Butter Potatoes

VEGETARIAN / GLUTEN-FREE / 7 INGREDIENTS

Hasselback potatoes are potatoes cut with lots of parallel slits across one side, slits that can get stuffed with little bits of aromatic herbs and thin slices of cheese. Hasselbacks are a bit of a (well) hassle in an air fryer because the convection currents dry out the potatoes, causing those slits to close up and squeeze out whatever's inside them, thereby depriving you of the pleasure of buttery goodness down in the crevasses.

We solve the problem by wedging a thin slice of mushroom into each slit. The mushroom adds plenty of flavor while keeping that slit open so that the butter and cheese can drip down into the potato.

Here's our best hack for making all those slits along the potato: Wedge it between two cutting boards, not thick boards, but thin plastic or glass boards. The boards can hold the spud upright and in place while you make all the cuts. Which you're doing because butter. Also garlic.

INGREDIENTS	2-quart or larger air fryer	3.5-quart or larger air fryer	5.25-quart or larger air fryer
8-ounce russet potatoes	2	3	4
Brown button or Baby Bella mushrooms, very thinly sliced	4	6	8
Olive oil spray	As needed	As needed	As needed
Butter, melted and cooled	2 tablespoons	3 tablespoons	4 tablespoons (¼ cup/½ stick)
Minced garlic	2 teaspoons	1 tablespoon	1½ tablespoons
Table salt	½ teaspoon	¾ teaspoon	1 teaspoon
Finely grated Parmesan cheese	2 tablespoons (about ⅓ ounce)	3 tablespoons (about ½ ounce)	¼ cup (about ¾ ounce)
MAKES	*2 servings*	*3 servings*	*4 servings*

1. With the basket (or basket attachment) in the air fryer, heat it to 350°F (or 360°F, if that's the closest setting).

2. Cut slits down the length of each potato, about three-quarters down into the potato and spaced about ¼ inch apart. Wedge a thin mushroom slice in each slit. Generously coat the potatoes on all sides with olive oil spray.

3. When the machine is at temperature, set the potatoes mushroom side up in the basket with as much air space between them as possible. Air-fry undisturbed for 45 minutes, or tender when pricked with a fork.

4. Increase the machine's temperature to 400°F (or 390°F, if that's the closest setting). Use kitchen tongs, and perhaps a flatware fork for balance, to gently transfer the potatoes to a cutting board. Brush each evenly with butter, then sprinkle the minced garlic and salt over them. Sprinkle the cheese evenly over the potatoes.

5. Use those same tongs to gently transfer the potatoes cheese side up to the basket in one layer with some space for air flow between them. Air-fry undisturbed for 3 minutes, or until the cheese has melted and begun to brown.

continues

6. Use those same tongs to gently transfer the potatoes back to the wire rack. Cool for 5 minutes before serving.

Then...

- Drizzle the finished potatoes with **Smoky Dipping Sauce** (page 33), **Fiery Sour Cream Dip** (page 44), or **Sweet-and-Sour Ketchup Dip** (page 71).

- Add a green salad like **Summery Watercress Salad** (page 91) or **Wilted Baby Spinach Salad** (page 199) on the side and call it "dinner."

See photo in insert.

Air-Fried Potato Salad

FAST / EASY / CAN BE GLUTEN-FREE / 9 INGREDIENTS

We don't make potato salad any other way these days. So what's changed our minds? This: The machine concentrates the flavors of the potatoes, offering better flavor than boiling the spuds does. At the same time, the air fryer caramelizes the onions for a sweet roasted finish.

And if you're pressed for time, here's a simple hack: Substitute an equal weight of frozen, unseasoned hash brown cubes for the potatoes. Do not thaw the cubes. Follow the recipe as it stands but increase the cooking time in step 3 to 20 minutes.

INGREDIENTS	2-quart or larger air fryer	3.5-quart or larger air fryer	5.25-quart or larger air fryer
Yellow potatoes, such as Yukon Golds, cut into ½-inch chunks	1 pound	1⅓ pounds	1¾ pounds
Sweet white onion(s), such as Vidalia, chopped into ½-inch pieces	1 medium	1 large	2 medium
Olive oil	1½ tablespoons	1 tablespoon plus 2 teaspoons	2 tablespoons
Thinly sliced celery	⅔ cup	¾ cup	1 cup
Regular or low-fat mayonnaise (gluten-free, if a concern)	⅓ cup	6 tablespoons	½ cup
Apple cider vinegar	2 tablespoons	2½ tablespoons	3 tablespoons
Dijon mustard (gluten-free, if a concern)	1 teaspoon	1½ teaspoons	2 teaspoons
Table salt	½ teaspoon	¾ teaspoon	1 teaspoon
Ground black pepper	¼ teaspoon	Rounded ¼ teaspoon	½ teaspoon
MAKES	*3 servings*	*4 to 5 servings*	*6 to 7 servings*

1. With the basket (or basket attachment) in the air fryer, heat it to 400°F (or 390°F, if that's the closest setting).

2. Toss the potatoes, onion(s), and oil in a large bowl until the vegetables are glistening with oil.

3. When the machine is at temperature, transfer the vegetables to the basket, spreading them out into as even a layer as you can. Air-fry for 15 minutes, tossing and rearranging the vegetables every 3 minutes so that all surfaces get exposed to the air currents, until the vegetables are tender and even browned at the edges.

4. Pour the contents of the basket into a serving bowl. Cool for at least 5 minutes or up to 30 minutes. Add the celery, mayonnaise, vinegar, mustard, salt, and pepper. Stir well to coat. The potato salad can be made in advance; cover and refrigerate for up to 4 days.

Then...

- Add even more to the potato salad: diced and seeded red or green bell pepper; minced drained jarred pimientos; sliced hard-boiled eggs; finely chopped dill pickles; and/or chopped fresh leafy herbs like parsley, lovage, or cilantro.

- Serve this potato salad alongside **Barbecue-Style Chicken Wings** (page 188) or **Baby Back Ribs** (page 251).

See photo in insert.

Sweet Potato Puffs

VEGAN / 7 INGREDIENTS

These little puffs are a sweet-potato version of our **Homemade Potato Puffs** (page 332). They are indeed made with a small amount of instant mashed potato flakes, if only to give them some starch so they'll stick together as they cook.

Even so, these puffs are pretty delicate. Take care getting them into the machine's basket. It's probably easier to remove the basket and work with it on your counter (provided your counter can handle a hot basket).

Enjoy the puffs pretty soon after they're out of the air fryer. They're crunchy for a few minutes, then soggy all too quickly.

INGREDIENTS	2-quart or larger air fryer	3.5-quart or larger air fryer	5.25-quart or larger air fryer
8- to 10-ounce sweet potatoes	2	3	4
Seasoned Italian-style dried bread crumbs	1 cup	1 cup	1½ cups
All-purpose flour	2 tablespoons	3 tablespoons	¼ cup
Instant mashed potato flakes	2 tablespoons	3 tablespoons	¼ cup
Onion powder	½ teaspoon	¾ teaspoon	1 teaspoon
Table salt	½ teaspoon	¾ teaspoon	1 teaspoon
Olive oil spray	As needed	As needed	As needed
MAKES	12 puffs	18 puffs	24 puffs

1. With the basket (or basket attachment) in the air fryer, heat it to 350°F (or 360°F, if that's the closest setting).

2. Prick the sweet potatoes in four or five different places with the tines of a flatware fork (not in a line but all around the sweet potatoes).

3. When the machine is at temperature, set the sweet potatoes in the basket with as much air space between them as possible. Air-fry undisturbed for 20 minutes.

4. Use kitchen tongs to transfer the sweet potatoes to a wire rack. (They will still be firm; they are only partially cooked.) Cool for 10 to 15 minutes. Meanwhile, increase the machine's temperature to

400°F (or 390°F, if that's the closest setting). Spread the bread crumbs on a dinner plate.

5. Peel the sweet potatoes. Shred them through the large holes of a box grater into a large bowl. Stir in the flour, potato flakes, onion powder, and salt until well combined.

6. Scoop up 2 tablespoons of the sweet potato mixture. Form it into a small puff, a cylinder about like a Tater Tot. Set this cylinder in the bread crumbs. Gently roll it around to coat on all sides, even the ends. Set aside on a cutting board and continue making more puffs: 11 more for a small batch, 17 more for a medium batch, or 23 more for a large batch.

7. Generously coat the puffs with olive oil spray on all sides. Set the puffs in the basket with as much air space between them as possible. They should not be touching, but even a fraction of an inch will work well. Air-fry undisturbed for 15 minutes, or until lightly browned and crunchy.

8. Gently turn the contents of the basket out onto a wire rack. Cool the puffs for a couple of minutes before serving.

Then...

- For an air-fryer Thanksgiving, serve these puffs with **Roasted Turkey Breast** (page 200) and **Perfect Broccoli** (page 345).

- Serve the puffs warm with toothpicks and **Creamy Harissa Dip** (page 75) or **Chipotle Salsa Dip** (page 262).

Simple Roasted Sweet Potatoes

EASY / VEGAN / GLUTEN-FREE / 1 INGREDIENT

Sweet potatoes don't need a thing to come out perfectly from the air fryer. Because they are loaded with sugars, they stay moist and tender inside while the skin gets crunchy and irresistible.

One important ingredient note: This recipe is for common, North American orange sweet potatoes, not white sweet potatoes, Japanese red-skinned sweet potatoes, or purple sweet potatoes, which are higher in natural sugars and do not work well as a substitution in this 1-ingredient recipe and timing.

INGREDIENTS	2-quart or larger air fryer	3.5-quart or larger air fryer	5.25-quart or larger air fryer
10- to 12-ounce sweet potato(es)	1 or 2	2	3
MAKES	1 or 2 servings	2 servings	3 servings

1. With the basket (or basket attachment) in the air fryer, heat it to 350°F (or 360°F, if that's the closest setting).

2. Prick the sweet potato(es) in four or five different places with the tines of a flatware fork (not in a line but all around).

3. When the machine is at temperature, set the sweet potato(es) in the basket with as much air space between them as possible. Air-fry undisturbed for 45 minutes, or until soft when pricked with a fork.

4. Use kitchen tongs to transfer the sweet potato(es) to a wire rack. Cool for 5 minutes before serving.

Then...

- Serve these sweet potatoes with **Cornbread-Crusted Chicken Breasts** (page 161), **State Fair Turkey Wings** (page 199), **Barbecue-Style London Broil** (page 214), **Crunchy Fried Pork Loin Chops** (page 236), or **Fried Spam** (page 262).

- Butter and salt may be the most common toppers. But we actually prefer Thai sweet chili sauce (with or without some butter) or **Pineapple Barbecue Sauce** (page 174).

Perfect Asparagus

FAST / EASY / VEGAN / GLUTEN-FREE / 4 INGREDIENTS

Asparagus spears work beautifully in the air fryer provided you 1) use very thin spears that can cook quickly without drying out and 2) oil the spears first to help protect them. Work a bit to get the spears fully coated. Otherwise, parts of the stalk can seem fibrous after air-frying.

INGREDIENTS	2-quart or larger air fryer	3.5-quart or larger air fryer	5.25-quart or larger air fryer
Very thin asparagus spears	¾ pound	1 pound	1½ pounds
Olive oil	1½ tablespoons	2 tablespoons	3 tablespoons
Coarse sea salt or kosher salt	½ teaspoon	1 teaspoon	1½ teaspoons
Finely grated lemon zest	½ teaspoon	¾ teaspoon	1 teaspoon
MAKES	2 to 3 servings	3 to 4 servings	5 to 6 servings

1. With the basket (or basket attachment) in the air fryer, heat it to 400°F (or 390°F, if that's the closest setting).

2. Trim just enough off the bottom of the asparagus spears so they'll fit in the basket. Put the spears on a large plate and drizzle them with some of the olive oil. Turn them over and drizzle more olive oil, working to get all the spears coated.

3. When the machine is at temperature, place the spears in one direction in the basket. They may be touching. Air-fry for 10 minutes, tossing and rearranging the spears twice, until tender.

4. Dump the contents of the basket on a serving platter. Spread out the spears. Sprinkle them with the salt and lemon zest while still warm. Serve at once.

Then...

- Although you used olive oil as a cooking medium, you can still put a pat or two of butter on the spears before you add the salt and lemon zest.

- Along with the salt and lemon zest, sprinkle the warm spears with finely grated Parmesan cheese, toasted sliced almonds, and/or red pepper flakes.

- For an easy dinner, top these spears with fried eggs, garnished with red pepper flakes.

See photo in insert.

Honey-Roasted Parsnips

EASY / VEGETARIAN / GLUTEN-FREE / 5 INGREDIENTS

Because of the way the air fryer works, you can roast parsnips whole—or in large pieces if the parsnips exceed certain dimensions, as you'll see. We brush the parsnips with a glaze for the last three minutes, balancing their earthy, savory flavor with a bit of honey. Use any type of honey you prefer, although a darker one, especially a tree or grain honey like eucalyptus, oak, or even buckwheat will give the vegetable a more sophisticated edge.

INGREDIENTS	2-quart or larger air fryer	3.5-quart or larger air fryer	5.25-quart or larger air fryer
Medium parsnips, peeled	1 pound	1½ pounds	2 pounds
Olive oil spray	As needed	As needed	As needed
Honey	2 teaspoons	1 tablespoon	1½ tablespoons
Water	1 teaspoon	1½ teaspoons	2 teaspoons
Table salt	¼ teaspoon	Rounded ¼ teaspoon	½ teaspoon
MAKES	2 to 3 servings	3 to 4 servings	5 to 6 servings

1. With the basket (or basket attachment) in the air fryer, heat it to 350°F (or 360°F, if that's the closest setting).

2. If the thick end of a parsnip is more than ½ inch in diameter, cut the parsnip just below where it swells to its large end, then slice the large section in half lengthwise. If the parsnips are larger than the basket (or basket attachment), trim off the thin end so the parsnips will fit. Generously coat the parsnips on all sides with olive oil spray.

3. When the machine is at temperature, set the parsnips in the basket with as much air space between them as possible. Air-fry undisturbed for 20 minutes.

4. Whisk the honey, water, and salt in a small bowl until smooth. Brush this mixture over the parsnips. Air-fry undisturbed for 3 minutes more, or until the glaze is lightly browned.

5. Use kitchen tongs to transfer the parsnips to a wire rack or a serving platter. Cool for a couple of minutes before serving.

Then...

- Here's the perfect accompaniment to **Rotisserie-Style Air-Roasted Chicken** (page 191). Prepare the parsnips first, then leave them at room temperature while the chicken cooks. Pop them back in the machine for 2 minutes at 350°F (or 360°F, if the closest setting) to warm them up.

- Cool the parsnips to room temperature, then thinly slice them and store them in a covered container in the fridge for up to 3 days to add to your next chicken salad or to add to **Chicken Club Sandwiches** (page 116).

Blistered Green Beans

FAST / EASY / VEGAN / GLUTEN-FREE / 7 INGREDIENTS

Here's a hybrid recipe: a high-heat way to cook green beans, familiar from Chinese-American stir-fries, but with a decidedly European flavor, given the pine nuts and balsamic vinegar. The blistered beans take on a range of flavors: sweet, but also savory, a little bitter, and quite sophisticated. Since they endure quite a bit of heat, it's best to remove the thin little "tail" on each bean, since it can easily burn.

For even more flavor, toast the pine nuts in a dry nonstick skillet set over medium heat for a few minutes, stirring often, until lightly browned and aromatic.

INGREDIENTS	2-quart or larger air fryer	3.5-quart or larger air fryer	5.25-quart or larger air fryer
Green beans, trimmed on both ends	½ pound	¾ pound	1 pound
Olive oil	1 tablespoon	1½ tablespoons	2 tablespoons
Pine nuts	2 tablespoons	3 tablespoons	¼ cup
Balsamic vinegar	1 tablespoon	1½ tablespoons	2 tablespoons
Minced garlic	1 teaspoon	1½ teaspoons	2 teaspoons
Table salt	½ teaspoon	¾ teaspoon	1 teaspoon
Ground black pepper	½ teaspoon	¾ teaspoon	1 teaspoon
MAKES	2 to 3 servings	3 to 4 servings	5 to 6 servings

1. With the basket (or basket attachment) in the air fryer, heat it to 400°F (or 390°F, if that's the closest setting).

2. Toss the green beans and oil in a large bowl until all the green beans are glistening.

3. When the machine is at temperature, pile the green beans into the basket. Air-fry for 10 minutes, tossing often to rearrange the green beans in the basket, or until blistered and tender.

4. Dump the contents of the basket into a serving bowl. Add the pine nuts, vinegar, garlic, salt, and pepper. Toss well to coat and combine. Serve warm or at room temperature.

Then...

- Serve these green beans with **Crunchy Vinegar-and-Salt Chicken Breasts** (page 157), **Glazed Meatloaf** (page 227), **Pesto-Rubbed Veal Chops** (page 232), or **Fried Scallops** (page 303).

- Or consider this dish your go-to for a Thanksgiving side dish.

Perfect Broccoli

FAST / EASY / VEGAN / GLUTEN-FREE / 3 INGREDIENTS

This recipe will yield still-crunchy broccoli, concentrated in its flavors but very straightforward. If you prefer softer broccoli, air-fry the florets for an additional 2 to 3 minutes.

Notice that this recipe only calls for broccoli florets, not the stems. These take much longer to cook and tend to burn in the convection currents before they're tender, even when they've been sliced into smaller segments.

INGREDIENTS	2-quart or larger air fryer	3.5-quart or larger air fryer	5.25-quart or larger air fryer
1- to 1½-inch fresh broccoli florets (*not* frozen)	3 cups (about 1 pound)	5 cups (about 1 pound 10 ounces)	7 cups (about 2¼ pounds)
Olive oil spray	As needed	As needed	As needed
Table salt	½ teaspoon	¾ teaspoon	1 teaspoon
MAKES	*2 or 3 servings*	*4 or 5 servings*	*6 or 7 servings*

1. With the basket (or basket attachment) in the air fryer, heat it to 375°F (or 370°F or 360°F, if one of these is the closest setting).

2. Put the broccoli florets in a big bowl, coat them generously with olive oil spray, then toss to coat all surfaces, even down into the crannies, spraying them in a couple of times more. Sprinkle the salt on top and toss again.

3. When the machine is at temperature, pour the florets into the basket. Air-fry for 10 minutes, tossing and rearranging the pieces twice so that all the covered or touching bits are eventually exposed to the air currents, until lightly browned but still crunchy. (If the machine is at 360°F, you may have to add 1 or 2 minutes to the cooking time.)

4. Pour the florets into a serving bowl. Cool for a minute or two, then serve hot.

Then...

- Toss the cooked florets with a little lemon juice.
- Or drizzle them with balsamic vinegar.
- Or melted butter.
- Or a nut oil, particularly toasted pecan oil.

Roasted Broccoli and Red Bean Salad

FAST / EASY / VEGAN / GLUTEN-FREE / 8 INGREDIENTS

This easy salad is a great side dish for almost any barbecue. By chopping the "roasted" broccoli florets, you'll get more varied ingredients in every bite (instead of a bite of a floret, then a bite of everything else).

Mincing the onion is key here. It should almost blend into the dressing—for which there's no oil. The broccoli florets will carry some from the air fryer forward into the salad. Any more will make it too heavy.

INGREDIENTS	2-quart or larger air fryer	3.5-quart or larger air fryer	5.25-quart or larger air fryer
1- to 1½-inch fresh broccoli florets (*not* frozen)	2 cups (about 10 ounces)	3 cups (about 1 pound)	4 cups (about 1¼ pounds)
Olive oil spray	1 tablespoon	1½ tablespoons	2 tablespoons
Canned red kidney beans, drained and rinsed	¾ cup	1¼ cups	1¾ cups (one 15-ounce can)
Minced yellow or white onion	2 tablespoons	3 tablespoons	¼ cup
Red wine vinegar	1½ tablespoons	2 tablespoons plus 1 teaspoon	3 tablespoons
Dried oregano	½ teaspoon	¾ teaspoon	1 teaspoon
Table salt	¼ teaspoon	Rounded ¼ teaspoon	½ teaspoon
Ground black pepper	¼ teaspoon	Rounded ¼ teaspoon	½ teaspoon
MAKES	2 or 3 servings	3 or 4 servings	5 or 6 servings

1. With the basket (or basket attachment) in the air fryer, heat it to 375°F (or 370°F or 360°F, if one of these is the closest setting).

2. Put the broccoli florets in a big bowl, coat them generously with olive oil spray, then toss to coat all surfaces, even down into the crannies, spraying them a couple of times more.

3. Pour the florets into the basket, spreading them into as close to one layer as you can. Air-fry for 12 minutes, tossing and rearranging the florets twice so that any touching or covered parts are eventually exposed to the air currents, until light browned but still a bit firm. (If the machine is at 360°F, you may need to add 1 or 2 minutes to the cooking time.)

4. Dump the contents of the basket onto a large cutting board. Cool for a minute or two, then chop the florets into small bits. Scrape these into a bowl and add the kidney beans, onion, vinegar, oregano, salt, and pepper. Toss well and serve warm or at room temperature.

Then...

- Add any of the following to the salad: thinly sliced celery, grated carrots, diced zucchini, or finely grated lemon zest.

Perfect Broccolini

FAST / EASY / VEGAN / GLUTEN-FREE / 3 INGREDIENTS

Broccolini ends up with two textures in an air fryer: soft flowery ends and al dente, slightly crunchy stems. In other words, it's got the best of both worlds in one vegetable. The flavor is mild if moderately herbaceous, as well as a little sweet with a few bitter notes.

INGREDIENTS	2-quart or larger air fryer	3.5-quart or larger air fryer	5.25-quart or larger air fryer
Broccolini	½ pound	1 pound	1½ pounds
Olive oil spray	As needed	As needed	As needed
Coarse sea salt or kosher salt	As needed	As needed	As needed
MAKES	2 or 3 servings	4 or 5 servings	6 or 7 servings

1. With the basket (or basket attachment) in the air fryer, heat it to 375°F (or 370°F or 360°F, if one of these is the closest setting).

2. Place the broccolini on a cutting board. Generously coat it with olive oil spray, turning the vegetables and rearranging them before spraying a couple of times more, to make sure everything's well coated, even the flowery bits in their heads.

3. When the machine is at temperature, pile the broccolini in the basket, spreading it into as close to one layer as you can. Air-fry for 5 minutes, tossing once to get any covered or touching parts exposed to the air currents, until the leaves begin to get brown and even crisp. Watch carefully and use this visual cue to know the moment to stop the cooking.

4. Transfer the broccolini to a platter. Spread out the pieces and sprinkle them with salt to taste.

Then...

- Drizzle the broccolini with **Buttermilk Dressing** (page 138) or **Blue Cheese Dressing** (page 172).

Moroccan-Spiced Carrots

FAST / EASY / VEGETARIAN / GLUTEN-FREE / 9 INGREDIENTS

No, we don't mean a dish served in Morocco. Rather, we mean a dish inspired by the country's spice blends.

The recipe requires you to use so-called baby carrots—not small, immature carrots (as you might find at a farmers' market) but the "baby" carrots that come in bags at the supermarket, the ones that are actually larger carrots cut down to a size just right for kids' hands.

Keep a close watch on the basket as the carrots cook. They should retain a bit of their natural crunch and not be soft. They should also be golden brown, not burned.

INGREDIENTS	2-quart or larger air fryer	3.5-quart or larger air fryer	5.25-quart or larger air fryer
Baby carrots	¾ pound	1¼ pounds	2 pounds
Butter, melted and cooled	1 tablespoon	2 tablespoons	3 tablespoons
Mild smoked paprika	½ teaspoon	1 teaspoon	1¼ teaspoons
Ground cumin	½ teaspoon	1 teaspoon	1¼ teaspoons
Ground coriander	½ teaspoon	¾ teaspoon	1 teaspoon
Ground dried ginger	½ teaspoon	¾ teaspoon	1 teaspoon
Ground cinnamon	¼ teaspoon	Rounded ¼ teaspoon	½ teaspoon
Table salt	¼ teaspoon	½ teaspoon	1 teaspoon
Ground black pepper	¼ teaspoon	Rounded ¼ teaspoon	½ teaspoon
MAKES	2 or 3 servings	4 or 5 servings	6 or 7 servings

1. With the basket (or basket attachment) in the air fryer, heat it to 400°F (or 390°F, if that's the closest setting).

2. Toss the carrots, melted butter, smoked paprika, cumin, coriander, ginger, cinnamon, salt, and pepper in a large bowl until the carrots are evenly and thoroughly coated.

3. When the machine is at temperature, scrape the carrots into the basket, spreading them into as close to one layer as you can. Air-fry for 30 minutes, tossing and rearranging the carrots every 8 minutes (that is, three times), until crisp-tender and lightly browned in spots.

4. Pour the contents of the basket into a serving bowl or platter. Cool for a couple of minutes, then serve warm or at room temperature.

Then...

- For a great pasta salad, slice the warm carrots into rounds and toss them with cooked and drained penne or ziti, as well as chopped walnuts, chopped raisins, and thinly sliced celery. Dress the salad with a drizzle of olive oil and balsamic vinegar. Add table salt and ground black pepper to taste.

Roasted Yellow Squash and Onions

FAST / EASY / VEGAN / GLUTEN-FREE / 5 OR 6 INGREDIENTS

Steamed squash and onions are a summertime treat, a sweet side dish to go with just about anything off the grill. But steaming the vegetables causes them to become soggy and lackluster. "Roasting" them in the air fryer makes them super sweet while they retain some of their fresh texture.

INGREDIENTS	2-quart or larger air fryer	3.5-quart or larger air fryer	5.25-quart or larger air fryer
Yellow or summer crookneck squash, cut into ½-inch-thick rounds	1 small (6-inch) squash	1 medium (8-inch) squash	2 small (6-inch) squashes
Yellow or white onion, roughly chopped	1 cup (1 medium onion)	1½ cups (1 large onion)	2 cups (2 medium onions)
Table salt	½ teaspoon	¾ teaspoon	1 teaspoon
Ground cumin (optional)	¼ teaspoon	Rounded ¼ teaspoon	½ teaspoon
Olive oil spray	As needed	As needed	As needed
Lemon or lime juice	1 tablespoon	1½ tablespoons	2 tablespoons
MAKES	*2 servings*	*3 servings*	*4 servings*

1. With the basket (or basket attachment) in the air fryer, heat it to 375°F (or 370°F or 360°F, if one of these is the closest setting).

2. Toss the squash rounds, onion, salt, and cumin (if using) in a large bowl. Lightly coat the vegetables with olive oil spray, toss again, spray again, and keep at it until the vegetables are evenly coated.

3. When the machine is at temperature, scrape the contents of the bowl into the basket, spreading the vegetables out into as close to one layer as you can. Air-fry for 20 minutes, tossing once very gently, until the squash and onions are soft, even a little browned at the edges.

4. Pour the contents of the basket into a serving bowl, add the lemon or lime juice, and toss gently but well to coat. Serve warm or at room temperature.

Then...

- Crumble soft goat cheese into the dish before serving.

- Or drizzle the dish with melted butter before serving.

- Or sprinkle toasted fresh bread crumbs all over the top of the dish before serving.

Crispy, Cheesy Leeks

VEGETARIAN / CAN BE GLUTEN-FREE / 5 INGREDIENTS

Leeks sweeten as they cook, losing some of their natural pungency and becoming quite mellow with surprisingly earthy notes. These are topped with a cheese-laced bread-crumb topping to give them a little crunch after they have softened.

INGREDIENTS	2-quart or larger air fryer	3.5-quart or larger air fryer	5.25-quart or larger air fryer
Medium leek(s), about 9 ounces each	1	2	3
Olive oil spray	As needed	As needed	As needed
Seasoned Italian-style dried bread crumbs (gluten-free, if a concern)	2 tablespoons	¼ cup	6 tablespoons
Finely grated Parmesan cheese	2 tablespoons (about ⅓ ounce)	¼ cup (about ¾ ounce)	6 tablespoons (a little more than 1 ounce)
Olive oil	1 tablespoon	2 tablespoons	3 tablespoons
MAKES	2 servings	4 servings	6 servings

1. With the basket (or basket attachment) in the air fryer, heat it to 350°F (or 360°F, if that's the closest setting).

2. Trim off the root end of the leek(s) as well as the dark green top(s), leaving about a 5-inch usable section. Split the leek section(s) in half lengthwise. Set the leek halves cut side up on your work surface. Pull out and remove in one piece the semicircles that make up the inner structure of the leek, about halfway down. Set the removed "inside" next to the outer leek "shells" on your cutting board. Generously coat them all on all sides (particularly the "bottoms") with olive oil spray.

3. Set the leeks and their insides cut side up in the basket with as much air space between them as possible. Air-fry undisturbed for 12 minutes.

4. Meanwhile, mix the bread crumbs, cheese, and olive oil in a small bowl until well combined.

5. After 12 minutes in the air fryer, sprinkle this mixture inside the leek shells and on top of the leek insides. Increase the machine's temperature to 375°F (or 380°F or 390°F, if one of these is the closest setting). Air-fry undisturbed for 3 minutes, or until the topping is lightly browned.

6. Use a nonstick-safe spatula to transfer the leeks to a serving platter. Cool for a few minutes before serving warm.

Then...

- Sprinkle the leeks with crumbled blue cheese, minced chives, and/or finely chopped walnuts.

- Serve them with **Steakhouse Filets Mignons** (page 209), **Garlic and Oregano Lamb Chops** (page 267), or **Salmon Croquettes** (page 288).

Roasted Fennel Salad

FAST / EASY / VEGAN / GLUTEN-FREE / 5 INGREDIENTS

There's no need for oil in this tasty, summery side salad because the fennel has been coated in olive oil before it's roasted, thereby giving the ensuing salad all the oil it needs.

To trim a fennel bulb, slice off about ¼ inch from the bottom where it may have dried out in storage. Also, slice off any green stalks and the fronds attached to them. If you've got extra bits from a fennel bulb, even the green stalks, save these in a sealed bag in the freezer for up to 4 months, adding them to vegetable, beef, or chicken soups for a rich, aromatic flavor.

INGREDIENTS	2-quart or larger air fryer	3.5-quart or larger air fryer	5.25-quart or larger air fryer
Trimmed fennel (see the headnote), roughly chopped	2 cups (about ½ pound)	3 cups (about ¾ pound)	4 cups (about 1 pound)
Olive oil	1 tablespoon	1½ tablespoons	2 tablespoons
Table salt	¼ teaspoon	Rounded ¼ teaspoon	½ teaspoon
Ground black pepper	¼ teaspoon	Rounded ¼ teaspoon	½ teaspoon
White balsamic vinegar (see page 203)	1 tablespoon	1½ tablespoons	2 tablespoons
MAKES	2 servings	3 servings	4 servings

1. With the basket (or basket attachment) in the air fryer, heat it to 400°F (or 390°F, if that's the closest setting).

2. Toss the fennel, olive oil, salt, and pepper in a large bowl until the fennel is well coated in the oil.

3. When the machine is at temperature, pour the fennel into the basket, spreading it out into as close to one layer as possible. Air-fry for 20 minutes, tossing and rearranging the fennel pieces twice so that any covered or touching parts get exposed to the air currents, until golden at the edges and softened.

4. Pour the fennel into a serving bowl. Add the vinegar while hot. Toss well, then cool a couple of minutes before serving. Or serve at room temperature.

Then...

- Add chopped tomatoes or even **Blistered Tomatoes** (page 310) to the salad.

- And/or add bits of crumbled **Bacon Candy** (page 41) to the salad.

- Or pile this salad onto a hamburger with lots of Dijon mustard spread on the bun.

See photo in insert.

Charred Radicchio Salad

FAST / EASY / VEGAN / GLUTEN-FREE / 5 INGREDIENTS

Here's a new, modern take on a classic Italian salad: a *warm*, comforting side dish made from this bitter vegetable. Charring radicchio adds lots of sweet notes to its sophisticated flavor. But watch the heads carefully. You want *some* blackened bits but not a giant patch of black across the leaves.

INGREDIENTS	2-quart or larger air fryer	3.5-quart or larger air fryer	5.25-quart or larger air fryer
Small 5- to 6-ounce radicchio head(s)	1	2	3
Olive oil	1½ tablespoons	3 tablespoons	¼ cup
Table salt	¼ teaspoon	½ teaspoon	Rounded ½ teaspoon
Balsamic vinegar	1 tablespoon	2 tablespoons	3 tablespoons
Red pepper flakes	Up to ⅛ teaspoon	Up to ¼ teaspoon	Up to ½ teaspoon
MAKES	2 servings	4 servings	6 servings

1. With the basket (or basket attachment) in the air fryer, heat it to 375°F (or 370°F or 360°F, if one of these is the closest setting).

2. Cut the radicchio head(s) into quarters through the stem end. Brush the oil over the heads, particularly getting it between the leaves along the cut sides. Sprinkle the radicchio quarters with the salt.

3. When the machine is at temperature, set the quarters cut sides up in the basket with as much air space between them as possible. They should not touch. Air-fry undisturbed for 4 or 5 minutes, watching carefully because they burn quickly, until blackened in bits and soft.

4. Use a nonstick-safe spatula to transfer the quarters to a cutting board. Cool for a minute or two, then cut out the thick stems inside the heads. Discard these tough bits and chop the remaining heads into bite-size bits. Scrape them into a bowl. Add the vinegar and red pepper flakes. Toss well and serve warm.

Then...

- Mix crumbled canned Italian tuna into this salad along with thinly sliced celery and sliced sun-dried tomatoes or **Tomato Candy** (page 311) for a quick lunch or dinner.

- Use this salad as a substitute for sauerkraut on hot dogs or in **Reuben Sandwiches** (page 126).

Roasted Belgian Endive with Pistachios and Lemon

FAST / EASY / VEGAN / GLUTEN-FREE / 5 INGREDIENTS

This side dish is fit for a dinner party—or maybe a holiday meal. The bittersweet Belgian endive mellows a bit in the air fryer. But because we can't cook the endive too long (it will burn and get really bitter), we add crunch with finely chopped pistachios.

Look for firm, tight heads of Belgian endive without squishy bits or any browning on the leaves.

For a holiday meal, make a platter of these endive spears, working in batches in the air fryer and serving them later at room temperature. They'll keep well for 2 or 3 hours, uncovered on their platter.

INGREDIENTS	2-quart or larger air fryer	3.5-quart or larger air fryer	5.25-quart or larger air fryer
Medium 3-ounce Belgian endive head(s)	1	2	3
Olive oil	1 tablespoon	2 tablespoons	3 tablespoons
Table salt	¼ teaspoon	½ teaspoon	Rounded ½ teaspoon
Finely chopped unsalted shelled pistachios	2 tablespoons	¼ cup	6 tablespoons
Lemon juice	Up to 1 teaspoon	Up to 2 teaspoons	Up to 1 tablespoon
MAKES	*1 serving*	*2 servings*	*3 servings*

1. With the basket (or basket attachment) in the air fryer, heat it to 325°F (or 330°F, if that's the closest setting).

2. Trim the Belgian endive head(s), removing the little bit of dried-out stem end but keeping the leaves intact. Quarter the head(s) through the stem (which will hold the leaves intact). Brush the endive quarters with oil, getting it down between the leaves. Sprinkle the quarters with salt.

3. When the machine is at temperature, set the endive quarters cut sides up in the basket with as much air space between them as possible. They should not touch. Air-fry undisturbed for 7 minutes, or until lightly browned along the edges.

4. Use kitchen tongs to transfer the endive quarters to serving plates or a platter. Sprinkle with the pistachios and lemon juice. Serve warm or at room temperature.

Then...

- Crumble blue cheese and/or finely chopped cooked bacon onto the endive with the pistachios. Omit the lemon juice and sprinkle with white balsamic vinegar (see page 203).

- Serve these spears with **Perfect Strip Steaks** (page 208), **Pretzel-Coated Pork Tenderloin** (page 246), **Crispy Lamb Shoulder Chops** (page 268), or **Butternut Squash–Wrapped Halibut Fillets** (page 283).

Roasted Eggplant Halves with Herbed Ricotta

VEGETARIAN / GLUTEN-FREE / 8 INGREDIENTS

You'll need quite small eggplants to make this dish. Larger eggplants won't fit in one layer and they'll take too long to get tender, burning (and turning bitter) before they're done.

Don't use round small eggplants but rather elongated eggplants, of either the Italian varietal or the Japanese. Make sure the vegetables are fairly "straight," not crooked, so they'll lie flat in the air fryer.

INGREDIENTS	2-quart or larger air fryer	3.5-quart or larger air fryer	5.25-quart or larger air fryer
5- to 6-ounce small eggplants, stemmed	2	3	4
Olive oil spray	As needed	As needed	As needed
Table salt	¼ teaspoon	Rounded ¼ teaspoon	½ teaspoon
Ground black pepper	¼ teaspoon	Rounded ¼ teaspoon	½ teaspoon
Regular or low-fat ricotta	⅓ cup	½ cup	⅔ cup
Minced fresh basil leaves	1 tablespoon	1½ tablespoons	2 tablespoons
Minced fresh oregano leaves	1 teaspoon	1¼ teaspoons	1½ teaspoons
Honey	As needed	As needed	As needed
MAKES	2 or 4 servings	3 or 6 servings	4 or 8 servings

1. With the basket (or basket attachment) in the air fryer, heat it to 325°F (or 330°F, if that's the closest setting).

2. Cut the eggplants in half lengthwise. Set them cut side up on your work surface. Using the tip of a paring knife, make a series of slits about three-quarters down into the flesh of each eggplant half; work at a 45-degree angle to the (former) stem across the vegetable and make the slits about ½ inch apart. Make a second set of equidistant slits at a 90-degree angle to the first slits, thus creating a crosshatch pattern in the vegetable.

3. Generously coat the cut sides of the eggplants with olive oil spray. Sprinkle the salt and pepper over the cut surfaces.

4. Set the eggplant halves cut side up in the basket with as much air space between them as possible. Air-fry undisturbed for 20 minutes, or until soft and golden.

5. Use kitchen tongs to gently transfer the eggplant halves to serving plates or a platter. Cool for 5 minutes.

6. Whisk the ricotta, basil, and oregano in a small bowl until well combined. Top the eggplant halves with this mixture. Drizzle the halves with honey to taste before serving warm.

Then...

- Add red pepper flakes to taste to the ricotta mixture.

- Drizzle sriracha over the eggplant halves along with the honey.

- Serve these eggplant halves as part of a mezze dinner with **Crunchy Falafel Balls** (page 146),

served with the **Tahini Sauce** we recommend (page 147); **Muhamarra** (page 25) with **Pita Chips** (page 24); and **Roasted Fennel Salad** (page 351); and **Roasted Pears** (page 404) for dessert.

See photo in insert.

Fried Eggplant Slices

FAST / VEGETARIAN / 5 INGREDIENTS

Rather than breading eggplant slices, we advocate for "frying" them in pulverized saltines. The crackers add lots of salt to the very crisp coating. Just don't make the coating too thick. A thinner layer of crust is better than too much coating, which would mask the fresh taste of the vegetable underneath.

INGREDIENTS	2-quart or larger air fryer	3.5-quart or larger air fryer	5.25-quart or larger air fryer
Saltine crackers	1 sleeve (about 40 saltines)	1½ sleeves (about 60 saltines)	2 sleeves (about 80 saltines)
Cornstarch	½ cup	¾ cup	1 cup
Large egg(s), well beaten	1	2	2
Eggplant, stemmed, peeled, and cut into ¼-inch-thick rounds	1 small (about ½ pound)	1 medium (about ¾ pound)	1 large (about 1 pound)
Olive oil spray	As needed	As needed	As needed
MAKES	*2 servings*	*3 servings*	*4 servings*

1. With the basket (or basket attachment) in the air fryer, heat it to 400°F (or 390°F, if that's the closest setting). Also, position the rack in the center of the oven and heat the oven to 175°F.

2. Grind the saltines, in batches if necessary, in a food processor, pulsing the machine and rearranging the saltine pieces every few pulses. Or pulverize the saltines in a large, heavy zip-closed plastic bag with the bottom of a heavy saucepan. In either case, you want small bits of saltines, not just crumbs.

3. Set up and fill three shallow soup plates or small pie plates on your counter: one for the cornstarch, one for the beaten egg(s), and one for the pulverized saltines.

continues

4. Set an eggplant slice in the cornstarch and turn it to coat on both sides. Use a brush to lightly remove any excess. Dip it into the beaten egg(s) and turn to coat both sides. Let any excess egg slip back into the rest, then set the slice in the saltines. Turn several times, pressing gently to coat both sides evenly but not heavily. Coat both sides of the slice with olive oil spray and set it aside. Continue dipping and coating the remaining slices.

5. Set one, two, or maybe three slices in the basket. There should be at least ½ inch between them for proper air flow. Air-fry undisturbed for 12 minutes, or until crisp and browned.

6. Use a nonstick-safe spatula to transfer the slice(s) to a large baking sheet. Slip it into the oven to keep the slices warm as you air-fry more batches, as needed, always transferring the slices to the baking sheet to stay warm.

Then...

- Top the slices with warmed marinara sauce.

- Or for a simple eggplant Parmesan, lay them in a baking dish, cover with a thin layer of marinara sauce, add lots of shredded semi-firm mozzarella, and bake in a 350°F oven until the cheese is melted and gooey.

- Or go simpler and serve the slices with **Sage Pesto** (page 111); purchased jarred caponata or **Caponata Salsa** (page 82); or warmed ratatouille on top. (We have a recipe for a very fast microwave ratatouille in *The Kitchen Shortcut Bible*.)

Fried Corn on the Cob

FAST / EASY / VEGETARIAN / CAN BE GLUTEN-FREE / 6 INGREDIENTS

Fried corn on the cob is a state fair staple: a crunchy coating over the warmed, sweet corn. Admittedly, it's also a greasy mess—except when you use an air fryer!

Frozen corn on the cob pieces come in just about exactly the size you'll need for this recipe. Thaw as many as you need on the counter for 30 minutes, then have at it!

If you're using fresh corn on the cob, look for thick, round ears that can be cut into even 4-inch segments. You'll want to discard the tapering ends or freeze them to add to vegetable soups down the road.

Increase the flavor of this dish by stirring up to 2 tablespoons finely grated Parmesan cheese into the bread crumbs. Or add dried herbs (up to 1 teaspoon each) like dried thyme and/or dried oregano.

INGREDIENTS	2-quart or larger air fryer	3.5-quart or larger air fryer	5.25-quart or larger air fryer
Regular or low-fat mayonnaise (*not* fat-free; gluten-free, if a concern)	1 tablespoon	1½ tablespoons	2 tablespoons
Minced garlic	1 teaspoon	1½ teaspoons	2 teaspoons
Table salt	¼ teaspoon	Rounded ¼ teaspoon	½ teaspoon
Plain panko bread crumbs (gluten-free, if a concern)	½ cup	¾ cup	1 cup
4-inch lengths husked and de-silked corn on the cob	2	3	4
Vegetable oil spray	As needed	As needed	As needed
MAKES	*1 or 2 servings*	*2 or 3 servings*	*2 or 4 servings*

1. With the basket (or basket attachment) in the air fryer, heat it to 400°F (or 390°F, if that's the closest setting).

2. Stir the mayonnaise, garlic, and salt in a small bowl until well combined. Spread the panko on a dinner plate.

3. Brush the mayonnaise mixture over the kernels of a piece of corn on the cob. Set the corn in the bread crumbs, then roll, pressing gently, to coat it. Lightly coat with vegetable oil spray. Set it aside, then coat the remaining piece(s) of corn in the same way.

4. Set the coated corn on the cob in the basket with as much air space between the pieces as possible. Air-fry undisturbed for 10 minutes, or until brown and crisp along the coating.

5. Use kitchen tongs to *gently* transfer the pieces of corn to a wire rack. Cool for 5 minutes before serving.

Then...

- Drizzle the warm corn with sriracha.

- Or serve the pieces with **Sweet-and-Sour Ketchup Dip** (page 71), **Ranch Dip** (page 293), or even **Rémoulade Sauce** (page 291).

- Seems like this side is a must with **Inside-Out Cheeseburgers** (page 132).

Mexican-Style Roasted Corn

FAST / EASY / VEGETARIAN / GLUTEN-FREE / 8 INGREDIENTS

This side dish is perfect for one offering among several on a buffet. Corn on the cob is air-fried with butter and spices, then garnished with cilantro leaves and crumbled cheese. If you're going to put this out on a platter for presentation, be generous with the garnishes!

One note: The pieces of corn on the cob must be cold. Set them in the fridge for at least 4 hours or overnight. When they're cold, the butter will partially solidify and stick to them.

Queso fresco is a Mexican cheese sometimes made from cow's milk, sometimes from a combination of cow's and goat's milk. It has a fairly mild flavor, a little salty-sour kick, and a smooth, velvety texture despite the fact that it's dry enough to crumble. If you can't track it down, substitute grated Parmesan cheese.

INGREDIENTS	2-quart or larger air fryer	3.5-quart or larger air fryer	5.25-quart or larger air fryer
Butter, melted and cooled	2 tablespoons	3 tablespoons	4 tablespoons (¼ cup/½ stick)
Minced garlic	1 teaspoon	2 teaspoons	1 tablespoon
Ground cumin	½ teaspoon	¾ teaspoon	1 teaspoon
Red pepper flakes	Up to ½ teaspoon	Up to ¾ teaspoon	Up to 1 teaspoon
Table salt	¼ teaspoon	Rounded ¼ teaspoon	½ teaspoon
Cold 4-inch lengths husked and de-silked corn on the cob	2	3	4
Minced fresh cilantro leaves	As needed	As needed	As needed
Crumbled queso fresco	As needed	As needed	As needed
MAKES	*2 servings*	*3 servings*	*4 servings*

1. With the basket (or basket attachment) in the air fryer, heat it to 400°F (or 390°F, if that's the closest setting).

2. Mix the melted butter, garlic, cumin, red pepper flakes, and salt in a large zip-closed plastic bag. Add the cold corn pieces, seal the bag, and massage the butter mixture into the surface of the corn.

3. When the machine is at temperature, take the pieces of corn out of the plastic bag and put them in the basket with as much air space between the pieces as possible. Air-fry undisturbed for 14 minutes, until golden brown and maybe even charred in a few small spots.

4. Use kitchen tongs to gently transfer the pieces of corn to a serving platter. Sprinkle each piece with the cilantro and queso fresco. Serve warm.

Then...

- Serve these with **Tamale-Style Chicken Breasts** (page 158), **Easy Carnitas** (page 256), or **Tex-Mex Fish Tacos** (page 276).

- Drizzle the ears with a hot red pepper sauce (gluten-free, if a concern), particularly the chipotle version of Cholula.

See photo in insert.

Roasted Corn Salad

EASY / VEGETARIAN / GLUTEN-FREE / 12 INGREDIENTS

By roasting corn in an air fryer, the kernels get a little charred, a nice contrast to their naturally sweet flavor. We then turn them into a fairly simple salad with the surprising combo of honey and olive oil.

INGREDIENTS	2-quart or larger air fryer	3.5-quart or larger air fryer	5.25-quart or larger air fryer
4-inch lengths husked and de-silked corn on the cob	2	3	4
Olive oil spray	As needed	As needed	As needed
Packed baby arugula leaves	¾ cup	1 cup	1⅓ cups
Cherry tomatoes, halved	8	12	16
Medium scallion(s), trimmed and thinly sliced	1 or 2	Up to 3	Up to 4
Lemon juice	1½ tablespoons	2 tablespoons	3 tablespoons
Olive oil	2 teaspoons	1 tablespoon	1½ tablespoons
Honey	1 teaspoon	1½ teaspoons	2 teaspoons
Mild paprika	¼ teaspoon	Rounded ¼ teaspoon	½ teaspoon
Dried oregano	¼ teaspoon	Rounded ¼ teaspoon	½ teaspoon
Table salt	¼ teaspoon, plus more to taste	Rounded ¼ teaspoon, plus more to taste	½ teaspoon, plus more to taste
Ground black pepper	¼ teaspoon	Rounded ¼ teaspoon	½ teaspoon
MAKES	2 or 3 servings	3 or 4 servings	5 or 6 servings

1. With the basket (or basket attachment) in the air fryer, heat it to 400°F (or 390°F, if that's the closest setting).

2. When the machine is at temperature, lightly coat the pieces of corn on the cob with olive oil spray. Set the pieces of corn in the basket with as much air space between them as possible. Air-fry undisturbed for 15 minutes, or until the corn is charred in a few spots.

3. Use kitchen tongs to transfer the corn to a wire rack. Cool for 15 minutes.

4. Cut the kernels off the ears by cutting the fat end off each piece so it will stand up straight on a cutting board, then running a knife down the corn. (Or you can save your fingers and buy a fancy tool to remove kernels from corn cobs. Check it out at online kitchenware stores.) Scoop the kernels into a serving bowl.

5. Chop the arugula into bite-size bits and add these to the kernels. Add the tomatoes and scallions, too. Whisk the lemon juice, olive oil, honey, paprika, oregano, salt, and pepper in a small bowl until the honey dissolves. Pour over the salad and toss well to coat, tasting for extra salt as needed before serving.

continues

Then...

- Serve this salad with **Easy Scallops with Lemon Butter** (page 302) or **Buttery Lobster Tails** (page 305).

- Mound (and overflow) this salad in avocado halves for an easy lunch.

- Use this salad as a bed for grilled shrimp or **Shrimp "Scampi"** (page 301).

- Or use this salad as a filling for omelets, for a new take on brunch.

Roasted Cauliflower with Garlic and Capers

FAST / EASY / VEGAN / GLUTEN-FREE / 6 INGREDIENTS

Capers, garlic, and red pepper flakes add an aromatic punch to air-fried cauliflower, which gets very sweet because its flavors concentrate in the convection currents. Alongside a salad of sliced tomatoes drizzled with balsamic vinegar and sprinkled with crunchy salt, this dish may well be a vegan main course. Have some crunchy bread on hand to mop up all the tasty juices.

INGREDIENTS	2-quart or larger air fryer	3.5-quart or larger air fryer	5.25-quart or larger air fryer
1-inch cauliflower florets	2 cups (about 10 ounces)	3 cups (about 15 ounces)	4 cups (about 1¼ pounds)
Olive oil	1½ tablespoons	2 tablespoons	3 tablespoons
Drained and rinsed capers, chopped	1 tablespoon	1½ tablespoons	2 tablespoons
Minced garlic	1 teaspoon	2 teaspoons	1 tablespoon
Table salt	⅛ teaspoon	¼ teaspoon	½ teaspoon
Red pepper flakes	Up to ⅛ teaspoon	Up to ¼ teaspoon	Up to ½ teaspoon
MAKES	2 servings	3 servings	4 servings

1. With the basket (or basket attachment) in the air fryer, heat it to 375°F (or 370°F or 360°F, if one of these is the closest setting).

2. Stir the cauliflower florets, olive oil, capers, garlic, salt, and red pepper flakes in a large bowl until the florets are evenly coated.

3. When the machine is at temperature, put the florets in the basket, spreading them out to as close to one layer as you can. Air-fry for 10 minutes, tossing once to get any covered pieces exposed to the air currents, until tender and lightly browned.

4. Dump the contents of the basket into a serving bowl or onto a serving platter. Cool for a minute or two before serving.

Then...

- These florets make a great filling for wraps. Cool the florets for 5 minutes, then chop them into small bits. Lay them in flour tortillas or flatbreads like lefse or lavash with hummus and sprouts, then roll closed. (For our **Lemony Hummus**, see page 24.)

General Tso's Cauliflower

VEGETARIAN / CAN BE GLUTEN-FREE / 10 OR 12 INGREDIENTS

A vegetarian main course or a big side dish, this one is modeled after a Chinese-American take-out favorite. Unfortunately, because cauliflower florets are so irregularly shaped, there's no way to get them coated with the standard dredging procedure in shallow soup bowls or small pie plates. You'll need three zip-closed plastic bags for the coating mixture, to which you add the florets. Seal the bags and shake them up. You'll need medium-size bags for the small or medium batches but very large bags for the large batch.

INGREDIENTS	2-quart or larger air fryer	3.5-quart or larger air fryer	5.25-quart or larger air fryer
All-purpose flour or tapioca flour	¼ cup	⅓ cup	½ cup
Large egg(s), well beaten	1	2	3
Plain panko bread crumbs (gluten-free, if a concern)	⅓ cup	⅔ cup	1 cup
1½-inch cauliflower florets	1½ cups (about ½ pound)	2½ cups (about 13 ounces)	4 cups (about 1¼ pounds)
Vegetable oil spray	As needed	As needed	As needed
Regular or low-sodium soy sauce or gluten-free tamari sauce	4 teaspoons	2 tablespoons	¼ cup
Hoisin sauce (gluten-free, if a concern; see page 180)	2 teaspoons	1 tablespoon	2 tablespoons
Unseasoned rice vinegar (see page 70)	2 teaspoons	1 tablespoon	2 tablespoons
Granulated white sugar	1½ teaspoons	2 teaspoons	1 tablespoon
Sriracha or other hot red pepper sauce (gluten-free, if a concern)	1 teaspoon	1½ teaspoons	2 teaspoons
Water	*Not* needed	*Not* needed	1 tablespoon
Cornstarch	*Not* needed	*Not* needed	2 teaspoons
MAKES	*1 or 2 servings*	*3 servings*	*4 servings*

1. With the basket (or basket attachment) in the air fryer, heat it to 400°F (or 390°F, if that's the closest setting).

2. Put the flour in one zip-closed plastic bag, the beaten egg in a second bag, and the bread crumbs in a third.

3. Put the cauliflower florets in the bag with the flour. Seal closed, then shake and turn to coat the florets completely. Open the bag and transfer the florets to the bag with the egg(s). (Do not just dump the florets from one bag into the other.) Seal the second bag and turn gently to coat the florets in the egg(s). Open the second bag and use kitchen tongs to transfer the florets to the third bag. Seal that bag; shake and turn it to coat the florets in the bread crumbs.

continues

4. Spread paper towels on your work surface. Gently transfer the florets to these paper towels, then coat them with vegetable oil spray on all sides.

5. Gently spread the florets in the basket in as close to one layer as you can. Air-fry undisturbed for 15 minutes, or until crisp and browned.

6. Meanwhile, stir the soy sauce or tamari sauce, hoisin sauce, vinegar, sugar, and sriracha in a small saucepan set over medium heat until smooth. Bring to a simmer, stirring often. Because of the small amount of liquid, the small and medium batches will not need to be thickened. Simply remove the saucepan from the heat.

For the large batch, whisk the water and cornstarch in a small bowl until smooth, then whisk this slurry into the soy or tamari mixture in the saucepan. Cook about 1 minute, whisking constantly, until thickened. Remove from the heat.

7. When the cauliflower florets are done, dump them into a large bowl. Pour the mixture in the saucepan over them. Toss well to coat. Serve warm.

Then...

- Garnish the servings with thinly sliced scallions, finely chopped unsalted peanuts, and/or chopped fresh cilantro leaves.

- Serve as a main course over cooked long-grain white or brown rice.

Tandoori Cauliflower

FAST / EASY / VEGETARIAN / GLUTEN-FREE / 5 INGREDIENTS

This recipe replicates the South Asian tandoori method to make a satisfying side dish—or even a main course with more accompaniments. The recipe's success will turn on the curry powder you use. Sure, you can use the standard yellow variety—or you can make homemade **CURRY POWDER** by whisking *1 tablespoon ground coriander, 2 teaspoons ground cumin, 2 teaspoons ground dried turmeric, 1 teaspoon ground dried ginger, ½ teaspoon ground cloves, ½ teaspoon ground cinnamon,* and *¼ teaspoon cayenne* in a small bowl. Save any extra in a sealed small container in a cool, dark pantry for up to 6 months.

   Notice that there's no salt in our curry blend. There may not be in a bottled blend you have on hand. In either case, add the optional salt as the recipe suggests. But check your blend. If it does have salt, omit the stated amounts in the recipe. You can always pass more at the table.

INGREDIENTS	2-quart or larger air fryer	3.5-quart or larger air fryer	5.25-quart or larger air fryer
Plain full-fat yogurt (*not* Greek yogurt)	⅓ cup	½ cup	⅔ cup
Yellow curry powder, purchased or homemade (see the headnote)	1 teaspoon	1½ teaspoons	2 teaspoons
Lemon juice	1 teaspoon	1½ teaspoons	2 teaspoons
Table salt (optional)	½ teaspoon	¾ teaspoon	1 teaspoon
2-inch cauliflower florets	3 cups (about ¾ pound)	4½ cups (about 1 pound 2 ounces)	6 cups (about 1½ pounds)
MAKES	*2 or 3 servings*	*4 or 5 servings*	*6 servings*

1. With the basket (or basket attachment) in the air fryer, heat it to 400°F (or 390°F, if that's the closest setting).

2. Whisk the yogurt, curry powder, lemon juice, and salt (if using) in a large bowl until uniform. Add the florets and stir gently to coat the florets well and evenly. Even better, use your clean, dry hands to get the yogurt mixture down into all the nooks of the florets.

3. When the machine is at temperature, transfer the florets to the basket, spreading them gently into as close to one layer as you can. Air-fry for 10 minutes, tossing and rearranging the florets twice so that any covered or touching parts are exposed to the air currents, until lightly browned and tender if still a bit crunchy.

4. Pour the contents of the basket onto a wire rack. Cool for at least 5 minutes before serving, or serve at room temperature.

Then...

- To serve Tandoori Cauliflower as a main course, offer chutney (even our **Blueberry Chutney**, page 73), raita (like our **Cucumber and Cilantro Raita**, page 179), purchased Indian pickles, sliced radishes, cooked long-grain white rice, and warmed or grilled flatbreads, particularly naan.

Crispy Cauliflower Puffs

FAST / VEGETARIAN / CAN BE GLUTEN-FREE / 8 INGREDIENTS

Riced cauliflower is now in almost all our supermarkets. It makes easy work of these crisp, light, tender puffs. The raw mixture is similar to that for falafel or bean burgers: thick and stable, not gooey, if still a tad sticky. The flour will help bind the batter, but you can use potato starch (not tapioca flour or other flour substitutes) for a gluten-free substitute because of the stickiness it will bring to the batter.

INGREDIENTS	2-quart or larger air fryer	3.5-quart or larger air fryer	5.25-quart or larger air fryer
Riced cauliflower	1 cup	1½ cups	2 cups
Shredded Monterey Jack cheese	⅔ cup (about 2½ ounces)	1 cup (about 4 ounces)	1⅓ cups (about 5½ ounces)
Seasoned Italian-style panko bread crumbs (gluten-free, if a concern)	½ cup	¾ cup	1 cup
All-purpose flour or potato starch	1½ tablespoons	2 tablespoons plus 1 teaspoon	3 tablespoons
Vegetable oil	1½ tablespoons	2 tablespoons plus 1 teaspoon	3 tablespoons
Large egg(s)	1	1 plus 1 large yolk	2
Table salt	½ teaspoon	¾ teaspoon	1 teaspoon
Vegetable oil spray	As needed	As needed	As needed
MAKES	8 puffs	12 puffs	16 puffs

1. With the basket (or basket attachment) in the air fryer, heat it to 375°F (or 370°F or 360°F, if one of these is the closest setting).

2. Stir the riced cauliflower, cheese, bread crumbs, flour or potato starch, oil, egg(s) and egg yolk (if necessary), and salt in a large bowl to make a thick batter.

3. Using 2 tablespoons of the batter, form a compact ball between your clean, dry palms. Set it aside and continue forming more balls: 7 more for a small batch, 11 more for a medium batch, or 15 more for a large batch.

4. Generously coat the balls on all sides with vegetable oil spray. Set them in the basket with as much air space between them as possible. Air-fry undisturbed for 7 minutes, or until golden brown and crisp. If the machine is at 360°F, you may need to add 1 or 2 minutes to the cooking time.

5. Gently pour the contents of the basket onto a wire rack. Cool the puffs for 5 minutes before serving.

Then...

- For a light lunch, set these puffs on top of **Simple Arugula Salad** (page 128).

- Or serve them as an alternative to fries with burgers or sandwiches of any sort.

- Or try them for a savory breakfast on the weekend alongside slices of Cheddar cheese.

Fried Okra

VEGETARIAN / CAN BE GLUTEN-FREE / 7 INGREDIENTS

The proper texture of fried okra is almost a matter of religious fervor in the South. The vegetable must be crunchy on the outside but tender inside, all while maintaining its distinctly grassy but sweet flavor.

For the best success, look for thin, small okra. (Large okra can be too fibrous.) And coat the pieces deliberately and carefully with the vegetable oil spray. In fact, coating them is the most time-consuming part of this process. But the results are just right for your next barbecue.

INGREDIENTS	2-quart or larger air fryer	3.5-quart or larger air fryer	5.25-quart or larger air fryer
Cornstarch	2 tablespoons	2½ tablespoons	3 tablespoons
Buttermilk	¼ cup	⅓ cup	½ cup
Yellow cornmeal	¼ cup	⅓ cup	½ cup
All-purpose flour or gluten-free all-purpose flour	¼ cup	⅓ cup	½ cup
Old Bay seasoning	1½ teaspoons	2 teaspoons	1 tablespoon
Small, thin fresh okra, cut into ¾-inch lengths	6 ounces	10 ounces	¾ pound
Vegetable oil spray	As needed	As needed	As needed
MAKES	2 servings	3 servings	4 servings

1. With the basket (or basket attachment) in the air fryer, heat it to 400°F (or 390°F, if that's the closest setting).

2. Set up and fill three shallow soup plates or small pie plates on your counter: one for the cornstarch; one for the buttermilk; and one for the cornmeal, whisked with the flour and Old Bay until well combined.

3. Set some of the okra pieces in the cornstarch, then toss them around to coat evenly and well. Pick the pieces up with a flatware fork (using the fork as a shovel, not a spear) and gently shake off any excess cornstarch. Set the pieces in the buttermilk and gently turn them to coat them on all sides. Use that fork to shovel up the okra once more, letting any excess buttermilk slip back into the rest. Set the okra pieces in the cornmeal mixture and gently turn them to coat them on all sides. Gently shovel them up and set aside. Continue coating the remainder of the okra in the same way.

4. Generously coat the okra pieces on all sides with the vegetable oil spray. Set them in the basket in as close to one layer as you can. Some may be touching—but the fewer that do touch, the better. Even a fraction of an inch between the pieces will work. Air-fry undisturbed for 8 minutes, or until crisp and brown.

5. Gently dump the contents of the basket onto a wire rack. Cool for a couple of minutes before serving.

Then...

- Make SPICY CAJUN DIPPING SAUCE for Fried Okra. Whisk *regular, low-fat, or fat-free mayonnaise (gluten-free, if a concern)* and *Thai sweet chili sauce* in a 4-to-1 ratio by volume until smooth, then whisk in a little *garlic powder, onion powder, dried thyme,* and *cayenne* to taste.

Roman Artichokes

FAST / EASY / VEGAN / GLUTEN-FREE / 5 INGREDIENTS

We modeled these crunchy artichokes on the ones sometimes found in Roman trattorias or their stateside incarnations. The leaves get crunchy in the air fryer, a wonderful treat alongside steaks, chops, and fish fillets off the grill.

Frozen artichoke heart quarters can be hard to track down in some parts of North America. If necessary, substitute a 14-ounce can of artichoke hearts packed in water for each 9-ounce box. The hearts must be drained and rinsed. If they're whole hearts, quarter them. In any event, blot them dry on paper towels.

For a more robust flavor, add up to 1 minced tinned anchovy fillet with the olive oil.

INGREDIENTS	2-quart or larger air fryer	3.5-quart or larger air fryer	5.25-quart or larger air fryer
9-ounce box(es) frozen artichoke heart quarters, thawed	1	2	3
Olive oil	1 tablespoon	1½ tablespoons	2 tablespoons
Minced garlic	1 teaspoon	2 teaspoons	1 tablespoon
Table salt	½ teaspoon	1 teaspoon	1¼ teaspoons
Red pepper flakes	Up to ¼ teaspoon	Up to ½ teaspoon	Up to ¾ teaspoon
MAKES	2 servings	4 servings	6 servings

1. With the basket (or basket attachment) in the air fryer, heat it to 400°F (or 390°F, if that's the closest setting).

2. *Gently* toss the artichoke heart quarters, oil, garlic, salt, and red pepper flakes in a bowl until the quarters are well coated.

3. When the machine is at temperature, scrape the contents of the bowl into the basket. Spread the artichoke heart quarters out into as close to one layer as possible. Air-fry undisturbed for 8 minutes. Gently toss and rearrange the quarters so that any covered or touching parts are now exposed to the air currents, then air-fry undisturbed for 4 minutes more, until very crisp.

4. Gently pour the contents of the basket onto a wire rack. Cool for a few minutes before serving.

Then...

- We skipped the breading on these artichokes for a lighter flavor. If you miss it, toast some plain dried bread crumbs in a skillet set over medium heat with a little olive oil, dried thyme, dried oregano, and a moderately generous amount of finely grated Parmesan cheese, stirring fairly often until crisp and fragrant. Season with salt to taste. Remove from the heat and sprinkle this mixture over these artichokes.

Crispy Brussels Sprouts

FAST / EASY / VEGAN / GLUTEN-FREE / 3 INGREDIENTS

By halving Brussels sprouts, we can expose more of their inner leaves to the heat in the air fryer and so render them extra crunchy. (Left whole, they soften inside before they burn outside. So, we ask you, what's the point?) Don't use giant, 3-inch-long Brussels sprouts—they tend to be too bitter. And very small ones blacken too quickly.

INGREDIENTS	2-quart or larger air fryer	3.5-quart or larger air fryer	5.25-quart or larger air fryer
Medium, 2-inch-in-length Brussels sprouts	¾ pound	1¼ pounds	1½ pounds
Olive oil	1 tablespoon	1½ tablespoons	2 tablespoons
Table salt	½ teaspoon	¾ teaspoon	1 teaspoon
MAKES	2 servings	3 servings	4 servings

1. With the basket (or basket attachment) in the air fryer, heat it to 400°F (or 390°F, if that's the closest setting).

2. Halve each Brussels sprout through the stem end, pulling off and discarding any discolored outer leaves. Put the sprout halves in a large bowl, add the oil and salt, and stir well to coat evenly, until the Brussels sprouts are glistening.

3. When the machine is at temperature, scrape the contents of the bowl into the basket, gently spreading the Brussels sprout halves into as close to one layer as possible. Air-fry for 12 minutes, *gently* tossing and rearranging the vegetables twice to get all covered or touching parts exposed to the air currents, until crisp and browned at the edges.

4. Gently pour the contents of the basket onto a wire rack. Cool for a minute or two before serving.

Then...

• To make a salad out of these Brussels sprouts, toss them with a little more olive oil, some pomegranate seeds, and some toasted walnut pieces or pepitas (pumpkin seeds).

• Or for another salad, mix them with diced cored apples, dried cranberries, and thinly sliced celery. Drizzle the salad with a little apple cider vinegar and toss with table salt and ground black pepper to taste.

See photo in insert.

Wilted Brussels Sprout Slaw

EASY / CAN BE GLUTEN-FREE / 7 INGREDIENTS

With bagged shredded Brussels sprouts, this warm salad is a breeze to make. Consider it a go-to side at the Thanksgiving or winter holiday table. If you can't find shredded Brussels sprouts, buy the equivalent weight of medium Brussels sprouts. Starting at the fat end (farthest from the stem), use a very sharp paring knife to cut the vegetable in very thin slices—which, when separated, become tiny threads. Discard the hard stem and soldier on with more Brussels sprouts.

INGREDIENTS	2-quart or larger air fryer	3.5-quart or larger air fryer	5.25-quart or larger air fryer
Thick-cut bacon strip(s), halved widthwise (gluten-free, if a concern)	1	2	3
Bagged shredded Brussels sprouts	3 cups (about ¾ pound)	4½ cups (about 1 pound 2 ounces)	6 cups (about 1½ pounds)
Table salt	⅛ teaspoon	¼ teaspoon	Rounded ¼ teaspoon
White balsamic vinegar (see page 203)	1 tablespoon	2 tablespoons	3 tablespoons
Worcestershire sauce (gluten-free, if a concern)	1 teaspoon	2 teaspoons	1 tablespoon
Dijon mustard (gluten-free, if a concern)	½ teaspoon	1 teaspoon	1½ teaspoons
Ground black pepper	¼ teaspoon	Rounded ¼ teaspoon	½ teaspoon
MAKES	2 or 3 servings	4 or 5 servings	6 or 7 servings

1. With the basket (or basket attachment) in the air fryer, heat it to 375°F (or 370°F or 360°F, if one of these is the closest setting).

2. When the machine is at temperature, lay the bacon strip halves in the basket in one layer and air-fry for 10 minutes, or until crisp.

3. Use kitchen tongs to transfer the bacon pieces to a wire rack. Put the shredded Brussels sprouts in a large bowl. Drain any fat from the basket or the tray under the basket onto the Brussels sprouts. Add the salt and toss well to coat.

4. Put the Brussels sprout shreds in the basket, spreading them out into as close to an even layer as you can. Air-fry for 8 minutes, tossing the basket's contents at least three times, until wilted and lightly browned.

5. Pour the contents of the basket into a serving bowl. Chop the bacon and add it to the Brussels sprouts. Add the vinegar, Worcestershire sauce, mustard, and pepper. Toss well to blend the dressing and coat the Brussels sprout shreds. Serve warm.

Then...

- For heat, sprinkle the salad with a very little cayenne before tossing.

- This slaw is great in wraps or on sandwiches with toasted rye bread, particularly with sliced turkey breast and a little smear of deli mustard.

- Divide the warm slaw on plates and top each serving with a poached egg. Have crunchy toast at the ready!

Brussels Sprout and Ham Salad

FAST / EASY / CAN BE GLUTEN-FREE / 6 INGREDIENTS

Because this substantial side salad—or even main-course salad—uses the brine from a jar of pickles as part of the dressing, it couldn't be much easier. Use any sort of brine you like. We tested this with the brine from a jar of garlic dills. You could even use the brine from a jar of pickled jalapeño rings if you wanted a salad to go with some sweet barbecue sauce on pork or chicken.

INGREDIENTS	2-quart or larger air fryer	3.5-quart or larger air fryer	5.25-quart or larger air fryer
2-inch-in-length Brussels sprouts, quartered through the stem	¾ pound	1 pound	1½ pounds
Smoked ham steak, any rind removed, diced (gluten-free, if a concern)	¼ pound	6 ounces	½ pound
Caraway seeds	¼ teaspoon	Rounded ¼ teaspoon	½ teaspoon
Vegetable oil spray	As needed	As needed	As needed
Brine from a jar of pickles (gluten-free, if a concern)	2½ tablespoons	¼ cup	⅓ cup
Ground black pepper	½ teaspoon	¾ teaspoon	1 teaspoon
MAKES	*2 or 3 servings*	*3 or 4 servings*	*5 or 6 servings*

1. With the basket (or basket attachment) in the air fryer, heat it to 375°F (or 370°F or 360°F, if one of these is the closest setting).

2. Toss the Brussels sprout quarters, ham, and caraway seeds in a bowl until well combined. Generously coat the top of the mixture with vegetable oil spray, toss again, spray again, and repeat a couple of times until the vegetables and ham are glistening.

3. When the machine is at temperature, scrape the contents of the bowl into the basket, spreading it into as close to one layer as you can. Air-fry for 12 minutes, tossing and rearranging the pieces at least twice so that any covered or touching parts are eventually exposed to the air currents, until the Brussels sprouts are tender and a little brown at the edges.

4. Dump the contents of the basket into a serving bowl. Scrape any caraway seeds from the bottom of the basket or the tray under the basket attachment into the bowl as well. Add the pickle brine and pepper. Toss well to coat. Serve warm.

Then...

- Add any or all of the following to the salad: thinly sliced celery, thinly sliced fennel, thinly sliced red onion, raisins, dried raspberries, and sliced almonds.

- This salad makes an excellent low-carb stuffing for a turkey at Thanksgiving.

Acorn Squash Halves with Maple Butter Glaze

EASY / VEGETARIAN / GLUTEN-FREE / 5 INGREDIENTS

Roasted acorn squash halves are a fall or early winter delight. They make a great dinner on their own, with a side salad in a vinegary dressing (like the **Classic Greek Diner Dressing** on page 90).

Our glaze is a simple mix of two ingredients: butter and maple syrup. Don't dare substitute pancake syrup or our New England souls will come haunt your house. But do feel free to substitute birch syrup for a savory, slightly bitter surprise against the sweet squash.

INGREDIENTS	2-quart or larger air fryer	3.5-quart or larger air fryer	5.25-quart or larger air fryer
Acorn squash	1 small (¾ to 1 pound)	1 medium (1 to 1¼ pounds)	2 small (each ¾ to 1 pound)
Vegetable oil spray	As needed	As needed	As needed
Table salt	¼ teaspoon	Rounded ¼ teaspoon	½ teaspoon
Butter, melted	1 tablespoon	1½ tablespoons	2 tablespoons
Maple syrup	1 tablespoon	1½ tablespoons	2 tablespoons
MAKES	2 servings	2 or 3 servings	4 servings

1. With the basket (or basket attachment) in the air fryer, heat it to 325°F (or 330°F, if that's the closest setting).

2. Cut a squash in half through the stem end. Use a flatware spoon (preferably, a serrated grapefruit spoon) to scrape out and discard the seeds and membranes in each half. Use a paring knife to make a crisscross pattern of cuts about ½ inch apart and ¼ inch deep across the "meat" of the squash. If working with a second squash, repeat this step for that one.

3. Generously coat the cut side of the squash halves with vegetable oil spray. Sprinkle the halves with the salt. Set them in the basket cut side up with at least ¼ inch between them. Air-fry undisturbed for 25 minutes for a small batch, 30 minutes for a medium batch, or 25 minutes for a large batch. (The medium batch has larger individual pieces that need longer in the air fryer.)

4. Increase the machine's temperature to 400°F (or 390°F, if that's the closest setting). Mix the melted butter and syrup in a small bowl until uniform. Brush this mixture over the cut sides of the squash(es), letting it pool in the center. Air-fry undisturbed for 3 minutes, or until the glaze is bubbling.

5. Use a nonstick-safe spatula and kitchen tongs to transfer the squash halves cut side up to a wire rack. Cool for 5 to 10 minutes before serving.

Then...

• For a crunchy coating, toast roughly ground walnuts or pecans in a dry skillet set over low heat for only a minute or two, stirring all the while, just until fragrant. Sprinkle the toasted nuts over the squash halves just before serving.

• For a main course or a more substantial side, set a small scoop of soft, creamy burrata (an Italian cow-milk cheese) in each half while still warm. Sprinkle the burrata with fresh thyme leaves and a dusting of cayenne, if desired.

Zucchini Boats with Ham and Cheese

EASY / 6 INGREDIENTS

These stuffed zucchini halves could make a light supper with a side salad, particularly a sweet one like our **Jicama and Mango Salad** (page 279). Hollow out the zucchini halves so they can hold a fair amount of stuffing but still hold together after air-frying.

Use any sort of *mini* croutons you like: plain, Italian seasoned, garlic, you name it. They'll change the character of the dish to fit your taste.

INGREDIENTS	2-quart or larger air fryer	3.5-quart or larger air fryer	5.25-quart or larger air fryer
6-inch-long zucchini	1	2	3
Thinly sliced deli ham, any rind removed, meat roughly chopped	1 ounce	2 ounces	3 ounces
Dry-packed sun-dried tomatoes, chopped	2	4	6
Purchased pesto	2½ tablespoons	⅓ cup	½ cup
Packaged mini croutons	2 tablespoons	¼ cup	6 tablespoons
Shredded semi-firm mozzarella cheese	2 tablespoons (about ½ ounce)	¼ cup (about 1 ounce)	6 tablespoons (about 1½ ounces)
MAKES	2 servings	4 servings	6 servings

1. With the basket (or basket attachment) in the air fryer, heat it to 375°F (or 370°F or 360°F, if one of these is the closest setting).

2. Split the zucchini in half lengthwise and use a flatware spoon or a serrated grapefruit spoon to scoop out the insides of the halves, leaving at least a ¼-inch border all around the zucchini half. (You can save the scooped out insides to add to soups and stews—or even freeze it for a much later use.)

3. Mix the ham, sun-dried tomatoes, pesto, croutons, and half the cheese in a bowl until well combined. Pack this mixture into the zucchini "shells." Top them with the remaining cheese.

4. Set them stuffing side up in the basket without touching (even a fraction of an inch between them is enough room). Air-fry undisturbed for 12 minutes, or until softened and browned, with the cheese melted on top.

5. Use a nonstick-safe spatula to transfer the zucchini boats stuffing side up on a wire rack. Cool for 5 or 10 minutes before serving.

Then...

- For an easy meal, try these stuffed zucchini boats with a pitcher of LIGHTNING JUICE PUNCH. Stir *1½ cups orange juice, 1½ cups pineapple juice, 6 ounces (¾ cup) coconut rum, 4 ounces (½ cup) melon liqueur (such as Midori)*, and *4 ounces (½ cup) Triple Sec* in a pitcher. Pour over lots of *ice* (even shaved or chipped ice) in tall glasses.

THIRTY-FOUR

Desserts
& Sweets

Desserts may be one of the more surprising things to come out of an air fryer. But we can put those convection currents to good use to make some pretty light cakes and cookies. And we can morph state fair favorites like **Fried Snickers Bars** into a *relatively* healthy treat with this machine (no joke—see page 380).

While timing has been important in the other chapters, it's actually less so here. We've given you timings based on multiple tests at our house. But your baking soda may be more or less active than ours; your butter, colder or warmer; and your flour, denser or airier because of the ambient humidity at your house. Always go by the *visual* cues in this chapter.

Check on things in the basket. Don't open it for cakes or cookies for the first three-quarters of their cooking time. The batter or dough needs a chance to begin to set. Then start checking, not obsessively but more often than you might for a chicken breast or a pork chop. Remember that everything's cooking more quickly in an air fryer; therefore, it can also burn or dry out more quickly. There's no reason to be scared, just watchful.

Scooping flour is a matter of concern in all recipes, since many cooks in the U.S. refuse to work by weight in the kitchen. (Don't even get us started.) The method we used in testing these recipes is to dip the measuring cup into the flour so that the cup overflows with no gaps inside. We do not press the cup against the side of the bag or the container. We then scrape the excess flour off the top of the cup with a flatware knife. Done.

Although a few more bread crumbs or even an extra teaspoon of a dried herb won't hurt a chicken thigh, more sugar or baking powder can ruin a dessert. Be more careful with amounts in this chapter and do not alter the size of the baking pans. You can't change these ratios without dramatically affecting the dessert.

And so we come to the last chapter of our air fryer book. Our great hope is that we've increased your understanding of the versatility of this kitchen tool. Frankly, after we got our first air fryer, within a week we both said, "How did we ever live without one of these?" We eventually ended up with fourteen of them as we were testing the recipes for this book. When the dust settled, we gave some away to friends but kept six! One is almost always out on the counter. That should tell you a lot about what we think of the promise of an air fryer.

Cinnamon Sugar Twists

EASY / VEGETARIAN / 5 INGREDIENTS

These twists are super easy with puff pastry—which the air fryer makes extra crunchy because of the dry air blowing around the dough. This recipe is one of the rare ones that assume you'll make the twists in batches, no matter the size of your machine. In fact, you can double the recipe, using the whole box of puff pastry and working in lots of batches.

You can add up to 1 teaspoon ground cardamom and/or ½ teaspoon grated nutmeg to the cinnamon sugar mixture. Add up to ⅛ teaspoon table salt for a more elegant finish to the dessert.

INGREDIENTS	2-quart or larger air fryer
Puff pastry sheet from a 17.25-ounce box of frozen puff pastry, thawed	1
Large egg	1
Water	2 tablespoons
Granulated white sugar	¼ cup
Ground cinnamon	2 teaspoons
MAKES	16 twists

1. With the basket (or basket attachment) in the air fryer, heat it to 400°F (or 390°F, if that's the closest setting).

2. Set the pastry sheet on a clean, dry work surface. Roll to a 12-inch square. Cut this square into four even 6 x 6-inch quarters.

3. Whisk the egg and water in a small bowl until uniform. Separate the puff pastry quarter-sheets and brush each with the egg mixture.

4. Stir the sugar and cinnamon in a small bowl until well combined. Sprinkle about 1 tablespoon of this mixture over each quarter. Cut each quarter into four even strips. Pick up one of the strips with an end in each hand, then twist the strip to form a corkscrew. Repeat with the remaining strips.

5. Set 4 twists in the basket of a small air fryer, 5 in a medium air fryer, and 6 in a large model, with as much air space between the twists as possible. They will puff as they cook, so ¼ inch or more between them would be best. Air-fry undisturbed for 7 minutes, or until puffed and crisp.

6. Use kitchen tongs to transfer the twists to a wire rack, then air-fry more twists in batches until all the twists are on the wire rack. Serve warm or cool to room temperature and store in a sealed container at room temperature for up to 2 days (provided the humidity's way down).

Then...

- These would be great with our easy VEGAN CHOCOLATE PUDDING. Put *1 cup (about 6 ounces) chopped bittersweet chocolate or bittersweet chocolate chips* in a medium microwave-safe bowl. Microwave on high in 6-second bursts, stirring after each, until the chocolate is about three-quarters melted. Cool for 5 minutes, then scrape the melted chocolate into a food processor. Add *1 pound 2 ounces soft silken tofu, 6 tablespoons unsweetened cocoa powder, ¾ cup granulated white sugar, 1 tablespoon vanilla extract*, and *½ teaspoon table salt*. Cover and process until smooth, scraping down the insides of the canister at least once. Divide between eight 1-cup ramekins or custard cups, then refrigerate for at least 4 hours or until set.

Peanut Butter S'mores

FAST / EASY / 4 INGREDIENTS

With these s'mores, you won't get that charred taste of marshmallows over a campfire. But you'll make s'mores in no time, even in the dead of winter, letting the marshmallows soften over the chocolate chips and peanut butter. Why peanut butter? Because it holds the chips in place. And because it is one of the major food groups (if not *the* major food group).

INGREDIENTS	2-quart or larger air fryer	3.5-quart or larger air fryer	5.25-quart or larger air fryer
Graham crackers (full, double-square cookies as they come out of the package)	8	10	12
Natural-style creamy or crunchy peanut butter	¼ cup	5 tablespoons	6 tablespoons
Milk chocolate chips	⅓ cup	½ cup	½ cup plus 1 tablespoon
Standard-size marshmallows (*not* minis and *not* jumbo campfire ones)	8	10	12
MAKES	*8 s'mores*	*10 s'mores*	*12 s'mores*

1. With the basket (or basket attachment) in the air fryer, heat it to 350°F (or 360°F, if that's the closest setting).

2. Break the graham crackers in half widthwise at the marked place, so the rectangle is now in two squares. Set half of the squares flat side up on your work surface. Spread each with about 1½ teaspoons peanut butter, then set 10 to 12 chocolate chips point side up into the peanut butter on each, pressing gently so the chips stick.

3. Flatten a marshmallow between your clean, dry hands and set it atop the chips. Do the same with the remaining marshmallows on the other coated graham crackers. Do *not* set the other half of the graham crackers on top of these coated graham crackers.

continues

4. When the machine is at temperature, set the treats graham cracker side down in a single layer in the basket. They may touch, but even a fraction of an inch between them will provide better air flow. Air-fry undisturbed for 45 *seconds*.

5. Use a nonstick-safe spatula to transfer the topped graham crackers to a wire rack. Set the other graham cracker squares flat side down over the marshmallows. Cool for a couple of minutes before serving.

Then...

- Make a s'more sundae by setting a completed s'more in a serving bowl, then topping it with vanilla ice cream and warmed caramel sauce.

- Cool the s'mores completely, then dip them halfway in melted dark or bittersweet chocolate, maybe mixed with a little butter. Set on a wire rack to cool until the chocolate hardens.

Cheesecake Wontons

VEGETARIAN / 8 INGREDIENTS

By stuffing wonton wrappers with a cream cheese mixture reminiscent of the filling in cheesecakes, you can make bite-size treats, best served on a platter so everyone can dig in.

This recipe requires you to use an egg yolk, rather than a pasteurized egg substitute—and you'll need to use less than a whole yolk for any batch except the large one. Save any remaining yolk in a small covered container in the fridge for up to 2 days to add to scrambled eggs or to add a little more richness to custards or puddings.

INGREDIENTS	2-quart or larger air fryer	3.5-quart or larger air fryer	5.25-quart or larger air fryer
Regular or low-fat cream cheese (*not* fat-free)	3 tablespoons	¼ cup	6 tablespoons
Granulated white sugar	1½ tablespoons	2 tablespoons	3 tablespoons
Egg yolk	1 tablespoon	1½ tablespoons	2 tablespoons (about 1 large yolk)
Vanilla extract	⅛ teaspoon	¼ teaspoon	½ teaspoon
Table salt	⅛ teaspoon	Rounded ⅛ teaspoon	¼ teaspoon
All-purpose flour	1 tablespoon	1½ tablespoons	2 tablespoons
Wonton wrappers (vegetarian, if a concern)	12	16	24
Vegetable oil spray	As needed	As needed	As needed
MAKES	12 stuffed wontons	16 stuffed wontons	24 stuffed wontons

1. With the basket (or basket attachment) in the air fryer, heat it to 400°F (or 390°F, if that's the closest setting).

2. Using a flatware fork, mash the cream cheese, sugar, egg yolk, and vanilla in a small bowl until smooth. Add the salt and flour and continue mashing until evenly combined.

3. Set a wonton wrapper on a clean, dry work surface so that one corner faces you (so that it looks like a diamond on your work surface). Set 1 teaspoon of the cream cheese mixture in the middle of the wrapper but just above a horizontal line that would divide the wrapper in half. (Or if you were a math nerd, at 0 on the x axis and at +1 on the y axis.) Dip your clean finger in water and run it along the edges of the wrapper. Fold the corner closest to you up and over the filling, lining it up with the corner farthest from you, thereby making a stuffed triangle. Press gently to seal. Wet the two triangle tips nearest you, then fold them up and together over the filling. Gently press together to seal and fuse. Set aside and continue making more stuffed wontons, 11 more for the small batch, 15 more for the medium batch, or 23 more for the large one.

4. Lightly coat the stuffed wrappers on all sides with vegetable oil spray. Set them with the fused corners up in the basket with as much air space between them as possible. Air-fry undisturbed for 6 minutes, or until golden brown and crisp.

5. Gently dump the contents of the basket onto a wire rack. Cool for at least 5 minutes before serving.

Then...

- Serve the wontons with strawberry jam that's been warmed for 10 seconds in the microwave on high, then stirred until smooth and pourable.

- Cool the wontons for 20 minutes, then toss them in a bowl with a mixture of ¼ cup confectioners' sugar and 1 tablespoon unsweetened cocoa powder.

Fried Oreos

FAST / VEGETARIAN / 5 INGREDIENTS

Well, why not? The air fryer can make a great crust on a fried cookie, a state fair favorite that can be a home treat anytime. We find that "regular" Oreos (or any creme-filled chocolate sandwich cookies) work best. The double-stuffed ones tend to get soggy because the filling runs. But feel free to substitute more exotic flavors beyond the standard: peppermint, chocolate-stuffed, you name it.

INGREDIENTS	2-quart or larger air fryer	3.5-quart or larger air fryer	5.25-quart or larger air fryer
Large egg white(s)	1	1	2
Water	2 tablespoons	2 tablespoons	2 tablespoons
Graham cracker crumbs	1 cup	1 cup	1½ cups
Original-size Oreos (not minis or king-size)	8	12	16
Vegetable oil spray	As needed	As needed	As needed
MAKES	8 fried cookies	12 fried cookies	16 fried cookies

1. With the basket (or basket attachment) in the air fryer, heat it to 375°F (or 370°F or 360°F, if one of these is the closest setting).

2. Set up and fill two shallow soup plates or small pie plates on your counter: one for the egg white(s), whisked with the water until foamy; and one for the graham cracker crumbs.

3. Dip a cookie in the egg white mixture, turning several times to coat well. Let any excess egg white mixture slip back into the rest, then set the cookie in the crumbs. Turn several times to coat evenly, pressing gently. You want an even but not thick crust. However, make sure that the cookie is fully coated and that the filling is sealed inside. Lightly coat the cookie on all sides with vegetable oil spray. Set aside and continue dipping and coating the remaining cookies.

4. Set the coated cookies in the basket with as much air space between them as possible. Air-fry undisturbed for 6 minutes, or until the coating is golden brown and set. If the machine is at 360°F, the cookies may need 1 minute more to cook and set.

5. Use a nonstick-safe spatula to transfer the cookies to a wire rack. Cool for at least 5 minutes before serving.

Then...

- Fried Oreos need vanilla ice cream. The easiest to make is NO-CHURN VANILLA ICE CREAM. Use an electric mixer at high speed to beat *2½ cups* chilled *heavy cream* in a *chilled* bowl until supple peaks form when the turned-off beaters are dipped in the beaten cream. Add *one 14-ounce can sweetened condensed milk, 2 teaspoons vanilla extract,* and *⅛ teaspoon table salt*. Fold gently with a rubber spatula, taking care not to deflate the whipped cream. Spoon this mixture into a 9 x 5-inch loaf pan. Cover with plastic wrap and freeze for at least 6 hours or up to 4 days. Scoop at will!

Fried Twinkies

FAST / 5 INGREDIENTS

Rather than a heavy batter on these famous little cakes, we coat them in ground gingersnap cookies. The results are something like a sugared cake donut—in fact, like the best sugared cake donuts you can make in an air fryer!

The one trick is to set the Twinkies flat side *up* in the air-fryer basket. If not, the filling begins to melt and run out the holes before the coating sets. Because the coating does get hot, the fried treats will need 10 minutes to cool and set up before kids can dive in.

INGREDIENTS	2-quart or larger air fryer	3.5-quart or larger air fryer	5.25-quart or larger air fryer
Large egg white(s)	1	2	2
Water	1 tablespoon	2 tablespoons	2 tablespoons
Ground gingersnap cookie crumbs	1 cup (about 6 ounces)	1½ cups (about 9 ounces)	2 cups (about 12 ounces)
Twinkies	4	6	8
Vegetable oil spray	As needed	As needed	As needed
MAKES	*4 fried Twinkies*	*6 fried Twinkies*	*8 fried Twinkies*

1. With the basket (or basket attachment) in the air fryer, heat it to 400°F (or 390°F, if that's the closest setting).

2. Set up and fill two shallow soup plates or small pie plates on your counter: one for the egg white(s), whisked with the water until foamy; and one for the gingersnap crumbs.

3. Dip a Twinkie in the egg white(s), turning it to coat on all sides, even the ends. Let the excess egg white mixture slip back into the rest, then set the Twinkie in the crumbs. Roll it to coat on all sides, even the ends, pressing gently to get an even coating. Then *repeat this process*: egg white(s), followed by crumbs. Lightly coat the prepared Twinkie on all sides with vegetable oil spray. Set aside and coat each of the remaining Twinkies with the same double-dipping technique, followed by spraying.

4. Set the Twinkies flat side *up* in the basket with as much air space between them as possible. Air-fry for 5 minutes, or until browned and crunchy.

5. Use a nonstick-safe spatula to *gently* transfer the Twinkies to a wire rack. Cool for at least 10 minutes before serving.

Then...

- Set the fried Twinkies on plates, drizzle them with maple syrup, and serve them with a knife and a fork.

Fried Snickers Bars

FAST / VEGETARIAN / 5 INGREDIENTS

Who could resist this converting this deep-fried treat into an air-fryer wonder? You must use the small "fun-size" bars. Larger bars will melt before the coating sets. And the candy bars must be frozen hard—not just a few hours in the freezer, but at least overnight, preferably more than 24 hours. Toss the bag of small bars into the freezer when you get it home from the store. That way, they'll be ready when you're ready to make a batch.

These bars don't have the standard, "batter-style" coating of those you'll find at state fairs. That sort of batter slips off them in an air fryer and makes a royal mess. Rather, we coat these with cookie crumbs so there's a little legit crunch factor in the decadence. You can buy those cookie crumbs already ground; the weight measure in the ingredient list tells you how many cookies you need to grind in a food processor to get (approximately) that amount of crumbs.

Take care as the candy bars cook. They start to melt. If you see structural failure in the coating of one bar, immediately remove the basket from the machine to cool all the candy bars.

INGREDIENTS	2-quart or larger air fryer	3.5-quart or larger air fryer	5.25-quart or larger air fryer
All-purpose flour	¼ cup	⅓ cup	½ cup
Large egg white(s), beaten until foamy	1	1	2
Vanilla wafer cookie crumbs	1 cup (4 ounces)	1½ cups (6 ounces)	2 cups (8 ounces)
Fun-size (0.6-ounce/17-gram) Snickers bars, frozen	6	8	12
Vegetable oil spray	As needed	As needed	As needed
MAKES	6 fried candy bars	8 fried candy bars	12 fried candy bars

1. With the basket (or basket attachment) in the air fryer, heat it to 400°F (or 390°F, if that's the closest setting).

2. Set up and fill three shallow soup plates or small pie plates on your counter: one for the flour, one for the beaten egg white(s), and one for the cookie crumbs.

3. Unwrap the frozen candy bars. Dip one in the flour, turning it to coat on all sides. Gently shake off any excess, then set it in the beaten egg white(s). Turn it to coat all sides, even the ends, then let any excess egg white slip back into the rest. Set the candy bar in the cookie crumbs. Turn to coat on all sides, even the ends. Dip the candy bar back in the egg white(s) a second time, then into the cookie crumbs a second time, making sure you have an even coating all around. Coat the covered candy bar all over with vegetable oil spray. Set aside so you can dip and coat the remaining candy bars.

4. Set the coated candy bars in the basket with as much air space between them as possible. Air-fry undisturbed for 4 minutes, or until golden brown.

5. Remove the basket from the machine and let the candy bars cool in the basket for 10 minutes. Use a nonstick-safe spatula to transfer them to a wire rack and cool for 5 minutes more before chowing down.

Then...

- These are terrific garnishes for ice cream sundaes of all sorts.

- While the candy bars are still warm, press one between two chocolate cookies (or even chocolate chip cookies) for a very unconventional take on s'mores.

Oreo-Coated Peanut Butter Cups

5 INGREDIENTS

Now we're getting silly. But haven't you ever wanted a chocolate sandwich cookie and a peanut butter cup in the same crunchy bite? No? You haven't dreamed big enough.

Grind the cookies until they're like fine bread crumbs so that you can make an even coating on the peanut butter cups—which *must* be frozen at least 12 hours (or better, for days) in advance. And get the coated peanut butter cups back in the freezer as the machine heats. The candies should be very cold when they start to cook. They are "meltier" than other candy bars.

You can even dip and coat the cups far in advance. Cover the plate with them in the freezer so the coating doesn't dry out in the low-humidity environment of the freezer. In fact, dip and coat the cups, then keep them covered in the freezer for up to 2 months, a treat ready whenever you're ready to fire up the air fryer.

INGREDIENTS	2-quart or larger air fryer	3.5-quart or larger air fryer	5.25-quart or larger air fryer
Standard ¾-ounce peanut butter cups, *frozen*	6	8	12
All-purpose flour	¼ cup	⅓ cup	½ cup
Large egg white(s), beaten until foamy	1	2	2
Oreos or other creme-filled chocolate sandwich cookies, ground to crumbs in a food processor	12	16	24
Vegetable oil spray	As needed	As needed	As needed
MAKES	*6 fried peanut butter cups*	*8 fried peanut butter cups*	*12 fried peanut butter cups*

1. Set up and fill three shallow soup plates or small pie plates on your counter: one for the flour, one for the beaten egg white(s), and one for the cookie crumbs.

2. Dip a *frozen* peanut butter cup in the flour, turning it to coat all sides. Shake off any excess, then set it in the beaten egg white(s). Turn it to coat all sides, then let any excess egg white slip back into the rest. Set the candy bar in the cookie crumbs. Turn to coat on all parts, even the sides. Dip the peanut butter cup back

continues

in the egg white(s) as before, then into the cookie crumbs as before, making sure you have a solid, even coating all around the cup. Set aside while you dip and coat the remaining cups.

3. When all the peanut butter cups are dipped and coated, lightly coat them on all sides with the vegetable oil spray. Set them on a plate and freeze while the air fryer heats.

4. With the basket (or basket attachment) in the air fryer, heat it to 400°F (or 390°F, if that's the closest setting).

5. Set the dipped cups wider side up in the basket with as much air space between them as possible. Air-fry undisturbed for 4 minutes, or until they feel soft but the coating is set.

6. Turn off the machine and remove the basket from it. Set aside the basket with the fried cups for 10 minutes. Use a nonstick-safe spatula to transfer the fried cups to a wire rack. Cool for at least another 5 minutes before serving.

Then...

- For a garnish, grind a little peanut brittle to a fine powder in a food processor, then sprinkle it over the fried peanut butter cups while they're still warm.

- Or for a sophisticated turn, dust them with a mixture of ground cardamom and ground cinnamon in equal proportions while the cups are still warm.

Fried Cheesecake

EASY / CAN BE VEGETARIAN / 3 INGREDIENTS

Here's the finale in our run of state fair–inspired treats that we think work best in the air fryer. Because you must cut a purchased cheesecake for this recipe, we set it up for all sizes of the machine, with the understanding that you'll have to work in batches for the small or medium models.

You can use any flavor cheesecake you like *as long as* the cheesecake doesn't have melted caramel or melted chocolate inside it or between the filling and the crust. Any of these will melt and run too quickly to work with this technique.

INGREDIENTS	2-quart or larger air fryer
18 x 14-inch phyllo sheets (thawed, if necessary; plus a few more, if needed)	6
6-inch round purchased cheesecake with a graham cracker crust (vegetarian cheesecake, if a concern; some crusts are made with animal fats)	1
Butter, melted and cooled	12 tablespoons (¾ cup/1½ sticks)
MAKES	*6 servings*

1. With the basket (or basket attachment) in the air fryer, heat it to 375°F (or 370°F or 360°F, if one of these is the closest setting). Set the phyllo sheets on a clean, dry work surface, covering them with a clean, dry kitchen towel. (It helps to have a few more than you need in case any tear.)

2. Cut the cheesecake into six equal wedges. Lay a sheet of phyllo on a clean, dry work surface. Brush it with melted butter. Fold it in half lengthwise, then brush it again. Place a slice of cheesecake at one narrow end of the sheet, with the cheesecake's crust nearest you but the whole wedge placed at a 45-degree angle to you. Roll the slice up by turning it on one side away from you with the phyllo dough covering it, then turn the wedge the other way, always bringing the phyllo with you as you roll it up in the sheet, just like folding a flag. Brush the entire package with melted butter, then set it aside to roll and brush the remaining wedges the same way.

3. Set the wedges in the basket in one layer. You'll fit 2 in a small air fryer, perhaps 4 in a medium one, and

maybe all 6 in a large model. Leave at least 1 inch of air space between the pieces. (Cover any wedges that didn't fit with a clean kitchen towel or a loose sheet of plastic wrap so they don't dry out while they wait.) Air-fry undisturbed for 4 minutes, or until golden brown and crunchy.

4. Use a nonstick-safe spatula, and perhaps kitchen tongs for balance, to transfer the wedges to a wire rack. Cool for at least 5 minutes but no more than 15 minutes before serving.

Then...

- Drizzle the fried wedges with **Easy Chocolate Drizzle** (page 386) while they're still warm.

- For a fancy presentation, put all the slices back in place as a whole cheesecake on a cake stand. Cover the top with fresh raspberries and dust it with confectioners' sugar.

See photo in insert.

Sweet Potato Pie Rolls

VEGAN / 6 INGREDIENTS

Sweet potato pie is a Southern classic, often served in the fall when sweet potatoes are in abundance. We've morphed that dessert into these crunchy rolls but kept them light by ditching the usual butter and condensed milk in the pie filling. Instead, we let canned yams in syrup do all the heavy lifting.

See the headnote to the recipe for **Cinnamon Sugar Banana Rolls** (page 385) for the exact sort of spring roll wrappers you need. We figure two rolls per person as a serving, but maybe we're saying too much about how much we liked these.

INGREDIENTS	2-quart or larger air fryer	3.5-quart or larger air fryer	5.25-quart or larger air fryer
Spring roll wrappers	4	6	8
Canned yams in syrup, drained	1 cup	1½ cups	2 cups
Light brown sugar	4 teaspoons	2 tablespoons	2 tablespoons plus 2 teaspoons
Ground cinnamon	¼ teaspoon	Rounded ¼ teaspoon	½ teaspoon
Large egg(s), well beaten	1	1	2
Vegetable oil spray	As needed	As needed	As needed
MAKES	*2 servings*	*3 servings*	*4 servings*

1. With the basket (or basket attachment) in the air fryer, heat it to 400°F (or 390°F, if that's the closest setting).

2. Set a spring roll wrapper on a clean, dry work surface. Scoop up ¼ cup of the pulpy yams and set along one edge of the wrapper, leaving 2 inches on each side of the yams. Top the yams with about 1 teaspoon brown sugar and a pinch of ground cinnamon. Fold the sides of the wrapper perpendicular to the yam filling up and over the filling, partially covering it. Brush beaten egg(s) over the side of the wrapper farthest from the yam. Starting with the yam end, roll the wrapper closed, ending at the part with the beaten egg that you can press gently to seal. Lightly coat the roll on all sides with vegetable oil spray. Set it aside seam side down and continue filling, rolling, and spraying the remaining wrappers in the same way.

3. Set the rolls seam side down in the basket with as much air space between them as possible. Air-fry undisturbed for 8 minutes, or until crisp and golden brown.

4. Use a nonstick-safe spatula and perhaps kitchen tongs for balance to gently transfer the rolls to a wire rack. Cool for at least 5 minutes or up to 30 minutes before serving.

Then...

• To make **EASY SALTED CARAMEL SAUCE** for these rolls, spread *1¼ cups granulated white sugar* across a medium skillet set over moderate heat. Cook, stirring a few times, until the sugar liquefies and begins to turn a golden, caramel brown; then stir well and continue cooking. Meanwhile, stir *¾ cup* heavy cream and ¼ cup light corn syrup in a small microwave-safe bowl until smooth, then microwave on high for 1½ minutes, stopping the second the mixture starts to boil up. Continue cooking the sugar on the stove until it's medium amber, about 4 minutes. Remove from the heat and carefully stir in the hot cream mixture with a wooden spoon. Return the skillet to low heat; add 5 tablespoons

butter and ¼ to ½ teaspoon coarse sea salt, stirring until any hardened caramel melts. Transfer to a heat-safe glass or other heat-safe nonreactive container and cool for at least 15 minutes before serving. The sauce can be covered and stored in this container for up to 5 days. Microwave batches on high for a minute or two to loosen it up and serve it.

See photo in insert.

Cinnamon Sugar Banana Rolls

FAST / VEGETARIAN / 7 INGREDIENTS

These dessert rolls are made with spring roll wrappers, usually found in the freezer case of a large supermarket. These wrappers are not the hard, translucent rice-paper wrappers that you must first soak to get them pliable. Nor are these egg roll wrappers, which are much thicker. These wrappers are thin squares, sort of like oversized egg roll wrappers, yet less opaque.

If you want to go over the top, brush the rolls with melted butter, rather than spraying them with vegetable oil spray.

INGREDIENTS	2-quart or larger air fryer	3.5-quart or larger air fryer	5.25-quart or larger air fryer
Granulated white sugar	¼ cup	¼ cup	⅓ cups
Ground cinnamon	2 teaspoons	2 teaspoons	1 tablespoon
Peach or apricot jam or orange marmalade	1 tablespoon	2 tablespoons	3 tablespoons
Spring roll wrappers, thawed if necessary	3	6	9
Ripe banana(s), peeled and cut into 3-inch-long sections	1	2	3
Large egg, well beaten	1	1	1
Vegetable oil spray	As needed	As needed	As needed
MAKES	3 rolls	6 rolls	9 rolls

1. With the basket (or basket attachment) in the air fryer, heat it to 400°F (or 390°F, if that's the closest setting).

2. Stir the sugar and cinnamon in a small bowl until well combined. Stir the jam or marmalade with a fork to loosen it up.

continues

3. Set a spring roll wrapper on a clean, dry work surface. Roll a banana section in the sugar mixture until evenly and well coated. Set the coated banana along one edge of the wrapper. Top it with about 1 teaspoon of the jam or marmalade. Fold the sides of the wrapper perpendicular to the banana up and over the banana, partially covering it. Brush beaten egg over the side of the wrapper farthest from the banana. Starting with the banana, roll the wrapper closed, ending at the part with the beaten egg. Press gently to seal. Set the roll aside seam side down and continue filling and rolling the remaining wrappers in the same way.

4. Lightly coat the wrappers with vegetable oil spray. Set them seam side down in the basket with as much air space between them as possible. Air-fry undisturbed for 8 minutes, or until crisp and golden brown.

5. Use kitchen tongs to gently transfer the rolls to a wire rack. Cool for at least 5 minutes or up to 30 minutes before serving.

Then...

• While still warm, coat these with EASY CHOCOLATE DRIZZLE. Put *semisweet or bittersweet chocolate chips* and *butter* in a 2-to-1 ratio *by weight* in a small saucepan set over low heat. (In other words, for every ounce of chips you'll use 2 tablespoons of butter.) Stir until about half of the chocolate has melted, then remove the pan from the heat and continue to stir until smooth. Drizzle this from a fork onto the rolls.

See photo in insert.

Chocolate Banana Turnovers

CAN BE VEGETARIAN / 6 INGREDIENTS

Unfortunately, because the air fryer cooks so quickly, a fresh fruit filling in a turnover won't cook before the pastry is done and crisp. And cooking a filling on the stove, then cooling it, and only *then* air-frying it was beyond the pale for this book. So we crafted a banana turnover that uses chocolate chips and nuts for a rich, creamy filling without any advance cooking.

We've set the ingredients to make six turnovers because even working in a large machine, you can only make four turnovers at a time—and a puff pastry sheet will make six. In other words, you'll have to work in batches no matter what size your machine.

INGREDIENTS	2-quart or larger air fryer
Large egg	1
Water	2 tablespoons
Puff pastry sheet from a 17.25-ounce box of frozen puff pastry, thawed	1
Large ripe banana, peeled	1
Milk chocolate chips	6 tablespoons
Very finely chopped walnuts or pecans	6 tablespoons
MAKES	*6 turnovers*

1. With the basket (or basket attachment) in the air fryer, heat it to 400°F (or 390°F, if that's the closest setting). Whisk the egg and water in a small bowl until foamy.

2. Set the puff pastry sheet on a clean, dry work surface. Roll it to a 12-inch square. Cut the square in half (that is, into two 12 x 6-inch rectangles). Cut each of these rectangles into thirds (that is, into 6 x 4-inch rectangles). Separate the pieces of dough from each other.

3. Cut the banana in half lengthwise, then cut each half into thirds.

4. Working with one puff pastry rectangle, set it so a long side is toward you. Set one banana piece along this long side, back about ¼ inch from the edge. Top the banana with 1 tablespoon chips and 1 tablespoon nuts. Brush all the edges of the dough with the egg mixture, then fold the "unused" long side, the side farthest from you, up and over banana toward you, to meet the other long side and make a rectangular packet. Seal the edges by pressing the tines of a flatware fork into them all around. Set aside and make more turnovers in the same way.

5. With as much air space between them as possible, set 2 turnovers in the basket of a small machine, 3 in the basket of a medium one, or 4 in the basket of a large one, covering the remaining turnovers with a clean kitchen towel or a loose sheet of plastic wrap. Air-fry undisturbed for 8 minutes, or until golden brown and puffed.

6. Use a nonstick-safe metal spatula to transfer the turnovers to a wire rack. Set more turnovers in the basket as before, and air-fry the next batch—then later, a third batch in a small machine. Cool the turnovers for 10 minutes before serving.

Then...

- Serve these turnovers with butter pecan or maple ice cream—or with **No-Churn Vanilla Ice Cream** (page 378).

- Drizzle these turnovers with **Easy Chocolate Drizzle** (page 386) or **Easy Salted Caramel Sauce** (page 384).

Chocolate Macaroons

FAST / EASY / VEGETARIAN / GLUTEN-FREE / 5 INGREDIENTS

We feel chocolate macaroons should be a little more sophisticated than the plain coconut ones. To that end, we use unsweetened cocoa powder *and* unsweetened shredded coconut (sometimes called desiccated coconut; see page 159) so that the cookies have a slightly bitter edge, the better to go with coffee, tea … or whiskey.

INGREDIENTS	2-quart or larger air fryer	3.5-quart or larger air fryer	5.25-quart or larger air fryer
Large egg white(s), at room temperature	1	2	3
Table salt	⅛ teaspoon	Rounded ⅛ teaspoon	¼ teaspoon
Granulated white sugar	¼ cup	½ cup	¾ cup
Unsweetened shredded coconut	¾ cup	1½ cups	2¼ cups
Unsweetened cocoa powder	1½ tablespoons	3 tablespoons	4½ tablespoons
MAKES	*8 macaroons*	*16 macaroons*	*24 macaroons*

1. With the basket (or basket attachment) in the air fryer, heat it to 375°F (or 370°F or 360°F, if one of these is the closest setting).

2. Using an electric mixer at high speed, beat the egg white(s) and salt in a medium or large bowl until stiff peaks can be formed when the turned-off beaters are dipped into the mixture.

3. Still working with the mixer at high speed, beat in the sugar in a slow stream until the meringue is shiny and thick.

4. Scrape down and remove the beaters. Fold in the coconut and cocoa with a rubber spatula until well combined, working carefully to deflate the meringue as little as possible.

5. Scoop up 2 tablespoons of the mixture. Wet your clean hands and roll that little bit of coconut bliss into a ball. Set it aside and continue making more balls: 7 more for a small batch, 15 more for a medium batch, or 23 more for a large one.

6. Line the bottom of the machine's basket or the basket attachment with parchment paper. Set the balls on the parchment with as much air space between them as possible. Air-fry undisturbed for 8 minutes, or until dry, set, and lightly browned.

7. Use a nonstick-safe spatula to transfer the macaroons to a wire rack. Cool for at least 10 minutes before serving. Or cool to room temperature, about 30 minutes, then store in a sealed container at room temperature for up to 3 days.

Then…

- If these macaroons sit around and get stale, toast them in a 350°F (or 360°F, if the closest setting) air fryer for 2 or 3 minutes, until very dry. Then crumble them over scoops of vanilla, chocolate, or butterscotch ice cream.

Coconut Macaroons

FAST / EASY / VEGETARIAN / GLUTEN-FREE / 7 INGREDIENTS

Coconut macaroons are a baker's dream: easy to make, impressive to serve. Most coconut macaroons are (in our opinion) unduly soft. These have a crisp exterior with that characteristic soft interior.

Because we don't want to call for portions of an egg, this recipe will only make a small or a large batch. As always, you can make the large portion for a small machine, so long as you're prepared to work in batches.

INGREDIENTS	2-quart or larger air fryer	5.25-quart or larger air fryer
Large egg(s)	1	2
Granulated white sugar	⅓ cup	⅔ cup
Sweetened shredded coconut	1¼ cups	2½ cups
Coconut flour	¼ cup	½ cup
Vanilla extract	½ teaspoon	1 teaspoon
Table salt	¼ teaspoon	½ teaspoon
Vegetable oil or coconut oil spray	As needed	As needed
MAKES	9 macaroons	18 macaroons

1. Using an electric mixer at medium speed, beat the egg(s) and sugar in a medium bowl until so thick that wide ribbons will fall from the turned-off beaters, ribbons that lie on top of the mixture below without immediately dissolving back in.

2. Scrape down and remove the beaters. Fold in the coconut, coconut flour, vanilla, and salt until evenly distributed. Set aside for 10 minutes at room temperature.

3. Meanwhile, with the basket (or basket attachment) in the air fryer, heat it to 325°F (or 330°F, if that's the closest setting).

4. Roll 2 tablespoons of the coconut mixture into a compact ball between your clean, dry palms and set aside. Continue making 8 more balls for the small batch or 17 more for the large one. Coat the bottom of each macaroon with vegetable oil or coconut oil spray.

5. Place the balls in the basket, spacing them at least ½ inch apart. Air-fry undisturbed for 10 minutes, or until lightly browned.

6. Use a nonstick-safe spatula, and perhaps a flatware fork for balance, to transfer the macaroons to a wire rack. Cool for at least 10 minutes before serving. Or cool to room temperature, about 45 minutes, and store in a sealed container at room temperature for up to 3 days.

continues

Then...

- Drizzle these macaroons with COCONUT GLAZE once they've cooled to room temperature. For the best results, stir the fat back into the liquid coconut milk in the can before measuring out what you need. To make enough for the small batch, whisk *2 cups confectioners' sugar, 3 tablespoons full-fat coconut milk or*

coconut cream (*not* crème de coconut), and *⅛ teaspoon table salt* in a bowl until smooth, adding more coconut milk in dribs and drabs until you have a thick, spreadable icing. Drizzle this mixture over the *cooled* macaroons. If desired, sprinkle shredded coconut over each while the glaze is still wet. Set aside at room temperature to dry for 1 hour.

Cheese Blintzes

EASY / VEGETARIAN / 6 INGREDIENTS

Blintzes are either fried or baked. These are a re-creation of the fried variety, made for the air fryer. And made simpler, too, since we've used square egg roll wrappers, rather than making crepes from a wet batter.

Our filling is fairly straightforward, a sweetened mix of farmer and cream cheese. The blintzes need a topper. We suggest two. Plan on two blintzes per person—or make more batches if you have enough willpower to stop from first snarfing down a plateful.

INGREDIENTS	2-quart or larger air fryer	3.5-quart or larger air fryer	5.25-quart or larger air fryer
7½-ounce package(s) farmer cheese	1	1½	2
Regular or low-fat cream cheese (*not* fat-free)	2 tablespoons	3 tablespoons	¼ cup
Granulated white sugar	2 tablespoons	3 tablespoons	¼ cup
Vanilla extract	⅛ teaspoon	¼ teaspoon	¼ teaspoon
Egg roll wrappers	4	6	8
Butter, melted and cooled	2 tablespoons	3 tablespoons	4 tablespoons (¼ cup/½ stick)
MAKES	*4 blintzes*	*6 blintzes*	*8 blintzes*

1. With the basket (or basket attachment) in the air fryer, heat it to 375°F (or 370°F or 360°F, if one of these is the closest setting).

2. Use a flatware fork to mash the farmer cheese, cream cheese, sugar, and vanilla in a small bowl until smooth.

3. Set one egg roll wrapper on a clean, dry work surface. Place ¼ cup of the filling at the edge closest to you, leaving a ½-inch gap before the edge of the wrapper. Dip your clean finger in water and wet the edges of the wrapper. Fold the perpendicular sides over the filling, then roll the wrapper closed with the filling inside. Set it aside seam side down and continue filling the remainder of the wrappers.

4. Brush the wrappers on all sides with the melted butter. Be generous. Set them seam side down in the basket with as much space between them as possible. Air-fry undisturbed for 10 minutes, or until lightly browned.

5. Use a nonstick-safe spatula to transfer the blintzes to a wire rack. Cool for at least 5 minutes or up to 20 minutes before serving.

Then...

- Whisk orange marmalade or apricot preserves in a small bowl until loosened, then spread over the warm blintzes to serve.

- Or serve them with SWEETENED SOUR CREAM. For every *½ cup regular, low-fat, or fat-free sour cream*, whisk in *1 tablespoon confectioners' sugar* and *1 teaspoon vanilla extract* in a bowl until smooth.

Giant Buttery Chocolate Chip Cookie

VEGETARIAN / 10 INGREDIENTS

Most of our air-fryer cookie recipes are made in a round cake pan. We find that cookies baked even on parchment in the machine turn out with overdone—even burned—edges and too-soft centers. What's more, you can only make two or three at a time on parchment to maintain the necessary space between the cookies for air circulation. With a baking pan, you can make a single large cookie, like the cookies at popular mall bake shops. This larger cookie can be cut into wedges to serve. Have milk on hand!

For all these cookies, it's best to work with a hand mixer because the amounts are so small, the paddle of a stand mixer won't be able to work with the batter or dough.

Also note that this recipe (along with some subsequent recipes) calls for *baking spray*, a mix of flour and oil. Along with coconut oil spray, baking spray is the other *aerosol* spray we recommend. Never spray it into the machine. And if you'd rather go old school, you can indeed coat the inside of the pan with vegetable oil spray, then add a small handful of all-purpose flour, turning the pan this way and that to coat it evenly and thoroughly before knocking out any excess. Whether you use baking spray or the more traditional method, the inside of the pan needs a generous coating so that the baked good will come loose after it cools a bit.

INGREDIENTS	2-quart or larger air fryer	3.5-quart or larger air fryer	5.25-quart or larger air fryer
All-purpose flour	½ cup plus 1 tablespoon	⅔ cup plus 1 tablespoon	¾ cup plus 2 tablespoons
Baking soda	¼ teaspoon	Rounded ¼ teaspoon	½ teaspoon
Table salt	¼ teaspoon	Rounded ¼ teaspoon	½ teaspoon
Baking spray (see the headnote)	As needed	As needed	As needed
Butter, at room temperature	3 tablespoons plus 1 teaspoon	4 tablespoons (¼ cup/½ stick) plus 1 teaspoon	5 tablespoons plus 2 teaspoons
Packed dark brown sugar	3 tablespoons plus 1 teaspoon	¼ cup plus 1 teaspoon	⅓ cup
Granulated white sugar	2½ tablespoons	3 tablespoons plus 1 teaspoon	¼ cup
Pasteurized egg substitute, such as Egg Beaters	2 tablespoons (or 1 small egg, well beaten)	2½ tablespoons	3 tablespoons (or 1 medium egg, well beaten)
Vanilla extract	¼ teaspoon	½ teaspoon	¾ teaspoon
Semisweet or bittersweet chocolate chips	⅔ cup	¾ cup plus 1 tablespoon	1 cup
MAKES	*2 or 3 servings*	*4 servings*	*4 or 5 servings*

1. With the basket (or basket attachment) in the air fryer, heat it to 350°F (or 360°F, if that's the closest setting).

2. Whisk the flour, baking soda, and salt in a bowl until well combined.

3. For a small air fryer, coat the inside of a 6-inch round cake pan with baking spray. For a medium air fryer, coat the inside of a 7-inch round cake pan with baking spray. And for a large air fryer, coat the inside of an 8-inch round cake pan with baking spray.

4. Using a hand electric mixer at medium speed, beat the butter, brown sugar, and granulated white sugar in a bowl until smooth and thick, about 3 minutes, scraping down the inside of the bowl several times.

5. Beat in the pasteurized egg substitute or egg (as applicable) and vanilla until uniform. Scrape down and remove the beaters. Fold in the flour mixture and chocolate chips with a rubber spatula, just until combined. Scrape and gently press this dough into the prepared pan, getting it even across the pan to the perimeter.

6. Set the pan in the basket and air-fry undisturbed for 14 to 16 minutes, or until the cookie is puffed, browned, and feels set to the touch.

7. Transfer the pan to a wire rack and cool for 10 minutes. Loosen the cookie from the perimeter with a spatula, then invert the pan onto a cutting board and let the cookie come free. Remove the pan and reinvert the cookie onto the wire rack. Cool for 5 minutes more before slicing into wedges to serve.

Then...

- This cookie is made for dunking. Consider whole milk, chocolate milk, strong coffee, red wine, aged rum, or whiskey as your best options.

See photo in insert.

Giant Vegan Chocolate Chip Cookie

EASY / VEGAN / 11 INGREDIENTS

We love these vegan cookies that use tahini as a flavorful replacement for butter. The addition of maple syrup balances that sesame flavor, giving the cookie a rich, sweet flavor with a cakey finish.

One note: Not all semisweet or even dark chocolate is vegan. Look for specifically vegan chocolate, if you want to maintain the animal-free quality of this cookie.

INGREDIENTS	2-quart or larger air fryer	3.5-quart or larger air fryer	5.25-quart or larger air fryer
All-purpose flour	½ cup	⅔ cup	¾ cup
Rolled oats (*not* quick-cooking or steel-cut oats)	¼ cup	5 tablespoons	6 tablespoons
Baking soda	¼ teaspoon	Rounded ¼ teaspoon	½ teaspoon
Table salt	¼ teaspoon	Rounded ¼ teaspoon	½ teaspoon
Granulated white sugar	¼ cup	5 tablespoons	6 tablespoons
Vegetable oil	3 tablespoons	¼ cup	4½ tablespoons
Tahini (see page 79)	2 tablespoons	2½ tablespoons	3 tablespoons
Maple syrup	2 tablespoons	2½ tablespoons	3 tablespoons
Vanilla extract	1½ teaspoons	2 teaspoons	2½ teaspoons
Vegan semisweet or bittersweet chocolate chips	½ cup	⅔ cup	¾ cup
Baking spray	As needed	As needed	As needed
MAKES	*2 or 3 servings*	*4 servings*	*5 or 6 servings*

1. With the basket (or basket attachment) in the air fryer, heat it to 325°F (or 330°F, if that's the closest setting).

2. Whisk the flour, oats, baking soda, and salt in a bowl until well combined.

3. Using an electric hand mixer at medium speed (see the headnote on page 392 for the rationale for this sort of mixer), beat the sugar, oil, tahini, maple syrup, and vanilla until rich and creamy, about 3 minutes, scraping down the inside of the bowl occasionally.

4. Scrape down and remove the beaters. Fold in the flour mixture and chocolate chips with a rubber spatula just until all the flour is moistened and the chocolate chips are even throughout the dough.

5. For a small air fryer, coat the inside of a 6-inch round cake pan with baking spray. For a medium air fryer, coat the inside of a 7-inch round cake pan with baking spray. And for a large air fryer, coat the inside of an 8-inch round cake pan with baking spray. Scrape and gently press the dough into the prepared pan, spreading it into an even layer to the perimeter.

6. Set the pan in the basket and air-fry undisturbed for 14 to 16 minutes, or until puffed, browned, and firm to the touch.

7. Transfer the pan to a wire rack and cool for 10 minutes. Loosen the cookie from the perimeter with a spatula, then invert the pan onto a cutting board and let the cookie come free. Remove the pan and reinvert the cookie onto the wire rack. Cool for 5 minutes more before slicing into wedges to serve.

Then...

- Serve this giant cookie with VEGAN NO-CHURN STRAWBERRY DELIGHT. Put the following in this order in a large blender: *2 tablespoons* cold *almond milk, 1 frozen peeled banana, ½ pound (8 ounces) frozen hulled strawberries, 1 tablespoon almond butter,* and *1 tablespoon agave syrup.* Cover and blend until icy but fairly smooth, occasionally shaking the canister and rearranging the ingredients, and adding *more almond milk* in small amounts to get the right texture. Scoop into bowls and serve at once.

Giant Buttery Oatmeal Cookie

VEGETARIAN / 12 INGREDIENTS

In our estimation, this cookie is the ultimate comfort food: rich, buttery, and soft. It will firm up as it sits, so if you prefer a soft cookie, enjoy it while it's warm. We chose nuts over raisins in this oatmeal cookie because the super-fast convection currents can burn any exposed raisins, giving them a bitter taste. The hot air toasts pecans for a gentler, more aromatic flavor.

INGREDIENTS	2-quart or larger air fryer	3.5-quart or larger air fryer	5.25-quart or larger air fryer
Rolled oats (*not* quick-cooking or steel-cut oats)	¾ cup	1 cup	1 cup plus 3 tablespoons
All-purpose flour	⅓ cup	½ cup	½ cup plus 1½ tablespoons
Baking soda	¼ teaspoon	½ teaspoon	¾ teaspoon
Ground cinnamon	¼ teaspoon	½ teaspoon	¾ teaspoon
Table salt	¼ teaspoon	½ teaspoon	¾ teaspoon
Butter, at room temperature	2½ tablespoons	3½ tablespoons	4 tablespoons (¼ cup/½ stick) plus 1 teaspoon
Packed dark brown sugar	¼ cup	⅓ cup	6 tablespoons plus 1 teaspoon
Granulated white sugar	1 tablespoon	1½ tablespoons	2 tablespoons
Pasteurized egg substitute, such as Egg Beaters	2 tablespoons plus 1 teaspoon	3 tablespoons (or 1 medium egg, well beaten)	3½ tablespoons
Vanilla extract	½ teaspoon	¾ teaspoon	1 teaspoon
Chopped pecans	¼ cup	⅓ cup	6 tablespoons
Baking spray	As needed	As needed	As needed
MAKES	*2 or 3 servings*	*4 servings*	*5 or 6 servings*

1. With the basket (or basket attachment) in the air fryer, heat it to 350°F (or 360°F, if that's the closest setting).

2. Stir the oats, flour, baking soda, cinnamon, and salt in a bowl until well combined.

3. Using an electric hand mixer at medium speed (see the headnote on page 392 for the rationale for this sort of mixer), beat the butter, brown sugar, and granulated white sugar until creamy and thick, about 3 minutes, scraping down the inside of the bowl occasionally. Beat in the egg substitute or egg (as applicable) and vanilla until uniform.

4. Scrape down and remove the beaters. Fold in the flour mixture and pecans with a rubber spatula just until all the flour is moistened and the nuts are even throughout the dough.

5. For a small air fryer, coat the inside of a 6-inch round cake pan with baking spray. For a medium air fryer, coat the inside of a 7-inch round cake pan with baking spray. And for a large air fryer, coat the inside of an 8-inch round cake pan with baking spray. Scrape and gently press the dough into the prepared pan, spreading it into an even layer to the perimeter.

6. Set the pan in the basket and air-fry undisturbed for 14 to 16 minutes, or until puffed and browned.

7. Transfer the pan to a wire rack and cool for 10 minutes. Loosen the cookie from the perimeter with a spatula, then invert the pan onto a cutting board and let the cookie come free. Remove the pan and reinvert the cookie onto the wire rack. Cool for 5 minutes more before slicing into wedges to serve.

Then...

- To make the best ice cream sandwiches, soften vanilla or butter pecan ice cream or gelato for a few minutes on the counter. Spread the ice cream or gelato on the flat side of one cookie wedge, then top with a second wedge flat side down. These ice cream sandwiches can be made well in advance; seal them in plastic wrap and store them in the freezer for up to 3 months (as if they'd last that long).

- Or if you make and cool two of these cookies but don't cut them into wedges, you can use this technique to make a giant ice cream sandwich cake.

See photo in insert.

Giant Oatmeal–Peanut Butter Cookie

VEGETARIAN / 11 INGREDIENTS

We didn't use butter for this cookie because its flavor competed with and even muted the peanut butter. We wanted a *peanut butter* cookie—or really, a cross between a peanut butter cookie and an oatmeal cookie.

Remember the rule for all cookie-making: Go ahead and overbeat the fat and sugars, but avoid working the flour too much or you'll end up with tough cookies. Fold the flour mixture in only until all the flour is moistened, not necessarily until the flour has dissolved into the dough.

INGREDIENTS	2-quart or larger air fryer	3.5-quart or larger air fryer	5.25-quart or larger air fryer
Rolled oats (*not* quick-cooking or steel-cut oats)	¾ cup	1 cup	1¼ cups
All-purpose flour	6 tablespoons	½ cup	⅔ cup
Ground cinnamon	Rounded ¼ teaspoon	½ teaspoon	¾ teaspoon
Baking soda	Rounded ¼ teaspoon	½ teaspoon	¾ teaspoon
Packed light brown sugar	¼ cup	⅓ cup	7 tablespoons
Solid vegetable shortening	3 tablespoons	¼ cup	5 tablespoons
Natural-style creamy peanut butter	1½ tablespoons	2 tablespoons	2½ tablespoons
Granulated white sugar	2 tablespoons plus ½ teaspoon	3 tablespoons	3 tablespoons plus 2 teaspoons
Pasteurized egg substitute, such as Egg Beaters	1½ tablespoons	2 tablespoons (or 1 small egg, well beaten)	2½ tablespoons
Roasted, salted peanuts, chopped	¼ cup	⅓ cup	7 tablespoons
Baking spray	As needed	As needed	As needed
MAKES	*2 or 3 servings*	*4 servings*	*5 or 6 servings*

1. With the basket (or basket attachment) in the air fryer, heat it to 350°F (or 360°F, if that's the closest setting).

2. Stir the oats, flour, cinnamon, and baking soda in a bowl until well combined.

3. Using an electric hand mixer at medium speed (see the headnote on page 392 for the rationale for this sort of mixer), beat the brown sugar, shortening, peanut butter, granulated white sugar, and egg substitute or egg (as applicable) until smooth and creamy, about 3 minutes, scraping down the inside of the bowl occasionally.

4. Scrape down and remove the beaters. Fold in the flour mixture and peanuts with a rubber spatula just until all the flour is moistened and the peanut bits are evenly distributed in the dough.

5. For a small air fryer, coat the inside of a 6-inch round cake pan with baking spray. For a medium air fryer, coat the inside of a 7-inch round cake pan with baking spray. And for a large air fryer, coat the inside of an 8-inch round cake pan with baking spray. Scrape and gently press the dough into the prepared pan, spreading it into an even layer to the perimeter.

6. Set the pan in the basket and air-fry undisturbed for 15 to 18 minutes, or until well browned.

7. Transfer the pan to a wire rack and cool for 15 minutes. Loosen the cookie from the perimeter with a spatula, then invert the pan onto a cutting board and let the cookie come free. Remove the pan and reinvert the cookie onto the wire rack. Cool for 5 minutes more before slicing into wedges to serve.

Then...

- Consider frosting this cookie with marshmallow Fluff or marshmallow creme.

- If you frost it, sprinkle it with even more chopped salted peanuts.

- Or if you miss the raisins in an oatmeal cookie, frost it, then sprinkle raisins on top.

Easy Churros

VEGETARIAN / 7 INGREDIENTS

We nixed piping this dough for churros in favor of shaping it by hand to make an overall easier-to-make treat, something like a cross between traditional churros (although not deep-fried) and a sugar-coated tube of cream puff pastry. The results are surprisingly light—which means you can eat several, right?

For more flavor (but hardly a traditional coating), add up to ½ teaspoon ground cardamom and/or ¼ teaspoon grated nutmeg to the cinnamon sugar mixture.

INGREDIENTS	2-quart or larger air fryer	3.5-quart or larger air fryer
Water	¼ cup	½ cup
Butter	2 tablespoons	4 tablespoons (¼ cup/½ stick)
Table salt	⅛ teaspoon	¼ teaspoon
All-purpose flour	¼ cup	½ cup
Large egg(s)	1	2
Granulated white sugar	¼ cup	¼ cup
Ground cinnamon	2 teaspoons	2 teaspoons
MAKES	6 churros	12 churros

1. Bring the water, butter, and salt to a boil in a small saucepan set over high heat, stirring occasionally.

2. When the butter has fully melted, reduce the heat to medium and stir in the flour to form a dough. Continue cooking, stirring constantly, to dry out the dough until it coats the bottom and sides of the pan with a film, even a crust. Remove the pan from the heat, scrape the dough into a bowl, and cool for 15 minutes.

3. Using an electric hand mixer at medium speed, beat in the egg, or eggs one at a time, until the dough is smooth and firm enough to hold its shape.

4. Mix the sugar and cinnamon in a small bowl. Scoop up 1 tablespoon of the dough and roll it in the sugar mixture to form a small, coated tube about ½ inch in diameter and 2 inches long. Set it aside and make 5 more tubes for the small batch or 11 more for the large one.

5. Set the tubes on a plate and freeze for 20 minutes. Meanwhile, with the basket (or basket attachment) in the air fryer, heat it to 375°F (or 370°F or 360°F, if one of these is the closest setting).

6. Set 3 frozen tubes in the basket for a small batch or 6 for a large one with as much air space between them as possible. Air-fry undisturbed for 10 minutes, or until puffed, brown, and set.

7. Use kitchen tongs to transfer the churros to a wire rack to cool for at least 5 minutes. Meanwhile, air-fry and cool the second batch of churros in the same way.

Then...

- Serve these churros with a sweet wine, like vin santo or chilled Eiswein.

- Dip the churros in **Hot Fudge Sauce** (page 418).

Sweet Biscuit Donuts

EASY / VEGETARIAN / 11 INGREDIENTS

We created this recipe so that it will yield a donut-like pastry in the air fryer without any yeast. Basically, these are very sweet biscuits that cook up like cake donuts in the machine. You'll need a 4-inch-round cookie cutter (or a very sturdy 4-inch-round drinking glass) and then a ½-inch round one to make the holes—or better yet, just a 4-inch round donut cutter.

INGREDIENTS	2-quart or larger air fryer
All-purpose flour	2 cups, plus more as needed
Granulated white sugar	⅔ cup plus 1¼ teaspoons
Baking powder	1 tablespoon
Table salt	½ teaspoon
Whole or low-fat milk (*not* fat-free)	½ cup
Large egg white	1
Lemon juice	1 tablespoon
Vanilla extract	1 teaspoon
Butter, melted and cooled	8 tablespoons (½ cup/1 stick)
Large egg yolk	1
Water	2 tablespoons
MAKES	*10 biscuit donuts*

1. With the basket (or basket attachment) in the air fryer, heat it to 375°F (or 370°F or 360°F, if one of these is the closest setting).

2. Whisk the flour, ⅔ cup sugar, baking powder, and salt in a medium bowl until well combined.

3. Make a well in the center of the flour mixture. Pour the milk, egg white, lemon juice, and vanilla in this well. Stir to combine, adding bits of the flour as you go. Then add the melted and cooled butter. Stir to form a soft dough.

4. Flour a clean, dry work surface. Turn out the dough onto it and press it to a circle about ½-inch thick. Cut 4-inch rounds out of the dough, then cut a ½-inch hole in the center of each of these. Gather the dough scraps together, including the cut-out holes, press out again to a ½-inch-thick circle, and cut more rounds and more holes. You should end up with 10 biscuit donuts.

5. Whisk the egg yolk with the water in a small bowl until uniform. Brush this mixture evenly over the biscuit donuts. Sprinkle each with ⅛ teaspoon sugar.

continues

6. Working in batches, put 2, 3, or 4 of the biscuit donuts in the basket with at least ½ inch between them. Air-fry undisturbed for 7 minutes, until puffed, lightly browned, and set. If the machine is at 360°F, you may need to add 1 minute to the cooking time.

7. Use a nonstick-safe spatula to transfer the biscuit donuts to a wire rack and cool for at least 5 minutes or to room temperature, about 45 minutes. Meanwhile, continue air-frying more of the biscuit

donuts in batches and cooling them as you did the first batch.

Then...

- Use the **Easy Chocolate Drizzle** (page 386) or **Coconut Glaze** (page 390) to frost the tops of these donuts.

- Serve them topped with **Sweetened Sour Cream** (page 391) and lots sliced strawberries for a new take on strawberry shortcake.

Donut Holes

EASY / VEGETARIAN / 9 INGREDIENTS

We should call these "donut holes without the donuts." You'll make small dough balls that you'll air-fry until crunchy, like cake donut holes but much simpler to prepare.

These are admittedly plain, best for dunking in a cup of hot coffee. If you want more pizzazz, check out the suggestions in the *Then* section for this recipe.

INGREDIENTS	2-quart or larger air fryer	3.5-quart or larger air fryer	5.25-quart or larger air fryer
Granulated white sugar	¼ cup	6 tablespoons	½ cup
Butter, melted and cooled	1 tablespoon	1½ tablespoons	2 tablespoons
Pasteurized egg substitute, such as Egg Beaters	1½ tablespoons	2 tablespoons (or 1 small egg, well beaten)	3 tablespoons (or 1 medium egg, well beaten)
Regular or low-fat sour cream (*not* fat-free)	¼ cup	6 tablespoons	½ cup
Vanilla extract	½ teaspoon	¾ teaspoon	1 teaspoon
All-purpose flour	1 cup plus 2 tablespoons	1⅔ cups	2¼ cups
Baking powder	½ teaspoon	¾ teaspoon	1 teaspoon
Table salt	¼ teaspoon	Rounded ¼ teaspoon	½ teaspoon
Vegetable oil spray	As needed	As needed	As needed
MAKES	*9 donut holes*	*13 donut holes*	*18 donut holes*

1. With the basket (or basket attachment) in the air fryer, heat it to 350°F (or 360°F, if that's the closest setting).

2. Whisk the sugar and melted butter in a medium bowl until well combined. Whisk in the egg substitute or egg (as applicable), then the sour cream and vanilla until smooth. Remove the whisk and stir in the flour, baking powder, and salt with a wooden spoon just until a soft dough forms.

3. Use 2 tablespoons of this dough to create a ball between your clean palms. Set it aside and continue making balls: 8 more for the small batch, 12 more for the medium batch, or 17 more for the large one.

4. Coat the balls in the vegetable oil spray, then set them in the basket with as much air space between them as possible. Even a fraction of an inch will be enough, but they should not touch. Air-fry undisturbed for 12 minutes, or until browned and cooked through. A toothpick inserted into the center of a ball should come out clean.

5. Pour the contents of the basket onto a wire rack. Cool for at least 5 minutes before serving.

Then...

- To coat the donut holes, melt 2 to 3 tablespoons butter, then cool for 5 minutes. Meanwhile, mix granulated white sugar and ground cinnamon in a ¼-cup-to-1-teaspoon ratio. Roll the cooled balls in the butter, then in the cinnamon sugar mixture.

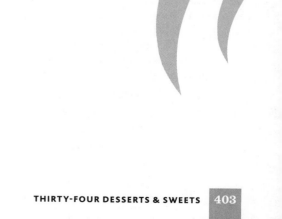

Roasted Pears

FAST / EASY / VEGETARIAN / GLUTEN-FREE / 6 INGREDIENTS

There's nothing like roasted pears for a simple dessert—or an easy breakfast—when the weather turns cool. Look for ripe pears that are still a bit firm to the touch. You can tell the texture by feel, but the only way to tell a pear's ripeness is with your nose. It must smell fragrant and sweet. An underripe pear won't have much smell at all—and will be hardly worth the effort of this recipe.

To shave Parmesan cheese, you can use a fancy cheese plane, although a vegetable peeler will work just as well, provided you cut the surface of the Parmesan so it's smooth, not scraggy.

INGREDIENTS	2-quart or larger air fryer	3.5-quart or larger air fryer	5.25-quart or larger air fryer
Ripe pears, preferably Anjou, stemmed, peeled, halved lengthwise, and cored	1	2	3
Butter, melted	1 tablespoon	2 tablespoons	3 tablespoons
Granulated white sugar	1 teaspoon	2 teaspoons	1 tablespoon
Grated nutmeg	As needed	As needed	As needed
Honey	2 tablespoons	¼ cup	6 tablespoons
Shaved Parmesan cheese	¼ cup (about ¾ ounce)	½ cup (about 1½ ounces)	¾ cup (a little more than 2 ounces)
MAKES	2 servings	4 servings	6 servings

1. With the basket (or basket attachment) in the air fryer, heat it to 400°F (or 390°F, if that's the closest setting).

2. Brush each pear half with about 1½ teaspoons of the melted butter, then sprinkle their cut sides with ½ teaspoon sugar. Grate a pinch of nutmeg over each pear.

3. When the machine is at temperature, set the pear halves cut side up in the basket with as much air space between them as possible. Air-fry undisturbed for 10 minutes, or until hot and softened.

4. Use a nonstick-safe spatula, and perhaps a flatware tablespoon for balance, to transfer the pear halves to a serving platter or plates. Cool for a minute or two, then drizzle each pear half with 1 tablespoon of the honey. Lay about 2 tablespoons of shaved Parmesan over each half just before serving.

Then...

- Offer plain Greek yogurt or **Sweetened Sour Cream** (page 391) as an accompaniment.

- And/or garnish the servings with minced fresh mint leaves.

- Although we suggest honey and Parmesan as the finish for these pears, unadorned they could become the base for an ice cream sundae, particularly with butter pecan, maple, or honey ice cream, as well as chopped pecans for a garnish.

Brown Sugar Baked Apples

FAST / EASY / VEGETARIAN / GLUTEN-FREE / 5 INGREDIENTS

"Baking" apples in the air fryer makes them almost impossibly sweet, their juices concentrated and the apples collapsed a bit in the hot air. The results are a little chewier than those made in the oven, better for a knife and fork than a fork alone.

For an extra crunchy topping, mix the brown sugar with 1 to 2 tablespoons plain dried bread crumbs (gluten-free, if a concern) before sprinkling it over the apple halves.

INGREDIENTS	2-quart or larger air fryer	3.5-quart or larger air fryer	5.25-quart or larger air fryer
Small tart apples, preferably McIntosh	2	3	4
Butter	8 teaspoons	4 tablespoons (¼ cup/½ stick)	5 tablespoons plus 1 teaspoon (⅓ cup)
Light brown sugar	¼ cup	6 tablespoons	½ cup
Ground cinnamon	As needed	As needed	As needed
Table salt	As needed	As needed	As needed
MAKES	2 servings	4 servings	6 servings

1. With the basket (or basket attachment) in the air fryer, heat it to 400°F (or 390°F, if that's the closest setting).

2. Stem the apples, then cut them in half through their "equators" (that is, not the stem ends). Use a melon baller to core the apples, taking care not to break through the flesh and skin at any point but creating a little well in the center of each half.

3. When the machine is at temperature, remove the basket and set it on a heat-safe work surface. Set the apple halves cut side up in the basket with as much air space between them as possible. Even a fraction of an inch will work. Drop 2 teaspoons of butter into the well in the center of each apple half. Sprinkle each half with 1 tablespoon brown sugar and a pinch each ground cinnamon and table salt.

4. Return the basket to the machine. Air-fry undisturbed for 15 minutes, or until the apple halves have softened and the brown sugar has caramelized.

5. Use a nonstick-safe spatula to transfer the apple halves cut side up to a wire rack. Cool for at least 10 minutes before serving, or serve at room temperature.

Then...

- These apple halves are best with ice cream. Try purchased butterscotch, caramel swirl, or butter pecan. Or plan in advance and make our **No-Churn Vanilla Ice Cream** (page 378).

Fried Pineapple Chunks

EASY / VEGETARIAN / 5 INGREDIENTS

We love frying *fresh* pineapple chunks. But because the wet chunks can be difficult to coat, we use a slightly different technique here, shaking them with flavored cookie crumbs in a large bag. We call for more cookie crumbs than you might need, but the increased amount is a bid to get the chunks evenly coated.

Use only regular cookies for the crumbs, not low-fat ones. Doing so means you don't have to coat the chunks with vegetable oil spray. It also keeps the pineapple bits crisp, since the fruit itself releases a little moisture into the coating as it cooks, moisture that can affect low-fat cookies more severely.

INGREDIENTS	2-quart or larger air fryer	3.5-quart or larger air fryer	5.25-quart or larger air fryer
Cornstarch	2 tablespoons	3 tablespoons	¼ cup
Large egg white, beaten until foamy	1	1	1
Ground vanilla wafer cookies (*not* low-fat cookies)	¾ cup (3 ounces)	1 cup (4 ounces)	1½ cups (6 ounces)
Ground dried ginger	¼ teaspoon	Rounded ¼ teaspoon	½ teaspoon
Fresh 1-inch chunks peeled and cored pineapple	12 (about 1½ cups)	18 (about 2¼ cups)	24 (about 3 cups)
MAKES	*2 or 3 servings*	*3 or 4 servings*	*4 or 5 servings*

1. With the basket (or basket attachment) in the air fryer, heat it to 400°F (or 390°F, if that's the closest setting).

2. Put the cornstarch in a medium or large bowl. Put the beaten egg white in a small bowl. Pour the cookie crumbs and ground dried ginger into a large zip-closed plastic bag, shaking it a bit to combine them.

3. Dump the pineapple chunks into the bowl with the cornstarch. Toss and stir until well coated. Use your cleaned fingers or a large fork like a shovel to pick up a few pineapple chunks, shake off any excess cornstarch, and put them in the bowl with the egg white. Stir gently, then pick them up and let any excess egg white slip back into the rest. Put them in the bag with the crumb mixture. Repeat the cornstarch-then-egg process until all the pineapple chunks are in the bag. Seal the bag and shake gently, turning the bag this way and that, to coat the pieces well.

4. Set the coated pineapple chunks in the basket with as much air space between them as possible. Even a fraction of an inch will work, but they should not touch. Air-fry undisturbed for 10 minutes, or until golden brown and crisp.

5. Gently dump the contents of the basket onto a wire rack. Cool for at least 5 minutes or up to 15 minutes before serving.

Then...

- Serve these fried pineapple chunks on top of vanilla or coconut ice cream.

- Dip them into plain Greek yogurt that's been sweetened with honey or maple syrup.

- Serve these pineapple chunks as dessert after any Asian recipe in this book!

Apple Dumplings

CAN BE VEGETARIAN / 4 INGREDIENTS

Soft apples wrapped in puff pastry—what could be better? You'll need to give the apples a head start, softening them a bit in the microwave before they get wrapped and go in the air fryer. Otherwise, the apples will not get done inside the pastry before it's browned and puffed. Also, plan on serving these within 30 minutes of making them. If they sit too long, the apples begin to turn the pastry soggy.

To core a whole apple, use an apple corer or melon baller to work up into the apple from the blossom end (opposite the stem), making as small a hole as possible in the apple while removing the seeds and keeping the apple otherwise intact.

INGREDIENTS	2-quart or larger air fryer	3.5-quart or larger air fryer	5.25-quart or larger air fryer
Small tart apples, preferably McIntosh, peeled and cored	2	4	6
Granulated white sugar	2 tablespoons	¼ cup	⅓ cup
Ground cinnamon	2 teaspoons	1½ tablespoons	2 tablespoons
A 17.25-ounce box frozen puff pastry (vegetarian, if a concern)	Two quarters of one thawed sheet (that is, a half of the sheet cut into two even pieces; wrap and refreeze the remainder)	1 sheet, thawed and cut into four quarters	1 sheet, thawed and cut into four quarters plus half a sheet, thawed and cut into two even pieces; wrap and refreeze the remainder
MAKES	2 servings	4 servings	6 servings

1. Set the apples (former) stem side up on a microwave-safe plate, preferably a glass pie plate. Microwave on high for 3 minutes, or until somewhat tender (but not soft) when poked with the point of a knife. Cool to room temperature, about 30 minutes.

2. With the basket (or basket attachment) in the air fryer, heat it to 400°F (or 390°F, if that's the closest setting).

3. Combine the sugar and cinnamon in a small bowl. Roll the apples in this mixture, coating them completely on their outsides. Also sprinkle this cinnamon sugar into each hole where the core was.

4. Roll the puff pastry squares into 6 x 6-inch squares. Slice the corners off each rolled square so that it's sort of like a circle (with four otherwise straight edges, of course). Place an apple in the center of one of these squares and fold it up and all around the apple, sealing it at the top by pressing the pastry together. The apple must be completely sealed in the pastry. Repeat for the remaining apples.

5. Set the pastry-covered apples in the basket with at least ½ inch between them. Air-fry undisturbed for 10 minutes, or until puffed and golden brown.

continues

6. Use a nonstick-safe spatula, and maybe a flatware tablespoon for balance, to transfer the apples to a wire rack. Cool for at least 5 minutes or up to 15 minutes before serving warm.

Then...

- Make **PRALINE SAUCE** to spoon over these dumplings. Stir *1½ cups granulated white sugar* and *1 cup water* in a medium saucepan set over medium heat until the sugar dissolves. Continue cooking until the mixture is a dark amber, about 15 minutes. Slowly whisk in *1 cup heavy cream,* stirring to dissolve any sugar clumps. Remove from the heat and stir in *2 cups toasted pecan pieces, 2 teaspoons vanilla extract,* and *¼ teaspoon table salt.* If desired, also stir in *2 tablespoons bourbon or whiskey.* Cool for at least 10 minutes but serve warm. The sauce can be stored in a covered glass or other nonreactive container in the refrigerator for up to 1 week. Microwave small portions in 10-second increments on high, stirring after each burst, until warm.

Blueberry Crisp

EASY / VEGETARIAN / 10 INGREDIENTS

The air fryer makes a decidedly wonderful fruit crisp. The topping dries out and becomes extra crunchy, more so than it would be from an oven.

This recipe uses instant tapioca, a throwback ingredient, probably more familiar to your grandmother than to you. Look for instant tapioca in the baking aisle of almost all supermarkets, often by the baking powder. It will give the filling a rich, smooth texture, much better than the jellied filling cornstarch would produce or the gummy one flour would make. Store the box of instant tapioca in a sealed bag in a cool pantry for up to 1 year.

INGREDIENTS	2-quart or larger air fryer	3.5-quart or larger air fryer	5.25-quart or larger air fryer
Fresh or thawed frozen blueberries	2½ cups	3 cups	4 cups
Granulated white sugar	¼ cup	⅓ cup	½ cup
Instant tapioca	2½ teaspoons	1 tablespoon	1½ tablespoons
All-purpose flour	¼ cup	⅓ cup	½ cup
Rolled oats (*not* quick-cooking or steel-cut)	¼ cup	⅓ cup	½ cup
Chopped walnuts or pecans	¼ cup	⅓ cup	½ cup
Packed light brown sugar	¼ cup	⅓ cup	½ cup
Butter, melted and cooled	4 tablespoons (¼ cup/½ stick)	5 tablespoons plus 1 teaspoon (⅔ stick)	8 tablespoons (½ cup/1 stick)
Ground cinnamon	½ teaspoon	¾ teaspoon	1 teaspoon
Table salt	¼ teaspoon	Rounded ¼ teaspoon	½ teaspoon
MAKES	*4 servings*	*6 servings*	*8 servings*

1. With the basket (or basket attachment) in the air fryer, heat it to 400°F (or 390°F, if that's the closest setting).

2. Mix the blueberries, granulated white sugar, and instant tapioca in a 6-inch round cake pan for a small batch, a 7-inch round cake pan for a medium batch, or an 8-inch round cake pan for a large batch.

3. When the machine is at temperature, set the cake pan in the basket and air-fry undisturbed for 5 minutes, or just until the blueberries begin to bubble.

4. Meanwhile, mix the flour, oats, nuts, brown sugar, butter, cinnamon, and salt in a medium bowl until well combined.

5. When the blueberries have begun to bubble, crumble this flour mixture evenly on top. Continue air-frying undisturbed for 8 minutes, or until the topping has browned a bit and the filling is bubbling.

6. Use two hot pads or silicone baking mitts to transfer the cake pan to a wire rack. Cool for at least 10 minutes or to room temperature before serving.

Then...

- The best WHIPPED CREAM is made by chilling the bowl, the beaters (or a whisk, if you're old school), and the *heavy cream.* The chill keeps the cream thick when whipped, rather than airy. Beat the cream in a bowl with an electric mixer at high speed (or that whisk) with *confectioners' sugar* in a 4-to-1 ratio by volume (for example, ½ cup cream to 2 tablespoons confectioners' sugar or 1 cup cream to ¼ cup confectioners' sugar). Beat in a little *vanilla extract,* if desired.

Easy Raspberry Tarts

EASY / CAN BE VEGAN / 6 INGREDIENTS

In fact, this is our version of Pop-Tarts. We opted to make it easy with purchased pie crust dough—which means the recipe makes three hand pies per circle of dough and can't easily be adjusted for various air fryer sizes. However, you can double—or triple—this recipe, working in even more batches for a party ahead.

And you can alter the jam. We like the tartness of raspberry jam, but you could use any jam you choose. We can even imagine these with ginger marmalade for a very adult treat. Just don't use jelly (which will melt and run) or preserves (which will result in lumpy hand pies with bits of fruit sticking this way and that).

INGREDIENTS	2-quart or larger air fryer
Purchased refrigerated pie crust, from a minimum 14.1-ounce box (vegan, if a concern)	1
Raspberry jam	3 tablespoons
Confectioners' sugar	1 cup
Lemon juice	1 teaspoon
Water	As needed
Nonpareils or sprinkles (vegan, if a concern)	1 tablespoon
MAKES	3 "tarts"

1. With the basket (or basket attachment) in the air fryer, heat it to 350°F (or 360°F, if that's the closest setting).

2. Unroll the pie crust, lay it on your work surface, and cut it into six even wedges. It's easiest to cut it in half first, then cut each of these halves into thirds.

3. Separate the wedges and spread 1 tablespoon of the jam over each of three of them, leaving a ¼-inch border all around the wedge. Set a not-topped wedge on top of each with jam. Seal by pressing the tines of a flatware fork all around the wedge edge.

4. Put the filled wedges in the basket in one layer with as much air space between them as possible. (You'll probably be able to fit only two in a small machine.) Air-fry undisturbed for 10 minutes, or until flaky and browned. Use a nonstick-safe spatula to transfer the hand pies to a wire rack. Air-fry additional pies, if

necessary. Cool for at least 15 minutes or to room temperature.

5. Stir the confectioners' sugar, lemon juice, and water in a small bowl until combined, adding more water 1 teaspoon at a time until you have a thick, spreadable glaze. Spread this glaze over the hand pies. Sprinkle each with about 1 teaspoon nonpareils.

Then...

- If you're making these for adults, not kids, skip the nonpareils. Instead, sprinkle the icing with ground cardamom, ground cinnamon, and/or grated nutmeg. Get really crazy and sprinkle a tiny pinch of cayenne over each hand pie. (A good balance for all these spices would be fig jam instead of the raspberry.)

Fried Fruit Pies

EASY / CAN BE VEGAN / 4 INGREDIENTS

As with our raspberry tarts, these fried pies are super simple with a refrigerated pie crust. The difference is in the coating of the crust with the brushed-on melted butter. The crust will then have a crisp, fried texture, more in keeping with a traditional hand pie.

Use any sort of canned pie filling you like. We went with cherry and blueberry in testing this recipe. You may need to cut apple slices to smaller bits in a canned apple pie filling to make sure you get enough fruit in every pie.

INGREDIENTS	2-quart or larger air fryer
Purchased refrigerator pie crusts, from a minimum 14.1-ounce box (vegan, if a concern)	2
Canned fruit pie filling, any flavor	1½ cups
Butter, melted and cooled	4 tablespoons (¼ cup/½ stick)
Granulated white sugar	2 tablespoons
MAKES	6 fried pies

1. With the basket (or basket attachment) in the air fryer, heat it to 350°F (or 360°F, if that's the closest setting).

2. Unroll the pie crusts and set them on a clean, dry work surface. Cut three 6-inch circles from *each* crust with a 6-inch cookie cutter or a *very* large, 6-inch-wide, sturdy glass. You may need to gather the dough together and reroll it after making two circles from each crust.

3. Put ¼ cup pie filling on the bottom half of a circle, leaving at least a ½-inch border at the edge. Fold the dough over the filling to seal it inside, making a half-moon. Seal the edges by pressing the tines of a flatware fork into the dough along its sealable edges. Continue filling, folding, and sealing 5 more half-moon pies.

4. Set 1 pie in a small air fryer, 2 in a medium, or 3 in a large. There must be at least ½ inch of air space between the pies. Cover any remaining pie(s) with a clean kitchen towel. Air-fry the pie(s) undisturbed for 7 minutes.

5. Remove the basket from the machine. Generously brush the top of the pie(s) with melted butter. Sprinkle 1 teaspoon sugar over a pie. Return the basket to the machine and continue air-frying undisturbed for 7 minutes, or until golden brown and glazed from the sugar.

6. Use a nonstick-safe spatula to transfer the fried pie(s) to a wire rack. Continue air-frying more pies as necessary, in the same amount as the original batch. Cool the pies for at least 10 minutes or to room temperature before serving.

Then...

- Go over the top by making LEMON CHEESECAKE DIP for these fried pies. With an electric mixer at medium speed, beat *lemon yogurt, marshmallow Fluff or marshmallow creme,* and *whipped cream cheese* in equal proportions by volume until smooth and light.

See photo in insert.

Vanilla Butter Cake

VEGETARIAN / 9 INGREDIENTS

Since an air fryer is essentially a mini convection oven, you can make light, airy cakes with little trouble—except you can't make more than one round layer at a time. While that may (or may not, depending on your patience) preclude layer cakes, the individual layers are perfect when cut into wedges and served with a cup of hot tea on an otherwise uneventful afternoon. (Do those ever happen? We can dream!)

INGREDIENTS	2-quart or larger air fryer	3.5-quart or larger air fryer	5.25-quart or larger air fryer
All-purpose flour	⅔ cup	¾ cup plus 1 tablespoon	1 cup
Baking powder	¾ teaspoon	1 teaspoon	1¼ teaspoons
Table salt	Rounded ⅛ teaspoon	¼ teaspoon	Rounded ¼ teaspoon
Butter, at room temperature	6½ tablespoons	8 tablespoons (½ cup/1 stick)	9½ tablespoons (1 stick plus 1½ tablespoons)
Granulated white sugar	6½ tablespoons	½ cup	½ cup plus 1½ tablespoons
Large egg(s)	1 plus 1 large egg white	2	2 plus 1 large yolk
Whole or low-fat milk (*not* fat-free)	1½ tablespoons	2 tablespoons	2½ tablespoons
Vanilla extract	½ teaspoon	¾ teaspoon	1 teaspoon
Baking spray (see page 392)	As needed	As needed	As needed
MAKES	*4 servings*	*6 servings*	*8 servings*

1. With the basket (or basket attachment) in the air fryer, heat it to 325°F (or 330°F, if that's the closest setting).

2. Mix the flour, baking powder, and salt in a small bowl until well combined.

3. Using an electric hand mixer at medium speed (see the headnote on page 392 for the rationale for this sort of mixer), beat the butter and sugar in a medium bowl until creamy and smooth, about 3 minutes, occasionally scraping down the inside of the bowl.

4. Beat in the egg or eggs, as well as the white or a yolk as necessary. Beat in the milk and vanilla until smooth. Turn off the beaters and add the flour mixture. Beat at low speed until thick and smooth.

5. Use the baking spray to generously coat the inside of a 6-inch round cake pan for a small batch, a 7-inch round cake pan for a medium batch, or an 8-inch round cake pan for a large batch. Scrape and spread the batter into the pan, smoothing the batter out to an even layer.

6. Set the pan in the basket and air-fry undisturbed for 20 minutes for a 6-inch layer, 22 minutes for a 7-inch layer, or 24 minutes for an 8-inch layer, or until a toothpick or cake tester inserted into the center of the cake comes out clean. Start checking it at the 15-minute mark to know where you are.

7. Use hot pads or silicone baking mitts to transfer the cake pan to a wire rack. Cool for 5 minutes. To unmold, set a cutting board over the baking pan and invert both the board and the pan. Lift the still-warm pan off the cake layer. Set the wire rack on top of the cake layer and invert all of it with the cutting board so that the cake layer is now right side up on the wire rack. Remove the cutting board and continue cooling the cake for at least 10 minutes or to room temperature, about 30 minutes, before slicing into wedges.

Then...

- Make a second cake, then slice off the rounded tops of each cake. The cake layers must be fully cooled to room temperature before you can frost them, stacking one on top of the other with frosting in between. The easiest way to make VANILLA BUTTERCREAM is to use an electric mixer at medium speed to beat *3 cups confectioners' sugar* and *8 tablespoons (½ cup/1 stick) room-temperature butter* in a medium bowl until smooth. Beat in *1 tablespoon whole or low-fat milk, 2 teaspoons vanilla extract* and *¼ teaspoon table salt*; then beat in *more milk in ½-tablespoon increments* until you have a spreadable frosting.

- Or split a single layer in half (that is, into two disks). Spread raspberry, apricot, or peach jam, or even orange marmalade on the cut half of one layer, then top with the other layer cut side down. Sprinkle confectioners' sugar over the cake.

Honey-Pecan Yogurt Cake

VEGETARIAN / 10 INGREDIENTS

Yogurt gives density to a cake batter, resulting in less of an airy crumb (even under the air fryer's convection currents) and a springy, almost chewy texture.

The flavor of this cake can be altered dramatically with the honey used. Sure, clover or wildflower honey will yield an aromatic, light cake. But eucalyptus honey will make it even more aromatic. And buckwheat, oak, or other dark-colored honeys will give the cake a slightly bitter cast, very sophisticated with a glass of vin santo on the side. (But avoid pine honey because of its cleaning solvent overtones.)

INGREDIENTS	2-quart or larger air fryer	3.5-quart or larger air fryer	5.25-quart or larger air fryer
All-purpose flour	1 cup	1 cup plus 3½ tablespoons	1½ cups
Baking powder	¼ teaspoon	Rounded ¼ teaspoon	½ teaspoon
Baking soda	¼ teaspoon	Rounded ¼ teaspoon	½ teaspoon
Table salt	¼ teaspoon	Rounded ¼ teaspoon	½ teaspoon
Plain full-fat, low-fat, or fat-free Greek yogurt	¼ cup	5 tablespoons	6 tablespoons
Honey	¼ cup	5 tablespoons	6 tablespoons
Pasteurized egg substitute, such as Egg Beaters	¼ cup (or 1 large egg, well beaten)	5 tablespoons	6 tablespoons
Vanilla extract	1½ teaspoons	2 teaspoons	2½ teaspoons
Chopped pecans	½ cup	⅔ cup	¾ cup
Baking spray (see page 392)	As needed	As needed	As needed
MAKES	4 servings	6 servings	8 servings

1. With the basket (or basket attachment) in the air fryer, heat it to 325°F (or 330°F, if the closest setting).

2. Mix the flour, baking powder, baking soda, and salt in a small bowl until well combined.

3. Using an electric hand mixer at medium speed (see the headnote on page 392 for the rationale for this sort of mixer), beat the yogurt, honey, egg substitute or egg (as applicable), and vanilla in a medium bowl until smooth, about 2 minutes, scraping down the inside of the bowl once or twice.

4. Turn off the mixer; scrape down and remove the beaters. Fold in the flour mixture with a rubber spatula, just until all of the flour has been moistened. Fold in the pecans until they are evenly distributed in the mixture.

5. Use the baking spray to generously coat the inside of a 6-inch round cake pan for a small batch, a 7-inch round cake pan for a medium batch, or an 8-inch round cake pan for a large batch. Scrape and spread the batter into the pan, smoothing the batter out to an even layer.

6. Set the pan in the basket and air-fry for 18 minutes for a 6-inch layer, 22 minutes for a 7-inch layer, or 24 minutes for an 8-inch layer, or until a toothpick or cake tester inserted into the center of the cake comes out clean. Start checking it at the 15-minute mark to know where you are.

7. Use hot pads or silicone baking mitts to transfer the cake pan to a wire rack. Cool for 5 minutes. To unmold, set a cutting board over the baking pan and invert both the board and the pan. Lift the still-warm pan off the cake layer. Set the wire rack on top of that layer and invert all of it with the cutting board so that the cake layer is now right side up on the wire rack. Remove the cutting board and continue cooling the cake for at least 10 minutes or to room temperature, about 30 minutes, before slicing into wedges.

Then...

- To make **CREAM CHEESE FROSTING** for this fully cooled layer, use an electric mixer at medium speed to beat *4 tablespoons (¼ cup/½ stick) room-temperature butter* and *4 ounces (¼ pound) room-temperature regular or low-fat cream cheese* in medium bowl until creamy and light, about 2 minutes. Beat in *2 cups confectioners' sugar* and *1 teaspoon vanilla extract* until creamy. If the frosting is too thin, add a little more confectioners' sugar. If it's too thick, thin it out with a very small splash of *milk*.

One-Bowl Chocolate Buttermilk Cake

FAST / EASY / VEGETARIAN / 9 INGREDIENTS

This simple cake doesn't even require a mixer. It's just stirred together in one bowl—which means the texture is something like a cross between a quick bread and a traditional cake. The top will be a bit uneven, sort of waggled, because of the hot air blowing across it in the machine. If this bothers you, turn the cake over. *Voilà*: a flat top!

INGREDIENTS	2-quart or larger air fryer	3.5-quart or larger air fryer	5.25-quart or larger air fryer
All-purpose flour	⅔ cup	¾ cup	1 cup
Granulated white sugar	6½ tablespoons	½ cup	⅔ cup
Unsweetened cocoa powder	2½ tablespoons	3 tablespoons	¼ cup
Baking soda	Rounded ¼ teaspoon	½ teaspoon	¾ teaspoon
Table salt	Rounded ⅛ teaspoon	¼ teaspoon	Rounded ¼ teaspoon
Buttermilk	6½ tablespoons	½ cup	⅔ cup
Vegetable oil	1 tablespoon plus 2 teaspoons	2 tablespoons	2 tablespoons plus 2 teaspoons
Vanilla extract	½ teaspoon	¾ teaspoon	1 teaspoon
Baking spray (see page 392)	As needed	As needed	As needed
MAKES	4 servings	6 servings	8 servings

1. With the basket (or basket attachment) in the air fryer, heat it to 325°F (or 330°F, if that's the closest setting).

2. Stir the flour, sugar, cocoa powder, baking soda, and salt in a large bowl until well combined. Add the buttermilk, oil, and vanilla. Stir just until a thick, grainy batter forms.

3. Use the baking spray to generously coat the inside of a 6-inch round cake pan for a small batch, a 7-inch round cake pan for a medium batch, or an 8-inch round cake pan for a large batch. Scrape and spread the chocolate batter into this pan, smoothing the batter out to an even layer.

4. Set the pan in the basket and air-fry undisturbed for 16 minutes for a 6-inch layer, 18 minutes for a 7-inch layer, or 20 minutes for an 8-inch layer, or until a toothpick or cake tester inserted into the center of the cake comes out clean. Start checking it at the 14-minute mark to know where you are.

5. Use hot pads or silicone baking mitts to transfer the cake pan to a wire rack. Cool for 5 minutes. To unmold, set a cutting board over the baking pan and invert both the board and the pan. Lift the still-warm pan off the cake layer. Set the wire rack on top of the cake layer and invert all of it with the cutting board so that the cake layer is now right side up on the wire rack. Remove the cutting board and continue cooling the cake for at least 10 minutes or to room temperature, about 30 minutes, before slicing into wedges.

Then...

- Serve wedges with **Sweetened Sour Cream** (page 391), **No-Churn Vanilla Ice Cream** (page 378), or **Whipped Cream** (page 409).

- Frost the fully cooled cake with a half-batch of **Vanilla Buttercream** (page 413) or even a smooth layer of **Sweetened Sour Cream**, the latter put on just as you serve the cake.

- Or drizzle pieces with **Easy Salted Caramel Sauce** (page 384).

Chewy Coconut Cake

VEGETARIAN / 10 INGREDIENTS

In effect, this cake is like a coconut blondie cookie without the chocolate chips. We kept those out because we wanted the cake to have an intense coconut flavor. It's also quite dense, thanks to all that coconut.

INGREDIENTS	2-quart or larger air fryer	3.5-quart or larger air fryer	5.25-quart or larger air fryer
All-purpose flour	¾ cup	¾ cup plus 2½ tablespoons	1 cup plus 1½ tablespoons
Baking powder	½ teaspoon	¾ teaspoon	1 scant teaspoon
Table salt	⅛ teaspoon	Rounded ⅛ teaspoon	¼ teaspoon
Butter, at room temperature	6 tablespoons	7½ tablespoons (1 stick *minus* ½ tablespoon)	8½ tablespoons (1 stick plus ½ tablespoon)
Granulated white sugar	⅓ cup	⅓ cup plus 1 tablespoon	½ cup
Packed light brown sugar	¼ cup	5 tablespoons	6 tablespoons
Pasteurized egg substitute, such as Egg Beaters	¼ cup (or 1 large egg, well beaten)	5 tablespoons	6 tablespoons
Vanilla extract	1½ teaspoons	2 teaspoons	2¼ teaspoons
Unsweetened shredded coconut (see page 159)	⅓ cup	½ cup	⅔ cup
Baking spray	As needed	As needed	As needed
MAKES	*4 servings*	*6 servings*	*8 servings*

1. With the basket (or basket attachment) in the air fryer, heat it to 325°F (or 330°F, if that's the closest setting).

2. Mix the flour, baking powder, and salt in a small bowl until well combined.

continues

3. Using an electric hand mixer at medium speed (see the headnote on page 392 for the rationale for this sort of mixer), beat the butter, granulated white sugar, and brown sugar in a medium bowl until creamy and smooth, about 3 minutes, occasionally scraping down the inside of the bowl. Beat in the egg substitute or egg (as applicable) and vanilla until smooth.

4. Scrape down and remove the beaters. Fold in the flour mixture with a rubber spatula just until all the flour is moistened. Fold in the coconut until the mixture is a uniform color.

5. Use the baking spray to generously coat the inside of a 6-inch round cake pan for a small batch, a 7-inch round cake pan for a medium batch, or an 8-inch round cake pan for a large batch. Scrape and spread the batter into the pan, smoothing the batter out to an even layer.

6. Set the pan in the basket and air-fry for 18 minutes for a 6-inch layer, 20 minutes for a 7-inch layer, or 22 minutes for an 8-inch layer, or until the cake is well browned and set even if there's a little soft give right at the center. Start checking it at the 16-minute mark to know where you are.

7. Use hot pads or silicone baking mitts to transfer the cake pan to a wire rack. Cool for at least 1 hour or up to 4 hours. Use a nonstick-safe knife to slice the cake into wedges right in the pan, lifting them out one by one.

Then . . .

- To make 4 to 6 servings of an easy HOT FUDGE SAUCE that doesn't even require you to melt chocolate, whisk *¾ cup granulated white sugar, ½ cup unsweetened cocoa powder,* and *½ cup half-and-half or whole milk* in a medium saucepan set over medium heat until the sugar melts. Cook, whisking very often, until the mixture comes to a simmer. Stir in *4 tablespoons (¼ cup/ ½ stick) butter* until it melts, then *2 teaspoons vanilla extract* and *¼ teaspoon table salt* until smooth. Cool in the pan for 10 minutes before drizzling over wedges of the cake—or over vanilla ice cream served on the side. Store any extra sauce in a sealed nonreactive container in the fridge for up to 1 week. Reheat small portions of the sauce in a microwave on high in 5-second increments, stirring after each burst.

Fudgy Brownie Cake

VEGETARIAN / 9 INGREDIENTS

It's not easy to make traditional brownies in an air fryer because of the size of the pan and the way the intense heat affects the batter. However, we can make a cake that's much like a fudgy brownie, dense and super chocolaty. The cake must cool a good while so it can set up; otherwise it will break apart when cut. The cake can also be made ahead and stored, once cooled to room temperature, in a sealed container or sealed in plastic wrap on the counter for up to 2 days.

INGREDIENTS	2-quart or larger air fryer	3.5-quart or larger air fryer	5.25-quart or larger air fryer
All-purpose flour	⅓ cup	6½ tablespoons	½ cup
Unsweetened cocoa powder	3½ tablespoons	¼ cup plus 1 teaspoon	⅓ cup
Baking powder	Rounded ¼ teaspoon	Rounded ½ teaspoon	1 teaspoon
Table salt	Rounded ⅛ teaspoon	Rounded ¼ teaspoon	½ teaspoon
Butter, at room temperature	5½ tablespoons	6½ tablespoons	8 tablespoons (½ cup/1 stick)
Granulated white sugar	7½ tablespoons	9½ tablespoons	¾ cup
Large egg(s)	1 egg plus 1 large egg yolk	1 egg plus 1 large egg white	2
Vanilla extract	½ teaspoon	¾ teaspoon	1 teaspoon
Baking spray (see page 392)	As needed	As needed	As needed
MAKES	*4 servings*	*6 servings*	*8 servings*

1. With the basket (or basket attachment) in the air fryer, heat it to 325°F (or 330°F, if that's the closest setting).

2. Mix the flour, cocoa powder, baking powder, and salt in a small bowl until well combined.

3. Using an electric hand mixer at medium speed (see the headnote on page 392 for the rationale for this sort of mixer), beat the butter and sugar in a medium bowl until creamy and smooth, about 3 minutes, occasionally scraping down the inside of the bowl.

4. Beat in the egg(s) and the white or yolk (as necessary), as well as the vanilla, until smooth. Turn off the beaters and add the flour mixture. Beat at low speed until thick and smooth.

5. Use the baking spray to generously coat the inside of a 6-inch round cake pan for a small batch, a 7-inch round cake pan for a medium batch, or an 8-inch round cake pan for a large batch. Scrape and spread the batter into the pan, smoothing the batter out to an even layer.

6. Set the pan in the basket and air-fry for 25 minutes for a 6-inch layer, 30 minutes for a 7-inch layer, or 35 minutes for an 8-inch layer, or until the cake is set but soft to the touch. Start checking it at the 20-minute mark to know where you are.

7. Use hot pads or silicone baking mitts to transfer the cake pan to a wire rack. Cool for at least 1 hour or up to 4 hours. Using a nonstick-safe knife, slice the cake into wedges right in the pan and lift them out one by one.

continues

Then...

- Serve this cake with SPICED STRAWBERRY SAUCE. For 4 to 6 servings, stir ½ pound hulled strawberries, ¼ cup dry white wine or white grape juice, 3½ tablespoons granulated white sugar, 2 teaspoons finely grated orange zest, 2 teaspoons lemon juice, ¼ teaspoon table salt, one 4-inch cinnamon stick, and 1 star anise pod in a medium saucepan set over medium heat until the sugar dissolves. Bring to a simmer, stirring occasionally. Reduce the heat to low and simmer slowly for 5 minutes. Cover and remove from the heat to set aside for 15 minutes. Remove the cinnamon stick and star anise pod before serving warm. The sauce can be stored in a sealed nonreactive container in the fridge for up to 1 week.

Banana Bread Cake

VEGETARIAN / 11 INGREDIENTS

Another hybrid, this cake isn't quite a true banana bread (the traditional loaf pan would never fit in most air fryers), nor is it a light cake layer. It's a cross between the two. Even so, the denser cake is exceptionally tender with enough structure that you can eat it as a snack cake on the go, rather than with a fork at the table.

The bananas should be quite ripe, with heavily mottled spots and maybe even some soft spots, certainly beyond the point where you'd slice them onto cereal in the morning. The ripest ones are often found on the sale rack in the supermarket's produce section.

INGREDIENTS	2-quart or larger air fryer	3.5-quart or larger air fryer	5.25-quart or larger air fryer
All-purpose flour	⅔ cup plus 1 tablespoon	¾ cup plus 2 tablespoons	1 cup plus 1 tablespoon
Baking powder	Rounded ¼ teaspoon	½ teaspoon	¾ teaspoon
Baking soda	Rounded ⅛ teaspoon	¼ teaspoon	Rounded ¼ teaspoon
Table salt	Rounded ⅛ teaspoon	¼ teaspoon	Rounded ¼ teaspoon
Butter, at room temperature	3½ tablespoons	4 tablespoons (¼ cup/½ stick)	5 tablespoons
Granulated white sugar	6½ tablespoons	½ cup	9½ tablespoons
Small ripe bananas, peeled	1½	2	2½
Pasteurized egg substitute, such as Egg Beaters	¼ cup (or 1 large egg, well beaten)	5 tablespoons	6 tablespoons
Buttermilk	3 tablespoons	¼ cup	5 tablespoons
Vanilla extract	½ teaspoon	¾ teaspoon	1 teaspoon
Baking spray (see page 392)	As needed	As needed	As needed
MAKES	4 servings	6 servings	8 servings

1. With the basket (or basket attachment) in the air fryer, heat it to 325°F (or 330°F, if that's the closest setting).

2. Mix the flour, baking powder, baking soda, and salt in a small bowl until well combined.

3. Using an electric hand mixer at medium speed (see the headnote on page 392 for the rationale for this sort of mixer), beat the butter and sugar in a medium bowl until creamy and smooth, about 3 minutes, occasionally scraping down the inside of the bowl.

4. Beat in the bananas until smooth. Then beat in egg substitute or egg, buttermilk, and vanilla until uniform. (The batter may look curdled at this stage. The flour mixture will smooth it out.) Add the flour mixture and beat at low speed until smooth and creamy.

5. Use the baking spray to generously coat the inside of a 6-inch round cake pan for a small batch, a 7-inch round cake pan for a medium batch, or an 8-inch round cake pan for a large batch. Scrape and spread the batter into the pan, smoothing the batter out to an even layer.

6. Set the pan in the basket and air-fry for 18 minutes for a 6-inch layer, 20 minutes for a 7-inch layer, or 22 minutes for an 8-inch layer, or until the cake is well browned and set even if there's a little soft give right at the center. Start checking it at the 16-minute mark to know where you are.

7. Use hot pads or silicone baking mitts to transfer the cake pan to a wire rack. To unmold, set a cutting board over the baking pan and invert both the board and the pan. Lift the still-warm pan off the cake layer. Set the wire rack on top of that layer and invert all of it with the cutting board so that the cake layer is now right side up on the wire rack. Remove the cutting board and continue cooling the cake for at least 10 minutes or to room temperature, about 40 minutes, before slicing into wedges.

Then...

- Consider serving the wedges with VANILLA YOGURT SAUCE. Whisk *plain full-fat or low-fat Greek yogurt* and *confectioners' sugar* in an 8-to-1 ratio by volume (so 1 cup of yogurt to 2 tablespoons confectioners' sugar) in a bowl until smooth. Whisk in *a little vanilla extract* and/or a very *little almond extract*. Cover and set the bowl in the fridge for at least 1 hour so the yogurt firms up a bit before serving.

Acknowledgments

Writing a cookbook is like giving a party. You get up early and do a lot of the work by yourself, then everyone shows up and the real fun begins.

Thanks to our editor cum laude, the helmsman of Voracious, Mike Szczerban, for his affable support, precision editing, and publishing know-how. And to Reagan Arthur, our publisher, for taking on another challenge from us. To Nicky Guerreiro, too, for working on so many of the details in this monster. And to Suzanne Fass for the unimaginable task of copyediting this huge book in, oh, a few weeks.

Thanks, too, to the whole team at Voracious and Little, Brown: Craig Young, our deputy publisher; Jules Horbachevsky and Elora Weil for this book's PR initiatives; Kim Sheu for marketing strategies; Lauren Hesse for the social-media outreach; Laura Palese for the book's design; Julianna Lee for the cover art; Nyamekye Waliyaya, the book's manufacturing coordinator; Ben Allen, its (terrific!) production editor (who seemed to glide around our crazy schedule); Dianne Schneider, its indexer; Leslie Cauldwell, Karen Wise, and Katy Isaacs, its (three!) proofreaders; Michael Gaudet for digital production; and Laura Mamelok for the sales of its foreign rights.

Thanks to Eric Medsker, hands down the best photographer. (We should know: He's shot our last eight books.) To Stephanie Yeh, one of the coolest prop stylists we've ever worked with. And to Alex Kikis, a fine assistant who worked tirelessly yet had the good graces to make the photo shoot fun.

Thanks (ever and ever) to Susan Ginsburg, at Writers House, our agent through thirty-some-odd cookbooks (or more, if you count the ghostwritten ones). And to Catherine Bradshaw, for understanding how panicked writers get over their statements.

Outside of publishing, this cookbook wouldn't have happened without the generous support of Joey Lozada and Colleen Cleary at OXO for so many tools and gadgets, Natasha Best and Emily Vox at Philips for lots of air fryers and even more information about the machine, Akirah Charles-Brown at Ninja for one of their air fryers, and Kaitlin Crocilla at Lotus823 Marketing for a Cuisinart air fryer.

Finally, it's safe to say there'd be no party without you, the reader. Thanks for picking up this book. You know where you can reach us. We'd love to hear from you.

Index

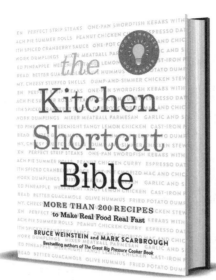
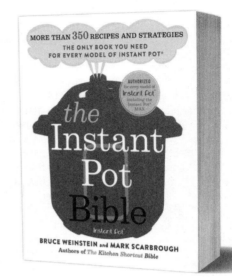